SPANISH CULTURE FROM ROMANTICISM TO THE PRESENT
STRUCTURES OF FEELING

LEGENDA

LEGENDA is the Modern Humanities Research Association's book imprint for new research in the Humanities. Founded in 1995 by Malcolm Bowie and others within the University of Oxford, Legenda has always been a collaborative publishing enterprise, directly governed by scholars. The Modern Humanities Research Association (MHRA) joined this collaboration in 1998, became half-owner in 2004, in partnership with Maney Publishing and then Routledge, and has since 2016 been sole owner. Titles range from medieval texts to contemporary cinema and form a widely comparative view of the modern humanities, including works on Arabic, Catalan, English, French, German, Greek, Italian, Portuguese, Russian, Spanish, and Yiddish literature. Editorial boards and committees of more than 60 leading academic specialists work in collaboration with bodies such as the Society for French Studies, the British Comparative Literature Association and the Association of Hispanists of Great Britain & Ireland.

The MHRA encourages and promotes advanced study and research in the field of the modern humanities, especially modern European languages and literature, including English, and also cinema. It aims to break down the barriers between scholars working in different disciplines and to maintain the unity of humanistic scholarship. The Association fulfils this purpose through the publication of journals, bibliographies, monographs, critical editions, and the MHRA Style Guide, and by making grants in support of research. Membership is open to all who work in the Humanities, whether independent or in a University post, and the participation of younger colleagues entering the field is especially welcomed.

SELECTED ESSAYS

Each title in *Selected Essays* presents influential, but often scattered, papers by a major scholar in the Humanities. While these essays will, we hope, offer a model of scholarly writing, and chart the development of an important thinker in the field, the aim is not retrospective but to gather a coherent body of work as a tool for future research. Each volume contains a new introduction, framing the debate and reflecting on the methods used.

Selected Essays is curated by Professor Susan Harrow (University of Bristol).

APPEARING IN THIS SERIES

1. *Enlightenment and Religion in German and Austrian Literature*, by Ritchie Robertson
2. *Perpetual Motion: Studies in French Poetry from Surrealism to the Postmodern*, by Michael Sheringham
3. *Putting it About: Popular Views of Social Rights and Wrongs in Spain in the Long Nineteenth Century*, by Alison Sinclair
4. *Perspectives on Culture and Politics in the French Antilles*, by Celia Britton
5. *Italian Rewritings: Subtexts and Reworkings in Italian literature from Dante to Calvino*, by Martin McLaughlin
6. *Dante, Petrarch, Boccaccio: Literature, Doctrine, Reality*, by Zygmunt G. Barański
7: *Creativity under Pressure: Essays on Antisemitism and the Achievements of German-Jewish Refugees*, by Edward Timms

Managing Editor
Dr Graham Nelson, 41 Wellington Square, Oxford OX1 2JF, UK

www.legendabooks.com

Spanish Culture from Romanticism to the Present

Structures of Feeling

Jo Labanyi

LEGENDA

Selected Essays 11
Modern Humanities Research Association
2019

Published by Legenda
an imprint of the Modern Humanities Research Association
Salisbury House, Station Road, Cambridge CB1 2LA

ISBN 978-1-78188-932-9

First published 2019

Copy-Editor: Richard Correll

CONTENTS

❖

ACKNOWLEDGEMENTS

The chapters in this volume have all been published previously as articles in journals or chapters in edited books.

Part I: Chapter 1 appeared in *Hispanic Research Journal*, 5.3 (2004): 229–43; Chapter 2 in *Culture and Gender in Nineteenth Century Spain*, ed. by Lou Charnon-Deutsch and Jo Labanyi (Oxford: Oxford University Press, 1995), pp. 8–26.

Part II: Chapter 3 appeared in *Studies in Honor of Vernon Chamberlain*, ed. by Mark Harpring (Newark, DE: Juan de la Cuesta, 2011), pp. 95–110; Chapter 4 is my translation into English of my article 'Las cosas de Galdós / Las cosas en Galdós' in *Actas del 8° Congreso Internacional Galdosiano (2005)* (Las Palmas de Gran Canaria: Casa Museo Pérez Galdós, 2009), CD-Rom; Chapter 5 in *Homenaje a Peter Bly*, ed. by Alan Smith, special issue of *Anales Galdosianos*, 42–43 (2007–08): 67–76; Chapter 6 in *Modern Spanish Women as Agents and Representatives of Change: Essays in Honor of Maryellen Bieder*, ed. by Jennifer L. Smith (Lewisburg, PA: Bucknell University Press, 2018), pp. 178–88; Chapter 7 in *Realism Revisited*, ed. by Lloyd Hugh Davies and Elizabeth Emery, special issue of *Romance Studies*, 30.3–4 (2012): 237–43; Chapter 8 in *Visualizing Spanish Modernity*, ed. by Susan Larson and Eva Woods (New York: Berg, 2005), pp. 64–80.

Part III: Chapter 9 appeared in *Journal of Romance Studies*, 8.3 (2008): 21–36; Chapter 10 in *Bulletin of Hispanic Studies* (Liverpool), 73 (1996): 377–87; Chapter 11 in *New Dangerous Liaisons: Discourses on Europe and Love in the Twentieth Century*, ed. by Luisa Passerini, Liliana Ellena, and Alexander C.T. Geppert (Oxford: Berghahn Books, 2010), pp. 197–212; Chapter 12 in *Cultural Encounters: European Travel Writing in the 1930s*, ed. by Charles Burdett and Derek Duncan (Oxford: Berghahn Books, 2002), pp. 87–103.

Part IV: Chapter 13 appeared in *Women's Narrative and Film in Twentieth-Century Spain*, ed. by Ofelia Ferrán and Kathleen Glenn (London: Routledge, 2002), pp. 75–92; Chapter 14 in *Mirrors and Echoes: Women's Writing in Twentieth-Century Spain*, ed. by Emilie L. Bergmann and Richard Herr (Berkeley: University of California Press / International & Area Studies, 2007), pp. 63–78; Chapter 15 in *Journal of the Institute of Romance Studies*, 5 (1997): 211–23; Chapter 16 in *Journal of Iberian and Latin American Studies*, 2.2 (1996): 145–63; Chapter 17 in *Constructing Identity in Contemporary Spain: Theoretical Debates and Cultural Practice*, ed. by Jo Labanyi (Oxford: Oxford University Press, 2002), pp. 206–21; Chapter 18 in *Europe and Love in Cinema*, ed. by Luisa Passerini, Karen Diehl, and Jo Labanyi (Bristol: Intellect, 2012), pp. 127–50.

Part V: Chapter 19 appeared in *Spanish Cinema: The Auteurist Tradition*, ed. by Peter Evans (Oxford: Oxford University Press, 1999), 76–92; Chapter 20 is my translation into English of my chapter 'Los fantasmas del pasado y las seducciones del psicoanálisis: *El desencanto* (Jaime Chávarri, 1976)' in *El cine y la transición política en España*, ed. by Manuel Palacio (Madrid: Biblioteca Nueva, 2011), pp. 73–85; Chapter 21 appeared in *Burning Darkness: Half a Century of Spanish Cinema*, ed. by Joan Ramón Resina, Andrés Lema-Hincapié, and Thomas C. Platt (Buffalo: SUNY Press, 2008), pp. 143–60.

Part VI: Chapter 22 appeared in *Disremembering the Dictatorship: The Politics of Memory in the Spanish Transition to Democracy*, ed. by Joan Ramon Resina (Amsterdam: Rodopi, 2000), pp. 65–82; Chapter 23 in *Unearthing Franco's Legacy: Mass Graves and the Recuperation of Historical Memory in Spain*, ed. by Carlos Jerez-Ferrán and Samuel Amago (Notre Dame: Notre Dame University Press, 2010), pp. 192–205; Chapter 24 in *The Witness and the Text*, ed. by Debra Kelly and Gill Rye, special issue of *Journal of Romance Studies*, 9.3 (2009), 23–35.

My thanks go to all the original publishers for granting me permission to reproduce these essays here.

I also thank the archives and museums that provided the images included in the book, and the copyright owners who granted me permission to include them in this volume. They are acknowledged individually in the List of Illustrations and captions.

LIST OF ILLUSTRATIONS

INTRODUCTION

The essays selected for this volume aim to provide an introduction to different ways of thinking about Spanish culture. In this respect, they are offered as examples of what has come to be known as 'cultural studies': the study of culture as a system of relations, integrated yet contradictory, in which cultural artefacts are shaped by — and may in turn shape — a range of concerns specific to a particular time and place. This approach to cultural analysis reaches across cultural production in different media. The time and place covered by this volume is Spain from the 1830s to the present, corresponding to the complicated process of the country's insertion into modernity — a process that has not been linear and has triggered considerable ideological conflict (not to mention the Civil War of the 1930s). The media covered are literature, cinema, painting and photography.

By 'cultural studies' I also understand a form of cultural analysis that is informed by cultural theory: that is, one that asks big questions of its material by considering its specificity in the light of wider issues. In putting together these essays — originally published between 1995 and 2018 — I have become aware of shifts of theoretical focus in my own work that have corresponded to shifts of theoretical focus within the humanities, and particularly within literary and visual studies. Thus, the focus on gender — which underlies much of the volume's contents — has moved from the feminist rethinking of psychoanalytic theory in the 1990s, with its critique of patriarchy, to a broader concern with the cultural construction of subjectivity, taking into account the post-structuralist deconstruction of fixed concepts of identity, including gender categories. This concern with the cultural construction of subjectivity has itself moved through different phases in my work, with a strong interest in memory studies from around the year 2000 when the debates on the memory of the Francoist repression in the Spanish Civil War and its aftermath began to occupy a significant space in the Spanish public sphere, on the back of a considerable corpus of theoretical reflection outside of Spain on the remembrance of the Holocaust. In recent years, my focus has shifted to the not unrelated field of the history of the emotions and affect theory, in this case corresponding to theoretical developments in the (mostly) Anglophone academy.

The fact that my career has spanned the UK and (since 2006) the USA has required me to reflect on the differences between the study of Spanish culture in each of those countries and in Spain. If in the UK the terms 'hispanism' or 'Hispanic Studies' are regularly used for the study of Spanish-speaking cultures anywhere in the world, those terms are not used in the USA, where 'Hispanic' refers to the population of Latin American extraction (predominantly Central American and Caribbean) that has made its home in the United States. Sensitivity to racial issues in the USA has made 'hispanism' a taboo word, associated — not without justification — with Spanish imperialism: that is, the assumption — strong in Spain until the late twentieth century and still found today — that Spain somehow 'owns' Spanish-language culture in other parts of the world. An embarrassing example is the tendency of the Spanish Government's institution for the promotion of Spanish language and culture, the Instituto Cervantes, to refer to the Spanish language as a 'gift' of Spain to the Americas and other parts of the world — Equatorial Guinea, the Philippines — where Spanish is or has been spoken. What in the UK tend to be called Departments of Hispanic Studies are, in the USA, called Departments of Spanish and Portuguese. This recognizes the importance of Portuguese-speaking Brazil for the study of Latin America but rarely includes the study of Portugal, while the study of Portuguese-speaking Africa (Mozambique, Angola) — vibrant in the UK among the small number of scholars of Portuguese-language culture — is only recently starting to attract scholarship in the USA. The subtext to all this is, of course, a much greater interest in the USA in what are called Hemispheric Studies — study of the Americas as a whole — than in the study of 'old' Europe. It is a humbling experience to discover, on moving from Europe to the USA, that Europe does not figure much in the US mindset. This means that, as a scholar of Spanish culture in the US academy, one's work has to engage with theoretical issues that have relevance beyond Peninsular studies (the term regularly used to distinguish the study of Spain from that of Latin America) in order to attract students. The result is positive inasmuch as it avoids provincialism, so long as one remains attentive to the historical and cultural specificity of the way those theoretical issues play out in Spain.

Nevertheless, the engagement of Peninsular studies with cultural theory has been slower in the USA than in the UK where the presence of public intellectuals such as Raymond Williams and Stuart Hall embedded cultural studies in the academy, including in Departments of Modern Languages. (The equivalent US term, Department of Foreign Languages, shows the hold still in the USA of the Cold War conception of Area Studies as the study of 'other' parts of the world.) The relative traditionalism of Peninsular studies in many US Departments of Spanish and Portuguese until quite recently has been attributed to the importance of the Spanish Republican intellectuals in exile who found a home in such departments during the Franco dictatorship; while their democratic credentials gave them prestige, they tended to perpetuate a somewhat elitist and narrow philological conception of literature which, it has to be said, continues to prevail in most Departments of Spanish (called 'Departamentos de Filología Española') in Spain today. I am fortunate in being located in a Department of Spanish and Portuguese (at New York University) that is known for its interdisciplinarity and broad theoretical approach to the study of culture. It must be noted that scholarship on Spain in the USA has changed considerably in the last twenty years as younger scholars have increasingly adopted a cultural studies approach that is more in line with scholarship on Latin America — and with scholarship, whether on Spain or Latin America, in the UK.

Sadly, however, there remains considerable tension — sometimes erupting into hostility — between the largely philological approach of scholars in departments of Spanish literature in Spain and the broad cultural approach of most Peninsular scholars in the UK and US, who study literature from an interdisciplinary theoretical perspective, alongside other cultural media. My own very productive relations with scholars in Spain over the last twenty years have been in the field, not of literary studies, but of cinema studies, which — in keeping with the transnationalism of the film industry — is (mostly) open to scholarship outside of Spain. While in the Anglophone academy film is often studied in Departments of Language and Literature, in Spain it tends to be studied in Departments of Communication Studies, receptive to cultural theory. Particularly enriching has been my longstanding relationship with the Department of Journalism and Communication at the Universidad Carlos III in Madrid, which, in addition to building up a superb team of film scholars, has made a point of involving overseas researchers (British, US and French) in its Spanish-government-funded projects. Chapter 20 of this volume is the product of one of those projects.

The other area of the Spanish academy with which I have enjoyed productive collaboration is that of women's studies — a field that is especially strong in Spain, with notable concentrations at the Universities of Barcelona, Valencia and Cadiz. My one collaboration with Spanish literary scholars has been with the Centre Dona i Literatura (Centre for Women and Literature) at the Universitat de Barcelona, whose graduate programme — now renamed 'Theory, Gender, Sexuality' — is impressively theoretical and cosmopolitan. Apart from this exception, my Spanish interlocutors in women's studies have been in the field of eighteenth- and nineteenth-century women's history, where dialogue with scholars such as Mónica Bolufer and Isabel Burdiel (Universitat de València), Gloria Espigado (Universidad de Cádiz) and Mónica Burguera (Universidad Nacional de Educación a Distancia) have inspired me to return in my recent work to study of the nineteenth century (as in Chapter 6 of his volume). Interestingly, several of these specialists in women's history draw on literary texts for their insights, producing work that is closer to cultural studies than that emerging from literature departments in Spain — something that I think tends not to happen in the generally empirically driven research of historians in the UK and US.

Reflecting on one's academic output over one's career is an interesting exercise that brings some surprises: it took me a while to realize that what holds all the essays in this volume together is a concern to explore what Raymond Williams famously called 'structures of feeling'. In this sense, my current interest in the history of emotions and affect theory was anticipated, without my realizing it until now, by much of my earlier work. This realization was unexpected since my university education at Oxford in the mid-1960s did not mention Raymond Williams but trained me in a mix of New Criticism and an incipient version of structuralism that had in common a focus on the text and nothing but the text, bracketing off the outside world and indeed the concept of the author. I remain grateful for this training in close reading, which I continue to find important. But

I now realize, retrospectively, that, regardless of my training as a student, Raymond Williams's writings were in the air everywhere in the humanities in Britain in the 1960s, and affected me without my being consciously aware of it at the time. In giving this volume the subtitle *Structures of Feeling*, I not only single out what I hope gives coherence to it at an implicit level, but also pay homage to Williams's pioneering theorization and analysis of how culture works as a system that is always contradictory and yet provides the social glue to any given period.

Perhaps the most valuable perception of Williams is his insistence that such 'structures of feeling' can be identified in the particularities of literary form. This insistence represented a break with orthodox Marxist criticism which, seeing the text as determined by economic forces, largely focused on subject matter rather than the formal properties of the text. For Williams, literary texts are not the result of forces outside the text but help to work out, and work through, still inchoate articulations of social concerns. Thus, for Williams, the structures of feeling that can be observed beneath the surface of the text are a key to emergent views and anxieties of the time; in this respect, they can help us understand processes of social change. Although Williams's most influential books study literature, his notion of 'structures of feeling' applies to any other kind of cultural text; indeed, it was first formulated in his early writing on film. Williams's formulation of culture as a mix of residual, dominant and emergent tendencies renders culture dynamic and invites readers to be attentive to the contradictions and incoherence that, perhaps even more than areas of consensus, put us in touch with the pulse of the time. This perception of Williams, together with the deconstructionist turn that took hold in the 1970s and 1980s, led to a stress in literary and visual studies on 'reading against the grain' as a way of revealing the tensions within a given text, on the assumption that such tensions tell us something about unresolved ideological conflicts operating in the society concerned. All the essays in this volume that deal with cultural texts are attempts to read against the grain, looking beneath the textual surface for tensions that trouble its overt meaning. The essays that analyse material culture or social phenomena (Chapters 4 and 24) have a similar aim.

The search for the 'trouble in the text' has its risks; one can become seduced by the pleasure of prising out contrary meanings, and can fall into the trap of supposing that all meanings that go against the grain are by definition subversive of dominant ideology. While I hope not to have succumbed to such temptations, I recognize that they are especially strong when one is studying a period like the Franco dictatorship, which did its best to impose a single, monolithic ideology that would keep the regime in power. I have included in this anthology only a small selection of my articles on cinema of the early Franco period, since these will be incorporated into a still unfinished monograph provisionally titled *Reading Films under Dictatorship*. But all my work on the early Franco period — whether on cinema or literature — has been motivated by a wish to correct a still strong tendency to treat Spanish culture of the time as overwhelmingly determined by regime ideology, on the tacit or explicit assumption that censorship succeeded in eliminating contrary views and in hiding the regime's own contradictions. Such a view does a disservice to those who lived through the regime's darkest period by implying that they were not capable of thinking for themselves. It is also inaccurate, as I was made acutely aware by my collective research project *Cinema and Everyday Life in 1940s and 1950s Spain: An Oral History*, the interviewees for which — elderly Spaniards who had gone to the cinema in those decades when young — made it clear that they themselves, knowing of the existence of censorship, were highly proficient readers against the grain. In the absence of direct engagement with audiences (impossible for earlier periods, and requiring substantial funding and logistical complexity for more recent periods), one cannot determine with certainty what meanings were read into cultural texts by audiences of the time. Nevertheless, I have come to believe that there is no text that does not have — or at least allow a perception of — moments of contradiction or incoherence, and that those moments are an indication of something important. Just as we have been trained to be attentive to the ways in which the off-frame leaves its traces on the photographic or cinematic image, so too, I suggest, such moments of contradiction or incoherence — in texts in any medium — point to the presence of an 'outside-the-text' that insists on intruding; an 'outside-the-text' that may be that of the author or that of the reader/viewer.

The essays in this volume could have been organized in many ways. It is probably only of interest to myself to read them in the order in which they were originally published, but, should that be felt useful as a way of observing evolving academic trends (no doubt assimilated by me in a not entirely coherent fashion), that order would be Chapters 2, 10, 16, 15, 19, 22, 12, 13, 17, 1, 8, 14, 5, 9, 21, 4, 24, 23, 11, 3, 20, 7, 18, 6. This order is partially skewed by the fact that one's publications sometimes respond not to one's latest interests but to invitations to write about a topic on which one has published previously. I have chosen to arrange the essays in chronological order of the material analysed, so that the book allows readers to work through a sequential cultural history of modern Spain — one that is far from comprehensive but that respects historical specificity. If I use the term 'cultural history' and not 'cultural studies' here, it is because, like Raymond Williams, I regard cultural studies as a way of understanding historical change.

For those interested in particular theoretical approaches and issues, it may be useful to note that the essays that draw on psychoanalysis (in some cases to reject it) are Chapters 2, 10, 19, 20 and 21. Gender lies at the heart of Chapters 2, 6, 10, 11, 13, 14, 15, 16, 17, 18, 19 and 20. Race is a significant factor in Chapters 1, 10, 11, 17 and 18. Nineteenth-century nation-formation forms the basis of Chapters 1, 7 and 8. Memory is the main focus in Chapters 4, 5, 12, 20, 22, 23 and 24. Place and material culture are discussed in Chapters 3, 4, 9 and 12. Popular culture — and, in the first two cases, its relation to high culture — is the topic of Chapters 8, 9, 13, 14 and 17. Chapter 6 (the most recently written) engages with emotion studies and affect theory.

In the first two essays on the Romantic period, I have wanted to stress the fluidity of the early stages of the nation-formation process in Spain, when a series of options were open before the consolidation of more conservative positions in the mid-century. This emphasis also drives my analysis in Chapter 3 of the first serialized novel (*folletín*) of Ayguals de Izco in the 1840s. It will be clear from the selection of essays that the second half of the nineteenth century has been one of my major interests, in great measure thanks to the opportunity to spend two years researching the period with a British Academy–Leverhulme Trust Senior Research Fellowship in 1993–95, which resulted in the monograph *Gender and Modernization in the Spanish Realist Novel* (Oxford University Press, 2000). In that book, I stressed the cultural repercussions of the consolidation under the Restoration of a capitalist market economy and of contemporaneous debates around social reform and individual and regional autonomy — topics which surface in Chapters 3, 4, 5, 7 and 8 of this volume. What I learned from extensive reading of economic, political and medical discourses of the time was that the Restoration period, often dismissed — I suspect thanks to its demonization by early twentieth-century writers, particularly Ortega y Gasset — as uniformly reactionary and corrupt, in reality enjoyed a lively public sphere in which many positions were aired. I hope that the chapters on this period included here show something of that plurality, as well as the importance of relating literary and artistic production to debates of the time. My recent work, motivated by an interest in the history of the emotions, has, as previously mentioned, returned to this period, as seen in Chapter 6. ⌐The realist novel can be seen as a kind of laboratory for talking about emotions, for it is by involving the reader affectively through the depiction of what the characters are feeling that reader identification — and thus what Barthes called 'the reality effect' — is secured.⌐

The chapters that cover the 1920s and 1930s reveal the contrast between the largely apolitical writing of the 1920s avant-garde and the politicization of culture that took place under the Second Republic of 1931–36. It is often forgotten that the blossoming of the Spanish avant-garde took place under the Primo de Rivera dictatorship, which closed down public debate; Ortega y Gasset's championing of an elitist art in which formal experimentation was privileged over content, expounded in his 1925 *La deshumanización del arte* (*The Dehumanization of Art*), is in keeping with his condoning of Primo de Rivera's coup of 1923 (only from 1929 would Ortega become a critic of the regime). In Chapter 9, however, I have wanted to show the limits of Ortega's influence by stressing the dialogue between elite and mass culture in much Spanish cultural production of the 1920s. The fusion of avant-garde aesthetics and the political was perhaps most successfully achieved by the fascist convert, Ernesto Giménez Caballero, studied in Chapter 10. Several chapters in this volume analyse the work of right-wing authors in order to counter a tendency to focus on writers whose politics makes them ethically acceptable. I consider it important to try to understand the mindset of those whose values one deplores — the far right, which triumphed in the Spanish Civil War, has after all played a major role in Spanish history. For that reason, Chapter 11 discusses the work of writers of a wide range of political persuasions, several of whom dramatically changed their political positions in the course of their lifetime. This chapter, together with Chapter 18, was written for the project *Europe: Emotions, Identities, Politics* (informally titled *Europe and Love*) directed in 2002–04 by the Italian cultural historian Luisa Passerini, whose work on subjectivity and memory has strongly marked my own. My debt to Passerini's work is evident also in the first and last chapters of this volume. The Spanish Civil War is treated indirectly through the photographs of two Central European women photographers working in 1930s Spain, which are analysed through the lens of Walter Benjamin's messianic view of history; like Benjamin, both of these photographers were Jewish.

As already mentioned, it is particularly in relation to the early Franco period that I have wanted to stress a cultural heterogeneity that, while severely curtailed, nevertheless existed. I have done this, in the chapters on this period, not by looking at manifestations of political dissidence (for obvious reasons, political dissidence could not be expressed publicly), but by prising out the contradictions in writing by Falangist women and in films that enjoyed official approval. What opens up these fissures is the representation of gender: of women and, surprisingly, of military masculinity. Chapter 13 ranges across political writing and novels by women members of the Spanish fascist party, Falange Española, while Chapter 14 focuses on the extensive production of romance fiction by pro-Falangist women. This fictional writing reveals a strand of Spanish fascism — quashed by Franco's imposition of National-Catholic values — that was grounded in a cosmopolitan modernity. This chimes with analyses of Mussolini's Italy as a form of fascist modernity. When I began to research Spanish cinema of the early Franco period, I was taken aback by the prevalence of strong female protagonists in a period when women had lost all the rights gained under the Republic. Chapters 15, 16 and 17 are an attempt to make sense of this contradiction. Unexpected contradictions are also explored in the discussion in Chapter 18 of a homosociality that comes near to condoning homosexuality and of a mixed-race sexual relationship that comes near to condoning miscegenation, particularly interesting for figuring protagonists from the Army of Africa, which had formed the hard core of Franco's military invasion of Republican Spain in the Civil War. Mixed-race liaisons, in this case between gypsy female protagonists and white establishment males, also form the curious basis of the folkloric musicals studied in Chapter 17. My stress on the contradictions of cultural production of the early Franco period is not intended to suggest that Francoist cultural repression was not after all so severe (my work on this period has been interpreted that way by some Spanish scholars). My point is, rather, that a focus on gender can reveal the 'trouble' in texts that are in other respects normative — though there is not much that is normative in the wild imagination of the fascist-sympathizing women writers of romance fiction that I have studied, apart from the obligatory 'happy end'. It is not coincidence that the novels and films analysed in my chapters on the early Franco period are popular cultural texts; popular culture, while it can reinforce stereotypes, has always enjoyed playing with gender categories.

The three chapters (19, 20 and 21) that discuss art cinema of the late Francoist and post-Franco era chart my changing relationship to psychoanalytic criticism over the period 1999 to 2011, when these essays were originally published. If the exiled director Buñuel's 1970 *Tristana* (filmed in Spain despite considerable obstacles created by the regime) is analysed through the lens of feminist writing on castration

anxiety, my discussion of Jaime Chávarri's 1976 cult film *El desencanto* attempts
to rescue the widow of the Francoist poet Leopoldo Panero, whose sons tear the
family apart before the camera, from the director's imposition of a psychoanalytic
framework that blames everything on the mother. My reading of Juanma Bajo
Ulloa's 1993 *La madre muerta* suggests that a material reading of the film may work
better than the psychoanalytic interpretation invited by its emphasis on loss of
the mother. In this respect, the essay charts the shift within film studies from a
psychoanalytically oriented gaze theory to a material concern with the haptic.

The last three essays in the volume contribute to memory studies. The first
comprises my earliest attempt in 2000 to theorize a spectral reading — one that has
since become commonplace — of the memorialization in fiction and film from the
1970s to the 1990s of the victims of the Francoist repression during and after the
Civil War. The last two essays were written in 2009–10, by when my attitude had
become more critical. The second questions the assumptions and methodologies of
the testimonial literature produced in the initial years of the twenty-first century,
while the third argues against the demonization of silence, and the supposition
that it is the opposite of memory, in memory discourses in contemporary Spain. In
critiquing contemporary Spanish memory discourses, I have not wanted to call into
question the need to remember and honour the victims of the Francoist reprisals
— Spain has more mass graves than any other country after Cambodia — but to
point to the need for nuanced understandings of how memory works and of what
memory can and cannot do.

The essays in this volume are thus offered not as a coherent body of work but
as a wide-ranging set of reflections on different cultural media from the 1830s to
the present that have in common a questioning of dominant interpretations. The
essays are printed as they first appeared, apart from the occasional correction or
updating of information and the addition of a few cross-references to link the
various chapters. Chapters 4 and 20 have been translated by myself from the original
Spanish in which I wrote them. Those essays published in the United Kingdom
follow the MHRA style guidelines; those that were published in the United States
(and the translations from Spanish) follow the style guidelines of the MLA. Readers
will thus find a mix of British and American spelling, corresponding to my career
change from the UK to the USA.

I am hugely honoured to have been invited to put together this anthology of
essays by Susan Harrow as editor of the *Selected Essays* series of Legenda, particularly
since it represents a sort of home-coming after crossing the Atlantic in 2006. Both
Susan Harrow and Graham Nelson as Managing Editor of Legenda have been
models of efficiency and I thank them both for their support of this project as well
as their work to make it happen.

J. L., New York, May 2019

PART I

Romanticism

CHAPTER 1

❖

Love, Politics and the Making of the Modern European Subject: Spanish Romanticism and the Arab World

This chapter arises out of my involvement in the collaborative research project *Europe: Emotions, Identities, Politics* (informally known as *Europe and Love*), directed by Luisa Passerini of the European University Institute, Florence, and funded by the Kulturwissenschaftliches Institut, Essen. The project is concerned with the intersection between the discourse on courtly and romantic love that has been elaborated from the Enlightenment on, and discourses on Europeanness. My role in the project has, in part, been to research the function that Spain has played in this intersection of discourses as an interface between Europe and the Arab world.

This particular piece of research was triggered by an increasing sense that something needs to be done about the 'black hole' in Spanish studies — that is, the eighteenth century and the first half of the nineteenth century, which are now barely taught. Academic specialization has led to a lack of dialogue, not only between those working in different disciplines, but also between those working in the same department on different periods: one 'does' early modern or modern culture, with no joined-up thinking about the moment of transition. We cannot do away with the division of history into periods, for historical specificity is hugely important; but perhaps we could institute a kind of historical 'border studies', that tries to think across the historical 'divides' produced by established schemes of periodization. I shall be arguing that the Spanish Romantics turn to the medieval period — specifically to the frontier dividing and joining the Christian and Muslim kingdoms — as a way of constructing what one might call a 'border subjectivity': that is, a notion of the modern liberal subject that is not — or not yet — rigidly bounded. I do not have space here to attempt a reading of these Romantic texts in terms of current Latino Studies border theory, but I think that might be a productive use of historical anachronism that could alert us to aspects of the past that have been ironed out by our respect for chronology, which makes us focus only on those aspects of the past that 'led to' later developments. This would mean applying a theoretical model that has been elaborated in relation to the 'post-modern' and the 'post-national' to a period — the early nineteenth century — when, in Spain as elsewhere in the West, the notions of the modern individual subject and of the nation state were being worked out but had not yet solidified.[1]

I have previously explored the role that culture — especially the novel — played in the nation-formation process in late nineteenth-century Spain, when nation-formation was at its height (Labanyi 2000). I tried there to show how, even in this period of consolidation, the nation-formation process consisted not just in what the state did, but in the many-sided debates that comprised the public sphere. The process was considerably more heterogeneous in the early nineteenth century, when — as Álvarez Junco has shown in his book, *Mater Dolorosa: La idea de España en el siglo XIX* (2001) — the idea that political sovereignty was invested in 'the nation' through a social contract between 'individual subjects' was still emergent and hotly contested by those supporting a dynastic model of sovereignty whereby political power derived from birthright. As Álvarez Junco argues, the adoption of the principle of 'the nation' as the basis of political power by the Spanish right — excepting Carlism — from around 1860 marked a sea-change (interestingly, Álvarez Junco suggests that the 1859–60 'Guerra de África' or invasion of northern Morocco functions as a catalyst in this process). In this chapter, I shall be interested in how the Spanish Romantics use Spain's Arab past as a way of trying out different models of the nation, at a time — the 1830s — when no one model of the nation state had gelled. For if one looks at the large amount of Spanish Romantic drama, poetry and narrative that deals with pre-1492 'Moorish' Spain (to use the contemporaneous term) or with the sixteenth-century Moriscos, it is hard to see any consistent pattern. The plurality of the models proposed is, precisely, what interests me.

Most of this chapter will set out a theoretical and historical framework, but in the last part I shall comment on three Romantic texts: Martínez de la Rosa's play *Aben Humeya o la rebelión de los moriscos* (*Aben Humeya or the Morisco Revolt*), written in exile in French and premièred in Paris in 1830, the Spanish version being premièred in 1836; Hartzenbusch's 1837 play *Los amantes de Teruel* (*The Lovers of Teruel*); and the Duque de Rivas's narrative poem *El moro expósito* (*The Moorish Foundling*), written 1829–33 in exile in Malta and France and published in 1834. The fact that the texts by Martínez de la Rosa and Rivas were, like many other Spanish Romantic works, written during a prolonged period of exile is likely to be a contributing factor to their particularly radical construction of a 'border subjectivity'. As is well known, Romanticism blossomed in Spain with the return in 1833 of the liberal political exiles, who had been forced to flee the country ten years earlier, in 1823, on Fernando VII's revoking of the liberal constitution. Older liberal intellectuals had also spent the period 1813–20 in exile, on the restoration of absolutism after the Napoleonic army's defeat — Martínez de la Rosa had spent these seven years

1   In this chapter I will be concerned only with the construction of a modern subjectivity in Spanish Romantic texts that depict Spain's Arab past, and not with the porous cultural border that joined and separated the Arab and Christian kingdoms in medieval Spain — a period on which I cannot pretend to be an expert. I am grateful to Alan Deyermond for taking the time to provide me with the bibliographical references included in the notes to this chapter, and for clarifying certain issues on which my original information was imprecise. I am, of course, responsible for any remaining inaccuracies in my reference to medieval Spain.

in a Spanish prison in North Africa. Border crossing was something that early nineteenth-century Spanish liberals knew a lot about.

The Italian historian Luisa Passerini, who directs the 'Europe: Emotions, Identities, Politics' project, has a particular interest in how the political is modelled and enacted via modes of intersubjectivity. The project explores Passerini's insight, developed in her book *Europe in Love, Love in Europe* (1999), that the discourse on courtly and Romantic love, elaborated in Europe from the Enlightenment on, is a discourse about the *superiority* of European identity, since only Europeans are seen as capable of such refined and complex — one might say 'contorted' — forms of loving. What interests me about this perception is that it constructs a model of European identity based on the notion of the superiority of 'impossible love'. Passerini mentions in her book the debate around whether courtly love, elaborated in Provence in the twelfth century, in fact had its origins in Arab culture, entering Provence via Arab Spain. This hypothesis remains a matter of debate today;[2] what interests me is not whether or not it is true, but what is at stake in such claims, and what cultural effects have resulted from them. For such claims were first coherently advanced by Spanish scholars in the late eighteenth century, and developed further by early twentieth-century Spanish Hispano-Arabists.

The Spanish Romantics are characterized by the confluence of an elaboration of extreme forms of impossible love, a political militancy that is for the most part lacking in the Romanticism of northern Europe, and their use of Hispano-Arabic culture. 'Oriental Spain' was a topos in European and indeed North American Romanticism, but its inflection in the Spanish case is especially complex since the 'Moors' and Moriscos are not simply picturesque 'others' but raise the central question of the extent to which they are part of the 'we in the past' that constitutes national history. The construction of a 'we in the past' is essential to nation-formation, for it produces those emotional identifications that determine who we include and who we exclude from national citizenship. The strong concern of Spanish Romantic writers with the medieval past (that is, with a past shared by Christians, Muslims and Jews) should not be seen as a sign of their traditionalism, for the point of this return to the distant past was to produce a new model of 'national history' that broke with the recent past — that of absolutism. Romantic writers are thus not worried about committing historical anachronisms — Rivas's erudite notes to *El moro expósito* are delightfully frank about how he has ignored chronology, having his Moorish heroine in tenth-century Córdoba tutored by Averroes who lived 150 years later — for the point is the construction in the past of a new national subject that provides the basis for the new concept of national sovereignty (that is, the idea that sovereignty is invested in the nation's citizens and not — or not exclusively — in the monarchy). This new national subject is constructed through romantic love.

I should like here to draw on Roger Bartra's theorization of melancholy in his book *Cultura y melancolía: Las enfermedades del alma en la España del siglo de oro* (*Culture and Melancholy: Maladies of the Soul in Golden Age Spain*, 2001), whose objectives are summarized in his earlier article 'Arabs, Jews, and the Enigma of Spanish

2   For an overview of this debate, see Boase (1977).

Imperial Melancholy' (2000). In his book, Bartra develops his earlier discussion of melancholy in relation to Mexican identity, focusing this time on the cultural consequences of the expulsion of the Jews and Arabs from Spain. (As we know, the Jews were expelled in 1492 at the same time as the Catholic Kings conquered the Muslim kingdom of Granada, and those Muslims who, at that time, chose to stay in Spain at the cost of an increasingly enforced assimilation were, after the 1568–71 Morisco Revolt in the Alpujarras, finally expelled between 1609 and 1614.) Bartra suggests that, if melancholy became 'one of the propelling forces of politics and society' (2000: 64) in Renaissance Europe, it was thanks to its elaboration in sixteenth-century Spanish discourse, going on to become *the* dominant cultural trope of Spain's Golden Age. Bartra notes that, in Renaissance Spain as elsewhere, melancholy — a medical concept — was seen as a particularly Jewish disease, both because in Spain most physicians were — or were assumed to be — Jewish converts, and because in Europe generally melancholy was associated with a condition of exile, regarded as inherent to the Jews as a diasporic people, especially after their expulsion from Spain in 1492, not to mention the internal exile resulting from the enforced suppression of Jewish cultural practices by the Inquisition. Bartra also includes the driving out of Islam and suppression of Islamic cultural practices in this melancholic configuration, since the Greek medical theorization of melancholy re-entered Renaissance Europe via Spain through Arabic as well as Jewish treatises. Bartra describes how, in the Spanish Golden Age, there was an increasing movement to 'de-arabize' Greek medical thought, with the prohibition of Avicenna's writings and the ending of the teaching of Arabic in university medical studies (2000: 68–69).

This Spanish melancholy, as described by Bartra, thus derives from the fact that the formation of the Spanish nation, via the political unification and cultural homogenization imposed in 1492, is founded on an irreparable loss. This would be a specifically Spanish version of the violence that, for Anthony Giddens (1985), lies at the origin of all state formation. As Bartra notes, melancholy can derive not just from the recognition of loss but also from its denial: indeed, the most corrosive melancholy is that which refuses to admit the object of loss to consciousness. This would be Freud's definition of melancholia, as opposed to mourning in which the lost object is acknowledged (Freud 1984). I shall come back to mourning because Spanish Romanticism is full of improperly buried or unburied bodies, as well as graves.

Bartra notes that during the Renaissance 'Spain obsessed over its borders' (2000: 68): the border with Islam in the Mediterranean, and that created by conquest in the New World, but also its internal borders since Arab medicine, while increasingly repudiated, was still practised, just as Jewish doctors continued to dominate the profession. As Bartra puts it:

> Melancholy was a border illness, a disease of transition and transformation. A sickness of displaced peoples, of migrants, associated with the fragile life of the people who suffered forced conversions [...]. An illness that attacked those who lost something and have not yet found what they look for [...]. (2000: 69)

Bartra suggests that analysis of the 'dense cultural and sentimental texture [of melancholy] that extended over Europe in the Renaissance [...] can help to explain the great transformations that the West lived in the dawn of modernity' (2000: 67). Looking forward to the moment when modernity in the form of political liberalism started to be negotiated in Europe, he also notes that 'the Romantics exalted melancholic sentimentalism as never before' (2000: 64). In this chapter I should like to read the notion of romantic love elaborated in my choice of 'border' texts from the 1830s, all of them set in Spain's Arab past, in the light of Bartra's theorization of melancholy as a mindset produced by the violently enforced cultural homogenization that founded Spain as a unified nation. Hobsbawm has noted that Spain was precocious in imposing the principle of a nation state based on 'one race, one language, one culture' from 1492, since this homogenizing principle did not become dominant in most of Europe until the mid-nineteenth century (1990: 16). In returning to the period prior to 1492, the Romantics — in a move Walter Benjamin would have approved of — are recuperating the unrealized potential of the ruins of the past (the Romantics love ruins) as the basis for future models of the nation.

It is important to stress that all the texts I shall discuss are resorting to Spain's Arab past to elaborate a *modern* notion of the nation on *European* lines; that is, one whose structures are based on individual merit and not on birthright. This rejection of birthright as a legitimizing principle is what allows Martínez de la Rosa and Rivas to propose a modern model of the nation via their Morisco or mixed-race protagonists. In other words, they are proposing a modern model of the nation that acknowledges cultural pluralism, which they figure through ethnic multiculturalism. (As we shall see, in Hartzenbusch's play Arab Spain plays a more negative role.) While all three works rehearse different models of the nation, they are all based on some notion of the rights of the individual subject as represented through Romantic love, whether this be love for a lover or for the nation. The liberal notion of rights is premised on the concept of individual freedom, incarnated in Romantic love which insists on asserting itself in the face of all obstacles. Romantic love is melancholic because, as obstacle love, it feeds on unfreedom. In Romantic love, loss is 'always already' installed within. Larra's 1834 historical novel *El doncel de don Enrique el Doliente: Historia caballeresca del siglo quince* (*Enrique the Sorrowful's Page: A Chivalric Tale of the Fifteenth Century*) is based on the recurrent motif '¡Es tarde! ¡Es tarde!' ('Too late! Too late!') — a lament uttered obsessively by the heroine Elvira, as previously by the ghost of the Moorish Zelindaja, to whom she is thereby linked.

The fatality at the heart of Romantic love can be seen as a model of the liberal social contract, by which the individual freely opts to relinquish freedom in the name of the collective good — freedom can be exercised positively only by installing unfreedom within it. Similarly, Romantic love recognizes no limitations (especially not limitations deriving from birthright) and yet defines itself as a form of 'captivity' or 'enslavement'. The crucial point is that the lovers *choose* their enslavement to each other; they may refer to it as their 'destiny' but they stick to it against all odds, refusing the easier options offered to them. Benedict Anderson has famously observed that nationalism replaces religion by offering the nation as a secular form of destiny (1983: 9): the social contract, like Romantic love, is a kind of *amor fati* which constructs subjectivity as the interiority of a subject who freely chooses subjection to something beyond the self. The social contract and Romantic love both limit the self and break it open, in the process of affirming it. This contradictory configuration — which I would call a 'border subjectivity' — allows the voluntary choice of death to be seen as the highest form of love — a sacrificial ethos that, while justifying the suicides that populate Romantic writing, comes dangerously close to the Christianity that those Romantics who were political liberals were combating in the name of a secular humanism. This dangerous confluence between Romanticism and Christianity, permitted by the exaltation of sacrificial love, would in mid- to late nineteenth-century Spain, as Álvarez Junco has shown, allow die-hard traditionalists to co-opt the originally liberal doctrine of nationalism, in the form of the new political phenomenon of national-Catholicism. Romantic love, by contrast, has a combative quality, allowing it to stand for political rebellion by signifying individual free choice in a world still determined largely by birthright: hence the Romantic idealization of the medieval courtly lover of humble birth who aspires to the love of a noble lady. When, from the mid-nineteenth century in Spain, capitalist modernization started to make the self-made man a viable possibility, no longer beset by insurmountable obstacles, Romantic love would lose its political force and would degenerate into a form of nostalgia. ⌐Romantic love is a transitional phenomenon that rejects absolutism but is not yet fully bourgeois. Its sense of the openness of borders and precariousness of the self installs melancholy within its affirmation of freedom.⌐This combination of rebellion and melancholy is central to the construction of medieval Spain as a 'border society' in the Romantic works I shall discuss.⌐

To appreciate these works, it is necessary to outline the revival of Arabic studies in late eighteenth- and early nineteenth-century Spain. I will not mention here the parallel, though less extensive, revival of Hebrew studies since I will not be discussing the representation of Spanish Jews in Romantic literature, where they are almost always — it has to be recognized — cardboard villains. The reason for the discrepancy between the literary treatment of Arabs and Jews is made clear in mid-nineteenth-century Spanish histories of the Jews, which insist on their diasporic condition (Rivière Gómez 2000: 646); consequently the Jews could not be seen as a nation in the modern sense of a nation state. Thus, unlike the Arabs who *had* formed a nation state in the Peninsula, they could not serve as a model for nation building. Aurora Rivière Gómez (2000: 21, 31–32) stresses that Spanish Orientalism differed from that of other European countries, where it was largely tied to colonial expansion, since in Spain the study of the Arabic intellectual tradition meant the study of the country's own national past for the purposes of nation formation. There was, however, a link to imperialism, since the state sponsorship of Arabic studies from the mid-eighteenth century coincided with Carlos III's and Godoy's political interest in Morocco (Monroe 1970: 60–61). Rivière Gómez insists, however, that it was only with the 1859–60 'Guerra de Africa' that the study of Arabic started to be used to construct the Arab world as Spain's negative 'other' (2000: 91–106). Álvarez Junco notes that it was around 1860 that the term 'race' — which had entered Spanish political vocabulary in the Romantic period — started to figure prominently in Western public discourse (2001: 394). As Monroe observes (1970: 82–83), the co-option of Arabic studies by a new national-Catholicism in the second half of the nineteenth century marked a return to the intolerance that had characterized the discipline — virtually dormant — prior to the mid-eighteenth century, when it had been in the hands of the Church. The mid-eighteenth century saw the start of a new secularized approach to Spain's Arab past with the change to state sponsorship, the postholders at this stage being liberal priests. The early nineteenth century saw a decisive shift with the emergence of secular, liberal scholars, and the institutional separation of Arabic studies from Theology, as new Humanities-based academic posts were created in state and secular institutions. The Universidad de Madrid created a Chair of Arabic in 1843. Its occupant, Pascual de Gayangos, had previously held the new Chair of Arabic created at the Madrid Ateneo in 1836, where he was succeeded in 1837 by his close friend and fellow Arabic scholar, the *costumbrista* writer Estébanez Calderón (Monroe 1970: 71; Manzanares de Cirre 1971: 108–09)

   I do not have space here to detail the scholars who, in the mid-eighteenth century, with state patronage, laid the foundations of a new brand of Arabic scholarship conceived on Enlightenment lines, or the considerable number of literary works set in Arab Spain produced in the late eighteenth century, except to note that the process began in 1735, with four Chairs of Arabic created between 1750 and 1786 (Rivière Gómez 2000: 30–31, 56–57). Monroe notes that Jovellanos looked to Spanish Arabic treatises on agriculture as more useful for his reform programme than contemporary English and French economic writings, including those of Adam Smith (1970: 44). This secularization of Arabic studies coincided with the rise of anthropology as a key Enlightenment discipline, concerned with the classification of cultures in evolutionary terms. This produced a concern to map the contours and origins of European civilization, now seen primarily in cultural rather than religious terms. This secularizing impulse is reflected in the Spanish Romantic representation of Arab Spain, which makes relatively little reference to Islam, the stress being on cultural difference. Study of Europe's defining 'others' was fundamental to the Enlightenment anthropological project, and Spanish scholars realized they had a golden opportunity to overcome Spain's 'black legend' by arguing that the splendours of Spain's medieval Arabic and Jewish heritage outshone the cultural achievements of the rest of Europe at the time — indeed, that medieval scholars had travelled from all over Europe to benefit from Arabic and Jewish philosophy and scientific knowledge. The suggestion that the twelfth-century Provençal courtly love lyric derived from Hispano-Arabic poetry transmitted to France via Castile, first mooted by a late sixteenth-century Italian scholar, was picked up by a number of Spanish Jesuits who settled in Italy after Carlos III's expulsion of the Jesuits, leading to a lively debate in the 1780s which crossed back into Spain (Monroe 1970: 39–44). As Monroe notes, this debate 'for the first time focused attention on Arab Spain as an essential element in the development of [...] European culture' (1970: 44). The point of this thesis of the Arab origins of European courtly love — as it would be again when it was revived by early twentieth-century Spanish Arabists (Monroe 1970: 154, 163–66) — was not to undermine the Europeanness of European culture, but to stake a claim to Spain's key role in the development of what was seen as the founding moment of European civilization.

One of the Spanish liberals who went into exile in 1813 was the Arabist José Antonio Conde, director of the Escorial library, which contained the largest collection of Arabic manuscripts in Spain. Condé's *Historia de la dominación de los árabes en España* (*History of Arab Rule in Spain*), published posthumously in 1820–21, is the source most cited by Rivas in his footnotes to *El moro expósito*. Conde, like other Spanish Arabists after him, distinguished between the superior civilization of Arab Spain, and the degenerate versions found in North Africa and the Middle East (Monroe 1970: 52). In Spanish Romantic texts, too, North African Muslims are vengeful fanatics, by comparison with the cultured, tolerant Arabs of the Peninsula. This splitting of Arab culture into 'our sort' and 'their sort' would permit the involvement of Hispano-Arabic enthusiasts in the mid-century colonial project in North Africa without contradiction.

Arabic studies were especially strong among the liberal exiles in London, where José Joaquín de Mora — who later wrote the liberal constitution in Chile (Monroe 1970: 59) — published his *Cuadros de la historia de los árabes, desde Mahoma hasta la conquista de Granada* (*Scenes from the History of the Arabs, from Mohammed to the Conquest of Granada*) in 1826. The previously mentioned Pascual de Gayangos, who would in the 1840s become Spain's leading Arabist and an internationally recognized scholar, also lived for many years in London, having trained in Arabic in Paris. On returning to Spain in 1828, he studied Arabic, together with Estébanez Calderón, with the Jesuit scholar Artigas, until the latter was murdered in the large-scale massacre of priests in 1843 (Monroe 1970: 67; Manzanares de Cirre 1971: 105–07). The strength of anti-clerical feeling in early and mid-nineteenth-century Spain should not be forgotten — the state nationalizations of Church property started in 1835, roughly coinciding with the Romantic texts I shall discuss.

Gayangos's studies in the late 1830s and 1840s stressed the debt of Spanish medieval literature to Arabic sources, and he was responsible for making known the existence of the hybrid Arabic-Spanish *aljamiado* texts (written in Castilian but using Arabic script) and *muwashashahat* (written in Classical Arabic with a Castilian or Vulgar Arabic *kharja* at the end). The latter became central to the hypothesis of the Arabic origins of the Provençal lyric (Monroe 1970: 71–72, 75). The *costumbrista* writer Estébanez Calderón was also an expert on *aljamiado* texts (Manzanares de Cirre 1971: 107, 115). Though Estébanez Calderón had joined the liberal political exodus in 1824, his various stories and novellas set in Arab Spain, published from 1837 to 1847, have none of the romantic rebelliousness of the texts that interest me but are cosy nostalgia or fantasy pieces, akin to those that Zorrilla would also write in the 1840s, confirming the conservative drift of both Romanticism and liberal politics in the mid-century. As is well known, Estébanez Calderón would, in the mid-century, be the political patron of his nephew, Antonio Cánovas del Castillo, who would become the conservative architect of the Restoration period which, from 1875, undid many of the liberal reforms of the 1868 Revolution. In the context of this drift to the right in the mid-century, we may note that, as early as 1831–36, Gayangos was employed by the Ministry of State to translate official correspondence with Morocco and the wider Arab world (Rivière Gómez 2000: 68); and that, in 1844, his friend and fellow Arabist Estébanez Calderón would publish a *Manual del oficial en Marruecos* (*Manual for Officers in Morocco*) (Manzanares de Cirre 1971: 117).

Turning now to my three Romantic texts: Martínez de la Rosa's historical drama, *Aben Humeya o la rebelión de los moriscos*, was — by a felicitous coincidence — premièred in Paris the week that the 1830 July Revolution broke out, allowing its Morisco rebels against the despotism of Felipe II to achieve acclaim as prototypes of the liberal struggle against absolutism (Sarrailh in Martínez de la Rosa 1972: 121–22). Throughout, the Moriscos are referred to as a 'nación', raising the question of how a 'nation' in the pre-modern sense of an ethnic group relates to the 'nation' in the modern sense of the nation state. Carolyn Boyd (1997: 65) has noted that the modern sense of the term 'nation', which triumphed generally in the West by the mid-nineteenth century, did not enter the *Diccionario de la Real Academia Española* (*Dictionary of the Spanish Royal Academy*) until its 1884 edition. However, Martínez de la Rosa's prologue shows that the old sense of the term as an ethnic group is already starting to take on its modern sense of a nation state, causing confusion in the process: 'De repente, como por encanto, vióse aparecer una nación muslímica en medio de una nación cristiana' ('Suddenly, as if by magic, a Muslim nation appeared in the midst of a Christian nation'; 1972: 132). The play charts the tragic overthrow and murder of the cultured, tolerant Morisco leader Aben Humeya by fanatical rivals, backed by North Africa. Aben Humeya is a neo-classical rather than Romantic hero, since he is torn between duty to his family (the need to avoid violence) and duty to his 'nation' (the need to defend them against the drastic new cultural restrictions imposed by the central Spanish state), compounded by the conflict between his love for his wife Zulema and his obligation to eliminate her father, wrongly accused by his fanatical rivals of treason. One of the major political effects of Romanticism would be its alignment of individual and political sentiment, since it conceives both as the rebellion of the individual against authority. Aben Humeya's wife Zulema is, however, a Romantic heroine, plagued by melancholy, against which Aben Humeya also has to fight — a melancholy arising from the loss of their former 'patria'. The play seems to be arguing for a tolerant, multicultural model of the nation, represented by Aben Humeya and betrayed equally by Felipe II and the North African backed Muslim fanatics. The Moriscos are portrayed as a border society in the sense of one with a double identity, exemplified by their dual names: the text refers to its Morisco protagonist and his wife and daughter as Aben Humeya, Zulema and Fátima, but they address each other as don Fernando, doña Leonor and Elvira. The play's elegiac lament for the tragic outcome of the Morisco

Revolt invites the early nineteenth-century audience to identify with the Moriscos' melancholy, recognizing the loss at the heart of the nation's enforced homogenization. It is worth mentioning that Martínez de la Rosa's most famous play, *La conjuración de Venecia* (published in French in 1830 during his exile), is an anti-Inquisition drama. It was first performed in 1835, the year that he became Spanish Prime Minister. By the time of *Aben Humeya*'s Madrid performance in 1836, Martínez de la Rosa had been forced to resign, though he continued to head the Moderate Party, drifting increasingly to the right. Between 1837 and 1846 he would publish the three volumes of his historical novel *Doña Isabel de Solís, reina de Granada* (*Isabel de Solís, Queen of Granada*), about the Christian wife of the penultimate King of Granada, whose foreword describes it as triggered by melancholy (Mayberry and Mayberry 1988: 95).

Hartzenbusch's 1837 *Los amantes de Teruel* uses Arab Spain in a more stereotypically Orientalist way, to define an 'other' against which the Aragonese Romantic hero and heroine are measured.[3] Of humble origins himself, Hartzenbusch is concerned with the self-making of his hero Marsilla, given a deadline of five years to get rich and return to claim the hand of his beloved, Isabel, the daughter of a wealthy *hidalgo* (squire). Set in the early thirteenth century, the play starts in the Arab kingdom of Valencia, where Marsilla is held captive. We do not see the King of Valencia, whom Marsilla saves from a conspiracy and who reciprocates by granting him freedom and wealth, but only the Sultana Zulima, an Orientalist tigress, involved in the conspiracy against her husband, who spends the rest of the play (cross-dressed as an Aragonese nobleman) vengefully ensuring that Marsilla, who had refused her adulterous advances, does not get to the church in time to marry Isabel. Arab Spain is thus constructed as a fabulously wealthy realm which has to be left behind, where men are loyal across religious divides, but where women are treacherous predators with a masculine appetite for sex and power. The melancholy here belongs to Isabel and Marsilla, prevented from consummating their love since he finally makes it home a few hours after the deadline to discover her father has married her to another man, precipitating their *Liebestod*. Marsilla's manliness and Isabel's womanly submission need the negative image of Zulima to affirm themselves. But, although the play sets up moral frontiers between Arab and Christian Spain, these are not absolute, as the Valencian King's loyal courtier Adel does his best throughout to aid Marsilla. The model of the nation being worked out here is that of an incipient bourgeois society based on the self-made man, where riches (gained in the Orient) are legitimized by being placed at the service of a superior, purely Christian model of love as sacrifice of the self.

Rivas's early tragedy *Aliatar* (1816) gives an even more negative view of Arab culture, with its lustful and barbaric Arab hero who takes his revenge on his luckless female Christian captive. Both Hartzenbusch and Rivas would contribute to the *Romancero de la Guerra de África* (*Ballad Book of the African War*), which celebrated the Spanish Army's Moroccan exploits in 1859–60. But in his 700-page narrative poem *El moro expósito*, published in 1834, Rivas created a highly complex and remarkably radical cultural scenario. The first five of the poem's twelve ballads (comprising

---

3   The play dramatizes a popular legend which may derive from a lost medieval romance. See Guardiola (1988).

Part I) are set in tenth-century Córdoba when the city was still the capital of a very substantial united Muslim kingdom at the height of its cultural achievements. Rivas apostrophizes the city (his birthplace) from exile at the start of Part I, as we are introduced to its glories, and again at the start of Part II, as we leave Córdoba for Castile with the protagonist Mudarra. This invites the reader to empathize with Mudarra's border-crossing to Castile, constructed as a journey of loss. The poem is, in fact, full of multiple border-crossings, in both directions, by a whole range of characters. The last seven ballads, comprising Part II, are set in a Christian Burgos that is explicitly described as barbaric and primitive, in which noblemen can barely read and the peasants are exploited by the clergy and tyrannical feudal lords, and ruled entirely by war (presented as heroic when against the Moors, but destructive when directed again fellow Christians) (Rivas 1982: II, 10–11). When Mudarra reaches Burgos, shocked by its poverty and backwardness, the narrator describes it as 'un Estado naciente' ('a nascent state'), by contrast with Córdoba, described as 'un imperio ilustrado' and 'grande nación' ('a cultivated empire', 'great nation'), whose power is about to wane (II, 12). For the monocultural, intolerant Castile has the makings of a modern nation state, unlike the pluri-ethnic Córdoba. The 'ignorancia' and 'rudeza' ('brutishness') of Castile (I, 149) contrast vividly with the superior education in both philosophy and war that is given to the hero Mudarra in Córdoba by his wise and generous tutor Zaide, not to mention the education in both philosophy and the sciences that is given to the heroine Kerima by Averroes. Indeed it will be her 'ciencia' ('knowledge') and 'amor' (II, 311) — in that order — that save Mudarra's life at the end, as, arriving in Burgos cross-dressed as a man, she applies her medical skills to his wounded body after he wins the jousting tournament against the Castilian traitor Ruy-González. Rivas distributes his traitors symmetrically between the two cultures: Ruy-González, together with Kerima's father Giafar, is responsible for the horrendous crime that Mudarra is avenging: the serving up to Mudarra's Castilian father, the Señor de Lara, of the heads of his seven sons who are Mudarra's step-brothers (the Infantes de Lara whose story was chronicled in Alfonso X's thirteenth-century *Estoria de España* [*History of Spain*]).[4]

The poem revolves around the Romantic trope of mysterious origins, necessary for the hero to prove his worth on his own terms. Mudarra and the reader are ignorant of his origins until the end of Ballad 4, and even after that he continues to be called 'el Expósito' or 'el Huérfano' ('the Foundling', 'the Orphan'). A sign of the racial instability in the text is the fact that, despite its title *El moro expósito*, Rivas refers to the poem in its English-language dedication to a British diplomat friend as 'my *Castilian foundling*' (I, 5; emphasis in the original). Mudarra does, in fact, turn out to be of mixed race: the illegitimate son of the Señor de Lara and the sister of the Arab ruler Almanzor, conceived during his father's captivity in Córdoba at a time when the city, in the benevolent Almanzor's absence, was under the control of its tyrannical governor, Giafar. We know from the start that Kerima is the mixed-race offspring of rape: that of the humble mozarabic — i.e. Christian — Gala by Giafar, who took her to his palace as a captive. Gala having died in childbirth, and

4   The evidence that this story derives from a lost epic is accepted by many scholars. See Menéndez Pidal (1971).

Giafar having no other surviving children, Kerima is brought up as his heir. The inverted symmetries are perfect: Mudarra as the illegitimate love child, conceived in a dungeon, of Christian father and Arab mother; Kerima as the now loved offspring of a violent encounter between Arab father and Christian mother. They are clearly meant for each other. Additionally, both mirror each other's androgynous qualities: both weep copiously and faint easily; both, in addition to being highly educated, are rebels (Kerima — unlike Isabel in Hartzenbusch's play — rebels against her father, 'el bárbaro Giafar', when he tries to marry her to a North African prince; consorting with North African princes is always in these texts a sign of barbarism). Kerima's charitableness likens her to Mudarra's mother Zahira (who died before being able to tell him she was his real rather than adoptive mother): the devotion of both Kerima and Mudarra to her grave brings them together and will bind them throughout. For both, as a result of the loss installed at their origins (Kerima never knew her mother; Mudarra grew up not knowing who his parents were), are marked by melancholy.

Given the obstacles that separate them as Romantic lovers (especially after Mudarra unknowingly kills Kerima's father, Giafar, and leaves for Burgos to avenge his newly revealed father), both devote a great deal of time to remembering the past. Their subjectivity is thus constructed as being subject to a past that is lost. In Mudarra's case, his objective becomes reparation for that loss, which he achieves by killing both traitors and restoring his father's honour, though he cannot restore his father's lost sight. The horrendous misfortunes suffered by the Señor de Lara, externalized in his Gothic ruined castle, serve to construct the poem's major Castilian figure as also ennobled by melancholy, thus avoiding a clear-cut opposition between superior Arab sensibility and brutish Castilian barbarism. Conversely, the poem's surprise ending pulls back from rescuing Mudarra and Kerima from their Muslim melancholy just at the moment when they seem to have been installed in a Christian happy end. With both of them baptized as Christians and about to exchange their wedding vows in Burgos Cathedral, Kerima refuses to go ahead with the marriage on the grounds that she cannot marry her father's murderer, opting instead for life in a convent. The preceding pages have explicitly denounced the 'ciego fanatismo' ('blind fanaticism'; II, 332) of Kerima's Christian slave María, into whose arms she falls at the end, and who has been working on converting her mistress since the end of Part I. After her conversion, Kerima is described as if she were a living corpse (II, 344) — paralleling the Señor de Lara's earlier description of himself as a 'frío cadáver' ('cold corpse'; I, 47) when imprisoned in Muslim Córdoba. It is impossible to read Kerima's renunciation as an edifying Christian end. Perversely, her over-successful conversion has induced her to reject a noble, now Christianized lover, in order to honour a treacherous Muslim father. The effect created by this unexpected ending is to re-install loss in what would otherwise be a concluding celebration of Christian cultural homogenization. The bathetic final reminder that Mudarra must later have married someone else since the chronicles record his descendants is a Byronic cynical note, which serves to construct domesticity as decidedly unheroic: this further strips the ending of any Christian triumphalism. Indeed, even after their baptism, Kerima and Mudarra continue to be called by their Muslim names by the poem's narrator. The poem also contains a massive satire of the greed and gluttony of the abbot who persuades the Christian villain, Ruy-González, to bequeath all his worldly goods to his monastery in exchange for absolving him of his crimes.

The poem's penultimate section preceding the final abortive wedding scene focuses on tombs. First, Mudarra's loyal tutor Zaide returns to Córdoba, charged by Mudarra with tending the grave of his Muslim mother, Zahira. Then, in a macabre scene typical of Romanticism, the heads of the Siete Infantes de Lara, which Mudarra had brought with him from Córdoba to Burgos, are given a Christian burial in the Cathedral. Shortly before, we have been told how, before bringing Kerima to Burgos, her mozarabic grandfather had returned from his wanderings in the Holy Land to his 'patria', Córdoba, to dig up the body of his violated daughter (Kerima's mother) and rebury her in a Christian grave. Unburied or improperly buried Christian bodies are being laid to rest; but the Muslim dead are also honoured: the whole poem is held together by Zahira's grave, representing the loss of the mother, and also the loss of Muslim Spain that is the price Mudarra has to pay for claiming his Christian inheritance. '[C]uánta memoria amarga' ('So many bitter memories'; I, 259), the narrator exclaims as Kerima returns to Zahira's grave at the end of Part I, on Mudarra's departure for Castile. These bitter memories are incarnated in the phantoms that beset the characters throughout, for the poem is the melancholy story of a haunting that no amount of 'proper' burial can cure. The mourning of the dead is not sufficient to allow Mudarra and Kerima happiness.

In his article 'Arabs, Jews, and the Enigma of Spanish Imperial Melancholy', Bartra frames his discussion in the context of the current historical amnesia in contemporary Spain that many have lamented, as (in Bartra's words) '[t]he end of Francoism and the reign of the socialists finished burying the melancholic past' (2000: 71). One of the problems of modernity is that its insistence on the need to break with the past in the name of progress caused historical memory to come to be seen as a form of traditionalism. Perhaps we should have another look at that early moment in modernity when melancholy — before it turned into nostalgia in the course of the 1840s — provided a way of opening oneself to the losses incurred in the past in order to propose an alternative to the present. Perhaps it could be argued that Romantic melancholy is a tragic vision not so much because its heroes and heroines are doomed to failure as because it keeps alive the hurt of the past as a motivating force — a Gothic haunting — unlike nostalgia which strips the past of pain, and in so doing constructs it as dead and gone for ever.

Works Cited

ÁLVAREZ JUNCO, JOSÉ. 2001. *Mater Dolorosa: La idea de España en el siglo XIX* (Madrid: Taurus)

ANDERSON, BENEDICT. 1983. *Imagined Communities: Reflections on the Origin and Spread of Nationalism* (London: Verso)

BARTRA, ROGER. 2000. 'Arabs, Jews, and the Enigma of Spanish Imperial Melancholy', *Discourse*, 22.3: 64–72

——. 2001. *Cultura y melancolía: Las enfermedades del alma en la España del siglo de oro* (Barcelona: Anagrama)

BOASE, ROGER. 1977. *The Origin and Meaning of Courtly Love: A Critical Study of European Scholarship* (Manchester: Manchester University Press)

BOYD, CAROLYN. 1997. *Historia Patria: Politics and National Identity in Spain, 1875–1975* (Princeton, NJ: Princeton University Press)

CIRUJANO, PALOMA, TERESA ELORRIAGA PLANES and JUAN SISINIO PÉREZ GARZÓN. 1985. *Historiografía y nacionalismo español (1834–1868)* (Madrid: Centro de Estudios Históricos, CSIC)

ESPRONCEDA, JOSÉ. 1966. *Articles et discours oubliés: La Bibliothèque d'Espronceda (d'après un document inédit)*, ed. by Robert Marrast (Paris: Presses Universitaires de France)

ESTÉBANEZ CALDERÓN, SERAFÍN. 1893. *Novelas, cuentos y artículos* (Madrid: Est. Tipográfico Sucesores de Rivadeneyra)

FREUD, SIGMUND. 1984. 'Mourning and Melancholia', in The Penguin Freud Library, II: *On Metapsychology: The Theory of Psychoanalysis* (London: Penguin), pp. 251–68

GIDDENS, ANTHONY. 1985. *The Nation-State and Violence* (Cambridge: Polity)

GUARDIOLA, CONRADO. 1988. *La verdad actual sobre los amantes de Teruel: Orientación crítica de los estudios amantísticos* (Teruel: Instituto de Etudios Turolenses)

HARTZENBUSCH, JUAN EUGENIO. 1989. *Los amantes de Teruel*, ed. by Carmen Aranzo, 4th edn (Madrid: Cátedra)

HOBSBAWM, E. J. 1990. *Nations and Nationalism since 1780: Programme, Myth, Reality* (Cambridge: Cambridge University Press)

LABANYI, JO. 2000. *Gender and Modernization in the Spanish Realist Novel* (Oxford: Oxford University Press)

LARRA, MARIANO JOSÉ DE. 1984. *El doncel de don Enrique, el Doliente. Macías*, ed. by Arturo Souto (Mexico: Porrúa)

MANZANARES DE CIRRE, MANUELA. 1971. *Arabistas españoles del siglo XIX* (Madrid: Instituto Hispano Árabe de Cultura)

MARTÍNEZ DE LA ROSA, FRANCISCO. 1972. *Obras dramáticas: La viuda de Padilla, Abén Humeya y La conjuración de Venecia*, ed. by Jean Sarrailh (Madrid: Espasa-Calpe)

MAYBERRY, ROBERT, and NANCY MAYBERRY. 1988. *Francisco Martínez de la Rosa* (Boston, MA: Twayne)

MENÉNDEZ PIDAL, RAMÓN. 1971. *La leyenda de los infantes de Lara*, 3rd rev. edn (Madrid: Espasa-Calpe)

MONROE, JAMES T. 1970. *Islam and the Arabs in Spanish Scholarship (Sixteenth Century to the Present)* (Leiden: E. J. Brill)

PASSERINI, LUISA. 1999. *Europe in Love, Love in Europe: Imagination and Politics in Britain between the Wars* (London: I. B. Tauris)

PÉREZ GARZÓN, JUAN SISINIO, EDUARDO MANZANO MORENO and AURORA RIVIÈRE GÓMEZ. 2000. *La gestión de la memoria: La historia de España al servicio del poder* (Barcelona: Crítica)

RIVAS, DUQUE DE (Ángel Saavedra). 1982. *El moro expósito*, ed. by Ángel Crespo, 2 vols (Madrid: Espasa-Calpe)

——. 1989 *Aliatar*, ed. by Manuel Ruiz Lagos (Seville: Editoriales Andaluzas Unidas)

RIVIÈRE GÓMEZ, AURORA. 2000. *Orientalismo y nacionalismo español: Estudios árabes y hebreos en la Universidad de Madrid (1843–1868)*, Biblioteca del Instituto Antonio de Nebrija de Estudios sobre la Universidad (Madrid: Universidad Carlos III)

ZORRILLA, JOSÉ. 1895. *Granada (Poema)*, 2 vols (Madrid: Imprenta y Tipografía de los Huérfanos)

—— 1946. *Antología de poesías líricas* (Buenos Aires: Espasa-Calpe Argentina)

—— 2000. *Leyendas*, ed. by Salvador García Castañeda (Madrid: Cátedra)

CHAPTER 2

Liberal Individualism and the Fear of the Feminine in Spanish Romantic Drama

Romanticism — in Spain and elsewhere — has long been seen as the literary expression of liberalism. Even Derek Flitter, who argues that Spanish Romanticism was largely traditionalist, concedes that the works of 1834–37 were exceptional in their liberal militancy (1992: 5–49, 184). In this essay I shall examine the ways in which four major Spanish Romantic plays first staged during those years — *La conjuración de Venecia* (*The Venice Conspiracy*, 1834) by Francisco Martínez de la Rosa, *Don Álvaro o la fuerza del sino* (*Don Álvaro or the Force of Fate*, 1835) by the Duque de Rivas, *El trovador* (*The Troubador*, 1836) by Antonio García Gutiérrez, and *Los amantes de Teruel* (*The Lovers of Teruel*, 1837) by Juan Eugenio Hartzenbusch — dramatize the contradictions inherent in liberal individualism. In particular I wish to show how the latter cannot be understood without reference to gender. Martínez de la Rosa and Rivas, both prominent liberal statesmen, had firsthand knowledge of Britain and France as political *émigrés*; it was in those countries that liberal political theory was developed.[1] Hartzenbusch and García Gutiérrez were not active in liberal politics and were too young to have gone into exile in 1814–20 and 1823–34 (being born in 1806 and 1813 respectively). But their plays show an

---

1   Martínez de la Rosa spent 1810–11 in London negotiating arms shipments for the Spanish Independence struggle and lived in exile in France from 1823 to 1831 (and again 1840–43). His political writings are based on the writings of Burke and Bentham: the latter, whom he met, was consulted by Spanish liberals over the drafting of the 1812 Cadiz Constitution. Martínez de la Rosa was parliamentary deputy for Granada 1812–14 and 1820–22, when he was appointed Prime Minister until exiled the following year. He was again Prime Minister 1833–35, and leader of the Moderate Party 1837–39. He subsequently served as Ambassador in Paris, Foreign Minister, Ambassador in Rome, President of Congress, and on his death in 1862 was President of the Council of State. Rivas fought in Wellington's army during the War of Independence, and lived in exile in London 1824–25, in British-controlled Malta 1825–30, and in France 1830–34. He was parliamentary deputy for Córdoba 1822–23, and in 1836 briefly served as Minister of the Interior. He would go on to serve as Senator for Córdoba, Ambassador in Naples, Prime Minister (briefly in 1854), and Ambassador in Paris. He resigned the post of President of the Council of State in 1864, a year before his death. Biographical information is given in Navas Ruiz 1982. For Spanish liberals' contacts with Britain see Llorens, who reminds us that the word 'liberal' was first used in its political sense in Cadiz in 1811, from there passing to England and France (1968: 13).

identical understanding of the construction of the individual subject, for liberal political theory was predicated on new models of the family and of sexual difference which became commonly accepted by the European bourgeoisie in the course of the eighteenth and nineteenth centuries. I am not concerned here with the writers' personal experience of family life, but with fantasies of the family that allowed the concept of the individual subject to emerge.

In a discussion which foreshadows many of the points made here, Stephen Hart persuasively reads the plots of Spanish Romantic plays as enactments of the Lacanian concept of the Name-of-the-Father, noting that the confrontation of the hero with his lover's father leads to the enforcement of paternal authority (1992: 11–12). Hart also notes that the father's tyranny is directed mainly against the daughter (1992: 8–9). In this essay I shall examine the four above-mentioned plays from a psychoanalytic perspective that is in disagreement with Lacanian theory, namely, the feminist critiques of ego psychology outlined by Nancy Chodorow in *The Reproduction of Mothering* (1978) and *Feminism and Psychoanalytic Theory* (1989) and developed by Jessica Benjamin in *The Bonds of Love* (1990).[2] I hope to build on Hart's perception that Spanish Romantic plays dramatize the oedipal scenario by arguing, with Chodorow and Benjamin, that any discussion of the latter must include not only father and son but also mother and daughter. The application to Romantic drama of oedipal theory is not fortuitous for, when Freud elaborated his final version of the Oedipus complex in which the sons overthrow the Father of the Primal Horde to institute a regime based on fraternal rights, he was describing the ideals of the French Revolution: liberty, equality, fraternity. The self that emerges from the Freudian oedipal trajectory is that of the autonomous individual posited by liberal political theory. The relevance of the Oedipus story to their own concerns did not escape Spanish Romantic playwrights and their contemporaries: Martínez de la Rosa wrote an *Edipo* during his exile in France just before writing *La conjuración de Venecia*, and Rivas's *Don Álvaro* was known to his friends as 'el *Edipo* del cristianismo' ('the Christian Oedipus').[3]

In her book *The Sexual Contract* (1988), Carole Pateman shows how liberal political theory arises out of the division between the public and private spheres first made by Locke in the late seventeenth century. Arguing against prevailing patriarchal theory, which maintained that both state and family were governed by paternal right transmitted by kinship, Locke claimed that this natural law applied only in the private sphere, and that the public sphere was subject to the law of contract. However, only free individuals could make legally binding contracts, and to be a free individual one had to be a property owner and thus one's own 'master'. The gender-specific term is not fortuitous, for women were legally defined as dependants and enjoyed limited property rights; as a result, only men had the right to make contracts that allowed entry into the public sphere. Liberal contract

2   Although published in 1989, Chodorov's *Feminism and Psychoanalytic Theory* consists of essays that appeared in article form before Benjamin's *The Bonds of Love*, first published in 1988.

3   See Sarrailh's introduction to Martinez de la Rosa 1972: xxv and Sánchez's edition of *Don Álvaro* (Rivas 1986: 27).

theory replaces patriarchal theory, but it reinforces patriarchy by confining women to the family. This ideological shift coincides with the beginnings of capitalist development, which takes away from the household its former economic function as a unit of production, creating a further split according to which production takes place in the public sphere, while the private sphere is reserved for the natural process of reproduction. The wife's role becomes limited to motherhood. The end of the household as a productive unit also means that the term 'family', which previously included all those involved in domestic output whether related by blood or not, now comes to refer to the minimum kinship unit of husband, wife and children. In the mid-eighteenth century, Rousseau modified this scheme, suggesting that the family, like the state, was governed by social contract: in this case, the marriage contract. But his notion of social contract as an improvement on nature confirmed the equation of the family with child-rearing: the difference for Rousseau was that women needed to be taught to fulfil their 'natural' duties as mothers.[4] The conceptual model of the family dominant by the end of the eighteenth century supposes that children will be brought up by one woman, their mother; and that the father's role is outside the family in the public sphere.

It is not necessary to prove that such family arrangements had become the norm in Spain by the 1830s; indeed, the greater the gap between theory and practice, the greater the insistence on the model is likely to be. Lilian Furst notes that the English Romantics laid less stress on individualism than their French counterparts, for they came from a political and religious tradition which took individualism for granted (1979: 60). Susan Kirkpatrick has suggested that the instability of the individual subject shown in *Don Álvaro* is a sign of Spain's lack of a Protestant individualist tradition (1989: 118). It seems logical to suppose that Spanish Romantic playwrights dramatize the individual's relation to the family unit so explicitly precisely because liberal values were not yet firmly established in Spain.

Ausencia de liberalismo

Raymond Williams notes that the term 'individual' (from the Latin *individuus* meaning 'indivisible') was first used to mean a single member of a species by Locke, and that it acquired the meaning of separateness from others only in the late eighteenth century; the term 'individualism' is an early nineteenth-century coinage (1990: 161–65). Liberal political theory equates selfhood with individuality in the sense of separateness. Chodorow (1989) and Benjamin (1990) argue that the modern Western concept of the individual born in the Romantic period is, in effect, that of the son who separates from the mother.[5] Such 'individuation' (to use the psychoanalytic term) is made desirable, even necessary, by the nuclear family in

4   Pateman notes that Freud writes his own version of social contract theory (1988: 12). For an excellent account of earlier concepts of the family as a unit of production, with frequent reference to Spain, see Casey 1989.

5   Chodorow and Benjamin have been accused of giving an essentialist account of mother–child relations. Although Chodorow regards mothering as some kind as a universal phenomenon, she makes it clear that the particular model of the family she is using is historically specific (1989: 4–5, 32, 53, 57). Benjamin is less clear on this point but notes that the individualism that she finds a problem is specific to modern culture (1990: 25). It is as a description of the nuclear family that becomes dominant at the end of the eighteenth century that I read their theories. For a summary of the arguments against Chodorow and Benjamin, see McNay 1992: 92–97.

which the child is reared exclusively by the mother, who thus appears to the child to be all-powerful and stifling. Freudian theory posits an initial oneness of the child with the mother; Chodorow suggests that Freud was here himself responding to fantasies of maternal omnipotence encouraged by a family structure in which mothers have sole responsibility for parenting. She also notes that Lacan perpetuates such fantasies with his notion that the child's entry into the Symbolic order through the agency of language (the Name-of-the-Father) marks its exit from an initial pre-linguistic undifferentiation represented by the mother–child dyad. For both Freud and Lacan, the Oedipus complex rescues the child from this lack of differentiation through the intervention of the father, who breaks the child's primary identification with the mother. The oedipal incest taboo declares sameness, associated with the feminine, to be a threat; and equates the self with difference in the guise of the father, whose role outside the home makes him an image of separateness. If the child is male, he will go on to assume the father's role as an individualized subject. There is, of course, a catch here, as Freud and Lacan acknowledge: by identifying with the father, the son internalizes paternal law and undermines the autonomy that identification with the father gave him in the first place. Freud and Lacan are mainly concerned with the father's role in the oedipal scenario, and consequently with the problem of authority; female psychoanalysts have stressed the pre-oedipal stage, where the mother's role is paramount and where the key issue is that of separation. We shall see how the two issues connect.

Chodorow's work is important for pointing out that Freudian oedipal theory equates individuation with rejection of the mother and consequently of the feminine. The logic of Freud's notion of primary unity with the mother is that both sexes originally identify with the feminine or, as Chodorow puts it are 'matrisexual'. Since, for Freud, individuation consists in the assumption of sexual difference this means that the boy can define his emergent masculinity only as not being like the mother. This turns upside down Freud's idea that both boys and girls start life as 'little men', and that the role of the Oedipus complex is to turn the girl away from primary masculinity. It also turns on its head the accepted notion, theorized by Simone de Beauvoir in *The Second Sex* (1972; French original 1949), that woman is defined as man's Other. Chodorow's analysis suggests that it is femininity that is primary, and masculinity that is constructed as the opposite of the feminine. As she puts it: masculinity, unlike femininity, has to be learnt. The precariousness of this negatively defined masculinity, based on not being like the mother, logically leads men to devalue activities and qualities labelled as feminine, in order to assert their own insecure sense of separate identity. This, Chodorow points out, means devaluing not only women but the primary feminine part of the male self. The modern Western concept of the autonomous individual, being based on the need to differentiate from the mother, opposes selfhood to femininity, and construes the latter as a dangerous regressive force threatening to engulf the male ego.

Girls, according to Chodorow, do not have the problem of needing to repudiate their primary gender identification in order to assume a heterosexual orientation; their problem is that of over-identifying with the mother to the point of not

achieving a separate sense of self at all. The problem for both men and women is
that our culture privileges the masculine values of independence, separateness and
differentiation, with the result that dependence, relationship and sameness are seen
as a threat to the autonomy of the self. Chodorow notes that the genuine experience
of difference involves the ability to recognize the other's subjectivity. It is only
when the sense of separate selfhood is not sufficiently strong that boundaries have
to be artificially erected and difference turned into an emotional, moral or political
imperative.

Benjamin takes up this last point of Chodorow, arguing that the oedipal model
needs to be reformulated so as to reconcile differentiation with recognition of
the other as a subject. She stresses the dangers of Freud's view of the mother as
a regressive, primitive force, pointing out that his reading of the Oedipus myth
suppresses the fact that Oedipus's father tried to kill him as a child, and projects
the negative qualities of the 'archaic, dangerous father' onto the mother (Benjamin
1990: 146). Benjamin notes that the regression to primary oneness with the feminine
that is feared by the male — what Freud called the 'oceanic feeling' or sense of
engulfment — is at the same time actively sought by him in the experience of love.
Sexual union becomes for the male an annihilation of the self that is both terrifying
and pleasurable. Benjamin quotes Bataille's contention that eroticism consists in the
violation of body boundaries in order to plunge into the 'sea of death' represented
by the loss of separateness (Benjamin 1990: 63–64).

Benjamin's main contribution is her analysis of the sado-masochistic tendencies
inherent in male–female relations, which she sees as the inevitable outcome of
our adherence to the Freudian oedipal scheme whereby selfhood is equated with
separation from the feminine. This produces a 'fault line' in both male and female
development, since the male can assert his individuality only by devaluing the
feminine, and the female can achieve subject status only by rejecting her original
same-gender identification and turning to the father; on being refused recognition
by the father (whose masculinity depends on his repudiation of femininity), the girl
is forced back to identification with the mother, now perceived through masculine
eyes as a devalued object. This, Benjamin observes, gives girls a propensity to fall
in love with idealized hero figures, through whom they can vicariously live out
their frustrated selfhood while at the same time confirming their feminine object
status. Conversely, men tend to turn the women they fall in love with into objects,
by degrading them or idealizing them.

Benjamin spends some time discussing Hegel's master–slave dialectic (elaborated
in 1806 at the time liberalism was consolidating itself as a political system), noting
that, like Freud, Hegel assumes that relations with others are a threat to individual
autonomy. As she points out, the master–slave dialectic — in which the master
denies the slave's subjectivity so as to assert his own autonomy, and the slave turns
herself into an object for the master so as to experience agency through him — is
self-defeating because they are locked in a form of bondage that denies the freedom
of both. Finally, Benjamin notes that, in the oedipal scheme, the male achieves
autonomy at the expense of a 'guilty identification' with paternal domination not just

because, as Freud and Lacan recognize, he limits his own freedom by internalizing paternal authority, but because he becomes a free subject by perpetuating a system that refuses recognition to women.

The use of masks and aliases in Spanish Romantic drama problematizes identity, as Hart notes (1992: 16–17), but at a more fundamental level it raises the issue of recognition. In particular, it relates identity to recognition of the other. Benjamin (1990: 78) observes that girls, in denying their own selfhood by identifying with a mother defined as object, learn to give recognition without receiving it. In these plays, when the hero is with the heroine, he takes his mask off, for she confers identity on him by looking at him. He adopts a mask or alias to protect himself from the gaze of other men, whose subjecthood makes them a threat to his autonomy. Kirpatrick points out that, in *Don Álvaro*, Leonor is fleeing the gaze of others (1989: 120): when a woman is looked at, she is reduced to object status. In *Los amantes de Teruel*, Isabel shuns Marsilla's gaze which confirms a negative image of her (Hartzenbusch 1989: 160). In *La conjuración de Venecia*, Laura is so terrified of being seen that she feels even the statues of the dead threaten her with their gaze (Martínez de la Rosa 1972: 269). Manrique's gaze in *El trovador* literally causes Leonor to lose consciousness (García Gutiérrez 1985: 141). At the end of *Don Álvaro*, Leonor's brother Alfonso sees only the degraded image of her he has formed in his mind. The use by Romantic playwrights of the conventions of the honour code stresses the debasement of the feminine that is the other side of the liberal concept of the autonomous individual.[6]

In a converse form of objectification, when Leonor's lover Álvaro is reunited with her in this final scene, he sees an idealized phantom: '¡Es un espectro!... ¡Imagen adorada!' ('It's a ghost!... Adored image!'; Rivas 1986: 168). When Isabel and Marsilla finally meet in *Los amantes de Teruel*, he likewise sees an idol: '¡Prenda adorada!... ¡Gloria mía!' ('Adored treasure!... My glory!'; Hartzenbusch 1989: 159). All the heroes of these plays repeatedly use the term 'angel', with its Victorian connotations of 'angel of the house', when addressing their lovers.[7] In *La conjuración de Venecia*, Rugiero explicitly says to Laura: 'tú no eres una mujer; eres un ángel' ('you're not a woman; you're an angel'; Martínez de la Rosa 1972: 277). When Laura finds Rugiero at the end of the play, her one act is to give him a portrait of herself: an objectified image (Martínez de la Rosa 1972: 335). It is in portrait form that Leonor's brother Carlos will 'recognize' her in *Don Álvaro*. The number of times the lovers see each other in these plays is extraordinarily limited, for their love is based not on recognition but on its lack. The recognition scenes that do take place are between the hero and his father (or, in *El trovador*, brother). Even in *Don Álvaro*, where the hero knows his identity from the start, it is the episode where Alfonso provides him with new information about his father that counts as the recognition scene, rather than the final encounter with Leonor, which, far from enhancing the subjecthood of either, leads to their death.

6   Kirkpatrick notes that the honour code turns Leonor in *Don Álvaro* into a 'signo degradado' (1989: 120).

7   For the use of the 'angel in the house' trope in nineteenth-century Spain, see Aldaraca 1992.

In this play and in *Los amantes de Teruel*, where the hero's identity is also known from the start, concealed identity takes the form of the cross-dressing of a female character. In *Don Álvaro* Leonor dresses as a man first when escaping from her brother Carlos, and second when she becomes a hermit wearing the Franciscan habit. Paul Johnson reminds us that strict gender differentiation in dress, with men wearing trousers and dark colours, only became standardized in Europe in the first two decades of the nineteenth century, and that it remained common for women to dress as men when travelling (1991: 457–59, 488–89). The plays discussed here, being set in earlier periods (from the thirteenth to the mid-eighteenth centuries), require costumes that would have given their heroes a feminine appearance in the eyes of the contemporary audience. By dressing as a man, Leonor visually confirms the fact that she has fled the home for the outside world. Separation from roots does not give her the autonomy it would give a man but makes her a non-being: her penance in the hermitage is described as an entombment. The cross-dressing of the Moorish Sultana Zulima in *Los amantes de Teruel* raises different issues: as an Oriental woman, she illustrates a powerful, primitive femininity from which Marsilla must extricate himself to become a free individual. Her cross-dressing ensures that her agency is read as a usurpation (at the start of the play, she literally usurps her absent husband's power). The play begins with Zulima in control and Marsilla languishing womanlike in her bed,[8] to make the point that the hero's freedom depends on his attainment of 'proper' sexual difference by escaping Zulima's feminizing clutches and marrying Isabel, whose submissiveness confers heroic status on him.

The medieval settings used in all these plays except *Don Álvaro* allow Islamic culture to be used as an image of threatening undifferentiated sexuality, as opposed to Christian Spain, where the roles of the sexes are clearly opposed. In addition, they offer the image of a society riven by frontier wars, whether with the Moors or Turks: this can be read as a symbolic representation of the need for boundaries to give definition to the self. In practice, both Moors and Christians move from one side of the frontier to the other with surprising ease, suggesting that it is largely a fiction. Part of *Don Álvaro* is set in eighteenth-century Naples, where the Spaniards were fighting Imperial German troops. The heroes need to assert their prowess in war and military conquest, for their subjecthood depends on their ability to subjugate or eliminate the Other. The statutory duel scenes reduce relationship to the violent penetration of body boundaries. The duels are between men who in normal circumstances would be friends, if not brothers or brothers-in-law: in this sense they are linked to the civil strife that also typifies these plays. In addition to the enemy without, there is the enemy within. The repeated motif of treachery poses the problem of the threat of sameness: the traitor is the ally turned enemy. In *La conjuración de Venecia*, the civil strife is between father and son; in *El trovador*, between brothers. The medieval Mediterranean world and particularly medieval Spain offer the perfect scenario of frontier war with an alien culture (Islam), plus

---

8   Kirkpatrick notes that, until 1800, Spanish women normally sat on 'Moorish' cushions while men sat on chairs, reinforcing the associations of Arab culture with a 'feminine' reclining position (1989: 65).

civil war against one's kin.[9] The self is defined in opposition to the Other, but also by combating sameness. Identity depends on the establishment and maintenance of difference.

The most striking common feature of these four plays is the separation of the hero from his parents: a separation which is felt as tragic, but which allows him to assert his independence. In *La conjuración de Venecia* and *El trovador*, the separation takes the form of an oedipal ignorance of origins, which leads the hero unwittingly to take up arms against his father and brother respectively (the brother having inherited the father's title). The implication is that the hero would not have challenged paternal authority had he recognized it as such. Indeed, *La conjuración de Venecia* ends with Rugiero pleading for his father's recognition, forgetting his lover Laura in the process. The fact that his father is the Grand Inquisitor makes it clear that final identification with the father is achieved at the cost of insertion into a system of domination. In this play as in *El trovador*, it is the father or father-substitute who, unknowingly but still unjustly, orders the son's death. This reversal of the oedipal story (in which the son unwittingly kills the father) suggests that the Romantic playwrights have a more negative view of paternal authority than Freud. But they concur with Freud in seeing identification with the father as the goal of the son's trajectory: all four plays end with the reunion of father and son, or the son's recognition of the father and/or the father's recognition of the son.

In *Don Álvaro* and *Los amantes de Teruel*, where separation from parents — though equally drastic — is not accompanied by ignorance of origins, there is no rebellion against the father (unless one counts as such Marsilla's refusal to obey his father's command to respect Isabel's marriage to another; the father however remains his ally). Don Álvaro's chief objective is to vindicate his father's name: before his death he learns that the latter, restored to authority and wealth, has named him his heir. In all four plays the stress is on separation from the father (or father-substitute) rather than on rebellion against his authority. And in each case, the final reconciliation is with a father (or father-substitute) whose wife is dead or never mentioned or, in *Don Álvaro*, racially alien. The paternal order is one in which women, if they exist at all, are of inferior status and at the same time idealized: Don Álvaro's mother, as an Inca princess, is a perfect example of this contradictory objectification which declares her both inferior and superior, but not a subject of equal standing. (An alternative rumour makes Álvaro the bastard of a grandee of Spain and a Moorish queen, which amounts to the same thing.) By ending with the son's rapprochement with the father and leaving the mother out of the picture, the plays make it clear that autonomy is achieved by final identification with the father while the primary bond with the mother remains severed.

The equation of the mother with the primitive found in *Don Álvaro* occurs even more dramatically in *El trovador* with Manrique's supposed mother Azucena, a gypsy whose mother was burnt at the stake for witchcraft and who herself is guilty of a

---

9   Flitter sees Spanish Romantic writers' medievalism and appeal to Golden Age drama as signs of their traditionalism. In these four plays at least, the medieval settings and use of the honour convention contribute to the dramatization of the liberal concept of the autonomous self.

horrendous crime. Manrique is saved — too late — from his primary identification with this monstrous mother, who has ruined his prospects by clinging to him as her son, by the revelation of his real parental origins. It does not matter that he does not live to benefit from the revelation, because the audience is liberated from this powerful incarnation of the Terrible Mother. Or is it? The play ends with Azucena's death, but her closing words 'Ya estás vengada' ('You are avenged at last') suggest alarmingly that her primary loyalty is to her mother, who can be avenged only by the sacrifice of her 'son'. We are left with the primary bond of two women, mother and daughter, who represent the dissolution of the family: neither has a father or husband; as gypsy nomads they negate the concept of home; both are guilty, by imputation or fact, of infanticide. The counterpoint to the Romantic hero's struggle for selfhood is the omnipotent, devouring, archaic mother. David Punter has noted the Romantic fascination with the possibility of self-authorship, in which the male writer appropriates the mother's reproductive powers (1989: 94, 141). In the plays discussed here, it is the hero who tries to exorcize the mother's powers by separating from origins and creating himself from zero, in an act of rebirthing that writes the mother out of the story.

If the incestuous threat of primary identification with the mother is successfully overcome, it nevertheless reasserts itself in *Los amantes de Teruel* and *La conjuración de Venecia* in the form of incest with a figurative sister or first cousin. Diane Long Hoeveler suggests that, in Romantic writing, figurative incest with a sister figure functions as a deflection of the incestuous identification with the mother.[10] This is clearly the case with the first cousins in *La conjuración de Venecia*: Laura insists that she was born to make Rugiero forget the loss of his mother (Martínez de la Rosa 1972: 277). Rugiero is horrified to discover his father and Laura's father are brothers, and from this moment his obsession with her is replaced by his obsession with his father: the female lover represents an incestuous sameness that must be replaced by the father as an image of separation. In *Los amantes de Teruel*, it is the fact that Marsilla and Isabel have been brought up together from the cradle that attracts them to each other. Marsilla describes them as 'un alma en dos partida' ('one soul split in two'). Their sameness is explicitly linked to an incestuous lack of differentiation not only between figurative brother and sister but also between infant and mother: Marsilla insists their embrace will be 'el abrazo | de un hermano dulcísimo a su hermana, | el ósculo será que tantas veces | cambió feliz en la maternal falda | nuestro amor infantil' ('the embrace | of a tender brother with his sister, | the kiss so many times | blissfully exchanged in the maternal lap | by our childhood love'; Hartzenbusch 1989: 162). But this bond of sameness is fatal to him because he literally cannot live without her: he dies when she repudiates him. Isabel utters the fatal words of rejection when Marsilla accuses her of putting her love for her mother before her love for him; as in *El trovador*, the mother–daughter bond is implicated in the hero's death.

___

10   Mellor suggests that the sister-bride motif found in Romantic writing is an attempt to turn the female lover into a mirror of the male self, thus incorporating her and denying her independence (1993: 25).

Perhaps the most remarkable feature of these plays is that they pay as much attention to the plight of the heroine as to that of the hero. The plot structure follows the hero's search for subjecthood, but in all four cases this is related to the heroine's reduction to object status. His proper attainment of masculinity is shown to be dependent on her proper attainment of femininity; as in the oedipal scenario, individuation is synonymous with sexual differentiation. But in practice individuation is achieved only by the male; the heroine attains femininity by identifying with the mother as devalued object and renouncing the self. It could be argued that the plays are concerned with the heroine's selflessness simply as the precondition for the hero's autonomy. But considerable attention is given to the painful process whereby the daughter's attempt to separate is thwarted by the father's refusal of recognition, which sends her back to a negative identification with the mother.

In all the plays except *Los amantes de Teruel*, the heroine's mother is dead and thus by definition lacks subjecthood. In *El trovador*, where the heroine's father is also dead, this forces her into dependence on a brother who regards it as his right to dispose of her. Leonor seems to hold her mother responsible for her brother's despotism: 'que me dio mi madre en vos | en vez de amigo un tirano' ('for my mother gave me in you | a tyrant instead of a friend'; García Gutiérrez 1985: 118). Refusal of recognition by the brother, as father-substitute, leads her to devalue the mother who is her model of femininity. In the other three plays, the relationship between daughter and father is more complicated. In *Don Álvaro* and *La conjuración de Venecia*, the father adores the daughter. In *Don Álvaro* this does not prevent him from refusing to recognize her independence — the right to dispose of herself as she wishes — for this adoration turns her into a semi-idealized substitute for his dead wife; he himself describes his devotion to his daughter as a form of 'gallantry' (Rivas 1986: 59). Leonor has internalized this attitude, identifying with an idealized image of her dead mother, which the maid makes clear bears no resemblance to the haughty, ill-tempered person she actually was (Rivas 1986: 63). This identification with a dead mother, coupled with her father's rejection of her as he dies, logically leads Leonor to opt for a life of entombment. A similar situation holds in *La conjuración de Venecia*, where the father adores his daughter so much that he forgives her for disposing of herself without consulting him (he was, after all, presumed dead at the time). But this does not constitute genuine recognition of her subjecthood because he persists in treating her as an objectified mirror-image (portrait) of his dead wife: 'En mi hija veía el retrato de mi pobre Constanza' ('In my daughter I saw the portrait of my poor Constanza'; Martínez de la Rosa 1972: 296). Laura in turn will identify with this idealized dead mother, who establishes an equation in her mind between femininity and suffering ('my poor Constanza'), indeed death. It is logical that she should suggest the family pantheon to Rugiero as the location of their amorous rendezvous. In all of these three plays the refusal (in differing degrees) of recognition by the father and consequent identification with a dead mother lead the heroines to subjugate their will to an idealized man of action, who confirms their own passivity by contrast, and allows them to live out their frustrated desire for agency by becoming his helpmeet. This idealization of the hero verges on the idolatrous in *Don Álvaro* and *El trovador*, where the two Leonors, on their lover's presumed death, replace him with God, opting for the religious life. The sacrilegious rivalry between love of God and love of the hero is explicitly recognized by Leonor in *El trovador* (García Gutiérrez 1985: 150): her idolatry leads her to the ultimate self-debasement of condemning herself to hell by committing suicide to save him.

The most interesting depiction of the heroine as daughter occurs in *Los amantes de Teruel*, where Hartzenbusch departs from previous versions of the legend by inventing a mother for Isabel. Here the mother is not dead but debased by having committed adultery.[11] This has led her to adopt a life of penance, renouncing motherhood to tend to the sick, leaving the home to live in a ruined Gothic hermitage at the bottom of the garden, and exchanging feminine dress for a penitent's habit. As when Leonor in *Don Álvaro* takes to the roads and renounces feminine dress, the result is not acquisition of masculine agency but simply loss of femininity. The relationship between mother and daughter is extremely complex. Isabel's love for Marsilla is clearly an extension of primary identification with the 'maternal lap' where both were reared. But at the start of the play she regards her mother as an enemy and ally of the father who refuses recognition of her independent will. Then, when her mother gives in to her maternal sentiments and promises to support Isabel against her father, Isabel prostrates herself at her feet, declaring that she had not known such happiness since even before Marsilla left: primary identification with the mother asserts itself over heterosexual love. When Isabel discovers Rodrigo is threatening to publish her mother's adulterous letters if she refuses him, she takes identification with the mother to the point of agreeing to marry a blackmailer, in a renunciation of self which she describes as going to the 'grave' (Hartzenbusch 1989: 129). What is interesting in this play is that it shows the different stages of Chodorow's and Benjamin's version of the oedipal trajectory, as the daughter moves away from primary identification with the mother, only to be forced back into it when the father refuses her recognition, the result being the loss of subjecthood that identification with a degraded feminine image entails.

The woman's loss of self is in these plays the necessary foil to a male autonomy achieved by separating from the feminine, but all four plays end with the death of both hero and heroine (*La conjuración de Venecia* condemns Laura to mere loss of consciousness). The male trajectory is ultimately as self-destructive as the female. The plays trace the hero's efforts to assert his independence, yet they are full of images of captivity. Favourite locations are castles, dungeons and tombs, not to mention prison cells, monk's cells and convent cells. In her book *Romantic Imprisonment*, Nina Auerbach notes that 'the Romantic imagination is in large part an imagination of confinement' (1986: 7).[12] Auerbach is chiefly concerned with the imprisonment

---

11   Iranzo notes that, in editions after the first, Hartzenbusch eliminated the actual word 'adultery'. See her edition of the play (Hartzenbusch 1989: 122 n. 23).

12   See Punter for an analysis of the entrapment of the female by the male in the Gothic novel (1989: 73–83). Mellor discusses the enslavement of the female lover by the male (1993: 26).

of women; in Spanish Romantic drama, while the heroine may spend some time in a convent cell, it is the male heroes who are repeatedly incarcerated or taken captive. Furst notes that Romantic heroes 'condemn themselves to a life sentence within the prison of their own egocentricity' (1979: 97). A concept of the self that is based on separation necessarily equates autonomy with solitary confinement. The incarcerations in these plays curiously seem to be the other side of the hero's independence, for they save him from the danger of relationship with others. In the case of *Don Álvaro*, it is the hero's parents who are imprisoned, with the result that he is separated from them; despite the fact that he is born in a dungeon, their captivity gives him autonomy. In *La conjuracion de Venecia*, the hero's mother is killed while being taken captive, freeing the son from primary maternal identification; as a result, he is brought up in captivity, but this allows him to separate from his Grand Inquisitor father. Manrique's kidnapping by Azucena in *El trovador* and Marsilla's captivity in Moorish Valencia in *Los amantes de Teruel* put them in the power of terrible, primitive women, but also give them the opportunity to separate from family origins and prove their own worth.

Marsilla's captivity in Valencia has the additional advantage of postponing his desired union with Isabel. The plots of all four plays take the form of as succession of impediments, mostly in the form of imprisonment, placed in the way of the hero's union with the heroine, to the extent that one feels the dramatists are trying to save their heroes from fusion with the feminine. Hart notes that Spanish Romantic plays are governed by the logic of obstacle love, the obstacle being for him the Name-of-the-Father (1992: 10–11). I suggest that it is not so much that the heroes desire what is forbidden as that they desire what they most fear: a return to the primary identification with the feminine from which they have separated to achieve subjecthood. The heroes are torn between desire to break out of the captivity of solitary confinement that is the other side of autonomy, and fear of falling captive to the feminine. Love offers the promise of a return to infantile undifferentiation, as is made explicit in *Los amantes de Teruel*, but at the cost of loss of self. To avoid engulfment, the heroes turn love into a form of conquest in which the female lover is emotionally enslaved, if not physically kidnapped as in *Don Álvaro* and *El trovador*. But, as Benjamin shows (1990), the master–slave dialectic is self-defeating. In reducing the heroine to subservience, the hero makes her an appendage, destroying the separateness that guaranteed his autonomy. Conversely, submission to the hero allows the heroine to live through him, at the expense of having no life without him. The bonds of love place both hero and heroine in a double bind.

Auerbach notes that Romantic narrative is structured in terms of 'the double prison, in which a journey of apparent liberation from captivity leads only to more implacable arrest' (1986: 6). Here, the heroes struggle to break free of the bonds of solitary confinement, only to fall prey to the bonds of love: a form of bondage that is particularly insidious because is consists in the dissolution, rather than erection, of boundaries. Love, as a dissolving agent, is what enables the heroes to break the chains of the self; it is described via destructive images of laceration, burning and drowning. In *Los amantes de Teruel* Marsilla, after ripping apart a series of chains and ropes, succumbs to love in the form of a 'mortal veneno [que] rompe, rompe, me rompe las entrañas' ('mortal poison [that] tears, tears, tears at my entrails'; Hartzenbusch 1989: 164). *El trovador* is dominated by fear of burning: being burnt at the stake, being consumed by passion. In *La conjuración de Venecia*, the boatman rowing Rugiero to his tryst with Laura sings of Leander drowning in the Hellespont: Rugiero and Laura appropriately embrace on a tomb. The water imagery intensifies towards the end of *Don Álvaro*: Álvaro talks of turning the river of blood that separates him from Leonor into a sea (Rivas 1986: 141); before the final holocaust Hermano Melitón comments, 'Va a llover a mares.... Hoy estamos de marea alta' ('There's going to be a deluge.... We're in for high water today'; Rivas 1986: 161). One is reminded of Bataille's previously quoted notion that eroticism, in violating body boundaries, plunges the individual into a 'sea of death'. The hero's and heroine's statutory death (or at least unconsciousness) as the curtain falls is not yet another obstacle frustrating their union: it is the only form that love can take in an individualistic ideology which regards fusion with the feminine as loss of the self. The violence of the various forms of *Liebestod* in these plays reinforces the sense of violation of body boundaries. (In *Los amantes de Teruel*, the violence is expressed solely at the level of language: appropriately, for the message of this play is that words can kill.) The fact that a large number of these deaths are self-inflicted — something deeply shocking in a Catholic culture — shows that the heroes and heroines desire their own annihilation. The plays illustrate Benjamin's analysis of the process that creates female masochism. But the view of heterosexual union as engulfment by the feminine leads the heroes also to equate desire with a masochistic urge to self-destruction. Love does indeed feminize the hero; and feminization means, for both hero and heroine, metaphorical if not literal suicide.

These plays give a terrible view of the dangers of relations between the sexes. But they also illustrate the destructiveness of the liberal notion that selfhood depends on separation from the feminine. The attention paid to mothers and daughters as well as to fathers and sons implies a subtle awareness of the gendered nature of subject formation. It would probably be a mistake to suppose that, in their attention to the daughter–parent relationship, Spanish Romantic dramatists are critiquing the equation of femininity with selflessness. Nevertheless, their depiction of the daughter's oedipal trajectory is in many ways more perceptive than that so hesitantly and unsatisfactorily attempted by Freud.

Works Cited

ALDARACA, BRIDGET. 1992. *'El ángel del hogar': Galdós and the Ideology of Domesticity in Spain* (Chapel Hill: North Carolina University Press)

AUERBACH, NINA. 1986. *Romantic Imprisonment: Women and Other Glorified Outcasts* (New York: Columbia University Press)

BEAUVOIR, SIMONE DE. 1972. *The Second Sex*, trans. by H. M. Parshley (Harmondsworth: Penguin)

BENJAMIN, JESSICA. 1990. *The Bonds of Love: Psychoanalysis, Feminism and the Problem of Domination*, 2nd edn (London: Virago)

CASEY, JAMES. 1989. *The History of the Family* (Oxford: Blackwell)

CHODOROW, NANCY. 1978. *The Reproduction of Mothering: Psychoanalysis and the Sociology of Gender* (Berkeley: University of California Press)

———. 1989. *Feminism and Psychoanalytic Theory* (New Haven, CT: Yale University Press)

FLITTER, DEREK. 1992. *Spanish Romantic Literary Theory and Criticism* (Cambridge: Cambridge University Press)

FURST, LILIAN R. (ed.). 1979. *Romanticism in Perspective*, 2nd edn (London: Macmillan)

GARCÍA GUTIÉRREZ, ANTONIO. 1985. *El trovador*, ed. by Carlos Ruiz Silva (Madrid: Cátedra)

HART, STEPHEN M. 1992. *The Other Scene: Psychoanalytic Readings in Modern Spanish and Spanish-American Studies* (Boulder, CO: Society of Spanish and Spanish-American Studies)

HARTZENBUSCH, JUAN EUGENIO. 1989. *Los amantes de Teruel*, ed. by Carmen Iranzo (Madrid: Cátedra)

HOEVELER, DIANE LONG. 1990. *Romantic Androgyny: The Woman Within* (University Park: Pennsylvania University Press)

JOHNSON, PAUL. 1991. *The Birth of the Modern World: World Society, 1815–1830* (London: Weidenfeld & Nicolson)

KIRKPATRICK, SUSAN. 1989. *Las Románticas: Escritoras y subjetividad en España, 1835–1850* (Madrid: Cátedra)

LLORENS, VICENTE. 1968. *Liberales y románticos: Una emigración española en Inglaterra, 1823–34* (Madrid: Castalia)

McNAY, LOIS. 1992. *Foucault and Feminism: Power, Gender and the Self* (Cambridge: Polity)

MARTÍNEZ DE LA ROSA, FRANCISCO. 1972. *Obras dramáticas*, ed. by Jean Sarrailh (Madrid: Espasa-Calpe),

MELLOR, ANNE K. 1993. *Romanticism and Gender* (New York: Routledge)

NAVAS RUIZ, RICARDO. 1982. *El romanticismo español*, 3rd edn (Madrid: Cátedra)

PATEMAN, CAROLE. 1988. *The Sexual Contract* (Cambridge: Polity)

PUNTER, DAVID. 1989. *The Romantic Unconscious: A Study in Narcissism and Patriarchy* (New York: Harvester Wheatsheaf)

RIVAS, DUQUE DE (Ángel Saavedra). 1986. *Don Álvaro o la fuerza del sino*, ed. by Alberto Sánchez (Madrid: Cátedra)

WILLIAMS, RAYMOND. 1990. *Keywords: A Vocabulary of Culture and Society*, 2nd rev. edn (London: Fontana)

PART II

The Realist Novel and Historical Painting

CHAPTER 3

Being There:
The Documentary Impulse from
Ayguals de Izco to Galdós

Alicia Andreu has demonstrated Galdós's unacknowledged debt to the melodramatic plotlines of the *novela por entregas* (serialized novel), despite his dismissal of the mid-century novel in his 1870 article 'Observaciones sobre la novela contemporánea en España' ('Observations on the Contemporary Novel in Spain'; Pérez Galdós, *Ensayos* 115–18). Indeed, *La desheredada* (*The Disinherited*), which will be discussed in this essay, was published in serialized form (Ribbans, '*La desheredada*'). In his valuable book on Ayguals de Izco, Russell Sebold proposes something different: that we should look to the mid-century novel for precedents for Galdós's realist project of a novel of contemporary life. The number of mid-century novels cited by Sebold which bear the subtitle *Novela de costumbres* (*Novel of Customs*) or *Novela de costumbres contemporáneas* (*Novel of Contemporary Customs*) is formidable (18–19). Sebold consequently names the 1840s the first decade of Spanish realism, pronouncing Gertrudis Gómez de Avellaneda the first Spanish realist writer, with her novels *Sab* (1841) and *Dos mujeres* (*Two Women*; 1842) (15–18). But he chooses to devote his monograph to the first two novels by the inventor of the serialized novel, Wenceslao Ayguals de Izco — *María o la hija de un jornalero* (*María or A Laborer's Daughter*; 1845–46) and its sequel *La marquesa de Bellaflor o el niño de la Inclusa* (*The Marquise of Bellaflor or the Boy from the Orphanage*; 1846–47) — since he sees them as paradigmatic examples of what, for him, is the defining feature of nineteenth-century realism: the aim of documenting contemporary national life across the whole social spectrum.

What is at stake here, we might add to Sebold's analysis, is the use of print culture to create an 'imagined community' which functions as a model of the modern nation, supplementing the mid- to late-nineteenth-century political nation-formation project — as Benedict Anderson showed so brilliantly in his analysis of the 1887 novel *Noli me tangere* by the hero of the Philippine Independence struggle, José Rizal (32–34). The nineteenth-century historical novel — a major genre, stretching from the romantic historical novel through the massive number of mid-century historical serialized novels to Galdós's *Episodios nacionales* (*National Episodes*) — played a huge role in creating a sense of identification with the nation, conceived as an entity existing over time. But, by definition, although it views the past from the perspective of present-day concerns, it cannot function as a model of the modern nation. Sebold's perception (18) that Ayguals de Izco's first two novels serve as an antecedent to Galdós's novels of contemporary life because they offer a broad vision of life in contemporary Madrid is crucial, both because it points to the fact that, in the mid-nineteenth century, the novel of modern life has to be urban, and, beyond that, to the fact that a novel of national modern life has to be set in the capital.[1]

In this essay, I coincide with Sebold's proposition that Ayguals's serialized fiction anticipates Galdós's aim of documenting contemporary life in the national capital across the full social spectrum. Where I differ from him is on the relation of the fictional plot to the description of actual places and public events. Sebold assumes that the desire to include a broad social and historical canvas, as well as contemporary historical events, poses a problem for the novelist, who has to integrate all this detail into a unified plot. Thus, Seebold sees documentation as subordinate to the creation of a story built around fictional characters. When he summarizes Agyuals's first two novels — necessary, as he notes, since their massive length means that there are no contemporary editions[2] — he omits any mention of this description, recounting only the fictional story. The result gives the impression of a text that is very different from what one encounters when one reads it. I would like here to see what happens if we examine Ayguals's *María* — I will limit myself to his first novel — in terms of what actually appears on its pages. Instead of viewing the mass of documentary detail as a 'problem' which Ayguals failed to solve, I will assume that it is there for a reason, and, indeed, that it provides a clue to Ayguals's aims. I propose, in other words, to view this documentary detail not as ancillary — as a series of 'interpolations' or 'digressions' — but as integral to the text. After all, Ayguals had to work extremely hard to include the lengthy descriptions of the places that he has his characters pass through, often lasting for several pages and sometimes for whole chapters, with extensive footnotes — some several pages long — from documentary sources, both historical and contemporary.

I take seriously Ayguals's claim, in his epilogue, that he has invented a new genre: 'Nos hemos ensayado en crear un nuevo género que puede calificarse de HISTORIA-NOVELA.' ('We have experimented with creating a new genre that can be called HISTORY-FICTION'; 2: 384) The word order is crucial: history comes first, and fiction second. The aim of this new genre is to insert a fictional narrative into a historical account, and not vice versa. Ayguals continues:

> Por lo que hace á la parte histórica, creemos no haber olvidado ninguno de los grandes sucesos ocurridos en Madrid durante el período del Estatuto real, y hasta nos hemos esmerado en detallar sus minuciosidades por órden de fechas, de días y de horas como el mas escrupuloso historiador, haciendo revelaciones importantes que no hemos leido en ninguna de las crónicas contemporáneas. (2: 384; original accentuation)

1   For a critical discussion of capitality, see Martí-López.
2   The four parts of *María o la hija de un jornalero* come to 821 pages in the original 2-volume 1845–46 book edition, set in double columns and small print.

(As for the historical part, we believe we have not forgotten any of the major events that took place in Madrid at the time of the Royal Statute, and we have even made a point of listing their details, ordered by date, day and hour, like the most rigorous historian, offering important revelations that we have not read in any of the chronicles of the time.)

Thus, the novel is, first and foremost, a contribution to the history of recent events in the capital, with Ayguals claiming to give his readers information that they will not find in historical records.

I take this to refer to the narrator's political explanations, throughout the novel, of the events described. These explanations are designed to support Ayguals's republican convictions, and particularly to exalt the National Militia, which he commanded in his native Vinaroz. The National Militia was a popularly-recruited local defense corps created during the 1820–23 *trienio liberal* (liberal interlude); Ayguals uses the term to subsume its later incarnations as Urban Militia and National Guard. It played a major role in combating Carlist insurrection in the rearguard — we should remember that in 1836, when *María* ends, the Carlist army was at the gates of Madrid: not for nothing is the novel's villain, Fray Patricio, a Carlist conspirator.

The novel's focus on the National Militia is significant, since, in its successive incarnations, this body saw its role as the defense of popular sovereignty. The novel starts with Martínez de la Rosa's 1834 Estatuto Real (Royal Statute): a timid return to constitutional rule that rejected the principle of national sovereignty enshrined in the 1812 Constitution. In summer 1835, armed revolt in the name of popular sovereignty by the Urban Militia (as the local defense corps was now called) placed much of Spain under the control of local *juntas*, eventually pacified by Mendizábal's progressive measures. These included reconstituting the local defense corps as the National Guard. With the change to conservative government in summer 1836, the National Guard mutinied, proclaiming the 1812 Constitution and again taking control of much of the country. The revolutionary process culminated in the August 1836 *Motín de La Granja* (La Granja Mutiny), which forced the Queen-Regent to recognize the 1812 Constitution, including the principle of popular sovereignty. This event closes the novel, coinciding with the marriage of the working-class María (whose father and brothers fight in the successive incarnations of the National Militia) to the liberal aristocrat (Marqués de Bellaflor) who is a National Guard commander. The historical events do not form a backdrop to María's Cinderella story; rather, by relating her so closely to the National Militia, Ayguals gives us an account of recent national history that makes his readers identify with a particular group of historical actors who are not the protagonists found in history books. The fictional characters' stories are fitted into historical events, in order to make a historical point, rather than the other way around. To see the historical documentation as supporting the fictional plot, but at the same time being poorly integrated into it, is to miss the point.

The novel's epilogue clarifies Ayguals's historical aims: (i) to develop 'amor de patria' ('patriotic love') by countering foreign slanders that Spain is not a civilized nation (meaning that the novel shows the existence in Spain, not only of a reactionary clergy — the villains of the novel — but also of progressive political forces drawn from all social classes); (ii) to argue a case for the 'clases menesterosas' ('needy classes'); (iii) to warn against hypocrisy (meaning that of a clergy and aristocracy involved in Carlist conspiracies); and (iv) to vindicate the National Militia (2: 360–61). Ayguals's reference in the epilogue to his own historical role as commander of the Vinaroz National Militia is illustrative of the complex and meticulous handling of documentary sources that characterizes the novel as a whole. First, a footnote prints the text of a 15 July 1837 article from the *Eco del Comercio* praising Ayguals's actions as National Militia commander. Then, the body of the text includes the 25 April 1840 speech by a deputy in the Cortes, praising the Vinaroz National Militia, followed by the text of a similar article from the Valencian *Diario Mercantil*. A footnote to this last article includes the military report to which it refers (2: 360–65). This accumulation of citations, with footnotes leading to further citations, makes the novel a historian's treasure trove, providing a mass of precisely-referenced documentary information. This covers not only Spanish history in this turbulent period, but also the urban history of Madrid, giving lengthy information about architecture, landscape gardening, and town planning — frequently citing the 1833 second edition of Mesonero Romanos's *Manual de Madrid* (*Guide to Madrid*), roughly contemporaneous with the novel's action.

The extent of this documentary impulse is particularly striking in the lead-up to the La Granja Mutiny, which itemizes not only the items in the art collection of the royal palace at La Granja, but also the statues and fountains in its grounds, citing their value and maintenance costs to make an explicit anti-monarchist point (2: 246–49, 252–56). It is presumably because the Museo del Prado allows the people access to what was previously the royal art collection that so much emphasis is placed on María's visit in Part IV, Chapter 4, which prints the catalogue number and entry for every painting she sees. (This can help us understand why Galdós finds it necessary to take Isidora round the Prado in *La desheredada*; Isidora damns herself in readers' eyes by declaring that public access to such treasures should not be allowed.) A repeated ploy in Ayguals's novel is to take the characters to sites in or around Madrid that have been rebuilt in the decade between the events described and the novel's publication, explaining what was there before. This impresses on readers the modernization that has recently taken place, largely as a result of Mendizábal's confiscation and sale of Church property, thus equating progress with the novel's strong anticlerical message. Not for nothing does the novel's prologue start by describing the Convento de San Francisco, subsequently turned into a barracks (1: 22–23). By attaching the novel's villain, Fray Patricio, to this now suppressed monastery, and having María's working-class family home live literally in its shadow, Ayguals aligns readers' emotions with a particular political account of recent history.

In the epilogue, Ayguals insists he has not wanted to produce a 'guía de forasteros' ('tourist guide'). Nonetheless, his text explicitly aims to show foreign and Spanish readers that Madrid has some impressive public buildings and parks, despite the squalor of its lower-class districts, which he has to highlight to get over his political reform message. The narrator's asides to the reader show his awareness of the tension between these two aims. The encyclopedic urge behind the novel becomes clear when, after stating that the novel could not include all of Madrid's sites, the epilogue proceeds to describe those that were omitted — lacking space to describe the Retiro, Ayguals sticks in a picture of it instead (2: 385). The same encyclopedic didacticism is seen in Ayguals's career as editor and publisher of several political magazines, as well as writing and publishing his own novels, translating and publishing the social novels of Eugène Sue, publishing the works of Voltaire and Feijoo, and compiling and publishing educational anthologies such as *La Escuela del pueblo: Páginas de enseñanza universal* (*School for the People: Pages of Universal Education*; 7 vols, 1852–53) or *Los verdugos de la humanidad desde el primer siglo hasta nuestros días: Cuadros históricos* (*Tyrants of Humankind from the First Century to Our Time: Historical Scenes*; 1855). Ayguals's serialized fiction has to be seen in the overall context of his *Sociedad Literaria* (*Literary Society*) publishing project, as a contribution to the dissemination of knowledge.

If Ayguals's characters are one-dimensional, it is because they are conceived as pretexts for the narrator to take his readers on a tour of Madrid encompassing its social extremes, in the course of which they witness, with the characters, the major political events of the day. As Sebold notes (39), only occasionally (as in María's visit to the Prado) do the characters function as focalizers, with events shown through their eyes; mostly they are simply described as 'being there,' whether as participants or bystanders. Sometimes, as Sebold also notes (38), the narrator takes readers to visit sites or witness events where no character is present, simply to provide additional information. The characters' inner lives are irrelevant to this pedagogical conception of the 'historia-novela.' Rather, the characters' function is to give a sense of a 'national society,' encompassing all classes, as analyzed so lucidly by Anderson in relation to Rizal's novel. If the historical novel gives a sense of the nation as an entity existing over time, Ayguals's contemporary 'historia-novela' gives a sense of the nation as an entity existing across space, through its depiction of the multifarious sites in and around the national capital, which are brought into relationship with each other by the characters who traverse them.

In this sense, the working-class María's fairytale marriage to the Marqués de Bellaflor is, I suggest, not an improbable allegory of national unity (the historical events described show nothing but turbulence), but part of a larger attempt to create an imagined community of sympathetic characters who, whatever their class position, ascribe to progressive liberal ideals. We should not forget here 'el negro Tomás' ('black Tom') the black former slave who repeatedly saves María, whose inclusion (four years after Gómez de Avellaneda's *Sab* and seven years before Harriet Beecher Stowe's *Uncle Tom's Cabin*, which Ayguals would later translate) allows the narrator to add a dose of anti-slavery rhetoric to this 'history' written from the viewpoint of the dispossessed. To enable this partisan account to serve as the basis for the construction of a national imagined community, it has to encompass as many spaces and social classes as possible. As Ayguals notes in the novel's dedication: 'Al presentar la historia de recientes acontecimientos políticos de Madrid, enlazada con incidentes dramáticos de pura invención, trato también de describir las costumbres de todas las clases del pueblo, costumbres españolas' ('In offering the history of recent political events in Madrid, interlaced with entirely invented dramatic incidents, I have also tried to describe the customs of all the classes that make up the nation, Spanish customs'; 1: 6).

To create such an 'imagined community,' the narrator needs also to persuade readers to ascribe to a common understanding of the political agenda the nation should address. María and her family are, at various points, confined to institutions of social control — the Hospital General (section for the insane), the Asilo de Pobres (Workhouse) de San Bernardino, the men's prison — allowing the documentation of institutions requiring reform. The narrator repeatedly describes conditions in these institutions as worthy of 'cafres' ('kaffirs'), equating civilization expressly with the creation of modern Foucauldian disciplinary and hygienic procedures designed to recycle the deviant or sick back into society (Foucault, *Madness*; *Birth*; *Discipline*). The documentation provided in the novel includes detailed statistics relating to beneficent associations and savings banks set up to help workers. The documentation of 'what is' is thus directly geared to generating in readers a common notion of what the nation 'might be' — and, indeed, 'must be' if it is to become a modern nation on a par with northern Europe (to which comparisons are regularly drawn). That Ayguals, in drawing readers' attention to the need for social reform, anticipates the contemporary novels of Galdós should be immediately obvious. This shows that modern discourses of social control were already circulating in 1840s Spain — and circulated further by Ayguals's novel, whose sales were boosted by his invention, through his *Sociedad Literaria* publishing venture, of the serialized novel.

I should like now to turn to Galdós's *La desheredada* (1881), to draw a comparison — and contrast — with the use of documentation in Ayguals's *María*. I have chosen this novel for the obvious reason that, like *María*, it takes readers on a tour of urban spaces in the capital, ranging from the aristocratic mansion to the outlying slums and giving priority to those spaces that require social reform (the rope factory, the lunatic asylum, the women's prison). Like *María* also, it allows readers — through the characters — to witness historical events (declaration of the First Republic, attempted assassination of Alfonso XII). I do not wish to suggest that Zola's naturalism played no part in Galdós's turn to a more documentary mode in *La desheredada*, but simply that Ayguals's novel provides an additional antecedent. It was, of course, in Galdós's interest to deny this antecedent, given the lack of cultural prestige of the mid-century serialized novel. It is also worth pointing out that, between 1873 and 1879, Galdós had written the twenty novels of the first two series of *Episodios nacionales*, which provided a massive apprenticeship in writing fiction based on documentation. Although Sebold excludes the historical novel from the realist project on the grounds that the latter has to represent contemporary life, there is clear overlap between the two in terms of methodology, since both claim to document 'the real.' We may note, with Ribbans (*History and Fiction* 57), that Galdós announced, at the start of the second series of *Episodios nacionales*, that their format would be closer to that of the *novela de costumbres*, with greater interaction between political and private events. *La desheredada*, the first novel Galdós would write after interrupting publication of the *Episodios*, marks a further development of this tendency.

In keeping with his supposition that the goal of any novelist who includes historical material in his text must be to integrate it into a unified fictional plot, Sebold suggests:

> Ayguals aborda algunos de los mismos problemas que Galdós tendría que solucionar en los *Episodios Nacionales* y en novelas contemporáneas como *Fortunata y Jacinta*: esto es, la integración inconsútil de conocidas accionas públicas y sus medios en una acción y un mundo creados. (38)

> (Ayguals tackles some of the same problems that Galdós would have to solve in the *Episodios nacionales* and in contemporary novels like *Fortunata y Jacinta*: that is, the seamless integration of well-known public events and their environments into an invented action and world.)

Elena Delgado reminds us (55–59) that Galdós's novels were criticized at the time for excessive detail, seen as jeopardizing the 'unity' of the literary text — the same 'failing' that Sebold finds in Ayguals's novels. Such criticisms started precisely with *La desheredada*, the first of Galdós's contemporary novels to include historical events and to cover the whole social spectrum. Delgado (57–58) notes how the Aristotelian concept of unity of action still prevailed in literary manuals of the day, despite the fact that writers had long since ceased to adhere to neoclassical rules.

And yet, in practice, Galdós's novels immediately strike the reader as more integrated than those of Ayguals, suggesting that Galdós's literary project for a novel of contemporary national life is differently conceived. The urban spaces and political events represented in *La desheredada* are systematically depicted through the mind of a character — usually the protagonist Isidora. Each chapter starts by focusing on a character, only then going on to describe their location. The reader is confronted with this narrative strategy forcefully at the start, which plunges straight into Tomás Rufete's insane ramblings relayed through interior monologue, the narrator subsequently stepping in to place him in the lunatic asylum at Leganés, and then taking us on a tour of the asylum's various sections. Another graphic example is the representation of the rope factory where Isidora's brother Mariano has been put to work, which we visit with La Sanguijelera and Isidora. By showing us the factory's interior through the eyes of Isidora, who — like most readers — has never witnessed industrial labor before, we are given a defamiliarized vision that turns the machinery into a terrifying, animate being. A similar technique of estrangement is found in the guided tour of the Aransis mansion, which we view through the eyes of an Isidora confronted for the first time with an aristocratic interior (she, of course, sees it through the lens of the novels she has read, with their rags-to-riches plotlines).

The novel uses a range of techniques for depicting urban spaces or political events through the mind of one or more characters: the characters' use as focalizers for the narrator's third-person account; interior monologue (direct or reported); dialogue; or, most often, a mix of these. Thus, when Isidora first ventures into Madrid's commercial center (Part I, Chapter 7), we move between the narrator's third-person account of her movements, and her thoughts and perceptions presented directly in interior monologue, passing increasingly to the indirect reporting of the latter. The result is a progressive blurring of the distinction between the narrator's and Isidora's perspectives — and, in the process, between what is inside the protagonist's head and what is outside it. In the famous chapter (Part I, Chapter 17) where Isidora wanders around the city center with José Relimpio, on the night when the First Republic is declared, we find the same mix (with a strong tendency to reported interior monologue), plus the addition of the spoken comments of both Isidora and José Relimpio, separately and in conversation. As a result, the historical events and urban spaces are knitted seamlessly into the mental experience of the characters.

However, what is produced is not a fusion of inner and outer, but a representation of the characters' misrecognition of what they are witnessing, as they transform it into a prop to support their own desires (as previously noted with regard to Isidora's tour of the Aransis mansion). Thus, on the night of the declaration of the First Republic, Isidora's thoughts travel as she moves through the streets, identifying as she passes a popular tavern with the republican slogan 'Todos somos iguales' ('We are all equal'), but as she passes the Royal Palace transferring her identification to the departing monarch (272–73). While this may be a comment on the political inconstancy of the Spanish people, it says much more about Isidora's tendency to project her own desires onto the outside world, failing to see what is actually going on. It is the narrator, and not Isidora, who notes the crowd's lack of political enthusiasm (275–76), for at this point in the chapter Isidora no longer sees anything, taken over by her 'idea' of acquiring wealth and status by becoming Joaquín Pez's mistress. There is a direct parallel with Mariano's obsession with his 'idea' of committing regicide at the end of Part II: in his epileptic fit, he blanks out on reality and obeys an inner compulsion. I have noted elsewhere (Labanyi 108) that Isidora's and Mariano's stories dramatize the debates on popular sovereignty that were reactivated in the *sexenio revolucionario* (revolutionary years) of 1868 to 1874, covered in the novel; both *María* and *La desheredada* focus on periods of revolutionary activity when the issue of popular sovereignty was at stake. Nevertheless, Galdós's novel is very different from Ayguals's literary project, in that it is not about Spain's recent history, but about the characters' misrecognition of it. We may note that, in the course of the first two series of *Episodios nacionales*, Galdós comes increasingly to focus on the gap between national perceptions of Spanish history and a much less palatable reality.

That Galdós's inclusion of historical events in his contemporary novels is not aimed primarily at giving readers historical information is shown by Mariano's attempted assassination of Alfonso XII, which does not map exactly onto either of the real-life assassination attempts that took place in 1878 and 1879. For a start, Mariano's visit to Juan Bou, shortly before, occurs in January 1877. In his edition of the novel (468 n. 239, 473 n. 241), Ricardo Gullón suggests that the description of Mariano's attempted regicide mixes Alfonso XII's wedding procession in January 1878 with the October 1878 assassination attempt committed (as in the novel) in the Calle Mayor, by a printer (Mariano had worked for the printer Juan Bou). Gordon, however, argues convincingly that it dramatizes the December 1879 assassination attempt by a nineteen-year-old lower-class epileptic, which gave rise to a major debate on the need for social reform, thanks to the intervention in the trial of the medical expert Dr José María Esquerdo,[3] who campaigned for more enlightened treatment of the insane: this maps clearly onto the novel's concerns.

This disregard for strict historical accuracy is taken further by the novel's occasional Cervantine spoof claims to be based on historical documentation — for example, when the narrator attributes the information he gives us about the style of Isidora's boots to alleged documentary sources (115). A similar parody of such documentary claims occurs at the start of Part II, in the mock chronicle ('Efémerides') whose month-by-month account of the years 1873–75 includes details of Isidora's private life alongside historical events, in an incongruous mix. Sebold (39) suggests that the frequent appeal to the authority of 'historiadores' ('historians') by Ayguals's narrator is equally a Cervantine dig at novelistic pretensions to historicity; I have to say that I see Ayguals's recourse to historical sources as totally serious. In this sense he could be said to be more of a professed realist than Galdós, whose love of Cervantine unreliable narration parallels his analysis of his characters' misrecognition of reality.

And yet there is a serious documentary claim in *La desheredada*. As in *María*, the plot is constructed so that the narrator can take the reader to spaces in and around Madrid that demonstrate the need for social reform. In addition to the lunatic asylum at Leganés and the rope factory south of the Ronda de Embajadores, we are shown the various sections of the women's prison in the Calle de Quiñones — though curiously, despite the novel's concern for child delinquency, we are not taken to visit Mariano when he is interned in the men's prison (twice), as well as in the Hospital General. We assume that Galdós is likely to have visited these spaces himself in order to document them, although footnotes and citations of documentary sources are avoided — as they are throughout the *Episodios nacionales* for which Galdós is known to have done considerable historical research. Even if he did not undertake ethnographic research, there was sufficient debate in the Spanish press and in intellectual circles (including among personal friends of Galdós like the advocate of child welfare, Manuel Tolosa Latour) for him to have been well informed (Gordon; Labanyi 122–23 n. 28; Fuentes Peris). In taking us to these urban spaces, the narrator of *La desheredada*, like that of *María* although more concisely, makes it explicit that his aim is to promote awareness of the need for social reform. Why, then, does he take us with the characters to witness real-life historical events, if his purpose is not to give us historical information but rather to show how the characters misrecognize national history?

The answer, I suggest, is a simple one, related to Anderson's fundamental perception that the aim of the realist novel was to instill in readers a sense of an 'imagined community.' By taking us inside the mind of the characters who observe these historical events, Galdós encourages us to identify with them: not

---

3   This is the same Dr. Esquerdo to whom Ballester suggests taking Maxi at the end of *Fortunata y Jacinta*.

in the sense that we lose our critical detachment, but in the sense that we engage affectively with the spaces they traverse and the events they witness. This affective engagement with spaces in the capital across the entire class spectrum, and with events from recent national history, binds readers together emotionally as Spanish citizens. In a sense it does not matter that much what the specific spaces and events are, so long as they are recognized by readers as real, contemporary, and Spanish. For that reason, I suggest that it is more important to analyze the ways in which Galdós makes his readers engage affectively with the real places and events depicted in his novel, than to try to work out what the precise symbolic relationship might be between Isidora's and Mariano's story and the particular historical events of the 1870s witnessed by them in the novel.

I hope to have shown the significant differences between the ways that Ayguals and Galdós represent real places and historical events. But they can be seen as subscribing to the same realist project in that, in both cases, they give readers a sense of 'being there' with the characters, that produces an emotional attachment to the places visited and the events witnessed. In the case of Galdós, this is done by taking us inside the characters so that, even as we perceive how they misrecognize what they see, we 'feel' those places and events to be part of our experience. In the case of Ayguals, we do not enter into the characters, for they have no interiority. But our affective engagement comes from the passion with which the narrator describes the places and events through which he leads them: that is, from the fact that he is not an impartial narrator — as it is generally assumed that realist narrators ought to be. Indeed, I suggest that, in the case of *María*, this affective engagement occurs, not despite the mass of information that the narrator crams into his novel, but because of the manic passion that drives his truly breathtaking pedagogical urge. Realism, then, in its concern to communicate knowledge about contemporary national life, depends ultimately on the text's ability to make readers engage affectively with that knowledge. As the examples of Ayguals and Galdós show, that can be done in a variety of ways. To call some of them realist, and others not, is to lose sight of the overall aim of the realist project: to make readers into Spaniards.

Works Cited

ANDERSON, BENEDICT. *Imagined Communities: Reflections on the Origin and Spread of Nationalism.* London: Verso, 1983.

ANDREU, ALICIA G. *Galdós y la literatura popular.* Madrid: SGEL, 1982.

AYGUALS DE IZCO, WENCESLAO. *María o la hija de un jornalero.* 2 vols. Madrid: Imprenta de D. Wenceslao Ayguals de Izco, 1845–46.

DELGADO, LUISA ELENA. *La imagen elusiva: Lenguaje y representación en la narrativa de Galdós.* Amsterdam: Rodopi, 2000.

FOUCAULT, MICHEL. *The Birth of the Clinic: An Archaeology of Medical Perception.* Trans. Alan Sheridan. London: Tavistock Publications, 1973.

——. *Discipline and Punish: The Birth of the Prison.* Trans. Alan Sheridan. London: Penguin, 1991.

——. *Madness and Civilisation: A History of Insanity in the Age of Reason.* Trans. Richard Howard. London: Tavistock Publications, 1971.

FUENTES PERIS, TERESA. *Visions of Filth: Deviancy and Social Control in the Novels of Galdós.* Liverpool: Liverpool UP, 2003.

GORDON, M. 'The Medical Background to Galdós's *La desheredada.*' *Anales Galdosianos* 7 (1972): 65–76.

LABANYI, JO. *Gender and Modernization in the Spanish Realist Novel.* Oxford: Oxford UP, 2000.

MARTÍ-LÓPEZ, ELISA. 'Autochthonous Conflicts, Foreign Fictions: The Capital as Metaphor for the Nation.' *Spain beyond Spain: Modernity, Literary History, and National Identity.* Ed. Bradd Epps and Luis Fernández Cifuentes. Lewisburg, PA: Bucknell UP, 2005. 148–67.

PÉREZ GALDÓS, BENITO. *La desheredada.* Ed. Germán Gullón. 2nd ed. Madrid: Cátedra, 2003.

——. *Ensayos de crítica literaria.* Ed. Laureano Bonet. Barcelona: Península, 1972.

RIBBANS, GEOFFREY. '*La desheredada,* novela por entregas: Apuntes sobre su primera publicación.' *Anales Galdosianos* 27–28 (1992–93): 68–75.

——. *History and Fiction in Galdós's Narratives.* Oxford: Clarendon Press, 1993.

SEBOLD, RUSSELL P. *En el principio del movimiento realista: Credo y novelística de Ayguals de Izco.* Madrid: Cátedra, 2007.

CHAPTER 4

Things in Galdós / Galdós's Things: Use Value and Exchange Value

This essay will look at the representation of things in Galdós's fiction, and at the things formerly belonging to Galdós displayed at his house-museum in Las Palmas de Gran Canaria. In both cases, I will be concerned with the materiality of things as a bearer of affect and memory.

As I have stressed in a previous study, the contemporary novels of Galdós, from *La desheredada* to *Miau*, depict a modern world ruled by the market in which the circulation of things turns them into objects of exchange. This supposes an abstract system of monetary value, determined not by the material qualities or function of things but by the law of supply and demand. The importance of things in Galdós's novels derives from his perception that the capitalist system, by fetishizing things on account of their abstract value as commodities, means a loss of respect for their materiality and functionality. In this respect, Galdós coincides with Marx's account of commodity fetishism. In the famous section of *Capital* entitled 'The Fetishism of Commodities,' Marx describes how the market value of the commodity, as the object that circulates on the market, represents a disavowal of the object's human value by suppressing the memory of the labor that produced it and its sentimental value as an object of everyday use.

If Galdós is the great chronicler of modernity, it is because he is an acute critic of its processes. The first part of this chapter will consider passages in his contemporary novels that critique the market system to which so many of his characters are in thrall, in certain cases countering that system by offering the reader an alternative vision in which things are valued for their materiality and shown to be embedded in human and social relations. We may note that, although some of Galdós's most notable female protagonists are seduced by the market, it is largely female characters who show sensitivity to the role of things in everyday life and to the material conditions of labor. This should not surprise us, given the contemporaneous association of men with the rational, which supposes a capacity for abstraction, and of women with feeling and materiality (the body). The notion of sexual difference, which so disadvantaged women, was consolidated with the modern division between the male world of work and female world of the home, which took place in Spain in the mid-nineteenth century. Men thus became identified with progress and women with conservation (reproduction) of the species.[1] The task of maintaining memories was consequently delegated to women, as guardians of the family album, for example.[2]

Before turning to Galdós's novels, I would like to outline the revisionary reading of Marx's theory of commodity fetishism undertaken by Peter Stallybrass in his brilliant article 'Marx's Coat.' Stallybrass insists that Marx was not against fetishism (giving value to things), but merely against the fetishism of commodities, which values things for their exchange value, makings us forget that things are central to social and human relations. Stallybrass describes Jenny Marx's repeated trips to the moneylender to pawn her husband's coat, which was thus stripped of its value as a garment that was loved and regularly worn, becoming reduced to its impersonal exchange value. Stallybrass notes that a used garment is worth less on the market than one that is new and unused. Observing that, without his coat, Marx could not go to the British Museum reading room to write *Capital* (because of the cold and because, if he was not well dressed, he would be denied entry), Stallybrass proposes that Marx's aim in writing *Capital* was 'to give back the coat to its owner' (187): that is, to give things back their human value as objects that are used and loved.

Stallybrass suggests that, in using the term 'fetishism' to describe contemporary bourgeois society's worship of things for their immateriality (exchange value), Marx was making 'one of his least understood jokes' (184). Stallybrass cites the anthropologist William Pietz's analysis of how the Enlightenment theorization of fetishism as the most primitive form of religion supported a colonial belief in the superiority of Europeans as subjects who know how to control objects, positing non-European peoples as inferior for respecting the power of things. As Stallybrass notes, the concept of the fetish (*fetisso*) coined by sixteenth-century Portuguese traders with West Africa was based on a misunderstanding: what the Portuguese traders interpreted as a primitive attribution of supernatural powers to things was, in reality, a refusal by the local inhabitants to trade (give a market value to) objects that for them had an unalienable social value. Marx's concept of commodity fetishism, Stallybrass argues, proposes that contemporary bourgeois society has regressed to the worship of things as bearers of a transcendental (market) value — that is, to the negative form of fetishism that Europeans have attributed to 'primitive peoples.' Bourgeois capitalists are thus the real 'primitives,' by contrast with non-European peoples' respect for the material and social value of things — a positive form of fetishism that Marx had in 1842 called a 'religion of sensuous desire' (Pietz 133). In *Capital* Marx noted that the conversion of a thing into a commodity meant that 'All its sensuous characteristics are extinguished' (cited in Stallybrass 184). This respect for the material and social value of things is, for Stallybrass, the basis of Marx's materialism. In proposing commodity fetishism as the hallmark of capitalism, Marx is inverting the European colonial belief that non-European peoples are inferior for

---

1   A classic statement of this argument is found in Leopoldo Alas's 1894 article 'Psicología del sexo' — disappointingly, given the subtle psychological portrayal of the female protagonist of his novel *La Regenta* (1884–1885). In this article, Alas argues, citing scientific 'evidence,' that men's biology makes them liberal while that of women makes them conservative.
2   See di Bello.

respecting the power of things and for supposing that 'history, memory, and desire might be materialized in objects that are touched and loved and worn' (Stallybrass 186).

Galdós's contemporary novels are full of characters who are dominated by things, while regarding themselves as superior because they appreciate their exchange value. By 'exchange value' I mean not just market value but also what Pierre Bourdieu calls 'symbolic capital': that is, the social prestige afforded by the possession of particular objects. Exchange value not only allows things to circulate on the market but also allows the social mobility of those who own things endowed with symbolic capital. When Galdós describes the tropical feathers that Rosalía de Bringas pins to the bodice of a new dress, he is echoing Marx's joke in proposing the term 'fetishism' to designate the bourgeois worship of exchange value.[3] Rosalía goes on accumulating new dresses that she cannot wear (since her over-spending has to be hidden from her frugal husband), because their value for her is symbolic rather than material. If Rosalía experiences a kind of sexual ecstasy when viewing the shawl in Sobrino Hermanos's store, it is because she is imagining its social impact. In this scene, Galdós shows how Rosalía is deceiving herself in thinking that she is in control of the object of her gaze. The narrator's humorous comparison of the shawl to 'una brava y corpulenta res' ('fierce, brawny bull'; Pérez Galdós, *La de Bringas* 98) confers animistic qualities on the garment, thereby evoking the primitive fetishism so despised by the modern bourgeois subject. In her study *The Culture of Cursilería*, Noël Valis suggests that, in *La de Bringas*, 'it is not so much that persons have undergone commodification as that things have become eroticized' (162). Galdós is here revealing the contradictions of bourgeois fetishism which, rather than confirming human control of things via their possession, shows how, in practice, people are seduced by things that are wrongly presumed to be inert.

In his famous essay on collecting, Walter Benjamin observed that the bourgeois collector tries to strip things of their commodity value by withdrawing them from the market but that, in so doing, he does not give them back their use value but rather confers on them a 'fancier's value' (168); that is, a symbolic value. This ambiguity is seen in Rosalía de Bringas's relationship to 'los trapos' (the sarcastic term for clothes used by the narrator), since she establishes an intensely physical relationship with her collection of dresses, but one that, since she cannot wear them, is not based on use value. The same occurs with her husband Francisco Bringas when he withdraws from the market the banknotes he keeps in his strongbox: he confirms his possession of them by taking them out to touch them, but without thereby giving them the human value of objects that are loved because they are used in everyday life. Here, Galdós anticipates Benjamin in showing how the collector seems to offer the possibility of converting commodity fetishism into a positive

---

3   The first volume of *Capital* was published in German in 1867. A Spanish translation of the first four sections was published in installments in 1886. The first complete translation to Spanish was not published until 1897–98. The ideas expressed in Marx's book were disseminated in Spain through French summaries, especially those of Deville published in 1883 and translated into Spanish in 1887. We do not know whether Galdós knew Deville's French summary when he wrote *La de Bringas* in 1883–84. See Labanyi 395 n. 5.

kind of fetishism that values things for their material qualities; but fails because his tactile relationship to things serves only to confirm his possession of objects desired by him because of their monetary or symbolic value. To desire clothes for their material rather than their symbolic qualities is difficult in a society governed by fashion; to desire banknotes for their material qualities is impossible. In this sense, Francisco Bringas is a 'purer' capitalist — seduced solely by symbolic rather than material value — than Rosalía.

This is seen in Francisco's attitude towards his own clothes. If Marx wrote *Capital* to 'return the coat to its owner,' Francisco Bringas, in the previous novel *Tormento*, loses his coat when it is stolen at the Palace ball. Bringas's overcoat is new; what upsets him is the money wasted in buying it, and not the loss of an item of clothing that is loved and used. His coat was bought solely to confirm his social status and had no practical function, because he doesn't even have to go outdoors to get to the Royal Palace, on whose upper floor the Bringas's apartment is located. Francisco's hair picture is more ambiguous: if, for him, it is a way of buying favors from the Pez family, for Carolina Pez is represents an object whose materiality — the hair of her dead daughter and of other deceased family members — makes it a sentimental memory.

The overly-pious Carolina's sentimentality is depicted negatively but there are other examples in Galdós's novels of a positive attachment to things for their sentimental value. The same Doña Bárbara who, in *Fortunata y Jacinta*, goes shopping every day to buy things she will never use is depicted at the novel's start as a young girl enamored of the Oriental objects in her father's textile store, which captivate her not because of their monetary value but thanks to their material appeal. These two stages of Bárbara's life mark the difference between the fetishism of things for their intrinsic qualities (dominant in a period prior to the consolidation of consumerism in Spain) and commodity fetishism (corresponding to a later period now governed by the market).[4] The young Bárbara grows up surrounded by her father's Oriental commercial goods because the separation between work and home has not yet taken place; the store occupies the ground floor of the family home. Thanks to the lack of a clear distinction between work and home — and thus between masculine and feminine sensibilities — her father Bonifacio Arnaiz is able to share the same material attraction to the Oriental objects he imports: his passion for 'mantones de Manila' (embroidered shawls) almost leads the family to bankruptcy as he orders more and more of them, mindless of declining market demand.

Because she grows up surrounded by imported Oriental goods in the family home, the young Bárbara loves and treats them like objects that form an intimate part of everyday domestic life, without thinking of their value as goods for sale. The

4   I thank Harriet Turner for her suggestion, in the debate following the panel where the original Spanish version of this essay was presented at the 8th International Galdós Conference of June 2005, that the young Bárbara's love of the objects in her father's shop can be read as an anticipation of her later consumerism. This explanation is valid provided one takes into account the fact that, in the years between Bárbara's girlhood and adulthood, Madrid commerce was transformed by its full integration into the modern capitalist market system, as the novel shows us in detail. This economic transformation involved a transformation of the relationship of people to things.

ivory miniatures and fans captivate her with their smell of sandalwood: an example of the 'religion of sensual desire' that for Marx was the positive basis of primitive fetishism. Indeed, Bárbara regards the two Oriental mannequins, and the portrait of the Chinese artist Ayún responsible for the designs of the embroidered shawls, as part of the family because of her cohabitation with them in her father's store. When, on her father's death, her brother Gumersindo takes over the family store, Bárbara will not let him throw out these Oriental figures 'porque dejar de verlos allí haciendo juego con la fisonomía [sic] lela y honrada del Sr. de Ayún, era como si enterrasen a alguno de la familia' ('because no longer seeing them there, keeping company with the honorable, expressionless physionomy of Mr. Ayún, would be like burying someone in the family'; Pérez Galdós, *Fortunata y Jacinta* I, 155–56). Bárbara's lifelong memory of those mannequins is matched by her continued attraction to ivory miniatures whose physical contact, still in middle age, 'le dan ganas de guárdarse[las] en el seno' ('make her want to hide them in her bosom'; I, 126–27, 136). Galdós's identification with Bárbara's attachment to these now outmoded objects is obvious; what makes them valuable — unalienable — for her is the sentimental value afforded by everyday contact.

However, the depiction of Bárbara's fetishistic love of Oriental artefacts is not just a celebration of material objects lovingly remembered. It also makes the reader aware of the history of imperial trade behind Madrid's incipient consumerism, and of the Chinese designers responsible for the 'mantones de Manila,' two of whom Galdós identifies by name. For Marx, commodity fetishism is negative because it relegates to oblivion the labor and economic exploitation that make capitalist consumerism possible. Before embarking on its narration of the progressive exhaustion of the primary energies of Madrid's new consumer society, *Fortunata y Jacinta* not only gives us a run through nineteenth-century global economic history but also takes us on a tour of Spain in which Juanito and Jacinta, on their honeymoon, visit a Barcelona textile factory. Jacinta expresses compassion for the female textile-workers whose working conditions reduce them to machines, exclaiming: 'Está uno viendo las cosas todos los días, y no piensa en cómo se hacen ni se le ocurre averiguarlo ('One sees things every day without stopping to think or find out how they are made'; I, 214).

In the first of Galdós's novels devoted to the critique of consumerism, *La desheredada*, we are given a similar admonishment. Before giving us the story of Isidora's seduction by commodities, the narrator has us accompany her, guided by her practical, hard-working aunt Encarna, to the rope factory where her brother Mariano works — rope factories were one of the small industries denounced for their unhealthy conditions by town planners of the time (Labanyi 121). The description of the industrial process dehumanizes the foreman — 'un "huso vivo" que lleva los hilos enrollados en su cintura, corriendo el peligro de destrozarse si la rueda se dispara' ('a "living spindle" with the strings coiled round his waist, risking being crushed if the wheel got out of control') — while animating the rope: 'la cuerda blanca gimiendo, sola, tiesa, vibrante' ('the white rope whining of its own accord, stiff, vibrating'; Pérez Galdós, *La desheredada* 982). Here the rope corresponds to the kind of fetish denounced by Marx, which seems to have an independent life only because the labor relations that create it are invisible. The wheel that twists the rope, and Mariano who turns it, are relegated to darkness until the reader, with Isidora and her aunt, penetrates deeper into the factory, finally being able to make out the 'invisible mecanismo' ('invisible mechanism'; 982) behind the factory's operations. That the hard-working, lower-class Encarna should be responsible for introducing us — and Isidora — to the mechanisms behind industrial manufacture is appropriate.

The previously cited passages are brief, but they offer a critique of, or counterpoint to, the consumerist ethos of the society depicted in Galdós's contemporary novels. Those novels were written at a time dominated by belief in progress, presumed to be male-driven, in which memory had no place or was delegated to women as guardians of the past. Even the nineteenth century's world exhibitions and museums were conceived not so much as spaces of commemoration, but rather as a celebration of progress in its double form of imperial trade and increasing technological 'mastery' (the gendered term is deliberate) of the material world (Bennett 177–209). For Benjamin, '[t]he fantasmagoria of capitalist culture attained its most radiant unfurling in the World Exposition of 1867' (166). As we know, the young Galdós visited this World Exposition in Paris shortly before embarking on his novelistic career. He returned from Paris not only with the works of Balzac, but also with some touristic souvenirs that are conserved in the Casa-Museo Pérez Galdós in Las Palmas de Gran Canaria: a set of Oriental masks. Tourist souvenirs are objects whose value is not monetary but sentimental; their materiality proclaims 'I was there.'

I will end this essay with some brief reflections on the function of the objects in Galdós's house-museum. Tony Bennett argues that nineteenth-century museums arrange their objects not to showcase their materiality but to convey an invisible narrative (that of human evolution or of the nation's history, for example). But house-museums obey a different impulse: their purpose is to display objects whose sole value consists in having been part of the life of the historical figure who lived there; that is, in having been touched and used by him (occasionally her). House-museums belong to a more recent period than that of the great national museums of the nineteenth century: specifically, to the second half of the twentieth century when belief in progress faltered, giving rise to a culture of commemoration (Huyssen). Galdós's house-museum in Las Palmas, one of the first house-museums in Spain, was inaugurated in 1964. In this respect, the Casa-Museo Pérez Galdós can be seen as the counterpart to the consumerist world depicted, from a critical perspective, in the best-known novels of the writer it commemorates.[5]

5   I would like to thank Rosa María Quintana and Miguel Ángel Vega for their assistance during my visit to the Casa-Museo Pérez Galdós to research this essay in April 2004. Although the museum was closed for refurbishment, Miguel Ángel managed to pull out from the piles of boxes numerous documents relating to the museum's creation, as well as providing me with a copy of the deed of sale by which Galdós's daughter conceded the personal objects from Galdós's villa 'San Quintín' in Santander to the Cabildo Insular of the Canary Islands, and of the script used by the museum guides when showing visitors round.

Only up to a point, however, since one of the functions of the Las Palmas house-museum is, inevitably, to convey to visitors the invisible message of the importance of culture, and specifically the importance of the work of a canonical national author, as well as establishing Las Palmas as his birthplace.[6] What interests me here, however, is the importance of the materiality of the objects displayed: fetishes in the positive sense of the term — that is, objects whose materiality serves to bring back to life the person who used and loved them. Appropriately, one of the most frequently-reproduced objects in the museum is the wooden cradle where Galdós and his nine siblings had lain as infants: a materialization of the story of origins that is the *raison d'être* of the conversion into a museum of the house where the writer was born. The script used by the museum guides explains that the various rooms are imperfect, incomplete reproductions of the sitting room, dining room, and bedroom of Galdós's villa in Santander, and of the bedroom of the house in Madrid where he died, but that most of the objects are authentic. Following the script, the guides warn the visitor that the only room that attempts to depict everyday life in the house where he grew up — the kitchen — is an entirely modern recreation. The script also offers the guides a number of possible responses to the inevitable question about Galdós's lack of physical contact with his native city, which he left in 1862 at the age of nineteen. For the story told by this birthplace converted into a museum is that of an absence. By not claiming to be anything else, the museum succeeds in bring the author back to life, through his embodiment in the authentic objects displayed in its rooms.

The displays give us an image of Galdós as a typical bourgeois collector. In the inventory of the objects sold to the Cabildo Insular de Gran Canaria by his daughter in 1959 we find listed, in addition to his library and a multitude of items of furniture and decorative objects, 'Dos espadas malayas' ('Two Malayan swords') and 'Varias espadas y flechas de indios' ('Several American Indian cutlasses and arrows'). These exotic objects confirm their owner as having possessed a certain level of cultural capital; nevertheless, their function is just to remind us that Galdós had them in his home. In her articles on the Casa-Museo, its director Rosa María Quintana stresses the care Galdós took to safeguard his personal privacy (Quintana Domínguez; Quintana Domínguez and Vega Martín). In recreating 'los ambientes cotidianos del entorno familiar del escritor' ('the everyday atmosphere of the writer's family environment'; Quintana Domínguez 1: 43), his house-museum promises to reveal a secret intimacy, embodied in the objects that were witnesses to his everyday life. Here, things are the subjects and the absent writer has become the object of their wordless story. The furniture occupies a special place on account of its material solidity — and because some of it, as the labels indicate, was designed by Galdós himself. A wardrobe from his bedroom in his Santander villa contains some shirts, a jacket, waistcoat, frock coat, and boots which belonged to — and were worn

6   In an excellent essay on the representation of public museums and private collections in Galdós's contemporary novels, Hazel Gold insists on this aspect of the Las Palmas house-museum. For Gold, museums are necessarily negative spaces that turn the objects displayed into commodities: fetishes in the negative sense of the word.

by — the writer. Especially striking is the purple-upholstered 'sillón del abuelo' ('grandfather's chair') that was used for the staging of Galdós's 1904 play *El abuelo*, subsequently given to Galdós by the actress María Guerrero whose theatre company premiered the work.

Indeed, quite a high proportion of the objects displayed comprise gifts to Galdós from his friends in the literary, artistic, and political spheres; many are signed photographs. This establishes the intimate space of his home as one governed not by the market but by a different kind of exchange based on personal relations — gifts are things whose value is not monetary but affective. The personal objects of Galdós on view in the Casa-Museo were, in some cases, donated by members of his family — in particular, his Madrid bedroom, bequeathed to the Cabildo Insular before the house-museum's creation and originally displayed in the Museo Canario. The cradle was also a gift to the house-museum. Most of the objects on display are a selection of the contents of Galdós's villa in Santander sold to the Cabildo Insular by his daughter; many more items from this purchase — including, of course, his library — are stored in its archives. Although the contents of Galdós's Santander summer home were sold at their market value (500,000 pesetas), the deed of sale states that the purchase is to enable the Cabildo to create a museum in the house where Galdós was born. This is a curious self-canceling commercial transaction, which certifies the sale of Galdós's personal objects while decreeing their withdrawal from the market. It thus turns them into commodities only to undo that conversion by giving them back their function as material memories of their owner.

These paragraphs devoted to the Casa-Museo Pérez Galdós are intended as a modest tribute to those responsible for its upkeep. For museums, like fetishes, are the visible face of the invisible labor relations that allow them to exist. House-museums, in particular, are complex spaces that, on the one hand, exist for the purpose of gaining cultural (and sometimes economic) capital, but we should remember that they also teach us, in a world infinitely more subordinated to abstract market value than the world inhabited by Galdós's characters, to appreciate things as material memories — to appreciate them, that is, for their affective value.

Works Cited

ALAS, LEOPOLDO ('Clarín'). 'La psicología del sexo.' *La Ilustración Ibérica* 12 (1894): 3, 6, 38, 231, 259, 262, 343.

BENJAMIN, WALTER. *Charles Baudelaire: A Lyric Poet in the Era of High Capitalism.* Trans. Harry Zohn. London: Verso, 1989.

BENNETT, TONY. *The Birth of the Museum: History, Theory, Politics.* London: Routledge, 1995.

BOURDIEU, PIERRE. *Distinction: A Social Critique of the Judgement of Taste.* Trans. Richard Nice. London: Routledge, 1996.

DI BELLO, PATRIZIA. 'The Female Collector: Women's Photographic Albums in the Nineteenth Century.' *Living Pictures* 1.2 (2000): 3–20.

GOLD, HAZEL. 'The Museum as Metaframe in the *Novelas contemporáneas*.' *The Reframing of Realism: Galdós and the Discourses of the Nineteenth-Century Spanish Novel.* Durham, NC: Duke UP, 1993. 123–47.

HUYSSEN, ANDREAS. *Twilight Memories: Marking Time in a Culture of Amnesia.* New York: Routledge, 1995.

LABANYI, JO. *Gender and Modernization in the Spanish Realist Novel.* Oxford: Oxford UP, 2000.

MARX, KARL. 'The Fetishism of Commodities.' *Selected Writings.* Ed. David McLellen. Oxford: Oxford UP, 1990. 435–43.

PÉREZ GALDÓS, BENITO. *La de Bringas.* Ed. Alda Blanco and Carlos Blanco Aguinaga. Madrid: Cátedra, 1985.

———. *Fortunata y Jacinta.* Ed. Fransico Caudet. 2 vols. Madrid: Cátedra, 1992.

PIETZ, WILLIAM. 'Fetishism and Materialism: The Limits of Theory in Marx.' *Fetishism as Cultural Discourse.* Ed. Emily Apter and William Pietz. Ithaca, NY: Cornell UP, 1993. 119–51.

QUINTANA DOMÍNGUEZ, ROSA MARÍA. 'El Museo Pérez Galdós, patrimonio cultural.' *Homenaje a Alfonso Armas Ayala.* Vol. 1. Las Palmas de Gran Canaria: Cabildo de Gran Canaria, 2000. 38–44.

———, and MIGUEL ÁNGEL VEGA MARTÍN. 'Los fondos documentales de la Casa-Museo Pérez Galdós.' *I Simposio de Biblioteconomía y Documentación de Canarias (Las Palmas de Gran Canaria, 16 y 17 de febrero de 1993): Actas.* Ed. Elisa Torres Santana. Las Palmas de Gran Canaria: Gobierno de Canarias, 1995. 201–10.

STALLYBRASS, PETER. 'Marx's Coat.' *Border Fetishisms: Material Objects in Unstable Spaces.* Ed. Patricia Spyer. New York: Routledge, 1998. 183–207.

VALIS, NOËL. *The Culture of Cursilería: Bad Taste, Kitsch, and Class in Modern Spain.* Durham, NC: Duke UP, 2002.

CHAPTER 5

❖

Time–Space Compression and Memory in Galdós's *Fortunata y Jacinta*

This essay was prompted by reflections on the relation of memory to modernity. If, on the one hand, modernity requires a break with the past, on the other hand, as Foucault (17–73) and Corbin have observed, one of the main tools for producing a modern sense of individual subjectivity is confession, which requires a review of one's past. The contradiction is only apparent, since the aim of confession — as Freud understood — is to allow the individual to 'unburden' himself of the past in order to 'progress' satisfactorily. I have been struck by the difference between the treatment of time in the work of Galdós and that of Alas. In the majority of Galdós's novels, time moves forward in a linear fashion (flashbacks explain the factors conditioning this forward-moving process, rather than undermining it), and interior monologues generally provide a running comment on the present rather than the past, as the character decides between alternative options for the future. There is little or no place for memory in this scenario. By contrast Alas's *La Regenta* is one of the great 'memory novels' of all time, second perhaps only to Proust's *À la recherche du temps perdu* — indeed, *Lost Time* would be an appropriate title for Alas's work. If Part I of *La Regenta* is framed by Ana Ozores's preparation for confession at its start and Fermín de Pas's review of his youth towards its end, Part II follows a complex temporal structure of overlapping loops as events are narrated via Ana's memories, ending with us back in the cathedral in October — the novel's starting point. Although the novel's end takes place three years after its start, readers are left with the sense that nothing has progressed; the only change is that the future possibilities open to Ana and to Fermín at the novel's start have by now all been closed off. Their tragedy is that they have run out of a future.

If Freud began to develop his theorization of neurosis as an affliction of memory in the 1890s (he was already working with Charcot at La Salpêtrière in 1885–86, just before *Fortunata y Jacinta*'s publication in 1886–87), it was because, from the late 1870s, belief in progress started to give way to an increasing concern with decadence. Morel's seminal *Traité des dégénérescences physiques, intellectuelles et morales de l'espèce humaine* (*Treatise on Physical, Intellectual, and Moral Degeneration*) — well known in Spain — was published in 1857. *La Regenta* (1884–85) betrays the influence of this concern, including the tendency to associate decadence with female transgression (Dijkstra). Galdós's work had been concerned with moral degeneration since at least

[marginalia:] Quizá esto explica el tema de la locura

La desheredada (1881), and his novels of the early 1890s — *Angel Guerra* (1890–91), *Nazarín* and *Halma* (1895) —depict failed attempts at correcting social degeneration. But in none of these novels — at least, in my reading of them to date — does the subject-matter affect the representation of temporality. *Fortunata y Jacinta*, however, has always struck me as an exception to Galdós's generally forward-looking perspective. The novel ends with a sense of moral restitution, as Jacinta receives the gift of Fortunata's child by her husband Juanito and gives Juanito his come-uppance. But the last third of the novel is marked by a sense of time running out as more and more characters decline and die, and the revitalization of the bourgeoisie represented by Fortunata's newborn child is achieved at the expense of the untimely death of Fortunata herself, eclipsing the symbolic source of the natural energies that bourgeois society has exhausted. *Fortunata y Jacinta* is also unusual among Galdós's novels in the attention it gives, at certain points in the text, to its characters' memories.

I have discussed elsewhere the novel's illustration of Herbert Spencer's principle of entropy — the progressive exhaustion of energy — which aggravated the pessimism generated by increasing concern at moral and social degeneration (Labanyi 165–208). As noted there (205), the young Don Baldomero Santa Cruz's mid-century belief in *laissez-faire* self-regulation — 'La naturaleza se cura sola; no hay más que dejarla' ('Nature provides its own cure; you just have to leave it alone'; Pérez Galdós I: 144) — is, by the novel's end in the late 1870s, replaced by a growing sense that society is a 'machine' that is incapable of repairing itself. In that discussion, I was concerned with the development of a market economy, and specifically of consumerism, as the cause of this exhaustion of energies. Here, I should like to focus on another contributing factor: the time-space compression that David Harvey has seen as a consequence of accelerated capitalist development from around 1848. My argument will be that a consequence of the novel's attention to time-space compression is a turn to memory.

Harvey sees the Europe-wide capitalist crisis of 1846–47 and the ensuing wave of political insurrections that swept across Europe in 1848 as responsible for a related crisis in the perception of time and space. Harvey argues that this economic and political crisis brought home the realization that capitalism had linked broad sweeps of the world in ways that made any idea of discreet, controllable units of space untenable, at the same time introducing a sense of living under a temporal order ruled by simultaneity rather than progress. Harvey sees this as calling into question earlier Enlightenment attempts to rationalize and standardize time and space in the name of progress — attempts that were based on the notion, fundamental to Renaissance perspective, that the individual stood at the center of a world laid out for his surveillance and command (258–59). As Harvey notes: 'The certainty of absolute space and place gave way to the insecurities of a shifting relative space, in which events in one place could have immediate and ramifying effects in other places' (261). One needs to add here that the Enlightenment's goal of rationalizing and standardizing time and space was never realized successfully in even the most technologically advanced Western societies, much less so in Spain; and that contradictory perceptions of time and space were thus not new in 1848. What was new was the sense that different spaces were bound up with one another, with the individual being affected by events occurring in distant places and beyond his control or understanding, decentering the individual and producing a new 'flattening' of time, as well as an awareness that all this was the result of the global expansion of the capitalist market system. Spain did not have an 1848 Revolution, but the second chapter of Part I of *Fortunata y Jacinta*, subtitled 'Vistazo histórico sobre el comercio matritense' ('Historical Survey of Madrid Commerce') makes it clear that, in the mid-century, Spaniards experienced a new consciousness of their involvement in the global reach of capitalist trade, which, thanks to the press and the availability of imported consumer goods, impacted widely on public consciousness. It might seem ironic that this global consciousness should have come into being *after* the loss in the 1820s of most of Spain's early modern empire, but this is not so illogical: Spain's loss of control of maritime trade — a process begun in the seventeenth century as Amsterdam took over from Seville as the seat of Atlantic traffic — placed it at the mercy of international circuits of commerce, which created a sense of being enmeshed in a global order that affected Spaniards without their being able to control it.

In their book *TimeSpace*, Jon May and Nigel Thrift insist that nineteenth-century capitalist expansion, made possible by faster communications, created a simultaneous sense of space expanding and shrinking, since awareness of the interconnectedness of different parts of the world expanded geographical horizons while making distant places seem nearer (8, 10, 12). The term 'time-space compression,' coined by Harvey and borrowed from him by May and Thrift, is the corollary of a new awareness of geographical expansion. This expansion is experienced as a compression since the individual becomes aware of his ensnarement in global networks that are beyond his control or understanding. What interests me particularly is Harvey's observation that this time-space compression is related to the late nineteenth-century obsession with world exhibitions and museums: institutions dedicated to the production of memory. These memory-factories contributed to the new awareness of the interconnectedness of the different parts of the world which they displayed to visitors, as well as resulting from it: 'The ideological labor of inventing tradition became of great significance in the late nineteenth century precisely because this was an era when transformations in spatial and temporal practices implied a loss of identity with place and repeated radical breaks with any sense of historical continuity' (Harvey 272).

Chapter 2 of *Fortunata y Jacinta* is a textbook illustration of Harvey's and May and Thrift's theorization of time-space compression.[1] It is precisely in 1848 that Juanito's father, Don Baldomero Santa Cruz, inherits his textile retail business from his father, the date that marks a shift from trade in 'géneros del país' ('domestic goods') to 'géneros *de fuera*' ('imported goods'; Pérez Galdós 1: 119–20; emphasis in original). Don Baldomero passes the business to his employees ('los *Chicos*') when this foreign

---

1   The historical implications of this chapter have been thoughtfully analyzed by Peter Bly (88–91).

commerce gets too complicated for him. If Don Baldomero dealt with both domestic and imported products, Madrid's other leading textile retailer, 'el gordo Arnaiz,' deals exclusively in imports, having banking connections in London. Don Baldomero's wife, Doña Bárbara (related to both 'el gordo Arnaiz' and to the Santa Cruz family) is the daughter of Bonifacio Arnaiz, a 'comerciante en pañolería de la China' ('Chinese textile merchant') and owner of a textile store popularly known as 'la tienda de Filipinas' ('the Filipino store') since its Chinese goods are imported via Manila (hence the name 'mantón de Manila' of the embroidered shawls that are the store's specialty) (1: 124–25, 132). It is at this point that the first reference in the novel to memory occurs, when we are told that Doña Bárbara remembered for the rest of her life the two Chinese mannequins in her father's store:

> Como se recuerda a las personas más queridas de la familia, así vivieron y viven siempre con dulce memoria en la mente de Barbarita los dos maniquís de tamaño natural vestidos de mandarín que había en la tienda y en los cuales sus ojos aprendieron a ver. (1: 126–27)

> (Just as one remembers the most beloved members of the family, so would those life-size mannequins dressed as mandarins in the store, through which her eyes learned to see, live on forever in Barbarita's memory.)

If the previous chapter picked up the young Bárbara's love of these Oriental objects as fetishes, adored not for their exchange value but for their sensuous characteristics, what concerns me here is the fact that these life-size figures, together with the portrait of the Chinese designer of the embroidered shawls, Ayún, become lodged in Bárbara's memory because of the loss of this Oriental trade when, on her father's death, the family firm is threatened with bankruptcy. This economic downturn results from a mix of capitalist over-accumulation (her father orders more 'mantones de Manila' than he can sell) and unpredictable changes of fashion. As the business passes into the hands of the next generation (Gumersindo Arnaiz, Bárbara's brother and the future father of Jacinta), Spanish trade with the Far East is thrown into crisis thanks to global geo-political changes: the growth of the British merchant navy, the establishment of the British trading port of Singapore, and the opening up of a new trade route to the East via the British-built railway across the Suez isthmus, the combination of which makes unviable the much longer and slower Spanish trade route round the Cape of Good Hope to Manila. As the narrator notes, the Arnaiz family business's contacts with China become redundant, when it is so much quicker and cheaper to buy imported Chinese fabrics from traders in Liverpool. The decline of Spain's Far Eastern trade is clinched by new fast steamship routes between Spain and northern Europe, leading to an influx in Spain of British, Belgian, and French merchants, and a new taste for Parisian imports which, with faster communications, can be guaranteed to be in fashion. Gumersindo Arnaiz's wife, Isabel Cordero, is the first to realize the consequences of these geo-political shifts. The narrator comments that these changes result from processes taking place in distant places about which she has no knowledge but which impact on her family's business nonetheless: 'Sin saber palotada de Geografía, [Isabel Cordero] comprendía que había un Singapore y un istmo de Suez' ('Without knowing a scrap of Geography, [Isabel Cordero] understood that there was a Singapore and a Suez isthmus'; 1: 153). Advised by his canny wife, Gumersindo Arnaiz abandons Far Eastern imports for textiles shipped from France, England, and Switzerland (1: 150–52, 155). The result for Spaniards is a sense of geo-political contraction that is the other side of an awareness of global spatial expansion and temporal acceleration: an expansion and acceleration achieved at Spain's cost. Doña Bárbara's lifelong memory of the Chinese figures in the store in which she grew up is the result of a complex reorientation of time and space on a global scale. Harvey insists on the paradox whereby faster communications between distant places, while opening up world trade, result in a sense of compression: 'as time horizons shorten to the point where the present is all there is ... so we have to learn how to cope with an *overwhelming sense of compression* of our spatial and temporal worlds' (240; emphasis in the original). To put this slightly differently: faster capitalist turnover time, with improved communications, produces a sense of simultaneity and instant gratification which eliminates the sense of a future. Consumerist growth not only exhausts natural energies, as *Fortunata y Jacinta* illustrates so well; it also eats up the future. In Spain's case, the loss of Far East trade to British competition further aggravates this sense of the loss of the future. What is left is memory: Doña Bárbara's memory of the Chinese figures in her father's store, which she insists remain there when her brother Gumersindo drops Far Eastern imports.

Although confession does not function in *Fortunata y Jacinta* as a device for the construction of subjectivity as it does in *La Regenta*, nevertheless Galdós's novel contains a significant number of confessions (unparalleled, I think, in Galdós's work). They are sufficiently symmetrically distributed to suggest that Galdós thought carefully about their role. In Part I, Juanito confesses his liaison with Fortunata to Jacinta; in Part II, Fortunata is interrogated about her past life by Maxi in his adopted role as 'misionero' ('missionary'); and in Part III, Feijoo not only encourages Fortunata to tell him about her past but reciprocates with his own erotic 'confessions.' I do not include here Fortunata's interrogation and 'absolution' by Maxi's priest brother, Nicolás Rubín, in Part II, since the focus is on Nicolás's incompetence, with Fortunata saying very little. The above-mentioned three confessions have the role of flashbacks, filling in the reader's gaps in knowledge about Fortunata's past, rather than being formative experiences for the confessant. In all three cases, the confessions are the result of prodding by another character, rather than spontaneous exercises in memory. As the equivalent of flashbacks, they largely underpin the novel's linear construction, and thus cannot be seen as a consequence of time-space compression. However, in all three cases these confessions reveal important information about the extensive spatial circuits into which the characters are inscribed. It is through Fortunata's 'confession' to Maxi in Part II that we hear the story of how prostitution — a form of market exchange — took her not only to Barcelona but even to Paris, something that is quite extraordinary for an illiterate, lower-class woman. Her 'confession' to Feijoo in Part III, which follows her genuinely spontaneous urge to go over her past in order to come to terms with her lapse into adultery, adds no new information for the reader (though it is new to Feijoo). It is Feijoo's erotic confessions to her that expand the novel's spatial horizons, as he tells of his amorous exploits 'en las cinco partes del mundo' ('in all five corners of the world'), particularly in the Far East with 'chinas, javanesas y hasta con joloanas' ('Chinese, Javanese and even Filipino native women'; 2: 107). He also recalls for her his military exploits in Cuba and Rome. Juanito's confession to Jacinta in Part I takes place in the course of their honeymoon tour of Spain, taking advantage of the new railway network which makes travel both easier and faster. This nationwide tour not only serves to inscribe them (and the Spanish reader) into a national framework, teaching them (and the reader) that Madrid is merely one part of a diverse tapestry of regions making up the nation; it also introduces them to the principal industrial and agricultural products of the various regions, showing that the nation is a network of commerce. It is important that they should tour Barcelona's textile factories: May and Thrift (14) note that factory production, with its strict timetables and routines, played a key role in changing the experience of time and space. As noted in the previous chapter, Jacinta expresses her compassion for the female factory workers trapped in the factory's mechanized rhythms, but she and Juanito are also learning that they form part of a wider system of interlocking networks, coordinated by the railway whose own timetables and mechanized rhythms alter perceptions of time and space. Jacinta prises Juanito's confession out of him at a point when they are feeling a sense of temporal dilation — 'Ni Jacinta ni su esposo apreciaban bien el curso de las fugaces horas' ('Neither Jacinta nor her husband had a clear sense of the passing of time'; 1: 201) — as well as an exhilarating expansion of spatial horizons as they speed through the landscape. The final and most substantial instalment of his confession occurs when Juanito gets drunk at the wedding party in Seville of some anglicized Spaniards from Gibraltar (1: 225): as his memories pour out uncontrollably, they experience the sensation of being bound up in networks crossing international frontiers as well as past and present.

Both Fortunata and Juanito want to escape their pasts but find themselves lapsing back into it, again and again. This oscillation not only reflects the U-turns of Spanish politics of the time,[2] but also embodies the flattening of linear time that Harvey has seen as a feature of the second half of the nineteenth century. This temporal experience is related to the characters' simultaneous sensation of being caught up in networks of relationships that collapse spatial difference. The term 'enredadera' (climbing plant or vine) is used repeatedly to refer to this simultaneous expansion and closing in of social networks. The more extensive the relationships — based on kinship and commerce — that bind the characters together, the more they (and we) are made aware of the plurality of spaces comprising Madrid society, and of their links to international banking and trade. At the same time, the characters experience the sensation of becoming ensnared in a web of lives and events beyond their control. The metaphor of the 'enredadera' first occurs in the context of the convoluted cross-class family and social relationships of the

2   For the parallels between Juanito's oscillation between attraction to the working-class Fortunata and attraction to his wife Jacinta and the historical vicissitudes of the period 1869–76, see Ribbans and Bly 87, 91–93.

Santa Cruz family, comprising a 'dilatado y laberíntico árbol que más bien parece enredadera' ('extended, labyrinthine tree that is more of a vine'; 1: 241; see also 245 and 403). The 'enredadera' is an apt metaphor, for these relationships proliferate like a fast-growing climbing plant which, the more it spreads, the more it threatens to strangle what it encompasses. The sprawling structure of the novel is itself that of an 'enredadera' which, the more it grows, the more it presses in on its characters, reducing their options through the very same process that appears to open them up.

True to this structure, the last third of the novel — from the start of Feijoo's decline in Part III, Chapter 4 — traces a series of deaths and snuffing out of possibilities. First Mauricia dies; then Moreno Isla; then Fortunata; then, finally, Feijoo. In Part IV, Chapter 3, titled 'Disolución' ('Dissolution'), Fortunata breaks first with Juanito and then with Maxi; at the end of the novel, Jacinta ends her marriage to Juanito in all but name. Harvey singles out Flaubert's *L'Éducation sentimentale* as an illustration of the new sensation of time-space compression, in which the characters' experience of multiple spaces as they '[glide] in and out of the differentiated spaces of the city' leads to a proliferation of infinite possibilities, but at the same to ensnarement in webs beyond one's control which close off one's options. The result is an overwhelming sense of wasted opportunities, of 'time lost' (to return to Proust's title). As Harvey puts is, referring to Flaubert's novel: 'Action is reduced to a set of paths that might have been but were not taken' (263). Unlike *La Regenta*, not all time is lost in *Fortunata y Jacinta*, for Fortunata does give birth to a son who will continue the Santa Cruz dynasty, and she does acquire social 'polish' in the course of her moves around Madrid's socially differentiated spaces. But the novel's overall spatial structure is cyclical, as she returns to the working-class quarters in the Cava de San Miguel where Juanito and the reader first met her in Part I. This return sparks off in her memories of her past life in that space, as she draws comparisons between its state of disrepair and the household comforts she has got used to in the petty-bourgeois Rubín home and the various love-nests that Juanito and Feijoo had set up for her:

> Aquel barrio y los sitios aquellos éranle tan familiares, que a ojos cerrados andaría por entre los cajones sin tropezar. ¿Pues y la casa? En ella, desde el portal hasta lo más alto de la escalera de piedra, veía pintada su infancia, con todos sus episodios y accidentes. ... '¡Las vueltas del mundo! — decía dando las de la escalera y venciendo con fatiga los peldaños — . ¡Quién me había de decir que pararía aquí otra vez! ... Ahora es cuando conozco que, aunque poco, algo se me ha pegado el señorío. Miro todo esto con cariño; ¡pero me parece tan ordinario...!' (2: 396; last two ellipses in original)

> (The neighborhood and those spaces were so familiar she could have picked her way through the crates [in the market] with her eyes closed, without stumbling. And the building? From the doorway to the top of the stone staircase, it offered her a gallery of images of her childhood, depicting every incident and detail. ... 'The twists of fate!' she reflected as she clambered up the twisting stairs. 'Who'd have thought I'd be back here! ... It makes me realize I've picked up some manners, though not a lot. I look at all this fondly, but it seems so common...!)

As she reflects (in free indirect style), in an eloquent recognition of time-space compression: 'Era como una red que la envolvía, y como pensara escabullirse por algún lado, se encontraba otra vez cogida.' ('It was like being caught in a net, and if she tried to escape, she found herself caught again'; 2: 398) Her return to her spatial origins means that the novel ends on a note of memory. This is not nostalgia for lost origins, but memory triggered by the unwanted return to origins resulting from failed opportunities. The narrative logic of this [cyclical structure] suggests that, despite the fact that she is about to give birth, there is nothing left for her but to die.

Feijoo's physical decline is experienced by him explicitly as a case of failed opportunities. On Fortunata's last visit to him, he emerges briefly from his senility to reflect: '¡Ah, qué tiempos aquellos! ¿Te acuerdas? Lástima que yo no hubiera tenido veinte años menos. Entonces sí que habríamos sido dichosos' ('Ah, what good times they were! Do you remember? If only I'd been twenty years younger. Then we'd really have been happy'; 2: 393). Fortunata says goodbye to him for the last time with a sense of irreparable loss. The chapter devoted to Moreno Isla — Part IV, Chapter 2, the only chapter in which he appears — has the sole function of reinforcing the theme of lost opportunities which is the novel's closing note. In his late forties, Moreno comes to regret never having married. The heart attack from which he dies represents the impossibility of reconciling the contradiction between the possibility of love which Jacinta has opened up, and the impossibility of satisfying it since she is married to someone else. It seems significant that the character whose sole function is to represent failed opportunity should be an international banker based in London, whose career has been devoted to extending the global financial networks that open up opportunities while producing time-space compression. His sudden pain is that of a terrible 'opresión' ('pressure'; 2: 363). His last few days are devoted to memories — memories of what he might have done but didn't, represented by the two beggars to whom he could have been generous but wasn't — as well as fantasies about what might have happened if he had married Jacinta. He feels intense empathy with Jacinta because her life too, as a childless wife who adores children, has been one of wasted opportunities. Moreno compensates for the impossibility of fathering children with Jacinta by turning to memories of his own childhood relationship to his father (2: 347–48). Moreno's death actualizes his acute sense of loss of the future; that is, his realization that the only future he can conceive of consists of what he might have done but didn't.

Moreno's retreat into memory, as he comes to realize that the past is all he has, is echoed by the sensation of loss of the future experienced by Juanito when he finally loses his wife's love: 'experimentó por vez primera esa sensación tristísima de las irreparable pérdidas y del vacío de la vida, sensación que en plena juventud equivale al envejecer ... y marca la hora en que lo mejor de la existencia se corre hacia atrás, quedando a la espalda los horizontes que antes estaban por delante' ('he felt for the first time that sorrowful sensation of irreparable loss and the emptiness of life, a sensation that, when experienced in the prime of life, is tantamount to growing old ... and marks the moment when the best times in one's life go into reverse, with the horizons that were previously ahead now being behind'; 2: 533). This statement is every bit as desolate as the sense of wasted opportunities left by the end of *La Regenta*, or by that of Flaubert's *L'Éducation sentimentale* — the example of the literary expression of time–space compression given by Harvey. The desolation is increased by the repeated reminders that even memories do not last: as Mauricia's body is taken away in the funeral carriage, the narrator comments: 'de Mauricia no quedó más que un recuerdo, todavía fresco; pero que se había de secar rápidamente' ('all that was left of Mauricia was a memory, still fresh, but that would quickly wither'; 2: 234). Feijoo's decline consists not just of loss of the future, in the form of his realization of wasted opportunities, but in his added loss of memory: 'El ayer se borró absolutamente del espíritu de aquel buen caballero' ('The past was completely obliterated from the good gentleman's mind'; 2: 392). Guillermina comforts the dying Fortunata by telling her she has left a 'buena memoria de sí' ('good memory of herself') by giving Jacinta her child; but, on his return from Fortunata's funeral, Segismundo Ballester (another character afflicted with a sense of lost opportunity, having never been able to express his love for Fortunata) declares: 'Esta imagen ... vivirá en mí algún tiempo; pero se irá borrando, borrando, hasta que enteramente desaparezca. Esta presunción de un olvido posible, aun suponiéndolo lejano, me da más tristeza que lo que acabo de ver...' ('Her image ... will live on in my mind for a while; but it will start to fade, and go on fading, until it has completely vanished. The thought of forgetting her, even if it doesn't happen for some time, makes me sadder than what I've just seen...'; 2: 535; last ellipsis in original).

Perhaps the most curious feature of the novel is that it ends, not just with the evacuation of the future and the threat of loss even of memory of the past, but with the creation of false memories. Jacinta starts to 'remember' her labor pains in giving birth to a son who is not her own (2: 534), at the same time as she takes to fantasizing about an 'if only' world in which the baby is her child with Moreno Isla, and Moreno Isla is still alive and has Juanito's good looks. Ironically, it seems that the only future left at the end of the novel is that provided by the projection of false memory. There is nothing new in signaling that this ending — together with the extraordinary depiction of Maxi's lucid derangement, not relevant to this discussion — anticipates the exploration of delusion in Galdós's novels of the 1890s. What I hope to have shown is that the novel's attention to memory, unusual in Galdós's work, is related to the bigger issue of time–space compression, whereby the expansion of global horizons simultaneously opens up limitless opportunities and creates a sense of being ensnared by events happening elsewhere. The result, to cite Harvey's phrase again, is the reduction of action to 'a set of paths that might have been but were not taken': belief in the future is replaced by an acute awareness of lost opportunities. The linear time of progress — living for the future — is replaced by memory not in its usual form of living in the past, but in the form of remembering what did not happen but might have happened. The future has become an empty time whose barrenness those characters still living at the end of the novel have to face. The future has been replaced by the future perfect.

Works Cited

BLY, PETER A. *Galdós's Novel of the Historical Imagination*. Liverpool: Francis Cairns, 1983.

CORBIN, ALAIN. 'Intimate Relations.' Trans. Arthur Goldhammer. *A History of Private Life*. Vol. 4: *From the Fires of Revolution to the Great War*. Ed. Michelle Perrot. Cambridge, MA: Belknap Press of Harvard UP, 1990. 549–613.

DIJKSTRA, BRAM. *Idols of Perversity: Fantasies of Feminine Evil in Fin-de-Siècle Culture*. New York: Oxford UP, 1986.

FOUCAULT, MICHEL. *The History of Sexuality: An Introduction*. Penguin: Harmondsworth, 1987.

HARVEY, DAVID. *The Condition of Postmodernity*. Oxford: Blackwell, 1989.

LABANYI, JO. *Gender and Modernization in the Spanish Realist Novel*. Oxford: Oxford UP, 2000.

MAY, JON, and NIGEL THRIFT. *TimeSpace: Geographies of Temporality*. London: Routledge, 2001.

PÉREZ GALDÓS, BENITO. *Fortunata y Jacinta*. 2 vols. Ed. Francisco Caudet. Madrid: Cátedra, 1992.

RIBBANS, GEOFFREY. 'Contemporary History in the Structure and Characterization of *Fortunata y Jacinta*.' *Galdós Studies*. Ed. John E. Varey. London: Tamesis, 1970. 90–113.

CHAPTER 6

The Obstinate Negativity of
Ana Ozores

This chapter is an attempt to explore alternative approaches to Leopoldo Alas's 1884–85 novel, *La Regenta*. It has become a commonplace to see the novel as an anticipation of psychoanalysis because of its synergies, not only with Freud's concept of the unconscious and attribution of neurosis to sexual repression, but also with his view of woman as lack. Feminist theorists have long had problems with Freud's notion of woman as defined by lack of a penis (castration), which equates agency with ownership of the (biological as well as symbolic) phallus. As a woman, I find such a notion illogical and untenable, though admittedly the equation of woman with lack works brilliantly for a novel whose protagonist, Ana Ozores, lacked a mother, lacks a child, lacks a sexual relationship with her husband, and has nothing to do. Worse still: Ana lacks an identity — she reflects more than once that her true self is the disintegration of the self that she feels within. Indeed, it is hard to write a character sketch of her, apart from the adjective *egoísta* (self-centered) that the narrator regularly applies to her — a negative affect not only because it is the reverse of the altruism or 'reciprocidad' (reciprocity) proposed as the ethical basis of society by the Krausist thinkers with whom Alas was closely associated, but also because it is precisely Ana's intense focus on her inner self that produces in her a sense of dissolution.[1] I have always been puzzled by how *La Regenta* succeeds in interesting us when its protagonist not only has no identity, but does not progress or learn anything in the course of the novel's seven hundred pages, in most of which nothing happens.

I would like to see if this can be explained by reading the novel through the theorization of negative affect that has emerged in the last decade as part of the 'affective turn.'[2] I am thinking particularly of Sianne Ngai's *Ugly Feelings*, which argues that negative affects have agency and critical productivity. I shall dialogue also with Sara Ahmed's *The Promise of Happiness* and Lauren Berlant's *Cruel Optimism*, which analyze how we come to desire what makes us unhappy. I have used the phrase 'obstinate negativity' in my title because what I find striking about

1   For a detailed discussion of Alas's relation to Krausism, see Lissorgues 156–87. A briefer account, relating specifically to *La Regenta*, is given in Labanyi, *Gender* 219–24.
2   For the affective turn, see in particular Brennan; Clough; Thrift. For a brief survey, see Labanyi, 'Doing Things.'

Ana Ozores is the obstinacy with which she clings to negativity. Stephanie Sieburth has chided the narrator of *La Regenta* for systematically cutting off Ana's options, but one can perhaps see negativity as a resource that enables Ana to endure. In this respect, my argument, while rejecting the psychoanalytic focus on the individual subject, is compatible with Alison Sinclair's psychoanalytical reading of the novel, which draws on the work of female psychoanalysts to argue that Ana's hysteria is not so much a response to female lack as strategic (33, 39, 219).[3]

⌐Ngai defines negative affects (what she calls 'ugly feelings') as those that allow no catharsis, no transcendence — unlike tragic or 'noble' forms of unhappiness such as grief or a sense of injustice or even anger. The 'ugly feelings' she analyzes are intransitive — turning away from, rather than toward, their object — and related to inertia, suspended agency, and inaction (1–14): concepts applicable to *La Regenta* as a novel about an introspective protagonist with no options, in which very little happens⌐ When things do happen, in the second part of the twenty-ninth chapter and first part of the final thirtieth chapter, the narrator rushes through them as if trying to get back as soon as possible, in the remainder of the last chapter, to the inertia, suspended agency, and inaction that have driven the rest of the novel. For Ana's inertia, suspended agency, and inaction are not a lack but what drives the novel. Ngai notes that negative affects are fundamentally non-narrative because they are about being stuck (25–26): ⌐*La Regenta* is an extraordinary example of a non-narrative novel whose 700 pages go nowhere.⌐ The fifteen chapters of its first part cover three days at such a slow pace that we feel we are not moving, while the fifteen chapters of its second part cover three years through a series of temporal loops that undo the sense of time progressing.[4] The novel ends as it starts: with Ana unsuccessfully seeking confession from the Magistral in the cathedral in October. In this chapter, rather than analyze the reasons for Ana's 'stuckness' (which only get us back to the conclusion that she is stuck), I would like to consider what her negativity does — for her, for her fellow Vetustans, and for us as readers.

⌐First, some introductory remarks on affect theory are in order. Affect theory departs from psychoanalysis in that it refuses a subject-centered view of the world, in which emotions are authentic expressions of the inner self. On the contrary, affect occurs at the interface of self and world: it is the result of an encounter. In its extreme form, propagated by Brian Massumi (2002, 2015), affect theory sees affect as a preconscious, subjectless force or energy produced through the encounter between self and world (including other selves and things, for the human and the non-human are not distinguished). According to this view, affect is a material process, distinct from the subjective experience of emotion which occurs once the subject acquires consciousness of this energetic charge and gives it a name: fear, joy, anger, pity, for example.[5] Berlant has criticized Massumi for stressing the preconscious impact

---

3   For Sinclair, the novel shows all the characters to be in flight from a more fundamental lack: that of an ontological formlessness or void.

4   A significant proportion of Part II is narrated via Ana's memories which fill the reader in on what has happened since the previous chapter. On several occasions, the temporal loops circle back over the same period of time twice.

5   Massumi (*Parables* 23–28) notes that there is a half second time-lag between the pre-conscious

of the world on the self to the point that, despite his insistence that affect is the capacity to affect as well as to be affected, human agency becomes diminished. Berlant is interested primarily in the active process of affective investment; for this reason, she prefers not to make a firm distinction between affect and emotion (14) — a practice followed also by Ahmed and Ngai. They are able to align affect and emotion (though seeing affect as characterized by a particularly intense energetic charge) because they see emotion too as occurring at the interface between self and world — as theorized in Ahmed's earlier study *The Cultural Politics of Emotion* (5–12).[6] This redefinition of emotion radically de-centers the Romantic notion of emotion as the seat of an authentic inner self. For the rest of this essay I will follow Ahmed, Berlant, and Ngai in using the terms 'affect' and 'emotion' interchangeably, and in regarding both as taking place at the point of contact of self and world.

Affect theory renders irrelevant the nineteenth-century debates around determinism — can subjects impose themselves on the world, or does the world determine them? — since affect, occurring at the interface between self and world, involves a two-way process in which self and world mutually constitute each other. For affect theory, self and world cannot be seen as separate entities for they are inextricably entangled — and affect is what binds them together. The debate on determinism versus free will was, of course, the context of the polemic in Spain over realism versus naturalism, which Zola had proclaimed as the literary equivalent of social medicine in its analysis of the material causes of human dysfunction. Alas's ambivalence in this polemic, supporting naturalism but rejecting determinism (Beser 108–53), perhaps signals that affect theory offers an appropriate reading of his novel, in which the same ambivalence exists. On the one hand, *La Regenta* places considerable stress on emotions as a response to the material world, rather than as residing in the inner self. On the other hand, the novel is also fundamentally about Ana's emotional investments, which suppose an active engagement with the world.

Affect theory is part of what has become known as the 'new materialism.'[7] The narrator of *La Regenta* goes into some detail about the reading of mid-nineteenth-century materialist thinkers by the local Don Juan, Álvaro Mesía. These thinkers include Büchner, Moleschott, Virchow, and Vogt, not to mention Lucretius (2: 360–61).[8] One of the devastating things about *La Regenta* is that Mesía's materialist

---

registration of an external stimulus on the body (affect), and conscious recognition of the feeling generated (emotion).

6   In *The Cultural Politics*, Ahmed argues that one does not 'have' emotions as a property of the self, nor do emotions enter us from the outside, but that 'emotions create the very effect of an inside and an outside' (8–10) — that is, the illusion that self and world are separate.

7   The 'new materialism' is concerned to question the binary oppositions between body and mind, self and world, human and animal, and the animate and the inanimate. The common inspiration is the monism of Baruch Spinoza, read via Gilles Deleuze, which sees all phenomena as part of a material continuum, in which everything is bound to everything else. For a clear exposition of the materialist reading of affect, based on Spinoza's definition of affect as 'the capacity to affect and be affected,' see Massumi, *Politics*. The ecological implications of the new materialism are explored in Bennett.

8   All page references to *La Regenta* are to Sobejano's edition. As Sobejano explains (360–61 nn.

diagnosis of Ana is proved right, despite the narrator's scathing depiction of him. Mesía sees himself as a 'máquina eléctrica de amor' ('electrical love machine') able to 'echar chispas' ('emit sparks'; Alas, *La Regenta* 2: 358). Ana's hysterical attacks are marked by her seeing 'chispas de fuegos artificiales' ('sparks like fireworks'; 1: 174). Given the similar terminology, we are invited to ask whether there is any difference between Mesía's materialist reading of the self and Ana's spiritual reading. The materialist doctor Benítez's maxim *Ubi irritatio ibi fluxus* ('Where the irritation, there the flow'; 2: 405) could be seen as an anticipation of affect theory, for it refers to an energetic process that takes place at the point of contact between self and world.[9]

There are many passages in *La Regenta* that depict emotions as resulting from the contact between self and world, rather than originating in the self. To cite a few examples: Ana's expansiveness towards Mesía at the Vegallanas' mansion is triggered by his masculine smell: 'un perfume ... que debía de tener algo de tabaco bueno y otras cosas puramente masculinas' ('a perfume ... that was no doubt a mix of good tobacco and other purely masculine things'; 2: 489, ellipsis added). Her receptivity to him can be triggered by the impact of physical objects, as when the sight of the uncleared table after lunch provokes the desolation that makes her welcome his subsequent appearance on horseback at her balcony: 'La insignificancia de aquellos objetos que contemplaba le partía el alma; se le figuraba que eran símbolo del universo, que era así, ceniza, frialdad, un cigarro abandonado a la mitad por el hastío del fumador' ('The insignificance of those objects displayed before her eyes struck at the core of her soul; she saw them as a symbol of the universe, which was like that too, ash, things gone cold, a cigar left half-smoked thanks to the smoker's lethargy'; 2: 10). The symbolism that Ana projects onto the objects on the table — the left-over coffee, the dirty liqueur glass, the cigar — is trite, but their material effect on her is real. Ana and Mesía's communication as they talk at the balcony takes place not through their verbal exchange but 'por efluvios' ('via emissions'; 2: 26).

The above examples involve emotional processes that originate in the physical imprint of the world on the self. But Ana is not just a recipient of external stimuli; so little happens in *La Regenta* because the novel is primarily concerned with her affective investments. And her affective investments are aimed at producing stasis. In my earlier *Gender and Modernization in the Spanish Realist Novel*, I read the late nineteenth-century Spanish novel as obsessed with the concept of blockage, which

---

18–22, 24), the philosopher of science Ludwig Büchner's best-known work, *Kraft und Stoff* (*Force and Matter*, 1854), cited by *La Regenta*'s narrator, argued that everything is matter in motion. The other German-language scientists mentioned by the narrator — the physiologist Jakob Moleschott, the founder of social medicine Rudolf Virchow, and the zoologist Karl Vogt — argued that thoughts and emotions are physiological processes. Mesía was too lazy to read beyond the first half of Lucretius's *De rerum natura* (1: 360–61). As the narrator wryly comments, Mesía tries to instill the notion that everything is energy and matter in his lovers because 'Cuando la mujer se convencía de que no había metafísica, le iba mucho mejor a don Álvaro' ('When women were persuaded that there was no such thing as metaphysics, things went much better for Don Álvaro'; 1: 361). Translations from *La Regenta* are my own.

9   For the medical history of this Latin phrase, see Sinclair 166.

I there related to contemporary medical and economic anxieties.[10] Here I wish to read the concept of blockage in terms of the 'stuckness' that is central to the theorization of negative affect. In her book on *La Regenta* (which has a wonderful section on mud as an image of being stuck), Alison Sinclair turns around Freud's reading of hysteria as being stuck in the past (viz. his maxim 'hysterics suffer mainly from reminiscences'), to argue that Ana resorts strategically to hysteria (whose physical symptom is a choking feeling) as an obstruction that allows her to avoid 'the reality of sexual life, sexual intercourse, and reproduction' (151).[11] According to this argument, Ana's enjoyment of being the object of Mesía's desire is a way of not acknowledging her desire for him. Indeed, by resisting the sexual temptation he offers but refusing to give the temptation up, she convinces herself that she does not need to confess her attraction to him, since a passive object is not guilty: 'La tentación era suya, su único placer. ¡Bastante hacía con no dejarse vencer, pero quería dejarse tentar!' ('The temptation was hers, her only pleasure. She was fulfilling her duty by not submitting, but she wanted to permit herself the temptation!'; 1: 363). Sinclair additionally observes (219) that Ana strategically opts for objecthood by imagining that her life may change because a savior will intervene without her having to abandon her object position. The irony of Mesía's name — as a profane Messiah — underscores Ana's view of love as the surrender of subjecthood to a savior. Ana explicitly describes her confessor, the Magistral, as her 'salvador' ('savior'; 1: 509); this invites a reading of her flirtation with mysticism in terms of Simone de Beauvoir's criticism of the female mystic for turning herself into the passive object of divine attention (679–87). In offering to be the Magistral's 'esclava' ('slave'; 2: 345) by walking in the Holy Week procession as a penitent, Ana will discover that her willed self-objectification only turns her into a semi-pornographic object of the collective gaze. She similarly treats her doctor Benítez as her savior, becoming his 'esclava' in turn (2: 378). By blindly following Benítez's instructions, she frees herself from guilt at her plunge into the pleasures of the natural life — Mesía's sexual charms included.

It can be productive to read Ana's strategic denial of her subjecthood through Ahmed's *The Promise of Happiness.* The result confirms Ana as a tragic figure, but one whose tragedy results not from transgression but from conformism. Indeed, the principal obstruction to Ana's happiness is that, despite her abnormal upbringing, she is the one 'normal' character in the novel who desires what society expects her to desire: the role of selfless wife and mother — what Ahmed has called the 'happiness script' proffered to women by society (15). As Ahmed notes, happiness is constituted by a "happiness archive': a set of ideas, thoughts, narratives, images, impressions about what is happiness' (32) — an archive that is historically specific. She notes also that 'happiness is crucial to the energy or 'forward direction' of narrative' (37). The search for happiness drives *La Regenta*, but the failure to get

10   The book argues that the Spanish realist novel subscribes to the economic and medical idea of 'free flow' that was fundamental to liberal political theory, and that it explores anxieties about what happens when 'free flow' is either too free or when it is blocked. For discussion of blockage in relation to *La Regenta*, see 236–40, 242.

11   For the discussion of mud, see Sinclair 45–58. For Freud's maxim, see Freud 7.

anywhere in the search for it accounts for the novel's non-narrative quality. One of the novel's great ironies is that everyone else in Vetusta is ignoring the appropriate happiness script by desiring what they are not supposed to desire — and faring much better as a result. All the men in Ana's life want to 'cure' her, but the problem is not her but the prescribed script that circumstances (her husband's lack of sexual interest in her and her resulting childlessness) make it impossible for her to follow. I would argue that Ana is following the prescribed female happiness script not only in trying to be the perfect wife, but also in desiring Mesía as the lover supposed to give her transcendental bliss, by contrast with the rest of Vetusta's mundane recourse to sexual activity. The ingenuousness of this belief in love as a means to transcendence is shown when, transported by Zorrilla's Romantic depiction of love in *Don Juan Tenorio*, Ana fails to notice Mesía's attempt to play footsie with her in the theatre box (2: 52).

Lauren Berlant has also analyzed how we construct our own unhappiness by insisting on desiring what we are supposed to desire when that desire cannot be fulfilled — a process that she calls 'cruel optimism.' By this she means the maintenance of an attachment to fantasies that hurt us because we have no hope of achieving them (23–24, 51). Berlant is referring primarily to the continued adherence in today's conditions of precarity to the post-World War II Western dream of the 'good way of life.' But, as she notes, cruel optimism is endemic to history since happiness scripts become obsolete over time and yet continue to be followed, inevitably producing an impasse or blockage. She sees the problem of historical obsolescence as one of genre (4, 6, 10). The theatre scene in *La Regenta* illustrates this point forcefully: Ana is stuck because she ascribes to a Romantic genre of happiness script, embodied by Zorrilla's 1844 play *Don Juan Tenorio* whose incommensurability with reality is aggravated by the fact that, as Mesía rightly notes (2: 49), it is anachronistic in the late 1870s. But the narrator is also right to show that the Romantic promise of transcendental love continued to endure long after its sell-by date (indeed, into the mid-twentieth century, if not beyond).

Ahmed notes that not getting what you want allows you to preserve the fantasy that it would make you happy (31–33). Accordingly, Ana persists in her unhappiness since the impossibility of obtaining what she wants confirms it as desirable; conversely, the confirmation of its desirability allows her to endure in her unhappiness. Berlant expresses the same idea in more negative terms, suggesting that happiness scripts are clung to, when it is clear that they are hurtful, because 'the loss of what's not working is more unbearable than the having of it' (27). This seems a good explanation of why Ana, despite knowing that Mesía is a serial seducer and that the Magistral's desire for her is carnal and not just spiritual, continues to oscillate between them in her search for transcendental love — to the point of going back to the Magistral at the end.

La Regenta can, then, be read not as the tragedy of a woman whose possibilities of self-fulfillment were denied, but as the tragedy of a woman who persisted in desiring what she was supposed to desire. That she should fall for a worthless Don Juan can be seen not as a flaw in the novel, as one might conclude from the narrator's imbalanced treatment of the two rivals for Ana's love (Mesía and the Magistral), but as the point, allowing a critique of the happiness script that offers women fulfillment through romantic love. Ahmed suggests that unhappiness can function as a critical tool: 'My suggestion is that we can read the negativity of such [unhappy female] figures in terms of the challenge that they offer to the assumption that happiness follows relative proximity to a social ideal' (53).[12] Judging by Alas's disappointingly traditional views on women expressed in his journalism, it is unlikely that he intended *La Regenta* to be a critique of the female happiness script that the novel exposes.[13] Ana, tragically, learns nothing. However, I do not find it anachronistic to suggest that at least some of Alas's contemporary female readers may have learnt the lesson. The novel's devastating end depicts Ana — rejected by Vetustan society and by the one person (the Magistral) able to appreciate her romantic desires — as an inert body awakening to the slimy contact of the homosexual Celedonio's kiss. This — homophobia apart — can be read as the narrator's punishment of Ana for committing adultery with a worthless Don Juan. But it can also be read, whether Alas intended it that way or not, as a warning to female readers that the pursuit of fulfilment through romantic love leads to the loss of subjecthood: happiness scripts produce objects and not subjects. We do not know whether Ana will, after she returns to consciousness, have the strength to abandon her cruel optimism, or whether she will cling to it as a lesser evil than having no optimism at all. Either way, the reader has been given a wake-up call about the cost of desiring what causes you damage.

Sianne Ngai's *Ugly Feelings* devotes a chapter to envy as a non-cathartic affect that is intransitive in that it turns away from, rather than towards, its object. As is well known, envy is what drives most of the inhabitants of Vetusta: the clergy and the members of the Casino who envy those who enjoy higher social status, and the women who envy Ana's status as the object of male desire.[14] Ngai draws on Melanie Klein's essay 'Envy and Gratitude' to argue that 'the ideal or good object envied and phantasmatically attacked is attacked precisely because it is idealized and good — as if the real source of antagonism is less the object than the idealization itself' (162). The envy of Ana by Vetusta's females can thus be read as providing a critique of the ideal of female virtue to which she clings. Indeed, Vetusta's womenfolk do not want to be like Ana; they want to destroy her reputation, to make her 'como todas' ('like other women'). Conversely, we can note that Ana's pleasure in

---

12   See also Ahmed, *The Promise* 50–87, 216–23.

13   See in particular Alas's substantial 1894 article 'La psicología del sexo', published in seven installments, which sees the female as suffering from a deficit of energy (hence women's need to 'hoard' energy, making them passive and egoistic) and the male as having a surplus of energy (allowing men to be active and outgoing). Thus, Alas concludes, women are congenitally 'conservative' and men congenitally 'liberal' — a definition of woman that was deeply threatening to a politically progressive thinker like Alas himself. Like other Krausist thinkers of his day, Alas supported education for women to equip them to be good educators of their children, on the supposition that they would cease working on marriage, and regarded women as incapable of a sense of justice, and hence unfit for civil rights, because they were able to think only in subjective terms (see Labanyi 221–22).

14   Sinclair (59) notes that envy is 'the most pervasive expression of desire in the novel.'

being an object of envy suggests a measure of complicity with her objectification. Another reason why her obstinate negativity cannot be seen simply in terms of lack is because it has agency, that is, it produces effects — affects — in others. Her persistence in unhappiness allows male fantasies of possessing her and provokes the female envy that wishes to destroy the ideal she represents. It is in this sense, above all, that Ana's negativity can be said to drive the novel. Ngai, discussing Melville's character Bartleby, talks of his 'powerful powerlessness'; we could say the same of Ana Ozores.

What fascinates Ngai about emotional negativity is what she calls its 'affective gaps and illegibilities' (1). Ana's descriptions of her negative feelings are full of ellipses, as, for example, when she struggles to define her illness to the Magistral: 'a veces se me figura que soy por dentro un montón de arena que se desmorona.... No sé cómo explicarlo ... siento grietas en la vida ... me divido dentro de mí ... me achico, me anulo ...' ('at times I feel as if my inner self were a pile of sand collapsing.... I don't know how to explain it ... I feel cracks in my life ... I splinter internally ... I shrink, I disintegrate ...'; 2: 107, ellipses in original). This is a description of emotional states that cannot be pinned down, that consist of not being rather than being, in an illustration of what Ngai calls 'a meta-feeling in which one feels confused about *what* one is feeling' (14). Ngai notes that this leads to doubts about whether what one is feeling is subjective or objective, coming from within or from without. In her analysis of *film noir*, she notes that this is expressed in the confusion between subjective and objective point of view (14–22). This seems a wonderful explanation of the extensive use of free indirect discourse in *La Regenta*. In one of the best examples, when Ana goes for a country walk after her first confession with the Magistral, we move from the narrator's description of the wagtail (observed by the narrator and by Ana) to her brief first-person reflections on 'estos animalitos' ('those little creatures'), giving way to six pages of free indirect discourse (Ana's thoughts presented directly but in the past tense and third person), ending with a return to the first person and present tense as Ana returns to reality and spots the toad beside her (1: 341–47).[15] The use of speech marks in the novel is erratic (including in the passage mentioned above), since they may be used for both direct speech and free indirect discourse (which at other times occurs without speech

15   This passage was used by me in a graduate seminar on 'Reading Spanish Culture through Raymond Williams,' inspired by Williams's attempt to trace the social circumstances that made possible the appearance in Elizabethan drama of the soliloquy as a dramatic mode; see Williams 139, 145–47. The idea was to see if we could work out what might be the social frame that allowed free indirect discourse to first appear in the Spanish realist novel of the 1880s. The students observed that this example of free indirect discourse began and ended with an observation of the outside material world; this led them to hypothesize that free indirect discourse may have been an expression of concerns at the time about the difficulty of establishing a boundary between the external and inner worlds, since free indirect discourse superimposes objective and subjective narration such that the two cannot be distinguished. I thank the students in the seminar for their acute observations, on which I have drawn here. The relationship between the self and the outside world is precisely what was at stake in the above-mentioned debates on naturalism in 1880s Spain. As previously noted, affect theory too is concerned with the relationship of the external to the internal, which it sees as mutually constitutive.

marks); this compounds the blurring of inner and outer worlds. In this and other passages that resort to free indirect discourse, not only can readers not determine whether what they are reading is Ana's thoughts or the narrator's reporting, since it is both at the same time, but this blurring of subjective and objective points of view could be interpreted as suggesting the impossibility for Ana — and perhaps also for the narrator — of disentangling what is subjective and what is objective. In this sense, free indirect discourse is a perfect expression of affect theory's insistence that emotions are not properties of the self but occur at the interface of self and world. This confusion makes Ana illegible even unto herself.

Ana's illegibility is what makes everyone in the novel — and us as readers — want to read her. This illegibility, with its ellipses and confusions between the subjective and objective, adds to the non-narrative quality of *La Regenta* as a text about a character who is stuck; the text gives the impression of being stuck too, particularly in Part II as the narrative keeps looping back on itself. In insisting on Ana's negativity, I have wanted to argue for the agency of negative affect, seeing Ana not as a victim of lack but as strategically opting for objecthood. Perhaps the ultimate meaning of Ana's 'egoísmo' is her obstinate persistence in a negativity that turns back on the self — a self that she can never pin down because it does not exist within her but at the point of contact between self and world.

Works Cited

AHMED, SARA. *The Cultural Politics of Emotion*. New York: Routledge, 2004.
——. *The Promise of Happiness*. Durham, NC: Duke UP, 2010.
ALAS, LEOPOLDO ('Clarín'). 'La psicología del sexo.' *La Ilustración Ibérica* 12 (1894): 3, 6, 38, 231, 259, 262, 343.
——. *La Regenta*. 1884–85. 2 vols. Ed. Gonzalo Sobejano. Madrid: Castalia, 1981.
BEAUVOIR, SIMONE DE. 'The Mystic.' *The Second Sex*. 1949. Trans. H. M. Parshley. Harmondsworth, UK: Penguin Books, 1972.
BENNETT, JANE. *Vibrant Matter: A Political Ecology of Things*. Durham, NC: Duke UP, 2010.
BERLANT, LAUREN. *Cruel Optimism*. Durham, NC: Duke UP, 2011.
BESER, SERGIO, ED. *Leopoldo Alas: Teoría y crítica de la novela española*. Barcelona: Laia, 1972.
BRENNAN, TERESA. *The Transmission of Affect*. Ithaca, NY: Cornell UP, 2004.
CLOUGH, PATRICIA TICINETO, ed. *The Affective Turn: Theorizing the Social*. Durham, NC: Duke UP, 2007.
DELEUZE, GILLES. *Spinoza: A Practical Philosophy*. Trans. Robert Hurley. San Francisco: City Lights, 2001.
FREUD, SIGMUND. *Standard Edition of the Complete Psychological Works*. Vol. 2: *Studies on Hysteria*. Trans. and ed. James Strachey. London: Hogarth Press, 1955.
LABANYI, JO. 'Doing Things: Emotion, Affect, Materiality.' *Journal of Spanish Cultural Studies* 11.3–4 (2010): 223–33.
——. *Gender and Modernization in the Spanish Realist Novel*. Oxford: Oxford UP, 2000.
LISSORGUES, YVAN. *El pensamiento filosófico y religioso de Leopoldo Alas 'Clarín.'* Oviedo: Grupo Editorial Asturiano, 1996
MASSUMI, BRIAN. *Parables for the Virtual: Movement, Affect, Sensation*. Durham, NC: Duke UP, 2002.
——. *Politics of Affect*. Cambridge, UK: Polity, 2015.
NGAI, SIANNE. *Ugly Feelings*. Cambridge, MA: Harvard UP, 2007.

SIEBURTH, STEPHANIE. 'La poética del sufrimiento en *La Regenta*.' *Leopoldo Alas, un clásico contemporáneo (1901–2001). Actas del congreso celebrado en Oviedo (12–16 de noviembre de 2001).* Ed. Araceli Iravedra Valea, Elena de Lorenzo Álvarez, and Álvaro Ruis de la Peña. 2 vols. Oviedo: Universidad de Oviedo, 2002. 2: 805–11.

SINCLAIR, ALISON. *Dislocations of Desire: Gender, Identity, and Strategy in 'La Regenta.'* Chapel Hill, NC: U of North Carolina P, 1998.

THRIFT, NIGEL. *Non-Representational Theory.* Abingdon, UK: Routledge, 2008.

WILLIAMS, RAYMOND. *The Sociology of Culture.* Chicago: U of Chicago P, 1995.

ZOLA, ÉMILE. *Le Roman expérimental.* 1880. Paris: Garnier-Flammarion, 1971.

CHAPTER 7

Modernity as Representation: The Self-reflexivity of the Spanish Realist Novel

In his article 'Realism: Model or Mirage?' in the founding issue of *Romance Studies* (1982), Brian Nelson linked nineteenth-century realism to relativism, by which he meant the representation of the real via the multiple perspectives of the characters, who discover in the course of the narrative that their perceptions are illusory. In this essay, I shall also insist on the relativism of nineteenth-century realism in the sense that it corresponds — at least in the Spanish case — to a loss of belief in fixed, inherent value, for political and economic reasons which I will explain. The depiction of the real as that which destroys illusion was, for Nelson, a mark of the nineteenth-century French novel's intellectual self-consciousness (1982: 2). In this respect, he noted a difference between Balzac and Zola's effort to 'reinforce the mimetic illusion' (1982: 4), and Flaubert's ironic questioning of the relation between representation and reality, which paved the way for the twentieth-century novel — specifically the *nouveau roman* (1982: 5). It is a commonplace of criticism of the work of Spain's major realist novelist, Benito Pérez Galdós, to note his Cervantine love of unreliable narrators, which introduce an explicitly self-reflexive dimension, making readers aware that what they are reading has at best a dubious relation to the real. This Galdosian self-reflexivity has been interpreted as contradicting his claim to be the chronicler of contemporary Spanish life. The implication is that Galdós is therefore not — or not entirely — a realist writer. In this essay I shall argue that the questioning of the relationship between representation and reality is, precisely, the core of Galdós's realism, for he is depicting a modernity which is constituted (and perceived as constituted) by representation. I shall also argue that Galdós's acknowledged debt to Cervantes can be attributed to the fact that Cervantes was responding, in his day, to similar concerns about the loss of fixed, inherent value. After all, the critique of 'appearances' is a staple of both Spanish Golden Age literature and of the late nineteenth-century Spanish realist novel. I will explain the historical circumstances that make this awareness that modernity is representation particularly acute in the Spanish case. It is common to suggest that Spain's belated and uneven development translates into cultural backwardness. I shall be suggesting that Spain's belated and uneven development is what allows it to be culturally precocious, anticipating the questioning of representation that we associate with twentieth-century modernism.[1]

What do I mean by suggesting that modernity — specifically as depicted in the Spanish realist novel — is constituted by representation? First, that the Spanish realist novel coincided with the Restoration period inaugurated in 1874, when the Spanish state embarked on an intensive project of nation formation bent on turning the inhabitants of the national territory into 'Spaniards'. This — as elsewhere (Anderson 1983) — was a programme of social homogenization designed to impose standardized norms of (bourgeois) conduct on citizens who, to maintain the fiction of the social contract, had to be induced to adopt those norms freely. The chief concern was with incorporating into the nation those inhabitants of the national territory who were considered marginal: the working-classes and women, both excluded from civil rights. This was a tricky process since they had to be incorporated into the national 'body' while acquiescing to their lack of rights, as C. B. Macpherson (1990) and Carole Pateman (1989) have brilliantly explained. The flowering of the realist novel in the Restoration period coincided with a burgeoning movement of liberal social reform designed to moralize the masses and women, the former largely through philanthropy (aimed especially at working-class women), the latter largely through medical manuals aimed at wives. Women were the target, since they were responsible for inculcating responsible citizenship into their children; women are also the key protagonists of most Spanish realist novels, as their titles often reflect. These liberal reformers were in direct competition with the Church, which responded through an intensified public morality campaign of its own, particularly after the influx into Restoration Spain of French religious orders following Jules Ferry's anticlerical legislation of 1881–82. The resulting intrusions into private life were insistently criticized by Spanish realist novelists (Galdós, Leopoldo Alas, Emilia Pardo Bazán), whose work precociously anticipates Judith Butler's insights (1990) that gender norms are not inherent but constructed; that is, representations. The heroine of Alas's La Regenta (1884–85), Ana Ozores, has a chronic sense of inner void and splintering of the self because her identity is the result of the contradictory prescriptions that her doctor, her confessor, and the local liberal political boss attempt to impose on her. Pardo Bazán's Los pazos de Ulloa (1886) shows the tragedy that ensues when a priest imposes gender norms on a wife; its sequel, La madre naturaleza (1887), depicts how an adolescent girl outwits the attempts of her uncle and would-be husband to mould her into a Rousseaunian Sophie. Galdós's Fortunata y Jacinta (1886–87) focuses on the working-class Fortunata's resistance to attempts to mould her by the various male and female Pygmalion figures in the novel. Relativism here does not (or not only) mean that reality is relayed via different characters' perspectives, but that femininity consists in a set of often contradictory and mostly male representations that have nothing to do with what women are.

Of course, Spain was not the only European country that, in the late nineteenth century, was attempting to mould the identity of its citizens. We have only to read

[1]   For a more detailed exploration of the ideas briefly outlined here, see Labanyi 2000.

Foucault's work to be aware that this was a process common to the Western nations (though Foucault is notoriously blind to the implications for female identity that are picked up so well in the Spanish realist novel). Eugen Weber's well-known study, *Peasants into Frenchmen: The Modernization of Rural France, 1870–1914* (1979), has documented the French state's attempt to 'nationalize' the rural populace in the same period. My impression, however, is that awareness of the resulting conversion of identity into representation is more intense in the Spanish realist novel than in that of other countries, perhaps because of the additional political and economic factors operating in the Spanish case, as we shall see.

One factor that the Spanish realist novel clearly shares with at least its French counterpart — a factor not unrelated to the awareness that gender identity is a construction — is the concern with imitation arising from the growth of consumer capitalism. In his 1890 book *Les Lois de l'imitation*, the French social theorist Gabriel Tarde suggested that modernity was based on imitation in the sense that consumer capitalism, through fashion, encouraged citizens to imitate the latest trends (Williams 1982: 346–84). As Tarde noted, this imitation process established Paris as cultural and not just political capital, through the provinces' imitation of the latest Parisian trends. The urge to imitate Madrid is evident in all Spanish realist novels set in the provinces — and satirized cruelly in Leopoldo Alas's *La Regenta* (1884–85) set in a fictionalized Oviedo — while Galdós has become accepted as Spain's major realist novel because he is the chronicler of life in the Spanish capital, assumed, by him and by critics, to stand for the nation. Fashion is the key theme of Galdós's novels of contemporary Madrid because in the modern city one is what one represents: hence his insistence on 'apariencias' ('appearances'). Luis Fernández Cifuentes has analysed how Galdós's *La desheredada* (1881), about a newcomer to the city seduced by fashion, depicts the capital as a city of signs for sale (1988: 310): signs that have become detached from their referents thanks to the circulation of goods in the market, which makes value relative — in the sense that it is determined by fluctuating relations between supply and demand — and not inherent. Fashion was, of course, also what seduced Emma Bovary, just as it seduces the heroine of Galdós's *La de Bringas* (1884).

The concern with (female) consumerism in the Spanish and French realist novels is well known. But in Spain this concern was aggravated by the fact that the consumerist phase of capitalism coincided with the country's incipient (and very patchy) industrialization, collapsing together what in northern Europe were two successive phases. This generated precocious ecological anxieties about the exhaustion of natural resources, since consumerism was not backed by solid production. Galdós's *Fortunata y Jacinta* expresses concerns about a modernity whose obsession with consumption is exhausting natural resources; Alas's *La Regenta* suggests that nature has been commodified to the point that the natural no longer exists (Labanyi 2000: 165–208, 247–51). There are other reasons why the awareness that, in the exchange economy, value is not inherent but determined by market relations was particularly acute in Spain. Anxieties at the increasing reliance on fiduciary (token) forms of money — banknotes, bills of exchange, credit — were exacerbated by the Bank of Spain's progressive reduction of the gold and silver content of coins from 1868 onwards. This meant that even coins — supposedly 'hard cash' — had a purely nominal value: that is, a value whose relation to the coins' metal content was arbitrary (Sardá 1948: 155–62). The start of the 1880s — the great decade of the Spanish realist novel — saw a massive increase in the Bank of Spain's issue of paper money, which replaced coins as the standard form of exchange, generating considerable public anxiety. This was compounded by the Barcelona stock market crash of late 1881, followed by the Bank of Spain's decision in 1883 to abandon the gold standard, which most other Western nations were at the time embracing (Sardá 1948: 175–93). This meant that banknotes — or coins for that matter — could no longer be exchanged for the equivalent of their nominal value in gold. The result was the definitive consecration of an entirely nominal system of monetary representation: a system of free-floating signs determined by market relationships, divorced from any kind of inherent value. Jean-Joseph Goux has argued (1988) that the early twentieth-century modernist abandonment of realism can be linked to the general abandonment of the gold standard by the Western nations from around 1914, which produced an awareness of modernity's dependence on a signifying system (money) based on the arbitrary relationship of signs to reality. But Spain's unstable late nineteenth-century economy had forced this to happen some thirty years earlier (1883): a notable case of uneven development leading to financial decision-making that was well ahead of its time. The following year (1884) saw the publication of *La de Bringas*, the work by Galdós which most explicitly deals with money and which, logically in these circumstances, has the highest degree of self-reflexivity. Galdós's interest in money in his fiction does not reflect worries about materialism, as is often argued, but an anxiety about the arbitrary relation between signs and their referents. We may note, in this context, that Cervantes — from whom Galdós undoubtedly took his love of self-reflexivity at least in part — was also writing in the context of a precocious economic debate in late sixteenth-century Spain that attempted to explain the rampant inflation produced by the influx of precious metals from the Americas. The fact that more gold and silver meant a drop in their value brought home forcefully to late sixteenth-century Spaniards the fact that monetary value is determined, not by inherent content, but by market relations.

One more factor specific to late nineteenth-century Spain needs to be brought into the picture, and here we return from economics back to politics. The Spanish realist novel pays a massive amount of attention to *caciquismo*: the network of local political bosses who, under the Restoration but notoriously in the 1880s, rigged elections to ensure that the conservative and progressive liberals alternated in power. Although this freed Spain from the succession of military coups which had marked the mid-century, it did so at the expense of subordinating democracy to clientelism. *Caciquismo* can be seen as another prong of the Restoration's nation-formation project, since its aim was to extend central government control to the rural areas. The result was that Spain was ruled by a form of representative government that was 'fictitious' — the adjective was frequently used in press debates — since it existed only in name ('on paper'). While attention to the effects of the market economy, which makes value relative, were logically most marked in novels with an urban setting (the work of Galdós, and Alas's *La Regenta*), *caciquismo* permeates the backdrop of all Spanish realist novels, whether set in the countryside where *caciquismo* was endemic (the novels of Pardo Bazán, Juan Valera or José María de Pereda) or in the city (where the urban electorate was anxious about its votes being swamped by the much larger percentage of rural votes controlled by the *caciques* of both political parties). José Varela Ortega (1977) has insisted that *caciquismo* was not a feudal relic but a product of modernity: an attempt to deal with the problem of uneven development in a rapidly modernizing society.

Thus late nineteenth-century Spaniards experienced modernity as a combination of increasingly fiduciary forms of monetary representation and a fraudulent system of political representation. On top of this, social reform campaigns aimed largely at women made it clear that gender identity was a construction: again, a form of representation. It should be stressed that, in questioning modernity's conversion of reality into representation, the late nineteenth-century Spanish realist novel was itself participating in the nation-formation process that sought to modernize the nation, inasmuch as it was part of the expansion of print culture that helped to 'nationalize' citizens by encouraging debate around a common fund of concerns, as Benedict Anderson has famously argued (1983). The realist novel, too, turned modernity into representation by writing about it. In critiquing modernity's conversion of reality into representation, the realist novel was thus commenting on its own procedures. But it was doing more than that, since the conversion of reality into representation was a process operating in the world beyond the text. I hope to have shown that, given its understanding of modernity as the conversion of reality into representation, the Spanish realist novel was able to engage in a self-reflexive questioning of representation without in any way contradicting its claim to be depicting the society of its time. It could be argued that, in this respect, the Spanish realist novel was not just anticipating early twentieth-century modernism's self-reflexive questioning of representation but doing something more complicated. For, if modernism is generally understood as exploring the gap between reality and representation (a fairly common-sense proposition, after all), the Spanish realist novel is depicting a world in which reality has become representation: a category collapse of major ontological significance.

Works Cited

ANDERSON, BENEDICT. 1983. *Imagined Communities: Reflections on the Origin and Spread of Nationalism*, 2nd rev. edn (London: Verso)

BUTLER, JUDITH. 1990. *Gender Trouble: Feminism and the Subversion of Identity* (New York: Routledge)

FERNÁNDEZ CIFUENTES, LUIS. 1988. 'Signs for Sale in the City of Galdós', *MLN*, 103.2: 289–311

GOUX, JEAN-JOSEPH. 1988. 'Banking on Signs', *Diacritics* 18.2: 15–25

LABANYI, JO. 2000. *Gender and Representation in the Spanish Realist Novel* (Oxford: Oxford University Press)

MACPHERSON, C.B. 1990. *The Political Theory of Possessive Individualism*, 13th edn (Oxford: Oxford University Press))

NELSON, BRIAN. 1982. 'Realism: Model or Mirage?', *Romance Studies*, 1.1: 1–17.

PATEMAN, CAROLE. 1989. *The Sexual Contract* (Cambridge: Polity)

SARDÁ, JUAN. 1948. *La política monetaria y las fluctuaciones de la economía española en el siglo XIX* (Madrid: CSIC)

VARELA ORTEGA, JOSÉ. 1977. *Los amigos políticos: Partidos, elecciones y caciquismo en la Restauración (1975–1900)* (Madrid: Alianza)

WEBER, EUGEN. 1979. *Peasants into Frenchmen: The Modernization of Rural France, 1870–1914* (London: Chatto & Windus)

WILLIAMS, ROSALIND H. 1982. *Dream Worlds: Mass Consumption in Late Nineteenth-Century France* (Berkeley: University of California Press)

CHAPTER 8

Horror, Spectacle, and Nation-Formation: Historical Painting in Late Nineteenth-Century Spain

On viewing the catalogue of the Museo del Prado's 1992 exhibition of nineteenth-century Spanish historical painting (Díez), I was struck by the frequency, in a pictorial genre promoted by the Spanish state as a tool of nation-formation, of melodramatic — even Gothic — sensationalism.[1] What kind of image of the nation, I wondered, would these scenes of death and madness have produced in the broad public who viewed these paintings at the Exposiciones Nacionales de Bellas Artes (National Art Exhibitions) mounted from 1856 by the Ministerio de Fomento (Ministry of Development), which included education in its modernizing agenda? My wonderment increased when I discovered, thanks to Agustín Sánchez Vidal's research into the Jimeno family (which pioneered cinema in Spain while running a flourishing waxwork business) that in the 1880s waxwork shows started to reproduce historical paintings shown at the National Art Exhibitions. The two examples cited by Sánchez Vidal (114–16) are, precisely, the two paintings that had most struck me as being at odds with any nation-formation mission: Francisco Pradilla y Ortiz's 1877 *Doña Juana la Loca* (*Queen Joan the Mad*) **(Figure 8.1)** and José Casado del Alisal's 1880 *Leyenda del rey monje* (*Legend of the Monk-King*) **(Figure 8.2)**, reproduced as wax tableaux by the Galería de Figuras de Cera La Universal at the Fiesta del Pilar in Zaragoza in 1883 (repeated 1884) and 1882, respectively.[2] That images produced as part of the state's attempt to foster a national school of painting of the highest quality, winning prizes at international as well as national

---

1   Gruesome subjects are too many to detail. Some fall into the *carpe diem* formula; most are scenes of unjust execution or slaughter. Particularly popular were the collective suicides of Sagunto and Numancia, which paralleled contemporaneous archaeological excavations designed to provide a myth of origins for a 'Spanish' spirit of independence, going back to the 3rd and 2nd centuries BC respectively (Álvarez Junco 267).

2   For the many paintings of Juana la Loca, see Reyero 326–33; Díez 250–53, 306–17; Salvá Herán 66. Pradilla's painting won first prize at the 1878 National Art Exhibition and was the only painting to be awarded the 'medalla de honor' between 1856 and 1895 (Pantorba 19). It won 'medallas de honor' also at the 1878 Paris and 1882 Vienna World Exhibitions. Casado's painting won prizes at the World Exhibitions of Vienna, Munich, and Düsseldorf in 1882 and 1883. See Díez 316, 360. For Pradilla's and Casado's careers, see García Loranca and García Rama; Portela Sandoval.

FIG. 8.1. Francisco Pradilla y Ortiz, *Doña Juana la Loca* (*Queen Joan the Mad*), 1877. Oil on canvas. 3.4 × 5.0 m. © Photographic Archive Museo Nacional del Prado.

exhibitions, should also be money-makers at fairground displays suggests that, in at least some cases, they held considerable potential for slippage between high-cultural and mass-cultural modes of spectatorship. In this essay I will focus on these two paintings, while discussing late nineteenth-century historical painting generally. I shall read these paintings through Mark B. Sandberg's thesis, in his book on waxworks and folk museums in 1880s and 1890s Scandinavia, that such spectacles constituted a pedagogy of spectatorship: that is, by exposing the public to representations of the past organized in a particular way, they schooled them in modes of viewing appropriate to modern citizens.[3]

I have argued previously (Labanyi) that the nation-formation process that occurred in Spain — as elsewhere in Europe — in the late nineteenth century, intensifying from 1875 under the Restoration, took the form not only of central state legislation but also of the debates on national life that took place in the public sphere. I use the term 'public sphere' in Habermas's sense of public opinion, whose role was to provide a forum for debate among members of civil society, in order to keep a democratic check on the actions of the state. The nation-formation project contained a considerable amount of heterogeneity, for public disagreement on what the nation was and should be was ample. As Carolyn Boyd notes, these debates were, among other things, a 'dispute over the right to define and transmit the

3   I thank Rebecca Haidt for introducing me to Sandberg's and Schwartz's work on wax museums.

FIG. 8.2. José Casado del Alisal, *La leyenda del rey monje* (*The Legend of the Monk King*), 1880. Oil on canvas. 3.56 × 4.74 m. © Photographic Archive Museo Nacional del Prado.

meaning of history' (xv). In his article in the catalogue of the 1992 Prado exhibition *La pintura de historia en el siglo XIX en España*, Alonso E. Pérez Sánchez observes that late nineteenth-century Spanish historical painting does not propose a single, celebratory model of the nation but a 'duplicidad interpretativa' ('interpretative duplicity'; Díez 35). The National Art Exhibitions were a site of struggle between competing interpretations of the national past in which artists, members of the jury that awarded the prizes, reviewers in the national press, and the educated and mass public all played a part. The stakes were considerable, in terms of both financial reward — the top prizes consistently went to historical paintings — and public dissemination — through engravings in the national press, not to mention school textbooks, postage stamps, calendars, and brand labels (Álvarez Junco 283).

Although these exhibitions were sponsored by the state and held in Madrid, and although many of the prize-winning paintings were bought by the state for the National Art Museum (amalgamated with the Prado when the latter passed from Crown to state ownership with the 1868 Revolution) or for the Congress or Senate, painters from the periphery increasingly won the major prizes (Gutiérrez Burón 1: 24–25). A high proportion of prize-winning entries were painted at the Spanish Academy in Rome by artists on state or local government scholarships. All writers on the subject stress the importance of historical painting in fostering local as well as national identities. Despite the overwhelming prestige of the National Art Exhibitions, local exhibitions — also privileging historical paintings — continued to be held in many provinces, sponsored by local governments or private cultural associations (Arias Anglés et al. 41, 50; Gutiérrez Burón 1: 147; Pantorba 3). Provincial Diputaciones, as well as the Congress and Senate, commissioned historical paintings — often on local topics — for display on their walls. The Valencian and Catalan local governments played a major role as patrons, commissioning many works that were awarded prizes at the National Art Exhibitions. Favorite subjects — with painters and patrons from other regions too — included Jaume I el Conquistador (who conquered Valencia and Mallorca from the Moors) and the Príncipe de Viana (heir to Juan II of Aragón, proclaimed King by the Catalans when he was arrested by his father under pressure from the latter's second wife, the mother of Fernando el Católico) (Reyero, *Imagen* 141–48, 213–20). Paintings on this last subject not only catered to Catalan regionalist sentiment but also disputed the legality of the Reyes Católicos' accession to the throne of a unified Spain. Private provincial cultural associations also commissioned works that celebrated a local past: for example, the painting of Abderrahmán III commissioned for Córdoba's Salón Liceo del Círculo de la Amistad (Reyero, *Imagen* 80), contrasting with the celebration of the Catholic Kings' conquest of Granada that was a favorite topic in paintings commissioned by the central state — for example, Pradilla's 1882 *La rendición de Granada* (*The Surrender of Granada*), contracted by the Senate in 1878 after the spectacular success of *Doña Juana la Loca* (Reyero, *La pintura* 23).

If historical painting in the 1850s and 1860s had largely followed French Republican neo-classical models, it was in order to construct a secular genealogy of the nation, countering the celebration of religious fervor found in, for example, the various paintings of Columbus's exploits (Reyero, *Imagen* 267–97). This secularizing classicism was developed from the early 1860s, by Antonio Gisbert in particular, into a statuesque hyper-realism that recreated the execution of martyrs fighting for local or liberal freedoms, in order to support progressive political agendas. Gisbert's famous painting of the execution of the leaders of the early sixteenth-century Comuneros' Revolt against Habsburg rule was bought by the Congress in 1861, and his equally famous 1888 painting of the Romantic revolutionary Torrijos facing the firing squad was commissioned for the Congress in 1886 by Sagasta's Progressive Government, as part of its campaign against Cánovas's centralizing measures (Reyero, *La pintura* 26). The role of the Republican leader Castelar in championing historical painting is notable: in 1873, as President of the First Spanish Republic, he set up the Spanish Academy in Rome which would produce so many prize-winning historical works (Pradilla painted his *Doña Juana la Loca* while studying there, and Casado was its President from its inception until his resignation in 1881 when his *Leyenda del rey monje* failed to win the top prize at that year's National Art Exhibition). Castelar headed the parliamentary commission that secured state funds to buy Pradilla's painting for a record 40,000 pesetas, and gave an impassioned speech to the Congress in defense of Casado's painting (whose depiction of Ramiro II of Aragón with the heads of the nobles he had slaughtered could be read as a statement of anti-monarchist sentiment), again securing state funds (35,000 pesetas, second only to the sum paid for Pradilla's painting) to buy it for the nation (Salvá Herrán 83–84; Gutiérrez Burón 1: 397; Arias Anglés et al. 55).

I will be most interested here in the dominant move in the late 1870s and 1880s to more expressive, dynamic artistic forms, which rendered history not in the guise of the statuesque but in that of the (often sensationalist) theatrical tableau. This new concern with theatrical spectacle does not seem to have been identified with any particular political agenda — it equally served the purpose of glorifying national unification (as in Pradilla's 1882 *La rendición de Granada*) or of denouncing the religious intolerance that formed its basis (as in Vicente Cutanda y Toraya's *¡A los pies del Salvador! (Episodio de una matanza de judíos en la edad media)* (*At the Savior's Feet! (Episode from a Massacre of Jews in the Middle Ages)*, awarded third prize at the 1887 National Art Exhibition). But its emphasis on dramatic effect produces a disconcerting freezing of time, which disturbs any providentialist notion of history moving inexorably towards a present thereby constructed as the realization of a manifest destiny. In many cases, the moment of time that is frozen is a scene of individual or (more often) collective death, presented not as stoic triumph (as so often in the earlier neo-classical paintings), but as a source of horror. The freezing of time eternally prolongs the moment of dying or the moment of horror of those who, within the painting, contemplate the already (but only just, or possibly not quite) dead. Any transcendental or redemptive message is undone by this very physical focus on gore and horror: the contorted or dismembered corpses, the bodily reaction of the diegetic onlookers. José Álvarez Junco titles a section of his major monograph on Spanish nation-formation 'La pintura histórica les pone rostro' ('Historical Painting Gives Them a Face'; 249–58), but what stands out in these historical paintings is not the faces but the bodies.

One must remember here the emphasis on physical mutilation in Christian religious painting: Spanish audiences (especially the illiterate, whose education was imparted largely by religious images) would have been used to contemplating gruesome scenes of martyrdom and would have been trained to inscribe these gory scenes into a teleological narrative of redemption. That Spanish popular audiences were schooled to read visual images in terms of religious allegory is shown by contemporary complaints that the lower classes who flocked to the Prado on Sundays — the only time that attendance was free, after it was opened to the public following its nationalization with the 1868 Revolution (Gil and Romea 119) — mistook Velázquez's *La rendición de Breda* (*The Surrender of Breda*) for St Peter proffering the keys to the pearly gates: a forgivable mistake given that the Prado did not display the titles of paintings until the start of the twentieth century (lower-class spectators could hardly be expected to buy the catalogue). Indeed, the restriction of free access to Sundays constructed a visit to the Prado as something one did after mass.[4] However, even the most gruesome Christian iconography contains signals that invite the degradation of the flesh to be read as

---

4   This information about lower-class responses to the Prado was given in Eugenia Afinoguénova's paper 'The Prado Museum and the Birth of the Spanish School' at the 2002 MLA, New York.

spiritual triumph: not least the omnipresent heavenwards gaze of the sufferer and/or bystanders. In Pradilla's painting, the upwards gaze of the seated ladies-in-waiting is trained on the vacant gaze of Juana la Loca looking downwards at the coffin of Felipe I; while, in Casado's painting, the 'rey monje' is looking up at the horrified nobles who are looking down at the severed heads of his victims. Any upwards gaze is redirected downwards to the spectacle of death. In Pradilla's painting, the priest's face, buried in his prayer book, is almost hidden by his cowl, as if disowning what is going on. In Casado's painting, the only representative of the Church is the bishop whose severed head forms the gruesome bell clapper proffered by the 'rey monje' to his rebellious nobles. Although the foremost noble has a Christ-like countenance and posture — the novelist Jacinto Octavio Picón, reviewing the 1881 National Art Exhibition, complained that he looked like a 'Cristo enfurruñado' ('grumpy Christ'; Díez 358) — his gaze is fixated on the bleeding heads on the ground (not even on the Bishop's head dangling to the left). A redemptive reading of either of these paintings requires considerable ingenuity.

Popular audiences were, however, used to forms of spectacle other than the religious. We should not forget the public executions that drew large crowds, albeit moved ever further to the city outskirts in the mid-century (Fernández de los Ríos 156). Marginally less gruesome but equally sensationalist were the mass cultural entertainments proliferating with the acceleration of urbanization from the 1870s on. This is precisely the time when the historical paintings exhibited at the National Art Exhibitions developed a penchant for the spectacular. If these paintings were reproduced in mass-cultural forms such as calendars and brand labels, it is because they shared the representational codes of contemporary mass culture — including waxworks and (from 1895) the cinema, which critics have seen as building on modern habits of mass-cultural consumption configured in an earlier period by the 'living pictures' of the wax tableaux (Charney and Schwartz; Schwartz; Singer; Sandberg). Indeed, several of these historical paintings were painstakingly recreated in a number of historical films of 1944–52, many (but not all) directed for Cifesa by Juan de Orduña with the prewar avant-garde stage designer Sigfrido Burmann as art director (Díez 113–18; Hernández Ruiz). The best-known example is Burmann's meticulous reproduction in tableau form of Pradilla's *Doña Juana la Loca* at the end of Orduña's *Locura de amor* (*Madness of Love*, 1948), massively popular as Pradilla's painting had been in its day.

The nation-formation project of early Francoism differed from that of the Restoration not only in that it did not allow debate in the public sphere, but also because its privileged vehicle was the mass-cultural medium of cinema — whereas painting is a high-cultural medium. With the development during the nineteenth century of forms of public exhibition, however, it became increasingly unclear who the public for paintings was — a problem that mirrored contemporary political debates about who exactly constituted the nation. The Academia de Bellas Artes de San Fernando had been founded in 1753 with the mission of educating national taste, so as to produce citizens worthy to be members of civil society (Álvarez Junco 81). It must be remembered that political liberalism was based on the notion of representative government, whereby elected representatives acted on behalf of the interests of the less able, who in turn voted for these representatives in the name of those who were excluded from suffrage on the grounds that they were not capable of independent judgement, because of lack of education or lack of economic independence. Late nineteenth-century Spanish politics were riven by disagreements about who constituted the nation. The 1869 Constitution, for instance, following the 1868 Revolution which deposed Isabel II, placed sovereignty in the nation rather than the Crown and introduced universal suffrage (meaning males over twenty-five). The draft constitution (never instituted) of the 1873–74 First Republic replaced national with popular sovereignty, opening the way for inclusion of the lower classes. The Krausist reformers of the 1870s and 1880s supported national rather than popular sovereignty, with suffrage based on a limited property qualification since they felt the masses needed to be educated before being enfranchised. The 1876 Restoration Constitution, drafted under the conservative liberal leader Cánovas del Castillo, revoked universal suffrage, re-introducing a substantial property qualification and placing sovereignty in the hands, not of the nation or the people, but of the monarchy and parliament. In 1890, universal suffrage was reintroduced by the progressive leader Sagasta (Labanyi 24, 108).

These re-negotiations of sovereignty find their cultural counterpart in the hesitations regarding the appropriate public for the National Art Exhibitions. The historical paintings showcased by these exhibitions constructed the nation not only by inviting citizens to internalize particular versions of the national past, but — more importantly — by developing certain kinds of taste, as Jesús Gutiérrez Burón has noted (1: 87). Pierre Bourdieu has argued that taste is not the product of class but constructs class in the first place. That is, one is labelled as belonging to a particular social class according to what cultural products one consumes and — especially — the manner in which one consumes them. Bourdieu's key insight is that cultural products are labelled 'high culture' or 'popular culture' (he uses the latter term in its late twentieth-century sense of 'mass culture') not because of their intrinsic qualities but because of the manner in which they are consumed. High-cultural products are those which are consumed in a detached, disinterested, 'aesthetic' manner; while popular-cultural products are those consumed through forms of emotional and bodily involvement. Bourdieu assumes that popular culture, unconcerned with aesthetic considerations, is largely realist, and that high culture is aligned with an avant-garde scorn for realism, since the latter supposes audience identification. Bourdieu is discussing France in 1963; his analysis overlooks the earlier history of taste. For, in the mid- to late nineteenth century, popular audiences mostly consumed a diet of spectacle (narrative and non-narrative), which in the growing urban centers, as it became enmeshed with a proliferating mass culture of commercial performance and mechanical reproduction, adopted increasingly sensationalist forms. Whereas realism was the privileged art form of the bourgeoisie, seen as a vehicle of nation formation since, on the one hand, it invited the audience identification necessary to construct national citizens as a 'we,' while, on the other, it served as a forum for public debate, parallel to the national press, airing a common fund of concerns about what 'national society' was and should be. Realism's combination of intellectual reflection with audience identification made it always prone to tip into the melodramatic sensationalism of popular culture, from which it partly extricates itself (in the case of the realist novel, at least) through self-reflexive critique. This ambivalence allowed realism to serve as the basis of nation formation, since the modes of response it permitted were all-inclusive: the realist novel could function as an apprenticeship in citizenship by emotionally engaging the untutored reader, who would then be invited to partake in intellectual reflection (and thus 'elevated' to a higher cultural plane) through its metafictional commentary on its own processes.

What, however, of the visual arts? Sandberg observes a complementary process whereby, in the 1880s, popular spectacles like waxworks started to mimic the representational techniques of realism in order to acquire a higher cultural status. Previously, waxworks were associated with sensationalist displays of diseased or dismembered bodies, of an often morbid or pornographic nature — as in the Venus figures that could be taken apart to show their inner organs (Pilbeam 1–16). This was true both of the 'anatomical cabinets' of wax figures that toured the fairground circuit (which proclaimed their wares among a motley assortment of freak shows) and of the anatomical collections, which included figures modeled in wax, of medical schools and anthropological museums (both open to public display for 'educational' but often prurient purposes).[5] Pamela Pilbeam has shown how Madame Tussaud, on inaugurating her show in England in 1802, trod a difficult path between the popular touring circuit and the more upmarket museum, building her reputation on the *frisson* of authenticity derived from the fact that she had, during the French Revolution, made casts of guillotined heads or murdered leaders *in situ* (Marat stabbed in his bath was, and still is, a favorite), while at the same time insisting on her respectable connections with the French royalty and aristocracy. Tussaud's wax 'museum' — as she called it even during its touring days — contained a mix of displays of great historical figures from the past and present, increasingly legitimized by authentic material props and costumes; and the 'Adjacent Room' which in 1846 became dubbed the 'Chamber of Horrors,' depicting the acts of notorious criminals. The concern with authentic props and costumes had, by the 1880s, developed into the creation of tableaux, sometimes arranged in a developmental narrative sequence, involving a number of wax figures arranged in a play of body movements and gazes that bound them together in an 'event,' set in a recreation of the original environment. This new vogue for tableaux

5   For a description of the Anatomical Museum of Madrid's Facultad de Medicina, see Gil and Romea's 1881 guidebook, which also notes the anatomical collection of the Anthropological Museum, inaugurated in 1875. For waxworks and popular entertainments in Spain, see Gil and Romea; Sánchez Vidal 19–132; and the sources used by the latter: Varey; Baroja; Gutiérrez Solana, *Madrid, escenas* (1st and 2nd series) and *Madrid callejero.* The current Madrid Museo de Cera was not created until 1972. Despite the tackiness of its displays (especially those where a jumble of historical figures line the walls, as in the early wax cabinets), those that are organized in tableaux form correspond exactly to its late nineteenth-century Parisian and Scandinavian counterparts, including the reconstructions of paintings and self-reflexive games (see the illustrations in Schwartz and Sandberg).

became the basis of the displays in the new Paris wax museum — the Musée Grévin — when it opened in 1882 (Schwartz 89–148).

As Sandberg argues in his discussion of how these techniques were developed by the upscale wax museums created in Scandinavia in the 1880s, these tableaux — whether recreating historical scenes or famous crimes — schooled spectators in causal logic (through their perception of the relations between figures and their environment), and in the limits of what constituted acceptable voyeurism (through visual jokes which subjected the unreflective viewer to private if not public embarrassment). Unlike Tussaud's earlier displays, which invited spectators to mingle with and touch the wax figures, the construction of these tableaux in the form of a self-contained environment, viewed through a glass or imaginary fourth wall, encouraged the spectator to gaze, but from a distance. Most importantly, such tableaux abandoned the emphasis on isolated body-parts typical of the disreputable early history of waxworks, insisting on the incorporation of bodies into a socially constituted whole. The pedagogy of spectatorship constituted by such tableaux functioned by inviting visitors to knowingly have it both ways: that is, to enjoy the sensationalism of the scenes depicted, but to reflect on the mechanics of the illusion created. Via a different route, the wax museums of the 1880s come to coincide with the contemporaneous strategies of the realist novel which, in Spain at least, borrows from sensationalist popular fiction while inviting the reader to reflect critically on its effects.

The other gentrification strategy used by wax museums in the 1880s was the construction of tableaux recreating scenes from realist novels (for example, those of Zola reproduced in the Musée Grévin) or — more frequently — historical paintings, showing that the popular-cultural medium of wax figures was capable of creating the effects of high culture. This was possible only because the high-cultural works that were imitated themselves contained the sensationalist effects on which popular culture relied. The 1880s can thus be defined as the period when realism (bourgeois culture) and spectacle (popular culture) come together, in a shifting and uneasy alliance that attempts to work through the various possible definitions of who is eligible for national citizenship (perhaps we should say 'national spectatorship'). As Sandberg notes (69–116), the modern nation-formation process takes place not only via the Foucauldian subjection of citizens to surveillance, but also via the construction of certain legitimate forms of looking. In urban modernity, to be is to look, as well as to be looked at. While 'being-looked-at' can construct one as an individual or as a member of the mass, looking necessarily constructs one as an individual. This is particularly true when the looking takes place within the confines of a high-cultural event like a state-run National Art Exhibition, with the paintings viewed at a distance on a wall. The massive dimensions of many of these historical paintings (the bigger canvases tended to win the prizes; Pradilla's *Doña Juana la Loca* measured 3.40 x 5 meters, Casado's *La leyenda del rey monje* 3.56 x 4.74 meters) forced a direct involvement in the painting — the human figures depicted are life size — while also obliging one to stand back to take the whole thing in.

It is clear that the organizers of the National Art Exhibitions were ambivalent about who their intended audience was (just as the Prado opened its doors to the masses on Sundays provided it was not raining, so they would not muddy the floor). Entry to the exhibitions was initially free to encourage cross-class attendance. From 1871 railway companies offered substantial discounts (45% in 1881) to people traveling to the exhibition from the provinces. In 1864 the press reported traffic jams in the surrounding streets and extra members of the Guardia Civil were brought in. To counter the threat of crowd disorder, from 1861 the state increasingly reduced the number of days with free entry; by 1884 it was limited to Sundays. The number of tickets sold in 1884 was 15,386, peaking at 21,396 in 1887, which was also the year when the largest number of historical paintings were exhibited (no attendance figures are available for days when access was free). In 1860 an anonymous reviewer in *La Época* had waxed lyrical about the innate artistic vocation of the 'pueblo español' ('Spanish people') that flocked to that year's National Art Exhibition, making it difficult to get in; and in 1864 even the conservative novelist Alarcón claimed that 'el pueblo por antonomasia, la plebe de la villa, la gente que habla a voces en las calles y plazas constituye, por decirlo así, la vanguardia de la opinion pública' ('the people by definition, Madrid's lower classes, the noisy crowds in the street and squares are, so to speak, at the vanguard of public opinion'). By contrast in 1884 Jacinto Octavio Picón complained about the ignorance of uneducated viewers (Gutiérrez Burón 1: 617–21, 625; 2: 703–04, 710; Reyero 100). Gutiérrez Burón cites two press articles of 1881 (the year when the refusal to award top prize to Casado's *Leyenda del rey monje* caused a public outcry, and when Sagasta's progressives returned to power, reinstating educational freedom) which defend popular taste against the decision of the jury, on opposing grounds. The first (in *La Gaceta Universal*) insisted that 'las obras de arte caen de lleno bajo la jurisdicción del *sufragio universal*' ('works of art fall squarely under the jurisdiction of *universal suffrage*'; emphasis in original), making it clear that the definition of who was fit to form the national art public was a definition of who was fit to enjoy civil rights: this supposes that artistic taste is based on a capacity for intellectual discrimination (Gutiérrez Burón 2: 622). The second (in the *Revista de Madrid*) defended the lower classes' artistic taste on the basis of their emotional response:

> En cuestiones de estética, el corazón es el que mejor juzga, es, por lo menos, juez inapelable. ¿Conmueve la obra? ¿Hiere las fibras ignoradas en que duerme el sentimiento? Pues la obra es buena, es hermosa, y merece aplauso incondicional.... ¿No conmueve? ¿No arranca un grito involuntario a los labios o una lágrima a los ojos? Pues entonces ¿Qué importa que la crítica la halle perfecta... ? (Gutiérrez Burón 1: 623; second ellipsis added)

> (In aesthetic matters, the heart is the best judge or, at least, its verdict is irrefutable. Does the work move us? Does it arouse our dormant emotions? Then the work is good and beautiful and deserves unconditional applause.... It doesn't move us? It doesn't produce an involuntary gasp or tear? Then what does it matter if the critics find it perfect...?)

The same defense of popular taste on the basis of its emotional engagement is found in an 1887 article in *La Ilustración Artística* (Gutiérrez Burón 1: 622–23).

These press articles suggest that popular and bourgeois taste, based on emotional involvement and intellectual discrimination respectively, had become inextricably entangled — and that the historical paintings privileged at the National Art Exhibitions played a role in this process. The requirement to appeal to a broad public seems to have produced a contamination of bourgeois art by the sensationalism characteristic of popular taste. As an 1867 article in *La España*, commenting on the mass attendance at the National Art Exhibitions, stated: 'donde quiera que haya un espectáculo allí está Madrid. El espectáculo es para Madrid absolutamente necesario' ('give me a spectacle and Madrid will be there. Spectacle is essential to Madrid's being'; Gutiérrez Burón 2: 719).

At this point it becomes necessary to discuss the implications of the fact that, in late nineteenth-century Spain, waxworks remained an itinerant fairground attraction, rather than being incorporated into bourgeois culture through the creation of elegant wax museums. While this did not stop Spanish waxworks from starting in the 1880s to recreate historical paintings, as happened contemporaneously in the wax museums of northern Europe, one cannot help wondering if the public exhibition of historical paintings took on in Spain some of the functions fulfilled by the new sophisticated wax museums elsewhere: specifically, the use of a sensationalist mode of realism that appealed to popular tastes while educating those tastes in bourgeois decorum — and conversely allowing bourgeois viewers to indulge popular tastes they might not confess to at home. Joaquín de la Puente notes that no bourgeois would have bought for his home paintings with the gruesome subject matter of those exhibited at the National Art Exhibitions (Arias Anglés et al. 28). Interestingly, the pre-1856 exhibitions of the Academia de San Fernando in the Calle de Alcalá had coincided with Madrid's September Feria celebrated in the same locality, producing a hugely mixed public. Indeed, there were complaints that the public for the September Feria regarded these exhibitions as an extension of the fairground stalls (Arias Anglés et al. 77). This led to the transfer of the exhibitions to the Ministerio de Fomento (now Teatro Calderón) in the Calle de Atocha, where they remained after their conversion into the National Art Exhibitions until their 1867 relocation to the Palacio de la Fuente de la Castellana (popularly known as the Barracón del Indo, since the pavilion was installed much like a fairground *barraca* (booth) in the garden of the private mansion of Señor Indo). This was the locale where Pradilla's and Casado's paintings were exhibited, in both cases attracting huge crowds (Díez 312; Pantorba 111; Gil and Romea 216). In 1887 the exhibitions were relocated to what is now the Museo de Historia Nacional (Pantorba 10). We may also note that, just as the gentrified wax museums of northern Europe located their 'Chamber of Horrors' in a different space from the respectable historical tableaux, so too the National Art Exhibitions had their 'Sala del Crimen' where paintings judged unworthy of acceptance were hung (Gutiérrez Burón 1: 575–77).

Bernardino de Pantorba, writing at the time of the early Francoist nation-formation project, notes the gruesome nature of the majority of historical paintings exhibited — and awarded prizes — at the National Art Exhibitions: 'Todas las notas negras de la historia de España, que no son pocas.... No se buscaba sino lo convulso

... cadáveres y féretros, puñales y fusiles, miradas de horror, ojos de llanto, ademanes amenazadores' ('All the black moments in Spain's history, which are more than a few.... The goal was to stir up violent emotions ... corpses and coffins, daggers and rifles, gazes of horror, tearful eyes, threatening gestures'; 35). Pantorba could be describing the contents of a wax museum. He rightly picks up the theatricality and play of gazes, again typical of the wax tableaux that came into vogue in the 1880s. Significantly, Pradilla — the painter of the most successful historical painting of them all: that of Juana la Loca gazing ashen-faced and blank-eyed (like a wax effigy) at the coffin of her husband Felipe I — had trained with a stage designer in Zaragoza and subsequently worked in Madrid with two Italian stage designers (Arias Anglés et al. 205). Just as contemporary wax museums elsewhere filled their tableaux with historically authentic accessories, so Pradilla worked from props and costumes constructed by him from descriptions of the time (Díez 313, 316). Casado also drew on his studio wardrobe of historical costumes to paint *Leyenda del rey monje*. And, if Madame Tussaud modeled wax figures from the heads of guillotine victims, so Casado painted the heads of Ramiro II's victims 'live' from the decapitated heads of corpses he had delivered to his studio from one of Rome's hospitals. According to a rumor that no doubt enhanced the painting's mass appeal, when the messenger emptied the sack of heads onto the ground, Casado nearly fainted — but took up his brush the following day (Díez 356–57).

Sandberg (92–95) notes how the new wax tableaux of the 1880s created a 'reality effect' by giving some of the figures the ability to look, mirroring the gaze of the spectator. This produced audience identification — indeed these diegetic spectators figured the emotional response that the non-diegetic spectator was expected to adopt. Pantorba (111) notes that the 'miradas de horror' ('gazes of horror') in the canvas were echoed by those on the faces of the crowds who flocked to see Casado's *Leyenda del rey monje*. What, one has to ask, might have been the function of that horror for the nation-formation project? Spectators would have known that the conservative statesman Cánovas del Castillo had, in his youth, written a historical novel *La campana de Huesca: Una crónica del siglo XII* (*The Bell of Huesca: Chronicle of the Twelfth Century*, 1854), published the same year as his *Historia de la decadencia de España* (*History of the Decadence of Spain*). The novel's illustrations included the Gothic scene of the king displaying his rebellious subjects' decapitated heads, fashioned into a bell clapper (the 'bell' of the novel's title), to the nobles who form the diegetic audience. Cánovas's text ends with the king absolved and spending the rest of his life in prayer; but one wonders what attracted the future architect of the Restoration's centralizing project to this gruesome subject matter, which he chose to foreground in his novel's title. The play of gazes within Casado's canvas ensures that one identifies with the horror of the nobles contemplating the massacre from the steps on the right, which encourages a reading of this painting as a condemnation of monarchical tyranny. Or does it? An eye-witness recounted hearing Casado, *incognito*, ask a bystander at the 1881 National Art Exhibition what he thought of the painting. Casado was appalled when the viewer replied that, in his view, the king ought also to kill the nobles in the picture for protesting at his dispensation of justice. Misreading was clearly possible (Díez 358–60). Indeed, the catalogue description of the painting explained the event as Ramiro II's revenge on 'los soberbios varones del Reino' ('the haughty nobles of the kingdom') for disregarding 'la autoridad rural y los fueros del pueblo' ('rural authority and popular common law'; Díez 352) — which makes Ramiro the champion of popular rights. I would suggest that the function of the painting was precisely to stir up debate about political rights and justice, and, at a more basic level, to trigger an emotional response of horror that filled spectators with a sense of the importance of responding to injustice, no matter how that injustice was defined. The painting could thus function as a training in citizenship, using horror to open — rather than close — debate.

It is even harder to determine how spectators might have responded to Pradilla's *Doña Juana la Loca*, except for the fact that we know from eye-witness reports that they were transfixed by it — that is, reduced to the same immobile staring that is enacted in Juana's figure. For these paintings are not so much historical representations as — like the contemporaneous wax tableaux — historical enactments. Like a wax tableau, Pradilla's painting gives the spectator the sensation of being an interloper contemplating a scene that is poised between life and death: wax being associated with embalming and yet producing a 'living image' (all the writers on waxworks comment on this uncanny quality of the medium). What this means is that the spectator internalizes Juana's own inability to determine whether Felipe I is really dead. This is not a 'mad' question for what is at stake is the status of the past as 'living dead': gone but still with us in its effects. This question, dramatized explicitly in Pradilla's painting, is effectively raised by all these historical paintings, whose status as 'living pictures' figures the past as hovering equivocally between life and death. It is an especially important question for nations on Europe's periphery anxious about their relation to modernity; that is, anxious about the pull of the past but also about the consequences of breaking free from it. Sandberg suggests that this explains the vogue for wax museums in 1880s Scandinavia. Tamayo y Baus's famous 1855 theatrical melodrama *Locura de amor* had picked up on this same anxiety: it ends with Juana asking her courtiers for silence so as not to wake Felipe's 'sleeping' corpse; this scene was reproduced in an 1866 painting by Lorenzo Vallés, whose simple grouping of figures and plain backcloth represents a stage in the history of the visual image prior to the development of the sophisticated wax tableaux of the 1880s. One may note here the popularity in wax museums of comatose figures — e.g. Sleeping Beauty — whose apparent death is belied by a mechanically-propelled heaving bosom.

I am not here arguing that Spanish historical paintings were influenced by the new wax tableaux: Pradilla's painting predates the 1880s, and we have very little information about waxworks in nineteenth-century Spain, where they remained an itinerant, ephemeral art form. What I wish to suggest is that these contemporaneous cultural phenomena correspond to similar visual developments, which in both cases express anxieties about whether the past is dead or alive, and use frozen dramatic re-enactments to train spectators in shared habits of looking that define them as national citizens. I would also suggest that, while these paintings produced certain inescapable emotional responses, they allowed these to be applied to a range of alternative readings of the visual configuration. In the case of Pradilla's painting, the spectator cannot help reproducing — that is, identifying with — the emotional response of Juana la Loca to the sight of Felipe's coffin. But how exactly does the spectator interpret this emotional response that he or she is forced to internalize? Juana's vacant look evokes an unspeakable trauma — and we may recall here Peter Brooks's observations on the melodramatic genre's ability to 'speak the unspeakable', frequently through the dramatization of muteness. On the one hand, Juana's madness — her fixation on her Habsburg husband — may have been read as an emblem of the 'disturbance' caused to Spain's historical destiny by the Habsburg dynasty, Felipe becoming King (with Juana's father Fernando el Católico's connivance) after having Juana declared mentally unfit to rule. Alternatively, female spectators especially may have interpreted Juana's traumatized figure as a mute protest against her husband's and father's unjust treatment of her (and they would surely have picked up the pathos of her clearly delineated advanced pregnancy). If Casado's painting reproduces a single emotion of horror in the spectators within his canvas, the onlookers in Pradilla's painting represent a range of emotional responses, from sympathy to dismissal. I suggest that the strength of Pradilla's painting is that, while binding spectators emotionally to its central figure (Juana), it forces them to try out a range of possible interpretations of the emotion they see dramatized in her figure, and which they internalize, without being able to articulate its contours. The painting thus provides a schooling in the need to think twice before claiming to understand the motivations of other people; that is, in responsible social relations. It is also a schooling in the need to reflect before coming to hasty conclusions about one's reading of the national past.

In her book *Democracy and the Foreigner*, Bonnie Honig has suggested that the nation is perhaps figured better not through the genre of romance, with its happy end, but through that of the Gothic (107–22).[6] Honig has in mind the female Gothic, which invites us to reflect on helplessness and our habit of invoking saviors which perpetuate the problem. Pradilla's painting can be read as an example of the female Gothic, but I wish to argue here for a reading of Spanish historical painting in general, with its emphasis on spectacles of horror, in the light of the Gothic genre in its broadest sense. For horror requires us to react empathetically, and its extremeness forces us to confront issues of injustice, while requiring us to reflect on what the nature of the injustice might be. Horror, which does not tell us what to think but requires us to feel, can thus be seen as a democratic genre: a schooling in responsible civic participation. I started this essay by wondering how Spanish spectators interpreted these gruesome representations of their national past. I end it by suggesting that the only thing we can know with any certainty is what they felt, and that was an intense involvement: this was a history that 'grabbed' you and made you part of it, like it or not. And, as Honig observes, democracy requires us to find ways of cohabiting with those we would rather not live with. As far as Spanish spectators' intellectual interpretations of these paintings are concerned, the point,

6   My thanks to Doris Sommer for drawing my attention to Honig's book.

I would argue, is that the paintings forced them to work these out for themselves; that is, they functioned as a schooling in democratic public debate.

Works Cited

ÁLVAREZ JUNCO, JOSÉ. *Mater Dolorosa: La idea de España en el siglo XIX*. Madrid: Taurus, 2001.

ARIAS ANGLÉS, ENRIQUE, and WIFREDO RINCÓN GARCÍA, eds. *Exposiciones nacionales del siglo XIX: Premios de Pintura*. Madrid: Centro Cultural del Conde Duque, 1988.

AVILÉS Y MERINO, ÁNGEL. *Catálogo de las obras de arte existentes en el Palacio del Senado*. Madrid: Est. Tip. Hijos de J.A. García, 1903.

BAROJA, PÍO. *Las figuras de cera*. 1924. Madrid: Editorial Caro Raggio, 1979.

BOURDIEU, PIERRE. *Distinction: A Social Critique of the Judgement of Taste*. Trans. Richard Nice. 1979. London: Routledge, 1996.

BOYD, CAROLYN P. *Historia Patria: Politics and National Identity in Spain, 1875–1975*. Princeton, NJ: Princeton UP, 1997.

BROOKS, PETER. *The Melodramatic Imagination: Balzac, Henry James, Melodrama, and the Mode of Excess*. New York: Columbia UP, 1985.

CÁNOVAS DEL CASTILLO, ANTONIO. *La campana de Huesca: Crónica del siglo XII*. 1854. Málaga: Instituto Cánovas del Castillo, Exma Diputación de Málaga, 1997.

CHARNEY, LEO, and VANESSA R. SCHWARTZ, eds. *Cinema and the Invention of Modern Life*. Berkeley: U of California P, 1995.

DÍEZ, JOSÉ LUIS, ED. *La pintura de historia en el siglo XIX en España*. Madrid: Museo del Prado, 1992.

FERNÁNDEZ DE LOS RÍOS, ÁNGEL. *Guía de Madrid: Manual del madrileño y del forastero*. 1876 (facsímile). Madrid: La Librería, 2002.

GARCÍA LORANCA, ANA, and RAMÓN GARCÍA-RAMA. *Vida y obra del pintor Francisco Pradilla y Ortiz*. Zaragoza: Caja de Ahorros de Zaragoza, Aragón y Rioja, 1987.

GIL, R. and T. ROMEA. *Guía de Madrid*. Madrid: Imprenta de Fortanet, 1881.

GUTIÉRREZ BURÓN, JESÚS. *Exposiciones nacionales de pintura en España en el siglo XIX*. 2 vols. Madrid: Universidad Complutense, 1987.

GUTIÉRREZ SOLANA, JOSÉ. *Madrid callejero*. 1923. Madrid: Castalia, 1995.

———. *Madrid, escenas y costumbres* (1ª serie). 1913. *Obra literaria*. Madrid: Taurus, 1961.

———. *Madrid, escenas y costumbres* (2ª serie). Madrid: Imprenta Mesón de Paños 8 bajo, 1918.

HABERMAS, JÜRGEN. *The Structural Transformation of the Public Sphere: An Inquiry into a Category of Bourgeois Society*. Trans. Thomas Burger and Frederick Lawrence. Cambridge, UK: Polity Press, 1989.

HERNÁNDEZ RUIZ, JOSÉ. 'Historia y escenografía en el cine español: Una aproximación.' *Ficciones históricas: El cine histórico español*. Spec. issue of *Cuadernos de la Academia* 6 (1999): 151–65.

HONIG, BONNIE. *Democracy and the Foreigner*. Princeton, NJ: Princeton UP, 2001.

LABANYI, JO. *Gender and Modernization in the Spanish Realist Novel*. Oxford: Oxford UP, 2000.

MIGUEL EGEA, PILAR DE, ed. *El arte en el Senado*. Madrid: Senado, 1999.

PANTORBA, BERNARDINO DE. *Historia y crítica de las Exposiciones Nacionales de Bellas Artes celebradas en España*. Madrid: Ediciones Alcor, 1948.

PILBEAM, PAMELA M. *Madame Tussaud and the History of Waxworks*. London: Hambledon Continuum, 2003.

PORTELA SANDOVAL, FRANCISCO. *Casado del Alisal 1831–1886*. Palencia: Excma Diputación Provincial de Palencia, 1986.

Reyero, Carlos. *La pintura de historia en España: Esplendor de un género en el siglo XIX.* Madrid, Cátedra, 1989.

——. *Imagen histórica de España (1850–1900).* Madrid: Espasa Calpe, 1987.

Salvá Herán, A. *Colecciones artísticas del Congreso de los Diputados.* Madrid: Fundación Argentaria, 1997.

Sánchez Vidal, Agustín. *Los Jimeno y los orígenes del cine en Zaragoza.* Zaragoza: Patronato Municipal de las Artes Escénicas y de la Imagen, 1994.

Sandberg, Mark B. *Living Pictures, Missing Persons: Mannequins, Museums, and Modernity.* Princeton, NJ: Princeton UP, 2003.

Schwartz, Vanessa. R. *Spectacular Realities: Early Mass Culture in Fin-de-siècle Paris.* Berkeley: U of California P, 1999.

Singer, Ben. *Melodrama and Modernity: Early Sensational Cinema and Its Contents.* New York: Columbia UP, 2001.

Varey, J. E. *Títeres, marionetas y otras diversiones populares de 1758 a 1859.* Madrid: Instituto de Estudios Madrileños, 1959.

PART III

Modernity and Politics in the 1920s and 1930s

CHAPTER 9

Cinematic City:
The Spanish Avant-garde,
Modernity and Mass Culture

References to the cinema occur in a huge number of Spanish avant-garde writers: I shall concentrate on the late 1920s, when this interest peaked. Some of the material I shall discuss is well known: Luis Buñuel and Salvador Dalí's *Un chien andalou* (*An Andalusian Dog*, 1929) and *L'Âge d'or* (*The Golden Age*, 1930); and Federico García Lorca's *Poeta en Nueva York* (*Poet in New York*, written 1929–30, published posthumously). Other material is less known: Lorca's film script *Viaje a la luna* (*Trip to the Moon*, written 1929 or 1930, published posthumously); Ernesto Giménez Caballero's film documentary *Esencia de verbena* (*Essence of the Fairground*, 1930); Maruja Mallo's fairground paintings (1927–28); Franciso Ayala's novella *Cazador en el alba* (*Hunter at Dawn*, 1929); and Ramón Gómez de la Serna's pastiche novel *Cinelandia* (1923). In two cases, the texts discussed are hardly known at all: Benito Perojo's silent film *El negro que tenía el alma blanca* (*The Black with a White Soul*, 1927) and César Arconada's literary biography *Vida de Greta Garbo* (*Life of Greta Garbo*, 1929).

Many cultural critics and film critics have pointed to the relationship between the 'ways of seeing' required by the modern city and those required by early cinema, suggesting that, if the cinema caught the imagination of popular as well as high-cultural audiences, it was because it capitalized on the visual training to which the inhabitants of the new urban agglomerations were subjected by their everyday bombardment with visual stimuli (Charney and Schwartz 1995; Levin 1993; Asendorf 1993). The theorists who have most imaginatively insisted on the experience of the modern city as the harnessing of spectacle and motion are, of course, Georg Simmel and Walter Benjamin; I am referring here specifically to Simmel's essay 'The Metropolis and Mental Life' (Harrison and Wood 1995: 130–35) and Benjamin's unfinished *Arcades Project* (1999). Unlike Simmel, Benjamin wrote not only about the city but also about cinema as a particularly complex modern means of mechanical reproduction (1992). James Donald, discussing Benjamin's writings on the city and on cinema, has gone so far as to argue that: 'This experience of remorseless visual stimuli is what, for Benjamin, created the *need* for the new medium' (1999: 74; emphasis in original). The proposition here is that the early moving pictures not only drew on the visual training of modern city dwellers but were a necessary outcome of it.

Susan Buck-Morss, also discussing Benjamin, proposes that '[f]ilm provides the audience with a new capacity — to study modern existence from the position of an expert' (Levin 1993: 323). By this she means both that, already before their exposure to cinema, the new city-dwellers had, through the practice of everyday life, become experts at dealing with multiple, fleeting, fragmentary visual stimuli that refuse narrative coherence; and also that film, by objectifying this process, allowed them to reflect critically on it, thus 'saving' them from the 'trauma' of urban alienation (her terms). This posits two modes of relating to the new forms of urban/cinematic perception: being overwhelmed (by implication negative) or distancing oneself (implying salvation). Buck-Morss's formulation betrays a high-cultural supposition that aesthetic detachment is superior to bodily engagement. The cinema necessarily calls into question bourgeois modes of cultural consumption because cinema audiences — except for private film clubs, about which more later — are by definition 'mass audiences', regardless of their social composition. In his classic study on the ways in which taste is used to construct systems of class discrimination, *Distinction*, Pierre Bourdieu (1996) emphasizes that cultural products are labelled 'high culture' or 'low culture' not according to their inherent qualities, or even according to the status of their producers, but according to who consumes them and their mode of consumption. Thus, the same product can shift from 'high' to 'low' cultural status, or vice versa, as it gets taken up by different audiences, which in turn supposes that it becomes consumed in a different way. It is, of course, perfectly possible for the same cultural object to be enjoyed simultaneously by elite and popular audiences, or by elite audiences in an ambivalent manner that mixes 'high' and 'low' cultural responses. It is this ambivalence that I wish to look at in relation to the late 1920s Spanish avant-garde.

Bourdieu makes a distinction between bourgeois aesthetic modes of consumption based on the establishment of a critical distance between spectator and object, thus privileging disinterested contemplation, and popular forms of consumption based on bodily involvement and functionality. This leads Bourdieu to equate popular taste with realism, which allows audience identification. Here Bourdieu is coinciding — though his class analysis is very different — with that notorious cultural snob, José Ortega y Gasset, whose 1925 essay *La deshumanización del arte* (*The Dehumanization of Art*) had insisted that 'the masses' could not appreciate 'art' because they were incapable of intellectual detachment, and, conversely, that modern art should opt for dehumanization in order to dissociate itself from the realism that was by definition a plebeian cultural form (Ortega y Gasset 1970). Bourdieu, who is analysing mid-twentieth-century French cultural taste, forgets something important here, as indeed does Ortega, namely, the strong tradition of popular spectacle (carnival, circus, musical hall, etc.) based on bodily involvement (through laughter, suspense and often audience participation) but where realism is a completely irrelevant category, for the enjoyment consists precisely in savouring the performance or masquerade. This is a popular cultural tradition that goes back to pre-modern oral culture, by definition based on live public performance, but it is one that remains a strong strand in modern urban mass culture, co-existing alongside a demand for realism that in fact is a hand-me-down from bourgeois culture, with its concern for individualized character. In fact, it would be more accurate to associate realism with the low-brow cultural tastes of members of the lower-middle or lower classes who have received a measure of education, than with the largely illiterate and unschooled peasantry who remained the norm in most of rural Spain in the 1920s, and who took their cultural tastes and habits to the cities as economic migrants, forming the mainstay of the growing urban working class. Lorca commented in an interview that he loved taking avant-garde productions of Spanish Golden Age theatre to illiterate rural audiences, with his travelling company La Barraca financed by the government of the Spanish Republic in the early 1930s, because they were much more responsive to the avant-garde sets and stage direction than bourgeois theatregoers (García Lorca 1966b). This responsiveness is not surprising, for these largely untutored popular audiences were versed in a popular cultural tradition of entertainment as spectacle. What this popular love of spectacle and the popular demand for realism described by Bourdieu and Ortega have in common is, of course, that both require a mode of consumption based on bodily engagement. Both these popular forms — spectacle, realism — come together in that enduring popular cultural form which came into existence in the late nineteenth-century modern city: the wax work (whose fascination lies in its ability to combine total realism with the freezing of motion; I shall come back later to the link between modernity as spectacle and death).[1]

The particularly brilliant Spanish avant-garde of the late 1920s is notable for the extent to which it mixes high-cultural, 'difficult' formal experimentation with the co-option of both pre-modern popular and modern mass-cultural forms. In his book *The Great Divide*, Andreas Huyssen (1988) has famously argued that the artistic and literary avant-garde that emerged after World War I should be distinguished from the rest of modernism, since the latter was generally characterized by the desire to distance 'art' from a newly proliferating mass culture, while the former was predominantly concerned — ultimately unsuccessfully — to break down the high/low cultural divide. It is unfortunate that Ortega y Gasset should be the only Spanish cultural theorist known in English translation, since his typically modernist scorn for mass culture is in fact untypical of the 1920s Spanish cultural scene, where artists of both political left and right coincided in their celebration of the cinema and other forms of mass or popular entertainment. The most famous

1   I am grateful to Luis Fernández Cifuentes for pointing out, after the presentation of an earlier version of this essay at Harvard University, that Ortega y Gasset hated wax works (see Ortega y Gasset 1970: 42). For the development and popularity of waxworks in late nineteenth-century Europe, see Schwartz 1998: 89–148 and Sandberg 2003. Schwartz (1998: 177) notes that Paris's famous wax museum, the Musée Grévin, installed a movie theatre on its premises in 1916; in Spain, the Jimeno family who opened the first cinema theatre in Spain in 1896, as well as making the first Spanish film in the same year, also ran a touring waxwork business (Sánchez Vidal 1994: 73–74). This, and the fact that early cinema and waxworks were both shown at fairgrounds (for Spain, see Sánchez Vidal 1994: 83–84), tells us much about the physicality of early cinemagoers' experience — not for nothing did Lorca call his experimental touring theatre company *La Barraca*, after the *barracas* (booths) that housed fairground attractions.

example of the co-option of popular culture is, of course, the use of the premodern oral ballad form by Lorca in his 1928 *Romancero gitano* (*Gypsy Ballads*; García Lorca 1989), closely related to Falla's eclectic musical syncretism mixing Spanish folk motifs with reminiscences of a wide range of cosmopolitan musical traditions. As is well known, in 1922 Falla and Lorca staged a flamenco competition in Granada, explicitly to 'save' flamenco from its 'degradation' by mass culture, where it was thriving in various hybridized forms in the music hall: here popular culture is seen as 'good' and mass culture as 'bad' (Mitchell 1994: 160–77). But Lorca's and Falla's co-option of flamenco rhythms, despite the primitivist rhetoric of 'pure', other-race (gypsy) origins, was always envisaged by them as a form of high-cultural plundering designed to create new aesthetic possibilities — the contrast with the non-experimental manner in which the ballad was used by Republican poets to create a genuinely popular poetry during the Spanish Civil War is notable.

If we turn to painting, those painters like Pablo Picasso and Juan Gris who left Spain for Paris are known for distancing themselves from low culture — apart from the incorporation via collage of certain low-cultural elements (for example, *anís* liqueur brand labels), lifted out of their original context. But in Madrid a large number of Spanish and Latin American painters were painting the fairground (Comisión Nacional 1998; Gubern 1999: 432), notably Maruja Mallo whose fairground canvases make self-avowed use of the cinematic technique of montage to create a sense of movement. Indeed, it became fashionable in the period for the members of the Madrid literary and artistic scene to get themselves photographed at Madrid's various popular festivals or *verbenas*, with their heads or upper bodies inserted into the stock cardboard cut-outs of motor cars or aeroplanes, or of figures in historical or traditional costume, that celebrated the fun of masquerade and, frequently, of cross-dressing.[2] This is cultural consumption as bodily participation in the most literal sense. One of the points I shall come back to is the tension, noted by Huyssen with regard to the northern European avant-garde, between a low-cultural celebration of the feminine and a high-cultural counter-tendency towards masculinization. Also noticeable in these photographs is the mixture of traditional and modern scenarios — the modern being represented by the car and aeroplane. I shall return to the use of aerial perspective as an avant-garde strategy for asserting dominion over the fragmentation of modern city life that is at the same time celebrated.

The fairground also formed the subject of an experimental short *Esencia de verbena*, made in 1930 by Ernesto Giménez Caballero, the editor of Spain's leading avant-garde art magazine, *La Gaceta Literaria* (*The Literary Gazette*), whose film column was written by Buñuel from Paris. The voice-over to the film's documentary montage stresses the dizziness (*mareo*) created by the constant whirling of the fairground, and literally represents the bodily involvement central to popular culture through its filming of the writer Ramón Gómez de la Serna masquerading as an animated

2   A number of these photographs, depicting Lorca, Buñuel, Maruja Mallo, Pablo Neruda, and others, are reproduced in the catalogue of the Centro de Arte Reina Sofía's exhibition dedicated to the centenary of Lorca's birth (Comisión Nacional 1998: 160–65).

fairground exhibit. Giménez Caballero was the founder of Spain's first film club, the Cineclub Español which ran from 1928 to 1931, with most members of the Madrid cultural elite subscribing, and with Buñuel responsible for programming in its initial stages. In 1928 Giménez Caballero also authored what is commonly regarded as the first Spanish surrealist text with the Freudian title *Yo, inspector de alcantarillas* (*My Self, Sewage Inspector*, 1975), as well as running an avant-garde art gallery. His Cineclub took over from the earlier film showings of 1927–28 at the elite Madrid university hall of residence, the Residencia de Estudiantes, which formed the breeding ground for the so-called 1927 Generation of avant-garde writers and artists, including Lorca, Dalí and Buñuel. The screenings at the Residencia were also organized by Buñuel from Paris, and included largely French experimental film, including René Clair's *Entr'acte* (1924), which supposedly prompted Ortega y Gasset to say that, if he were younger, he would devote himself to the cinema (Gubern 1999: 265) — an indication that the object of these screenings was the promotion of film as an elite aesthetic medium.

The films shown at Giménez Caballero's Cineclub were also unrelentingly avant-garde and impressively cosmopolitan, including Soviet and some Chinese cinema; to get past the censor (Spain was under military dictatorship from 1923–31) the first showing of Soviet cinema was held at the Ritz Hotel. Despite the political reasons for this venue, it indicates the select nature of the film club's subscribers: very little Hollywood cinema was shown at the Cineclub precisely because it was popular (Gubern 1999: 271–377). The first screening in Spain of Sergei Eisenstein's 1925 political classic *Battleship Potemkin* was at the Cineclub's last session in 1931, three years after Giménez Caballero's conversion to fascism in Italy. Despite being a founding member of the Spanish fascist party in 1933 and a virulent ideologue of fascism until his death in 1988, Giménez Caballero published work by writers of all political persuasions in *La Gaceta Literaria* (until 1930, from when he wrote the whole journal himself), and had no problem with showing Soviet cinema at his film club. It must of course be remembered that Mussolini was an ardent believer in the instrumental value of cinema; in his 1935 fascist tract *Arte y Estado* (*Art and the State*), Giménez Caballero sang the praises of cinema as the new 'profane cathedral' of modern civilization, because of its ability as a visual medium to reach the illiterate masses. In this book Giménez Caballero rejected European avant-garde attempts at abstract cinema, but praised German, Soviet and French avant-garde cinema for its 'cult of the object' (Gubern 1999: 84–85). In his impressively documented book on the Spanish avant-garde and the cinema (1999), on which my discussion relies heavily, Román Gubern notes that this same rejection of cinematic abstraction in favour of an avant-garde celebration of the material object was reiterated by most members of Madrid's avant-garde elite. In *Arte y Estado*, Giménez Caballero singled out for praise two Hollywood popular genres: the western for its epic qualities, and silent comedies. As is well known, the latter were immensely popular among the Spanish avant-garde, inspiring Lorca's one-act sketch *El paseo de Buster Keaton* ('Buster Keaton's Promenade'; García Lorca 1966a),[3] and Rafael Alberti's poems

---

3   First published in 1928 in the second (and last) number of Lorca's Granada-based magazine,

dedicated to the stars of Hollywood silent comedies — Keaton, Harold Lloyd (most people's favourite), Chaplin (who went out of favour for his sentimentality after his early films), Harry Langdon, Louise Fazenda, Bebe Daniels, Ben Turpin, Stan Laurel and Oliver Hardy, Wallace Beery, Charles Bowers — under the title *Yo era un tonto y lo que he visto me ha hecho dos tontos* (*I Was a Fool and What I've Seen Has Made Me Two Fools*; Alberti 1981).[4] The poems dedicated to Keaton, Lloyd, and Chaplin were 'performed' by Alberti during the interval of the May 1929 Cineclub session devoted to Hollywood comedies — the only session devoted to American movies (Gubern 1999: 308).

There are, then, a variety of positions adopted by the Spanish avant-garde with regard to popular and mass culture, and the preceding remarks do not claim to give a complete overview. What I should like to explore here is the relationship of this tension between an elitist impulse and a fascination with popular and mass culture to another tension that exists within modernism: that is, the tension between, on the one hand, a stress on the gap between reality and representation, and, on the other hand, an insistence that in urban modernity reality *is* representation. These two different contradictions do not map exactly onto one another, but they can be seen as related. The supposition of a divorce between reality and representation coincides with Bourdieu's analysis of the detachment and aestheticization of high-cultural taste, while the supposition that reality is representation coincides with the popular love of spectacle as masquerade.

I have argued elsewhere (Labanyi 2000) that the late nineteenth-century Spanish realist novel is so remarkably self-reflexive because its authors, whether they are pro- or anti-modern, coincide in supposing that urban modernity consists in the loss of fixed essential meaning, since, in the modern exchange economy, the value of things lies not in their intrinsic material worth but in an arbitrary system of representation (money) dictated by fluctuating demand (desire). As explained in Chapter 7, although Spain's modernization was belated and very patchy, public debate in late nineteenth-century Spain had a remarkably modern understanding of value thanks to the fact that Spain abandoned the gold standard in 1883, at precisely the time when the rest of the Western world (with the exception of Russia) had adopted it. If the European modernist awareness of the gap between signs and things can be related to the abandonment of the gold standard by the Western nations after 1914, exacerbated by the 1929 Wall Street crash (Goux 1988), in the case of late nineteenth-century Spain the abandonment of the gold standard, which leaves value entirely free-floating, does not produce a sense of a gap between signs and things so much as a sense that things (reality) are nothing but signs (representation).

In practice, early twentieth-century modernism does not entirely conform to the usual view of it as a break with realism resulting in a highlighting of the

---

Gallo (*Cockerel*), whose title refers to the crowing cockerel that appeared at the start of Pathé films. *El paseo de Buster Keaton* also starts with a crowing cockerel (see Gubern 1999: 17).

4   Most of these poems were published in numbers 58–66 (15 May–15 November 1929) of Giménez Caballero's magazine *La Gaceta Literaria*, illustrated with drawings by Maruja Mallo (at the time, Alberti's girlfriend) (Morris 1980: 87). The only complete edition remains that by C. B. Morris (Alberti 1981).

divorce between reality and representation. Indeed, there is a considerable strand that is concerned to capture the materiality of things through the image (whether cinematic or literary), in the supposition that, in urban modernity, things have the status of images, that is, representation. The visual image, particularly the photographic or cinematic image, can convey the materiality of objects especially well, and the only way to process the difficult tropes of much avant-garde writing is to treat them as visual complexes: this means that, despite the elitist difficulty of the work, it demands not an intellectual response, but one based on embodiment. We have already seen that the Spanish avant-garde by and large rejected abstract film for a cinema of the object. Buñuel and Dalí always insisted that their early surrealist films were concerned to show the 'thingness' of things; their method in selecting the images to be filmed in *Un chien andalou* was to reject any image for which they could find a meaning (Buñuel 1983: 104), for they wished to liberate objects from human subjectivity. In looking to dream images, they were not — like Freud — seeking to explore subjectivity but trying to reach something close to what Benjamin would later call 'unconscious optics' (1992: 230), whereby things would speak for themselves: what Dalí termed 'Santa Objetividad' ('Holy Objectivity'; Dalí 1927). In this sense, their films, while unrelentingly avant-garde, look back to the early moving pictures of cinema's beginnings — what Tom Gunning (1990) has called the 'cinema of attractions' — whose lack of narrativity foregrounds pure matter in motion: a busy street scene, waves breaking against a jetty.

There is an irony in the avant-garde revolt against capitalism, for it was triggered by an awareness of the arbitrariness of representation systems that was itself a product of the capitalist exchange economy. One of the few avant-garde films produced in Spain in the 1920s was the experimental short, *Historia de un duro* (*Story of a Five-Peseta Coin*, 1928), by Sabino Antonio Micón who had studied film production in Germany and France where similar films had been made (Gubern 1999: 165–75). The coin's circulation from one owner to the next is represented through disconnected shots of objects, arms, feet or shadows, but no faces: money reduces human beings to an abstract system of relations. Georg Simmel's lengthy 1900 study *The Philosophy of Money* (Simmel 1978) — less read than his essays on the modern city as visual spectacle — argues that the modern monetary economy marks a giant leap in intellectual development because it represents a new capacity for abstraction, since things are related to each other via a third term: money. It should be noted that, in Simmel's analysis, as in *Historia de un duro*, it is the relationships that are abstract, not their components which are material objects and bodies. The modern monetary economy thus combines abstraction and materiality in a complex way.

Lorca's stay in New York from 1929–30, which produced his most outstanding surrealist work (including *Poeta en Nueva York* and the film script *Viaje a la luna*) coincided with the Wall Street crash which he witnessed, writing home some wildly exaggerated accounts of bankers throwing themselves out of hotel windows (García Lorca 1990: 249). I do not think the difficult imagery of *Poeta en Nueva York* should be read as an indication of a divorce between words and things — this is not an 'unreal city', to use T. S. Eliot's phrase from *The Waste Land* — but rather as an indication of a city which, standing at the centre of the capitalist system, is governed by abstract relations between material things and bodies. The evacuation of things and bodies through images of wounding, maiming and vomiting suggests a world reduced to surface, but one whose materiality and carnality is striking. Nor am I sure that Lorca's New York poems should be read as a simple indictment of a city that has repressed nature, which consequently returns to take its revenge, as if the two were in opposition. In some cases, at least, the use of natural imagery suggests a cinematic technique of animation whereby things — set in motion by the circulation of the modern city as well as by the cinema — acquire a life of their own. Many critics seem to suppose that, as a Spaniard from Andalusia, Lorca must have hated New York and longed for the countryside he was used to, which is patronizing, to say the least. In practice, Lorca's letters home from New York show him to have been having a terrific time, fêted by the cultural elite of Manhattan and taken up by protagonists of the Harlem Renaissance (Lorca 1990: 201–56). The Latin American cultural critic Néstor García Canclini, following Perry Anderson, has argued that the avant-garde was most brilliant, not in advanced capitalist countries, but in those (like France, Italy, Spain or Latin America) where modernization was belated and uneven, thus producing a particularly violent 'shock of the new' (García Canclini 1989).[5] Almost all the members of Spain's avant-garde came to Madrid from the rural periphery, consequently perceiving modernity as a 'shock': one that was as exhilarating as it was traumatic.

A dominant theme in Lorca's letters home from New York is how he is getting better and better at finding his way around the city. His poems can be seen as an expression of vertigo at the frantic movement of modern city life, but also of the poet's desire to control that movement via a structured system of imagery. In other words, the abstract relations that govern the imagery arise out of those that govern urban experience, but they also allow the poet to position himself as all-controlling god. Thus, in the poems, the poet is bodily inscribed in the network of material images while at the same time positioned outside — and above — it. In the poem 'Paisaje de la multitud que vomita (Anochecer de Coney Island)' ('Landscape of the Vomiting Multitude [Dusk at Coney Island]'), it is through the gaze — an alienated gaze that is his but not his ('Esa mirada fue mía, pero ya no es mía' ['This gaze was mine but is mine no more']) — that the poet distances himself from the masses returning from a day out at the Coney Island amusement park: 'Me defiendo con esta mirada' ('I defend myself with this gaze'; García Lorca 1990: 54).[6] The superior distancing gaze is here linked explicitly to a horror of mass commercial culture, in the form of the amusement park; but we should remember those photos taken at Madrid fairgrounds, where Lorca literally puts himself into the spectacle.

Something different happens in the poem 'Danza de la muerte' ('Dance of Death') where an African mask invades Wall Street, resurrecting the dead objects of

5   For the historical avant-garde as a response to the 'shock of the new', see Robert Hughes's classic book of the same title (1991).
6   All translations from Spanish given in this essay are my own.

the city in a kind of final judgement by setting them in motion through dance. Tom Gunning has noted that the fascination with automata in early twentieth-century popular culture tips into the suggestion that modernity is a *danse macabre*; that is, a dance of animated mechanical corpses, but at the same time a magical infusion of life into the inanimate, making apocalypse and resurrection coterminous: the 'living dead' in all senses of the term.[7] As Lorca puts it in 'Danza de la muerte': 'El ímpetu primitivo baila con el ímpetu mecánico' ('The primitive beat dances with the mechanical beat'; García Lorca 1990: 47). In this spectacle or masquerade, things are dead, empty representations in the capitalist exchange economy, but they are also living, bodily participants in a magic ritual. This poem remains a difficult high-cultural text, but the rhythms of African-American dance — there is an incantatory quality to the verse — restore a non-realist functionality to art: dance is something that bodies do. This ritualistic physicality helps explain why Lorca's poetry, despite its difficulty, should be so popular, for it produces a bodily and not an intellectual response: that is, its very resistance to meaning allows it — perhaps requires it — to be consumed in a low-cultural manner. Indeed, Lorca is especially popular with students starting to learn Spanish, who have only a flimsy grasp of the language and therefore are forced to respond bodily to the sound of his words, rather than intellectually to their meaning. Lorca did of course prefer to read his poems rather than publish them; and *Poeta en Nueva York* was known in his lifetime only through his live recitals of certain poems.

In 'Danza de la muerte' Lorca includes himself in the scenario, not distanced by the gaze this time but 'en la terraza luchando con la luna' ('on the terrace struggling with the moon'; García Lorca 1990: 48). The moon recurs throughout Lorca's work, normally being interpreted as a force of nature. However Gubern takes as the title of his above-mentioned book (1999) the phrase 'proyector de luna' ('projector of moonlight'; the phrase is from Arconada's 1929 *Vida de Greta Garbo*, the last text I shall discuss), noting that the cinema was in the work of the 1920s Spanish avant-garde repeatedly associated with the moon, not only because of Méliès's 1902 film *Voyage dans la lune* (*Journey on the Moon*), but because the shaft of light coming from the projector in the dark above the audience's head was like a moonbeam. The word 'luna' in Spanish in fact not only means 'moon' but is also used for a large mirror, as in a wardrobe door, or for the glass of a shop-window. 'La luna' is both projector and reflector. It is thus an appropriate metaphor for the cinematic image which is and is not real: both because it depicts something real that is not there, and because it originates out of the spectacle of modern city life in which reality is representation. I would not like to suggest that whenever Lorca uses the word 'luna' he means the cinema; but I would argue that an association with the cinema invites itself on many occasions. The frequency of references to the moon in Lorca's major collection of poems of city life, *Poeta en Nueva York*, is striking (in this case the term also evokes the Luna Park fairground attractions on Coney Island). The reader of these poems often feels that the poetic 'I' is literally an 'eye' occupying

---

7   Keynote lecture to the conference 'Literature, Film and Modernity 1880–1940' given at the Institute of English Studies, University of London, on 13–15 January 2000.

the moon's position with regard to the objects and bodies depicted: a device for releasing things from human subjectivity. One might call this the replacement of the poet's viewpoint by the moon's viewpoint — the interplay between moon and eye famously opens Buñuel and Dalí's *Un chien andalou* as a metaphorical statement about the cinema.

Lorca's 1929 film script — whose title *Viaje a la luna* echoes that of Meliès's film *Voyage dans la lune* — was written during two days in New York, sometime between December 1929 and February 1930, spent with the Mexican filmmaker and painter Emilio Amero. Amero had made an abstract short titled *777* about cash registers, which he showed to Lorca; one notes again the focus on money as the mark of abstraction. Amero never got round to filming Lorca's script as was intended, and it was found by his widow in Oklahoma in 1989 (Monegal in García Lorca 1994: 9–10). The moon occurs three times in the script, in a highly self-reflexive manner. The first time, reminiscent of the chain moon-eye-cutting at the start of *Un chien andalou*, is fairly near the beginning as a sky with a moon emerges from the head of a dead body, and the moon splits in two, giving way to a drawing of a vomiting head opening and shutting its eyes. The second time is in the middle of the script: a man looks up at the moon, the moon appears on screen, another man looks up at the moon, and a close-up appears on screen of a bird's head which is strangled before the camera, a third man looks up at the moon, and the screen fills with a moon drawn on a white backcloth, which dissolves into genitals (it is not clear from the syntax whether these are meant to be male or female), which dissolve into a screaming mouth. The third time the moon appears in *Viaje a la luna* is in the last shot, of a moon and trees in the wind, whose 'naturalness' is called into question by the preceding image of 'un beso cursi de cine' ('a clichéd film kiss'; García Lorca 1994: 63, 70, 76). The film script has no narrative sense but makes its impact as a sequence of concrete images of material objects and human bodies with rapid cuts, multiple dissolves, and double or triple superimpositions, with alternating or simultaneous contrary horizontal or vertical movements, particularly the latter (repeated scenarios are stairs and elevators). The film is unremittingly experimental, but its use of speed and shock produces a bodily response that is more akin to the notion of art as spectacle than to high-cultural aesthetic detachment.

There is also a shot near the beginning of *Viaje a la luna* of 'Broadway de noche' ('Broadway at night'), which means a shot of neon signs (Lorca 1994: 60). In *The Film Sense*, Eisenstein noted that the spectacle of the modern city at night eliminated perspective and depth:

> The modern urban scene, especially that of a large city at night, is clearly the plastic equivalent of jazz. [...]
>   All sense of perspective and realistic depth is washed away by a nocturnal sea of electric advertising. Far and near, small (in the *foreground*) and large (in the *background*), soaring aloft and dying away, racing and circling, bursting and vanishing — these lights tend to abolish all sense of real space, finally melting into a single plane of coloured light points and neon lines moving over a surface of black velvet sky. [...] Headlights on speeding cars, highlights on receding rails, shimmering reflections on the wet pavements — all mirrored in puddles that

destroy our sense of direction (which is top? which is bottom?), supplementing the mirage above with a mirage beneath us, and rushing between these two worlds of electric signs, we see them no longer on a single plane, but as a system of theatre wings, suspended in the air, through which the night flood of traffic lights is streaming. (Eisenstein 1968: 82–83)

For the proliferation of signs in the city turns the city into just that: signs. This is a loss of the real which at the same consists of real material phenomena, collapsing reality and representation, while at the same time verging on abstraction. The artistic cult of the fairground in late 1920s Madrid included the stunning photographs of fairground lights in movement at night by Lorca's close friend, the Granada artist Hermenegildo Lanz (Comisión Nacional 1998: 163). The documentary *Les Nuits électriques* (*Electric Nights*, 1928) by the Paris-based Ukrainian Eugène Deslaw was shown at the second session of the Cineclub Español in January 1929; its fifth session, in April 1929, showed Deslaw's *La Marche del machines* (*March of the Machines*, 1929), which consisted entirely of images of machines in motion, with no human figures; Lorca — a subscriber to the Cineclub — is known to have been at this session.

Images of neon lights and machines are central to the 1930 surrealist novella by Francisco Ayala, *Cazador en el alba*. The neon lights of Madrid which the protagonist experiences for the first time as a rural military recruit are real, whereas the machines are metaphorical as he and his new city girlfriend become machines perfectly synchronized with modern city life. There is here a dual movement between the depiction of the city as spectacle, where reality itself is representation (neon lights), and a tendency towards abstraction as the characters' bodies become inanimate objects. In the former case, objects (the neon lights) are animated yet also the source of dehumanization, as we saw before in Lorca's 'Danza de la muerte': 'Ninguna [de las generaciones de dioses locales], sin embargo, procuraba a Antonio Arenas esa trémula emoción de lo heroico tanto como la — ya no superhumana — inhumana especie recién salida de los huevos eléctricos que las grandes avenidas incubaban' ('However, no generation of local gods evoked in Antonio Arenas that quivering sense of the heroic as much as the not so superhuman as inhuman species recently emerged from the electric eggs incubated in the great avenues'; Ayala 1971: 48). Interestingly, Antonio and his new city girlfriend decide not to have their photo taken since only photographs of dead people appear in the press. Despite the dominant tendency of this text to work towards abstraction (dehumanization), nevertheless it celebrates its rural hero's successful integration into the city, as he not only adapts to the mechanized rhythms but becomes a boxer: a popular sport par excellence, where bodily participation — including that of the audience — is everything.

José del Pino (1995: 164) has pointed out that Antonio Arenas's conquest of the city is the conquest of a woman, and that the moment of sexual triumph is narrated, not as bodily participation, but through his aerial view of her body, which turns it into an abstract pattern 'de triángulos, de planos, de líneas, de interferencias, de reiteraciones, de pliegues' ('of triangles, planes, lines, intersections, duplications, folds'). This can be read as a parable of the modernist desire for (masculine) control over the threatening (but seductive) proliferation of mass culture (conceived as feminine) in the modern city. Del Pino notes that the aerial perspective used in this passage recurs frequently in Spanish avant-garde fiction of the late 1920s. Before going on to the last two texts I wish to mention, I should like to contrast the handling of the city in two film sequences. The first is the sequence from Buñuel's *Un chien andalou*, when the characters look down from the upstairs apartment at the commotion in the street, as an androgynous figure toys with a severed hand. The aerial perspective that introduces and punctuates this sequence is matched by literal disembodiment: the severed hand. The androgynous figure also pokes the hand dispassionately. The use of point of view constructs the city as a spectacle for high-cultural detached, aesthetic contemplation, though also as a place of danger where nasty things can happen to bodies — a hesitation between high and low forms of cultural response mirrored by Buñuel's alternation in the soundtrack of Wagner and that most bodily of popular dances, the tango.[8] It is instructive to compare this scene to a short but telling sequence from Benito Perojo's little-known but extraordinary silent feature film *El negro que tenía el alma blanca* (1927) — a popular rather than avant-garde film, though containing a stunning experimental section (only the shorter 1929 French version, titled *Le Danseur de jazz* [*The Jazz Dancer*], survives). In the sequence that interests me, the Madrid theatre doorman and his daughter arrive in Paris, the latter having been 'discovered' and signed up as dancing partner by an internationally successful black dancing star, Peter Wald. This time we get a view of the city from below as the new arrivals find themselves at the bottom of their first escalator. Although the camera positions itself alternately behind/below them and above/in front of them, we are invited to identify with their position as they clumsily move from the bottom up (they learn to 'ride the city'): no detached aesthetic contemplation here, but physical involvement by the characters as they are knocked about and by the spectators through laughter. This film was immensely popular with audiences but at the same time it is technically brilliant, through its self-reflexive use of spectacle: it is, like so much early popular cinema, a film about performers. In these two films, there is a clear polarization between high-cultural and popular modes of representation, and yet both films show the impossibility of completely separating 'high' and 'low' modes of consumption.

To illustrate the ambivalence towards the city, and the way in which it relates to an ambivalent attitude towards high and low culture, I should like to finish by discussing two fictional representations of a very specific modern urban environment, Hollywood itself, depicted as an autonomous city by authors who had never visited it and for whom it was a purely imaginary location. The first, which I shall mention very briefly, is an earlier text, from 1923: the novel *Cinelandia* by the same Ramón Gómez de la Serna who posed as an animated fairground attraction in Giménez Caballero's *Esencia de verbena*. Here Hollywood is from start to finish represented as an 'unreal city', consisting entirely of cinematic clichés. The interesting bit is the end when, after the lead female star's rape and murder, Hollywood is closed down, and the star's films enjoy a posthumous success because

---

8   When originally screened as a silent film in 1929, the sound was provided by Buñuel playing records on a gramophone. In 1960, Buñuel added a musical soundtrack that attempted to reconstruct the acoustic effects of the original screening.

of the *frisson* of seeing 'live' on screen the body of someone who is known to be dead. Again, we have the tension between cinema as resurrection of the dead and as animated corpse. Audiences also get a kick out of watching films by a Hollywood that no longer exists; the point made here is that, as an 'unreal city', it was never real anyway. The other, more interesting text is Arconada's 1929 literary biography *Vida de Greta Garbo*: Arconada was Managing Editor of Giménez Caballero's magazine *La Gaceta Literaria* and a member of the original committee of his Cineclub. In a 1928 article in *La Gaceta Literaria* he declared: 'Para mí, el cinema es la expresión de lo moderno, del espíritu moderno. Vemos que el cinema es un espectáculo de juventudes. Y más aún, de juventudes femeninas.' ('For me, cinema is the expression of the modern, of the modern spirit. It is evident that the cinema is a spectacle that attracts youth. Particularly female youth'; Gubern 1999: 87). Accordingly, Arconada declared: 'La única literatura que existe — la nueva — está al servicio del cine, de los deportes, de la vida' ('The only literature today — the new literature — puts itself at the service of the cinema, sport, life'). The article continues: 'El cinema es la afirmación de las cosas. Flotación. Superficie. La música es un arte vertical. De ascensión, de vaga estructuración. El cinema es un arte horizontal. De asiento, de volumen, de estructuración concreta.' ('The cinema is an affirmation of things. Flotation. Surface. Music is a vertical art. Ascension, vague structuration. The cinema is a horizontal art. Solidity, volume, concrete structuration'). For this reason, Arconada adds, the notion of 'pure cinema' advocated by certain avant-garde filmmakers is a contradiction in terms (Gubern 1999: 126). Arconada went on in the 1930s to become a social novelist, joining the Communist Party in 1931 and after the Civil War living for the rest of his life in exile in Moscow. In 1931 he also wrote a book on Chaplin, Clara Bow and Harold Lloyd, called *Tres cómicos del cine* (*Three Comic Film Actors*; Arconada 2007). In 1928 he had written a book of poems titled *Urbe*: an erudite term for 'city' indicating the text's high-cultural pretensions, although the book is a celebration of everyday life in the modern city, in which the cinema plays a significant part.

Arconada's *Vida de Greta Garbo* is so interesting because it dramatizes in a particularly evident way its author's hesitations about positioning himself in relation to high and mass culture. His treatment of Hollywood as 'cinema city' is very different from that of Gómez de la Serna: this is not an 'unreal city' but just one more industrial town, the only difference from Chicago (to take the author's example) being that, instead of manufacturing cars, it manufactures films. There is huge emphasis on the materiality of the production studios and their electrical equipment. Paradoxically, this very material emphasis makes this a high-cultural text because, in demystifying the 'dream factory', it creates critical distance. Conversely, there is a sense in which one could argue that the text's literary excess (this is purple prose with a vengeance), while making it a high-cultural product through the self-reflexive attention to form, at the same time colludes with a popular delight in spectacle and fantasy. The text deconstructs the cinematic production process, but it also mimics it: each of its three sections is prefaced by a 'Primer plano lírico' ('Lyrical close-up').

The cause of the 'trouble' in the text is Greta Garbo's body, for the eroticized body of the female star engages the male avant-garde artist's bodily response (the narrator is a 'biógrafo' ['biographer'] called César Arconada), no matter how much he may wish to position himself as superior detached observer. In this sense, Garbo's function in the text is to illustrate the ambivalent relationship of the avant-garde (Arconada as biographer) to a mass culture (Hollywood) conceptualized as female. Garbo is the perfect star to mediate the contradiction between high-cultural aesthetic detachment and popular bodily engagement, for her sexiness emanates from her aloofness. It seems significant that Garbo should be the Hollywood star most mentioned by 1920s Spanish avant-garde writers (I refer here to male writers, of course). However, Garbo's refusal, in Arconada's biography, of all the men who fall in love with her not only positions her as the distant object of aesthetic contemplation, but also leaves her available for the male reader's not-so-detached erotic pleasure — and that of the author, for this is a self-reflexive text in which the author-narrator Arconada constantly enters as character. It seems interesting that Arconada does not mention the Spanish Latin lover, Antonio Moreno, who played opposite Garbo in one of the films he discusses — *The Temptress* (Fred Niblo, 1926)[9] — for that would introduce a competitor. Indeed, it is noticeable that no Spanish avant-garde text that I know mentions the considerable number of Spanish actors and actresses who made it in 1920s Hollywood silent movies, when it did not matter if you spoke English with a thick accent (García de Dueñas 1993; Armero 1995) — not even Conchita Montenegro who was nicknamed 'the Spanish Garbo'. This was no doubt because these Spanish stars played in popular films with no claim to artistic status, but perhaps also because their 'Spanishness' produced for Spanish spectators an identification that undercut high-cultural aesthetic contemplation: their role, after all, was that of 'Latin lover'. Arconada's biography ends with the 'biógrafo de sombras' ('biographer of shadows'), as the intruding author's visiting card describes him, going to Stockholm to meet Garbo during a trip back to Sweden. After trying to get rid of him, Garbo warms to him, invites him to sit down in a chair next to her, and asks him to read her his biography: the text ends with its opening words in a kind of film loop. This ending, with its self-conscious fictional games, 'rescues' the text for high culture, and it does so by reversing the gender dynamics, putting Garbo in the thrall of the male author. But it does this at the expense of a dangerous bodily proximity, as the chairs are pulled up closer. I would like to end with this image of Arconada sitting next to Garbo, as an embodiment (with all the physicality that the term implies) of the ambivalence and tensions that characterize the attitudes of late 1920s Spanish (male) avant-garde artists towards women, towards the cinema, towards the city, towards modernity, and — involved in all these ambivalences — towards high and mass culture.

---

9   *The Temptress* was based on the 1923 novel by the Valencian novelist Blasco Ibáñez, *La tierra de todos* (*Everyman's Land*; Blasco Ibáñez 1984), building on the massive success of two of the numerous Hollywood adaptations of his work: *The Four Horsemen of the Apocalypse* (Rex Ingram, 1921), starring Rudolph Valentino; and *Blood and Sand* (1922), also directed by Niblo and starring Valentino.

Works Cited

ALBERTI, RAFAEL. 1981. *Sobre los ángeles; Yo era un tonto y lo que he visto me ha hecho dos tontos*, ed. by C. B. Morris (Madrid: Cátedra)

ARCONADA, CÉSAR M. 1928. *Urbe* (Málaga: Imp. Sur)

———. 1929. *Vida de Greta Garbo* (Madrid: Ulises)

———. 2007. *Tres cómicos de cine* (Seville: Renacimiento)

ARMERO, ÁLVARO. 1995. *Una aventura americana: Españoles en Hollywood* (Madrid: Compañía Literaria)

ASENDORF, CHRISTOPH. 1993. *Batteries of Life: On the History of Things and their Perception in Modernity* (Berkeley: University of California Press)

AYALA, FRANCISCO. 1971. *Cazador en el alba y otras imaginaciones* (Barcelona: Seix Barral)

BENJAMIN, WALTER. 1992. 'The Work of Art in the Age of Mechanical Reproduction', in *Illuminations*, ed. by Hannah Arendt, trans. by Harry Zohn (London: Fontana), pp. 211–44

———. 1999. *The Arcades Project*, trans. by Howard Elland and Kevin McLaughlin (Cambridge, MA: The Belknap Press of Harvard University Press)

BLASCO IBÁNEZ, VICENTE. 1984. *La tierra de todos* (Barcelona: Plaza & Janés)

BOURDIEU, PIERRE. 1996. *Distinction: A Social Critique of the Judgement of Taste*, trans. by Richard Nice (London: Routledge)

BUÑUEL, LUIS. 1983. *My Last Breath*, trans. by Abigail Israel (New York: Alfred Knopf)

BUÑUEL, LUIS, and SALVADOR DALÍ (dirs). 1929. *Un chien andalou* (prod. Luis Buñuel)

—— (dirs). 1930. *L'Âge d'or* (prod. Vicomte de Noailles)

CHARNEY, LEO, and VANESSA R. SCHWARTZ. 1995. *Cinema and the Invention of Modern Life* (Berkeley: University of California Press)

CLAIR, RENÉ (dir.). 1924. *Entr'acte* (prod. Rolf de Maré)

COMISIÓN NACIONAL ORGANIZADORA DE LOS ACTOS CONMEMORATIVOS DEL CENTENARIO DEL NACIMIENTO DE FEDERICO GARCÍA LORCA. 1998. *Federico García Lorca (1898–1936)* (Madrid: Ministerio de Educación y Cultura)

DALÍ, SALVADOR. 1927. 'San Sebastián', *L'Amic de les Arts*, 31 July: 52–54

DEL PINO, JOSÉ M. 1995. *Montajes y fragmentos: Una aproximación a la narrativa española de vanguardia* (Amsterdam: Rodopi)

DESLAW, EUGÈNE (dir.). 1928. *Les Nuits électriques* (prod. Eugène Deslaw)

—— (dir.). 1929. *La Marche des machines* (prod. Eugène Deslaw)

DONALD, JAMES. 1999. *Imagining the Modern City* (London: Athlone Press)

EISENSTEIN, SERGEI (dir.). 1925. *Battleship Potemkin* (prod. Yakov Bliokh)

———. 1968. *The Film Sense* (London: Faber & Faber)

GARCÍA CANCLINI, NÉSTOR. 1989. *Culturas híbridas: Estrategias para entrar y salir de la modernidad* (Mexico: Grijalbo)

GARCÍA DE DUEÑAS, JESÚS. 1993. *¡Nos vamos a Hollywood!* (Madrid: Nickelodeon)

GARCÍA LORCA, FEDERICO. 1966A. *El paseo de Buster Keaton*, in *Obras completas*, 11th edn (Madrid: Aguilar), pp. 893–96

———. 1966B. 'Teatro para el pueblo', in *Obras completas*, 11th edn (Madrid: Aguilar), pp. 1747–49

———. 1989. *Poema del cante jondo; Romancero gitano*, ed. by Allen Josephs and Juan Caballero (Madrid: Cátedra)

———. 1990. *Poet in New York*, ed. by Christopher Maurer, trans. by Greg Simon and Steven F. White, bilingual edn (London: Penguin)

———. 1994. *Viaje a la luna*, ed. by Antonio Monegal (Valencia: Pre-Textos)

GIMÉNEZ CABALLERO, ERNESTO (dir.). 1930. *Esencia de verbena* (prod. Ernesto Giménez Caballero)

——. 1935. *Arte y Estado* (Madrid: Gráfica Universal)

——. 1975. *Yo, inspector de alcantarillas* (Madrid: Turner)

GÓMEZ DE LA SERNA, RAMÓN. 1995. *Cinelandia* (Madrid: Valdemar)

GOUX, JEAN-JOSEPH. 1988. 'Banking on Signs', *Diacritics*, 18.2: 15–25

GUBERN, ROMÁN. 1999. *Proyector de luna: La generación del 27 y el cine* (Barcelona: Anagrama)

GUNNING, TOM. 1990. 'The Cinema of Attractions: Early Film, its Spectator, and the Avant-Garde', in *Early Cinema: Space, Frame, Narrative*, ed. by Thomas Elsaesser (London: British Film Institute), pp. 56–62

INGRAM, REX (dir.). 1921. *The Four Horsemen of the Apocalypse* (Rex Ingram Productions)

HARRISON, CHARLES, and PAUL WOOD (eds). 1995. *Art in Theory, 1900–1990: An Anthology of Changing Ideas* (Oxford: Blackwell)

HUGHES, ROBERT. 1991. *The Shock of the New: Art and the Century of Change* (London: Thames & Hudson)

HUYSSEN, ANDREAS. 1988. *After the Great Divide: Modernism, Mass Culture, Postmodernism* (Basingstoke: Macmillan)

LABANYI, JO. 2000. *Gender and Modernization in the Spanish Realist Novel* (Oxford: Oxford University Press)

LEVIN, DAVID MICHAEL (ed.). 1993. *Modernity and the Hegemony of Vision* (Berkeley: University of California Press)

MELIÈS, GEORGES (dir.). 1902. *Voyage dans la lune* (Star Film Company)

MICÓN, SABINO ANTONIO (dir.). 1928. *Historia de un duro* (Luna Film)

MITCHELL, TIMOTHY. 1994. *Flamenco Deep Song* (New Haven, CT: Yale University Press)

MORRIS, C. B. 1980. *This Loving Darkness: The Cinema and Spanish Writers, 1920–1936* (Oxford: Oxford University Press)

NIBLO, FRED (dir.). 1922. *Blood and Sand* (Paramount Pictures)

—— (dir.). 1926. *The Temptress* (Metro-Goldwyn-Mayer)

ORTEGA Y GASSET, JOSÉ. 1970. *La deshumanización del arte*, 10th edn (Madrid: Revista de Occidente)

PEROJO, BENITO (dir.). 1927. *El negro que tenía el alma blanca* (Goya Producciones Cinematográficas)

SÁNCHEZ VIDAL, AGUSTÍN. 1994. *Los Jimeno y los orígenes del cine en Zaragoza* (Zaragoza: Patronato Municipal de las Artes Escénicas de la Imagen)

SANDBERG, MARK. 2003. *Living Pictures, Missing Persons: Mannequins, Museums, and Modernity* (Princeton, NJ: Princeton University Press)

SCHWARTZ, VANESSA. 1998. *Spectacular Realities: Early Mass Culture in Fin-de-Siècle Paris* (Berkeley: University of California Press)

SIMMEL, GEORG. 1978. *The Philosophy of Money*, trans. by Tom Bottomore and David Frisby (London: Routledge)

CHAPTER 10

Women, Asian Hordes and the Threat to the Self in Giménez Caballero's *Genio de España*

The work of Ernesto Giménez Caballero has been excluded from the Spanish literary canon both for his politics and for his crossing of generic boundaries. His best-known work, *Genio de España* (*Genius of Spain*, 1932) is as much a text of the literary avant-garde as it is a political tract; its hybrid nature can be understood only in the context of its author's multifaceted activities. Spain's most explicit and talented literary exponent of fascism, to which he was converted in 1928, Giménez Caballero was a leading cultural entrepreneur in the late 1920s and early '30s. Critics have mostly focused on his contribution to the avant-garde through his foundation and editorship of *La Gaceta Literaria* (*The Literary Gazette*, 1927–32), which published Lorca, Alberti and Buñuel among others, texts in Spain's minority languages, and articles on Judeo-Spanish culture.[1] By 1929 the magazine had swung to the right, causing the defection of many of its contributors. Yet in the same year, 1929, Giménez Caballero founded a modern art gallery, La Galería, specializing in the applied arts; and the Cineclub Español (Spanish Film Club), which he founded in 1928, continued to function until 1931, at its last session showing Eisenstein's *The Battleship Potemkin* in Spain for the first time. A perceptive film theorist, in 1930 Giménez Caballero made two avant-garde documentaries exploiting the potential of montage: the self-celebratory *Noticiario del Cineclub* (*Film Club Newsreel*) and (with the painter Maruja Mallo as art director) the brilliant *Esencia de verbena* (*Essence of the Fairground*), celebrating popular carnival and the modern city. Interestingly, given the demands by many Spanish fascists for a return to an anachronistic rural, feudal order, he was one of the few Spanish avant-garde writers to embrace urban modernity unreservedly. He also experimented with collage in his witty *Carteles literarios* (*Literary Posters*; literary criticism in poster form), exhibited at the Dalmau Gallery, Barcelona, in 1927 and dedicated 'A la era industrial del mundo. Nada

---

1 See Tandy and Sferrazza 1977; Hernando 1974, 1975a, 1975b; Geist 1980. Peña Sánchez (1995: 179–263) studies the magazine's links with Italian fascism. Foard 1975 gives a largely uncritical overview of Giménez Caballero's work. Rodríguez-Puértolas 1986 is an invaluable source for Giménez Caballero's political thought and involvement. See also López-Vidriero's bibliography (1982).

menos' ('To the industrial era of the world. Nothing less.').[2] One of the first Spanish writers to read Freud seriously, his overtly Freudian prose fiction *Yo, inspector de alcantarillas* (*My Self, Sewage Inspector*, 1928) has been called the first Spanish surrealist text (Hernando 1975a).

His avant-garde prose cocktail *Julepe de menta* (*Mint Julep*, 1929) aggressively exalts mass culture: the cinema, seen as the modern equivalent of the *aleluya* (broadsheets telling a story in captioned images), and the dance-hall (tango, charleston, jazz).[3] More obviously prefiguring his fascism, his celebration of myth and modernity *Hércules jugando a los dados* (*Hercules Rolling the Dice*, 1928) proposes a modern Nietzschean superman who is an amalgam of the Hellenic athletic ideal and the Hollywood hero Douglas Fairbanks. All the works listed here celebrate the avant-garde, especially the cinema, as a new mass art, capable of combining heterogeneous and dissonant cultural ingredients. ⌐Like many other Spanish avant-garde writers, Giménez Caballero refused the split between high and low culture for which European modernism has been held responsible, and which was so notoriously propounded in Spain by Ortega y Gasset⌐ But, unlike most of his Spanish contemporaries, Giménez Caballero's interest lay not in popular culture (produced by the pre-modern rural populace) but in mass culture (aimed at the masses through modern mechanical means of reproduction). Ortega thought the masses incapable of understanding modernism, which he saw as the product of intellectual abstraction; for Giménez Caballero, modernism was defined by the appeal to the irrational, allowing it to reach the masses by speaking to the unconscious. ⌐This hierarchical, irrationalist concept of mass culture formed the basis of his 1935 fascist artistic credo *Arte y Estado* (*Art and the State*), first published in the far-right magazine *Acción Española*, which turned art into state propaganda while celebrating the state as art form. One is reminded of Walter Benjamin's definition of fascism as the 'aestheticization of politics' (1992: 234).⌐

Giménez Caballero's 1928 conversion to fascism took place during a visit to Rome (his wife was Italian). In 1929 he translated Malaparte's *Italia Barbara* (*Barbarous Italy*), and in 1930 was received by Mussolini; throughout the 1930s he lectured and published in Italy. In 1941, invited to a writers' congress in Nazi Germany (where he gave Hitler a dedicated copy of *Genio de España*), he was a house guest of Goebbels. In his autobiography *Memorias de un dictador* (*Memories of a Dictator*, 1979: 152), he claimed that he proposed to Goebbels's wife the idea of marrying Hitler to Pilar Primo de Rivera, sister of the leader of the Spanish fascist party, Falange Española, but that she dismissed the idea on the grounds that Hitler was 'incapacitated' for marriage by his World War I injuries. In 1931, a year before the publication of *Genio de España*, Giménez Caballero was a signatory to Ramiro Ledesma Ramos's fascist manifesto *La conquista del Estado* (*The Conquest of the State*), and in 1933 was a founding member of Falange Española, serving on its first National Council. On the Nationalist uprising against the Republic in 1936, he joined Franco's

---

2   See the exhibition catalogue *'Carteles literarios'* 1994, which also discusses Giménez Caballero's two avant-garde films, shown at the exhibition.

3   The prose poem 'Oda al bidet', which ends *Julepe de menta*, is discussed in Dennis 1995: 42–43.

headquarters, playing an active role in the Nationalist propaganda apparatus. In addition to founding the front-line magazine *Los Combatientes (Combatants)*, he drafted the text of the decree unifying the Falange with the Carlists. A member of the Political Secretariat of the new unified party, he continued to serve on the Falange's National Council after the war. In the period 1958–70 he was Spanish Ambassador in Stroessner's Paraguay. His autobiography (Giménez Caballero 1979) shows him to have remained an unrepentant fascist to the last. The embarrassment produced by the political orientation of Giménez Caballero's literary and artistic modernism should, I suggest, be faced and not ignored. Spain is not the only country in which modernism appealed to writers of the right as well as of the left. The most embarrassing feature of Giménez Caballero's work is its use of often lurid sexual images: it is his sexual politics, as expressed in *Genio de España*, that concerns me here.

Genio de España constitutes a passionate incitement to a fascist 'rebirth' through violence, drawing in time-honoured modernist fashion on Nietzsche, Sir James Frazer and Spengler. Its exclamatory style — it bears the subtitle *Exaltaciones a una resurrección nacional y del mundo (Exaltations towards National and World Resurrection)* — masks a confused but acute analysis of the 'crisis of modernity'. Giménez Caballero's insistent use of sexual terminology is linked to his obsession with the Oriental, here in the guise of communism, seen as the invading 'Asian hordes'. Andreas Huyssen has suggested that, by the end of the nineteenth century, 'the male fear of women and the bourgeois fear of the masses become indistinguishable', (1986: 53). My frame of reference is Klaus Theweleit's classic two-volume study of German fascism, *Male Fantasies* (1987, 1989), which psychoanalyses novels, letters and autobiographical writings by members of the Freikorps who went on to figure prominently in the SA (Sturm Abteilung). Theweleit's central thesis is that these men remained at the pre-oedipal stage, never successfully separating from the mother. Their precarious sense of ego boundaries led them, he suggests, to erect a literal and metaphorical body armour to defend them against the threat of women and the masses, perceived as a projection of the fluidity and formlessness feared within. Theweleit was writing in 1977–78, prior to the development of gender studies. Today his thesis could usefully be reformulated in the light of Nancy Chodorow's and Jessica Benjamin's suggestion that post-Enlightenment Western culture, in privileging a concept of individual autonomy achieved by separating from the pre-oedipal mother–child dyad, almost inevitably equates individual maturity with rejection of the feminine, perceived — as in Freud — as an 'oceanic' formlessness that threatens to engulf the individual ego. This means both that women can never be full individuals, for they cannot wholly repudiate the feminine, and that success is measured for men in terms of their debasement of women (Chodorow 1978; Benjamin 1990). At the same time, as Theweleit also notes, men retain a nostalgia for the original union with the feminine that has had to be sacrificed. It is no surprise that Jessica Benjamin should be co-author of the introduction to the English translation of Theweleit's second volume. This revision to Theweleit's argument avoids the pitfalls of his implied suggestion that the members of the Freikorps became fascists because of a defective upbringing, and instead puts the emphasis on the collective representations of gender to which fascist writing appeals. The most valuable contribution of Theweleit's stress on the pre-oedipal is its rejection of the commonplace view of fascism as an oedipal fear of/desire for paternal authority, for, as he notes, the texts he analyses insist not on fathers but on mothers. Despite Giménez Caballero's repeated demand for a national 'hero', this is also true of *Genio de España*.

At this stage, a word of caution is needed. Theweleit is writing about post-World War I Germany, whose political situation, social and family structures, and moral and religious values, were very different from those of Spain in the same period. Giménez Caballero makes it clear that he is proposing the Catholic, Mediterranean Italy of Mussolini, and not Hitler's Germany, as a model for Spain. He also notes that Spain, unfortunately in his view, did not fight in World War I; Theweleit stresses the importance of the experience of war for the German Freikorps. Theweleit's analysis offers a way of reading Giménez Caballero's text, but the differences are revealing. In his book *Nationalism and Sexuality*, George Mosse notes that the insistence on a continent virility found in Nazi Germany was much less strictly adhered to in Mussolini's Italy (1988: 56–57, 174). *Genio de España*, which sets up Don Juan as the national superman, confirms that the male sexual complexes to which fascism appealed in Spain, though equally based on a fear of women and the masses, differed in important respects from those which underlay German fascism. The extent to which such differences account for the ideological and organizational differences between German and Spanish fascism is a matter of speculation; I would be wary of any explanation that failed to consider economic and political factors. But, as Theweleit notes, fascism had an emotional appeal that went beyond material interests. As he also notes, this emotional appeal operated at a conscious as well as unconscious level: fascists, he insists, knew what they wanted and what they were doing (1987: 89, 432; 1989: 189, 361). The highly structured rhetoric of *Genio de España* shows Giménez Caballero consciously manipulating psychological complexes for political effect.

Theweleit insists that the bodily metaphors used by his 'soldier males', as he calls them, should be taken seriously. In their introduction to his second volume, Jessica Benjamin and Anson Rabinbach note that these metaphors are explicitly sexual (Theweleit 1989: xii) As is well known, the topos of the nation as a diseased body was central to the debate on national 'regeneration' that had monopolized Spanish intellectual life since the mid-1880s. In *Genio de España*, the stress is not so much on disease (posing the need for what Giménez Caballero calls the 'desintoxicación' ['detoxification'] of the body politic) as on 'desmembramiento' ('dismemberment'), in an overtly Freudian play on castration anxiety, 'miembro' meaning 'member' in the sense of both 'limb' and 'penis'. Giménez Caballero's schematic run through Spanish history reduces it to a series of thirteen 'dismemberments', in which the nation lost part of its territory. The last of these comprises Spain's disastrous military defeat in Morocco in 1921, seen as the prelude to Alfonso XIII's abdication in 1931 and the declaration of the Second Republic, which that same year granted political autonomy to Catalonia. Giménez Caballero's first book *Notas marruecas de un soldado*

(*A Soldier's Moroccan Notes*, 1923), for which he was court-martialled, had recounted his experiences as a conscript in the Moroccan war. These thirteen 'dismemberments' function much like the historic dates that Theweleit's 'soldier males' repeat so as to turn the threatening chaos of history into a series of fixed 'memorial stones' (1989: 261–63). Giménez Caballero's text plays constantly on the associative links between 'genial' (brilliant), 'genesíaco' (genesial), 'genético' (genetic), 'genital' (genital); also repeated insistently are the words 'fecundar' (fertilize), 'fecundo' (fertile), 'fecundidad' (fertility). The emphasis on dismemberment on the one hand, and fertility on the other, suggests a castration anxiety that is not so much to do with fear of authority as with fear of loss of potency in the sense of sterility. We shall come back to this and its relation to the desire for 'rebirth' later.

The most interesting chapter of *Genio de España*, titled 'Los tres genios del mundo' ('The Three World Geniuses'), explicitly relates the crisis of modernity to a Freudian crisis of the ego. The first two geniuses — the 'Genio de Oriente' ('Genius of the Orient') and the 'Genio de Occidente' ('Genius of the West') — represent two converse threats to the individual self. Edward Said's argument (1985) that the Orient functions in Western discourse not as a discrete historical and geographic entity but as a symbolic projection of Europe's dark 'Other' is confirmed by Giménez Caballero's use of the term to refer indiscriminately to the USSR, China, India, North and Sub-Saharan Africa, Mexico, Peru and even Australia. For Giménez Caballero, the 'Genio de Oriente' is incarnated in Soviet communism which, making a huge imaginative leap, he sees as the expression of a Buddhist or Hindu negation of the individual: "La anulación del *Ego*, la supresión de la *Libido*, la *muerte del Deseo* [...], el *Nirvana*' ('The annihilation of the *Ego*, the suppression of the *Libido*, the *death of Desire* [...], *Nirvana*'; 1983: 144). The 'dios bolchevique' ('Bolshevik god') is the god of 'el Hombre-Masa' ('Mass-Man'), who invites collective suicide in the waters of the Ganges (1983: 145). The 'Genio de Oriente' — the Asian hordes who comprise the non-individualized communist masses — is represented on Giménez Caballero's world map by the colour yellow (for 'yellow peril') rather than red (for socialism), because the latter is, curiously, seen as the modern manifestation of the 'Genio de Occidente'.

The genius of the West is posited as the polar opposite of its Oriental counterpart, namely, the hyper-valorization of the individual ego, regarded as equally problematic. If the Orient is 'El Todo sobre el Hombre' ('All above Man'), the West is 'El Hombre sobre Dios' ('Man above God'), from the classical Greek myth of Prometheus through to modern liberal individualism. Giménez Caballero sees the liberal proclamation of equal rights for all as an extension of Caesarism since, if the latter confers sovereignty on one individual, the former makes all individuals sovereign. Here again, Giménez Caballero is making some huge imaginative leaps. The 1929 Wall Street crash and socialism are seen by him as the final apocalypse of this individualist tradition:

> Suena por todo el ámbito occidental el ¡crac! de los negocios. El grito de las masas en paro y sin amparo [...]. El suicidio vuelve a la moda [...]. El surrealismo hace un culto de ellos [los suicidios]. El arte se ha descompuesto, como el

> hombre [...]. Todo es relatividad, fenomenologismo, atomística [...]; vida de
> los sueños, de las larvas. ¿Y el hombre dónde está? Ése es, ése: el drama de lo
> moderno. El drama del humanismo. (1983: 151)

> (The financial crash reverberates throughout the Western world. The shouts
> of the unemployed, defenceless masses [...]. Suicide is back in fashion [...].
> Surrealism makes a cult of them [suicides]. Art has disintegrated, like man [...].
> Everything is relativity, phenomenology, atomism [...]; the life of dreams, of
> larvae. And where is man? That, yes, that is the drama of the modern. The
> drama of humanism.)

The humanistic overvaluing of the ego has led to the latter's demise, with the
revenge of the unconscious ('vida de los sueños, de las larvas'). Giménez Caballero
justifies his arbitrary inclusion of communism under the Orient and socialism
under the West by arguing that Lenin, for whom he shows tremendous admiration,
was the vulture that devoured the Western Promethean myth from within,
misappropriating Marxism's original promise to extend individual rights to the
masses and instead instituting a mass society that denies individualism. This analysis
allows Giménez Caballero to come to the controversial conclusion that both the
genius of the Orient and the genius of the West have culminated in the same
destruction of the individual ego.

Giménez Caballero's freudianization of what Ortega y Gasset, in his famous book
of that name published two years before, had called 'la rebelión de las masas' ('the
rebellion of the masses') accords with Theweleit's suggestion that fascism offered
itself as an answer to men who felt their egos threatened with dissolution. I say
'men' because, in *Genio de España* as in the texts analysed by Theweleit, this fear
of ego boundaries dissolving is explicitly related to a fear not just of the masses but
also of women. For Giménez Caballero, the Spanish Republic represents the threat
not only of socialism but also of 'la separación de la mujer del hombre' ('woman's
separation from man'; 1983: 47), an obvious reference to the February 1932 Divorce
Law. It is no longer men who are separating from women (their mothers), but
women who are separating from men. A parallel is established between the granting
of autonomy to Catalonia — 'la desmembranza de Cataluña' ('the severance of
Catalonia'; 1983: 55) — and 'la separación de la mujer del hombre', implying
that the latter, too, is a castrating dismemberment or loss of potency, for without
women man cannot 'fecundar' ('sow their seed'). In a note to the 1939 edition,
Gimenez Caballero describes autonomous Catalonia as being 'divorciada de España'
('divorced from Spain') and compares the victorious Nationalist troops' entry into
Barcelona, in which he participated, to a jealous husband punishing his unfaithful
wife. With Franco's military victory, Catalonia has been forced back into the 'yoke'
of marriage: 'bajo el yugo de otras nupcias con España' ('into the yoke of another
marriage to Spain'; 1983: 190). In his later book, *Amor a Cataluña* (*Love for Catalonia*,
1942), Giménez Caballero would state bluntly:

> Cataluña: te habla un español que te quiere. Y te quiere, como los españoles
> de la meseta castellana desde siglos te aman: con *pasión*. Con la misma pasión
> que se quiere a una mujer. Y la pasión, ya lo sabes: va [...] hasta el crimen, que
> por eso se ha llamado *pasional*. 'Quien bien te quiera, te hará llorar', dice el

profundo adagio nuestro. 'La maté porque era mía', dice también otro hondo y apasionado decir de nuestro pueblo. (cited in Rodríguez-Puértolas 1986: 689)

(Catalonia: I speak to you as a Spaniard who loves you. And who loves you as the Spaniards of the central Castilian plain have loved you for centuries: with *passion*. With the passion one feels for a woman. And passion, as you know so well, can lead [...] to crime, not for nothing do we talk of 'crimes of passion'. 'You have to be cruel to be kind,' as a profound Spanish saying goes. Or 'I killed her because she was mine,' to cite another deeply passionate Spanish popular maxim.)

The quotation makes it clear that, for Giménez Caballero, men show their love for women by possessing and debasing them: love for women means proving one's masculinity. In 1937 Giménez Caballero caused a sensation with a hysterical speech from the pulpit of Salamanca Cathedral, denouncing Madrid as a whore and medusa (Rodriguez-Puértolas 1986: 291): both recurring images in the German texts analysed by Theweleit (1987: 68–69, 79–84, 138–83, 187–202). *Genio de España* attacks Western modernity in general, and Spain's history since the Enlightenment in particular, as a form of bastardy, defined — in a curious phrase borrowed from the Italian fascist writer Bontempelli — as being an 'hijo de dos madres' ('son of two mothers'). In all this imagery women are getting out of control, as indeed they were in Spanish public life of the time: in addition to the 1932 Divorce Law, the Republican Constitution of December 1931 had granted the vote to women. This last image of modernity as an 'hijo de dos madres', blaming the lack of an integrated identity onto a proliferation of mothers, implies that Giménez Caballero's fear of women is rooted in a pre-oedipal terror of the all-powerful mother.

Theweleit notes that his German soldier males might have been expected to express their aggression towards women through rape, but that this does not happen in their texts. They eliminate women by killing them, or through the establishment of a ritualized, militarized all-male order which permits the desired/feared union of self with other — for example, in the mass parade — while retaining hierarchical (phallic) structure (Theweleit 1987: 155, 429–32; 1989: 25, 87, 213). It is precisely this notion of union through a structure of domination that Giménez Caballero proposes as his solution to the crisis of modernity. His third genius — the 'Genio de Cristo' ('Genius of Christ') — combines the individual ego of the West with the 'Dependencia de un todo' ('Dependence on a Whole') of the Orient, in a fusion of 'Libertad' ('Freedom') with 'Absolutidad' ('Absolutism') or totalitarianism (1983: 154). This structured fusion, which overcomes the alienation of the ego while protecting it against the threat of formlessness, is — he argues — offered by Christianity which, having originated in Jerusalem and made its home in Rome, fuses the Eastern and Western traditions. And it is as a son of Rome, and more specifically as an ex-Marxist follower of Moscow who fought in the 'European War' (World War I), that Mussolini is seen as able to offer present-day salvation by bringing together East and West. Giménez Caballero insists that Spain, with its Oriental as well as Western past, is even more ideally placed to fulfil this role, following in Mussolini's footsteps. This at least partially positive evaluation of the Islamic contribution to Spanish culture, and recognition of Christianity's Middle-

Eastern roots, contrasts with the total denigration of the Oriental in later National-Catholic historiography. In Giménez Caballero's words:

> *En lo politico*, el Fascimo representaba la *Libertad* frente al Bolchevismo. Y la *Jerarquía* frente al Capitalismo. Defendía al mundo de los dos monstruos: el Yo del Capital [...]: Genio de Occidente. Y la *Masa* del Proletariado [...]: Genio de Oriente. (1983: 159)

> (*In political terms*, Fascism represented *Freedom* versus Bolshevism. And *Hierarchy* versus Capitalism. It defended the world from the two monsters: the Ego of Capital [...]; Genius of the West. And the *Mass* of the Proletariat [...]: Genius of the East.)

The fascist Caesar is a Hero because he organizes the masses into a militarized structure: 'conductor de tropas y milicias, de masas encuadradas en *falanges entusiastas*' ('a conduit for troops and militias, for masses organized in *enthusiastic phalanxes*'; 1983: 160). A year later, in 1933, the Word 'falange' ("phalanx") would provide the name of the newly founded Spanish fascist party, as Giménez Caballero proudly comments in a footnote to the 1938 edition (1983: 160). In this same footnote, he observes that the Greek 'phalanx' meant a truncheon: an explicitly phallic symbol exalted in his earlier *Hércules jugando a los dados* and here related to Mussolini's 'manganello'; the Spanish term 'porra', of course, also means 'prick'. For all its avant-garde play, this virile posturing is meant to be taken seriously.[4] Theweleit notes that his German soldier males constantly clutch rigid phallic objects — mostly weapons, held upright at the cost of considerable physical discomfort — to defend their sense of self (1989: 264).[5] Vertical imagery, central to Falangist rhetoric, recurs throughout *Genio de España*.[6]

Giménez Caballero picks up the emblem of the Catholic Kings — the 'haz y yugo' (bound arrows and yoke) that would at his suggestion be adopted as the Spanish fascist emblem — as an image of bonding/binding (the Roman *fasces* adopted by Italian fascism) through subordination (the yoke). The image of Catalonia returned to the 'yoke' of marriage is just one example of Giménez Caballero's repeated use of the metaphor of enforced heterosexual coupling to describe the fascist organization of the masses into a structure of domination. Unlike Theweleit's

---

4   Rodríguez-Puértolas (1986: 693–94) quotes a 1979 interview with Giménez Caballero in which, asked to give his views on homosexuality, he replied: 'El fascista es justamente contrario del homosexual en cuanto pretende continuar el gran símbolo viril de Hércules y de su maza o basto o falo que los mussolinianos llamaban "el manganello"' ('The fascist is the exact opposite of the homosexual in that he aims to continue the great phallic symbol of Hercules and his mace or truncheon or phallus, which Mussolini's supporters called "the manganello"').

5   See also the section 'The Mass and Culture: The "Upstanding" Individual' (Theweleit 1989: 43–61).

6   A suggestive example of the falangist emphasis on vertical imagery is the definition of the Spaniard (presumed to be male) given by the psychiatrist Juan José López Ibor, a member of the Falange's National Council: 'hombre vertical [...] Posición erecta, dura y difícil ante la vida, raíz de sus heroísmos y madre de sus desgracias' ('vertical man [...] Erect, hard, and arduous attitude to life, the root of his heroisms and mother of his misfortunes'; 1951: 128). Masculine 'hardness' is achieved through self-inflicted suffering as a way of imposing oneself on the negative 'maternal' aspects of experience.

soldier males, Giménez Caballero expresses his desire for fusion without dissolution not just through appeal to all-male ritual (the 'falanges entusiastas') but, much more obviously, through repeated images of heterosexual rape. Don Juan is proposed as the Spanish national hero:

> Cuando [...] se enamoraba de una *mujer*, no era para convertirse en su *amigo y colaborador*, sino en su *adversario*. Para *vencerla, derribarla* y — ¡admirable enemiga! — en el supremo éxtasis del triunfo genital, imprimirla un inolvidable beso ardiente sobre la boca. (1983:140)

> When [...] he wooed a *woman*, it was not to become her *friend* and *partner*, but her *adversary*. To *conquer* her, *force her to the ground* — admirable enemy! — and in the supreme ecstasy of genital triumph, stamp an unforgettable, ardent kiss on her mouth (emphases in original).

Or as he revealingly puts it in another passage:

> Todo pueblo es en el fondo una querencia de amor de mujer. Cuando encuentra su hombre, se entrega. [...] Es todo pueblo, asimismo, como una arcilla que sufre la tortura de lo informe hasta que una mano lo salva en forma, en estatua. (1983: 103)

> (Every people is at heart driven by a female longing for love. When it finds its man, it surrenders. [...] So too, every people is like a clay suffering the agony of formlessness until a hand saves it by sculpting it into form, into a statue.)

The nation is a threatening, formless, feminine mass that needs to be bounded and fixed in a rigid, phallic structure; turned into a kind of stone erection, like the Nazi monuments analysed by Theweleit (1989: 203–04).

Giménez Caballero's predilection for images of heterosexual rape leads to his major disagreement with German fascism: his text explicitly rejects Hitler's doctrine of racial purity for that of miscegenation. Despite isolated antisemitic remarks in *Genio de España* attacking capitalists as Jews, Giménez Caballero had in fact campaigned actively for the re-establishment of links with the Sephardic Jews expelled from Spain in 1492. In 1922 he visited Sephardic Jewish communities in Morocco with his teacher Américo Castro; in 1929 and 1931 he undertook Spanish state-sponsored tours of the Balkans to study the situation of Spanish Jews, making a short documentary film, *Los judíos de patria española* (*Jews of the Spanish Fatherland*, 1929), of the visit.[7] His concern to 'incorporate' Spanish Jews into the Hispanic 'fatherland' parallels his view of Spain's imperial history as the incorporation of other races through the white male's fertilization of women of colour. As he puts it, in the unashamedly hyperbolic style that typifies *Genio de España*: 'País fecundo, genital: genial. Somos raceadores, donjuanes, magníficos garañones varoniles de

---

7   I have updated the information about Giménez Caballero's tours of the Balkans in the light of Friedman's informative article (2011), published after this essay originally appeared. Rodríguez-Puértolas (1986: 128) notes that, although Giménez Caballero's 1934 essay 'Pío Baroja, precursor del fascismo' ('Pío Baroja, fascist precursor') was included as the prologue to the virulently antisemitic 1938 anthology of writings by Baroja, *Comunistas, judíos y demás ralea* (*Communists, Jews, and other Scum*) published in the Nationalist zone during the Civil War, Giménez Caballero was not the volume's editor as is often stated.

pueblos' ('A fecund, genital nation: a nation of genius. We are race-makers, Don Juans, magnificent virile studs engendering peoples'; 1983: 105). This history of rape represents the taking into the (male) body politic of alien (female) elements, as opposed to the 'dismemberments' that have led to Spain's imperial demise. The male, in raping the female, makes *himself* fertile. This scenario has evident parallels in Greek classical mythology, on which Giménez Caballero, like many other European modernist writers and fascist sympathizers, freely draws throughout his work. *Genio de España* is full of images of male procreation, whereby the man — like Zeus giving birth to Athene — appropriates the female maternal role. The 'genialidad' ('capacity for genius') or 'fuerza genital' ('genital energy') that Spain is urged to recover is explicitly described as a 'genio matriz' ('matrixial genius'; 983: 168) or 'maternidad' ('maternity'; 1983: 14).[8] If Theweleit's German soldier males acknowledge/defuse the mother's power by placing her on a pedestal as an asexual ideal, Giménez Caballero — coming from a Catholic, Mediterranean culture where the Virgin and Child comprise an erotic icon and the ideal of motherhood is highly sensualized — internalizes the mother as sexual object. Fear of engulfment by the female is neutralized by recasting man's penetration of woman as his appropriation of her. Fear of the mother is conquered by taking the mother's, and not the father's, place.[9]

At the same time, since the male has appropriated the maternal procreative role, he becomes his own son, in an act of rebirthing that makes the mother unnecessary. This, I suggest, is the meaning of the multiple references to rebirth in Giménez Caballero's text, as in Spanish fascist rhetoric generally. Theweleit notes that this same fantasy of fathering oneself occurs in his German texts, though in their case it is accompanied by a de-eroticization of the mother:

> What we are dealing with here is what structural anthropology calls 'direct filiation'; an attempted specification of origins in which any human line of descent is eradicated. In direct filiation, a single man sets himself up independently as son of God and his mother as nature. The filiative power that thereby accrues to him supersedes all other forms of social power; the ego it engenders is massive, its limits measured only by the limits of the world. Fascism produces a construction of rebirth that is similar in structure to direct filiation, but involuted; the new-born ego is not the son of God, but the son of himself and history. (Theweleit 1989: 241)[10]

Giménez Caballero's first chapter, titled 'Filiaciones' ('Filiations'), is a repudiation of his literary 'fathers'. By equating the Fascist Hero with Christ, he effectively makes him both son of God and son of himself as part of the Godhead; either way, son of

8   In *Arte y Estado* (1935), Giménez Caballero proposed the poet as 'el macho de la historia' ('the macho of history') whose role is to fertilize the politician, who comprises the 'elemento feminéo' ('feminine element'): here procreation takes place between two men. See Selva Roca de Togores (1988: 35).
9   Theweleit notes that his German soldier males dispense with the father because he is seen as having abdicated his role, just as Kaiser Wilhelm II abdicated his (1987: 108). Giménez Caballero sees Alfonso XIII's abdication of his role as national leader as the culminating aspect of the last of his thirteen national 'dismemberments'.
10   See also Theweleit 1989: 95, 243.

man and not of woman. Giménez Caballero stresses the Spanish male's devotion to the Immaculate Conception and the Spanish female's devotion to St Joseph, because both cults permit this megalomaniac fantasy of direct filiation. Theweleit notes that 'Though childbirth has become masculine, it still requires a body — the body of the earth' (1989: 88). Giménez Caballero describes his own text as his 'hijo' ('offspring'; 1983: 12) which 'me asciende desde las entrañas de esta tierra que son mis propias entrañas' ('arises from out of the entrails of this land which is my own entrails'; 1983: 195).

The Christian doctrine of the 'incarnation' thus fuses with Mussolini's doctrine of 'corporación', the term Giménez Caballero uses for 'corporativism': that is, the incorporation of the formless, feminine masses into the male body politic (the state), allowing a rebirthing or resurrection. Mussolini's Rome is seen not as a patriarchal order but as 'Roma, madre' ('mother Rome'). In his 1938 book *España y Franco* (*Spain and Franco*), Giménez Caballero would describe Franco's smile — something for which he was not noted — as 'paternal y maternal' ('paternal and maternal'; cited in Rodríguez-Puértolas 1986: 289). This appropriation of the maternal procreative role allows the fascist to live out the pre-oedipal mother–son bond in a scenario made safe by male domination. Giménez Caballero insists on the 'childishness' of his discourse (1983: 75), and also on its 'mystical' quality (1983: 15, 129, 162, 164), mysticism traditionally being seen as a form of feminine discourse. One could also argue, though for obvious reasons Giménez Caballero does not, that the ecstatic or ranting style of his 'exaltaciones' ('exaltations'), as he calls them, mimics another form of feminine discourse: that of the hysteric.[11] Theweleit notes that the purple prose of his German soldier males, like that of Nazi leaders' speeches, provides a ritual enactment of the dissolution of the ego that is both feared and desired: an enactment that is safe precisely because it is staged (1989: 124–29, 184–85). The Spanish fascist party Falange Española was founded, by Giménez Caballero and others, in a Madrid theatre; during the Civil War, he became notorious for his histrionic political speeches.[12] In *Genio de España*, he describes his text as a 'visión sagrada' ('sacred vision') and 'oráculo' ('oracle'; 1983: 15): its incantatory quality allows it to fulfil the ritual function of fascist discourse by enacting a dissolution of the ego that defuses the threat of feminine formlessness by appropriating its linguistic effects.[13]

Genio de España ends with its author's apocalyptic vision at sunset on the day of Corpus Christi, as he stands on the Monte de El Pardo, described as Spain's

---

11 For the classic analyses of mysticism and hysteria as forms of feminine discourse, see Irigaray 1985 and Kahane and Bernheimer 1985.

12 See the previously mentioned information given by Rodriguez-Puértolas (1986: 291) on Giménez Caballero's 1937 speech from the pulpit of Salamanca cathedral. Jorge Campos, in his story 'El jerarca' ('The Hierarch'; 1985) narrating his experiences as a prisoner in a Nationalist concentration camp during the Civil War, relates how Giménez Caballero, visiting the camp, delivered a harangue from a truck and was driven into an apoplectic rage when the prisoners, disappointed to discover that his speech was not an announcement about rations, turned their backs on him.

13 Interestingly, Kristeva bases her analysis of 'abject' writing (1982), which she sees as a mimicking of the formlessness of the feminine (and specifically maternal) body in order to defuse its terror, on the French fascist writer, Louis-Ferdinand Céline.

Mount Tabor. The closing image of transubstantiation and transfiguration offers a staged death-rebirth of the self, couched in the all-male imagery of war. The apocalyptic vision takes the form of red storm clouds looming on the horizon 'en rangos de batallas y tormentas': a repeated phrase in Giménez Caballero's text, as it is in the German texts analysed by Theweleit, which draw on the experience of war as the ultimate permissible 'controlled explosion' of the self. Theweleit notes that war allows the soldier male to identify with his 'primitive' interior without being devoured by it (1989: 22–23). In a suggestive passage in *Genio de España*, Giménez Caballero talks of the primordial 'grito de la sangre' ('call of the blood') he experienced at a Colonial Exhibition on seeing a young African tribesman: 'al contemplarle, sorprendido vagamente el corazón me dio un brinco de transcendencia. Me acababa de reconocer yo mismo' ('as I gazed at him, my heart, vaguely startled, made a transcendental leap. I had just recognized myself'; 1983: 91). Giménez Caballero cannot look back to the experience of World War I, but he does draw on his Moroccan experience. His book is an explicit incitement to war as a redemptive, transformative, 'mystical' experience: a 'Crusade' less concerned with subduing the enemy without than with finding acceptable forms of release for a male ego fearful of dissolution. What distinguishes his text from those studied by Theweleit is its overt emphasis on fascism as the incorporation into the male body (whether that of the individual or that of the state) of the eroticized mother. As Giménez Caballero puts it, in a particularly lurid passage describing his conversion to fascism in Rome: 'Encontraba en Roma el olor a madre que nunca había olido en mi cultura, que es peor que el olor a hembra, porque enloquece de modo más terrible' ('I found in Rome the smell of the mother that I had never smelt in my own culture, a smell worse than that of the female because it produces a more terrible madness'; 1983: 92). Giménez Caballero's explicit use of sexual imagery proposes fascism as an antidote to the male fear of annihilation of the ego. His politics, in keeping with the fascist appeal to irrational forces, is sexual rather than social or economic. What remains unclear is how this rhetoric of sexual violence appealed — if it did appeal — to the many Spanish women who were drawn to fascism.

Works Cited

BENJAMIN, JESSICA. 1990. *The Bonds of Love: Psychoanalysis, Feminism and the Problem of Domination* (London: Virago)

BENJAMIN, WALTER. 1992. *Illuminations* (London: Fontana)

CAMPOS, JORGE. 1985. 'El jerarca', in *Cuentos sobre Alicante y Albatera* (Barcelona: Anthropos), pp. 112–15

'Carteles literarios' de Gecé. 1994. Catalogue of exhibition held at Balmes 21 / Universitat de Barcelona 15 June–7 July 1994 and Museo Nacional Centro de Arte Reina Sofía 26 July–14 October 1994 (Barcelona: Balmes 21)

CHODOROW, NANCY. 1978. *The Reproduction of Mothering: Psychoanalysis and the Sociology of Gender* (Berkeley: University of California Press)

DENNIS, NIGEL. 1995. 'Writers in the Bathroom: Readings in the Spanish Avant-Garde', in *The Spanish Avant-Garde*, ed. by Derek Harris (Manchester: Manchester University Press), pp. 40–53

FOARD, DOUGLAS W. 1975. *Giménez Caballero o la revolución del poeta* (Madrid: Instituto de Estudios Políticos)

FRIEDMAN, MICHAL. 2011. 'Reconquering "Sepharad": Hispanism and Proto-Fascism in Giménez Caballero's Sephardist Crusade', in *Revisiting Jewish Spain in the Modern Era*, ed. by Daniela Flesler, Tabea Alexa Linhard and Adrián Pérez Melgosa (special issue of *Journal of Spanish Cultural Studies*, 12.1: 35–60)

GEIST, ANTHONY LEO. 1980. *La poética de la generación del 27 y las revistas literarias: De la vanguardia al compromiso (1918–1936)* (Madrid: Guadarrama)

GIMÉNEZ CABALLERO, ERNESTO. 1979. *Memorias de un dictador* (Barcelona: Planeta)

——. 1983. *Genio de España: Exaltaciones a una resurrección nacional y del mundo*, 8th edn (Barcelona: Planeta)

HERNANDO, MIGUEL ÁNGEL. 1974. *'La Gaceta Literaria' (1927–1932): Biografía y valoración* (Valladolid: Universidad de Valladolid)

——. 1975A. 'Primigenia plasmación del superrealismo castellano: *Yo inspector de alcantarillas* (1928)', *Papeles de Son Armadans*, 236 (November): 137–59

——. 1975B. *Prosa vanguardista en la generación del 27 (Gecé y 'La Gaceta Literaria')* (Madrid: Prensa Española)

HUYSSEN, ANDREAS. 1986. *After the Great Divide* (Bloomington: Indiana University Press)

IRIGARAY, LUCE. 1985. 'La Mystérique', in *Speculum of the Other Woman*, trans. by Gillian C. Gill (Ithaca, NY: Cornell University Press), pp. 191–202

KAHANE, CLAIRE, and CHARLES BERNHEIMER (eds). 1985. *In Dora's Case: Freud, Hysteria, Feminism* (London: Virago)

KRISTEVA, JULIA. 1982. *Powers of Horror: An Essay on Abjection*, trans. by Leon S. Roudiez (New York: Columbia University Press)

LÓPEZ IBOR, JUAN JOSÉ. 1951. *El español y su complejo de inferioridad* (Madrid: Rialp)

LÓPEZ-VIDRIERO, MARÍA LUISA. 1982. *Bibliografía de Ernesto Giménez Caballero* (Madrid: Universidad Complutense)

MOSSE, GEORGE. 1988. *Nationalism and Sexuality* (Madison: University of Wisconsin Press)

PEÑA SÁNCHEZ, VICTORIANO. 1995. *Intelectuales y fascism: La cultura italiana del 'ventennio fascista' y su repercusión en España* (Granada: Universidad de Granada)

RODRÍGUEZ-PUÉRTOLAS, JULIO. 1986. *Literatura fascista española*, vol. I (Madrid: Akal)

SAID, EDWARD W. 1985. *Orientalism* (Harmondsworth: Penguin)

SELVA ROCA DE TOGORES, ENRIQUE (ed.). 1988. *E. Giménez Caballero: Prosista del 27 (Antología)*, supplement to *Anthropos* (May).

TANDY, LUCY, and MARIA SFERRAZZA. 1977. *Ernesto Giménez Caballero y 'La Gaceta Literaria' (1927–1932)* (Madrid: Turner)

THEWELEIT, KLAUS. 1987. *Male Fantasies*, vol. I: *Women, Floods, Bodies, History*, trans. by Stephen Conway, Chris Turner and Erica Carter (Cambridge: Polity)

——. 1989. *Male Fantasies*, vol. II: *Male Bodies: Psychoanalyzing the White Terror*, trans. by Stephen Conway, Chris Turner and Erica Carter (Cambridge: Polity)

CHAPTER 11

Political Readings of Don Juan and Romantic Love in Spain from the 1920s to the 1940s[1]

Walter Mignolo (2000) has argued that the 1898 Spanish-American War in the Caribbean and the Philippines marked an epochal shift in the world system, ending the period of Western European hegemony instituted in 1492, as the United States entered the world stage as an imperial power. Spanish intellectuals were quick to recognize this shift since Spain had been the direct victim of US aggression. In fact, Spain had already lost its place as the centre of Western European hegemony in the seventeenth century, as Amsterdam took over from Seville as the centre of Atlantic trade (Mignolo 2000: 58). The early twentieth century saw a proliferation of Spanish publications responding to this shift in the world system; these writings have been seen as a bout of soul-searching about Spain's relation to the rest of the modern world, but they can also be read as part of a wider discussion on the relative values of 'Old Europe' and 'New America'. Spanish intellectuals — assigned to a marginal position for the previous three centuries — were well placed to appreciate Mignolo's insight that loss of hegemony means loss of cultural credibility: this epochal shift was a challenge not just to Western Europe's political and economic hegemony but to the 'universality' of Western European culture. It could be argued that at least some of the numerous essays written in Spain from 1905 — the tercentenary of the *Quixote* — through to the 1940s about Spanish literary types associated in various ways with love (Don Quixote, Don Juan, Celestina) are not defending a Spanish exceptionalism but positing Spain as a repository of a universal European culture based on love, which the more economically successful European nations are felt to have abandoned. The claim often made in these essays that Spain can offer a model to northern Europe has been interpreted in existing criticism, including my own (1989), as a sour-grapes justification of Spain's economic backwardness. They can perhaps be read more interestingly as echoes — and in some cases anticipations — of the crisis of European values that would become a major cultural issue in northern Europe with the carnage of World War I.

1   I have left the quotations in this essay in English translation only, as in the original publication written as part of the European research project *Europe: Emotions, Identities, Politics* (2002–04), with an international team directed by Luisa Passerini, whose aim was to explore the centrality of conceptions of love to conceptions of Europe.

It is no coincidence that two of the three Spanish intellectuals whose writings on Don Juan will be examined here — Ramiro de Maeztu, who swung from guild socialism to the Spanish equivalent of Action Française, and the liberal humanist Salvador de Madariaga — had been war correspondents in the United Kingdom during World War I (in which Spain did not participate). The third intellectual examined — the avant-garde writer and convert to fascism, Ernesto Giménez Caballero — witnessed the immediate aftermath of World War I in Strasbourg, recently returned from German to French control, at whose university he taught in 1920–21 and 1923–24. It is also not coincidental that Madariaga — the only one of these writers who championed liberal humanism — should propose Romantic love as an ideal; for this reason, in addition to his writings on Don Juan, this discussion will include the exploration of Romantic love in his historical romance on the conquest of Mexico.

This essay will not consider those Spanish intellectuals — notably, Unamuno and Azorín — who turned to Spanish literary figures, especially Don Quixote, in order to idealize Spain's supposed failed modernity, since this has been much discussed. I have preferred to focus on less studied intellectuals who were political figures. Consequently, this discussion will also exclude the considerable number of writers — literary and medical — who drew on Don Juan not for political purposes but to elaborate views on gender and sexuality.[2] Another reason for choosing these three writers is that all three married women from another European country, whose intellectual life would impact significantly on them. Their lives thus mirror the fusion of ideas with feeling that is the key strength of their recourse for political ends to literary figures associated with love.

This essay will stress that these three thinkers are concerned not just with Spain but with a wider geopolitical scenario, including both Europe and the Americas. It is useful to start with brief biographical sketches in order to show how the physical, intellectual, and amorous trajectories of these three writers crossed European (and Atlantic) boundaries.

Three Political Biographies

Maeztu (1874–1936) was born to an English Protestant mother (whose first language was French, having grown up in France) and the owner of a Cuban sugar plantation who had returned to Spain. In 1891–94 the young Maeztu worked on a sugar plantation and in the tobacco industry in Cuba, which impressed on him the belief — prior to reading Weber's *The Protestant Ethic and the Spirit of Capitalism* (1904), whose linkage of capitalism and religion would deeply influence him — that capitalism was perfectly compatible with Catholicism: a point which he felt was also demonstrated by the industrialization of his native Basque Country and Catalonia. He lived in London as foreign correspondent 1905–19, studying

2   For discussion of psychological and medical analyses of Don Juan's sexuality, see Sinclair 2010. For an overview of the Don Juan theme in early twentieth-century Spanish literature, see Johnson 2003 (chs 3 and 4) and Pérez-Bustamante 1998.

philosophy at Marburg University in 1911. In the UK, he established close contacts with the thinkers associated with the journal *The New Age*, and with Catholic intellectuals. He returned to Spain in 1919 with an English wife, Alice Mabel Hill, and their British-born son. The 1926 book studied here, *Don Quijote, Don Juan y la Celestina: Ensayos en simpatía (Don Quixote, Don Juan and Celestina: Essays in Collective Sentiment)* was begun during a 1925 lecture tour of the United States. From 1927 to 1930, he was Ambassador to Argentina. In 1931, reacting to the declaration of the Spanish Republic, he founded Acción Española, based on Maurras's Action Française, becoming editor of its journal. In October 1936, three months into the Spanish Civil War, he was arrested by the Spanish Republican authorities and, despite the British government's intercession on his behalf, was executed for having, since 1931, openly supported military insurrection against the Republic.

Giménez Caballero (1899–1988) married Edith Sirone, sister of the Italian consul in Strasbourg, in 1925. Two years later, he converted to fascism after a trip to Rome, establishing long-term links with Italian fascist intellectuals — especially Bottai, editor of *Critica fascista (Fascist Critique)*, and Malaparte, whose work he translated (Carbajosa and Carbajosa 2003: 54). In 1928, he undertook a European lecture tour as a fascist intellectual. A major avant-garde cultural entrepreneur in the late 1920s, he is regarded as the first Spanish surrealist writer to draw on the theories of Freud. As editor of Spain's leading arts magazine *La Gaceta Literaria (The Literary Gazette)* and founder of Spain's first film club, he played a key role in introducing into Spain the work of European avant-garde writers and filmmakers of all political persuasions, including Eisenstein. Giménez Caballero himself directed two avant-garde films, plus a documentary on Spanish-speaking Sephardic Jews in the Balkans and Middle East, made during the first of his two tours of the region, with Spanish state sponsorship, in 1929 and 1931.[3] In 1933, he became a founding member of the Spanish fascist party, Falange Española. A leading figure in the Francoist propaganda apparatus during and after the Civil War, he visited Hitler and Goebbels in Germany in 1941. An unrepentant fascist to his death, he became an embarrassment to the Franco regime as it strove to court US support after 1945 and was shunted off to Stroessner's Paraguay as Ambassador from 1958 until his retirement in 1969. The main work I shall discuss here, *Dialoghi d'amore tra Laura e Don Giovanni o Il Fascismo e l'Amore (Love Dialogues between Laura and Don Juan or Fascism and Love)*, was delivered orally by him in Florence on 25 May 1935, at the Maggio Fiorentino cultural festival, and published in September of that year in the Rome-based fascist journal *AntiEuropa* (Giménez Caballero 1935: 567; 1936: 9).

Madariaga (1886–1978) — who wrote equally easily in Spanish, French and English — was educated in Paris and moved to the UK in 1916, recruited by the

3   See Friedman 2011, whose detailed study has enabled me to correct information given in the original version of this essay, published in 2010. Despite his fascist politics, Giménez Caballero maintained a lifelong interest in reintegrating Sephardic Jews, expelled from Spain in 1492, back into their Spanish 'homeland'. In the 1920s, he had toured Sephardic Jewish communities in Morocco with the cultural historian Américo Castro, who in the 1940s and '50s, as a Republican exile in the United States, made his scholarly reputation as a defender of the medieval Jewish contribution to Spanish culture.

British Foreign Office to write pro-Allied war reports for the Spanish press, having married the Scottish political economist Constance Archibald in 1912. In 1927 he was appointed to the newly created King Alfonso XIII Chair of Spanish at Oxford, returning to serve the Spanish Republic on its election to power in 1931 — among other things, as Ambassador in Washington (1931) and Paris (1932). Although Oxford remained his family home until his death, he was based for much of his life in Geneva, working for the League of Nations 1921–27 and again as Spanish Republican representative 1931–36. In 1936 he broke with the Republic on account of what he saw as its drift towards totalitarianism, and went into lifelong exile in the UK, from where he worked to denounce the Nationalist uprising and subsequent Franco dictatorship.[4] In this capacity, he undertook repeated lecture tours of the United States and Latin America. After World War II, Madariaga continued to work for European unity through the European Movement and as founder and first President of the Collège d'Europe, created to form a European intellectual elite; from 1946 to 1952 he was President of the newly founded Liberal International, and chaired the Cultural Section of the 1949 Congress of Europe at The Hague. In his concluding speech at The Hague, Madariaga declared his faith in a Europe based on love: 'Above all, let us love Europe' — by which he meant love for Europe's cultural heritage (Victoria Gil 1990: 288). The 1943 historical romance *El corazón de piedra verde* (*The Heart of Jade*) which will be analysed here was written in Oxford, based on research conducted by the Hungarian Emilia Rauman, whom he had met at the Spanish Embassy in Vienna in 1934, and whom he had helped escape Nazi-occupied Austria in 1938, with her Austrian Jewish husband, offering her work as his literary secretary. Madariaga married Emilia in 1970, at the age of 84, on the death of his Scottish wife — Emilia by this time also being widowed. Through the coyness of Madariaga's biographers (Victoria Gil 1990; Fernández Santander 1991), one deduces that this was a love of a lifetime.

It is crucial to bear in mind the distinct biographical trajectories of these three political figures when considering their writings, to which we will now turn.

Maeztu: The Critique of Don Juan as Modern Egoist

As Villacañas argues (2000), Maeztu's reading of Weber clinched his lifelong attempt to encourage the construction of a Spanish industrial bourgeoisie driven by an ethic of labour rather than consumption. His youthful admiration for Nietzsche, which nourished an equally lifelong dislike of state control, led him in the late 1890s and early 1900s to reject Marxism for a version of social democracy. His political evolution while in the UK follows that of the journal *The New Age*, with which he was associated, moving from Fabianism to guild socialism, with an increasingly strong religious dimension.[5] In this last respect he was influenced by his

---

4   For a politically acute account of Madariaga's career, which stresses his role in keeping alive international opposition to the Franco regime, see Preston 1987.
5   For the intellectual trajectory of Alfred R. Orage, editor of *The New Age*, who in 1922 would become a disciple of Gurdjieff, see Passerini 1999: 107–18.

contacts with British Catholic intellectuals, including Chesterton and Belloc, and particularly his close friend T. E. Hulme, whose death in World War I reinforced his belief that liberal humanism was in crisis. Maeztu's *Authority, Liberty and Function in the Light of the War*, published in English in 1916 (*The New Age* printed an extract in 1915), championed a modern industrial version of the medieval guild system, based on a spiritually informed notion of mutual responsibility rather than the liberal notion of individual human rights, which he saw as having led to a selfish, competitive and destructive consumerism, whose consequence was the expenditure of lives in World War I. The 1919 Spanish version of this book was explicitly titled *La crisis del humanismo* (*The Crisis of Humanism*): from now on, Maeztu became an advocate of a curious mix of modern industrialism within a premodern Catholic framework, which he saw Spain as particularly well placed to develop, leading the way illuminated by the contemporary European Catholic Right. This mix is summarized by the phrase 'the reverential sense of money' which he coined, adapting Weber, in a series of 1926 press articles, coinciding with the publication of *Don Quixote, Don Juan and Celestina*. From 1927 Maeztu flipped politically, espousing a retrograde authoritarianism based on a pre-modern notion of the Divine Right of Kings, while continuing to advocate capitalist industrialism. His political activism became openly counter-revolutionary with the 1931 declaration of the Republic. Villacañas (2000) rightly sees him as the unacknowledged precursor of the Opus Dei technocrats who would clinch the Franco dictatorship's fusion of National-Catholicism and capitalism in the 1960s.

Don Quixote, Don Juan and Celestina — Maeztu's most famous book — is a brilliant exercise in cultural-historical analysis. Central to it is Maeztu's critique of Don Juan, viewed as an embodiment of the hedonistic individualism that Maeztu sees as the outcome of modern humanism, culminating in a narcissistic capitalist consumerism. He notes, rightly, that northern Europe has turned Don Juan into a Faustian idealist — the restless hero in pursuit of impossible love — but that this is completely lacking in the Spanish dramatizations of his story: not only in Tirso de Molina's 1630 play, *El burlador de Sevilla* (*The Trickster of Seville*), which created the figure, but even in Zorrilla's 1844 Romantic version, *Don Juan Tenorio*.[6] The Spanish Don Juan mocks divine and earthly authority, caring only for instant gratification through sexual conquest. Maeztu notes that Zorrilla's Romantic Don Juan finally falls in love only when he encounters the innocent Doña Inés who satisfies his egocentric power drive by surrendering to him totally — he is incapable of love in the sense of altruism. Maeztu sees Don Quixote as an embodiment of altruistic love; Celestina (the procuress in Rojas's 1499 tragicomedy of the same name), of knowledge; and Don Juan, of power, noting that they represent a splitting and humanist abrogation of the attributes of God. That is, they represent the modern separation of spheres that Maeztu wishes to counteract by returning to a

---

6   A key factor in the northern European 'misreading' of Don Juan is the 'discovery' and subsequent dissemination of Spanish Golden Age literature by the German Romantic critic, August Wilhelm von Schlegel, for whom it represented a primitive energy untamed by Classicism — Don Juan being seen as a prime example.

medieval corporatism in which the various capacities work in unison, driven by a religious sense of communal responsibility. Maeztu sees Don Juan as an option only for socially irresponsible egoists in a godless world. What is needed is a marriage of Don Quixote's capacity for selfless love and Celestina's practical skills, infused with the power and energy that Don Juan has monopolized and squandered. Here Maeztu is advocating the severing of US-style capitalism (power harnessed to practical skills) from liberal humanism and its injection into an Old-World pre-modern belief system built on divinely ordered communal love (as illustrated by Don Quixote's fusion of chivalric love with social justice). Without power and practical skills, Don Quixote's capacity for love makes him a figure of ridicule; with them, he becomes a blueprint for a new universal order that combines the best of the New World with the best of the Old. Villacañas (2000) argues that we should not see this eclectic ideological mix as pre-determined by Maeztu's subsequent political evolution but should value it — while recognizing the naivety of its reading of medieval corporatism — as a major contribution to the theorization of a conservative modernity.

Giménez Caballero: Don Juan as Fascist Superman

Giménez Caballero is also a critic of liberal humanism but takes up the figure of Don Juan as a revolutionary antidote to what he sees as a debilitating European courtly love tradition that places men in the service of women. The title of his 1935 fascist tract *Love Dialogues between Laura and Don Juan or Fascism and Love* is a critical reference to the sixteenth-century Neoplatonic text *Dialoghi d'amore* published in Italy by the Spanish Jewish humanist Leo Hebraeus, expelled from Spain with other Jews in 1492. Giménez Caballero's text was reissued in Spanish in 1936 with the title *Exaltación del matrimonio* (*Exaltation of Marriage*), for in it he subjects Petrarch's Laura and Don Juan to a forced marriage.

   Giménez Caballero's best-known work, *Genio de España* (*Genius of Spain*, 1932; see Chapter 10), is a Freudian analysis of the malaise of Western individualism.[7] The ideal of love that he proposes in *Love Dialogues* is likewise an antidote to the Western individual subject. The book stages an imaginary love encounter between Laura and Don Juan, immodestly declaring that he, as a Spaniard, is Don Juan and his Florentine wife is Laura. Giménez Caballero insists that he has fallen in love with fascism as a result of falling in love with his Italian wife: fascism is for him a passionate stance. In *Love Dialogues*, he sees Laura and Don Juan as embodying two conflicting European models of love, both products of the modern Western individualism that first developed in the Renaissance, bound on a collision course. For, if Don Juan represents the anarchic male hero who subjects women to his will, Laura represents the Petrarchan inaccessible female who spurns her male lover. Both Don Juan and Laura are admirable in their massive egos but both are sterile: Laura because she refuses to surrender to a man; Don Juan because he

---

7   Curiously, Madariaga's first book, published in English, was called *The Genius of Spain* (1923). Giménez Caballero makes no reference to it.

moves on rather than found a family (and indeed is hardly ever depicted as leaving his female victims pregnant). In a famous 1924 article, 'Notes towards a Biology of Don Juan', published in Ortega y Gasset's magazine *Revista de Occidente*, the Spanish medical specialist Gregorio Marañón had noted this fact, suggesting that Don Juan's failure to adopt the paternal role was a sign of effeminacy.[8] By contrast, Giménez Caballero denounces as effeminate the courtly lover who is in thrall to his disdainful lady. There are clear male anxieties in this denunciation of the woman who refuses to subject herself to a man, while Don Juan is criticized, not because he subjects women to his will, but because he does not get them pregnant. Both types, Giménez Caballero suggests, are leading the West to sterility. His answer is to force Don Juan and Laura to marry, discovering love in perpetual conflict and through the self-sacrifice of having children. (If this is autobiographical, as he claims, one wonders what his wife thought about it.) The Petrarchan figure of Laura is thus forced into the mould of the Madonna and Child — though she is not a virgin but subjected to ongoing violation by Don Juan.

Giménez Caballero is explicitly advocating a Christian marriage based on procreation and the self-sacrifice of both parties as an antidote to what he sees as the threat of female emancipation (women no longer agreeing to submit sexually to men). He thus describes Laura as a '"femme fatale", Greta Garbo of the Renaissance. Nordic and blonde, like Greta' (1936: 45). Although both Don Juan and Laura have to sacrifice their individual freedom, their forced marriage means that Don Juan will subject Laura to lifelong sexual conquest, to which Laura has to consent: the self-sacrifice is not an equal one. Hence Giménez Caballero declares that his text is a treatise on fascism and love, since it expounds a notion of love based on hierarchy and violent subjection — but love nonetheless. It should be said that there is a surrealist aspect to this project of marrying two irreconcilable opposites — Laura and Don Juan — not least in the rejection of the Neoplatonic *amor intelectualis* of Leo Hebraeus for an explicitly sexual notion of union. Giménez Caballero describes Hebraeus's Neoplatonism as deriving directly from 'the most refined casuistry of the Provençal troubadours' together with 'the subtlest ardours of the Jewish Cabbala' (1936: 17). While this may seem to have antisemitic overtones, we should note — in addition to Giménez Caballero's positive attitude to the Sephardic Jewish diaspora, mentioned above — that in this passage he breaks with the stereotyping of Jews as carnal by aligning them with the Neoplatonic tradition that he is critiquing. Giménez Caballero's concept of fascist love is overtly based on sexual conquest and not on mystical transcendence. He explicitly praises Don Juan's sexual prowess because it represents an urge to 'punish woman' (1936: 31). As he puts it in *Genius of Spain* (cited in Chapter 10): 'When *Don Juan* [...] fell in love with a *woman*, it was not to become her *friend* and *partner*, but her *adversary*. To *conquer* her, *force her to the ground — admirable enemy! —* and in the supreme ecstasy of genital triumph stamp an unforgettable, burning kiss on her mouth' (1983: 103; emphases in

---

8   For Marañón's various essays on Don Juan, see Johnson 2003: 186–89; Pérez-Bustamante 1998: 317–33. Marañón's crucial point was that, in devoting himself to love, Don Juan was shirking his male responsibilities in the public sphere, in which men legally participated as heads of family.

original). Elsewhere in *Genius of Spain*, Giménez Caballero corroborates this notion of fascism as violent sexual subjection, the important point being that the fascist hero, like Don Juan, incites undying love in the women he conquers: 'Every people is at heart driven by a female longing for love. When it finds its man, it surrenders' (1983: 103).

In *Love Dialogues*, Giménez Caballero insists that Don Juan is quintessentially Spanish, and that the Petrarchan idealization of woman is alien to the Spanish tradition. At this point he links his discussion of Don Juan to Spain's conquest of its American empire. How, he asks, could Petrarchism exist in the 'ardent, virile atmosphere' of a Seville (Don Juan's home town) 'ringing with the virile, macho tones of a recently discovered America, smelling of recently expelled Africans, Moors, jealous passions, conquest, rape, war, adventure, heroism' (1936: 61)? His blatantly racist apology for imperial violence is at least honest in its transparency. Empire is explicitly equated with sexual violence (rape) and with the conquest of racial others. Giménez Caballero is here arguing that Spain can offer something to fascist Italy, since Don Juan — who knows how to conquer empires — could not have been born in Italy, the land of unconquerable Petrarchan Lauras. We should remember that this is written at the time of Italy's invasion of Ethiopia, as Giménez Caballero observed when recycling chunks of this text in his *Roma madre* (*Mother Rome*; 1939: 120), which won an Italian fascist prize (as the author, never modest, notes in his introduction). In highlighting Don Juan's Andalusian origins in this passage, Giménez Caballero is also proposing him as an amalgam of West and East. A key feature of his earlier *Genius of Spain*, as seen in Chapter 10, had been his suggestion that fascism amalgamates the strengths of both cultural systems (Lenin being the Eastern 'superman'), thus again placing Spain, with its eight centuries of Arab rule from 711 to 1492, in a privileged position to take a leading role in European fascism.

Don Juan represents for Giménez Caballero an embodiment not only of the cultural miscegenation of West and East but also of the mixing of races in Spanish America. The 4th edition of *Genius of Spain* (1939) again links the sexual violence of Don Juan to empire, whose goal is seen as miscegenation: 'as a people we are makers of races but never racist [...]. We are race-makers, Don Juans, magnificent virile studs' (1983: 105; partially cited in Chapter 10). In the case of imperial conquest, it seems that, in order to produce children, Don Juan does not have to be settled in a forced marriage. Indeed, Don Juan's restless urge constantly to move on is necessary to make him a figure of empire, always pushing at the boundaries: *Plus Ultra*, as Charles V's imperial motto put it. In an earlier fascist tract, *Circuito imperial* (*Imperial Circuit*; 1929), Giménez Caballero had proposed Don Juan as the image of a fascist modernity because of his sportive attitude, always trying to beat records: 'Splendid *performances* of Don Juan! [...] Don Juan, *recordman*' (1929: 18–19; italicized words given in English in original). When, in his 1942 text *Amor a Cataluña* (*Love for Catalonia*), Giménez Caballero advocates this same kind of love based on violent subjection as a way of dealing with Republican Catalonia on its fall to Franco's army (Giménez Caballero had entered Barcelona with the victorious Nationalist troops in January 1939), he speaks of subjecting Catalonia to the 'yoke' of marriage to the Spanish state. In *Mother Rome*, he similarly talks of Mussolini's march on Rome as 'a Don Juan, a virile tyrant' taking Italy by force: 'But Mussolini did not rape Italy. He married her in Rome!' (1939: 125, 128). It seems that, in a European context, Don Juan needs to be made productive via the straitjacket of marriage but that, in the context of empire, the more women he can violently fertilize, the better.

Madariaga: Political Union via Romantic Love

Giménez Caballero and Madariaga disliked each other intensely. The two men met at least twice as political antagonists: in fascist Italy in July 1934, during Madariaga's visit to Venice representing the League of Nations' International Institute of Intellectual Cooperation, Giménez Caballero being one of the fascist intellectuals invited by the Italian host delegation; and at the Council of Europe's Strasbourg sessions in 1949–50, when Giménez Caballero was sent by the Franco regime (not recognized by the Council) as unofficial observer to obstruct debate on Spain (Victoria Gil 1990: I, 191; Giménez Caballero 1950a and 1950b). In his reports on these sessions (1983: 62), Giménez Caballero recounts how, at a reception, the wife of the US Head of Intelligence asked him: 'Is it true that the Aztecs are so cruel?' because she was having nightmares after reading Madariaga's historical novel, *The Heart of Jade*. The US Head of Intelligence tried to bring Giménez Caballero and Madariaga together to pursue the topic but they avoided each other. Giménez Caballero refers to the League of Nations, for which Madariaga worked for two decades, as 'that cesspit in Geneva' (1983: 62). Madariaga's role as head of the League of Nations' Disarmament Committee in 1922–27 and his continued efforts to secure a peaceful Europe throughout the 1930s, particularly via his role as Chairman of the League of Nations' Committee of Five that in 1935 vainly tried to halt Italian aggression in Ethiopia, clashed directly with Giménez Caballero's open calls for a fascist politics of violence to renew what he saw as a decadent, liberal Europe.

Madariaga wrote about Don Juan in two texts. In his 1952 *Bosquejo de Europa* (*Sketch of Europe*), he named Don Juan as one of Europe's four major cultural archetypes (with Faust, Don Quixote, and Hamlet). Like Giménez Caballero, but more ambivalently, he sees Don Juan as an incarnation of European individualism and imperial conquest: 'Don Juan embodies the spirit of expansion, discovery and conquest that has made Europe the creator of America. And the torch-bearer of universal culture. It is true that Don Juan is also the source of the crimes and excesses that sully the history of Europe's empires' (1969: 79). Madariaga notes that, in Zorrilla's Romantic version, Don Juan is, like Faust, saved by the love of a woman (contrary to Tirso de Molina's original in which he goes unrepentant to hell). Unlike Giménez Caballero, who has no truck with romantic love, Madariaga clearly privileges Zorrilla's version. In Madariaga's earlier 1948 radio play, *La don-juanía o seis don Juanes y una dama* (*Don-Juanism or Six Don Juans and a Lady*) — written for the BBC Latin American Service for broadcast to Latin America at Halloween,[9] and published with a substantial essay (1950) — he had brought together six different European versions of Don Juan, whose brawling — an implicit allegory of World War II — is stopped by a veiled Doña Inés, who declares herself to be the eternal feminine. Only Zorrilla's Romantic Don Juan is capable of appreciating her message of redemption through love. Madariaga's writings on Don Juan largely echo those of Maeztu in seeing him as a negative image of brute male force — except that he uses the Romantic redemption of Don Juan to argue for a Western individualism tempered by love: that is, the taming of the masculine by the feminine. We may note that, in Madariaga's radio play, it is the Spanish Don Juan and Doña Inés who offer a model of redemptive love that brings peace to Europe.

Given Madariaga's preference for Zorrilla's play in which Don Juan is redeemed by romantic love, it is not surprising that his 1943 novel about the conquest of Mexico, *The Heart of Jade*, should be cast in the form of a historical romance. The novel proposes an inter-racial marriage based on mutual love and respect as a model for empire — one which the novel makes clear is an ideal not borne out by the Spaniards' general behaviour in New Spain (as the Vice-Royalty of Mexico was called) or in the Old Spain of the Inquisition. In keeping with Madariaga's critique of Don Juan as the prototype of the imperial plunderer in *Bosquejo de Europa*, the novel describes Cortés as the greatest womanizer among the Spanish conquistadors. The novel's Spanish hero, Alonso Manrique, is clearly meant as a utopian antidote to the donjuanesque behaviour of the novel's real-life (and some of its fictional) male characters. This is popular romance fiction in the utopian form of 'history as it might have been'. Thanks to its popular fictional format, *The Heart of Jade* is one of the few texts by Madariaga still in print, reissued in 2004.

The novel was conceived as an antidote to Cortés also in that it was written as a way of using the vast amount of historical research — chiefly into indigenous Mexican customs and beliefs — undertaken for Madariaga's 1941 biography of Cortés, which he had not been able to include in the 'factual' account. Because Madariaga turned to the popular genre of the historical romance for pleasure, after the efforts of writing a serious biography, he can allow himself a freedom of imagination that he does not permit himself in his more overtly political works. The result is a text that provides insights into his political assumptions precisely because they are betrayed indirectly, through his treatment of the love plot. The novel was a labour of love also in the sense that, as noted above, the research for it was undertaken by Emilia Rauman whom he would later marry and to whom he dedicated a volume of dreadfully clichéd love poetry (1989: 143–58). *The Heart of Jade* is dedicated to her as its 'godmother' (*madrina*). Given that she had already published studies on Spanish history before she met Madariaga (Victoria Gil 1990: I, 170), one wonders whether she was in fact responsible for some of its writing.

The Heart of Jade is notable for its efforts to get inside the indigenous mindset prior to the arrival of the Spaniards, who only reach Mexico City at the end of the second of its three parts. The whole of the first two parts are an anticipation

---

9   It was traditional in Spain until relatively recently for Zorrilla's *Don Juan Tenorio* to be performed on Halloween because of its ghost scene.

of Alonso's meeting with the Aztec princess Xuchitl on the very last page of Part 2, for they have both dreamed of each other for years: this is a love foretold. This legitimizes the Spanish conquest as something that was 'meant to be'. The fact that Alonso is not part of Cortés's army allows him to be untainted by the generally violent behaviour of the Spaniards in Mexico; he consistently refuses to participate in their looting and raping, similarly refusing the offers of women by local chiefs. His chastity is that of the courtly love hero, driven by desire for an inaccessible ideal — something that as an adolescent back in Spain he had sought in religious faith, becoming disillusioned by his experience of the Spanish clergy.

Consistent parallels are drawn between the Old World and the New. The chapters of Part 1 and Part 2 alternate between Xuchitl and Alonso (she comes first), until their two stories converge at the end of Part 2. Both New and Old World societies are shown to be riven by contradictions, and ethnically and culturally diverse. Madariaga gives Alonso an Arab great-grandmother, a converted Jewish mother, and an Arab nurse; he is brought up to read Hebrew and Arabic texts. He is born the day that Granada falls to the Catholic Kings, in a southern Spain where Jews are generally respected but where antisemitic pogroms are starting. The novel depicts in tragic terms the departure for exile of the Jews expelled in 1492, including Alonso's Rabbi grandfather ha-Levy, though this tolerance of religious diversity is attenuated by the fact that ha-Levy has come to believe in the Christian faith (like his daughter before him). Both he and his daughter convert out of rational conviction; this could not be more different from Giménez Caballero's passionate conversion to fascism.

The novel contains a large amount of rational questioning by Alonso and Xuchitl of their respective societies' religious beliefs. Both Christian and Aztec belief systems are shown to be based on rigid binary oppositions, which Alonso and Xuchitl discover do not hold, since opposites can coincide, and the same thing can have a positive and a negative side. This is especially true of sexuality: both Xuchitl and Alonso — she particularly — are brought up with an open, natural attitude to the body, later complicated by their exposure to a religion based on the notion that the body must be chastised. If, as previously recounted, the wife of the US Head of Intelligence was horrified by Madariaga's descriptions of Aztec sacrifice, she had missed the point, because the novel draws explicit parallels with Christian practices: when Xuchitl, converted and married to Alonso, witnesses an auto-da-fé in Spain, it reminds her of the smell of burning flesh of the Aztec human sacrifices she had so deplored. While these parallels put Aztec and Spanish culture on a par, they also show Madariaga's inability to think outside the secular rationalism that the European Enlightenment disseminated as a universal category.[10] The novel's romance format is undercut by Part 3 when Xuchitl and Alonso return, married, to Spain, only to find Alonso's converted Jewish mother arrested by the Inquisition: she will die, after release, from the effects of torture, before Alonso, who has been arrested in turn, can be reunited with her. Xuchitl finds herself not at the heart of civilization but alone and pregnant in a hostile, primitive land.

10   See Chakrabarty 2002: 20–37.

Notwithstanding its negative depiction of Spain, the novel takes it for granted that Christianity is a superior religion of love, albeit imperfectly practised by most Christians. Like Giménez Caballero — despite their vast political differences — Madariaga appeals to the image of the Madonna and Child as the emblem of this religion of (maternal) love. The difference is that, for Giménez Caballero, the female is the conduit for producing the son, whereas Madariaga shows the female's need for love and succour, as well as that of the male. Despite Madariaga's clichéd love poetry, in this historical romance he creates female characters who are as much agents as their male counterparts, and who are equally capable of intellectual reflection and growth. The ethnocentric representation of Xuchitl's ecstatic discovery in Christianity of the religion of love she had always intuited but never known is tempered by immediately plunging her into an intolerant Spain in the Inquisition's grip. The last page, however, holds out the possibility of a happy end as she and Alonso set sail back to the New World with their newborn son, whose string of names — Rodrigo Manrique ha-Levy ben-Omar Nezahualpilli[11] — proclaims racial fusion, albeit hierarchically ordered.

This happy end is, however, disturbed by the novel's final words which describe the mixed-race infant trying to put in his mouth the jade heart that provides the novel's title. The jade heart's presence in the novel complicates the Enlightenment secular rationalism that pervades its pages, for it is a magic amulet representing the contradictory nature of love: it brings a perfect experience of love to the person who has a healthy attitude to the body, but sexual torment to the person who regards sexuality as sinful. The jade heart has passed from Xuchitl's mother, on her death, to her father, for whom it signifies the torment of his sexual desire for the Bad Queen: an exotic *femme fatale* with a penchant for killing her lovers after love-making. What is going on in this extraordinary strand of the story is not clear, except that through it Xuchitl, who steals into the Bad Queen's secret chambers, learns that love has its dark side. Alonso has a similar induction through the brazen Marta, the daughter of the Jewish Esquivel family who are the novel's villains: converted Jews who denounce other Jews to the Inquisition, and who dog Alonso in both Old and New Worlds, father and son finally meeting their end in the auto-da-fé that Xuchitl and Alonso witness. The depiction of the Bad Queen and Marta Esquivel introduces some unfortunate ethnic and sexual stereotypes, despite the novel's generally positive depiction of Aztec and Jewish (and Arab) women.

Nonetheless, the novel's hero — who represents the ideal, humane, loving colonizer, though a colonizer for all that — is presented as a mixture of the three races that made up early modern Spain, and is shown to be capable of romantic love for a woman of yet another race — just as she, importantly, is shown to be capable of the romantic love that has so often been seen as an exclusively European phenomenon. Both Giménez Caballero and Madariaga exalt miscegenation as the major achievement of Spain's empire — as would Maeztu in his last book, *Defensa de la hispanidad* (*Defence of Hispanic Values*, 1934), which proposed the Spanish model

---

11   'Rodrigo Manrique' and 'Nezahualpilli' are the names of Alonso's and Xuchitl's fathers respectively.

of colonial relations as the basis for a new world system embracing all peoples, regardless of race, by contrast with the northern European segregationist model. It is striking that all three of the very different writers discussed in this essay should be united by belief that the miscegenation practised in Spain's early modern empire signified a political order based on love. This view has regularly been advanced under modernity to justify Spain's imperial project, by both Spanish Right and Left — and is still heard in Spain today to argue that Spaniards are not racist.[12]

Conclusion

The three writers we have analysed all use the trope of love to position Spain in relationship to the Americas as well as to Europe. Maeztu rejects the hedonistic egoism of Don Juan for Don Quixote's chivalric notion of altruistic service, allied to Don Juan's energy and Celestina's practical skills, as a way of harnessing the strengths of capitalism to those of medieval corporatism, in order to establish an alliance with the European Catholic Right that will allow Europe to confront the new hegemony of the United States. The implication is that the Spanish legacy in Spanish America, which implanted medieval corporatist structures in the New World, will allow the latter to do the same.

Giménez Caballero's work is more closely focused on Europe, Don Juan being proposed as the charismatic leader of a Spanish-Italian fascist alliance. When Giménez Caballero proposes Don Juan as the prototype of the Spanish conquistador, he is not concerned with the future of the Americas but is arguing that Spain's past capacity for imperial conquest allows it to play a leading role in European fascism. The United States comes into this political scenario only by implication, via Giménez Caballero's Spenglerian belief in European decadence, requiring an injection of virile energy from the fascist Don Juan. His defence of fascism represents a desire to re-establish a threatened European pre-eminence, achieved by drawing on Europe's position (and particularly that of Spain) as a meeting point of West and East. It is often forgotten that the subtitle to his fascist tract *Genius of Spain* is *Exaltations towards National and World Resurrection*: the goal is the creation of a new world order.

Madariaga, as an upholder of liberal Enlightenment values, rejects Don Juan as sexual predator — seen as the unacceptable face of European (and not just Spanish) imperialism — for a romantic notion of love, represented by Zorrilla's version of the Don Juan story, which can unite Europe after World War II. Romantic love is similarly used by him to figure the fusion of races in both Spain and Spanish America. Although his use of love as political trope does not address the question of

---

12   There is not space here to go into the complexities of Spanish racial discourse, which has varied hugely over time as well as being massively contradictory. Suffice it to say that the Inquisition's obsession with 'blood purity' was concerned more with religious deviance than with miscegenation and was based on the notion that racial 'others' could be 'saved' via their assimilation (voluntary or enforced) into Christianity. Mixed-race alliances in the Americas were often justified, particularly under modernity, as 'whitening' the race. Giménez Caballero's support for the repatriation of Spanish Jews formed part of this project for 'saving' racial others via their incorporation.

Europe's relation to the United States, it should be remembered that a major drive behind the movement to create a united Europe, to which Madariaga devoted his political career, was to counter a growing US hegemony.

Love means very different things to these three writers, but they all see it as something that derives from European culture. Even the liberal Madariaga, despite his positive depiction of his Aztec heroine, grants her the possibility of romantic love only via union with a Spaniard. For Maeztu, US capitalism needs to be redeemed by an 'Old European' chivalric altruism. For Giménez Caballero and Madariaga, the United States simply does not figure in their explorations of love as political allegory. If these writers draw on Spanish literary models — or, in the case of Madariaga's historical novel, incarnate romantic love in a multiracial Spanish hero — it is in order to suggest, explicitly or implicitly, that Spanish culture and history offer models for rethinking Europe.

We should remember here that not all the models of love explored by these three writers are positive: all of them reject at least certain aspects of the Don Juan figure, and the writer who most valorizes Don Juan — Giménez Caballero — proposes him as the fascist superman: a model that cannot be regarded as positive by any reader with a concern for ethics. Perhaps one of the most important points to emerge from this discussion is that the northern European idealization of Don Juan as restless hero in search of an impossible ideal is not supported by the Spanish representations of him, whether Tirso de Molina's and Zorrilla's source texts, or the works by the early twentieth-century Spanish political thinkers we have studied in this essay. We have here a key example of how northern Europe has appropriated southern European culture for its own ends, turning a character whose egoism can indeed be seen as a figure of the negative side of modern individualism into a tragic hero, thereby idealizing the pursuit of self-interest as Promethean curse — what one is tempted to call 'Don Juan's burden'.

Works Cited

Carbajosa, Mónica, and Pablo Carbajosa. 2003. *La corte literaria de José Antonio: La primera generación cultural de la Falange* (Barcelona: Crítica)

Chakrabarty, Dipesh. 2002. *Habitations of Modernity: Essays in the Wake of Subaltern Studies* (Chicago, IL: University of Chicago Press)

Fernández Santander, Carlos. 1991. *Madariaga, ciudadano del mundo* (Madrid: Espasa-Calpe)

Friedman, Michal. 2011. 'Reconquering "Sepharad": Hispanism and Proto-Fascism in Giménez Caballero's Sephardist Crusade', in *Revisiting Jewish Spain in the Modern Era*, ed. by Daniela Flesler, Tabea Alexa Linhard and Adrián Pérez Melgosa (special issue of *Journal of Spanish Cultural Studies*, 12.1: 35–60)

Giménez Caballero, Ernesto. 1929. *Circuito imperial* (Madrid: La Gaceta Literaria)

——. 1935. 'Dialoghi d'amore tra Laura e Don Giovanni o Il Fascismo e l'Amore', *AntiEuropa: Rassegna dell'Expansione Fascista nel Mondo*, 5 (1935): 567–99

——. 1936. *Exaltación del matrimonio: Diálogos de amor entre Laura y Don Juan* (Madrid: Giménez Caballero)

——. 1939. *Roma madre* (Madrid: Ediciones Jerarquía)

——. 1942. *Amor a Cataluña* (Madrid: Ruta)

———. 1950A. *La Europa de Estrasburgo (Visión española del problema europeo)* (Madrid: Instituto de Estudios Políticos)

———. 1950B. *Informe sobre el Consejo de Europa* (Madrid: Ministerio de Asuntos Exteriores)

———. 1983. *Genio de España: Exaltaciones a una resurrección nacional y del mundo*, 8th edn (Barcelona: Planeta)

JOHNSON, ROBERTA. 2003. *Gender and Nation in the Spanish Modernist Novel* (Nashville, TN: Vanderbilt University Press)

LABANYI, JO. 1989. *Myth and History in the Contemporary Spanish Novel* (Cambridge: Cambridge University Press)

———. 1995. 'Women, Asian Hordes and the Threat to the Self in Giménez Caballero's *Genio de España*', *Bulletin of Hispanic Studies* (Liverpool), 73: 377–87

MADARIAGA, SALVADOR DE. 1923. *The Genius of Spain and Other Essays on Contemporary Spanish Literature* (Oxford: Clarendon Press)

———. 1941. *Hernán Cortés* (Buenos Aires: Editorial Sudamericana)

———. 1950. *Don Juan y la don-juanía* (Buenos Aires: Editorial Sudamericana)

———. 1969. *Bosquejo de Europa* (Buenos Aires: Editorial Sudamericana)

———. 1988. *El corazón de piedra verde*, 2 vols (Madrid: Austral). English trans. 1944. *The Heart of Jade* (London: Collins)

———. 1989. *Poemas a Mimí*, in *Poesía* (Madrid: Austral), pp. 143–58

MAEZTU, RAMIRO DE. 1919. *La crisis del humanismo: Los principios de autoridad, libertad y función a la luz de la guerra* (Barcelona: Editorial Minerva)

———. 1934. *Defensa de la Hispanidad* (Madrid: Gráf. Universal)

———. 1957. *El sentido reverencial del dinero* (Madrid: Editora Nacional)

———. 1981. *Don Quijote, Don Juan y la Celestina: Ensayos en simpatía* (Madrid: Espasa-Calpe)

MARAÑÓN, GREGORIO. 1924. 'Notes towards a Biology of Don Juan', *Revista de Occidente*, 2.7: 15–53

MIGNOLO, WALTER D. 2000. *Local Histories / Global Designs: Coloniality, Subaltern Knowledges, and Border Thinking* (Durham, NC: Duke University Press)

PASSERINI, LUISA. 1999. *Europe in Love, Love in Europe* (London: I. B. Tauris)

PÉREZ-BUSTAMANTE, ANA SOFÍA (ed.). 1998. *Don Juan Tenorio en la España del siglo veinte: Literatura y cine* (Madrid: Cátedra)

PRESTON, PAUL. 1987. *Salvador de Madariaga and the Quest for Liberty in Spain* (Oxford: Clarendon Press)

SINCLAIR, ALISON. 2010. 'Love, Again: Crisis and the Search for Consolation in the *Revista de Occidente*, 1926–1936', in *New Dangerous Liaisons: Discourses on Europe and Love in the Twentieth Century*, ed. by Luisa Passerini, Liliana Ellena, and Alexander C.T. Geppert (Oxford: Berghahn Books), pp. 178–96

THEWELEIT, KLAUS. 1987. *Male Fantasies*, vol. I: *Women, Floods, Bodies, History*, trans. by Stephen Conway, Chris Turner and Erica Carter (Cambridge: Polity)

———. 1989. *Male Fantasies*, vol. II: *Male Bodies: Psychoanalyzing the White Terror*, trans. by Stephen Conway, Chris Turner and Erica Carter (Cambridge: Polity)

VICTORIA GIL, OCTAVIO. 1990. *Vida y obra trilingüe de Salvador de Madariaga*, 2 vols (Madrid, Fundación Ramón Areces)

VILLACAÑAS, JOSÉ LUIS. 2000. *Ramiro de Maeztu y el ideal de la burguesía en España* (Madrid: Espasa)

CHAPTER 12

❖

The Politics of the Everyday and the Eternity of Ruins: Two Women Photographers in Republican Spain (Margaret Michaelis 1933–37, Kati Horna 1937–38)

I should like to start by putting together three quotations from disparate sources, all of them on the subject of ruins.

In her travel book *Farewell Spain*, written in London between October 1936 and February 1937 (that is, in the early months of the Spanish Civil War), Kate O'Brien, in her first chapter titled 'Adiós, turismo', lamented the end of the sentimental tourist in a world of 'forward marchers, who read no epitaphs' (1985: 13):

> let us reflect with sadness that Macaulay's New Zealander, so exciting to us all at school, will almost certainly never stand on Westminster Bridge to view the ruins of St Paul's [...] because in his day [...] ruins will not be tolerated, for reasons of physical and mental hygiene. (1985: 14–15)

I shall come back to O'Brien at the end of this essay, for in many ways her travel writing provides a verbal analogue to the photographs of Republican Spain — also by women — that I shall be discussing.

The second quotation is from the Spanish anarchist leader Durruti. When interviewed shortly before his death in 1936 during the Civil War by a foreign journalist who remarked that, even if victorious, the workers would be sitting on a pile of ruins, Durruti magnificently replied:

> We've always lived in slums and holes in the wall. We'll manage. You mustn't forget, we can also build. It was the workers who built these palaces and cities [...]. We can build others to take their place. [...] We're not afraid of ruins. (cited by Cleminson in Graham and Labanyi 1995: 117)

Margaret Michaelis, one of the two Central European women photographers discussed in this essay, photographed Durruti's funeral in Barcelona. The other photographer studied here, Kati Horna, photographed Durruti's portrait in a Valencia shop window in October 1937 **(Figure 12.1)**. The portrait, mass-produced

FIG. 12.1. Kati Horna, *Escaparate (Shop Window)*, Valencia, October 1937. © Spain, Ministerio de Educación, Cultura y Deporte, Centro Documental de la Memoria Histórica, ES.37274.CDMH/22/2/Fotografías Kati Horna, Foto 56.

for public consumption, is displayed amid a jumble of cultural relics which mix the political (the Marianne-like embodiment of the Spanish Republic) and the personal (the portrait of a baby, a sentimental landscape, a mallard). Both Michaelis and Horna were anarchists; I shall return to the significance of this for their attitude to ruins, and to photography.

My third quotation, the most famous, is Walter Benjamin's passage on the 'angel of history' in his 'Theses on the Philosophy of History' (Benjamin was, of course, a key commentator on the historical significance of photography):

> This is how one pictures the angel of history. His face is turned towards the past. Where we perceive a chain of events, he sees one single catastrophe which keeps piling wreckage upon wreckage and hurls it in front of his feet. The angel would like to stay, awaken the dead, and make whole what has been smashed. But a storm is blowing from Paradise; it has got caught in his wings with such violence that the angel can no longer close them. This storm irresistibly propels him into the future to which his back is turned, while the pile of debris before him grows skyward. This storm is what we call progress. (1992: 249)

I should like to explore the ways in which the photographs of Republican Spain of Michaelis and Horna, by focusing on the debris and incompleteness of everyday experience, 'blast open the continuum of history' (Benjamin 1992: 254) in order to produce 'a past charged with the time of the now' (Benjamin 1992: 253). As Hannah Arendt notes in her preface to Benjamin's collection of essays *Illuminations*, Benjamin had wanted to write a book that consisted solely of a montage of quotations (Benjamin 1992: 51), true to his unorthodox notion of historical materialism as the juxtaposition of motley fragments from the debris of the past, lifted out of their context in order to release them from the grip of tradition, thereby creating new constellations of meaning or what he called 'the transfiguration of objects' (Benjamin 1992: 46). Benjamin's refusal of causal explanation in order to liberate the 'materiality' of things is based on the idea that the past reveals itself in those things that have been forgotten and thus elude incorporation into grand causal narratives of progress. As Arendt puts it (Benjamin 1992: 45), for Benjamin 'the past spoke only through things that had not been handed down'. Benjamin's fascination with the imagery of ruins is a fascination with that which refuses the notion of history as a sequential continuum; that is, as progress. In similar fashion, Benjamin noted that photography can liberate things from our preconceived notions of them by drawing our attention — through the freezing of the image in a moment of time, and its isolation from its context — to elements that elude the notice of those present at the time. Thus, as he notes, 'The camera introduces us to unconscious optics as does psychoanalysis to unconscious impulses' (Benjamin 1992: 230). The reference to Freud should be taken seriously, for, in Benjamin's analysis, the past — as revealed by photography — obeys the structures of the dream logic: a materialist dream logic ruled not by subjective fantasy projections but by the capacity of objects to interpellate us: to make us theirs. Like Benjamin's collector, the excavator of the debris of history does not 'possess' the past but is 'possessed' by it. The historical excavator — likened by Benjamin to a ragpicker or *bricoleur* — is thus driven not by a desire for rational mastery but by personal engagement.

Benjamin's major essays were, of course, written in exile from the threat of fascism in the 1930s, as befits a 'nomadic' thinker in Deleuze and Guattari's sense of the term (1998) as one who refuses to be 'territorialized' by 'master narratives'. Benjamin's unorthodox version of historical materialism, which aims to release the multiple potential of the past by freeing it from the 'master narratives' of historicist causal explanation (whether orthodox Marxist or liberal), in some senses shares with anarchism its refusal of a single, rational authority and its celebration of the heterogeneous: history at the micro- rather than the macro-level. Michaelis and Horna were also refugees from Nazism, who had sought refuge in Republican Spain from Austria and Hungary respectively.

Margaret Michaelis, of Jewish origin, was born in Austria in 1902, and had worked as a photographer in Vienna, Prague and Berlin since 1929. In December 1933, she fled Berlin for Barcelona with her husband after both had been separately arrested for their involvement with the anarcho-syndicalist Freien Arbeiter-Union Deutschlands (FAUD), all of whose members ended up in Republican Barcelona. Her husband, Rudolf Michaelis, was head of the FAUD's cultural branch, as well as an archaeologist who had worked on excavations in the Middle East (and hence an expert on ruins). She separated from him in Barcelona in 1934, thereafter earning her living as a professional photographer. She had photographed the Barrio Chino (red-light district and old popular quarter) of Barcelona during a previous stay in 1932. Her 1932 photographs and those taken during her later stay in Barcelona from 1933–37 were published in the magazine *AC* of the architectural group GATCPAC,[1] which included the famous Bauhaus-linked modernist architect Josep Lluís Sert. These published images included a large number of architectural photographs commissioned by GATCPAC, as well as photographs of southern Spanish popular architecture taken on a trip with Sert and the painter Joan Miró. She also did some commercial photography for advertising. In October 1936 she accompanied Emma Goldman, of whom she took an impressive portrait, on a tour of the anarchist collectives in Aragon. Between 1936 and 1937 she was commissioned by the Propaganda Commissariat of the Catalan Autonomous Government (Generalitat) to take photographs for its magazine *Nova Iberia*. In 1937, as the tide turned against the Republic in the Civil War, she left Spain, settling in Australia in 1939. Her photographs of Republican Spain remained forgotten or unknown until, on her death in 1985, they were donated to the National Gallery of Australia.

Kati Horna (née Deutsch), also Jewish and born in Hungary in 1912, came to Barcelona from Paris with her Hungarian anarchist first husband, Paul Partos, in early 1937, where both were employed by the Foreign Propaganda Office of the anarchist trade union CNT (National Workers' Confederation), she being placed in charge of its photographic agency. In this capacity she produced a 1937 brochure, illustrated with her own photographs, for international circulation, illustrating positive aspects of life under anarchist control in Catalonia and Aragon. Many of her photographs were published in anarchist magazines such as *Mujeres Libres*, *Libre Studio*, *Tierra y Libertad*, *Tiempos Nuevos*, and *Umbral* (of which she was graphic editor from July 1937 to the war's end). Some of her photographs also appeared in foreign magazines, such as the British *The Weekly Illustrated*, and after the war's end, in exile in Paris, she recycled some of her photographs in the 1939 brochure *L'Enfance* produced with her Spanish second husband, José Horna, to raise awareness of the plight of Republican children following Nationalist victory.[2] Many of her photographs taken in Spain have been lost; the only negatives to survive are the 270 she took with her in a box when she left Paris for Mexico in October 1939. In 1979, after Spain's return to democratically elected government, she donated her Civil War photographs to the Spanish Ministry of Culture.

As Vicent Monzó notes in his introduction to the exhibition catalogue of Horna's photographs (Horna 1992: 10), the work of women photographers in Republican Spain has been eclipsed by that of better-known male photographers, such as Henri Cartier-Bresson or Robert Capa, who photographed Republican Spain before and during the Civil War respectively. While I do not wish to suggest that female photographers have an essentially 'feminine' vision, it is noticeable that both Michaelis and Horna stress the everyday, with particular — but not sole —

---

1   Grup d'Arquitectes i Tècnics Catalans per al Progrés de l'Arquitectura Contemporània (Group of Catalan Architects and Technicians for the Progress of Contemporary Architecture).
2   The information about Horna has been updated thanks to the extensive research on her work conducted by Michel Otayek for his 2019 PhD dissertation at New York University, 'Photography, Mobility and Collaboration: Kati Horna in Mexico and Grete Stern in Argentina'.

emphasis on women and children caught in the midst of some banal (but, for that reason, expressive) activity. However, this emphasis on women and children is not a privileging of the private over the public; on the contrary, these women and children are captured in the course of public interchange in the street, or in some cases in public institutions such as refugee centres. I prefer to read these photographs through Benjamin's insistence on everyday material culture as that which, precisely because it is not handed down through official records and discourses but is forgotten, thus forms the 'stuff' of the past. As Benjamin notes (1992: 248), historicism — which stands back from the past in order to produce a supposedly rational account of it — in practice empathizes with the victors by editing out the multiple potential of the everyday which, at the time, is experienced as a 'now' and not as part of a causal chain. The order in which I shall discuss the photographs is not that of their publication, which in turn does not follow the sequence in which they were taken; in keeping with Benjamin, and with the anarchist rather than Marxist orientation of Michaelis and Horna, I prefer to concentrate on their photographs as single statements, irreducible to causal explanation as part of a grand historical narrative, but revealing the material 'stuff' of history in all its triviality and specificity. Their concentration on individualized human figures (particularly in the work of Horna) also matches the visual style of Spanish anarchist posters produced during the Civil War, by contrast with the constructivist-influenced communist posters which represent the human body in the mass as machine. Many of Michaelis's photographs were taken before the Civil War, and she photographs the effects of war only at a distance via its refugee camps, Red Cross workers, demonstrations, and posters; but if war tells us anything about history, it is that it does not make sense at the time (or after) and is perceived in a fragmentary, partial manner, for in the midst of war one simply does not know what is going on elsewhere. Thus, in their insistence on the everyday moment interrupted in midstream — suspending any possibility of explanatory narrative — the photographs of Michaelis and Horna capture a sense of the materiality of history (objects that are used; bodies engaged in social exchange) and of its impermanence (as in those photographs where humans beings are absent but implicit in the object captured within the frame).

Benjamin argues that:

> Thinking involves not only the flow of thoughts, but their arrest as well. Where thinking suddenly stops in a configuration pregnant with tensions, it gives that configuration a shock, by which it crystallizes into a monad. [...] In this structure, [the historical materialist] recognizes the sign of a Messianic cessation of happening, or, put differently, a revolutionary chance in the fight for the oppressed past. He takes cognizance of it in order to blast a specific era out of the homogeneous course of history [...]. (1992: 254)

The fact that so many of Michaelis's and Horna's photographs capture social encounters in mid-flow allows us to perceive the past moment not as a 'fact' but as a crystallization of tensions whose outcome is still undecided. In this sense they can be seen as constituting what Benjamin calls 'a politics of remembrance' that is not geared towards prophecies of the future, but towards producing an experience of the past as a 'now' that stands outside of time and yet forms the 'matter' of history.

Benjamin has talked of this 'resurrection' of the past in the now as a Messianic project, as opposed to historicism which constitutes the past as dead and immutable: hence his insistence that the historicist notion of history as a causal continuum does not, in fact, link the past with the present except insofar as it subjects the past to a providentialist vision that legitimizes the victors (1992: 248). It is possible, I think, to relate Benjamin's concept of Messianic time (in his case, derived from Jewish thought) to an anarchist tradition strongly influenced by millenarianism. I would also suggest that Benjamin's insistence on wrenching the fragments of the past out of their context — explicitly described by him as a form of creative destruction — maps quite closely onto the anarchist concept of the need to destroy the old in order to usher in a new dawn that is not so much a destruction of the past, as a destruction of those contextual configurations that prevented the potential of the past from realizing itself. Benjamin's angel of history, blown towards the future while facing the wreckage of the past, sounds remarkably like the anarchist Messiah — incarnated for many in Spain in the figure of Durruti, especially after his sacrificial death in the defence of Madrid.

In effect, Benjamin replaces the historian — in the historicist sense — with the figure of the collector, whose passion he describes as 'anarchistic' and 'destructive' because he destroys the context of the objects which he collects at random (Benjamin 1992: 49). Unlike the historian, the collector is driven by passion for the objects which he assembles in new arbitrary configurations that infuse them with a personal meaning or 'transfiguration' (Benjamin 1992: 47–48). As Hannah Arendt comments:

> The figure of the collector [...] could assume such eminently modern features in Benjamin because history itself — that is, the break in tradition which took place at the beginning of this century — had already relieved him of this task of destruction and he only needed to bend down, as it were, to select his precious fragments from the piles of debris. (Benjamin 1992: 49)

One may note here that the Spanish Civil War played a decisive role in the destruction of the grand historical master narratives — as Orwell's *Homage to Catalonia* (1961) shows so well — not just because liberalism and socialism were defeated, but because both found it necessary to turn on the anarchists, and on the anti-Stalinist Catalan communist party POUM that supported anarchist insurrection in Barcelona in May 1937, as a prerequisite for fighting fascism. Both Michaelis and Horna were in Spain during the May 1937 events in Barcelona, though they did not photograph them. Their focus on the trivial and the everyday allows a 'resurrection' of that which lies forgotten beneath the debris of history, at a time when history seemed to be constituted by ruins — for what else does one think of when one conjures up an image of the Spanish Civil War?

This was, of course, the first war to see the systematic aerial bombardment of civilian targets, by the Nationalist forces aided by the German Condor Legion and Italian Legionary Air Force. Horna returned repeatedly in her photographs to the ruins left by the Nationalist bombing of Barcelona. In the photograph reproduced here as **Figure 12.2**, the mound of debris on the right comprises a miscellany of

FIG. 12.2. Kati Horna, *Vigilando después del bombardeo* (*On Guard after the Air Raid*), Barcelona, March 1938. © Spain, Ministerio de Educación, Cultura y Deporte, Centro Documental de la Memoria Histórica, ES.37274.CDMH/22/2/Fotografías Kati Horna, Foto 143.

domestic appurtenances from which protrudes what appears to be a truncated female shop-window mannequin. The Republican soldiers keeping guard look the camera directly in the eye, interpellating us; while the statue of the Virgin carefully placed to one side of the debris is reminiscent of Benjamin's angel of history: unlike the latter, her back is turned on the rubble but she nonetheless stands a forlorn image of redemption which, rather than reject the past for the future, takes the burden of the past on its shoulders. Such photographs invite us to occupy the position of Benjamin's ragpicker who confronts us with the materiality and immediacy of the past precisely by refusing to order and explain it. It is the fact that the debris in the picture is wrenched out of his context by war that makes it speak to us so eloquently.

Michaelis did not photograph ruins but she photographed a great deal of rubbish. Her major project was her photographs for GATCPAC's 1934 exhibition *Nova Barcelona*, whose aim was the reconstruction of Barcelona's old popular quarters on rational modernist lines. In practice, Michaelis's photographs document the chaotic heterogeneity of Barcelona popular street life, stressing its rubbish for sanitary reasons — as in the aerial view of an inner courtyard in the Barrio Chino reproduced here as **Figure 12.3** — but in effect replicating Benjamin's excavation of the debris

FIG. 12.3. Cover of book *La municipalització de la propietat urbana* (*The Municipalization of Urban Property*) by J. Grijalbo and F. Fàbregas, 1937, with untitled photograph by Margaret Michaelis, Barcelona, 1933–34. COAC (Col·legi d'Arquitectes de Catalunya), Fondo GATCPAC.

of history. These photographs could not be more different from her architectural photographs of new modernist apartments in Barcelona, whose functionalist structures appear dehumanized in their geometric lines and uniformity, and whose very cleanness has a spartan quality; indeed, with one exception these photographs of 'model' modernist housing show no signs of human habitation. By contrast, it is the filth of the working-class kitchen in the Barrio Chino photographed by her (**Figure 12.4**) that betrays the traces of human presence.

Michaelis's emphasis on street life makes her a female version of the Baudelairean *flâneur* who provided Benjamin with a model for the historian of everyday material culture. Her photographs of the Barrio Chino create a sense of arrested narrative, of random constellations that exist entirely in the now. Loaves are caught about to be shovelled into the bakers' oven; meat is captured about to be carved in a bar as

FIG. 12.4. Margaret Michaelis, *24 San Rafael Street, Kitchen*, Barcelona, *c.* 1933–34. Gelatin silver photograph. 23.6 x 17.5 cm. National Gallery of Australia, Canberra. Gift of the estate of Margaret Michaelis-Sachs, 1986. © Estate of Margaret Michaelis-Sachs.

a guitarist plays; one extraordinary photograph 'arrests' a pickpocket in the act of snatching a handbag from a table where a woman and a man sit engaged in animated conversation: the thief is fixed forever at the edge of the frame trying to steal out of it into oblivion. In a large number of these street photographs, as in **Figure 12.2** by Horna discussed above, at least one human figure is looking at the camera: that is, at Michaelis and at us. These figures looking at us are not communicating any message — we cannot guess what they are thinking — but their function is simply that of interpellating the spectator. A particularly poignant photograph of a sick-looking boy (suffering from rickets?) is shot from above (from a balcony?), with his crooked head staring vacantly up at us as if interrogating us: this photograph was used on the cover of volume 6 of *AC*, next to a statistic indicating the 20% mortality rate in the Barrio Chino. In the photograph reproduced here as **Figure 12.5**, the two

FIG. 12.5. Margaret Michaelis, *No Title (Woman in Apron, Barrio Chino, Barcelona)*, *c*. 1934. Photograph. 23.6 x 17.5 cm. National Gallery of Australia, Canberra. Gift of the Estate of Margaret Michaelis-Sachs, 1986. © Estate of Margaret Michaelis-Sachs.

FIG. 12.6. Margaret Michaelis, *No Title*, Barcelona, 1932. COAC (Col·legi d'Arquitectes de Catalunya), Fondo GATCPAC. © Estate of Margaret Michaelis-Sachs.

FIG. 12.7. Margaret Michaelis, *Comissariat de Propaganda Postcard 'Refugiats a l'estadi de Barcelona. Joves professors saben ensenyar, tot jugant amb els infants* (*Refugees in Stadium in Barcelona. Young Teachers Know How to Offer Instruction by Playing with the Children*), *c*. 1936–37. Gelatin silver photograph. Printed image 8.2 × 13.1 cm. National Gallery of Australia, Canberra. Gift of the Estate of Margaret Michaelis–Sachs, 1986. © Estate of Margaret Michaelis–Sachs.

boys peering at us, flanking the male figure engaged in an unexplained, arrested encounter with the central female figure, draw us into the photograph, resurrecting the past in the present. The female foot and skirt bottom right further involve us because their owner is concealed from view. In the street-life scene reproduced as **Figure 12.6**, parts of bodies are cut off by the frame, producing a sense of the fleeting moment captured in its arbitrary materiality. The lack of unity in the photograph's composition (the various figures are each involved in some individual activity) creates a sense of the heterogeneity of history as it is experienced at the time. This immediacy is increased by the fact that we do not know what the child in the middle and the woman seated with her back to us on the right are looking at outside the picture's frame: the historical moment is not explained but is reproduced as an interrogation. Similarly, **Figure 12.7** gives us a high-angle shot of a teacher leading a trail of refugee children across the stadium in Barcelona to an unknown future, present in the photograph through their various gazes at the unrepresented (unrepresentable) space ahead (positioned somewhere behind us). The ragged line formed by their shadows contrasts with the geometric formations found in fascist (and in many Spanish communist) pictorial representations: this is history left ragged at the edges (and, in many of these photographs, literally in rags).

FIG. 12.8. Kati Horna, *Comité de Refugiados 'Alcázar de Cervantes'* (*Refugee Centre 'Alcázar de Cervantes'*), Alcázar de San Juan, undated. © Spain, Ministerio de Educación, Cultura y Deporte, Centro Documental de la Memoria Histórica, ES.37274. CDMH/22/2/Fotografías Kati Horna, Foto III.

In Horna's photographs, we have a similar sense of the 'now' interrupted in mid-flow. Again many of the photographs contain one or more human figures looking at us, or looking at something that is beyond representation off frame. The photograph of a group of children in a refugee centre reproduced as **Figure 12.8** combines both modalities, with one girl and one boy interpellating us, and the boy in the centre of the picture looking at something off frame to the right, while the boy on the far right hides his gaze altogether. In **Figure 12.9**, the nursing mother photographed at a maternity centre for women evacuated from a besieged Madrid gazes anxiously at something off frame to the left: an image of new life undercut by the impossibility of knowing the future. In another photograph, the crowd (mostly women and girls) are shot staring expectantly at something off frame to the left, with the camera held at a tilt as if tipping the figures into the uncertainty ahead. In another photograph — reminiscent of Michaelis's photograph of the teacher and children in the Barcelona Stadium but bleaker — a small group of refugees, clutching infants and suitcases, marches towards us round a bend in a desolate country road, in a landscape empty save for a few pollarded trees, bound for an unknown future that exists off frame somewhere to our rear. As spectators, we find ourselves occupying the position of Benjamin's angel of history, our gaze fixed on

Fig. 12.9. Kati Horna, *Centro de acogida destinado a mujeres embarazadas de Madrid* (*Centre for Pregnant Women from Madrid*), Vélez Rubio, August 1937. © Spain, Ministerio de Educación, Cultura y Deporte, Centro Documental de la Memoria Histórica, ES.37274.CDMH/22/2/Fotografías Kati Horna, Foto 103.

the human relics and ruins, and impelled with them into the future to which our backs are turned.

Horna frequently chooses as subjects situations of impermanence and incongruity. One photograph portrays a makeshift hospital installed in a requisitioned church, with the letters CNT for the anarchist trade union painted on the bare wall where the altar once stood. Another depicts piles of furniture in the street after a bombing raid in Valencia in 1937: the centre of the picture is occupied by a large framed photograph of twin little girls who are staring directly at us. This interpellating gaze from within the 'photograph within the photograph' draws us not only into the 1937 street scene represented, but also further back into the earlier private historical moment when this family portrait was taken. Here, as in the first photograph by Horna discussed (**Figure 12.1**), the jumble of randomly assembled objects recalls the collages of *objets trouvés* so beloved of the surrealists, and through them by Benjamin. Several of Horna's photographs use montage, superimposing a human face over a street scene or, on an anti-fascist poster produced for the Federación

FIG. 12.10. Kati Horna, *Hospital de campaña en Grañeu (Field Hospital at Grañeu)*, March–April 1937. © Spain, Ministerio de Educación, Cultura y Deporte, Centro Documental de la Memoria Histórica, ES.37274.CDMH/22/2/Fotografías Kati Horna, Foto 19.

Anarquista Ibérics (FAI), over the ruined shell of a house destroyed by bombing. This use of montage has the effect of giving human figures a spectral quality, as ghosts of the past who return to haunt the present. A similar effect is produced in several photographs shot through shop windows, where the reflection on the glass superimposes a ghostly outside world onto the objects displayed — which always represent human figures: photographic portraits, busts of Durruti. Perhaps nowhere is this sense of a haunting human presence stronger than in the photograph of a field hospital in Grañeu taken by Horna in March–April 1937 (**Figure 12.10**), where the human presence is felt all the more poignantly because of its absence from the photograph, present only through its traces: the suitcases, the pin-ups on the wall, and the imprint of a body still left on the empty bed. Here it is not the human figure that interpellates us, but its absence, evoking the fragility of the moment and recognition of the fact that the historian can never fully recover the past but only its fragmentary traces.

The isolation of a human figure interpellating us, who is not symbolic of anything but simply 'there' as a guarantee of presence, is found similarly in Kate O'Brien's *Farewell Spain*. Writing in London provoked by a newspaper photograph of Irún burning, she evokes a vision of the sight of Irún on crossing into Spain from

France, which corresponds to no particular date but is emblematic without being symbolic:

> There was apparently nothing else to see at Irún — except just beyond the bridge, a man in black. He was standing quite still in the roadway, with his back to the train. A solid man of fifty, of respectable mien, and wearing his black overcoat slung as if it were a cape. Wearing a black beret, too. Apparently unaware of the train and indifferent to the weather.
>
> They saw this identical man that morning, because wherever or however one enters Spain, he is the first living object that catches the eye. (1985: 8)

If this testimonial figure has his back turned, on other occasions, O'Brien singles out a human figure who is looking at her and who thus also interpellates us: for example, the six-year-old Enrique in Santiago de Compostela who, as 'the type of all these little boys', is seen by her and her companion Mary every day, and is seen again by Mary the following year. O'Brien ends her chapter on Santiago: 'So Rome of the Middle Ages fades from me again, its baroque towers clear and noble in the background and in the foreground a little smiling boy' (1985: 88).

Just as Benjamin exalts the idle wanderings of the *flâneur* (he notes the particular advantages of being transient in another country), so O'Brien exalts what she calls 'pottering memory': 'Santander is comparatively safe for pottering memory' (1985: 20), she nicely writes. And just as Benjamin insists on the random encounter, wrenched from its context, that produces the 'shock' of the real, so O'Brien seeks 'the quickened sense of life, the accidents that jab imagination' (1985: 16); she writes repeatedly of how the places she visits do not fit her expectations, almost always focusing not on the predictability of place but on some chance encounter that throws things awry. Like Benjamin, too, she refuses linear sequence and historicist accuracy:

> my journey will be a composite one, made up of many, and without unnecessary chronological reference. The route will be a plaiting together of many routes; seasons and cities will succeed each other here in reminiscence as almost certainly they did not in fact [...]. (1985: 21)

Knowing that Spain is in flames as she writes, she remembers and mourns 'the new ruins', recalling 'a million things not set down in this book or anywhere — moments and places without name or date' but filled with the everyday: 'Rich in sun, children and acacia-trees' (1985: 226–27) and with:

> the junk we have accumulated and so obstinately loved and sought to increase. Temples, palaces, cathedrals; libraries full of moonshine; pictures to proclaim dead persons; [...] odds and ends of two thousand silly years [...]. (1985: 5)

That is, a vision of history based on the everyday which does not fit the grand master narratives of 'the forward marchers, the right-minded' (1985: 6) whose rational vision is set on the future. By contrast O'Brien insists: 'Let us praise personal memory, personal love', insisting that 'our protective dullness is only really penetrated, our nerves only really ache when that which we have personally known, that which has touched ourselves, takes the centre of the stage awhile'

(1985: 7). O'Brien is convinced that she has lived the last decade — the 1930s — when it was possible to be a 'sentimental tourist', for the 'hour of full authority' of the scientific vision is dawning: 'There will be no point then in going out to look for a reed shaken in the wind' (1985: 4). She was wrong because, as Benjamin predicted, despite his dislike of prophecy, there are still plenty of ruins and we are still fixated on them while being blown backwards into the future. If the Spanish Civil War still arouses such passions it is perhaps because it figures so tangibly the possibility that history could have been otherwise; that is, as the photographs of Michaelis and Horna show, it provides an emblem of the eternity of ruins — not in the sense of a universalist belief in timeless essences, but in the sense that ruins, if one looks among the debris, contain the unrealized potential of forgotten material lives and objects.

Works Cited

BENJAMIN, WALTER. 1992. *Illuminations*, intro. by Hannah Arendt, trans. by Harry Zohn (London: Fontana)
DELEUZE, GILLES, and FÉLIX GUATTARI. 1988. *A Thousand Plateaus: Capitalism and Schizophrenia*, trans. by Brian Massumi (London: Athlone)
GRAHAM, HELEN, and JO LABANYI (eds). 1995. *Spanish Cultural Studies: An Introduction. The Struggle for Modernity* (Oxford: Oxford University Press)
HORNA, KATI. 1992. *Fotografías de la guerra civil española (1937–1938)* (Salamanca: Ministerio de Cultura)
MICHAELIS, MARGARET. 1998. *Fotografía, vanguardia y política en la Barcelona de la República* (Valencia: IVAM Institut Valencià d'Art Modern)
O'BRIEN, KATE. 1985. *Farewell Spain* (London: Virago)
ORWELL, GEORGE. 1961. *Homage to Catalonia* (Boston, MA: Beacon Press)

PART IV

Popular Fiction and Film in the
Early Franco Dictatorship

CHAPTER 13

Resemanticizing Feminine Surrender: Cross-Gender Identifications in the Writings of Spanish Female Fascist Activists

In an article on the difficulties of writing about the Sección Femenina (Women's Section of the Spanish Fascist Party, Falange Española), Victoria Lorée Enders notes that feminist historians have tended to assume that women of the political right cannot have chosen their right-wing stance freely and thus cannot have agency (389). This is tantamount to saying that right-wing women cannot be feminists. Enders asks how this supposition can be squared with the testimony of women activists of the Sección Femenina, who unanimously portray themselves as having championed the cause of women, and as having themselves broken with conventional notions of womanhood by entering the public sphere. In this essay I wish to consider what might have attracted certain Spanish women to fascism — for I am assuming that their political allegiances *were* chosen by them. My theoretical framework is drawn from Klaus Theweleit's study of diaries and novels written by German male fascists, *Male Fantasies* (1987, 1989) and from Louise Kaplan's *Female Perversions* (1991).[1] My historical evidence is based on novels, autobiographies, speeches, and handbooks by Spanish female fascist activists, mostly founding members of the Spanish fascist party Falange Española's Student Union (SEU) in 1933 and of its Women's Section in 1934.[2] My intention is to move beyond the usual concentration by historians on male fascist pronouncements on sexual difference, to examine the more complex picture that emerges from female fascists' representations of their own sex.

The question of why women as well as men should have been attracted to join Falangist organizations is especially vexed, given the Falange's notoriously

---

[1]   An earlier version of this article was published in the *Journal of the Institute of Romance Studies* 7 (1999): 145–56.

[2]   Women normally joined these organizations rather than the Falange proper, whose recruits were required to declare in writing that they had a "bicycle" (code for pistol), after which they were given a *porra* (meaning both a prick and a truncheon) — a gendered double-entendre that was exploited in Falangist rhetoric (Preston 114). In practice, as the texts studied here make clear, the women habitually carried on their persons the pistols of their male comrades (not, it seems, their truncheons).

machista rhetoric (Labanyi, 'Women'). I am not thinking here of those women who joined the Sección Femenina in the Nationalist zone during the Civil War, or after the Nationalist victory in 1939, when the pressures to throw one's lot in with the winning side were massive. My concentration on women founders of the SEU and the Sección Femenina requires us to suppose that their actions were based on conscious choice, for to be a Falangist in the organization's early days meant putting one's person at considerable risk. Women historians of the Sección Femenina (Scanlon; Gallego Méndez; Sánchez López; Graham) have noted that its activists, while publicly advocating a domestic role for women, themselves enjoyed considerable public power. Indeed, the organization's leader, Pilar Primo de Rivera, was appointed a Procurador in the Francoist Cortes (Parliament, whose members — *procuradores* — were appointed and not elected); as head of the Sección Femenina from 1934 to 1977, she beat even Franco's record for clinging to office. As Enders notes (387–88), it is generally assumed that this was, at best, an unintended contradiction between principle and practice; at worst, a case of hypocrisy. My hypothesis is that the Falangist rhetoric of submission was embraced by at least some female activists because it afforded them a measure of empowerment.

In particular, I should like to ask why the Falange's stress on virility and phallic erectness or verticality was accompanied by a rhetoric of service and submission — a rhetoric that was applied equally to men and to women. Service and submission are, of course, qualities traditionally associated with women; so, what is going on when these qualities are also demanded of men, in a way that clearly is seen as enhancing their virility? Service and submission are, it must be remembered, military as well as feminine virtues. Presumably these values meant different things when applied to men and to women; but at the same time the coincidence allows considerable slippage between ideals of male and female behavior. My argument is that this slippage could be, and in many cases was, exploited by female Falangists for their own ends. The slipperiness of the Falange's mixture of traditionalist and revolutionary political rhetoric extends, I argue, to the sphere of gender.

There is one crucial difference between the feminine and the military ethos: both sacrifice the self by serving and submitting to superiors, but the soldier, unlike woman, never surrenders, even in defeat or death. Falangist rhetoric was based on the cult of fallen heroes (female as well as male) who remained 'firm' to the last. Indeed, when the word *entrega* is used in Falangist discourse (of male and female activists), it does not have its normal meaning of 'surrender' but signifies the opposite: unswerving dedication to a cause such that, if one has to go down, one goes down fighting. The appropriation of this militaristic rhetoric by women allows them to re-semanticize traditional feminine *entrega* as masculine 'firmness'. Conversely, men's adoption of a masculinized version of the feminine virtues of service, submission, and *entrega* allows them too to have it both ways, claiming to be at their most masculine when behaving as women are supposed to.

Surprisingly, my suggestion that Spanish fascism was based on the application to both men and women of traditional feminine values has the backing of none less than Falange Española's founder, the charismatic *supermacho* José Antonio Primo de

Rivera. Historians usually sum up his views on women by quoting out of context his statement, made in a speech to female Falangists in Badajoz province on 28 April 1935: 'Tampoco somos feministas. No entendemos que la manera de respetar a la mujer consista en sustraerla a su magnífico destino y entregarla a funciones varoniles.' ('We are not feminists. We do not think the way to respect woman is to take her from her magnificent destiny and devote her to manly functions.'; José Antonio Primo de Rivera n. pag.).[3] In *Las tres Españas del 36*, Paul Preston extends the quotation to include José Antonio's preceding dismissal of the concept of woman as a mindless object of male sexual attentions — 'tonta destinataria de piropos' ('silly object of catcalls') — and his succeeding remark, startling in its negative representation of masculinity:

> El hombre — siento, muchachas, contribuir con esta confesión a rebajar un poco el pedestal donde acaso le teníais puesto — es torrencialmente egoísta; en cambio, la mujer casi siempre acepta una vida de sumisión, de ofrenda abnegada a una tarea. (Preston 148)

> (Men — I am sorry, girls, if this confession dislodges them somewhat from the pedestal on which you may have placed them — are overwhelmingly egoistic; by contrast, women almost always accept a life of submission, of selfless devotion to a task.)

Preston does not quote the opening words of this speech: 'Y acaso no sabéis toda la profunda afinidad que hay entre la mujer y la Falange' ('You may not be aware of the deep affinity that exists between woman and the Falange'; quoted in Rodríguez Puértolas 893). Nor does he quote its extraordinary end, which I have never seen cited anywhere: 'Ved, mujeres, cómo hemos hecho virtud capital de una virtud, la abnegación, que es, sobre todo, vuestra. Ojalá lleguemos en ella a tanta altura, ojalá lleguemos a ser en ésto [sic] tan femeninos, que algún día podáis de veras considerarnos ¡hombres!' ('So, you [women] can see how we have made a supreme virtue out of a virtue, selflessness, that is above all yours. May we be capable of taking this virtue to such heights, may we succeed in becoming so feminine in this respect that one day you will genuinely be able to consider us men!'; José Antonio Primo de Rivera n. pag.). The fascist *hombre nuevo* or 'New Man' is, it seems, a woman. And he is an emancipated woman: in another provocative statement, cited by his sister Pilar, José Antonio declared his wish to create 'una España alegre y faldicorta' (a carefree, short-skirted Spain) (Pilar Primo de Rivera, *Recuerdos* 346).[4]

I propose to take José Antonio's cross-gendered rhetoric seriously. I am, of course, aware that, in exalting feminine self-sacrifice as a model for men to follow, José Antonio was, in a typically seductive ploy, flattering his female audience

---

3   All translations from the Spanish in this article are my own.
4   José Antonio would perhaps not have been displeased by the attempt by two of the female Falangists discussed here, Carmen Werner and Mercedes Formica, to get him out of the Republican prison in Alicante where he would eventually be executed, by having him exchanged for the Republican film star Rosita Díaz Jimeno (daughter-in-law of the Republican politician and future prime minister Juan Negrín), who had been taken prisoner by the Nationalists while filming in Seville. This idea was rejected by their fellow Falangists as frivolous (Formica, *Visto y Vivido* 243–44).

into submission. But, regardless of his condescension, his female audience could internalize and use such statements to their advantage, as a strategy for legitimizing their public activism. In fact, it can be argued that this cross-gendered rhetoric held a degree of attraction for male activists too. In his analysis of German male fascist writing, Theweleit suggests that fascism was the result not of a fixation with paternal authority, but of a failure to separate from the pre-oedipal stage of bonding with the mother, resulting in a precarious sense of ego-boundaries. This, he suggests, led to a defensive need to construct 'body armour,' but at the same time to a longing for the pre-oedipal dissolution of self: an ambivalence catered for by military discipline, which allows loss of self within safely rigid, hierarchical structures. Hence the attraction to men, as well as women, of a notion of discipline based on feminine *entrega*.

Theweleit is concerned only with the male fascist, whom he sees as terrified by the soft, permeable body boundaries of women, figuring his own inner formlessness resulting from the failure to separate from the mother. I have elsewhere examined the ambivalent disavowal (appropriation/repudiation) of the feminine, and specifically of the mother, in the work of the Spanish male avant-garde writer and founding fascist, Ernesto Giménez Caballero (Labanyi, 'Women,' published as Chapter 10 of this volume). Giménez Caballero's combination of a misogynistic rhetoric of sexual violence with the appropriation of a 'feminine' capacity for 'exaltación' frequently borders on the hysterical (I use here advisedly a term originally — and still commonly — applied to women). The 1941 film *¡Harka!* by the Falangist director Carlos Arévalo, which depicts the Spanish *harkas* (shock troops comprising Arab mercenaries led by Spanish officers) fighting Arab rebels in Spanish Morocco, is similarly based on a misogyny that, through its exaltation of military *entrega*, allows feared feminine impulses to be projected on to male–male relations, tipping at moments into an overt homoeroticism (Evans 219; see also Chapter 18 in this volume). In this discussion I wish to explore the ways in which such cross-gendered identifications might have worked for women. For the scenario that Theweleit describes is all too familiar to women, who by definition cannot fully separate from the feminine embodied by the mother; and who, even if one does not accept oedipal explanations of gender construction, almost inevitably have to cope with a precarious sense of ego-boundaries, with the aggravation that the terror of formlessness is represented by their own female bodies. For women, the adoption of a militaristic ethos could not only provide them with a sense of bodily definition through physical discipline but could also turn female lack of self into a virtue, allowing women to outdo men at their own game.

What we seem to have here is an internalization of masculine agency in the guise of classic femininity. I do not think masochism is an appropriate term. More useful is Louise Kaplan's definition of perversion as same-sex impersonation allowing the disavowal (simultaneous denial/satisfaction) of inadmissible urges associated with the other sex. That is, male perversion consists in mimicking phallic mastery in such a way as to deny/indulge a desire for 'feminine' submission; while female perversion consists in a masquerade of 'feminine' submission in order to deny/

indulge a desire for 'masculine' control (Kaplan). This seems a good description of what female Falangists were doing. Indeed, one could read Theweleit's analysis of male fascism as an illustration of Kaplan's notion of male perversion, denying/ indulging a desire for 'feminine' formlessness under a mask of 'masculine' rigidity. The sheer excessiveness of the protestations of feminine submission by members of the Sección Femenina makes one feel that something else is going on. A classic case is Pilar Primo de Rivera's speech to the Spanish Parliament in 1961 presenting the Law on Women's Political, Professional, and Labor Rights drafted by the Sección Femenina, which marked a major step in redressing early Francoism's massive reneging on women's rights. The speech is a masterpiece of ambiguity, insisting on her 'anti-feminist' belief in the doctrine of separate spheres while arguing rigorously for women's right to work and noting that the 1938 Fuero de los Españoles (Bill of Rights), while proclaiming equal rights for men and women, had led to regressive measures (*Palabras* 7). In this speech as elsewhere, she insists that women's entry into the public sphere is a heroic sacrifice of their domesticity (*Palabras* 6): a brilliant argument allowing women to have it both ways by claiming that their sense of public service is a manifestation of feminine selflessness while also a sacrifice of natural femininity.[5] Having it both ways is the basis of Kaplan's definition of perversion.

In this, as in all of Pilar Primo de Rivera's speeches and writings, her dead brother José Antonio is constantly invoked.[6] While this could be seen as female deference to his superior male intelligence, it is also a canny manipulation of dynastic credentials and, on a personal level, the introjection of a masculine other who speaks 'through her,' allowing her a public voice while disclaiming ownership of it. One thinks here of Freud's theory of mourning and melancholia, whereby the bereaved person introjects the dead loved one, temporarily in the case of the mourning process, permanently and pathologically in the case of melancholia. Many female Falangists lost husbands and brothers in the war. Given Spanish widows' traditional inheritance of their deceased husband's business and property rights, and given the opportunities for cross-gender identification offered by the introjection process, this could offer strategic advantages. Pilar Primo de Rivera's autobiography notes that the wives of 'fallen comrades' gave girl children born after their husband's death a feminine version of a male name in their memory, as was the case with her niece Fernanda (*Recuerdos* 99). Apart from Pilar, who lost her brother Fernando as well as José Antonio, there is the case of the founding Falangist and Nazi sympathizer Carmen Werner, appointed head of the Sección Femenina's Youth Movement in

5   A similar double argument is used by Pilar Primo de Rivera in her autobiography when commenting on Giménez Caballero's plan to marry her to Hitler, which she disclaims by, on the one hand, humbly declaring herself unworthy of such a mission and, on the other, stating firmly that "mi vida privada era sólo mía" ("my private life was mine alone") (*Recuerdos* 210). The first appendix to her autobiography consists of the testimony of a graphologist, whose analysis of her handwriting results in a formidable list of parallel "masculine" and "feminine" qualities — no doubt chosen for inclusion as another strategy for having it both ways, conveniently placed in the mouth of a male expert.
6   Her autobiography, written in a self-effacing style, has whole chapters devoted entirely to José Antonio; its second appendix (355–81) consists of 27 sonnets to him by various writers.

1938, whom even Pilar recognized was particularly close to José Antonio (*Recuerdos* 148). On the exhumation of José Antonio's corpse in 1939, Werner was given one of the religious medals found round his neck (I shall discuss a text by Werner later). The most gruesome example of this introjection of the dead male is that of Mercedes Sanz Bachiller, widow of the founding fascist Onésimo Redondo and herself founder of the Falangist Auxilio de Invierno (Winter Aid, modelled on the Nazi aid organization, Winterhilfe, also run by women), subsequently re-named Auxilio Social (Social Aid). In her autobiography, Mercedes Formica — one of the female Falangist activists discussed in this essay — describes how Sanz Bachiller continued her political activism while not only mourning her husband, shot at the war's start, but while carrying in her body the dead fetus of his child, which doctors would not let her abort (*Visto y vivido* 11).[7] It also seems significant that Pilar Primo de Rivera lost her mother as an infant and had a twin sister who died young: enough to give anyone a precarious sense of ego-boundaries likely to lead to over-compensation through appeal to rigid forms of discipline, not to mention the introjection of masculine others.[8] In her autobiography, Pilar tells how her largely absent father, General Miguel Primo de Rivera, later in the 1920s military dictator, would, on his rare stays at home, pin timetables on the wall organizing the children's life 'like that of a regiment' (*Recuerdos* 18).

It seems understandable that certain Spanish women, wanting but lacking a secure sense of self, should have found advantageous the extreme submission to discipline that paradoxically grants self-definition while confirming selflessness. The wearing of the fascist blueshirt and adoption of the fascist salute, forcing the body into a rigid, erect position, also permitted a mimicry of male body language. The gymnastics displays and regional dancing (Coros y Danzas) for which the Sección Femenina was famous were, above all, a form of body training designed to give girls a paradoxical sense of ego-boundaries through the submission of self to a greater whole; a public exhibition of the female body in which the self is denied and affirmed. The novelist Carmen Martín Gaite has famously commented on the *pololo* or long bloomers with tight elastic, simultaneously restricting the body and producing an intense bodily self-consciousness, which girls had to wear during gymnastics sessions with the Sección Femenina (61–62). Not for nothing was the Sección Femenina's headquarters, where its 'officers' or *mandos* (a military term) were trained, a castle (the Castillo de la Mota) complete with fortifications and tower. And while it is true that most of the Sección Femenina's rhetoric was aimed at instilling domestic values into women — an enormous amount of its publications

---

7   Sanz Bachiller lost her battle with Pilar Primo de Rivera for political control of Auxilio Social when she remarried and thus could no longer legitimately claim to carry her dead husband's mantle.

8   Paul Preston argues that she was also probably put off marriage by her mother's death from a pregnancy she embarked on despite doctors' warnings that it would kill her (144–45). In her autobiography, Pilar notes that her mother's death was described at her funeral in military terms as a heroic "muerte en campaña" ("death in active service"; 17). Preston also notes that Pilar was obsessed with hygiene, which Louise Kaplan singles out as a classic female way of exercising power by impersonating stereotypical femininity.

bear titles such as *Puericultura posnatal* (*Postnatal Childcare*), *Manual de cocina* (*Cookery Manual*), *Muñecos de trapo* (*Making Soft Toys*) — it could be argued that, by turning even family life into an act of patriotic service requiring rigid discipline and training, it aimed to give women a sense of public selfhood that was significantly different from traditional bourgeois wifely domesticity.[9]

I have singled out for analysis two novels by Carmen de Icaza, from the early 1940s, and one by Mercedes Formica, from 1950, because they show different representations of femininity by authors who, in both cases, were important Falangist activists. A considerable number of other novels were written in the 1940s by female Falangist sympathizers who were not activists and whose depiction of women is much more traditional. I do not have space to discuss these here, except to comment that, even in these cases, where fascist allegiance takes the form of submission through love to a Falangist hero, the women have a 'masculine' active past, or their love for a Falangist converts them from female frivolity and egoism to a sense of love as public service and sacrifice of self. This is romance not as refuge in the private but as heroic insertion into the public, in which *entrega* is resemanticized as a kind of *milicia* or military service.[10]

Carmen de Icaza, a best-selling writer of romances, was born to a Mexican diplomat and poet father, and brought up in Germany and other European countries. On her father's death in 1925, she started work as a journalist on Spain's top liberal daily *El Sol* (which serialized her first novel) in order to support the family; she also wrote for the national newspapers *Blanco y Negro*, *ABC*, and *Ya*, where she started a campaign in support of unmarried mothers. In 1945 she was declared the 'most

9   The 1969 summary of the Sección Femenina's activities appended to Pilar Primo de Rivera's autobiography states: "el principio de nuestro quehacer será el formar a la niña y a la mujer en todas sus dimensiones e incorporarla, activa y políticamente, al servicio de la Patria" ("the basis of our activities will be the formation of girls and women in all areas and their active, political incorporation into service of the Fatherland"; 402). Pilar expressly noted that the six months' "social service" which all unmarried women not qualifying for an exemption had to undertake with the Sección Femenina was the female equivalent of military service (103); indeed, it was first instituted during the war. In the same militaristic vein, girls as well as boys belonging to the Falangist youth organization were called *Flechas* (Arrows), contrasting with the cloyingly feminine name of the Carlist youth organization, the *Margaritas* (the word means "daisy" as well as "Margaret"). The name *Flecha* comes from the Falangist symbol of the yoke and arrows (again pairing submission with phallic verticality), while the *Margaritas* were named after the wife of the Carlist pretender to the throne. On Franco's 1937 forced merger of the Falange with the Carlists, under protest from Pilar Primo de Rivera, the name *Margaritas* was assigned to girls under 11, while the name *Flechas* was given to the 11 to 17 age group, implying that girls' passage from childhood to maturity consisted in the masculinization, via militaristic discipline, of an originary femininity (the reverse of Freud's hypothesis, one may note).
10   Novels that fall into this category, all of them set in the Civil War, are: Concha Espina's *Retaguardia (imágenes de vivos y de muertos)* (*Rearguard [Images of the Living and the Dead]*; 1937), *Las alas invencibles: novela de amores, de aviación y de libertad* (*Invincible Wings: A Novel of Love, Aviation and Freedom*; 1938), *Princesas del martirio: perfil histórico* (*Martyred Princesses: A Historical Account*; written 1938, published 1941); Concha Linares Becerra's *¡A sus órdenes, mi coronel!* (*At Your Orders, My Colonel!*; 1938); Rosa María Aranda's *Boda en el infierno* (*Wedding in Hell*; 1942, filmed the same year by Antonio Román). Linares Becerra was a prolific writer of romances from 1934 through the 1940s, several of them filmed but, apart from the one mentioned above, devoid of political reference. See Chapter 14 in this volume.

read novelist of the year.' In 1936 she co-founded Auxilio Social in Valladolid, and with it entered Madrid at the head of the victorious Nationalist army; she remained National Secretary of Auxilio Social for eighteen years.[11] She visited Nazi Germany and Fascist Italy (being received by Mussolini) with Pilar Primo de Rivera and Carmen Werner (Pilar Primo de Rivera, *Recuerdos* 209–10). Most of her novels, despite their romance format, end with their resourceful heroine going off on her own to a hopeful future; when they do end in marriage — as in her best-known novel, *Cristina Guzmán, profesora de idiomas* (*Cristina Guzmán, Language Teacher*) (1935) — it is as a reward for a lifetime of independence. I shall discuss two novels: one set in the Civil War, *¡Quién sabe...!* (*Who Knows... !*) (1940), and one set in its wake, *Soñar la vida* (*Dream of Life*) (1941). I shall take the second novel first.

   The heroine Teresa of *Soñar la vida* is, like Icaza, a female journalist who on her intellectual father's death works to support her brothers and sisters, becoming editor of a women's magazine, *Feminidades* (*Women's World*), as well as a successful writer of romances under the male pseudonym Juan Iraeta. In this last capacity she receives fan mail, including love letters, from women addressed to her as a man. This creates in her a split male/female self: the former public and successful; the latter private and unrecognized. On the success in (then fascist) Rumania of the film version of one of her romances, Juan Iraeta is invited by a Rumanian aristocratic poetess and Teresa accepts the invitation, announcing on arrival that Iraeta has sent her in his place. As the Rumanian who meets her at the airport announces, 'El señor es una señora' (The gentleman is a lady'). Her hosts then take her to Istanbul, where she strikes up a romantic friendship with a millionaire aristocrat Alfonso/ Alí of Spanish-Turkish origin, who has spent his fortune financing fascism in various European countries, including Spain, and whose split Western/Oriental identity mirrors her split male/female persona. Ataturk's attempts to modernize and secularize Turkey are described in explicitly fascist terms, with 'los campos de deportes llenos de obreros jóvenes, los alegres desfiles de las juventudes y las mujeres encuadradas dignamente en la vida nacional' ('young workers out in the sports fields, youth groups parading jauntily, and women incorporated nobly into national life'; 194); the word *encuadradas* used here of women is a military term, meaning 'incorporated' but also 'formed in cadres'. Alfonso/Alí previously nearly lost both legs in an accident and thus represents a heroic spirit imprisoned in an emasculated body, mirroring her male/female duality. Indeed, she comes to regard her female persona as the impersonation concealing her 'true' masculine identity; what this effectively means is that both of her differently gendered selves are impersonations. Most interestingly, her masculine self is the sentimental writer of romances, while her female self is the pragmatic worker who does not believe in dreams. She cannot bring herself to tell Alfonso/Alí that she is the admired Juan Iraeta because she is

11   This biographical information is taken from her daughter Paloma Montojo's edition of her novel *Cristina Guzmán* in Castalia's Biblioteca de Escritoras series (1991). Montojo notes that Icaza was proud of the fact that Franco ordered the women activists of Auxilio Social, with their bread lorries, to enter Madrid at the head of the military parade: a classic example of how the use of women for male political ends, presenting the victors as charitable benefactors, could be, and was, internalized by female activists as a mark of their own public importance.

afraid to abandon her gray, female existence for the public limelight. Finally, his non-phallic, supportive form of love (she is nursing him in his wheelchair) allows her to pluck up courage to announce publicly in the closing line that she is Juan Iraeta: 'Juan Iraeta soy yo.' It is her avowal of her masculine persona that clinches her fairy-tale romance with her fascist (if mutilated) prince.

If in *Soñar la vida* we have psychological transvestism, in *¡Quién sabe... !* we have actual transvestism. Its spy story format, where no one is who they seem, allows it to explore the notion of identity as impersonation in a particularly interesting way. The novel is dedicated 'A mis camaradas, las mujeres de la Falange.' ('To my comrades, the women of the Falange'). Its epigraph — 'Lo irreal ¿dónde empieza...? ¿dónde acaba...?' (The unreal: where does it start... ? where does it end... ?) — refers to the Falangist political dream and to gender identity, both of which represent the triumph of will and imagination. It starts with a Republican questioning the reasons for the execution of a female Falangist, for how could a pretty girl be dangerous? — a warning to the reader not to make the same mistake. The hero of Part 1 is José María Castell, a young, slight but immensely daring *falangista*, entrusted with a special mission by the Falange's leader José Antonio from his prison cell. In addition to successfully infiltrating the Republican Headquarters as a double agent, José María leads his band of Falangists across Spain on a secret mission, bluffing his way out of a series of sticky situations through sheer bravado. All the members of the band are known by numbers (José María is Number 7), for they have sacrificed their private selves to a higher cause. José María is characterized by his passionate love of risk: his unconditional *entrega*, described as a feminine quality, is what earns him the admiration of his male comrades. Part 1 ends with him in Genoa boarding a liner bound for New York, where he changes places with a girl who has got a cabin ready for him: we leave him going through the female underwear in the wardrobe and the make-up on the dressing-table, as he says goodbye to his male image in the mirror.

Part 2 starts with the 'slender female figure' of Marisa Castell, posing as an Argentine widow,[12] checking her image in the mirror on the way to dinner: '¿Es ella esa mujer pálida y fina, de sienes demacradas bajo una diadema de trenzas? No se reconoce. No se conoce, mejor dicho. La mujer frente a ella es nueva' ('Is she that pale, fine-featured woman, her brow drawn beneath the coils of hair? She doesn't recognize the person she was. Rather, she doesn't recognize the person she is. The woman facing her is new'; 140). In the following sequence, José María recreates the past of his sister Marisa, a university student who rebelled against her military general father by becoming a SEU activist, gun-running for her male comrades and frequently replacing her brother José Luis as the contact relaying orders from José Antonio in prison. As the flashback continues, we gradually realize that the character we thought was José María impersonating his sister Marisa is in fact the twenty-year-old Marisa who, having lost her whole family in the 'red terror' in Republican Madrid, has taken the identity of her brother José Luis, adopting the

---

12   Pilar Primo de Rivera escaped Republican Alicante by ship, masquerading as the Argentine wife of a German citizen (*Recuerdos* 78–79).

androgynous name of José María. As she lapses momentarily into self-pity at her sacrifice of 'normal' girlhood, a male stranger (Lord Aberdeen) takes her in his arms. From now on she is torn between a new desire for submission to a male protector, and her masculine persona — 'the secret agent' — which she describes as her real self but which is enacted by Marisa Castell, Argentine widow. It is becoming impossible — for her and the reader — to distinguish between her 'real' identity and the multiple, cross-gendered impersonations, particularly when Marisa takes to using female seduction for the purposes of spying, such that her 'true' feminine nature is a deception. As she says, it was much easier being a man back in wartime Madrid (203). She gets increasingly annoyed with her male Falangist fellow-activist, who starts behaving patronizingly towards her now that she is no longer José María; but the narrator alternately refers to her in the feminine and the masculine, implying that she is both. After many complicated episodes, for in this spy story the identity of everyone is suspect, Marisa ends up in New York devastated to discover that Lord Aberdeen's attentions were not personal but political, because he is a Soviet spy. However, it turns out that his love was genuine as well as feigned, for he kills himself and the master-criminal (a New York dentist plotting germ warfare against the Nationalists), sending Marisa a secret chemical formula in a bunch of flowers. The object of Marisa's secret mission (the secret formula) is a red herring in this novel where the real enigma — the 'who knows ...' of the title — is gender identity.

In the novels of Mercedes Formica, we find neither this kind of male/female split personality nor the notion of masquerade, but what I think can be called a genuinely feminist depiction, within Falangist parameters, of the politically engaged woman. Formica, a founding member of Falange Española, was the only female Falangist in Madrid's Law Faculty, which she represented on the Falange's first National Council, in a photograph of which she figures as the only woman. Just before his arrest in 1936, José Antonio appointed her to the party's Junta Política (Political Council) as National Delegate for the Falangist Female University Students' Union (SEU Femenino) (Formica, *Visto y vivido* 147, 158–59, 205). In Málaga she was a close associate of Carmen Werner who effectively ran the Falange in Málaga province due to the imprisonment of its male delegates. Nevertheless, Formica notes that Werner (whose grandmother had corresponded with Georges Sand) believed that women's role should be confined to the private sphere, whereas Formica championed their right to work in the professions (*Visto y vivido* 177, 179, 198, 243). Formica's autobiography makes a point of listing other female Falangists who held actual or *de facto* office in the Falange. She laments the massification of the Falange during the war, as people joined out of fear rather than revolutionary conviction (*Visto y vivido* 205–19, 234–36), and criticizes the Sección Femenina for opposing women's university education after the war (*Visto y vivido* 248; Ruiz Franco 31). However, she praises the Sección Femenina for turning the old Catholic concept of charity into a social right, savagely attacking the Carlists' 'theocracy' and arguing that things went wrong for the Falange (particularly for women) when it got mixed up with the Church (*Escucho* 11–13). Indeed, the more traditional romances written by female Falangist sympathizers have a clear Catholic emphasis. In 1950 Formica completed her law degree, and became one of three Spanish women lawyers at the bar, devoting herself to women's rights. In 1950 she started to work, alongside other disaffected Falangist intellectuals, at the Instituto de Estudios Políticos, where, on Pilar Primo de Rivera's request, she prepared a paper on women's professional rights, which was confiscated. Much of it resurfaced unacknowledged in the text of the 1961 law, mentioned above, presented to the Cortes as Pilar Primo de Rivera's own. In 1953 Formica started a campaign for legal reform of married women's rights (the subject of her 1955 novel *A instancia de parte* [*The Lawsuit*]),[13] which led to minor reforms of the Civil Code in 1958 (Formica, *A instancia* 35–38; Ruiz Franco 36–37).[14] In the 1970s, she turned to writing historical novels about women. Her legal activism has recently begun to be recognized by female historians (Ruiz Franco).

Formica's first full-length novel, *Monte de Sancha* (1950), describing the 'red terror' which she experienced at first hand in Málaga in 1936 (much of it occurring in the wealthy outlying district of Málaga which gives the novel its title), explicitly relates the need for a new model of womanhood to Falangism. The novel is focalized through a mindless high-society girl, Margarita, who thinks women are made for flirting and that politics is men's business. The narcissistic Margarita, who has to keep looking in the mirror to convince herself that she exists, is contrasted with the self-possessed Julia, converted to Falangist activism after the killing of her Falangist boyfriend in a clear-cut case of introjection: as she touches the still-warm hand of his corpse, it transmits into her body the message that she must continue his political work. Julia, and Margarita's former boyfriend, Eduardo, who has dropped her for Falangist activism, talk of the need to tackle social inequality, not out of charity but out of social justice. The novel shows the inability of most of the girls to understand their politically active fiancés and in particular Julia, whom they see as talking 'like a man' (59). Julia rejects her religious mother in a Falangist version of 1960s generational revolt: 'Cada uno de nosotros de quien primero tiene que huir es de su propia familia. Nuestro ambiente no desea cambiar sino conservarse. Conservarse es su palabra favorita.' ('The first thing we all have to escape from is our families. Our social milieu doesn't want change but self-preservation. Self-preservation is its favorite word.'; 61–62) That all these young Falangists are from a high-society background is obvious; their concern for social justice is motivated by the need to impose a revolution from above before the workers take revolution into their own hands.

When Margarita argues that women should stay out of politics to save their skins, Julia retorts that, in the coming social conflict, women will get killed anyway. The

---

13   Re-issued in Castalia's Biblioteca de Escritoras (1991). My translation of the title is an approximation.
14   During this campaign, Pilar Primo de Rivera secured her an interview with Franco who, traumatized as Preston notes (31) by his father's abandonment of his mother, was sympathetic to her demand that the abandoned wife should have the right to the marital home (Ruiz Franco 37). Formica was also motivated here by her experience as a child of her mother's forced expulsion from the marital home and separation from her son on her parents' divorce, under the Republic, after her father left for another woman.

self-centered Margarita is also contrasted with the traditionally self-sacrificial Inés, inferior to Julia because her self-sacrifice is motivated only by love for her husband, not by a desire for the collective good. Margarita goes some way to snapping out of her narcissism by falling in love with a working-class would-be sculptor, Miguel, but is still limited by her inability to see beyond the personal. Conversely, Miguel's working-class aspirations are limited by his preference for art and beauty (including Margarita, who models for him, as art object) over politics and social justice. Their illusion that they can live in a world of private pleasure is shattered by the political violence after the outbreak of Civil War on 18 July 1936; the privacy of the home is further shattered by the discovery that the household servants are communists. Margarita witnesses Julia's death in the massacre of Falangists detained in Málaga prison. In trying to save Margarita, Miguel shoots her former boyfriend Eduardo, who in turn reveals that he shot the killer of Julia's Falangist boyfriend. In this world where all find themselves with dirty hands, the bourgeois dream of beauty and privacy is exploded. The novel ends with Margarita shot by a Republican thug, fulfilling Julia's prophecy that one is involved in politics whether one likes it or not.

Although Formica is the better writer, the gender ambivalence of Icaza's romances is perhaps more interesting than Formica's straightforward demonstration that the personal is political. That a Falangist woman writer should explore transvestism is less surprising than it might seem, if one accepts my reading of fascist gender ambivalence in the light of Kaplan's theory of perversion: that is, same-sex impersonation designed to deny/allow the satisfaction of urges associated with the other sex. Should the female Falangists discussed, then, be regarded as 'perverse'? In Formica there are no double games. In Icaza's novels, the heroines do seem to be trapped in a perverse duplicity, but nevertheless are lucid about their impersonations and split identities. As we have seen, *Soñar la vida* ends with its heroine's final avowal of her masculine persona. What of Pilar Primo de Rivera? The answer here depends on whether one believes her to have been consciously manipulating contrasting notions of womanhood for strategic ends or disavowing her inner contradictions. Given her political longevity, the former seems likely.

I shall conclude by turning to one final text: a handbook for 'officers' of the Sección Femenina by Carmen Werner, from around 1942. Most striking here is the repeated stress on the need for dissimulation (*disimulo*). Section 2 is titled: 'De la higiene o disimulo de la vida animal' ('On hygiene or the dissimulation of animal life'); Section 3 'On food' starts 'Cómo disimulamos o decoramos la comida' ('How we dissimulate or decorate food'); Section 4 'On discretion' starts 'De la ocultación o disimulo de nuestra intimidad' ('On the concealment or dissimulation of our inner feelings').That this is subalternist strategy rather than unconscious disavowal is made clear in a long passage which starts by citing Madame de Staël's riposte to Napoleon, when the latter objected to women talking about politics, that in a country where women were guillotined they needed to know why (this is much like Formica's point in *Monte de Sancha*). Werner goes on to say that, in all historical periods, 'por muy legítima que haya sido la intervención femenina en la acción política e histórica, [la mujer] ha tenido que usar de toda su gracia femenina para hacerlo perdonar de los hombres (me refiero a las pugnas que se suelen establecer entre el elemento femenino y masculino de una Jefatura Provincial)' ('no matter how legitimate women's political and historical activism may have been, they have had to deploy all their feminine charms so that men would forgive them for it [I am referring here to the bickering that so frequently occurs between male and female officials at a Provincial Headquarters]'). Werner is here clearly talking from experience. She continues by arguing that, although men and women have different spheres of action:

> cada vez que las circunstancias nos sacan de nuestra esfera e invadimos el campo de la acción, aunque sea por motivo legítimo ... encontramos tremendos defensores de los derechos del hombre... .
>
> Por eso, disimulemos o disminuyamos nuestra presencia física en el trabajo. Seamos hormiguitas, hormiguitas graciosas y amables. Envolvamos en femenidad [sic] nuestras formas de trabajo, nuestro uniforme, nuestro andar, nuestra propaganda... . (53–54)

> (whenever circumstances take us out of our sphere and we invade the field of action, even if for a legitimate reason ... we come across the most passionate defenders of the rights of man... .
>
> So, let's dissimulate or minimize our physical presence at work. Let's be little ants — charming, amiable little ants. Let's cast a veil of femininity over our work activities, our uniform, our deportment, our propaganda... .)

She then launches into a homily about women's pleasure lying in submission and men's in action, the whole of which takes the form of a quotation from a German male author (Axel Muntche), which starts by saying that actually women are superior to men but men should never tell them that. This is clever use of rhetoric: not only does Werner put the statement of women's subordination in a male mouth, dissociating herself from it, but she exposes male self-interest in putting women down. With regard to Formica's previously mentioned quarrel with Werner over the latter's belief that women should operate in the private sphere, one feels, after reading the above, that the disagreement was purely over tactics. While it may be humiliating for women to have to pretend to be 'little ants,' I would argue that female Falangists knew what they were doing when they prefaced their public statements with expressions of self-abasement. Indeed, their lucid understanding, for the most part, of femininity as a form of impersonation designed to secure masculine empowerment contrasts with the general lack of recognition by male Falangists of the cross-gender identifications implied by the equation of military discipline with feminine selflessness. If perversion entails disavowal, then it is male, rather than female, fascists who should be called perverse.

Enders calls for ways of thinking feminism outside of its usual progressive frameworks. My contention that the female Falangists discussed here resemanticized feminine surrender to their advantage implies that at least those women who joined Falangist organizations at their start should be seen as representing a conservative feminism. Lest this sound a fanciful conclusion, it is worth noting that the Falangist Carlos Arévalo's previously mentioned misogynist film ¡Harka! (1941), which dramatizes a male military ambivalence towards femininity (within and without), was followed, in his next film *Rojo y negro* (1942; the title refers to the red and black of the Falangist flag) by the apparent anomaly of an overtly Falangist feminist film, in which masculine heroic values are enacted by its female *falangista* protagonist (played by Conchita Montenegro, known at the time as 'the Spanish Garbo') who provides an example of public *entrega* to the male characters of both political right and left.[15]

It is not entirely surprising that two men — José Antonio, Arévalo — should have explicitly proposed woman as the embodiment of the fascist doctrine of service, while Falangist women themselves continued to claim a subordinate role (which is of course what 'service' means). Icaza and Werner, at least, knew that the way to empowerment was via the impersonation of stereotypical femininity (Formica's feminist stance is more overt; one notes that she was the least successful in gaining positions of authority). It should be remembered that traditional female deviousness is another term for good Gramscian subalternist practice: that is, using a position of weakness to gain a measure of power.

Works Cited

ARANDA, ROSA MARÍA. *Boda en el infierno*. Madrid: Afrodisio Aguado, 1942.

ARÉVALO, CARLOS, dir. *¡Harka!*. Cifesa, 1941.

——, dir. *Rojo y negro*. Cepicsa, 1942.

ENDERS, VICTORIA LORÉE. 'Problematic Portraits: The Ambiguous Role of the *Sección Femenina* of the Falange.' *Constructing Spanish Womanhood: Female Identity in Modern Spain*. Ed. Victoria Lorée Enders and Pamela Beth Radcliff. New York: SUNY Press, 1999. 375–97.

ESPINA, CONCHA. *Las alas invencibles: Novela de amores, de aviación y de libertad*. Burgos: Imprenta Aldecoa, 1938.

——. *Princesas del martirio: Perfil histórico*. Madrid: Gráfica Informaciones, 1941.

——. *Retaguardia (imágenes de vivos y de muertos)*. Córdoba: Colección Nueva España, 1937.

EVANS, PETER. 'Cifesa: Cinema and Authoritarian Aesthetics.' *Spanish Cultural Studies: An Introduction*. Ed. Helen Graham and Jo Labanyi. Oxford: Oxford UP, 1995. 215–22.

FORMICA, MERCEDES. *A instancia de parte*. 1955. Ed. María-Elena Bravo. Madrid: Castalia, 1991.

——. *Escucho el silencio*. Barcelona: Planeta, 1984.

——. *Monte de Sancha*. Barcelona: Luis de Caralt, 1950.

——. *Visto y vivido 1931–1937: Pequeña historia de ayer*. Barcelona: Planeta, 1982.

FREUD, SIGMUND. 'Mourning and Melancholia.' 1915. *On Metapsychology*. The Penguin Freud Library, 11. London: Penguin, 1984. 245–68.

GALLEGO MÉNDEZ, MARÍA TERESA. *Mujer, falange y franquismo*. Madrid: Taurus, 1983.

GRAHAM, HELEN. 'Gender and the State: Women in the 1940s.' *Spanish Cultural Studies: An Introduction*. Ed. Helen Graham and Jo Labanyi. Oxford: Oxford UP, 1995. 182–95.

ICAZA, CARMEN DE. *Cristina Guzmán, profesora de idiomas*. 1935. Ed. Paloma Montojo. Madrid: Castalia, 1991.

——. *¡Quién sabe... !* Madrid: Afrodisio Aguado, 1940.

——. *Soñar la vida*. Madrid: Afrodisio Aguado, 1941.

---

15   *¡Harka!* and *Rojo y negro* are discussed in Chapters 18 and 16 of this volume, respectively.

KAPLAN, LOUISE J. *Female Perversions*. London: Penguin, 1991.

LABANYI, JO. *Gender and Modernization in the Spanish Realist Novel*. Oxford: Oxford UP, 2000.

———. 'Women, Asian Hordes and the Threat to the Self in Giménez Caballero's *Genio de España*.' *Bulletin of Hispanic Studies* (Liverpool) 73 (1996): 377–87.

LINARES BECERRA, CONCHA. *¡A sus órdenes, mi coronel!* Córdoba: Colección Nueva España, [1938].

MARTÍN GAITE, CARMEN. *Usos amorosos de la postguerra española*. Barcelona: Anagrama, 1987.

PRESTON, PAUL. *Las tres Españas del 36*. Barcelona: Plaza & Janés, 1998.

PRIMO DE RIVERA, JOSÉ ANTONIO. 'Palabras a la mujer.' [1935]. Pamphlet, no publication details. Biblioteca Nacional cat. V/Cª 8899–5.

PRIMO DE RIVERA, PILAR. *Palabras de Pilar Primo de Rivera, condesa del Castillo de la Mota, Delegada Nacional de la Sección Femenina, en el Pleno de las Cortes Españolas del día 22 de julio de 1961*. Madrid: Almena, 1961.

———. *Recuerdos de una vida*. Madrid: DYRSA, 1983.

RODRÍGUEZ PUÉRTOLAS, JULIO. *Literatura fascista española*. Vol. 2: *Antología*. Madrid: Akal, 1987.

RUIZ FRANCO, ROSARIO. *Mercedes Formica (1916–)*. Madrid: Ediciones del Otro, 1997.

SÁNCHEZ LÓPEZ, ROSARIO. *Mujer española: Una sombra de destino en lo universal (trayectoria histórica de Sección Femenina de Falange, 1934–1977)*. Murcia: U de Murcia, 1990.

SCANLON, GERALDINE M. *La polémica feminista en la España contemporánea (1868–1974)*. Madrid: Akal, 1976.

THEWELEIT, KLAUS. *Male Fantasies*. Trans. Stephen Conway, Erica Carter, and Chris Turner. 2 vols. 1977–78. Cambridge: Polity Press, 1987, 1989.

WERNER, CARMEN. *Breves reglas de convivencia social o Pequeño tratado de educación para las alumnas de 'Medina'* (Sección Femenina de FET y de las JONS). Madrid: Afrodisio Aguado, [1942].

CHAPTER 14

❖

Romancing the Early Franco Regime: The *novelas románticas* of Concha Linares-Becerra and Luisa-María Linares

This article complements an earlier discussion of Spanish female fascist activists who were also novelists (Labanyi, *Resemanticizing*; published as Chapter 13 in this volume). In this case, the material studied will be the romantic fiction (*novelas rosa*) of two popular women writers of the early Franco regime, who — to my knowledge — had no political role, though it is clear from references in their texts to the Civil War that they had Nationalist sympathies. The two writers concerned — Concha Linares-Becerra and Luisa-María Linares — were sisters, daughters of the playwright Luis Linares Becerra (1887–1931), author of popular comedies, melodramas, zarzuelas, operettas, and music dramas, and inventor in the early 1920s of the new genre of the 'película hablada' ('spoken film'): dramatizations of silent film melodramas (Dougherty and Vilches 30). According to the *Encyclopedia Espasa-Calpe*, Luis Linares Becerra's dramatizations included an adaptation of Blasco Ibáñez's novel *Los cuatro jinetes del apocalipsis*, which had been filmed in Hollywood in 1921 (*The Four Horsemen of the Apocalypse*, dir. Rex Ingram). Linares Becerra's cousin was the prolific playwright Manuel Linares Rivas y Astray, who in 1924 co-scripted Manuel Noriega's highly successful film adaptation of Alejandro Pérez Lugín's novel *La casa de la Troya* (*The Boarding House*; recently restored by Filmoteca Española); in the same year, Noriega made a film version of Linares Rivas y Astray's play *La mala ley* (*A Bad Law*; Gómez Mesa 150).[1] These links with cinema would be continued by both Concha and Luisa-María, with a large number of their novels being made into successful film comedies.

The novels of both women can still be bought in Spanish bookstores and over the internet — seventeen novels by Concha are still in print, and twenty-two by Luisa-María. Since their first editions, they have continued to be published by Editorial Juventud in Barcelona, which issued the older Concha's prewar fiction (she started publishing in 1933) in its La Novela Rosa (Romance) series. Other writers published in this prewar collection were Rosalía de Castro, Armando Palacio Valdés, Concha

---

1   Biographical information on the Linares sisters given on their publishers' websites is contradictory. I have updated the biographical details given here since more data has become available since 2007 when this essay was originally published.

Espina, and Edith Wharton. Several of Concha's fictional works are set in the Civil War; these are no longer in print. The younger Luisa published her first novel in 1939, and her work refers to the war only occasionally; one novella set in the war, 'Ojos azules' ('Blue Eyes'), is still available in the volume *Una aventura de película* (*A Movie Adventure*; 59–87). The vast majority of their works in print have no temporal reference, allowing them to be reissued over successive decades. I have found one clear case of updating: the current edition of Luisa-María's 1940 novel *Un marido a precio fijo* (*Husband with a Price Tag*) includes in its closing 'Manual del perfecto marido' ('Manual of the Perfect Husband') — an ironic reference to Fray Luis de León's sixteenth-century *La perfecta casada* (*The Perfect Wife*), which young women under the early Franco dictatorship were encouraged to read — a mention of cozy winter evenings watching television.[2] Current editions of the older Concha's work give only the date of the recent reissue, as if wanting to deny their age. The covers of her novels are blatantly anachronistic in their modernity. For example, the cover of the still available 1988 edition of *Maridos de lujo* (*Luxury Husbands*) — originally published in 1941 as *Maridos de Coral* (*Coral's Husbands*) — features, in between color photographs of a chauffeur with limousine and the Alhambra, that of a smart young woman with fashionable short haircut that might have featured on the cover of a recent issue of *Elle* magazine. The cover of the current edition (dated 1986) of *La novia de la Costa Azul* (*Girlfriend on the Côte d'Azur*) contains a bizarre collage of color photographs of an elegant couple in evening wear, a yachting marina, and a fragment from a Spanish newspaper article on The Rolling Stones, including a picture of Mick Jagger in pink trousers and sleeveless T-shirt — despite the fact that the novel was published in 1943 and there is no equivalent of a rock concert anywhere in the novel. The romances of the younger Luisa mostly have anodyne modern female faces on their covers but, curiously, are issued with the original date of publication preceding the date of the current edition.

Both writers — especially Luisa-María[3] — were spectacularly successful in selling the film rights to their novels. Ángel Luis Hueso's catalogue of Spanish films for 1941–50 lists only one adaptation of Concha's fiction: *Una chica de operetta* (*Operetta Star*), filmed by Ramón Quadreny in 1943 from her novel *Opereta* of the same year. But a 1944 feature on the two sisters in the state-published, Falangist-run film magazine *Primer Plano* (García Viñolas), states that the film rights to three more novels have been sold — *Por qué me casé con él* (*Why I Married Him*, 1933), *La novia de la Costa Azul* (1943), and *Vendrá por el mar* (*He'll Arrive by Sea*, 1943) — with two more — *Sanatorio de amor* (*Love Sanatorium*, 1945) and *Maridos de Coral* (*Coral's Husbands*, 1941) — under consideration. A prewar novel, *Diez días millonaria* (*Ten Days a Millionairess*, 1934), was filmed by José Buchs in its year of publication (Gasca 165).

The same 1944 *Primer Plano* article tells us that all of Luisa-María's novels to date have been or are about to be adapted for the screen: *En poder de Barba Azul* (*In Bluebeard's Power*, 1939, adapted by Buchs in 1940 and with an additional Italian film

---

2   Spanish television started broadcasting, for a few hours a day, in 1956.
3   An advertisement for Luisa-María's novels placed in *ABC* on June 2, 1944 bills her as "La escritora más 'cinematográfica' de España."

version); *Escuela para nuevos ricos* (*School for the New Rich*, 1939); *Un marido a precio fijo* (1940, adapted by Gonzalo Delgrás in 1942); *Mi enemigo y yo* (*My Enemy and I*, 1940, adapted by Quadreny in 1943); *Doce lunas de miel* (*Twelve Honeymoons*, 1941, adapted by Ladislao Vajda in 1943); *La vida empieza a medianoche* (*Life Starts at Midnight*, 1943, adapted by Juan de Orduña in 1944); *Tuvo la culpa Adán* (*It Was Adam's Fault*, 1944, also adapted by Orduña in 1944); and *Napoleón llega en el Clipper* (*Napoleon Will Arrive on the Clipper*, adapted by Delgrás in 1945 with the new title *El viajero llegó en el Clipper* [*The Traveler Arrived on the Clipper*], also known as *El misterioso viajero del Clipper* [*The Mysterious Traveler on the Clipper*]). Gómez Mesa adds to the list *Detective con faldas* (*Detective in Skirts*, adapted by Ricardo Núñez in 1941) and *Mi novio el emperador* (*My Emperor Boyfriend*, 1943, adapted by Vajda in 1944 with the title *Te quiero para mi* [*I Want You for Myself*]).[4] The 1944 *Primer Plano* article tells us that she is currently writing the film script for *Ella y él al cincuenta por ciento* (*She and He 50:50*; filmed by Delgrás in 1944, also known as *Ni tuyo ni mío* [*Neither Yours nor Mine*]), and that Delgrás is signed up to film her 1943 novella 'Una aventura de película.'

A French website still selling translations of her work (www.livrenpoche.com) says that around twenty films were made of her novels, in Spain, Italy, and Mexico, as well as three theatrical and several television adaptations. Galerstein (178) states that her novels, in addition to being translated into French, German, Italian, Portuguese, Swedish, Dutch, and Finnish, have been adapted for television in France and Argentina as well as Spain. We may note that two 1944 film versions of her novels, *La vida empieza a medianoche* and *Tuvo la culpa Adán*, were made by the period's top director Juan de Orduña, reminding us that his output does not consist only in the patriotic epics with which he is associated, but additionally includes a significant number of light-hearted romantic comedies. For this is *literatura lite*: I do not wish to claim otherwise, though I will note some features shared with high-cultural texts. I am interested in examining these novels as a cultural phenomenon. If so many of them still sell today, and if they were so successful in attracting film adaptations (particularly the work of Luisa-María), I think we ought to consider what their appeal might be.

Like all romance fiction written for a publisher specializing in the genre, these novels are written to a formula. Here we may bear in mind Homi Bhabha's obser-vation, made in a totally different context, that stereotypes are a way of managing contradiction. Tania Modleski and Janice Radway have written persuasively about romance fiction as a coping mechanism, allowing women readers to deal with dissatisfaction resulting from their disadvantaged life situations, though not provi-ding a way of solving the problem. I shall not suggest that the romances studied here contain a feminist subtext, for they ritually end with the heroine's capitulation to the hero's embrace, resulting in the loss of her previous independence. But I am interested in looking at the plot twists that occur along the road to love, since there are some fairly extraordinary things going on — and the end is seen as a capitulation.

---

4   I have been unable to trace the date of her novels *Napoleón llega en el Clipper* and *Detective con faldas*.

I am particularly interested in how these romances deal with women's relation to modernity. This is where the link with cinema becomes relevant for, in the 1930s and '40s, cinema represented the most modern art form. In the previously-mentioned 1944 *Primer Plano* interview, Luisa-María stated that her novels have a cinematographic quality not because she writes them with film adaptation in mind, but because 'somos de la generación actual, es decir, ... la generación del cine' ('we belong to today's generation, which is ... the generation of cinema'; García Viñolas). In a June 1, 1944 feature in the popular film magazine *Cámara*, 'Los espectadores opinan' ('Spectators Give Their Views'), Concha was one of seven people invited to reply to a questionnaire on their tastes in cinema (36). Her reply demonstrates this same association of cinema with the modern and with movement: 'La conceptúo una de mis mayores aficiones. Porque plasma los gustos y aspiraciones de la generación a que pertenezco. Hay movimiento, variedad, amplitud de horizonte... .' ('I regard it as one of my favorite activities. Because it embodies the tastes and aspirations of my generation. It offers movement, variety, broad horizons....'). She names the romantic actor Charles Boyer as her favorite star, and Franz [sic] Capra as her favorite director because his style is 'ágil' ('agile') and 'dinámico' ('dynamic'). The stress on modernity remains as strong in those novels published by both of them after the Civil War as in those by the older Concha published under the Republic. In the collaborative project 'An Oral History of Cinema-Going in 1940s and 50s Spain' which I directed,[5] we found that cinema provided a cultural continuity between the prewar and postwar periods, giving it a key role at a time when people had suffered so much dislocation. I would extend this perception to popular culture in general. Given that so many people's love lives had been broken by the war, the continuity represented by the romance fiction genre is likely to have been especially important. This is something that Luisa-María was in a position to understand since she started to write to earn a living for herself and her two infant daughters at the age of 21, when her Nationalist navy officer husband was killed in the Civil War three years after she married him at the age of 18 (www.editorialjuventud.es). I have chosen to discuss five books by Concha published between 1933 and 1943, and five by Luisa-María published between 1939 and 1943, since I want to show how the continuities of popular culture cut across historical periodization.

I would support the historian Michael Richards' insistence (7–8) that the Franco dictatorship should be seen as a period of conservative modernity, breaking with the Republic by rejecting a certain kind of modernity rather than breaking with modernity as such. The key motifs in Falangist propaganda were, after all, youth, dawn, and spring. The modern quality of both Concha's and Luisa-María's romances is stressed in the jacket blurbs as well as in the text. Many of their novels start with the young orphaned protagonist, who has made herself independent through work, arriving in the capital — whose modernity is signaled by the cinema theatres —

5   Co-researchers for the project, funded by the Arts and Humanities Research Board of the UK, were Kathleen Vernon, Susan Martin-Márquez, Eva Woods, Vicente Sánchez Biosca, Steven Marsh, and María José Millán. A co-written volume, *Cinema and Everyday Life in 1940s and 50s Spain: An Oral History*, is in preparation.

seeking upwards social mobility and, above all, excitement. This is ritually described as an escape from provincial 'vulgarity' to the 'distinction' represented by life in the modern city. This 'distinction' is conceived in terms of fashion: several heroines have friends who have become successful fashion designers. As in cinema, speed is a constant motif. The jacket blurb for Luisa María's *La vida empieza a medianoche* highlights its 'ritmo modern' ('modern rhythm') with a vertiginous succession of 'intensas y singulares aventuras' ('intense, extraordinary adventures') happening 'en espacio de breves horas' ('in the space of a few hours'). The chapter headings are 'Nueve de la noche,' 'Nueve y veinte de la noche,' 'Nueve y media de la noche' ('9:00 p.m.'; '9:20 p.m.'; '9:30 p.m.') through to 'Cuatro menos diez de la madrugada' ('3:50 a.m.'). Cars (including the stock film motif of the car chase, sometimes with a female driver) figure prominently in these novels, as do train and plane journeys, plus the more leisurely, high-class travel afforded by transatlantic liner and yacht. Grand hotels — as places of transit and impermanence — are also (as in the movies) favorite locations. These are heroines on the move, crossing national frontiers and oceans as the normal stuff of life, contrasting with the difficulty of leaving the country under the early Franco dictatorship. Being on the move geographically represents being socially mobile in terms of career advancement: almost all the heroines are successful professionals (ranging from journalist to film star). The heroine of Concha's *Maridos de Coral* (the new title *Maridos de lujo* given to the 1951 and later editions is that of the film within the novel) is an international figure-skating and ski-jump champion, explicitly embodying speed and risk. The novel starts with her recovering from a sporting accident; by the end she has got back to the height of her sporting fame and additionally become a film star. In their overall tone, all of these novels put into practice Ortega y Gasset's identification of the modern with the sportive (63–64).

Two extraordinary texts by the older Concha — both of which have Falangist resonances — have female air pilots as protagonists. *La conquista del hombre* (*The Conquests of Man*, 1936) figures the poor orphan Alicia Gor, an air pilot hired by a high-class Madrid beauty salon to scatter publicity leaflets over the city. Alicia has a poor childhood sweetheart but is corrupted when the daughter of the beauty salon's White Russian owner, the spoilt heiress Tatiana, pays her to go to Paris to seduce the tedious fiancé her mother wants her to marry. Alicia ends up marrying the Mexican adventurer from whom Tatiana's mother was divorced, and they go off to Hong Kong where they live off the opium trade. Her husband having been murdered by the Chinese gangster who was pursuing her, Alicia returns to Paris where she makes money as a stunt pilot, loses it gambling at the horse races, and takes off in her plane to fly away from her failure — she was previously described as an angel with 'alas de hierro' ('wings of steel'; 34). The novel ends with Tatiana, now married to the boring fiancé and pregnant, reading in the paper that Alicia has crashed having sought a 'bella muerte' ('beautiful death') in the skies, 'luciendo al sol de primavera' ('gleaming in the spring sun'; 108). Alicia is a female Icarus, punished for her pride; but the married, pregnant Tatiana's admiration for Alicia's spectacular death creates an intense ambivalence.

The phrase 'luciendo al sol de primavera' associated with Alicia's self-inflicted death explicitly echoes the line 'volverá a reir la primavera' ('spring will smile again') from the Spanish fascist anthem *Cara al sol* (*Face to the Sun*). The same line is echoed by the title of Concha's 1939 volume *Mientras llega la primavera* (*Waiting for Spring to Come*). In its closing novella 'La patrulla del arco iris' ('The Rainbow Patrol'; 85–96), we have another female air pilot Vic — not a man, as we originally suppose, but the name by which the risk-loving María Victoria is known. Her ambition to fly seems to be a substitution process whereby she takes on the destiny of her brother who died at birth together with her mother — it being assumed that the only male child in the family would automatically continue the military prowess of the father, blinded when serving as a pilot in the German air force during World War I. María Victoria finds herself increasingly attracted to the equally risk-loving Republican pilot Carlos who is engaged to her domestic sister Isabel. When the Civil War breaks out, Carlos supports the Nationalist military coup (referred to, as in Francoist discourse, as an 'alzamiento' ['uprising']), but it emerges that, in addition to betraying Isabel with Vic, he is a Republican spy preparing to fly Nationalist war planes out to the Republican command. On discovering this, Vic — who had agreed to elope with him — takes off in her plane and crashes it into his, in a kamikaze attack which foils Carlos's treachery. It seems that women air pilots are doomed to a self-inflicted spectacular death but, in this story, Victoria becomes a war hero (hence her name). The long-suffering domestic Isabel is presented as noble but as obviously not capable of arousing the passion of a dashing, if treacherous, hero like Carlos.

We may note that long-suffering domestic females in these novels never get the romantic hero. The heroines who get their man are always independent women: a large number are orphans who have made their way in the world through their own efforts, comprising unusual female examples of the autonomous self-made individual.[6] They routinely claim not to be interested in men — putting career or pride first, for not all the heroines are sympathetic — and end up falling in love *despite themselves*. The repetition of this formula deserves some thought for these novels are not simply advocating domesticity. As Carolyn Galerstein notes with respect to Luisa-María's novels (Concha is not listed in her *Women Writers of Spain*), they frequently feature a taming-of-the-shrew format (178). Within this format, the language of war — siege, defense, conquest — is frequently deployed. These novels are explicitly aimed at a female public, so what is the attraction for female readers of seeing these competent heroines capitulate, despite themselves, to the hero's attentions? Different readers are likely to have responded differently, but generally the reader seems to be invited to have it both ways: to identify with the modern, independent woman while simultaneously identifying with the woman who puts domesticity above everything. Through being encouraged to identify with these heroines who choose to give up career and often fame for love, female readers are also invited to indulge in the contradictory fantasy that they are in control of their

6   In this sense, these heroines are female versions of the orphaned/foundling heroes of early nineteenth-century Romantic drama (see Chapter 2 in this volume).

'destiny' (another much-used word). At a more basic level, this formula of the heroine capitulating after a prolonged pursuit offers female readers the gratifying spectacle of dashing heroes on their knees before women who have the power to grant or deny them happiness.

Janice Radway, in her fieldwork with female readers of romance fiction, notes that the appeal of the heroes to whom the romantic heroines finally capitulate is that they represent masculine authority softened by emotion (81–85). Their role is that of protective guardian, offering the nurturing that many female readers, trained to nurture others, do not receive themselves. In this sense, the hero is not so much a father figure as a kind of male mother. This is extremely evident in the endings of the romances discussed here. It constructs a significant variant on the Freudian oedipal scenario, for the hero replaces not the heroine's lost father but her lost mother. As a result — as Radway notes (81–85) — the heroine is not obliged to obey the oedipal injunction to separate definitively from the feminine (represented by the mother) but, after a period of separation, rediscovers the feminine in the male lover. This also means that the feminine is not devalued, as in the classic oedipal scenario, first because it is lost through the mother's death and not through the heroine's choice to separate from her, and second, because it reappears in the form of the strong, protective hero who lends feminine nurturing qualities his authority — the words most used to describe these androgynous Romantic heroes are 'firmeza' ('strength') and 'energía' ('energy'). If the heroines end up with maternal, caring men, there is a sense in which they too are allowed to keep a limited androgyny — though this will now be confined to the private sphere since in almost all cases these nurturing heroes expect their women to give up work on marriage. An exception is Concha's *La novia de la Costa Azul*, whose end supposes that its journalist heroine Regina will go on writing. The nurturing hero of this novel, Miguel, is an interesting mix of the man of action (he wins Regina's love at the masked ball dressed as the bandit protagonist of the film *The Mark of Zorro*) and the carer (he turns out not to be a compulsive gambler, as everyone had thought, but a brilliant doctor who has put about the rumor that he spends his days at the casino so as not to upset his aristocratic mother who thinks that work is shameful). We should remember that this model of marriage, in which the heroine will, for the first time in her life, be looked after rather than having to struggle for survival, is an affluent bourgeois model in which servants will do all the housework and the heroine will be rewarded with a leisure she has never known. The feminist equation of women's emancipation with their right to enter employment on the same terms as men sometimes forgets that, for many working women (this was certainly true in the so-called years of hunger of the early 1940s), work was not a choice but a necessity, and that the idea of becoming a lady of leisure could be a highly attractive one.

I hope to have shown that both heroine and hero have split personalities — the heroine simultaneously wanting independence and protection, the hero (who we can see as a projection of the heroine's desires) simultaneously representing strength and nurture. There is a similar splitting at the level of narrative. Most of the romances by Concha discussed in this essay are narrated by the heroine in the first person but frequently slip into third-person narration referring to the heroine by her name. The protagonist-narrator thus splits herself into an 'I' and a 'she.' Modleski notes that, although Harlequin romances are required to be written to formula in the third person, nevertheless this is a personalized third person such that the reader internalizes it as an 'I' (55–56); Luisa María's romances adopt this format. The slippage between first- and third-person narration found in Concha's romances produces a more radical destabilization. When avant-garde writers like Diamela Eltit exploit a similar slippage between the first and third person, it is hailed by feminist critics as a strategy for subverting the notion of a stable, unified female 'essence.'[7] Should we assume that, when this strategy occurs in a popular genre like romance fiction, it is doing something less interesting?

Diane Elam, in her book *Romancing the Postmodern*, argues that the romance genre has many features in common with postmodern fiction, given their shared rejection of realism: that is, their rejection of causal logic for plotlines driven by chance, coincidence, and spatial and temporal dislocation. The romances of the two Spanish women writers studied here are not failed realist texts but are governed by laws quite other than those of causality — more akin to the Byzantine novel. The traveling between different countries that occurs in many of them is a mark not only of cosmopolitanism but also of dislocation: the locations covered by the ten volumes discussed here are Spain, USA, England, France, Monaco, Italy, Germany, Switzerland, Hungary, a fictitious Sylvania, Kenya, and Hong Kong, with characters additionally from Ireland, Austria, Russia, Cuba, Mexico, and Japan if we count the dog that narrates Concha's 1939 novella 'Memorias de una "gheisha"' ('Memoirs of a "gheisha"'; *Mientras llega la primavera* 72–84).

As Elam notes, postmodern culture is also characterized by its frequent pastiche of popular forms, which in turn produces an intense self-reflexivity. There is a sense in which the romances of Concha Linares-Becerra and Luisa-María Linares, with their self-conscious reworking of formulae, become a pastiche of themselves: characters and events are frequently described as 'novelescos' ('novelesque'). They also offer a pastiche of popular film comedy, with its farcical situations dependent on mistaken identities: the writers appear to be anticipating the conversion of their plots into films with characters frequently exclaiming 'Parece de película' ('It's just like a film'). Both writers liberally pepper their texts with quotations from canonical writers, from Aristotle to Nietzsche. Several characters are writers. The considerable number of female journalist-heroines function as investigators, overlapping with the thriller genre. The heroine of Concha's *La novia de la Costa Azul*, Regina, is a top journalist for a gossip magazine who, because of her investigative skills, gets hired — disguising herself as a maid — by a Cuban millionaire as a private eye to investigate the thefts taking place in his Gothic villa on the Côte d'Azur. It turns out that the millionaire, an unhinged detective-fiction fan, is in fact setting up the crimes himself, basing them on his latest reading (we may note that with this plot device Linares-Becerra is imitating the *Quijote*, thrillers having replaced novels of chivalry as the staple popular fictional diet of the era). Regina's investigation

---

7   See, for example, Labanyi 1996.

of these fake crimes becomes supplanted by her investigation of the millionaire's grandson, Miguel, with whom she falls in love while suspecting him to be the criminal (as previously mentioned, he turns out to be a successful doctor devoted to his caring profession). The novel ends with Regina announcing that she will write a novel about the experience, which has the title of the novel we are reading. The screen kiss with which the novel ends — true to genre — is Miguel's answer to her question to him about how to end her future novel. Such overt metafictional touches are a trademark of Concha Linares Becerra. Her romance *Maridos de lujo* (as *Maridos de Coral* was subsequently retitled) ends with the cast list for a film of the same title, which the female protagonist is billed to star in, but which — in a Borgesian twist — she discovers she has been acting out for the greater part of the novel while thinking she was responsible for the script of her impersonations. Concha's 1939 novella 'Como las estrellas' ('Like the Stars'; *Mientras llega la primavera* 15–30) depicts the romance between the German manager of a timber factory in the Black Forest and a film set designer looking for a scenario for her next film: she will of course find it in the events that she lives through in the forest. Although Luisa-María's novels do not play these metafictional games, their narratives constantly point to their own ficticity: as, for example, in the title of the previously-mentioned 1943 novella 'Una aventura de película', used as the title of the 1943 collective volume in which it appears. We should not assume, as is so often done, that self-reflexivity is the mark of quality literature. Popular culture, with its love of *double-entendre*, pastiche, and impersonation, has self-reflexivity built into its system.

It is in their reliance on impersonation as a plot device that these romances most approximate to postmodern fiction. I have already mentioned the impersonations by both heroine and hero of Concha's *La novia de la Costa Azul*. In the same author's *Maridos de lujo*, the sports-champion heroine Coral agrees to impersonate the Mexican adventuress who has married by proxy one of the three aristocratic brothers Juan (since they have the same name and she has never met them, she does not know which one) who run the film studios where both women want to get a part. The proxy marriage has been arranged so that the adventuress can acquire the family title, and so that the brothers can save their film studios from financial ruin by acquiring part of her fortune. Coral will discover that the story of the proxy marriage is itself a fake, contrived in connivance with the three brothers so as to test Coral's acting talents for the star role in the film which turns out to be the novel we are reading. The ultimate plot twist is that Coral and the brother to whom she thinks she is married (in her faked role) really fall in love and marry. A similar plot line, based on a proliferation of assumed identities, structures Concha's first novel, *Por qué me casé con él*, published in 1933 under the Republic. Its urban heroine, Marián (note the cosmopolitan name), is a modern, emancipated young woman who drives her own car but whose life suffers a radical break at the start of the novel when her aristocratic father dies (she had never known her mother) and it is revealed that she was adopted from an orphanage. Although legally entitled to her adoptive father's inheritance, she refuses it out of pride, whereupon her wealthy *novio* and her father's sister — who inherits the title and fortune in her place — drop her (the aunt spreads rumors that she is 'un poco bolchevique' ('a bit of a bolshevik'; 78)). Desperate after a succession of jobs in which she is sexually harassed by her boss, she answers an advertisement from an English Lord looking for a wife for reasons he cannot declare. Initially ashamed, she marries him on condition that it remain a marriage of convenience (they both comment repeatedly that lots of people do it). He whisks her off to his Tudor mansion, inhabited by a suitably Gothic cast of relatives, where it finally emerges that his Spanish mother (appropriately called Carmen), repudiated by his jealous father, is not dead but is the 'madrina' ('godmother') to whom he had introduced Marián in Madrid. Carmen is finally reconciled to her husband, and Marián and Lord Fourbridges admit they have fallen in love (Marián's aunt conveniently dies at this point, leaving Marián the title and inheritance she had 'usurped' from her). In a crowning plot twist, Lord Fourbridges reveals that he did not place the lonely hearts advertisement, which printed his telephone number in error, but was so taken by Marián's voice on the phone when she responded — it reminded him of his mother — that he went along with the mistake. In this case, true love blossoms from a printing error.

A similar plot twist, whereby a fake marriage becomes real, structures four of the five romances by Luisa-María studied here. The exception — her first novel, *En poder de Barba Azul* — is equally dependent on impersonation. A New York heiress, Myriam, runs away on the eve of her loveless wedding to an ageing tycoon, stowing away in a ship that she thinks is bound for Argentina where she plans to join her Argentine grandmother. It turns out to be the ship of a Spanish count returning to Europe; he has banned women from his presence having been jilted by a French ballerina with a fake Polish name (more impersonation). On discovering Myriam aboard, he orders her to don cabin-boy uniform; there are some wonderful instances of *double-entendre* as they find themselves falling for each other. The novel ends with them setting sail back to New York together, with Myriam, having stowed away again, now taking the role of 'capitana' ('ship's captain'). Moving to the other four novels: in *Un marido a precio fijo*, the spoilt heiress heroine Estrella, having been tricked into marriage by an Austrian con-man and serial bigamist who absconds after getting money out of her, persuades a journalist (who has hidden in her railway carriage in the hope of getting a news scoop) to pretend to be her new husband, to avoid losing face since she has already announced her marriage to her adoptive millionaire father back in Paris. The journalist in turn pretends that he entered her carriage as a thief, so as not to blow his cover. The condition of the fake marriage (following a fraudulent marriage) is that the journalist will not touch her. The intrigue climaxes with the journalist — a former Nationalist pilot in the Civil War — flying her off to a snowbound log cabin in the Pyrenees where he teaches her the art of home-making to punish her arrogance. In the process, they both discover that they have, against their will, fallen in love. They separate, to discover that her adoptive millionaire father has died and left his fortune to the journalist, thinking he is her husband and will administer the money for her. The journalist persuades Estrella to marry him in a marriage of convenience (after annulling the previous fraudulent marriage) as the only way of enabling her to enjoy the inheritance destined for her. After the church ceremony, they part — but both are now hopelessly in love and the novel ends with her coming to find him in Madrid to turn their marriage of convenience into a 'matrimonio de verdad' ('true marriage').

A similar scenario occurs in *Doce lunas de miel*, as the 'wannabe' film star orphan heroine and the unrecognized inventor hero literally bump into each other trying to get through the swing doors of Madrid's Hotel Palace for important career interviews. Both interviews being unsuccessful, they overhear that elsewhere in the hotel a widowed benefactress is interviewing candidates for twelve dowries which she is offering to deserving couples who cannot afford to get married (it is impossible not to read this as a hilarious spoof of the pious charitable activities encouraged in the early Franco period). They decide to pretend they are *novios* (engaged) and tell such a heartrending story that they are chosen as one of the twelve winning couples. They go through with the required marriage so that they can claim the money, and then part, splitting the proceeds. Five years later, Julieta has become a famous film star in Italy, while Jaime has had no luck. By coincidence Jaime ends up getting a job as butler at the villa Julieta is renting back in Spain for the summer. This reverses gender roles, with her giving the orders and him cast in the role of nurturer who provides for her needs. The novel ends, again, with them falling in love and — Jaime's invention having conveniently found recognition at long last — Julieta giving up her film career to be wife to the man she had previously married for money. The 1943 novella 'Una aventura de película' brings together by chance a desperate orphan heroine Celia, who has lost yet another job after being harassed sexually by her boss (a recurring situation in several novels by both writers), and the also recently sacked Enrique. He takes her to a nearby Exposición del Hogar Perfecto (Perfect Home Exhibition), where they buy the winning lottery ticket for an ideal modern home. To claim the prize, they pretend to be man and wife. Once installed, they agree to live in the chalet in alternate weeks, to maintain decorum. After the usual twists and turns, they recognize that they love each other and — Enrique having got his job back — their feigned marriage becomes a true marriage. (These romances are quite hard-nosed about the need for the hero to acquire money before the heroine will agree to marry him.)

The plot of *La vida empieza a medianoche* is even more bizarre. The orphaned journalist heroine Silvia arrives in Madrid to stay at the apartment of her former school friend — who has made her way in the world, becoming a successful fashion-designer — only to discover that the friend has to leave that same night. An old man, his handsome grandson, and a young boy enter the apartment claiming to be Silvia's grandfather, husband, and son respectively. It emerges that the grandson — a famous composer of dance-band music who, as a child, was taken in by the old man as his adoptive grandson — wants to spare the old man, half blind and deaf, from knowing that his married real grandson has died in an accident, and so is impersonating him, having hired a fake son and wife — the role of wife was to have been played by the fashion designer's flat-mate, who has failed to get there on time. Sylvia, moved by the story, agrees to act out the part. After a night packed with complicated events involving a famous woman novelist whose novels turn out to be forgeries (more fakes), Sylvia and the composer fall in love and, once again, the faked marriage becomes real.

One has to ask what is going on with these repeated scenarios of fraudulent marriages that become 'the real thing.' The frivolous treatment of marriage is extraordinary given the moral puritanism of the early Franco regime (there is a complete lack in all these romances of any mention of religion). It is possible to read this plot structure in two directions: as saying that love is so real that it can emerge even from the fake; or as suggesting that the ontological status of love is fraudulent. Either way, we have a postmodern notion of identity — particularly gender identity — as performance, with the characters getting so engrossed in the impersonation that it becomes the real.

What, then, might these novels tell us about the periods in which they were written (the Republic in the case of Concha's early novels; the early Franco dictatorship in the case of Concha's later work and Luisa's entire output)? First and foremost, that there is no necessary correlation, at the level of content, between culture and political context. I would, however, argue that at a structural level these novels do tell us something about these two periods which, despite their vast differences, have in common the fact that they were characterized by political and personal upheaval. The temporal and especially spatial dislocations in these novels, their reliance on chance and coincidence, and their collapsing of the distinction between impersonation and the real, speak to us of a popular imaginary that has to process events that it cannot control or explain, and that has a keen sense of the importance of dissimulation as a strategy for survival.

Dissimulation has always been a female tactic: a classic example of what Certeau, distinguishing tactics from strategy, has called 'the art of the weak' (37). But it takes on a particular importance in times of political tension and repression. In the earlier essay on Spanish female fascist activists mentioned at the start of this essay and included as Chapter 13 of this volume, I argued that the stress on dissimulation in texts authored by such women can be read as a perverse strategy for exercising agency while appearing to be stereotypically feminine (Labanyi 2002). Given the evident Nationalist sympathies of the authors of the romances discussed here, we can assume — despite the lack of information about their readership — that they will have been popular with women of the right who, during the Republic or when living in areas under Republican control during the Civil War, would have felt a greater or lesser need to dissimulate. The success of both authors in securing film adaptations of their novels suggests that they held an appeal also for popular audiences, for in the 1930s and 1940s the lower classes formed the bulk of the cinema-going public. For female readers of a left-wing political persuasion — here we should remember that political affiliation during the Civil War, although largely class-based, could cut across class lines — dissimulation would have become a daily tactic after Nationalist victory. Both categories of female readers would have understood the emphasis on impersonation in these novels. Perhaps we should view these romances not just as coping mechanisms — as Radway and Modleski concluded from their studies of English-language romantic fiction — but as training manuals for women, teaching them to survive in a hostile environment.

Works Cited

BHABHA, HOMI. 'The Other Question: Stereotype, Discrimination and the Discourse of Colonialism.' *The Location of Culture*. London: Routledge, 1994. 66–84.

CERTEAU, MICHEL DE. *The Practice of Everyday Life*. Trans. Steven Rendell. Berkeley: University of California Press, 1988.

DOUGHERTY, DRU, and MARÍA FRANCISCA VILCHES. *La escena madrileña entre 1918 y 1926*. Madrid: Fundamentos, 1990.

ELAM, DIANE. *Romancing the Postmodern*. London: Routledge, 1992.

GALERSTEIN, CAROLYN L., ed. *Women Writers of Spain: An Annotated Bio-Bibliographical Guide*. New York: Greenwood Press, 1986.

GARCÍA VIÑOLAS, PÍO. 'Concha Linares Becerra y Luisa María Linares han llegado al cine a través de sus novelas.' *Primer Plano* 172 (30 January 1944): 17.

GASCA, LUIS. *Un siglo de cine español*. Barcelona: Planeta, 1998.

GÓMEZ MESA, LUIS. *La literatura española en el cine nacional*. Madrid: Filmoteca Nacional de España, 1978.

HUESO, ÁNGEL LUIS. *Catálolo del cine español: Películas de ficción 1941–1950*, vol. F-4. Madrid: Cátedra, 1998.

LABANYI, JO. 'Resemanticizing Feminine Surrender: Cross-Gender Identifications in the Writings of Spanish Female Fascist Activists.' *Women's Narrative and Film in Twentieth-Century Spain*. Ed. Ofelia Ferrán and Kathleen M. Glenn. New York: Routledge, 2002. 75–92.

——. 'Topologies of Catastrophe: Horror and Abjection in Diamela Eltit's *Vaca sagrada*.' *Latin American Women's Writing: Feminist Readings in Theory and Crisis*. Ed. Anny Brooksbank Jones and Catherine Davies. Oxford: Clarendon Press, 1996. 85–103.

LINARES, LUISA-MARÍA. *Una aventura de película*. 1943. 7th ed. Barcelona: Editorial Juventud, 1986.

——. *Doce lunas de miel*. 1941. 12th ed. Barcelona: Editorial Juventud, 1990.

——. *En poder de Barba Azul*. 1939. 7th ed. Barcelona: Editorial Juventud, 1961.

——. *Un marido a precio fijo*. 1940. 11th ed. Barcelona: Editorial Juventud, 1990.

——. *La vida empieza a medianoche*. 1943. 7th ed. Barcelona: Editorial Juventud, 1983.

LINARES-BECERRA, CONCHA. *La conquista del hombre*. La Novela Rosa 310. Barcelona: Editorial Juventud, 1936.

——. *Maridos de lujo*. 1951. Barcelona: Editorial Juventud, 1988. (Originally published as *Maridos de Coral*. Barcelona: Editorial Juventud, 1941.)

——. *Mientras llega la primavera*. La Novela Rosa, Nueva Época, Año de la Victoria. Barcelona: Editorial Juventud, 1939.

——. *La novia de la Costa Azul*. 1943. Barcelona: Editorial Juventud, 1986.

——. *Por qué me casé con él*. La Novela Rosa 228. Barcelona: Editorial Juventud, 1933.

'Los espectadores opinan.' *Cámara* 34 (1 June 44): 36.

'Luisa María Linares: La escritora más "cinematográfica" de España.' Advertisement for Editorial Juventud. *ABC* (2 June 1944): 10.

MARTÍNEZ MONTALBÁN, JOSÉ LUIS. *La novela semanal cinematográfica*. Madrid: CSIC, 2000.

MODLESKI, TANIA. *Loving with a Vengeance: Mass-Produced Fantasies for Women*. New York: Routledge, 1990.

ORTEGA Y GASSET, JOSÉ. *La deshumanización del arte*. 1925. 10th ed. Madrid: Revista de Occidente, 1970.

RADWAY, JANICE. *Reading the Romance: Women, Patriarchy, and Popular Literature*. Chapel Hill: University of North Carolina Press, 1991.

RICHARDS, MICHAEL. *Un tiempo de silencio: La guerra civil y la cultura de la represión en la España de Franco, 1936–1945*. Barcelona: Crítica, 1999.

CHAPTER 15

Gender and History: Spanish Cinema in the Early Franco Period

This essay, part of an on-going project on early Francoist cinema, is the result of viewing some 160 films made between 1938 and 1952.[1] The experience has shown me that prevailing views of the monolithic nature of early Francoist culture, cinema in particular, are based on a fallacy, namely, the supposition that, under totalitarian government, culture is uniformly 'determined' by official forms of control.[2] This is a simplification which underestimates the creative capacity and varied concerns of film directors and audiences alike. Indeed, it could plausibly be argued that 1940s Spanish cinema is more varied that that of the 1950s, when the emergence of a relatively coherent cultural opposition imposed neo-realism as a dominant mode. The only production company to have been studied in any depth is Cifesa, which enjoyed official favour in the 1940s (Fanés 1989; Evans 1995). Cifesa is, however, just one of many production companies functioning at the time, and films explicitly transmitting Nationalist ideology are a minority. The awfulness, particularly with regard to gender, of *Raza* (*Race*, 1941; scripted by Franco under the pseudonym Jaime de Andrade), is mercifully unparalleled, except perhaps by Orduña's holier-than-thou biopic of Columbus, *Alba de América* (*Dawn of America*, 1951): it is unfortunate that *Raza* has received more critical attention, particularly from non-Spanish scholars, than any other 1940s Spanish film.

With heavy censorship of mass culture in the immediate postwar period, there is of course nothing that one could call opposition cinema. But several 1940s directors, of varying political persuasions, had previously worked under the Republic, when an attempt was made to produce a popular national cinema. The slippage between left- and right-wing notions of 'the popular' is notorious; this slippage helps to explain Buñuel's prewar collaboration with the later director of *Raza*, Sáenz de Heredia. A surprising number of postwar directors had made propaganda films for the Republic during the Civil War: for example, Rafael Gil, best known for his religious dramas of the late 1940s and '50s; Carlos Serrano de Osma, who in the

---

1   My thanks to Margarita Lobo, Juan Peña (on my first visit) and Trinidad del Río (on my second visit), at the Filmoteca Española, Madrid, for making nearly 100 of these films available to me.

2   In this respect, John Hopewell (1986: 33–34) warns: 'Early cinema under Franco was, in fact, very rarely fascist, never monolithic, and not even "Francoist" if the term is to suggest a large, homogeneous corpus of para-governmental production.'

late 1940s attempted to create a Spanish art cinema; Antonio del Amo; Ignacio F. Iquino; and Arturo Ruiz-Castillo, who had also worked as stage designer for Lorca's touring company La Barraca.[3] The brilliant art director of Cifesa's big budget historical epics, Sigfrido Burmann, had designed the stage-sets for the Madrid premières of Lorca's *La zapatera prodigiosa* (*The Prodigious Shoemaker's Wife*, 1930) and *Yerma* (1934).[4] Edgar Neville, perhaps the best of all 1940s Spanish directors, had worked on Hollywood's Spanish-language productions in 1929–30: despite having supported the Nationalists, his 1939 propaganda film *Frente de Madrid* (*Madrid Front*), made in Mussolini's Cinecittà studios, was banned for ending with the embrace of a dying Nationalist and Republican, and his films from then on eschewed politics; they are notably radical in their depiction of active, intelligent, witty heroines (played by his Vassar-graduate common-law wife, Conchita Montes).

The influence of Hollywood is evident throughout 1940s Spanish cinema. It must be remembered that Hollywood was also subject to censorship by the Production Code Administration, which outdid Franco's censors in prudishness by requiring marital bedrooms to be furnished with twin beds. Hollywood influence is particularly striking in the use of *film noir* techniques; *film noir* was shown and reviewed in Spain from at least 1945, a year before it was 'discovered' and given its name in France. Indeed, *film noir* techniques are evident from the start of the 1940s, deriving — as in Hollywood — directly from German expressionist cinema; a number of Central European Jewish cameramen had sought refuge from Nazism in Republican Spain, and several stayed on to work in the Spanish film industry in the 1940s, most notably Enrique Guerner (born Heinrich Gaertner); he trained the next generation of Spanish cameramen who, in the 1950s, would create neo-realist opposition cinema (Llinás 1989: 45–50, 57, 62). Critics of *film noir* have suggested that it arose in the United States in the 1940s, peaking from 1945 to 1950, as the expression of anxieties about masculinity resulting from the difficult transition from wartime to peacetime. Spain was, of course, suffering an infinitely more acute postwar crisis.

What I should like to suggest here, by analysing a range of films, is that 1940s Spanish cinema, like that of 1940s Hollywood, serves to mediate uncertainties about gender roles resulting from the contradiction between the immediate postwar exaltation of military values and the increasing recourse to family values as a way of stabilizing — literally 'domesticating' — the populace, male as well as female. I do not have space here to examine the ways in which the representation of gender is problematized in several 1940s Spanish films by the use of *film noir* conventions (see Labanyi 1995). Instead, I shall limit myself to brief comments on three cinematic moments. First, films about the Civil War made from 1940–42 (it is often said that the Civil War could not be mentioned in Spanish films until 1948; this is not true). Second, the spate of historical epics made between 1944 and 1952, several, but not all, by Cifesa. And third, the vogue for films about missionaries and priests from

3   For information on the contribution of these directors and others to the Republic's wartime propaganda effort, see Sala Noguer 1993.
4   See the photographic documentation in Fundación Federico García Lorca 1995.

1946 to the early 1950s. The films I have chosen are those which explicitly voice Nationalist ideology; I hope to show how even these contain contradictions and ambiguities that allow deconstructive or contrary readings, particularly for female spectators.

First, films about the Civil War made in its immediate aftermath. These form part of an explicit project for legitimizing military values, which effectively means the values of an all-male world from which women are — or should be — excluded, except in the ancillary function of desexualized 'ministering angel' or nurse. A typical example is the Spanish-Italian co-production, directed by Augusto Genina, made in Mussolini's Cinecittà studios in 1940, *Sin novedad en el Alcázar* (*All Quiet at the Alcázar*; discussed in detail in Chapter 16), where the wartime heroics of the Nationalist defence of the Toledo military academy are offset by a cloying sentimental plot in which love for a Nationalist officer teaches a frivolous city girl the virtues of an ethos based on service. More complicated is the depiction of gender in Antonio Román's *Escuadrilla* (*Squadron*, 1941), made with the collaboration of 'la gloriosa aviación española' ('the glorious Spanish air force') Here, too, we have a frivolous young girl, Ana María, English-educated in this case, played by Luchy Soto, who arrives back in wartime Spain to find women working in the fields because the men are at the front: women's work is a heroic sacrifice required by abnormal circumstances. Ana María's mere presence creates emotional rivalries between the fighter pilots billeted in her father's Andalusian *cortijo*, destroying their *esprit de corps* and causing military mishap. The long scenes of the *escuadrilla* flying in formation function as a counterpart — a kind of counter-quadrille — to the frivolity of the scenes where they dance with women, as well as an obvious metaphor for sexual prowess — or rather, anxieties about sexual prowess for they can 'perform' only when in the air safely away from women. This is made blatantly clearly when Ana María's and the hero Miguel's awkward attempts to get close enough to kiss are interrupted by a cut to a huge cannon moving into erect position, followed by a row of bombs, followed by soldiers loading the cannon and firing, as the battle sequence — with repeated close-ups of the pilots in the air — begins.

As one would expect in a war film, the physical contact is between men: the squadron leader Pablo's paternalistic protectiveness towards the new young recruit; Pablo's devotion to his fellow-pilot Miguel, whom he rescues from the Republicans, dying in a *Liebestod* as he collapses on Miguel's shoulder in the escape plane. Here male bonding overcomes the divisions between the two men produced by their rivalry for Ana María's attentions. Ana María has meanwhile become a nurse, thus deserving Miguel's love. The most curious part of the film is the subplot, which presents the squadron leader Pablo as emotionally weakened by his love for a mysterious Elena; it turns out that this is not a lover but his father's illegitimate daughter, for whose upbringing he has taken responsibility, keeping her existence a secret so as not to shame his father's name. His love is thus ennobled: love between men and women is, it seems, most admirable when within the family. But this is an illegitimate half-sister ambiguously outside and inside the family. And the Nationalist hero's function is that of redeeming his errant father's ways:

the Nationalist spiritualization of male–female relations is clearly based on a view of sexuality as shameful. No wonder that, in this film, the male pilots find flying planes easier than handling women.[5]

The dependence of the military ethos on a fear of women is most explicitly enacted, as several critics have noted (Evans 1995: 218–19; Hopewell 1986: 35–36), in Carlos Arévalo's 1941 film ¡Harka! (discussed in detail in Chapter 18), about the North African Regular Indigenous army units used to divide the local tribes against each other. The film's Orientalist ambivalence makes its hero superior for his ability to control the natives and also for his ability to internalize their 'barbarian' virility; European civilization, represented by the dance-floors of grand hotels where men are in the arms of women, is decadent because feminized. At the end, the new Spanish *harka* officer rejects his fiancée (Luchy Soto) and Europe simultaneously, in order to assume the persona of the now-dead hero (a stunningly good-looking Alfredo Mayo) to whom he is clearly homoerotically attracted. It is Alfredo Mayo, and not Luchy Soto, who is turned into an object of desire by the camera's positioning and focus. The film explicitly enacts that strand of Falangist ideology that promoted a Nietzschean return to a lost 'barbarian' virility, as opposed to the strand that advocated a return to classical order. The latter tendency triumphed historically with Franco's 'emasculation' (the word seems unavoidable) of the Falange's radical elements.

Arévalo's next film *Rojo y negro* (*Red and Black*, 1942), titled after the colours of the Spanish fascist party Falange Española's flag, was inexplicably banned after release, despite approval by the censors. It frustrates any theory about Arévalo's supposed Nietzschean misogyny, for it is the anomaly of a Falangist feminist film — a contradiction in terms that possibly explains why its run was curtailed. An explicit apology for Falangist heroics before and during the Civil War, its protagonist is a female *falangista*, Luisa, played by Conchita Montenegro, known at the time, on account of her starring roles in Hollywood silent movies, as the Spanish Greta Garbo. Like Garbo in the role of female spy, she never loses her cool, is always in command of herself and others (men and women), and uses her feminine charms to seduce her way into the enemy stronghold — here, the Republican Dirección General de Seguridad (General Security Headquarters) in wartime Madrid. Most significantly, the camera insists on her wide-eyed stare, which persists even when she is being raped: she is the woman who owns the gaze, contrasted with satirical shots of male public figures wearing blindfolds, in a montage sequence clearly influenced by Eisenstein (there is no space here to comment on the film's brilliant use of avant-garde visual and musical effects). At the end, her communist childhood sweetheart Miguel, discovering her corpse with that of other female *falangistas* in a field where they have been shot by firing squad, realizes that he has been blind — 'engañado' ('deceived') — and turns on his communist comrades, who shoot him.

The only times that Luisa lowers her eyes are as a seductive gesture to get her way, or in order to dismiss those who oppose her. Her superior intelligence and clear-sightedness are contrasted throughout with the doubts and indecision of her

5   For a classic analysis of the dependence of fascism on a fear of women, see Theweleit 1987, 1989.

boyfriend Miguel. It is she who goes to get the hidden pistol of the male *falangista* she is hiding, who calls her 'una camarada imponente' ('an awesome comrade'). The film's feminist slant is made explicit by its prologue, in which Luisa and Miguel as tiny tots have an argument about whether she can come with him in his pirate ship. He insists that women are not allowed because 'los barcos de piratas que dejan llegar a una mujer, se pierden' ('pirate ships that take a woman on board founder'); whereupon she retorts, 'Es que yo me vestiría de hombre y haré todo lo que sea' ('But I'll dress as a man and do whatever is needed'), and she'll get herself tattooed because she is braver than him (her words here contrast with her little-girl frock and Shirley Temple ringlets). The female spy is a cinematic stereotype, but Arévalo's use of it to exalt Falangist bravery could not be more different from the Sección Femenina's casting of women in the role of maternal, charitable nurturer; indeed, Luisa bosses her mother around as much as anyone else.

The last of these early films about the Civil War that I wish to discuss is Juan de Orduña's *Porque te vi llorar* (*Because I Saw You Cry*, 1941), which has been dismissed by Román Gubern (1986: 92) because of its 'silly' plot. It is precisely its plot's outlandishness that makes one ask what is going on. A marquis's daughter is raped during the Civil War and her fiancé killed; she gives birth to a son, who is rejected by her aristocratic parents. She prays to the Virgin Mary, represented as another single mother. A worker watching her pray insists he is the father of her child. To escape the worker's pursuit, she asks her father to arrange a marriage of convenience to legitimize her child retrospectively, whereupon she plans to go abroad and start a new life. By chance, the husband found for her is the same worker, who happened to be fixing her father's radio. After the marriage, he withholds his permission for her to leave the country (wives throughout the Franco regime could not get a passport without their husbands' permission) and sets about winning her over by inviting her and her child to tea parties in his humble cottage with his loving, elderly mother (in clear contrast to the lovelessness of her aristocratic home).

What is interesting so far is that we are persuaded that a Republican worker can be loving, as a husband and father. In a final twist, we discover that he is in fact a Nationalist 'mutilado de guerra' ('war-wounded veteran'), who has pretended to be the Republican who raped her because he wanted to take on himself all the hatred she felt, in order to turn it to love. Several things are going on here. At an explicit level, we have the stock National-Catholic message of redemptive sacrifice attempting to heal the divisions of war (a war which the Nationalists started, of course). Then we have the 'relief' of discovering that the worker who seemed to be the ideal husband and father is not a Republican after all but a Nationalist war hero. More ambiguously, he is positioned in the role of St Joseph as surrogate rather than actual father, completing the earlier image of the Virgin Mary as single mother: his name is José (Joseph). This makes the ideal husband and father not the phallic hero but the saint-like figure who takes on another man's child and indeed is impotent: it is because of his war wound that José is attracted to a woman who can provide him with a ready-made family. The message seems to be that the ideal husband and father is a castrated Nationalist. *Porque te vi llorar* is, I suggest, a particularly interesting film because it is an early example of the use of cinema in the postwar period to mediate the conflict between militaristic notions of masculinity and the domestic ideal of the 'family man' more suited to peacetime: a conflict represented cinematically also by NO-DO newsreel footage alternately showing Franco in military dress and as a 'family man' surrounded by women (his wife Carmen Polo and daughter Carmencita). Orduña's film shows that this 'domestication' requires the 'castration' of the Nationalistic military ethos that brought the Nationalists to power in the first place.

If the early 1940s saw a series of film about the Civil War, the second half of the decade saw a vogue for historical epics where the battle scenes (Orduña's speciality) take place in the Middle Ages, the sixteenth century, or the early nineteenth-century War of Independence against Napoleonic occupation. In the case of the sixteenth century and the War of Independence, the battles are conveniently against foreigners; but in the Middle Ages they are struggles of Spaniard against Spaniard (in *Reina santa* and the Spanish-Portuguese co-production *Inés de Castro*, displaced onto civil war in Portugal). All but two of these historical epics have heroines rather than heroes; and, with the exception of *Locura de amor* (*The Mad Queen*; Orduña, 1948) and the Spanish–Portuguese coproduction *Inés de Castro* (José Leitão de Barros, 1944), these heroines play an active political and/or military role: something hardly ever, if at all, found in Hollywood historical epics.[6] One has to ask why these films concentrate on female heroism, at a time when women were being forced back into the home after the emancipatory measures of the Republic and the experience of war, which on the Republican side took women into the munitions factories and, until May 1937, to the front, and, on the Nationalist side, pressed them into service as nurses and helpers in soup kitchens.

It has been noted that the women's section of the Spanish fascist party, Sección Femenina, with its obligatory Servicio Social (Social Service), while theoretically confining women to unpaid charitable work nevertheless gave middle-class women on the winning side a public role in postwar Spain. Those on the losing side, and the lower classes in general, were in practice forced by economic hardship to work in the black market, despite the 1938 Labour Charter's 'freeing' of women from the workplace. As Helen Graham has commented (1995), it was women, as family providers, who most of all perceived the glaring contradictions between official 'spiritual values' and the realities of a society governed by an officially created black market. It seems unlikely that the historical epics of the late 1940s were aimed at female viewers, though the idea of the war film as woman's movie is an appealing one. But these films must have afforded female viewers some compensations, and perhaps helped mediate the contradictions they experienced between theoretical confinement to domesticity and practical involvement in the market or charity. How male viewers viewed — or were intended to view — these active female heroines is harder to gauge, for the representation in these films of both masculinity and femininity is complex.

6   The two historical epics with male heroes (which are also the dullest) are *El capitán Loyola* (José Díaz Morales, 1948) and *Alba de América* (Orduña, 1951). For the Hollywood (and Italian) historical epic, see Elley 1984.

Several films set in the Middle Ages have poet-musician kings, feminized by their preference for artistic over military pursuits; their decadence also manifests itself in sexual debauchery, seen as an effeminate love of sensual delights rather than as phallic prowess. In *Reina santa* (*Queen and Saint*; Rafael Gil, 1946), the thirteenth-century Portuguese poet-musician king, Dionís, causes civil war by neglecting affairs of state and spawning bastards. As one of his songs says, 'soy el hombre más servicial... rendido siempre' ('I am the most compliant of men... always submissive'); love for him means feminine surrender. But, as several characters note, the superior moral values of his horribly pious Aragonese queen, Isabel, are directly responsible for causing civil war: by taking her husband's bastards into the palace to be brought up as her own children, she, not surprisingly, makes her own son by Dionís (Fernando Rey) feel slighted, leading him to rebel against his father. Whereupon Isabel rides into battle to stop them warring, in a traditional gesture of feminine domestic mediation — 'quiero ser mediadora entre dos pedazos de mi corazón' ('I want to be the mediator between two parts of my heart') — that is at the same time an active intervention in matters of state. She counteracts her husband's neglect of his subjects by clandestinely taking food to the poor, in an attempt to turn the nation into one big family in which citizens are in the position of children as, of course, they were in 1940s Spain. Feminine values here both heal and cause discord: perhaps a message to over-zealous members of the Sección Femenina to keep their charitable activities within bounds.

In *Doña María la brava* (Luis Marquina, 1947), set in the early fifteenth century, the Castilian poet-musician king's effeminacy is again to blame, putting power in the hands of his young Portuguese wife, who successfully plots to remove his capable Constable, Don Álvaro de Luna.[7] The feminine counterpart to the vamp-like queen is Doña María la brava, an amalgam of maternal devotion and masculine valour who, unlike the king in *Reina santa*, never surrenders, not even to love. The film opens with the heroine striding across the screen in full armour, having won a jousting tournament; later she fights a duel with her son's murderer, killing him and handing his sword to Don Álvaro de Luna, in a symbolic admission of the love she feels for him but to which she will never surrender. Her masculine physical and moral strength is, as she says, a necessity since she is a widow, as is the heroine of *La leona de Castilla* (Orduña, 1951), the wife of the leader of the early sixteenth-century Comuneros' Revolt against Austrian Habsburg rule, Padilla, who carries on the defence of Toledo after his execution. The implication is that women are forced into masculine roles when men put private pleasure before their public duties or are not there, and that this is both heroic and tragic, for, in adopting a masculine role, they have to sacrifice normal feminine fulfilment through love. The depiction of Padilla's widow (played by a pouting Amparito Rivelles) is, however, less positive. She heroically insists on watching her husband's execution but faints when his head is held up to the crowds. She takes on the role of Regidor of Toledo, noting that

---

7   The film is based on the 1909 play by the director's father Eduardo Marquina, raising the issue of how 1940s cinema used texts from earlier periods to mediate current historical issues. Literary adaptations account for a high percentage of 1940s Spanish cinematic productions.

'el que manda no se pertenece a sí mismo' ('he who rules gives up his personal feelings'), referring to herself in the masculine; but she persuades the city council to continue the fight in what is more of a hysterical tantrum than reasoned argument. Indeed, her political judgement becomes more and more clouded by her attraction to the Duke of Medina-Sidonia, a 'goodie' but on the enemy side; her insistence on sparing his life causes her only son to rebel against her and die in a suicidal act of heroism. This can be read either as an example of the lack of an impartial sense of justice traditionally attributed to women, or as an example of superior feminine desire for reconciliation between enemies which, as in *Reina santa*, backfires by fuelling discord.

Catalina de Inglaterra (*Catherine of Aragon*; Arturo Ruiz-Castillo, 1951) is played more spunkily by Maruchi Fresno who turns the role of discarded wife into a defiant assertion of political as well as personal rights. Even so, one of her ladies-in-waiting is made to observe that she has 'todas las virtudes necesarias para aburrir a un hombre' ('all the virtues needed to bore a man'), a comment that would have been more appropriately directed at the same actress's earlier pious rendering of the 'reina santa'. On one level *Catalina de Inglaterra* is an anti-divorce tract, encouraging female spectators to see divorce as a legalization of men's abandonment of women, as well as a foreign (English) plot against Spanish interests. But the film's nationalistic emphasis requires it to defend a woman's right to power: Catherine bases her legal defence, which she conducts herself, on her political rights and duties as Queen of England, and on the right of her daughter Mary to be Queen, attacking Henry VIII's argument that he needs to remarry to produce a male heir. Once again, a woman is shown to be a better ruler than a man, but in this case feminine virtues have no counter-productive negative effects. When, early in the film, Henry VIII goes off to war, he nominates Catherine ruler in his absence and we see her giving military orders on horseback, repelling the Scots (sending in her Castilian soldiers, of course), and on victory knighting the youngest soldier by girding him with his phallic sword (a gesture she repeats on her deathbed). When Wolsey congratulates her on her military successes, she replies: 'Es que estamos en guerra, canciller. La única compensación que tenemos las pobres mujeres es ser un poquito valientes' ('Well, we are at war, Chancellor. The only compensation we poor women have is to show a little bravery'): a nicely sarcastic diminutive. The Spanish Ambassador comments that a strong princess is worth more than a weak prince, provoking Wolsey to reply that women may have governed England centuries ago but now times are different. The English are thus presented as objecting to a female ruler while the Spanish are shown to support a women's right to power.

Nationalistic reasons also explain the glorification of the military exploits of Agustina de Aragón (Orduña's 1950 film named after her never tells us that Zaragoza eventually fell to Napoleon's French troops). The predominance of strong Aragonese women in these films is noticeable; the 'reina santa' was also Aragonese and Catherine of Aragon is described as 'obstinate like the Aragonese are supposed to be'. In fact, as has been noted, Agustina was Catalan — something the film ignores (De España 1993: 53). Here, too, the adoption of a masculine role requires the sacrifice of love, in this case Agustina's fiancé whom she rejects on discovering he is collaborating with the French. Throughout, Agustina takes the lead figuratively and literally, whether followed by spies or by the crowds. General Palafox (Fernando Rey) says to her uncle, whom she had disobeyed in order to deliver to Palafox news of the French attack: '¿Te sorprende que una mujer sirva para algo?' ('Are you surprised to find that a woman can make herself useful?') As in the other historical epics discussed, Agustina takes the reins of power because the men are failing in their patriotic duty. She rallies the defence on hearing a soldier say that the French are entering Zaragoza with the words: '¿No te da vergüenza escucharte?... Hoy las mujeres ocupamos vuestro sitio... Dame tu fusil... no hay hombres, no hay hombres, no hay hombres en Zaragoza' ('Aren't you ashamed to hear your words?... Today the women will take your place... Give me your gun... There are no men, no men, no men in Zaragoza'). 'Cobardes' ('Cowards'), she will shout at the men before rushing to fire the cannon in the famous shot that opens and ends the film. This shot, with Aurora Bautista at her aggressive best, is however not quite the end of the film, which has a frame story that 'emasculates' Agustina, restoring her to demure, unthreatening femininity. After the opening credits, following on from the shot of her firing the cannon, we cut to her now grey-haired and wearing a lace veil, remembering her heroic past; the end of the film picks up from this point as she receives a medal from Fernando VII, literally and figuratively bowing to one of the most tyrannical examples of male authority in Spanish history. This schizophrenic depiction of Agustina as both fighter outdoing the men and demure matron was reproduced on the poster for the film, where both images are juxtaposed, with the demure matron (here retaining her youthful black locks) occupying the top position. Male spectators may have been relieved to see her return in later life to a subservient role, but Aurora Bautista's spirited performance allows female spectators the possibility of identification with an altogether different image of womanhood. It was the image of Agustina firing the phallic cannon, reproduced on commercial calendars of the period, that passed into the collective imaginary (Pérez Rojas and Alcaide 1992: 110–11).[8]

The late 1940s vogue for historical epics empowering women, however problematically, was matched by a simultaneous vogue for films about missionaries and priests, replacing the early 1940s films about the military discussed above. This shift obviously reflects the increasing influence of the Catholic Church after the Falange's relegation to a subordinate position on Axis defeat in 1945, after which date the regime strove to present a more civilian face. The historical epic no doubt contributed to this process by relegating war to the past, and subordinating men's involvement in war to that of women. It has been noted that José Antonio Nieves Conde's *Balarrasa* (*Daredevil*, 1950), whose *roué* military hero (Fernando

---

8   Pérez Rojas and Alcaide (1992) give interesting information about the painstaking recreation of famous nineteenth-century Spanish historical paintings by film directors, Orduña in particular. It is not a coincidence that the episodes of national history treated in early Francoist cinema should have been those exalted in historical painting of the second half of the nineteenth century. Both periods, in different ways, were concerned with consolidating state formation through the regulation of the family and particularly of women.

Fernán Gómez) reforms by becoming a missionary in Alaska, charts the Church's replacement of the Falange as the dominant ideological influence (Gubern 1986: 113).[9] I should like to go further by suggesting that the new stress on missionary and priest heroes is part of the process of accustoming men to a domestic role as heads of the family.

This signifies a feminization of the male role; if citizens were not allowed to participate in public affairs except nominally as heads of family, there was a need to make domestic values attractive to men as well as to women. Priests are, of course, men in skirts, who turn the other cheek rather than resort to violence, and who function as nurturing 'mothers' as well as protecting 'fathers'. At the same time, as celibates, priests move in an all-male world. Films about priests and missionaries thus cater to the same male fear of women expressed in early 1940s films about the military, with the added advantage of allowing men to incorporate feminine values. This means that feminine, 'domestic' values can be privileged while at the same time allowing women to be dispensed with.[10] I should like to end by briefly considering two films that present the missionary and priest as a positive feminizing influence while stressing all-male relationships: *Misión blanca* (*White Mission*; Orduña, 1946) and *Cerca de la ciudad* (*On the City's Outskirts*; Luis Lucia, 1952).

In *Misión blanca*, the missionary hero in Guinea Española (where the outdoors locations were shot, the native population providing the 'background' local colour) turns out to be motivated in his vocation by the desire to redeem his wayward father, a former banker (relics of Falangist anti-capitalist sentiment surface here) who in 1910 had absconded after the discovery of his fraudulent dealings, abandoning and robbing the wife whom he had married for money and whom we see him abuse physically. As he leaves, he looks wistfully at his baby son, implying that the father–son bond is his one humanizing feature. Under the false name Brisco, he settles in Spanish Equatorial Guinea, exploiting the natives and using violence against his fellow Spanish settlers. The mission's function is explicitly to pacify the violent behaviour of the white settlers which the voice-over admits 'used to exist' in Spain's African colonies; the use of male 'voice-of-God' authoritarian voice-over appropriately characterizes all these missionary films.

Brisco's abusiveness is represented by his enslavement of a native girl (played by a Cuban mulata actress with long black hair, flower behind one ear and demure sarong making her look like a Polynesian; the audience is presumably expected not to be able to tell the difference between one kind of 'native' and another). The missionary hero Padre Xavier rescues her so that she can marry her native lover Minoa (a Tarzan figure played by the Spanish star Jorge Mistral with body blacked).

9   Heredero (1993: 54–58) notes the Church's financial investment in this wave of films about missionary and priest heroes, particularly through the creation in 1950 of the production company Aspa (responsible for *Balarrasa*).
10   Modleski (1991: 7, 10, 76–89) notes that, in several 1980s films, the feminization of men takes the form of a male appropriation of the female maternal function, further marginalizing women. Despite the obvious historical differences, parallels could be drawn between the 1980s cultural 'backlash' against feminism analysed by Modleski, and the early Franco regime's attempt to obliterate the advances made by women under the Second Republic and in wartime.

The most erotic scene in the film is when Brisco whips Minoa, with the camera focusing on his writhing oiled, naked torso in a masochistic confusion of suffering and ecstasy. Xavier's concern with redeeming his father leads him to take several decisions that, as other characters comment, privilege Brisco as an abusive white settler over the natives, introducing a troubling note. Indeed, Xavier admits that his real 'mission' is not to 'save' the natives but to 'salvar a mi padre' ('save my father'). There are several close-ups of Brisco's and Xavier's faces gazing at each other homoerotically.[11] It is made clear that Brisco is a 'baddie' because he is a man unable to admit to emotion, represented by the attraction he evidently feels towards Xavier whom he, and we, do not yet know is his son. His masculine 'hardness' is contrasted with Xavier's capacity for compassion. When Brisco whips Xavier on the face (whipping and homoeroticism again being linked), he tells him to defend himself 'like a man'; Xavier replies, tears rolling down his cheeks, that he can't because he is a priest and because he made a vow to his now dead mother. The priest is thus proposed as a superior image of masculinity associated with the capacity for emotion and with the maternal, by contrast with Brisco as the violent, abusive father figure. This scene, where Xavier reveals that he is Brisco's son, and Brisco, still reluctant to believe the truth, says his son was the one thing he ever loved, is filmed as if it were a love scene, complete with raging storm outside, providing the emotional climax to the narrative. In the ensuing storm sequence, which sets the spectators' emotions racing as Brisco speeds through the jungle to save Xavier from the assassin he had previously contracted to murder him, Brisco is accidentally hit by a falling tree and dies in Xavier's arms crying '¡Hijo mío, perdóname!' ('My son, forgive me!'), having just had time to make his confession and receive Xavier's absolution as priest and son. Again, we have an all-male *Liebestod*; the film ends with the new young missionary, to whom Xavier's story has been recounted by the father superior in the film's narrative frame, going off to continue Xavier's role in an alternative form of generational transmission whereby the father–son continuity makes the woman's role in the reproductive cycle redundant.

Luis Lucia's *Cerca de la ciudad* (1952) was, at the time, seen as the Catholic reply to Nieves Conde's *Surcos* of the previous year, generally regarded as the first postwar opposition movie. I do not have space here to discuss Lucia's extraordinarily interesting metafictional engagement with neo-realism, both parodied and appropriated. The priest hero's attempts to relieve the poverty in Madrid's *chabolas* (shanty towns) explicitly cast him in the role of missionary. The film confirms the regime's treatment of the working classes as barbarian 'other' while arguing for the 'other' to be incorporated into the nation: a dual manoeuvre which replicates the colonization process. The film's most noticeable feature is its appeal to feminine family values, portraying the priest hero (brilliantly played for laughs by the young Adolfo Marsillach) as a father figure who takes on the maternal function of nurturer, contrasting with the stony heart (finally redeemed through his influence)

---

11   The film's director, Orduña, was homosexual, as was widely known in film circles but of course not mentioned publicly. That did not prevent him from being the regime's most favoured filmmaker in the late 1940s.

of the only female character, a caricaturesque *beata* (over-pious spinster). The priest, called José and posted to the Parroquia del Niño Jesús (Parish of the Christ Child), is another St Joseph or surrogate father. Indeed, one of the film's running jokes is that almost all the males in the film are called José, including the doctor whom the priest persuades to give his services as 'ministering angel' for free. The working-class men in the local bar taunt Padre José, saying he has a 'vocación de niñera' ('nanny's vocation'): he also turns the comic sacristan into a 'niñera' ('nanny'), as the latter notes. For Padre José's aim is to give the slum children an alternative 'hogar' ('home'), taking them into his own house, feeding them and procuring medical care, sending the sacristan out with a housewifely shopping basket, and finally founding an institutional 'home' for them. This construction of social welfare as the incorporation of the socially marginalized into one big collective family positions the slum dwellers in the role of minors: indeed, they are represented by a family of young boys with no mother, whose criminal father is in jail. Quite extraordinarily, there is not one girl among the slum children whom Padre José takes under his wing; indeed, in the film's many shots of the slums I have identified only one girl, hidden behind the credits. Although the occasional adult female slum dweller crosses the screen, none of them enters the narrative. This is an all-male world, but one in which fathers — until the nurturing Padre José comes along — provide negative role models.

The criminal activities of the eldest boy in the foregrounded family are 'redeemed' by the fact that he steals to feed his younger brothers, placing him in the role of maternal provider. In the film's climax, the boy's father, released from jail, enters the church during the Christmas Eve midnight mass, won over by Padre José's example: the camera focuses on the nativity scene in the church, confirming the film's recurrent parallel between the slum boys and the infant Jesus — also born in a *chabola*, as Padre José repeatedly remarks. The church is crowded with fathers and sons from the shanty town, but again not a single girl child, though three unknown women are briefly glimpsed in the background. The nearest thing to a girl in this scene — indeed, in the whole narrative — is the statue of the boy Jesus on the altar, foregrounded by the camera, whose blonde curls and calf-length frock provide a feminized model of masculinity. Throughout this sequence, Padre José bridges the divide between masculinity and femininity by impersonating the 'cura ta...ta... tartamudo' ('stu... stu... stuttering priest') of his favourite joke, stuttering here with emotion, showing the need for the man to voice emotion but also the constraints on his doing so. The scene ends with the camera closing on the repentant criminal father (the 'good thief') in a male version of the weeping Magdalene image that closes so many contemporary Spanish film melodramas, cutting to Padre José writing to his mother. For this is an all-male world where men redeem themselves and others by taking on the maternal caring function, literally and figuratively writing women out of the picture.

Interestingly Padre José has a 'son', also called José (Pepito), born not of woman but of man, in the form of the ventriloquist's dummy inherited from his father which he manipulates effectively throughout the film to win the slum boys over. The motif of ventriloquism posits another form of all-male generational transmission whereby the father gives his own voice to his sons, denying them (in this case, the working classes; one of the slum boys is significantly dumb) a voice of their own. In appropriating the maternal role, Padre José eliminates both gender and class difference. The feminized man functions as a brilliant strategy for imposing the Law of the Father. Or perhaps, in this film where almost everyone is called José, one should say 'for imposing the Name of the Father': the name, that is, of St Joseph, the non-phallic family man.

To conclude: early 1940s films about the Civil War, with the exception of the banned *Rojo y negro*, construct an all-male brand of heroism based on the exclusion of a threatening femininity. By the second half of the 1940s a shift has taken place whereby, in the historical epic, heroism is largely displaced onto women and, in films about missionaries and priests, women are excluded by men taking over their maternal function. In all cases, despite the regime's obvious repudiation of the gains made by women under the Republic and in wartime, the problem seems to be not so much women as men, contradictorily seen as not masculine enough and as too masculine. The contradiction is perhaps inevitable in a period when traditional gender roles were being re-imposed while at the same time men were being denied an active public role and forced into 'feminine' passivity.

Works Cited

ARÉVALO, CARLOS (dir.). 1941. *¡Harka!* (Cifesa)

—— (dir.). 1942 *Rojo y negro* (Cepicsa)

DE ESPAÑA, RAFAEL. 1993. 'Cataluña y los catalanes vistos por el cine del franquismo', in *El cine en Cataluña: Una aproximación histórica* (Barcelona: PPU)

DÍAZ MORALES, JOSÉ (dir.). 1948. *El capitán Loyola* (Producciones Calderón)

ELLEY, DEREK. 1984. *The Epic Film* (London: Routledge)

EVANS, PETER. 1995. 'Cifesa: Cinema and Authoritarian Aesthetics', in *Spanish Cultural Studies: An Introduction*, ed. by Helen Graham and Jo Labanyi (Oxford: Oxford University Press), pp. 215–22

FANÉS, FÉLIX. 1989. *El cas Cifesa: Vint anys de cine espanyol (1932–1951)* (Valencia: Filmoteca de la Generalitat Valenciana)

FUNDACIÓN FEDERICO GARCÍA LORCA. 1995. *Federico García Lorca: Vida y obra en fotografías y documentos* (Granada: Fundación Caja de Granada)

GENINA, AUGUSTO (dir.). 1940. *Sin novedad en el Alcázar* (Film Bassoli / Ulargui Films)

GIL, RAFAEL (dir.). 1946. *Reina santa* (Filmes Albuquerque / Suevia Films)

GRAHAM, HELEN. 1995. 'Gender and the State: Women in the 1940s', in *Spanish Cultural Studies: An Introduction*, ed. by Helen Graham and Jo Labanyi (Oxford: Oxford University Press), pp. 182–95

GUBERN, ROMÁN. 1986. *1936–1939: La guerra de España en la pantalla* (Madrid: Filmoteca Española)

HEREDERO, CARLOS. 1993. *Las huellas del tiempo: Cine español, 1951–1961* (Valencia: Filmoteca de la Generalitat Valenciana)

HOPEWELL, JOHN. 1986. *Out of the Past: Spanish Cinema after Franco* (London: British Film Institute)

LABANYI, JO. 1995. 'Masculinity and the Family in Crisis: Reading Unamuno through *Film Noir*', *Romance Studies*, 26: 7–21

LEITÃO DE BARROS, JOSÉ (dir.). 1944. *Inés de Castro* (Faro Producciones Cinematográficas / Filmes Lumiar)

LLINÁS, FRANCISCO (ed.). 1989. *Directores de fotografía del cine español* (Madrid: Filmoteca Española)

LUCIA, LUIS (dir.). 1952. *Cerca de la ciudad* (Goya Producciones Cinematográficas)

MARQUINA, LUIS (dir.). 1947. *Doña María la brava* (Manuel del Castillo)

MODLESKI, TANIA. 1991. *Feminism without Women: Culture and Criticism in a 'Postfeminist' Age* (New York: Routledge)

NIEVES CONDE, JOSÉ ANTONIO (dir.). 1950. *Balarrasa* (Aspa Producciones Cinematográficas)

NEVILLE, EDGAR (dir.). 1939. *Frente de Madrid* (Film Bassoli)

ORDUÑA, JUAN DE (dir.). 1941. *Porque te vi llorar* (Producciones Orduña Films)

—— (dir.). 1946. *Misión blanca* (Colonial AJE)

—— (dir.). 1948. *Locura de amor* (Cifesa)

—— (dir.). 1950. *Agustina de Aragón* (Cifesa)

—— (dir.). 1951. *La leona de Castilla* (Cifesa)

PÉREZ ROJAS, JAVIER, and JOSÉ LUIS ALCAIDE. 1992. 'Apropiaciones y recreaciones de la pintura de historia', in *La pintura de historia del siglo XIX en España*, ed. by José Luis Díez (Madrid: Museo del Prado), pp. 103–18

ROMÁN, ANTONIO (dir.). 1941. *Escuadrilla* (Productores Asociados)

RUIZ-CASTILLO, ARTURO (dir.). 1951. *Catalina de Inglaterra* (Balcázar Producciones Cinematográficas)

SÁENZ DE HEREDIA, JOSÉ LUIS (dir.). 1941. *Raza* (Cancillería del Consejo de la Hispanidad)

SALA NOGUER, RAMÓN. 1993. *El cine en la España republicana durante la guerra civil* (Bilbao: Ediciones Mensajero)

THEWELEIT, KLAUS. 1987, 1989. *Male Fantasies*, trans. by Stephen Conway, Erica Carter and Christ Turner, 2 vols (Cambridge: Polity)

CHAPTER 16

Three Nationalist Film Versions of the Civil War: *España heroica* (Reig, 1937), *Sin novedad en el Alcázar* (Genina, 1940), *¡El Santuario no se rinde!* (Ruiz-Castillo, 1949)

The Spanish Civil War was the first to be fought after the introduction of the synchronized sound film. The interaction of image and sound dramatically increased the propaganda potential of the medium, allowing the possibility of re-inflecting visual images for particular purposes. During the Civil War both sides produced a considerable number of documentary films, mostly shorts, though the location of film studios in Republican-held Madrid and Barcelona made the Nationalists heavily reliant on Berlin, Rome and Lisbon. For obvious political reasons, Republican films about the war have received considerably more attention than those produced on the Nationalist side. But cinema was one of the few aspects of modernity enthusiastically embraced by the Nationalists, as it was by Hitler and Mussolini, for its capacity to reach the masses. In this essay I will discuss three Nationalist films — one documentary and two features, all full length — depicting the Civil War. In each case the reading of the war is somewhat different. The first was made in Berlin during the Civil War; the second, in Rome one year after the war's end; the third, in Spain in the late 1940s. The first shows the Nationalists rampantly triumphant; the second shows them under siege but eventually liberated; the third shows them besieged and — despite its title *¡El Santuario no se rinde!* (*The Sanctuary Will Not Surrender!*) — defeated.

I shall pay particular attention to the ways in which all three films permit counter-readings that subvert the surface message. It must be remembered that Spanish cinema audiences during and after the Civil War were anything but homogenous. Despite the Nationalists' attempt to create a 'national cinema' as an instrument of national unification, the class, gender and regional affiliations that colour audience response were intensified by the various forms of repression to which a major part of the population was subjected. The first film discussed is a textbook illustration of how an image's meaning depends on what the director does with it and on who is viewing it. Its juxtaposition of Nationalist and Republican newsreel footage resemanticizes the latter for Nationalist ends, but for pro-Republican viewers this

Republican footage is likely to produce contrary identifications which, in a reverse process, contaminate the Nationalist narrative. The two feature films discussed also incorporate extraneous material, causing interpretive slippage. Both supplement their reconstructions of historical events (respectively, the 1936 siege of the Toledo Alcázar, and the 1936–37 siege of the Santuario de Nuestra Señora de la Cabeza in the Sierra Morena) with fictional narratives whose conventions belong to the romance genre. While the sentimental plots are resemanticized through their incorporation into a military narrative, the latter is also affected by the presence of the former. This interpenetration of masculine and feminine narratives is particularly interesting in ¡El Santuario no se rinde! where the feminine narrative predominates since, unusually for any 1940s Spanish film but exceptionally for a war film, events are narrated by a female voice-over.

Before analysing the representation of the war in these three films, it is necessary to set them in their contexts. The first, España heroica/Helden in Spanien (Heroic Spain, 1937), was made in Nazi Berlin by the Spanish-German film company Hispano Film Produktion, founded in 1937 by the head of Cifesa's distribution division in Cuba, Norberto Soliño, and the German Johann Ther, who provided the capital and technical resources. The aim was to make co-productions, in double Spanish and German versions, in the hope of breaking into the huge Spanish American film market (Gubern 1986: 73–77; Torres 1989: 156–58). Joaquín Reig's proposal for España heroica was submitted to the German Ministry of Propaganda, under Goebbels, who approved the project but gave it to two successive German directors, whose products displeased him. On the creation of Hispano Film Produktion, Goebbels passed the project to the company, with Reig as director, backed by a team of German technicians. Reig had been employed in Berlin since late 1936 to edit Spanish and German newsreels shot in the Nationalist zone. In this capacity, he was authorized by the German Ministry of Propaganda to view Republican news footage regularly intercepted by the German police at Berlin airport on its way to Moscow, and sometimes copied. Goebbels's role in commissioning the film must be borne in mind when considering its propaganda message. It was shown at the Nationalist headquarters in Burgos to a delegation of the International Non-Intervention Committee, whose resolve to maintain the arms embargo on the Republic was apparently influenced by it (Fernández Cuenca 1972: I, 467–68). It must also be remembered that the film was made at a time when Nationalist victory was not yet certain; it was not until April 1938 that they reached the Mediterranean coast, dividing the Republican zone in two. The film therefore needed to exaggerate Nationalist military prowess: Hopewell (1986: 23) notes the contrast between the dynamic editing used for the Nationalist assault on the Basque Country, and the long, drawn-out takes used for the Republican withdrawal.

Sin novedad en el Alcázar (All Quiet at the Alcázar, 1940; the reference to Lewis Milestone's 1930 Hollywood film of Erich Maria Remarque's novel All Quiet on the Western Front is intentional) belongs to the cycle of films set wholly or partly during the Civil War that were produced in the immediate postwar years. These fall into two phases: those made from 1939 to 1940 in the Cinecittà studios in Mussolini's

Rome, and those made from 1940 to 1942 in Spain. In October 1936, the Head of Nationalist Propaganda, Dionisio Ridruejo, visited the Italian Minister of Popular Culture to discuss creating a joint Spanish-Italian production company, finally founded in 1939 by Renato Bassoli (head of Italian Metro-Goldwyn-Mayer) and his brother Carlo, who since 1938 had produced films for the fascist cause. Only two of these Spanish-Italian co-productions depicted the Civil War. The first, *Frente de Madrid/Carmen fra i rossi* (*Madrid Front*, 1939), was by the Spanish director Edgar Neville, who had made three wartime documentaries for the Nationalists, including the 1939 short *¡Vivan los hombres libres!* which staged torture scenes in newly conquered Barcelona's supposed Republican *chekas* (Gubern and others 1995: 177). As mentioned in the previous chapter, the Francoist censors forced Neville to change the ending of *Frente de Madrid*, in which the Nationalist hero and a Republican militiaman die in a shell crater embracing each other (Gubern 1986: 78–80). The other co-production depicting the Civil War was *Sin novedad en el Alcázar/L'assedio dell'Alcazar* (1940), made with an all-Italian crew but a mixed Spanish-Italian cast, by the Italian director Augusto Genina, known as fascist Italy's 'war bard' (Hay 1987: 54–55, 185; Landy 1986: 149–52, 218–22). Shot shortly after Nationalist victory in Spain but at a time when Mussolini was under pressure from the Allied war effort, the film had different propaganda functions in Spain and Italy. To engage both national audiences, the role of Colonel Moscardó, the defender of the military academy housed in the Toledo Alcázar, under siege by Republican troops, was given to the Spanish actor Rafael Calvo, while the sentimental hero Captain Dávila was played by the Italian star Fosco Giachetti, known for his heroic military roles, notably in Genina's *Lo squadrone bianco* (*The White Squadron*, 1936) about the Italian army in Africa. The film won the Copa Mussolini at the 1940 Venice Film Festival despite the Italian censors' disquiet, in their report on the original script, that it showed no concern with 'recuperating and integrating' the enemy (Gubern 1986: 86). If Italian audiences were meant to read 'the enemy' as the Allies, 'recuperation and integration' were out of the question; for Spanish audiences, however, the 'enemy' was not allegorical and foreign but a tangible presence at home. The film's depiction of a fight to the last, which in Italy served as a plea for national unity, in Spain meant the opposite.

I have singled out *Sin novedad en el Alcázar* for analysis rather than any of the films about the Civil War made in Spanish studios from 1940 to 1942, since I have discussed several of those elsewhere (see Chapter 15). Only three of the films made in Spanish studios make the war their main focus: the notorious *Raza* (1941), directed by José Luis Sáenz de Heredia and scripted by General Franco under a pseudonym; *El crucero Baleares* (1940) made by the Mexican Nationalist spy, Enrique del Campo; and Carlos Arévalo's Falangist apologia *Rojo y negro* (Arévalo, 1942; discussed in Chapter 15). The last two, although approved by the censors, were banned: in the first case, on the orders of the Navy who had all copies of the film destroyed before release; in the second case, a few days after release in unclear circumstances. The remaining films — Juan de Orduña's *Porque te vi llorar* (1941; discussed in Chapter 15), Antonio Román's *Escuadrilla* (1941; also discussed in Chapter 15) and *Boda en el infierno* (1942) — use the war as a prop for a sentimental or melodramatic plot. The last of these, based on the novel *En un puerto seguro* by Rosa María Aranda, is an interesting example of the contamination of the war film by the female genre of melodrama, in this case written by a woman as well as for women. That this cycle of war films should end in 1942 is logical since, as Gubern has noted (1986: 103), from that date, sensing Allied victory in World War II, the Franco regime played down its fascistic, militaristic origins. A July 1942 article in the Falangist film magazine *Primer Plano* observed that the 'cine de Cruzada' ('Crusade cinema') ran the risk of degenerating into 'patriotería' ('empty patriotism'), but nevertheless rebutted suggestions that the subject of the war was a box-office loser and had been exhausted, and that such films were preventing the wounds of war from healing (Luján 1942).

The use of the Civil War as a historical setting resumed in 1947–51, in a series of films by directors whose links with the regime were ambivalent or tenuous. Lorenç Llobet-Gràcia's *Vida en sombras* (*A Life in Shadows*, 1947), which had to be re-written and re-edited several times to satisfy the censors (Gubern 1986: 109), provides a critical comment on the role of the war photographer, as the hero holds his obsession with filming the Barcelona barricades responsible for his wife's death from snipers' gunfire in his absence. The film ends with him relegating the memory of his wife's death to the past. As Gubern notes (1986: 113), the post-1945 shift of political influence from the military to the Church is charted in *Balarrasa* (*Daredevil*, 1950), by the disaffected Falangist José Antonio Nieves Conde whose *Surcos* the following year marked the beginning of neo-realist opposition cinema. The film's roué military hero reforms by becoming a missionary in Alaska, implying that the war is something one has to repent of and leave behind. The issue of returning exiles was tackled in two films. In the now lost *En un rincón de España* (*In a Corner of Spain*, 1948), by Jerónimo Mihura, who collaborated on several films with his humourist brother Miguel as well as contributing to Miguel's much-fined satirical magazine *La Codorniz* (founded 1941), a group of refugees bound for Marseilles fleeing Soviet-occupied Poland, including a Spaniard who had gone into exile, are shipwrecked on the Costa Brava; the exile decides to stay. A similar narrative of an exile who returns to Spain disillusioned with communism is found in Carlos Serrano de Osma's extraordinary *Rostro al mar* (*Face to the Sea*, 1951), by a director who had made shorts for the Communist Party during the Civil War (Sala Noguer 1993: 458, 463), not as a Communist Party member but thanks to friends who fixed him up with the work to protect him from persecution in Republican Madrid. The film focuses sympathetically on a communist who flees to France on the fall of Catalonia and on the plight of the heavily pregnant wife he is forced to abandon, who rejects her kind but unsexy Nationalist suitor for her communist husband when he finally returns to Spain. The message in both films is that it is safe for (repentant) Spanish exiles to return, but in the case of Serrano de Osma's film this entails rejection of the 'upright', sexually repressed Nationalist model of masculinity for the more human and desirable model embodied by the communist hero.

The only film of this period to take the Civil War as its central focus is *¡El Santuario* *no se rinde!* (1949), which I discuss here for that reason. Its director Arturo Ruiz-Castillo had worked as stage designer for Lorca's travelling theatre company under the Republic, La Barraca, and during the Civil War had made documentaries for the pro-communist production company Film Popular, the Alianza de Intelectuales Antifascistas, and the Republican Estado Mayor Central (Sala Noguer 1993: 129–31, 146–47, 170, 174, 179–80). Gubern (1986: 111–12) has seen *¡El Santuario no se rinde!* as 'una neta alegoría de la resistencia del franquismo ante el cerco político de las democracias occidentales, cuando tal reto beligerante no resultaba ya peligroso' ('a clear allegory of the Franco Regime's holding out under political siege by the Western democracies, at a moment when that bellicose challenge was no longer a threat'), noting that 1949 marked the beginnings of international recognition of the Franco regime. This reading does not explain why the film should end with Nationalist defeat. The film was made with the help of military assessors, using the same kinds of guns, tanks and planes as had been used during the siege, and actual grenades (Fernández Cuenca 1972: II, 551–52). It was given the top rating 'de interés nacional' ('In the National Interest'), which had been introduced in 1944 as an incentive to ideological conformism since it was rewarded with dubbing licences for remunerative foreign (effectively American) films; it also received the second prize of the Nationalist Sindicato del Espectáculo (Entertainment Trade Union; Falquina and Porto 1974). The critic José Luis Gómez Tello, reviewing the film (1949), found it strange that there had been no films about the Civil War in recent years, since there had been over three hundred literary works on the subject and Hollywood was now making a lot of films about World War II: this suggests that the return to the war in late 1940s Spanish cinema may have been triggered, at least in part, by the influx of imported war movies. Gómez Tello was not wholly smitten by Ruiz-Castillo's film: he found its military narrative an 'hermoso palmetazo a los nudillos de muchos olvidadizos' ('a magnificent rap on the knuckles for all those who have short memories') but its love plot unmemorable. This criticism, spotting the disturbance caused by the mixing of war film and romance, reminds us that the function of films about the Civil War in postwar Spain was to negotiate a difficult path between remembering and forgetting. Gubern is surely right to suggest (1986: 112) that the film provides a bridge between the earlier belligerent 'cine de Cruzada' (Crusade cinema) and the later mid-1950s topos of national reconciliation. Its narrator-heroine is not suffering from amnesia as Gubern claims (1986: 122); a leitmotif of her narration is the phrase 'Lo recuerdo bien' ('I remember it well.'). But she returns to the scenario of war to relive a love affair with a Republican who, for her sake, joined the Nationalist side: the romance plot permits a re-vision of the war in which old hostilities are laid aside. If *Sin novedad en el Alcázar* presented events in unmediated, dramatic form, as if happening in the present, the use throughout *¡El Santuario no se rinde!* of a voice-over recalling events from an unspecified date after the war's end makes it clear that the war belongs to the past; indeed, that it is dead and buried, like the siege's hero, Captain Cortés, whose tomb opens and closes the film. This voice-over needs to be female because it is the film's romance plot that recasts enmity as love. This involves admitting that the war, initiated by the Nationalists allegedly to end divisions, had only exacerbated them. All of these films of 1947–51 unearth the wounds of war in order to lay its ghost to rest.

Moving now to textual analysis, the first of the three films I will discuss in detail, *España heroica*, uses the classic documentary device of male voice-over. As a piece of war propaganda, it is anything but conciliatory; its message is the need for national unity in the sense of the fascist demand for a totalitarian state to counter the 'failure' of the multi-party system. Like *Raza* and *Rojo y negro*, the film satirizes politicians, filming them against Catalan or communist posters to associate them with separatism or foreign influence. Its voice-over has to be male because its function is to impose a single, godlike 'truth' that disallows any form of cultural difference. Throughout, this male voice-over is used to incorporate Spain's cultural 'Others' into a monolithic account of national history. The opening voice-over narrates how, through the ages, Spain has been the victim of the 'garras de expansion imperialista' ('claws of imperialist expansion') of a series of aggressors: Phoenicians, Greeks, Carthaginians, Romans, Goths and Arabs. The inclusion of Romans and Goths as 'aggressors' is interesting, given Italian and German military support for the Nationalists, plus the fact that the film was made in Germany. The voice-over swiftly recasts this historical dependence on outside cultural influences as Spain's colonization of 'the Other', claiming that 'la fuerza étnica del suelo espanol ha sido siempre tal que todos sus dominadores acabaron por ser absorbidos por ella' ('the ethnic potency of the Spanish earth has ensured that all its conquerors have ended up being absorbed by it'). The cultural difference of the film's opening frames of palm trees and Arab and Roman architecture is thus resemanticized as a vision of 'Spanishness', culminating in the image of the Escorial monastery. This allows the voice-over to describe the ensuing shots of Republican politicians as a 'lapse' into 'un mundo inmoral escindido por toda suerte de diferencias' ('an immoral world riven by all manner of differences') which are incompatible with the nation's 'psicologia étnica' ('ethnic mindset'). We then cut to Republican newsreel footage of crowds and lorries crammed with popular militias, with clenched fists and a significant presence of women, made ominous with suspense music. The incorporation of Republican footage mirrors the voice-over's imperialist rhetoric of the 'incorporation of the Other'.

Throughout, soundtrack and montage are used with considerable skill to appropriate Republican images for Nationalist ends. Reig has clearly learnt the art of the propaganda film from Eisenstein, in another appropriation of 'the Other'. The head-on shots of Nationalist warships advancing on Málaga, to music that gets faster and faster, is a virtual retake of *The Battleship Potemkin*. The depiction of Republican Madrid echoes Eisenstein's use of satirical effects, with comic chase music over scenes of street fighting, and shots of International Brigaders carousing to trombones simulating farting. The juxtaposition of images of dishevelled, unshaven Republican troops, crammed into lorries or moving chaotically, with images of impeccably uniformed Nationalists in military formation, equates the Republic with disorder and the Nationalists with efficiency and discipline. The many scenes of arms being handed out to the Republican crowds (including women) create the sense of an uncontrolled escalation of violence, reinforced by accelerating music. By contrast, the scenes of Nationalist troops and crowds (in which men and women are always shown in separate images) are set to crisp military marches. Throughout, a hysterical quality is given to the Republican images by the use of stridently repeated notes and rising crescendos. Other Republican images have no music but a 'real-life' soundtrack of crowd noises or soldiers' voices in battle: this creates a sense of disorganization, but also makes the Republicans seem human by comparison with the militarized Nationalists. The emphasis on Republican crowd scenes also makes it clear that the Republic enjoyed massive popular support.

Despite the voice-over's reference throughout to Nationalist troops as 'nuestros muchachos' ('our boys'), it is hard to imagine many working-class Spaniards, particularly women, identifying with the film's closing shots of a Nationalist mass rally, with its smartly uniformed, sexually segregated male and female blueshirts, and ladies with *mantillas*. This follows a sequence depicting Falangist voluntary work, which clearly establishes differentiated roles for men and women. Its opening shot of young male blueshirts with spades and picks is succeeded by a vast nursery with toddlers eating at tables set with white cloths and flowers, to the male voice-over: 'En el auxilio de invierno, con su extensa trama de beneficiencia social, encuentra la mujer española un campo de acción ideal para las maravillosas virtudes femeninas que la adornan' ('In Winter Aid [the original name, taken from the Nazi Winterhilfe, of what would after the war become Auxilio Social], with its extensive social welfare system, Spanish woman finds an ideal sphere of action for the splendid feminine virtues that embellish her'). That women's place is with the infants is implied by the order of the ensuing shots of figures marching in military formation: first female blueshirts, then male tiny tots, then young boys, then male youths. These images do, however, give Nationalist women a public role. It is thus necessary for the film to end with the male voice-over (seemingly a real-life recording) asserting supreme control as it harangues the Nationalist rally, finally giving way to the image of Franco arriving.

This visual equation of the Republicans with disorder and of the Nationalists with order creates the impression that the former caused the war. There is no mention of the Nationalist uprising. The war's start is narrated through a dramatic montage sequence in which the screen is split, with the outer images comprising a sequence of scenes of violence, and the central one alternating shots of seigneurial and religious buildings with banners of the anarcho-syndicalist organizations CNT (Confederación Nacional del Trabajo / National Labour Federation) and FAI (Federación Anarquista Ibérica / Iberian Anarchist Federation) and with footage of rifles being handed out to the crowds, the latter finally taking over the screen. This is followed by a series of superimpositions and dissolves of images of buildings (particularly churches) burning, with the flames getting progressively higher. Inserted into this sequence is newsreel footage, staged for a Nationalist cameraman and much used for propaganda purposes in the United States, of a supposed Republican firing squad 'shooting' the statue of Christ at the Cerro de los Ángeles (Gubern 1986: 13). Throughout, footage of buildings destroyed by the Nationalists is included in such a way that the Republic looks responsible. A sequence of shots of village streets riddled with bullet holes ends with the camera cutting to the graffiti 'Para la seguridad de vuestras casas ingresad en el PC' ('To ensure your homes' safety, join the Communist Party'): beyond the ironic demonstration of the ineffectiveness of communist protection lies the suggestion that the residents have made their homes legitimate targets of Nationalist aggression by labelling them as communist. We see 'la aviación republicana marxista' ('the Marxist Republican Air Force') flying in formation, punctuated by air raid sirens and people rushing for cover: the montage makes it look as if the air raid damage were caused by Republican bombing, when in fact the bombing of civilian targets was almost exclusively carried out by the Nationalists, chiefly by German or Italian fighter planes acting on their behalf. This tactic is particularly evident in the long sequence narrating the fall of the north to Nationalist troops. Oviedo is called 'la mártir' ('the martyr'), as if besieged by the Republicans who were in fact defending it against the Nationalists. The many shots of Basque and Asturian villages in flames, which can only be the result of attack by the advancing Nationalist troops, are attributed by the voice-over to 'la tea incendiaria de los republicanos' ('the torches of Republican incendiaries') or 'los dinamiteros del norte' ('the explosive experts of the north'; a reference to the Asturian miners whose 1934 insurrection had been put down savagely by General Franco).

The Basque country clearly presents a problem in the film, since its regionalist aspirations made it strongly Republican, but it was also, with Navarre, the traditional home of the Carlists who formed part of the Nationalist military alliance. The voice-over bends over backwards to distinguish 'el legítimo forismo vasco' ('the legitimate defence of Basque foral rights'; i.e. Carlism) from the illegitimate 'separatismo' ('separatism') of the Republic, which had passed the Basque autonomy statute (not the same thing as separatism) in October 1936. The tricky subject of Guernica, traditional symbol of Basque cultural identity, bombed by the German Condor Legion on 26 April 1937, is introduced by reference to the Basque Country's 'pintorescos pueblos' ('picturesque hamlets') whose music and folklore make it 'uno de los más ricos joyeros del tesoro espiritual de España' ('one of the richest treasures of Spain's spiritual heritage'). Again, the nation is constructed through the appropriation of 'the Other'. German documentary footage shot in Spain focused almost exclusively on the exploits of the Condor Legion (Fernández Cuenca 1972: I, 471; Álvarez Berciano and Sala Noguer in Torres 1989: 157); the bombing by German planes of a civilian target could not, however, be admitted in a film commissioned by the German Ministry of Propaganda. The voice-over acknowledges rumours 'en cierta prensa' ('in certain newspapers') that Nationalist bombing destroyed the town but, in keeping with Nationalist press accounts (Preston 1993: 245–47), places the blame for the destruction of Guernica squarely on 'Republican incendiaries', showing oil drums outside churches as 'proof'. At no point in the film is German or Italian military support for the Nationalists mentioned, despite its depiction of the conquest of Málaga, in which Italian troops played a leading role. By contrast, foreign aid to the Republic is exaggerated out of all proportion: besieged Madrid is made to look like a city under occupation by the International Brigades, with graffiti written in Russian; Republican weapons captured in Asturias are said to be 'de todos los calibres y procedencias' ('of all calibres and origins').

The concern with incorporating 'the Other' into the nation forces the film to focus on the defeated enemy, presented as the object of a programme of 'recuperation and integration' (what the censors found missing in *Sin novedad en el Alcázar*). The shots of refugee trails leaving Málaga and Bilbao are shown to complete silence, as if they were a disturbance in the film for which no adequate soundtrack could be found. With no voice-over or music to give a Nationalist slant to the images on screen, it is impossible not to be overwhelmed by pity. The lengthy footage of Asturian prisoners — first 'mujeres y niños en espera de ser internados' ('women and children awaiting internment'); then male prisoners 'llegados a campos de concentación para ser empleados en reconstruir todo lo que destruyeron' ('taken to concentration camps to work on the reconstruction of everything they destroyed') — is set to elegiac violin music. This temporarily changes to ominous chords as the camera closes on the internees' faces, then back to elegiac violins over the succeeding images of abject prisoners in a wood, a concentration camp with watchtower, and the interior of a jail, its upper and lower galleries crammed with prisoners. What this elegiac violin music is meant to signify to Nationalist viewers is not clear: maybe, given the film's later focus on Falangist social work, we are meant to be impressed with the Nationalists' 'humanitarian' concern to re-educate their enemies. In practice, we know that most of these prisoners were shot, just as we know that Nationalist planes bombed the refugee trails. With this knowledge, only one response to these images is possible. There is some solace to be drawn from the fact that the film is in the end unable to incorporate the defeated into its monolithic narrative of the nation.

If Reig appropriates Eisenstein's use of montage for Nationalist objectives, Genina (1940) explicitly stated that he made *Sin novedad en el Alcázar* to counter *The Battleship Potemkin*'s celebration of 'la revolución destructora' ('destructive revolution'). The shooting of the film's exterior scenes in the spectacular ruins of the Toledo Alcázar explicitly equates the besieging Republicans with destruction. The closing shot of Colonel Moscardó, the head of the military academy in the Alcázar who led its defence, saluting the Nationalist General Varela as he enters the ruins to lift the siege is like an apocalyptic scenario. However, Genina's film makes no use of Eisensteinian montage; the nearest we get to it is the cutting from one side in battle to the other which is the war film's equivalent of the shot/reverse shot basic to continuity editing. *Sin novedad en el Alcázar* is a straightforward realist narrative, aiming to create audience identification with the Nationalists.

The film's realism is designed to distract attention from its mythographic function. The credits, in acknowledging the 'help' of members of the military, including Moscardó's aide, allege historical veracity while making the film's propaganda purpose evident. The legendary telephone conversation between Moscardó and the Republican militia chief, in which the former allegedly refused to surrender the Alcázar in exchange for his son being spared execution, is filmed with an understated naturalness that belies its fictional status: Eric Southworth has established that phone links with the Alcázar were almost certainly cut at the time, and that Moscardó's son was shot a month later in Republican reprisals for a Nationalist aerial bombardment, not as part of an attempt to bargain with Moscardó (Southworth 1963: 49–63). The film also depicts the women and children in the besieged Alcázar as Nationalist supporters voluntarily seeking refuge, when in fact most of them were hostages taken by the Nationalists at the start of, and during, the siege (Southworth 1963: 56–60). As late as 1972, Carlos Fernández Cuenca (I: 474–45, 481) defended the film's historicity against Southworth's evidence, admitting however that there were only seven military cadets in the Alcázar, since the siege started during the summer vacation: the film's glorification of army heroics ignores the fact that almost all the Alcázar's one thousand defenders were Civil Guards and Falangists. The film omits the mythical comparison, made in 1940s school textbooks, between Moscardó's supposed sacrifice of his son and that of Guzman el Bueno defending Tarifa against the Moors in the thirteenth century, but it is full of Christ parallels, constructing the Nationalist cause as a 'Crusade'. On one occasion, as Leif Furhammer and Folke Isaksson note (1971: 48–51), the film works into its apparently realist narrative a quotation from William Dieterle's 1938 pro-Republican film, *Blockade*. Dieterle's film ends with its Republican officer hero (Henry Fonda) addressing the viewer: 'This war is not war but murder' (referring to the Nationalist blockade cutting off food from the civilian population). In Genina's film, when a Republican officer expresses doubts about the Republican plan to mine the Alcázar since there are women and children inside, a fellow officer replies in a verbatim translation of Henry Fonda's words, here turned against the Republicans: 'Esto no es una guerra, es un asesinato'. As Furhammer and Isaksson also note, Genina has a Nationalist officer appropriate La Pasionaria's rallying cry '¡No pasarán!', encouraging subliminal identification from politically recalcitrant viewers.

The film may not depict the 'recuperation and integration' of the enemy as part of its narrative, but its realist mode is itself an attempt at 'recuperation and integration' through the process of audience identification. For 'recuperation and integration' means the elimination of divergent viewpoints. The function of the romance plot, involving two of the female refugees in the Alcázar, Conchita and Carmen, is to secure identification at an emotional level regardless of the viewer's conscious political beliefs. Genina (1940) stressed the importance of the film's foregrounding of the women characters. The repeated close-ups of Conchita and Carmen are clearly intended to make the audience identify with their love for the male military heroes, Antonio and Captain Dávila respectively. But, as we shall see, this specular process, whereby viewers are invited to see the male heroes through female eyes, is problematic.

The realist depiction of the Nationalists contrasts with the satirical treatment of the Republicans, none of whom is singled out as an individual. Gubern (1986: 87) has suggested that the film's typically Nationalist Manicheism mimics the 'goodies versus baddies' format of the Western. In fact, the film constructs the Republicans, with their *cartucheras* (cartridge belts) and straw *sombreros* (broad-rimmed hats), much like Mexican bandits as depicted by Hollywood. They are treacherous liars: Antonio is shot by a Republican sniper in breach of a truce; the Republican radio broadcasts false reports of the Alcázar's surrender. The Republican militia chief who phones Moscardó to say he will shoot his son if he does not surrender sounds drunk; and throughout this scene we cut to shots of Republicans grossly eating and drinking beer. And the Republicans treat women like whores, taunting a Nationalist by mauling his wife at the facing window. Only one Republican is exempted: the envoy who asks to shake Moscardó's hand, whose function is to show that even a Republican admires Moscardó's courage. As in *España heroica*, the cutting back and forth between the Nationalists and the Republicans constructs the latter as unruly and dishevelled, by contrast with the Nationalists who are impeccably uniformed, disciplined and courteous to women — which is another way of saying that they are stiff and repressed.

The film's opening sequence, in which Moscardó addresses the cadets, organizes the human figures in typically fascist geometric lines crossing the screen at a diagonal, filmed from above to create a sense of vertical hierarchy. In one shot, the diagonal lines of men are intersected by their shadows at right angles, reducing them to a dehumanized abstract pattern in which the individual dissolves in the hierarchically organized mass. As discussed in Chapter 10, Klaus Theweleit (1987–89) has analysed the ways in which Nazi writing sublimates a fear of loss of ego boundaries, expressed as a fear of intimacy with women, by subordinating the self to military forms of organization — typically, the mass parade — that permit dissolution of the self within tightly controlled, all-male parameters. The film's romantic plot highlights the characters' difficulties in expressing their emotions. Here the love story intermeshes with the heroic refusal of emotion of Moscardó's telephone exchange with his son. In an interview, Rafael Calvo, who played Moscardó, said he wanted to convey his 'hombría' ('manliness'): 'Lo he visto como hombre que ha sabido disciplinar perfectamente sus gestos, sin que por ello tenga encadenados sus sentimientos' ('I saw him as a man who has learnt how to discipline his gestures perfectly, without that meaning that his feelings are suppressed'; Luján 1940). In practice, the discipline and not the sentiment comes over. By contrast, the soft-focus lighting in the close-ups of the two romantic heroines emphasizes emotion. Nevertheless, the narrative denies them and their male lovers the possibility of communicating their feelings to each other. Indeed, we rarely see the couples together; the camera cuts from Conchita talking to Carmen about her love for Antonio, or from Carmen confessing to Conchita her attraction to Captain Dávila, to shots of the male under discussion and back again, emphasizing their physical distance. On one occasion the camera moves back and forth between Carmen looking at Dávila and Dávila looking at Carmen as they move separately through the crowd, to the national anthem over, as if the latter were a sublimation of their personal emotion. Conchita and Antonio are married *in articulo mortis*: death makes 'consummation' of their relationship permissible. The one attempt at amorous dialogue, as Dávila finally declares his love to Carmen, is excruciating. It takes place after they have accompanied Conchita at Antonio's bedside, as if his dying gave them permission to express their feelings. Even during this brief love scene, Carmen calls the hero by his surname; there is no physical contact. The one exception to this Nationalist emotional repression is Carmen's 'dissolute' former boyfriend Pedro, who has danced with her and kissed her, and freely talks to her about it. He is 'reformed' by his experience in the Alcázar — too late, because Carmen's encounter with Dávila has introduced her to a 'superior' model of masculinity. As Pedro dies wounded, he tells Dávila to marry Carmen, 'redeeming' himself through renunciation.

However, the film does not end with Carmen and Dávila's union — they are not even seen together in the film's closing sequences — but with the embrace of two men: Moscardó and General Varela. For the film is about the need to sacrifice the personal to the political. Women are clearly a problem here, as they are in most war films. The main source of disturbance is Carmen, initially depicted as a spoilt city girl always looking at herself in the mirror. Like Pedro, she too is re-educated through her experience in the Alcázar. When she asks Dávila if he can find her a private space, he tells her she will have to throw her lot in with everyone else, additionally taking away her bed since it will be needed by the wounded. She falls in love with him because of his superior ethos based on the renunciation of private pleasure for the public good, subsequently apologizing to him for her selfishness and offering her services as a nurse. However, it seems that only men can wholly sacrifice the personal to the political. For women, renunciation remains at the personal level of romance: sacrificing oneself for a man. On learning that Carmen has become a nurse, Conchita says that proves that she has fallen in love 'de veras' ('for real'). Carmen replies that it is the same for all women: 'es un hombre que nos gusta y nada más' ('it's a man we're attracted to and that's it'). For Carmen is clearly serving the Nationalist cause to win Dávila's attentions; relatively late in the film, she still prefers to use her water ration to wash her face rather than drink it. The woman is expected to transcend the personal but at the same time is regarded as incapable of doing so. It is only after Antonio's death that Conchita too becomes a nurse, as if her love for him previously involved her completely in the personal. The scene where Carmen and Dávila are shown moving towards each other, without meeting, as the national anthem is sung makes it clear that the 'noblest' relationships are those in which the personal is sublimated through service to the nation. Significantly, he is singing but she is not. The end of the film leaves the romance plot behind to concentrate on Moscardó, the male hero who, in sacrificing his son, proved himself able to subordinate the personal to the political in a way that neither Carmen nor Conchita are able to do. Female viewers, invited to identify with Carmen and Conchita, may have found their preference for the personal more human than Moscardó's stifling of emotion. Indeed, the repeated close-ups of Carmen and Conchita may have encouraged male spectators too to identify with the feminine values of romance at the expense of masculine military discipline.

¡El Santuario no se rinde! also leaves its romance plot behind at the end, but the effects are different. The film is striking for its lack of resolution. Its hero, Luis

Aracil, blurs political oppositions. A Republican lawyer under surveillance by the Civil Guard for his political activities, he is played by Alfredo Mayo, the Spanish equivalent of Fosco Giachetti known for his roles as military hero in various 1940s films, including *Raza*. At the war's start, he stops the peasants from breaking into the heroine Marisa's ancestral home in Jaén, later rescuing her after Republican militias have abducted her marquis father. Wounded while helping Marisa to safety, she gets him to the Nationalist refuge in the local religious shrine (the Santuario de Nuestra Señora de la Cabeza, in the Sierra Morena), where he receives medical treatment. His gratitude to Marisa, plus admiration for the heroism of the besieged Nationalists led by the local Civil Guard commander, Captain Cortés, make him convert to the Nationalist side. The film ends with the Republicans taking the Sanctuary, but we do not know if Luis is alive or dead. He was last seen wounded in the trenches. We are shown the thirty-eight surviving male defenders of the Sanctuary, wounded and bandaged, being led off across country by the victorious Republicans, but even with repeated viewings it is impossible to identify Luis among them. (Twenty-two of the surviving defenders were played by real-life survivors of the siege, wearing identical clothes and bandages to those they had worn at the time [Fernández Cuenca 1972: II, 551–52].) Nor do we see Marisa as the Republicans enter the Sanctuary. We cut from this episode in April 1937 to a map of Madrid and assorted war scenes, with Marisa's female voice-over rapidly summing up the rest of the war. The film closes with the famous words of the last Nationalist war communiqué — 'Los Nacionales han alcanzado el último objetivo. La guerra ha terminado' ('The Nationalists have achieved their ultimate objective. The war is over.') — superimposed as an intertitle over shots of Nationalist flags flying, intercut with the image of Captain Cortés's tomb shown at the start. We know nothing of Marisa's life after the war.

Writing about the film, Gubern (1986: 112) says that Marisa and Luis (whom he wrongly describes as one of the besieging Republicans) 'sellarán su unión en la posguerra, en el escenario de la vieja fortaleza' ('will seal their union after the war, on the site of the former fortress'), but this is not depicted. All we have is an oblique suggestion of a possible reunion in the film's opening narrative frame. In this, we see Marisa picking some cistus blossom, to her voice-over: 'el tiempo había borrado las huellas de la guerra, pero yo sentía nostalgia de otras horas de miseria y de miedo [...]. Algo que no sabía explicarme me atraía fuertemente' ('time had erased the traces of the war, but I felt nostalgia for other times of hardship and fear [...]. I was powerfully attracted by something I couldn't explain to myself'). This implies that the postwar period has brought disillusionment. The camera travels with Marisa through the gates to Captain Cortés's tomb, as her voice-over recalls a 'mañana de primavera' ('spring morning') that changed her life for ever. We then cut from the flowers in her hand to an identical but dead bunch of flowers on the tomb, which her voice-over says could have been put there by only one person. She picks the flowers up and joins them with those in her hand. Although the conventions of romance make us assume that this 'one person' is a man, we have to wait until quite late in the film for the key to this enigma. The 'mañana de primavera' must be the April morning when the final Republican assault began, interrupting an idyllic sequence in which Luis picks some cistus blossom and gives it to Marisa. The opening narrative frame of Marisa visiting Cortés's tomb in the postwar period makes us expect to return at the film's end to the same present moment from which the story is narrated, but this closure is denied. And the flowers on the tomb are dead: they may represent hope of a future union with Luis, but they may also represent a love that, like the past, is dead. This opening symbolic scene suggests that love between a man and a woman who belonged to different sides in the war cannot, in the postwar period, be expressed directly but has to be mediated through, and sanctioned by, the tomb of a Civil Guard commander.

This, perhaps, is the source of Marisa's nostalgia. For during the war, she and Luis were able to express their love, despite belonging to opposing sides. The wartime period is shown to have been characterized by a tolerance that, after Nationalist victory, would not be permitted. This tolerance is both personal and political. The depiction of the love relationships differs notably from that in *Sin novedad en el Alcázar*. Marisa and the other female lead, Marcela, work as nurses not to get a man but to make themselves useful. Indeed, it is through working as a nurse that Marcela becomes involved with the medical student acting as surgeon, not the other way around. We see them embrace and kiss passionately, albeit briefly, and, even if he waits until she is off screen to say 'Pase lo que pase... te quiero, dios mío' ('No matter what happens... I swear to God I love you'), it is the man who voices his love rather than the woman. Marcela is not a conventional romantic heroine but is efficient, cool, and in control; she becomes the spokesperson for the civilian refugees in the Sanctuary, voicing their decision not to leave the soldiers to their fate. Her refusal to play the traditional female role is shown by her wish to be a pilot: 'debe ser bonito volar, a mí me gustaría morir allí arriba, como mueren los aviadores' ('it must be beautiful to fly, I'd like to die an aviator's death up in the sky'). Her conversations with Marisa are never about their love relationships but always about the siege. Marisa and Luis are also shown embracing and kissing, with no apparent inhibitions about physical contact. This occurs in the scene when Luis considers crossing enemy lines to re-join the Republicans, but turns back out of love for Marisa. Here, it is the man whose political commitment is motivated by love. In this film, the genres of romance and war film are mixed in order to assert the superior 'feminine' values of love, values most explicitly articulated by the two heroines' male lovers. The use throughout of Marisa's female voice-over means that what we have is not the insertion of a romance plot into a war film, as in *Sin novedad en el Alcázar*, but the insertion of a war film into a romantic narrative.

We do twice get Captain Cortés's voice-over reading out the letters he is writing. But, on one occasion, his military orders are articulated by Marisa's female voice-over. Her final summing-up of the war's progress makes her responsible for a military narrative. When we first see Marisa in the past, after the opening postwar narrative frame, she is wearing jodhpurs and talking vivaciously to her father about how her fiancé and cousin Fernando cannot live without her. Her father, an aristocrat but far from a patriarchal authority figure, replies benevolently: 'Eres de una independencia salvaje' ('You're ferociously independent'). We have to assume that Marisa dragged or carried the wounded Luis to safety in the Sanctuary, since he seemed to be unconscious; she is as active in saving his life as he is in saving hers. When they first meet, they are both on horseback, putting them on a par. Throughout Marisa is offered cigarettes by Luis and Captain Cortés, as if this were entirely normal; once, she initiates the request. When her voice-over says, referring to Luis, 'sabía que sus sentimientos eran los míos' ('I knew he felt the same as me'), this is not just a sentimental line but the expression of a relationship where the man and the woman treat each other as equals. The comic Andalusian *gracioso* figure, Curro, greets the news that only forty men are left in the Sanctuary with two hundred women with the exclamation '¿tú te imaginas nada más horrible?' ('can you imagine anything worse?'); but he goes on to say that 'his type of woman' is Marlene Dietrich, noted for being cool and in command.

The mutual respect shown by men and women towards each other is echoed by the mutual respect between political enemies. Throughout, Luis and Captain Cortés, as Republican lawyer and Civil Guard commander, treat each other as equals. Cortés expresses his understanding of Luis's Republican beliefs, saying: 'Yo también tengo un concepto de lo social, de lo justo y de lo injusto, del poder, y de la religión, y aquí mando yo [...]. Es una pena que no mande Vd allá abajo [en la zona republicana]' ('I too have a sense of the social, of justice and injustice, of power, and of religion, and I'm the one in charge here [...]. It's a shame you aren't in charge down there [in the Republican zone]'). Whatever one feels about the Civil Guard's concept of justice, what matters here is that a Civil Guard commander expresses respect for the ideas of others. When Luis asks to be imprisoned since he cannot fire on his fellow Republicans, Cortés refuses, offering his hand: 'Sentiría que no estuviéramos juntos al final [...] no somos enemigos' ('I'd be sorry if we weren't together at the end [...] we aren't enemies'). Luis takes his hand, replying, 'No, no podemos serlo' ('No, we can't be'). Captain Cortés tells Marisa that, if he were Luis, he would defect to the Republicans; he does nothing to stop him from doing so, but leaves him to decide for himself. When Luis brings news that the Nationalist troops are abandoning the Sanctuary to its fate, he says to Cortés (referring to the decision to fight on): 'Yo pienso como Vd' ('I think the same as you'), in a line echoing Marisa's declaration of emotional reciprocity.

The Republican militias do break a truce but they are never made grotesque. Indeed, the two caricaturesque characters — Curro and a fat, moustachioed Civil Guard — are Nationalists, in this case for pathos since we see them both shot. The International Brigaders who take the Sanctuary express their admiration for the survivors ('Bloody hell!', 'C'est incroyable'). When an International Brigader raises his gun to shoot the wounded Captain Cortés, a Spanish Republican soldier stops him, saying: 'A ése no, es español, tú no entiendes de eso' ('No, not him, he's Spanish, that's something you don't understand'). This shows Spaniards fighting for the Republic to be decent, as well as showing that the International Brigades are under their orders, and not the other way around as *España heroica* had implied. Cortés dies melodramatically, uttering the single word 'España' as his hand scrapes the plaque commemorating the Civil Guard's foundation in 1844, inscribed with the motto 'La Guardia Civil muere, pero no se rinde' ('The Civil Guard may die, but it never surrenders'). Before the Nationalist uprising, we see him refuse to obey the Republican Provincial Governor, but we see ordinary Civil Guards hesitate as to where their allegiance lies.

The Church's role in the film is surprisingly low profile, given that the Nationalists are holding out at a religious shrine and that the late 1940s was the peak period of Church influence, with a vogue for religious films. The two monks glimpsed have minimal roles, one playing the organ, the other (aged and ineffectual-looking) speaking only when celebrating Midnight Mass and when praying to the Virgin as the women and children gather in the chapel during the final attack. On this last occasion, it is Marcela who leads the singing to drown out the sound of gunfire. This 'duel' between a hymn to the Virgin, led by a woman, and the sounds of war is a contest between feminine and masculine values. The latter win out, as the gunfire eventually engulfs the singing, but this is presented as a tragedy.

At the gala première of ¡El Santuario no se rinde! on 15 December 1949, attended by the Director General of the Civil Guard, Ruiz-Castillo said that his film was a replay of 'la grandeza y el sacrificio de los habitantes de Numancia como demostración de la permanencia del espíritu españolista' ('the greatness and sacrifice of the inhabitants of Numantia [who committed collective suicide rather than surrender to the Romans] as a demonstration of the permanence of the Spanish patriotic spirit'), marked by 'el profundo sentido fatalista ante la muerte, que tiene tanto de vocación heroica cuanto de elevación mística' ('a profoundly fatalistic attitude to death, which is as much a heroic vocation as a mystical exaltation'; Fernández Cuenca 1972: II, 549). Despite this conventional Nationalist rhetoric and the official acclaim awarded the film, it can be read as the expression of nostalgia for a time before Nationalist victory when women and men and political opponents treated each other as equals, and there was no difficulty in reconciling war and romance. Made in wartime, España heroica has no place for feminine values except inasmuch as they can be mobilized for the war effort: military values reign triumphant. Sin novedad en el Alcázar, filmed in wartime Italy and in a still intensely militarized postwar Spain where men were starting to return to family life, has some trouble reconciling the military requirement to sacrifice the personal with its romance plot's feminine assertion of the primacy of emotion. This is perhaps not unrelated to the fact that it shows the Nationalist military temporarily under siege: the film's end, with Moscardó's and General Varela's all-male embrace, represents both Nationalist military triumph and the triumph of masculine values. If, in ¡El Santuario no se rinde!, the Nationalists are shown not only besieged but defeated, it is perhaps because the experience of the 1940s had shown the bankruptcy of militaristic values that had no place for love. The political importance of the move from the male voice-over of España heroica to the female voice-over of Ruiz-Castillo's film goes far beyond questions of gender.

Works Cited

ARÉVALO, CARLOS (dir.). 1942. Rojo y negro (Cepicsa)
DEL CAMPO, ENRIQUE (dir.). 1940. El crucero Baleares (Radio Films Española)

FERNÁNDEZ CUENCA, CARLOS. 1972. *La guerra de España y el cine*, 2 vols (Madrid: Editora Nacional)

FURHAMMER, LEIF, and FOLKE ISAKSSON. 1981. *Politics and Film* (London: Studio Vista)

GENINA, AUGUSTO (dir.). 1936. *Lo squadrone bianco* (Roma Film)

—— (dir.). 1940. *Sin novedad en el Alcázar* (Film Bassoli / Ulargui Films)

——. 1940. 'Por qué he realizado *Sin novedad en el Alcázar*', *Primer Plano*, 3 (3 November): n.pag.

GÓMEZ TELLO, [JOSÉ LUIS]. 1949. Untitled review of *¡El Santuario no se rinde!*, *Primer Plano*, 480 (25 December): n.pag.

GUBERN, ROMÁN. 1977. *'Raza': Un ensueño del general Franco* (Madrid: Ediciones 99)

——. 1986. *1936–1939: La guerra de España en la pantalla* (Madrid: Filmoteca Española)

GUBERN, ROMAN, and OTHERS. 1995. *Historia del cine español* (Madrid: Cátedra)

HAY, JAMES. 1987. *Popular Film Culture in Fascist Italy: The Passing of the Rex* (Bloomington: Indiana University Press)

HOPEWELL, JOHN. 1986. *Out of the Past: Spanish Cinema after Franco* (London: British Film Institute)

LANDY, MARCIA. 1986. *Fascism in Film: The Italian Commercial Cinema, 1931–1943* (Princeton, NJ: Princeton University Press)

LLOBET-GRÀCIA, LORENÇ (dir.). 1947. *Vida en sombras* (Castilla Films)

LUJÁN, ADOLFO. 1940. 'El héroe y su "doble"' (interview with Rafael Calvo), *Primer Plano*, 2 (27 October): n.pag.

——. 1942. 'Presencia de la Cruzada en el nuevo cine español', *Primer Plano*, 92 (19 July): n.pag.

MIHURA, JERÓNIMO (dir.). 1948. *En un rincón de España* (Emisora Films)

NEVILLE, EDGAR (dir.). 1939. *¡Vivan los hombres libres!* (Departamento Nacional de Cinematografía)

—— (dir.). 1939. *Frente de Madrid* (Film Bassoli)

NIEVES CONDE, JOSÉ ANTONIO (dir.). 1950. *Balarrasa* (Aspa Producciones Cinematográficas)

—— (dir.). *Surcos* (Atenea Films)

ORDUÑA, JUAN DE (dir.). 1941. *Porque te vi llorar* (Producciones Orduña Films)

PINGREE, GEOFFREY B. 1995. 'Franco and the Filmmakers: Critical Myths, Transparent Realities', *Film-Historia*, 5: 183–200

PRESTON, PAUL. 1993. *Franco: A Biography* (London: Harper Collins)

REIG, JOAQUÍN (dir.). *España heroica* (Hispano Film Produktion)

ROMÁN, ANTONIO (dir.). 1941. *Escuadrilla* (Productores Asociados)

—— (dir.). 1942. *Boda en el infierno* (Hércules Films)

RUIZ-CASTILLO, ARTURO (dir.). 1949. *¡El Santuario no se rinde!* (Centro Films / Terramar Films / Valencia Films)

SÁENZ DE HEREDIA, JOSÉ LUIS (dir.). 1941. *Raza* (Cancillería del Consejo de la Hispanidad)

SALA NOGUER, RAMÓN. 1993. *El cine en la España republicana durante la guerra civil* (Bilbao: Mensajero)

SERRANO DE OSMA, CARLOS (dir.). 1951. *Rostro al mar* (Titán Films)

SOUTHWORTH, HERBERT RUTLEDGE. 1963. *El mito de la Cruzada de Franco* (Paris: Ruedo Ibérico)

THEWELEIT, KLAUS. 1978, 1979. *Male Fantasies*, trans. by Stephen Conway, Erica Carter and Christ Turner, 2 vols (Cambridge: Polity Press)

TORRES, AUGUSTO M. (ed.). 1989. *Cine español (1896–1988)* (Madrid: Ministerio de Cultura/ ICAA)

CHAPTER 17

Musical Battles:
Populism and Hegemony in the
Early Francoist Folkloric Film Musical

This article will analyse the Spanish cinematic genre of the folkloric film musical, which enjoyed massive popularity with lower-class and especially female audiences in the early Franco period, through Gramsci's key concepts of the 'national-popular' and 'hegemony'. The genre has generally been dismissed by Spanish film directors and critics, reflecting the unfortunate tendency in Spanish film criticism to scorn popular cinema. The proliferation of folkloric film musicals in the 1940s and early 1950s has encouraged perceptions of it as mindless escapism serving the early Francoist political project. Of the two books on the subject, Pineda Novo (1991) consists in trivializing anecdote about its hugely popular female stars; while Moix (1993) lays the ground for a contestatory reading by reclaiming the genre for gay spectators. I should like here to develop the possibilities for a different contestatory reading — without forgetting the genre's obviously conservative plot structures — on the assumption that the popular and especially female audiences who enjoyed these films were not simply duped by them but found in them resonances that struck a chord with their own life-experiences, needs or aspirations. Gramsci's theories have formed the basis of British cultural studies, as developed by Raymond Williams and the Birmingham Centre for Contemporary Cultural Studies, because — unlike Adorno's and Horkheimer's tendency to view popular culture as the culture industries' manipulation of the masses — they credit popular audiences with discrimination and the ability to resemanticize the cultural products they consume for their own ends.[1] One of the unfortunate cultural consequences of Francoism is that it encouraged opposition critics to adopt an orthodox Marxist position that viewed popular culture as little more than ideological manipulation — a view which at the time was excusable given state censorship and control of the media (though one must remember that the film industry remained in private hands). Curiously, the acknowledged debt of the Spanish opposition cinema that developed in the 1950s to Italian neo-realism, itself based on Gramsci's theories of

---

1   A good outline of the development of cultural studies as a discipline is given by During (1993: 1–25).

the 'national-popular', did not lead to the assimilation of Gramsci's unorthodox Marxist analysis of culture, which to this day remains largely ignored by critics of Spanish culture.[2]

There are, in fact, many reasons why Gramsci's theories should be applied to Spanish culture. First, Gramsci was analysing another Mediterranean culture (Italy), marked by the dominant influence of popular and official Catholicism, and by a north–south divide. Coming from underdeveloped Sardinia, Gramsci was keenly aware of the divorce between the state and the mass of the southern Italian peasantry, whose incorporation into the nation he regarded as a political priority. Here Gramsci was rejecting what he called bourgeois 'voluntarism', that is, the co-option of select individuals moulded in the image of their 'superiors' — a cultural strategy that has typified Spanish liberalism, Ortega y Gasset's emphasis on the need to create 'select minorities' being the clearest example. Instead, Gramsci sought to empower the peasantry through an inter-active process of cultural alliances and contestation: what he famously termed 'hegemony'. It is important to remember that, for Gramsci, hegemony was not so much a negative description of the way the dominant classes used culture to manipulate the people as a political theory designed to enable the Italian Communist Party, of which Gramsci was leader when arrested in 1926, to secure a mass political voice. For, even when hegemony is exercised by the traditional ruling classes, the need to negotiate consent by cultural means leaves a space for subaltern groups. It is also important to remember that Gramsci's concept of hegemony insists on culture as a plural site of struggle between competing constituencies, which are internally heterogeneous and fragmented, and which relate to each other through a double process of collusion and contestation. Indeed, Gramsci notes that collusion can be a strategy for survival: subversion and subordination overlap. There is no place in this cultural map for binary oppositions.[3]

Gramsci's theories are particularly salutary when dealing with early Francoism, whose Manichaean rhetoric has tended to fool critics into supposing that the period was one of relatively straightforward opposition between victors and vanquished. This is what Gramsci suggestively calls a 'melodramatic' representation of history, according to which the oppressors simply impose their rule on the oppressed, constituted as passive victims. In her book *Film, Politics, and Gramsci*, Marcia Landy (1994: 32) notes that this melodramatic conception of history characterized fascism. Despite its rhetoric of exclusions, fascism was as concerned with incorporating the people into the nation as was Gramsci. Indeed, Gramsci developed his notion of the 'national-popular' as a cultural strategy for securing hegemony through his analysis of Italian fascism during his years in prison under Mussolini from

2   Addition to original article: Gramsci's political theories were introduced into Spain by Manuel Sacristán in the 1960s but seem not to have influenced opposition views on culture, which remained largely indebted to Lukács. See Sacristán 1983 for his 1967 study of Gramsci, plus his 1970 anthology of Gramsci's writings, published in Mexico thanks to the Francoist censorship.
3   My account of Gramsci's theories is taken from Forgacs and Nowell-Smith's anthology of his cultural writings (1985), and from Landy (1994) who is particularly helpful in showing the relevance of Gramsci's writings for the analysis of cinema (specifically Italian cinema under Mussolini).

1926 to 1937. Gramsci's theories are thus directly relevant for an analysis of early Francoism. Spanish fascism had always been ideologically closer to Mussolini than to Hitler, and the fact that Francoism was an alliance of disparate extreme-right forces, of which the Spanish fascist party Falange Española was one, confirms Gramsci's insistence that even power blocs which present themselves as monolithic are a precarious amalgam of competing groups. A significant feature of Gramsci's writings is his understanding of the ideological strength of fascism because, contrary to the bourgeois capitalist exclusion of the masses and particularly of the rural populace which had no place in the capitalist scheme, fascism sought to construct an all-inclusive national culture based on an organic concept of 'the popular'.

The repressive effects of early Francoism — which like the Italian fascist state sought to manufacture consent through the manipulation of popular culture, especially cinema — must not, however, be underestimated. As Landy notes, the fascist concept of the 'national-popular' is a hegemonic tool for incorporating the nation's diverse constituencies into a monolithic state; it is an 'organic' concept because it aims to subsume difference into wholeness. Whereas the Gramscian notion of the 'national-popular' is concerned with incorporating the masses through a hegemonic process that allows the expression of cultural differences. But no matter how 'melodramatic' the fascist conception of history, in practice fascist populism sought to manufacture consent by dramatizing, in its cultural products, complex bargaining processes between dominant and subaltern groups, in which collusion and contestation coexist or blur. The romance plots of the early Francoist folkloric film musical (*folklórica*) are just such an example of manufactured consent, with the lower-class gypsy heroine who figures the people surrendering to the higher-class male protagonist (usually a landowner) only after using her seductive powers to secure his capitulation to her cultural values

Gramsci is especially relevant to study of the *folklórica* because of the centrality in his writings of folklore. Gramsci rejects the prevailing 'picturesque' concept of folklore, produced by intellectuals who view the peasantry as 'foreign' and who frequently are themselves foreigners.[4] Instead he argues for an 'organic' concept of folklore whereby the intellectual allies himself with the peasantry by identifying with their way of looking at the world. The fact that the heroines of the early Francoist *folklórica* are overwhelmingly 'other-race', usually gypsy, on the one hand perpetuates the picturesque idea of the 'pueblo' as foreign; but the point of the plot is to assimilate her, in return for her higher-class suitor assimilating, and being enriched by, her values; indeed, in several films, the higher-class suitor has been educated abroad, constructing *him* as foreign.[5]

Gramsci notes that, while folklore — in this sense of the peasant worldview — is largely opposed to officialdom, it incorporates elements from official culture,

4   Hobsbawm (1990: 103–04) notes that the folkloric 'rediscovery' of 'the people' that typified the rise of European nationalism from the late eighteenth century through the nineteenth century was largely 'the work of enthusiasts from the (foreign) ruling class or élite'.
5   For a more detailed analysis of the racial dynamics of the *folklórica* than can be given here, see Labanyi 1997 and 1999, and particularly Woods Peiró 2012, published after the original version of this essay.

including cultural relics from the past. Indeed, as he acutely observes, it is 'a repertory of clichés' (1991: 378) bordering on pastiche. The lower-class heroine of the early Francoist *folklórica* is, without exception, a performer, who expresses herself by mimicking a mixture of popular and high cultural forms. This is both because the popular cultural traditions represented are already hybrid mixes of high and low (as well as mixes of traditional rural culture and modern urban mass culture), and also because the bargaining process that secures her final marriage to the landowner involves her mimicking his habits and speech. However, it also involves her higher-class suitor, despite the fact that he is not a performer and is acted in a 'straight' if not wooden acting style, to an extent mimicking the cultural signs of *her* class. The populist use of folklore in the early Francoist *folklórica*, despite some ethnographic touches, makes relatively few gestures to the 'purist' concept of folklore cultivated by 1920s' avant-garde artists like Falla and Lorca and by 1950s Francoist intellectuals, for, in opting for the modern mass-cultural medium of film as a tool for manufacturing national consensus, early Francoism is accepting a concept of the 'national-popular' marked by hybridity and by modernity.[6] The genre thus echoes Gramsci's insistence that popular culture is always touched by official culture and by historical change. Indeed, the lower-class heroines frequently triumph in the modern city (in Spain and abroad) as performers. The resourcefulness of the genre's lower-class female protagonists, and even of the caricaturesque work-shy gypsy males, supports Gramsci's view that folklore contains 'various strata: the fossilized ones which reflect conditions of past life and are therefore conservative and reactionary, and those which consist of a series of innovations often creative and progressive [...] which are in contradiction to or simply different from the morality of the governing strata' (1985: 190). Above all, the *folklórica*'s use of hybrid forms of popular song and dance as the subaltern's strategy for seducing the dominant classes, in a double process of collusion and subversion, illustrates Gramsci's view that all forms of popular song, whether or not composed by or for the people, are 'adopted' by the people 'because they conform to their way of thinking and feeling' (1985: 194) and thus serve as a strategy for survival. Gramsci also notes that popular songs are commonly recycled for different purposes (1985: 352); this recycling is a characteristic of the *folklórica* genre, with many films of the early Franco period being built around a song that had enjoyed previous popularity, often under the Republic, thus carrying over considerable cultural ambivalence.

The romance plot of the *folklórica* is an attempt to secure, with the final marriage, the fascist dream of a society transcending capitalist class conflict, which differs from the egalitarian socialist dream of Gramsci (or indeed of the Spanish Republic which first promoted the *folklórica* as a 'national-popular' genre) in its vertical ordering: higher-class male marries lower-class female. Nevertheless, in the process, class relations are shown to be complex, inter-active bargaining processes between different cultural groups that are internally heterogeneous and contradictory. In an article drawing parallels between Gramsci's notion of hegemony and Bakhtin's

6   For a critique of the primitivist co-option of flamenco for the purposes of high culture by Lorca and Falla, and by 1950s intellectuals, see Mitchell 1994: 160–77.

notion of heteroglossia, Craig Brandist (1996: 103) notes that Bakhtin outlines two hegemonic principles whereby discourses seek to bind other discourses to themselves 'either by establishing a relation of authority between the enclosing and target [i.e. subaltern] discourses or by facilitating the further advancement of the target [i.e. subaltern] discourse *through* the enclosing discourse'. In principle, the former ('establishing a relation of authority between enclosing and subaltern discourse') corresponds to the populist project of the early Francoist *folklórica* and the latter ('facilitating the further advancement of the subaltern discourse *through* the enclosing discourse') to Gramsci's Marxist political project. In practice, the *folklórica* blurs the difference between Bakhtin's two categories, since the lower-class heroine's surrender to the embrace or 'enclosing authority' of the higher-class male protagonist takes the form of her seduction of him and of the spectator.

For Bakhtin, like Gramsci a linguistics scholar, hegemony is effected via the negotiation process that he termed 'dialogism' or 'heteroglossia'; that is, a contest of voices. In a large number of *folklóricas*, the romance plot takes the form of a contest between popular music (personified by the heroine, usually a gypsy flamenco singer) and either some form of classical music (associated with the male protagonist) or else nineteenth-century operetta or modern cabaret, represented as urban, bourgeois and foreign-influenced (sometimes personified by the male suitor but more often by a treacherous female rival). There is space here only to outline these musical battles but it should become clear that the transactions involved are complex and by no means a knock-out competition between cultural opposites. What emerges is a view of culture that, far from being monolithic, is inter-active and dynamic. By representing relations between popular and bourgeois musical forms as a contest — which necessarily involves contestation — the *folklórica* genre provides a self-reflexive comment on early Francoist populism as an attempt to secure hegemony through a process of cultural negotiation. In a 1997 paper, John Kraniauskas described the Peronist populist promotion of Evita as lower-class movie star as a case of 'the state meets the culture industry'; the same could be said of the populist project enacted in the early Francoist folkloric musical.

This contestation process is particularly well illustrated by a key sequence from *Estrella de Sierra Morena* (*Estrella of the Sierra Morena*; Ramón Torrado, 1952) which runs through a gamut of flamenco performance styles. The sequence starts with a spectacularly choreographed formal display of eighteenth-century-style classical flamenco, performed by a dance ensemble at the Provincial Governor's ball, where Lola Flores (brought up by bandits and not knowing she is his daughter) is impersonating his niece as a ploy to get her bandit adoptive father freed from jail; in the process she falls for an army officer in the Provincial Governor's entourage. Bored by this aestheticized high-cultural entertainment and incapable of the piano-playing expected of a bourgeois lady, Lola first performs a mildly saucy song, typical of music hall's assimilation of flamenco into its repertoire. In the course of her rendition of the song, we see her wink at a comic bandit disguised as a bourgeois, showing that her performance is a strategy of collusion for subversive ends; indeed, she weaves her clandestine message to him — 'meet me in the garden' — into the lyrics. At the end of the sequence, she bursts into an openly defiant performance of popular flamenco dance (*bulerías*) whose provocative physicality leaves the assembled bourgeois guests shell-shocked. The bourgeois ladies present — whose crass stereotyping constitutes a send-up of bourgeois taste — comment in horror that her unrestrained dancing style shows she had been educated abroad. The stock comedy here conceals a serious critique of bourgeois culture's dismissal of popular culture, which the ladies regard as 'foreign'. Lola Flores's flamboyant, seductive performance ensures that audience identifications are entirely on the side of popular culture, as they are in another of her films, made with the same director the previous year, *La niña de la venta* (*The Girl at the Inn*; Torrado, 1951). Here Lola dances 'spontaneously' at the tavern of her *padrino* (adoptive father), contrasting with the suave, modern cabaret singer Raquel, billed as 'La Venus de Tánger' ('The Venus of Tangiers'), hired to distract the police chief from the locals' smuggling operations. Predictably Raquel turns out to be a spy. She is Lola's rival in song as well as love; the local audience is un-enthused by her cool jazz-inspired crooning which constructs them as passive audience, unlike Lola's folkloric singing and dancing which fires them all to join in: popular music constructs community. There is a third musical scenario in the film: the gypsy camp, whose inhabitants are filmed almost ethnographically as a 'native tribe'. This serves to construct Lola as a musical hybrid: 'spontaneous' by comparison with the cabaret singer but a performer by comparison with the 'raw' dancers at the gypsy camp. Like most *folklóricas*, this film promotes flamenco as a source of national-popular identifications not so much in the sense of a return to natural, rural origins as in that of popular culture as performance. While this could be viewed as an Orientalist reduction of the lower classes to spectacle, it can also be seen as a demonstration of how performance can be used by the subaltern as a strategy for their own ends: the innkeeper and Lola put on a performance to put the police off the scent; Lola gets her higher-class man by performing a stunning drum routine on oil cans outside his window.

In *El sueño de Andalucía* (*The Dream of Andalusia*; Luis Lucia, 1950), the star Carmen Sevilla is similarly pitted against a treacherous female rival in the form of a Viennese operetta star, who performs to an entourage of ballet dancers dressed in tutus and hussars' uniforms, the pretentiousness of which is exposed by a comic chase scene, reminiscent of musical-hall bawdy, when the Andalusian *gracioso*, dressed in female costume to evade pursuit by a jealous Mexican, gets mixed up with the performers on stage, finally triumphing with a flamenco *zapateado*. Andalusian song and dance are in this film promoted as a source of national-popular identifications, not because they are 'natural' by contrast with the tackiness of Viennese operetta, but because they are *more* polished and glitzy: Carmen Sevilla's hairdo and toothpaste-advert smile are straight out of Hollywood; the male singing lead Luis Mariano was a star of French operetta. The self-reflexivity of this film — typical of its director Luis Lucia — is notable, with its outer narrative frame converting the drama into a 'film within the film'. The film opens with Luis Mariano playing himself as acting star in his Paris theatre dressing room, signing the contract for *El sueño de Andalucía* and starting to read the script, which slips into voice-over as the start of the film proper appears on screen. At the narrative's climactic moment, we cut to the actors in the Paris film studio; on finishing filming, they decide to go off to Andalusia to see 'the real thing' and we follow them touring Seville, ending in the film-set version of the city used in the main narrative. The effect is to construct Spanish popular culture — figured by an exotic Andalusia staged explicitly for the benefit of foreigners — as performance. Indeed, the resolute lack of realism of the folkloric musical genre as a whole can be seen as promoting an almost postmodern notion of the performance of everyday life, with everyone assuming roles for different tactical ends.

In *Gloria Mairena* (Lucia, 1952), Juanita Reina plays an internationally successful performance artist, who performs polished versions of Andalusian song to her husband's classical guitar accompaniment. When she dies, he becomes a priest and music teacher in the school attached to Seville Cathedral where he had been a choirboy, bringing up their daughter (also played by Juanita Reina) in an all-male environment where she is forbidden to sing. However, the unconscious memory of her mother's singing asserts itself in Gloria Junior and she triumphs as a singer, winning the love of a successful pianist who, having failed as a classical musician, has turned to the mambo; the Carmen Miranda look-alike who performs with him is the treacherous rival in this film. Juanita Reina is left cold by the mambo, and converts him to 'Spanish song' by getting him to perform with her the song her father had written for her mother to the music of Granados's fifth *Danza Española*. The film ends with the couple triumphing worldwide, after a rapid cut to the seminarist previously in love with Gloria sublimating human passion by conducting a choir of turbaned little boys as a missionary overseas. This colonial scenario throws another kind of music into this film's particularly complex contest of musical styles, whose function is to raise popular Andalusian song to high-art status. The fact that Gloria 'cannot help singing' despite the paternal prohibition does not so much construct Andalusian song as natural as construct her as a 'born performer'; the pull of maternal origins is the pull of performance.

In *Canelita en rama* (Eduardo García Maroto, 1942) Juanita Reina plays a somewhat similar role as a gypsy girl (whose nickname gives the film its title), who has lost her mother and who is educated to be a lady by the landowner who has been tricked by her gypsy family into thinking he is her father. Again, she 'can't help singing' because it is in the blood. However, here the rural setting of her father's Andalusian estate is filmed with ethnographic precision, constructing her song as tied to the land. She sings mostly in the open air, though on the first occasion she says she'd like the pony-trap to have a radio but, since it hasn't, *she* will be the radio; later we hear her singing along to jazz music on the radio or record-player: 'natural song' is linked with modern means of mass reproduction. The film is an indictment of the upper classes' dismissal of popular song as in bad taste; Juanita Reina's singing wins everyone over, including the landowner's Oxford-educated son, to the extent that he starts taking guitar and singing lessons from her stereotypically work-shy male gypsy relatives. Here we have a double carnivalesque reversal, as the work-shy gypsies mimic the lifestyle of the *señorito*, reclining in armchairs, smoking cigars, and commenting that as gentlemen they wouldn't dream of working, while he mimics their musical prowess, provoking the nicely subversive comment from one of the gypsies speaking in thickest 'andalú': 'hombre, que no, que me destroza el castellano' ('no, that's not how to do it, you're ruining the Castilian language'). What is important in this carnivalesque scene is that lower and upper classes are both engaged in a process of cultural negotiation; the *señorito* may have the land and he gets Juanita Reina (only after his conversion to flamenco, which she lays down as a condition), but the film shows that she and her trickster relatives are able to use the stereotypes associated with popular culture to considerable advantage.[7]

Carnival features explicitly in *Bambú* (José Luis Sáenz de Heredia, 1945), set in Cuba during the independence struggle.[8] The film's protagonist, a failed Spanish avant-garde composer, finds musical regeneration through his love for a Cuban mulatto singer Bambú, whose song, proclaiming the fruit she sells, constructs her as the nourishment provided by the colonies to a decadent bourgeois Europe. In this capacity, she is contrasted on the one hand with the Pay-Pay cabaret where the singers prostitute themselves for money, and on the other with the composer's initial Spanish upper-class fiancée who wants him only for the prestige expected of him as a classical composer. One of Bambú's musical appearances is with the Afro-Cuban carnival singers who 'invade' the Governor's palace singing 'El Gobernador no permitió el carnaval' ('The Governor banned the carnival') in a tolerated ritual of subversion, which recurs in the final syncretic musical masterpiece — choreographed and filmed like a Busby Berkeley fantasia — which the male protagonist composes in his head as he dies in a *Liebestod* with Bambú, both shot by the rebel Cuban troops. No matter how seductive Bambú's singing, the only kind of subversion permitted here is, it seems, that which colludes — as she does — with Spain's colonial presence: the function of Afro-Caribbean music is to enrich the Western classical musical tradition. Bambú is, of course, played by a Spanish star (Imperio Argentina, who was actually half-English) and the film's wonderful musical score is by Ernesto Halffter, the principal composer of the 1927 Generation who developed Falla's syncretic brand of cultural nationalism.

A similar plot occurs in *Serenata española* (*Spanish Serenade*; Juan de Orduña, 1974), a fictionalized biopic of the classical composer Albéniz based on the play by Eduardo Marquina, which has the composer derive his inspiration from his love for a gypsy singer (Juanita Reina), conveniently murdered by a jealous gypsy suitor so that Albéniz can go on to triumph unencumbered by her presence. This entirely spurious plot allows Albéniz to be rescued from his multinational musical formation (and from his Jewish origins, never mentioned), by giving him an indigenous source of inspiration. Juanita Reina's musical and amorous rival is a foreign classical

---

7   González-Medina (1997), in an otherwise excellent analysis, sees the film as a mouthpiece of Francoist populist ideology, failing to appreciate the complexity of the bargaining processes dramatized in it.

8   Sáenz de Heredia, a cousin of the founder of the Spanish fascist party José Antonio Primo de Rivera, had in 1941 been chosen to direct the Nationalist panegyric *Raza*, scripted under a pseudonym by Franco. At the same time that he was making *Raza*, Sáenz de Heredia was writing the lyrics for Celia Gámez's musical revues: an indication of the cultural complexity — particularly in terms of the relations between high and low culture — of the early Franco regime.

singer. In another syncretic musical fantasia, Albéniz imagines Juanita Reina performing a balletic version of flamenco against a theatre backcloth depicting the Giralda, an iconic representation of Andalusianness. Here the balance between ballet and flamenco is on the side of the latter, albeit staged. By contrast, flamenco metamorphoses completely into ballet in the climactic moment of *Lola la piconera* (*Lola the Coal Girl*; Lucia, 1951), again with Juanita Reina, set in Cadiz during the Spanish War of Independence against Napoleonic occupation. In this sequence, the performance-artist heroine (a product of urban mass culture, since she runs a *colmado* or cabaret) and her French officer lover first watch the highly choreographed but raw dancing of some gypsy nomads, which then slips into their 'dream' of a world where national enmities can be overcome by love; that is, where cultural heterogeneity can be turned into homogeneity. At this point, the costumes and choreography become balletic, with non-diegetic choir and orchestra taking over from the previous diegetic guitars and drums, climaxing in a spectacular musical fantasia set against tropical plants and exotic backcloth. In this film too, Juanita Reina dies, showing the utopian dream of syncretic fusion to be a mere fantasy; the narrative dramatizes, not the achievement of fusion, but the tensions and conflicts that occur along the way. The film is based on a play by José María Pemán, head of the early Francoist Comisión Depuradora which purged Republican teachers and cultural workers. The film's patriotic exaltation of flamenco as a popular cultural form associated with 'spontaneous' female emotion (the heroine dies a martyr to the Spanish cause) betrays Pemán's anti-intellectual stance, but the film's elevation of popular song and dance to high art also betrays his association with official culture: the credits bill him as 'D. José María Pemán de la Real Academia Española' (he was in fact the President of the Spanish Royal Academy).

In the last film I wish to discuss, *Torbellino* (*Whirlwind*; Luis Marquina, 1941), the contest between popular and classical music is weighted in the opposite direction. Estrellita Castro plays a humble girl from Seville who dreams of being a radio star: we see her singing to a parrot perch functioning as makeshift microphone, foregrounding the mimicry involved in the hegemonic process of cultural negotiation and contestation. In a complicated intrigue where collusion and subversion blur, she impersonates the niece of the dour director of a Madrid radio station, which is floundering thanks to his insistence on broadcasting gloomy classical music. He hates 'la alegría' (gaiety) and 'lo populachero' (vulgarity), despite his involvement in the modern mass media: his luxury flat combines an art-deco mural of a gigantic radio transmitter with a portrait of Beethoven. The plot revolves around a competition between radio stations, figuring hegemony as a struggle between competing cultural claims. Estrellita Castro saves the day for her supposed uncle (converting him to 'lo andaluz' as well as winning his hand) by exposing the treacherous defection to a rival radio station of the Italian opera *diva* he had contracted, and by fixing the controls so her own performance of Andalusian song goes out on the air for the competition — winning, of course — instead of the programmed classical broadcast. A particularly interesting sequence occurs midway through the film, as Estrellita Castro breaks into the radio station at night to enact her fantasy of being a radio star. As she manipulates the radio controls, her fantasy image as singing star (also played by Estrellita Castro) materializes and performs before her eyes, separated from her by the glass window of the control room. This sequence is interesting on several counts. First, because it throws into relief the film's self-reflexivity as a film about the radio; that is, the culture industry commenting on itself. Secondly, because in this fantasy sequence the mass media invest her popular 'andalucismo' with an aura of glamour, as she appears with ball gown and full orchestra, dramatizing the hybridization process resulting from the meeting of popular and mass culture.[9] Here the song is popular while the orchestration is classical: in a telling shot, Estrellita Castro as fantasized radio star is filmed with the orchestra's harp — a visual icon denoting classical music — in the foreground. Popular culture is here subsumed into high culture, in a populist move typical of early Francoism; but this process allows the underclasses (Estrellita Castro as 'little poor girl') considerable scope for agency: she takes the plot entirely into her hands, manipulating and outwitting everyone as a popular trickster figure (hence her nickname 'Whirlwind'). Thirdly, this sequence is significant because it illustrates the 'double-voiced discourse' which Bakhtin opposed to 'the verbal and semantic dictatorship of a monologic, unified style' (Brandist 1996: 103). We see Estrellita Castro reacting as stage-manager and spectator to the spectacle of her persona as performer: her two incarnations as 'little poor girl' and radio star alternate on screen in classic shot/reverse-shot mode, constructing them as in dialogue with one another. The sequence ends with a travelling shot going a full 180°, as the camera sweeps from Estrellita Castro in the control room to her fantasy persona performing before her eyes in the studio. It is important that a travelling shot and not a dissolve is used here: the two class personae do not merge but form a continuum in which they retain separate identities. Indeed, the precariousness of this populist fantasy of cross-class alliance is immediately exposed as the controls start to smoke and then blow a fuse, bringing the fantasy to an abrupt end. Estrellita may at the end of the film win the hand of the radio station's owner, but she does so on her terms: his conversion to popular culture is also figured as his conversion from misogyny to an appreciation of the feminine. The romance 'happy end' of marriage is one in which the partners will clearly continue to bargain and negotiate (we see them still arguing), and in which the woman — representing popular culture — will be the driving force.

The films I have discussed share fascism's melodramatic vision of history with their sudden reversals, ethos of sacrifice, and virtue recognized whether in marriage or death (there are no other options). But their attempt to create a national-popular imaginary through their dramatization of contests between competing musical forms is anything but Manichaean or monologic. In all of them popular song is privileged, but the alignment with the varied repertoire of other musical forms is different in each case. What is common to all these films, as musicals about musical contests, is their self-conscious dramatization of the hegemonic process. It is commonly said that early Francoism did not have a coherent cultural project. I would reformulate

---

9   Rowe and Schelling (1991: 8) note that, when the culture industry coincides with the nation-formation process, as it has in countries where modernization occurred late, the former takes on some of the 'aura' of high culture.

this to argue that early Francoism had a sophisticated understanding of hegemony, precisely because it appreciated that this involves complex, shifting negotiations between heterogeneous cultural forms.

Works Cited

BRANDIST, CRAIG. 1996. 'Gramsci, Bakhtin and the Semiotics of Hegemony', *New Left Review*, 216: 94–109

DURING, SIMON (ed.). 1993. *The Cultural Studies Reader* (London: Routledge)

GARCÍA MAROTO, EDUARDO (dir.). 1942. *Canelita en rama* (Rafa Films)

GONZÁLEZ-MEDINA, JOSÉ LUIS. 1997. 'E. G. Maroto's *Canelita en rama* (1943): The Politics of Carnival, Fascism and National(ist) Vertebration in a Postwar Spanish Film', *Journal of Iberian and Latin American Studies*, 3: 15–29

GRAMSCI, ANTONIO. 1970. *Antología*, ed. and trans. by Manuel Sacristán (Mexico: Siglo XXI)

——. 1991. *Selections from Cultural Writings*, ed. and trans. by David Forgacs and Geoffrey Nowell-Smith (Cambridge, MA: Harvard University Press)

HOBSBAWM, E. J. 1990. *Nations and Nationalism since 1780: Programme, Myth, Reality* (Cambridge: Cambridge University Press)

KRANIAUSKAS, JOHN. 1997. '*El fiord*: The State and Literary Form', paper to LASA conference, Guadalajara, Mexico (April 17–19)

LABANYI, JO. 1997. 'Race, Gender and Disavowal in Spanish Cinema of the Early Franco Period: The Missionary Film and the Folkloric Musical', *Screen*, 38: 215–31

——. 2000. 'Miscegenation, Nation Formation and Cross-Racial Identifications in the Early Francoist Folkloric Musical', in *Hybridity and its Discontents: Politics, Science, Culture*, ed. by Avtar Brah and Annie F. Coombes (London: Routledge), pp. 56–71

LANDY, MARCIA. 1994. *Film, Politics, and Gramsci* (Minneapolis: University of Minnesota Press)

LUCIA, LUIS (dir.). 1950. *El sueño de Andalucía* (Compagnie Commerciale Française Cinematographique / CEA)

——(dir.). 1951. *Lola la piconera* (Cifesa)

——(dir.). 1952. *Gloria Mairena* (Producciones Reina)

MARQUINA, LUIS (dir.). 1941. *Torbellino* (Cifesa)

MITCHELL, TIMOTHY. 1994. *Flamenco Deep Song* (New Haven, CT: Yale University Press)

MOIX, TERENCI. 1993. *Suspiros de España: La copla y el cine de nuestro recuerdo* (Barcelona: Plaza & Janés)

ORDUÑA, JUAN DE (dir.). 1947. *Serenata española* (Colonial AJE)

PINEDA NOVO, DANIEL. 1991. *Las folklóricas y el cine* (Huelva: Festival de Cine Iberoamericano)

ROWE, WILLIAM, and VIVIAN SCHELLING. 1991. *Memory and Modernity: Popular Culture in Latin America* (London: Verso)

SACRISTÁN, MANUEL. 1983. 'La formación del marxismo en Gramsci', in *Sobre Marx y marxismo* (Barcelona: Icaria), pp. 62–84 (first published in 1967)

SÁENZ DE HEREDIA, JOSÉ LUIS (dir.). 1941. *Raza* (Cancillería del Consejo de la Hispanidad)

—— (dir.). 1945. *Bambú* (Suevia Films)

TORRADO, RAMÓN (dir.). 1951. *La niña de la venta* (Suevia Films)

——(dir.). 1952. *Estrella de Sierra Morena* (Suevia Films)

WOODS PEIRÓ, EVA. 2012. *White Gypsies: Race and Stardom in Spanish Musicals* (Minneapolis: University of Minnesota Press)

CHAPTER 18

Love and Colonial Ambivalence in Spanish Africanist Cinema of the Early Franco Dictatorship

This chapter examines two Spanish colonial films set in Spanish Morocco and Spanish Sahara respectively: *¡Harka!* (Carlos Arévalo, 1941) and *La llamada de África* (*The Call of Africa*; César Fernández Ardavín, 1952). Any discussion of these films has to ask how these two films were able, at a time of strict censorship under the Franco dictatorship of 1939–75, to offer a positive depiction of unorthodox same-sex and mixed-race love relationships — in both cases triangulated by a love for Arab culture on the part of the Spanish male protagonists. It is also necessary to ask why both films, while explicitly exalting the Spanish colonial enterprise in North and North-West Africa, give a negative representation of a white woman, newly arrived from Spain, who attempts to break up these unorthodox relationships. To answer these questions — insofar as they can be answered — requires an understanding of Spanish fascist ideology and of the specificity of Spanish colonial discourse. It also involves asking how these films relate to a longstanding European tradition that equates Europeanness with forms of love that transcend the body and find their highest realization in death: a Christian paradigm which in these films is expressed in terms of military values.

Given the high degree of ambivalence shown in both films towards Arab culture — subjected to colonial control yet passionately loved — my discussion will draw on the postcolonial critic Homi Bhabha's (1994) work on the conflictive nature of the colonizer's attitude to the colonized. Bhabha's analysis of colonial mimicry will be set against the somewhat different concept of colonial mimesis elaborated by the anthropologist Michael Taussig (1993). The complex relation between sameness and alterity is central to both films, not only in terms of the colonial relationship between Spaniards and Arabs, but also in terms of gender: both replace heterosexual reproduction with a process of same-sex reproduction whereby males reproduce themselves in other men. Above all, both films offer a model of colonial relations as love: a love that is sincerely felt but is able to further empire because it is based on structures of domination and the surrender of self to a higher cause. In this respect, the chapter will further draw on Klaus Theweleit's (1989) psychoanalytical discussion of the psychology of Nazi 'soldier males', as well as on film scholar

Richard Dyer's (1997) examination of the relation of whiteness to embodiment — the notion that the body is inhabited by a spirit that is separate from it — and to death. The unorthodox love relationships in both films have to be terminated through death because, while furthering empire, they also threaten it. What makes the colonial enterprise possible is impossible love.

Spanish-Arab Relations and Spanish Colonial Film Production

In a 1936 interview, given in the year he launched his military occupation of Republican Spain from Spanish Morocco, General Franco declared: 'Without Africa, I can scarcely explain myself to myself' (cited in Rein 1999: 197). Franco's meteoric military career had been made in the Spanish Protectorate of Morocco, where he served for most of the period 1912–26 (from 1923 as Commander of the Spanish Foreign Legion), coinciding with the violent colonial war of 1909–27.[1] It was as Commander of the Army of Africa — comprising the Foreign Legion and the Regular Indigenous Forces (units of local mercenaries commanded by a Spanish officer, known in Morocco as *harkas*) — that he announced the July 1936 military rebellion. Although the ensuing Civil War of 1936–39 was seen by the Nationalist insurgents as a Christian crusade, they relied on around 70,000 Moroccan mercenaries — a contradiction Franco smoothed over by stressing the common cause of Christian and Muslim believers against atheism (Madariaga 2002: 345–64). In the immediate postwar, Franco made a point of appearing in public escorted by his mounted 'Moorish Guard'. This colonialist stance went together with a policy, during the Civil War, of Arabizing education in the protectorate, building mosques and supporting Muslim festivals (including contracting a ship for the annual pilgrimage to Mecca), and favouring Moroccan nationalists (Elena 2004: 19–21; Madariaga 2002: 347–56, 360–61). Once installed in power, Franco courted Arab support to relieve ostracism by the Western democratic nations, while at home enforcing an aggressive National Catholicism which demonized Spain's medieval Islamic past (Aidi 2006: 72–74; Rein 1999).

This ambivalent attitude towards Arab culture is reflected in cinematic production of the early Franco dictatorship. It should be clarified that, unlike fascist Italy and Germany, the Spanish film industry remained in private hands, though subject to stringent state censorship. The Moroccan War of 1909–27 triggered an appetite in the mainland for documentary reportage, especially after Abd el-Krim's victory at Annual in 1921, which left over 8000 Spanish troops dead. Morocco's importance in the Spanish Civil War would revive this documentary production, most notably with the Flaherty-influenced ethnographic film *Romancero marroquí* / *Der Stern von Tetuan* (*Moroccan Ballad*; Domínguez Rodiño and Velo, 1939), edited in Nazi Germany and aimed at maintaining Moroccan recruitment for Franco's

1   In addition to its long-standing control of the urban enclaves of Melilla and Ceuta (held since 1497 and 1580 respectively), Spain had had a colonial presence in Morocco since the 1859–60 'African War'. In 1912, the Berlin Conference divided Morocco between France and Spain. In 1956, both Spain and France ceded independence to their Moroccan territories.

rebel army (Elena 2004; 2010: 26–31, 45–49). The peak period of documentary production on the Spanish Protectorate of Morocco was 1946–51, coinciding with a similar boom in French documentary films on its North African possessions, and with the United Nations' boycott of Franco's Spain, which led Franco to increase his efforts to procure Arab support (Elena 2001: 120–22). The period 1938–52 saw the parallel and related production of fiction films set in Spain's African possessions (Spanish Morocco, Spanish Sahara, and Equatorial Guinea).

The first of the two fiction films discussed in this essay — Arévalo's ¡Harka!, filmed mostly in Spain's Moroccan protectorate — was accused of 'stealing' ethnographic footage from *Romancero marroquí*. While this is not true (Elena 2004: 65), certain scenes do have an ethnographic 'look': the panning of the Moroccan mercenaries making tea in their encampment; the Arab market, with untranslated dialogue in Arabic, as Moroccan mercenaries try to procure new *harka* recruits; and the tour of Tetuán, capital of Spanish Morocco, that Arévalo offers spectators as the camera follows the Spanish officer Carlos (Luis Peña) as he courts the newly arrived Amparo (Luchy Soto). This last sequence is notable for its use of montage, with the couple's image superimposed on scenes of Arab life in Tetuán's streets in a way that stresses the mediation of their relationship by Arab culture, while at the same time depicting them as ghostly presences hovering over the Arab city. As Elena notes (2010: 103), Arévalo's prior directing experience had been in documentary film. Unused ethnographic footage from the second film examined here — Fernández Ardavín's *La llamada de África*, shot entirely in the Protectorate of Spanish Sahara — was used by the director for his 1953 documentary short *Con los hombres azules* (*With the Blue Men*), a reference to the blue veils worn by male Tuaregs (the nomadic Berber inhabitants of Spanish Sahara).[2] The ethnographic sequences of *La llamada de África* — which follow the nomadic camel trains, and depict a Tuareg festival with its oral storyteller, snake-charmer, kohl-painted female dancers, and javelin-throwing contest — are dramatic, enhanced by the film's repeated use of dialogue in untranslated Hassaniya (the local dialect of Arabic).

Several Spanish fiction films set in an Arab or Berber context involve a love interest between a Spanish male and an indigenous female. One film, the Spanish-German coproduction *La canción de Aixa / Hinter Haremsgittern* (*Aixa's Song*; Rey, 1939), depicts the love triangle comprised by a mixed-race female (with Spanish father and Arab mother) and two Arab males (both princes and cousins). *La canción de Aixa* is exceptional not only in focusing on a half-white female's marriage to an indigenous male, but also in allowing its mixed-race romance a happy ending, achieved by having the heroine renounce a wayward cosmopolitanism (she is a cabaret singer in Tetuán) for Islamic female submission. On the surface an Orientalist musical fantasia, the film is a parable about the need for Spanish women to abandon the emancipation granted by the Republic and return to patriarchy (spectators are

---

2   Spain first established a protectorate in the coastal strip of Western Sahara, south of Morocco, in 1884, subsequently expanded and its boundaries defined as 'Spanish Sahara' in 1924. In 1975, shortly before Franco's death, as independence was about to be granted, Spanish Sahara was annexed by Morocco.

aware that the actors are Spanish, especially in the case of the female lead, Imperio Argentina, Spain's biggest-grossing star of the time). What is extraordinary about this film is that it was made in Nazi Berlin by the Spanish-German production company Hispano Film Produktion, created in 1937 with Goebbels's approval. Its Moroccan setting no doubt fed both Spanish and German dreams of colonial expansion in North Africa: the following year (1940) Spain would occupy Tangiers (an international zone since 1923) and Franco attempted to negotiate with Hitler significant expansion in North-West Africa and the Gulf of Guinea, unsuccessfully since Hitler had African designs of his own (Goda 1999; Martin-Márquez 2008: 250–51). But, curiously, the film's mixed-race plot, in which a half-white woman's love is won by an Arab who rejects Western civilization (thereby proving superior to his decadent, Westernized cousin), supports the fascist rejection of a degenerate capitalist modernity at the expense of flouting Nazi racial policies.[3]

Susan Martin-Márquez has noted that Spanish foreign policy influences several romantic film narratives of the early Franco period that have African settings (2008: 224). ¡Harka!, set in contemporary Spanish Morocco, was made just six months after Spain's occupation of Tangiers in June 1940, on the fall of Paris to the Nazis (Martin-Márquez 2008: 250). Shot with assistance from the Spanish colonial authorities and regular indigenous forces, the film dramatizes the central trope used to underscore Francoist claims to Morocco: that of a Spanish-Moroccan blood brotherhood — as explicitly stated by the film's opening title. For the rest of 1940, Franco attempted to negotiate with Hitler the annexation by Spain of part or all of French Morocco (Goda 1999). The subtext of ¡Harka! is justification of an expanded Spanish role in Africa. The plot dramatizes the intense bond between two officers in the Army of Africa, triangulated by their mutual love of Arab culture. Like the documentary Romancero marroquí, it shows the Spanish military's reliance on Arab foot soldiers. And like La canción de Aixa, it rejects a decadent Western modernity, in this case — even more extraordinarily — for an Arab culture that sanctions love between men. The action of La llamada de África, although made in 1952, also starts in June 1940, coinciding not only with France's fall to Germany but also with the start of World War II's North African Campaign, though this did not reach North-West Africa until two years later. In late 1940, Franco's Foreign Minister offered to enter World War II on Germany's side in return for multiple territorial concessions in Africa, including an extension of Spanish Sahara southwards into French territory (Goda 1999: 74). Thwarted by Hitler's own expansionist claims in the area and as the war turned in the Allies' favour, Franco switched to courting US support and — alarmed by the claim Hitler had made on one of the Canary Islands during their 1940 failed negotiations — in 1944 granted the US military use of Spanish Saharan coastal installations, including Cape Yubi where the airstrip in La llamada de África

---

3   Imperio Argentina was invited to Berlin on a contract with Hispano Film Produktion partly because she was one of Hitler's favourite stars, although this has been somewhat mythologized (he granted her a private audience). An additional curiosity is that, in the first film she made in Berlin, Carmen, la de Triana (Carmen from Triana; Rey, 1938), she played the gypsy Carmen, again flouting Nazi racial policies. For discussion of both films, see Labanyi 1997; for La canción de Aixa, see Martin-Márquez 2008: 234–49.

is located (Goda 1999: 176–77; Martin-Márquez 2008: 251, 253–55). The film's adventure plot hinges on the attempt by unspecified 'Nordic' gangsters operating from the French colony of Mauritania to the east and south (at the time under the collaborationist Vichy Government) to sabotage the airstrip which is being built to allow Spanish military protection of communications with the nearby Canary Islands.[4] The intertwined romance plot depicts the love relationship between a Lawrence of Arabia figure — a mixed-race but white-skinned officer in the nomadic police (the camel-riding equivalent of Spanish Morocco's *harkas*) who has 'gone native' — and a Tuareg princess who will, after the film's end, have his child. In April 1952, a month before the film's première, Franco's Foreign Ambassador had toured the Middle East, extolling the common blood, culture and destiny shared by Spain and the Arab world, and offering Franco as an ally against a socialist Israel (Rein 1999: 206–09; Aidi 2006: 72–73).

¡*Harka!* was generally well received by critics and audiences, though some critics found the plot development unconvincing (Elena 1997: 134). While there are conflicting reports of audience response to *La llamada de África*, it played for 43 days at Madrid's central Cine Callao — the third longest-running film of the year (Elena 2010: 113; Martin-Márquez 2008: 252–53). It was criticized by reviewers for lack of clarity in its exposition but — after lobbying by Luis Riera Ferrer, a former aide to the Governor of Spanish Sahara and military advisor for the film — was awarded the top state rating 'In the National Interest' (Zumalde Arregi 1997: 310). Critics' unease about both plots suggests that the character relationships were found problematic, though there were no specific complaints about the male–male or mixed-race liaisons. However, as we shall see, the original script of *La llamada de África* contains several scenes involving the mixed-race couple that are eliminated from the film — presumably because of censors' objections. (Directors had to submit filmscripts to the censors before being allowed to start shooting; most changes or cuts were made at this stage. Once the film was made, it required the censors' approval for release.) The two sections that follow will consider the implications of the fact that, despite the elimination of certain scenes in *La llamada de África*, both films appear — extraordinarily — to condone their male–male and mixed-race love relationships.

¡*Harka!*: Homoeroticism, Sacrificial Love and the Colonial Reproduction of the Same

Scripted by a former member of the Spanish Foreign Legion, Luis García Ortega, ¡*Harka!* explicitly postulates a bond between the Spanish military male and the Arab warrior, whose hierarchical symbiosis is exemplified by the *harka* units' structure of native mercenaries under Spanish command. This bond is linked to the repudiation of women, which the film's two Spanish officer heroes learn from the Arab world,

---

4   Goda stresses that Hitler's expansionist plans in Africa should be seen as the context to his October 1940 meeting with Franco at Hendaye, noting that, just before this meeting, Franco had raised Spanish troop levels in the Canaries as well as Morocco (1999: 179).

constructed in the film as an all-male culture. The poster for the film **(Figure 18.1)** foregrounds the romantic relationship between the junior officer Carlos Herrera and his fiancée Amparo, but places above them the image of the senior *harka* officer Santiago Balcázar (Alfredo Mayo), in Arab dress, with whom Carlos establishes an intense homoerotic bond. The dramatization of Carlos's ditching of Amparo to return to Africa to take up the mantle of the now dead Santiago cannot be attributed to misogyny on the director's part: Arévalo's next film, *Rojo y negro* (*Red and Black*, 1942; discussed in Chapter 15), is the contradiction-in-terms of a Falangist feminist apologia, in which the Falangist heroine surpasses the men in daring and courage).[5] Amparo, however, far from sacrificing the self to the nation, is the modern liberated woman who lives for pleasure, enjoying sport and luxury hotel ballrooms. As an embodiment of the egoistic individualism of a decadent, 'feminized' Western modernity, she thinks only of what Carlos' military role in Africa will do to her, incapable of appreciating his needs or those of the fatherland. This indictment of a 'feminized' modernity is typical of Spanish fascist rhetoric, as of fascist rhetoric elsewhere. It also corroborates Klaus Theweleit's analysis of the terror of women expressed in the writings of Nazi soldiers, which he reads as a fear of loss of male body boundaries: a fear countered by constructing impermeable body armour through military discipline (1989: 143–252).

The film's exaltation of the fascist ideal of service to the nation is illustrated most clearly by the principal hero Santiago's refusal not only of relationships with women but of all forms of intimacy: he repeatedly refuses leave, for he has no private life. When Carlos — upbraided by him for leaving the Army of Africa to marry Amparo — retorts by asking if he has never felt a need for affection and tenderness, Santiago responds by violently grabbing a prostitute and dancing with her stiffly. His body language is rigidly erect throughout, in keeping with Spanish fascist rhetoric's emphasis on verticality: the conversion of the male body into a permanently erect phallus that is never allowed discharge, as analysed by Theweleit (1989: 43–61). This verticality is based on self-control as well as the domination of others. The actor who plays Santiago, Alfredo Mayo, was typecast as the fascist warrior hero in Spanish cinema of the early 1940s. By contrast the younger officer Carlos is played by Luis Peña, known for his roles as romantic lover: his soft features contrast strikingly with Mayo's sculptural profile — a contrast that detracts from the verisimilitude of Carlos taking on Santiago's mantle after his death, but which shows Santiago's need to find some kind of outlet for his self-imposed emotional rigidity. The male–male relations permitted — indeed, required — by the army, and condoned by Arab culture, provide such an outlet for Santiago because they are sanctioned by military discipline. Theweleit notes that the Nazi soldiers whose writings he analyses find release through battle and military drill (1989: 143–206). This is a form of emotional release characterized by a sacrificial ethos because it is marked by non-fulfilment: that is, the continued maintenance of body boundaries — or so we assume, since, although Santiago and Carlos are shown sharing a tent, Carlos is at the time leaving to marry Amparo back in Madrid. The film's

5   The Falange was the Spanish Fascist Party, founded in 1933.

FIG. 18.1. Poster for *¡Harka!* (Carlos Arévalo, 1941; prod. Arévalo P.C. / Cifesa). Filmoteca Española. © Video Mercury Films.

glamorization of Santiago as *harka* leader — through repeated close-ups and takes of him riding ever upwards against the skyline — comes close to fusing the fascist ideal of service to the nation with what is represented as an Arab tribal notion of personal allegiance. The film is here picking up on one of the ambiguities of fascism, whereby the abstract notion of service to the state is channelled through devotion to a charismatic leader. Carlos's final return to Africa to assume the role of the now dead Santiago allows this personal devotion to be elevated to an abstract level. Specifically, Santiago's death allows Carlos to express his devotion to him without risk of consummating a homosexual relationship.

Bhabha has argued, in *The Location of Culture*, that the colonizer is torn between fear and desire towards the colonial Other — an ambivalence that involves juggling opposing emotions (1994: 66–84). In *¡Harka!*, the Moroccans are both enemies and allies: the *harkas* were the instrument of a colonial divide-and-rule policy whereby the Spanish military formed alliances with particular warlords so as to recruit their men to fight against rival warlords. The potential of the local populace to swing between the roles of enemy and ally is illustrated in the scene when Santiago engages in a psychological duel with the warlord who had previously injured him in battle in order to pursuade him to provide men for the new *harka*. In this episode, the relationship between the two men is shown, through the interplay of gazes, to be one of mutual respect between enemies: a relationship of chivalry. Nonetheless, Santiago is in this scene placed higher in the frame.

Bhabha's analysis of colonial ambivalence is based on his personal experience of the British colonial legacy in his native India, which maintained racial segregation while encouraging the colonized to 'mimic' British culture. For Bhabha, the objective of this colonial mimicry is to construct the colonized as 'white but not quite' — that is, Anglicized rather than English (1994: 85–92). In *¡Harka!* — unlike *La llamada de África*, as we shall see — there is no mimicry of Spanish culture by the colonized, who are depicted as wholly Other, rarely individualized, and on the battlefield not even given a face (Elena 2010: 104). Although Spanish colonial discourse was generally characterized by a policy of enforced incorporation of the Other through evangelization — developed under Spain's early modern empire in America and Asia (1492–1898) — this was not the case in Spain's twentieth-century North African protectorates, where, as noted above, Islamic practices were tolerated, particularly in the late 1930s. Martin-Márquez notes that, if Spain's colonial war in Morocco was in the 1920s marked by extreme brutality, in the late 1930s and early 1940s Spanish texts set in North Africa — including *¡Harka!* — become suffused with 'a dreamy Orientalism that exalted and eroticized fraternal relations between Spaniards and Moroccans' (2008: 206). In *¡Harka!*, the mimicry is that of the colonial army officers Santiago and, less visibly, Carlos through their attraction to Arab culture. What characterizes Santiago is not so much a conflictive attitude towards the Arabs he is commanding or fighting — as in Bhabha's theorization of colonial ambivalence — but rather a hierarchical symbiosis of both Spanish and Arab cultures: Arab culture is harnessed for Spanish colonial ends. In Santiago's case, this symbiosis takes the form of his imitation of Arab horsemanship, customs (tea-drinking rituals), and dress (wearing a *djellaba* over his Spanish military uniform for much of the film). Santiago is also the only army officer depicted as wearing the Army of Africa fez rather than a standard officer's cap. These imitative practices, while expressing a passionately felt identification with Arab culture, allow him to win Arabs over to the Spanish cause, represented by the army uniform he wears next to his skin.[6]

In this context, the theorization of colonial mimicry by Taussig in his book *Mimesis and Alterity* (1993) — published the year before Bhabha's *The Location of Culture* and treating the very different context of hemispheric relations in the Americas — may be more helpful as an interpretive tool than Bhabha's conflictive model of colonial ambivalence. Taussig is concerned with mimicry largely from the perspective of the colonizer, both in the sense of the colonizer's fascination with the colonized's mimicry of himself (something we will explore in the analysis of *La llamada de África*), and in the sense (relevant particularly to *¡Harka!*) that mimicry and alterity, far from being in conflict, reinforce each other in a specular fashion: the greater the Otherness, the greater the impulse to mimicry, while conversely mimicry of the Other confirms sameness. In *¡Harka!*, Santiago's and Carlos's mimicry of Arab culture is thus not in conflict with the perpetuation of the colonial project but, paradoxically, what allows it. Bhabha and Taussig concur in seeing the colonized's mimicry of the colonizer as clinching his construction as Other. Taussig's contribution is to suggest that, conversely, the colonizer's mimicry of the colonized (the Other) is what reinforces the colonizer's sense of self (the same). This defines the colonial project as the reproduction of the same through the mimicry of alterity.

This colonial reproduction of the same is clinched when, at the end of *¡Harka!*, Carlos becomes Santiago. The film dramatizes two kinds of mimesis: Santiago's imitation of male Arab culture (the Other), and Carlos's imitation of Santiago (the same). In imitating Santiago, Carlos is imitating his imitation of Arab culture (that is, imitating the same imitating the Other). Although we never see Carlos wear Arab dress or imitate Arab warrior prowess on a horse, he tells Santiago, during their first intimate encounter, that he too feels partly Arab (an identification based on a structure of domination):

> Vine a África [...] buscando eso que Vd acaba de decir: riesgo [...]. Poco a poco comenzaron a interesarme las costumbres de esta gente, aprendí unas nociones de árabe, deseé mandarlos, y ahora estoy aquí, tal vez porque me siento un poco semejante a ellos.
>
> (I came to Africa [...] seeking what you've just said: risk [...]. Gradually I started to get interested in the people's customs, I learnt a smattering of Arabic, I wanted to command them, and now I'm here, perhaps because I feel a bit like them.)

It is significant that, of the four newly arrived *harka* officers, Carlos is the only one who has not come from Spain but from the Foreign Legion: his Africanist vocation

---

6   Viscarri sees Santiago's *djellaba* as unimportant since he wears his Spanish officer's uniform underneath (2002: 413). I agree that Santiago's Spanishness is paramount, but would argue that, paradoxically, it is his imitation of Arab culture that allows him to further Spanish interests.

made him opt for service in Africa immediately on graduation. As Peter Evans has noted (1995: 219), the scene in which Carlos makes this profession of love for Arab culture to a Santiago decked in *djellaba* and fez is filmed like a love scene, the two men's heads framed so they almost touch. As Carlos says 'tal vez porque me siento un poco semejante a ellos', we cut to an extreme close-up of Santiago's face, illumined by soft-focus lighting recreating the play of light from the camp fire, as he lowers his eyelids. At this point, Oriental rhythms take over the musical soundtrack. The shot reverse shot sequence then cuts to a similar extreme close-up of Carlos.[7] This is the moment of bonding, mediated by Arab culture as internalized Other. As Carlos leaves, asking if 'mi capitán' ('my captain') has any orders for him, Santiago replies, 'Sí, que me tutees' ('Yes, stop addressing me formally'). This is a complicated kind of intimacy, legitimized by being granted in the form of a military command, and made possible by the triangulation afforded by Arab culture as the third term in the relationship. In this triangulation process, public and private forms of love merge. For this *is* love. Santiago is first introduced to us, before he appears on-screen, via his fellow officers' conversation about his love for Africa:

> Noble, leal, desprendido hasta la exageración, valiente hasta la temeridad, pero incomprensible. / ¡África! Balcázar es un enamorado de esta tierra. Vive en ella y para ella. [...] Nadie comprende mejor la psicología del marroquí, tan identificado está con él. Sidi Absalam Balcázar, así le llaman. Y sin embargo nadie tan español como Santiagao Balcázar.

> (Noble, loyal, selfless to the point of exaggeration, brave to the point of recklessness, but incomprehensible. / Africa! Balcázar is in love with this land. He lives in it and for it. No one understands better the psychology of the Moroccan, so identified with it is he. Sidi Absalam Balcázar, they call him.[8] And yet no one is more Spanish than Santiago Balcázar.)

This symbiosis of Spanish and Arab qualities is presented as strange and mysterious, for the mimesis reinforces the alterity that obtains between the two cultures. The power relations are complex because the surrender to the lure of Africa is what allows Santiago to control the indigenous inhabitants, just as Carlos's identification with them takes the form of a desire to command them. In incorporating the culture of the Moroccan natives into themselves, both Santiago and Carlos are incorporating them into empire without requiring them to mimic Spanish customs.

The incorporation of the Other is a typically Francoist rhetorical trope, found in the more conventional sense of cultural assimilation through evangelization in

---

7   This shot, including the play of light, replicates a scene in the Italian colonial film, *Lo squadrone bianco / The White Squadron* (Genina, 1936), set in Libya, in which the profligate junior officer bonds over a camp fire with his fascist military captain. In Genina's film, premièred in Spain in May 1940, the junior officer also rejects his decadent Westernized female lover from the metropolis, to assume the fascist warrior role of his military superior on the latter's death. See Hay 1987: 188–92 and Landy 1998: 194–97. I thank Liliana Ellena for pointing out this intertextual reference, also noted in Elena 2010: 106.

8   González Alcantud notes references to General Franco in Spanish Africanist discourse as 'Sidi Franco', appropriating the Arabic honorific 'My Lord' (2003: 167–68; 202). The Spanish military hero of *La llamada de África* is similarly acclaimed as 'Sidi Andrade' (see below).

Spanish missionary films of the time. These films — despite Franco's alliance with Hitler in the Spanish Civil War — contradict Nazi policies of the exclusion if not extermination of racial others, by dramatizing a kind of spiritual miscegenation that reinforces hierarchy (Labanyi 1997). In this spiritual miscegenation, the relationship is not between man and woman but between figurative father and son: an all-male bond that makes women unnecessary to the reproductive process since the father reproduces himself in the son.[9] Klaus Theweleit has analysed this megalomaniac fantasy of male self-reproduction in the writings of Nazi soldiers, seeing it as a way of avoiding the heterosexual relations that are feared as a breach of body boundaries (1989: 95, 241, 243). The same rhetorical trope, based on a homoerotic act of mimesis that permits the reproduction of the same, is found in both *¡Harka!* and *La llamada de África*. In the missionary film genre, the homoerotic nature of this trope — as 'love of the same' — is attenuated since, although it is enacted between two men, they are usually from different races (colonizer and colonized); as we shall see, this scenario is dramatized in *La llamada de África*. In *¡Harka!* the homoerotic implications of the trope are taken to their logical conclusion, as the sacrifice of the individual self to secure the reproduction of the same is enacted between two military officers in the colonial army — one senior, one junior — with the colonized 'Other' relegated to the sidelines as a third term. This homoerotic reproductive pact is at least as much about the need to incorporate the Arabs into a Spanish imperial design as it is about the relationship between Santiago and Carlos. For their homoerotic pact signals the continuation of the colonial mission, whereby the alterity of Arab culture is rendered part of the colonial self. The words of induction to the new *harka* officers uttered by the commander at the start, and repeated at the end by Carlos as he assumes Santiago's role, are:

> Para ser un buen oficial de harka, hay que comprender al marroquí, identificarse en cierto modo con él, y quererlo. [...] Para ser un buen oficial de harka, hay muchas condiciones, pero sólo una indispensable: tener más corazón que el harqueño más bravo de la harka.

> (To be a good *harka* officer, you have to understand the Moroccan, identify with him in a way, and love him. [...] To be a good *harka* officer, there are many requirements but only one is indispensable: to have a greater heart than the fiercest *harka* warrior.)

This trope of homoerotic symbiosis between colonizer and colonized makes it possible to believe that empire is based on love: a paternalistic love by the father for his wayward children. Carlos tends a wounded Arab boy soldier with the solicitous gestures of a father. The trope of the father's love for the wayward child is reproduced in Carlos's homoerotic relationship with Santiago, for the former succumbs to a life based on self-gratification (sport and ballroom dancing in Spain with Amparo), only to learn the error of his ways and to return to Africa to continue the colonial process of reproduction of the same. The turning point for Carlos is when, in a frivolous gesture, Amparo puts on a party hat in the form of a fez at the end of a montage sequence in which scenes of modern Western decadence

9   For this trope in Spanish fascist writing, see Chapter 10 in this volume.

in Madrid (represented by jazz playing on the dance floor) are rapidly intercut with scenes of the fighting back in Morocco. In one of these intercut scenes, the warlord who had agreed to provide men for Santiago's *harka* (his former enemy) insists on remaining at his side to die with him: a colonial, homoerotic *Liebestod* that seals the mimetic pact. Carlos is now honour-bound to take up Santiago's previous injunction to assume his role as Sidi Absalam Balcázar by becoming Sidi Absalam Herrera. On issuing this injunction, Santiago had insisted, 'te he querido como a un hermano, casi como a un hijo, porque creí que eras como yo' ('I've loved you like a brother, almost like a son, because I thought you were like myself').

In the film's final scene, Carlos tears up his photo of Amparo precisely as he inducts the new *harka* officers who reproduce his own position as a new recruit at the film's start. In so doing, he replaces modern Western heterosexual love (based on self-gratification) with colonial homoerotic reproduction (based on sacrifice of the self). This sacrificial form of love transcends the personal in order to provide the affective underpinnings of empire. *¡Harka!* occupies a key role in the prehistory of representations of homosexuality in Spanish cinema, but it should not be forgotten that its depiction of love between men is a political exploration and justification of the nature of colonial power. The film's investment in the equation of love with renunciation ensures that the love between Santiago and Carlos marks them out as superior to the Arab culture they seek to emulate. Indeed, the film coyly suggests, in its depiction of two pubescent boys flanking the Arab warlord whose military aid Santiago solicits, that in Arab culture love between men is not an impossible ideal but a mundane reality. The film constructs the superior male as the Spaniard who rejects Western modernity by incorporating the Arab 'Other' into the self, but he must not become an Arab: European-but-not-quite and Arab-but-not-quite, at one and the same time — to adapt Bhabha's terminology (1994).

La llamada de África: 'Going Native' and the Seductive Power of Western Technology

The mixed-race hero of *La llamada de África*, born of a Spanish military father killed at Annual and a distinguished Moroccan mother from Tetuán, was acted by a former Nazi officer, Gérard Tichy, who after World War II had escaped from a French prisoner-of-war camp and sought refuge in Spain. Tichy's first film role had been as the German submarine captain in the 1949 film *Neutralidad* (*Neutrality*), now lost, scripted by Fernández Ardavín and directed by his veteran filmmaker uncle, Eusebio Fernández Ardavín. This film depicted the rescue by Spaniards of survivors from battling German and American submarines in World War II, attempting to dissociate Spain from support for fascism at a time of international boycott by stressing the Spaniards' non-partisan rescue of crew members from both vessels. While we could criticize Tichy's lead role in *La llamada de África* as a piece of miscasting, it is more productive to consider the effects of having a blond Aryan play the role of the mixed-race Lawrence of Arabia figure, Captain Andrade. This casting certainly complicates the relation between sameness and alterity: Andrade becomes 'Other' (non-Spanish) both in his imitation of Saharawi culture and in his whiteness, represented by a German actor. Tichy's Aryan looks make us ever conscious of Andrade's whiteness, despite his assumption of Tuareg clothing and his mixed-race origins (revealed only towards the film's end). At the same time, we are made aware that race is a matter of performance; indeed, the spectacle of a Lawrence of Arabia figure of mixed origins played by an escaped Nazi officer could be seen as something of a joke. Imanol Zumalde Arregi has noted that Andrade's Galician family name is that taken by General Franco (himself Galician) as his pen name for the script he wrote for the 1941 film *Raza* (*Race*; directed by José Luis Sáenz de Heredia), and that, like Andrade in *La llamada de África*, Franco was reputed to be miraculously immune to Arab bullets (Zumalde Arregi 1997: 311). As an officer in the nomadic police (made up of natives under Spanish command), Andrade occupies much the same position that Franco had held in Spanish Morocco as *harka* commander. While Franco did not 'go native',[10] there is a similar camouflage going on with his overtures to the Arab world as their 'blood brother' at the time the film was made. When one considers Franco's chameleonic shifts of foreign policy during World War II, the idea of a Nazi playing a Lawrence of Arabia figure starts to sound less far-fetched.

The film stresses the good relations between the Spanish military and the local nomads: when Andrade first appears, in Tuareg dress on camelback, he is hailed by a series of Tuareg herders as '¡El kaid bueno!' (The good chief!'), '¡el hijo del sol!' ('the son of the sun!'), '¡Sidi Andrade!' The nomads speak in Hassaniya, mostly left untranslated, as do Andrade and the other Spanish officers, Lieutenant Ochoa and Lieutenant Hurtado, when addressing them.[11] Andrade's mimicry of Tuareg culture, like Santiago Balcázar's mimicry of Arab culture in *¡Harka!*, makes him a mystery to the other characters (both Spanish and Saharawi), constructing Andrade's 'marriage' of the two cultures, embodied in his love relationship with the Tuareg princess Halima, as exceptional. Although Ochoa has not 'gone native' like Andrade, he too is in Africa's thrall, and refuses his leave. When the newly arrived ensign Gelmírez, fascinated with Africa since childhood, says 'Parece esto tan distinto' ('It seems so different'), Ochoa replies that he needs to:

> Comprender esta tierra y su gente. Recucerda siempre aquella frase que decía San Agustín el africano: 'Deshacer las tinieblas que están sobre el abismo de mi entendimiento para que entendiendo os vea y comprendiendo os conozca y conociendo os ame, porque cualquiera que os conoce, os ama.'

> (Understand this land and its people. Remember the words of St Augustine the African: 'Undo the dark that covers the abyss of my understanding, so that understanding I may see you and understanding I may know you and knowing you I may love you, for anyone who knows you loves you.')

The similarity of this induction into military service in Africa to that which occurs

---

10   However, one contemporary report alleges that Franco flew from the Canaries to Morocco, the day before he launched his military uprising, dressed in an Arab cape, *djellaba* and turban (González Alcantud 2003: 167).

11   The script has inserts giving Spanish translations, presumably for the censor's benefit.

near the start of ¡Harka! is striking: both emphasize the need to love Africa, thereby inducting spectators into the same sentiment. Ochoa reminds us that St Augustine was a North African; in quoting St Augustine out of context, he puts Africa in the place of God. If Augustine converted to Christianity, it is implied that the Spanish colonizers need to convert to an appreciation of African culture — a notable reversal of Spanish missionary rhetoric.

When Andrade rejects Magda — the Spanish journalist niece of the Spanish commander, arrived from the mainland, and an epitome of modern woman (in addition to her career, Germanic-sounding name, and short blonde hair, she is described throughout the script as 'the European woman') — he insists that his love for the Tuareg princess Halima is part of something bigger: his love for Africa. What triggers his rejection of Magda (shared by viewers, given the film's idealization of him) is Magda's overt racism — that is, her failure (like Amparo in ¡Harka!) to love Africa. She upbraids Andrade uncomprehendingly:

> ¿Qué encuentra en estas tierras miserables, en estas almas tan distintas a nosotros, tan incomprensibles? ¿Cómo pudo querer a una mujer que es igual a todas ellas, que entre las demás apenas se la reconoce?
>
> (What do you find in these wretched lands, in these souls so different from us, so incomprehensible? How could you love a woman who is like the rest of them, barely distinguishable from the others?)

The film's fetishization of the figure of Halima — played by Mexican actress Irma Torres — is exoticist (she looks like a darker-skinned version of Vivien Leigh's Cleopatra in Gabriel Pascal's 1945 Hollywood blockbuster, Caesar and Cleopatra), positioning her clearly in the role of racial Other (**Figure 18.2**). In her first encounter with Andrade in the film, she is stretched catlike on the luxurious rugs in her Tuareg nomad's tent, in a dark tunic baring one shoulder, gazing avidly up into the eyes of Andrade, who sits cross-legged in Arab fashion and placed higher in the frame, the light playing on his dazzling white Arab cape. The script primitivizes her by describing her movements as feline, indolent and statuesque; and by stressing her sexual availability (she initiates the kisses) and her 'dulce' ('gentle') yet 'terrible' and 'inquietante' ('disturbing') beauty. But, contrary to Magda's allegations, she stands out as highly individualized, not only through her spectacular looks but also through her characterization: viewers enter into her subjectivity through use of point-of-view shots and empathize with her fears for Andrade's safety. In a key scene, she is juxtaposed with Magda, wearing jodhpurs and flexing a whip, filmed with low-angle shots as she towers over Halima crouched tiger-like on the floor of her tent. Throughout this scene the script refers to them as 'la europea' ('the European woman') or 'la blanca' ('the white woman') and 'la saharauí' ('the Saharawi woman') respectively. Magda's imperiousness is visually critiqued through her masculinization (almost always a negative sign in Spanish cinema of the Franco period), particularly since the low-angle shots depict her from Halima's level, though not always from her point-of-view. Her evident sense of superiority — which the script describes as making her 'despiadada' ('merciless') — is further undermined when she holds out her hands for Halima to read. Halima replies: 'No sé leer en

FIG. 18.2. *La llamada de África* (César F. Ardavín, 1952; prod. Hesperia Films). Filmoteca Española. © César F. Ardavín.

esas manos; son blancas. ¡Nunca he visto unas manos tan blancas! Tienen el color de la muerte. [...] No tienes más fuerza que el color de tu piel.' ('I can't read those hands, they're white. I've never seen such white hands! They're the colour of death. [...] Your only strength is the colour of your skin.') Here Halima not only intuits the association between whiteness and death that Dyer (1997) theorizes, but also perceives that this, far from being a liability, is what gives Europeans their power.

In the ensuing dialogue, Magda and Halima argue over whether Andrade's hands are white like Magda's or darker: the script clarifies that here Halima is painfully remembering an earlier dialogue with Andrade, when they had discussed the likely colour of the child Halima is expecting by him.[12] When Halima had insisted that the baby would be dark like herself or a bit lighter like the palms of her hands, he had interjected, 'Más blanco, mucho más blanco' ('Whiter, much whiter'). At that point Halima, visibly upset, had spotted the religious medallion round his neck which Magda had given him when he had said it was like the medallion his father was wearing when killed at the Battle of Annual. As Halima moved to touch it, he had chided her, 'Deja, tú no sabes de estas cosas' ('Leave that alone; you don't understand such things'). Beneath Andrade's 'going native' there appears to be a belief in the superiority of the white man, embodied in his father who gave his

12   Martin-Márquez also discusses the white hands/dark hands motif in the film (2008: 252–68).

life for Spain. Indeed, his brief attraction to Magda seems to have been motivated by her whiteness: 'No creía que tuvieras las manos tan blancas' ('I didn't think your hands could be so white'), he says to her. When, later in the film, we learn of Andrade's mixed-race parentage — Ochoa tells Madga 'hay algo oscuro en su nacimiento' ('there is something dark, obscure about his birth'), upon which, in keeping with her racist views, she stops pursuing him — we start to suspect that Andrade's motivation in 'going native' may be shame at his mixed-race origins, driving him to embrace African culture and an African woman as a form of self-punishment. Here we have a complex example of mimesis of the Other in order to denigrate the Other within the self, thus confirming the superiority of the same. However, this desire for self-punishment is not presented as undermining Andrade's passion for Africa (and for Halima) but, on the contrary, as justifying it. Again, we have an exaltation of love as self-renunciation — as in ¡Harka! allied to a military sacrificial ethos. Lieutenant Ochoa tells the engineer, who had previously deserted the military, that 'sólo de verdad llega al servicio aquel que sabe rebajarse, porque el soldado entrega para siempre no solo su cuerpo sino todos sus pensamientos y sus pasiones' ('those who truly serve are those who are able to abase themselves, because the soldier surrenders for good not only his body but all his thoughts and passions'). In La llamada de África, this military ethos takes on an explicit religious dimension through the medallion round Andrade's neck.[13] As he dies at the film's end, machine-gunned by the 'Nordic' gangsters (the Saharawis, who revere him, refuse to fire), he asks Lieutenant Hurtado to tell the chaplain he thought of him in his last moments. Andrade rides alone towards certain death, filmed in medium shot against the dawn sky, with a Christ-like sense of mission; he dies in the Spanish commander's arms in an all-male Pietà. Interestingly, his last words enquire not after Halima, but after his white she-camel, Jedha, with whom, throughout the film, he has been depicted as having a symbiotic relationship.

Whenever Andrade and Halima appear together, the script refers to him as 'el hombre blanco' ('the white man'): his apparent self-abasement through his relationship with a Saharawi woman has the additional merit of affirming his whiteness by contrast. Here, the sameness confirmed by mimesis of the Other is evident. But we should not forget Andrade's rejection of the white Magda for despising Halima as a woman of colour. The film clearly represents Magda's modernity as threatening; she is the white woman who cannot understand Africa because she is incapable of renunciation. In the script, the scene of Magda leaving to go back to Spain is preceded by a scene in which Halima, in profile and visibly pregnant, looks down from a hilltop at Andrade's burial, then rides off slowly with her camel train into the desert. This scene does not appear in the film, nor does the earlier scene when Andrade comes to say goodbye to Halima, kissing her tenderly, before going on his military mission to save the airstrip.[14] The effect is that Halima

---

13   ¡Harka! was made at a time (1941) when the Falange dominated Francoist propaganda. La llamada de África (1952) coincides with the period (1945–59) of maximum Church influence in the regime.

14   Martín-Márquez also notes the excision of the pregnant Halima at the film's end (2008: 268).

is airbrushed out of the narrative halfway through the film, her last appearance being the scene when Magda, with her whip and masculine riding attire, humiliated her. It appears that the censors needed to rid the film's second half of Halima's presence so that it would not complicate the Christ-like depiction of Andrade's self-sacrifice, and that they particularly needed to eliminate the final reminder to viewers that Halima will bear Andrade's child after his death.

Andrade dies saving the airstrip from the 'agentes blancos' ('white agents') originating from Vichy-controlled Mauritania. Here the colour white is associated with evil: the 'agentes blancos' — in black leather jackets, shot against dark backgrounds — are dressed and filmed as gangsters. In a key scene, Lieutenant Ochoa tries to uncover the 'agentes blancos' who have infiltrated the Tuareg camel caravan by asking the riders to show their hands: dark hands signify loyal Saharawis, white hands signify the enemy (who open fire, killing Ochoa). In the film it is unclear what nationality the 'agentes blancos' are: Zumalde Arregi assumes they are Nazis, given the film's mention of the 'trouble' likely to come from Mauritania after the German occupation of France (1997); Martin-Márquez describes them as speaking a German-sounding language (2008). The script specifies that they are speaking French with a 'Nordic' accent, and gives their names as Stasser, Vajda, Massaryk, and Radlyz (seemingly German, Polish, and Czech). Goda shows that Franco's 1940 negotiations with Hitler were marked by fear of Gaullist activity in France's African colonies (1999: 178; 180). Goda also notes repeated Spanish complaints in 1940 about German agents operating covertly in Spanish Morocco (1999: 183–85). The plot is indeed incoherent, as contemporary critics noted, but it corresponds to the multiple rumours about undercover political activity in North Africa at the time of the film's setting. What is clear is that the goal of these Nordic whites is destruction of the Spanish airstrip designed to protect communication with the Canaries. The whitest characters in the film — the gangsters, Magda — are the most negative. We might then say that Andrade is idealized because, despite his extreme whiteness (played by a German actor), he carries Africa within, though not it seems without a sense of racial stigma.

Whiteness is viewed negatively also by Halima's little brother Ahmed, the bugle boy for the Spanish military. When Lieutenant Hurtado shows him a photo of an officer's wife back in Spain, he responds, 'Es blanca, demsiado blanca' ('She's white, too white'). And yet the dark-skinned Ahmed's goal is to be like Lieutenant Ochoa; on finding Ochoa's dead body, he takes his place, risking his life for Spain by going on a lone mission to warn the airstrip of the impending attack. If Andrade's 'going native' ultimately reinforces his Spanishness — a Spanishness placed precariously between the white and the African — Ahmed's identification with Ochoa merely confirms his assimilation into the colonial order. Unlike Andrade, poised conflictively between alterity and sameness, Ahmed has to live at the film's end to ensure the Other's reproduction of the same: that is, the male–male reproduction process whereby the Spanish military reproduce themselves in the colonized. Ochoa had previously told little Ahmed, in a direct reference to the words of the Spanish fascist anthem,[15] that fallen Spanish soldiers go to a star in the sky. The film's last words consist of Ahmed telling the engineer that one day he will join Ochoa on a neighbouring star. He does this after handing the engineer the officer's stars bequeathed to him by the dead Andrade: the engineer, redeemed from his former desertion by his newly acquired spirit of self-sacrifice, now takes Andrade's place. Ochoa similarly reproduces himself at the end with the arrival of his younger ensign brother. The fact that Ochoa reproduces himself in both little Ahmed and his younger brother allows him, in a complicated way, to reproduce himself as both Berber and Spanish. The arrival of Ochoa's younger brother is a replay of the earlier arrival of the ensign Gelmírez to whom Ochoa had quoted St Augustine to induct him into the need for the Spanish military to love Africa: Gelmírez repeats verbatim to the young ensign Ochoa the older Ochoa's previous words to himself. As in ¡Harka!, the injunction to love Africa is replayed in a cyclical structure whereby fallen colonial heroes reproduce themselves in younger men. Although La llamada de África, unlike ¡Harka!, does not explore homoeroticism, it replicates the same structure of male–male reproduction associated with love for Africa. In the case of La llamada de África, the film ends with multiple examples of men reproducing themselves in other men. The pregnant Halima had to be removed from the film's end so that reproduction can be presented as an exclusively male process. But this is not an excision of mixed-race reproduction, for her little brother Ahmed becomes Ochoa: a male–male reproduction process whereby the Other becomes the same.

While both ¡Harka! and La llamada de África depict the colonizer's mimicry of the culture of the colonized, effectively confirming both alterity and sameness through mimesis, La llamada de África additionally portrays the Western fascination with the indigenous population's fascination with Western culture, as manifested through technology; the theme which Taussig develops progressively throughout his book (1993). The specularity of this process — as the white man looks at the 'native' reflecting back at him his own whiteness — is suggested by the play with Halima's hand mirror in La llamada de África, particularly the disconcerting shot which shows us Andrade and Halima via their reflection upside down in the mirror lying on the tent floor: they are both looking at us looking at them (reproduced in Martin-Márquez 2008: 264). Although Halima, unlike her little brother Ahmed, does not assimilate (she reproaches Ahmed for using the Spanish first name Ignacio given him by the military; the film always calls him by his Arab name), she is depicted as fascinated by the Western gadget that Andrade brings her as a present in her first scene: a musical box that, when its lid is lifted, plays Western dance music, and which terrifies her when the music gives way to a human voice. This scene enacts what Taussig sees as the classic colonial moment when the colonizer (in this case, the Spanish viewer as well as Andrade) sees the superiority of his own culture reflected back at him through the colonized's view of it as 'primitive' magic.

---

15   'Cara al sol [...] me hallará la muerte [...] junto a mis compañeros que hacen guardia sobre los luceros' ('Face to the sun [...] death will find me [...] in the ranks of my comrades standing sentinel over the morning stars'.

The scene is especially curious since, later, Andrade brusquely stops the Western music that Magda is playing on a gramophone, saying, as he goes on to flirt with her, that he hates civilization. Yet he is not averse to using the musical box with its Western music to reflect back at him, through Halima's fascinated play with it, the superiority of a whiteness about which he seems to feel ambivalent. Halima, reputed to have magic powers, concedes defeat in the face of this 'magic' box whose workings she cannot fathom. By contrast, for the acculturated little Ahmed, the musical box holds no mystique. A related trope with a self-reflexive twist is performed when the engineer tells Magda that the sound of the Sirocco is like 'ese murmullo que hace la gente a la salida de los cines' ('the babble of people coming out of the cinema'): here viewers are asked to recognize the 'magic' power of the cinema through analogy with an unstoppable African force of nature (the Sirocco is blowing through much of the film's violent finale). In both cases, Spanish viewers are reassured of the superiority of their own culture, by seeing it reflected back at them in the form of primitive magic and nature. Andrade's seduction of Halima with his musical box is cinema's seduction of Spanish viewers by affording them the pleasurable spectacle of the colonized's seduction by superior Western technology. Spanish viewers are thus seduced by Halima's seduction. In the process, cinema is confirmed as a kind of 'modern magic'. Elena has suggested that the hinging of the film's plot on the military's attempt to save the airstrip represents an exaltation of Spain's *mission civilisatrice* (2010: 111). Perhaps the point is that the military are exalted by being aligned with a technology — they are throughout the film shown using radio transmitters — that has the power to seduce both the colonized and the colonizer into accepting Western superiority. Technology too is an object and instrument of love.

Death in the Desert

La llamada de África closes with an image of the stars which can be read as little Ahmed's point-of-view shot, following his closing words which announce that one day he will join Ochoa on a neighbouring star. We now realize that the voice-over at the film's start, over an aerial shot of the Spanish fort in the desert 'en el que viví cerca de tres años antes de vivir aquí' ('where I spent nearly three years before I lived here'), is that of the dead Ochoa speaking from his star.[16] This materialization of the Spanish fascist anthem opens a story in which miscegenation is presented positively, but at the same time as a form of self-abasement akin to the self-denial required by military service. In the same way, *¡Harka!* shows love between men to be noble provided it is — again in a military context — based on renunciation. The self-punishing urges evident in both Santiago and Andrade drive them to find release in death. Both films relate this association of fulfilment with death explicitly to the Spanish army in Africa: the soldiers of the Spanish Foreign Legion were notorious for calling themselves 'los novios de la muerte' ('death's bridegrooms'). Although religion is absent in *¡Harka!* and minimally present in *La llamada de África*, there is an

---

16   This narrative frame is not present in the script.

evident Christian substratum to this notion of fulfilment in death, exemplified in the description of the fascist warrior as 'mitad monje, mitad soldado' ('half-monk, half-soldier') by the founder of the Spanish Fascist Party, José Antonio Primo de Rivera. This chimes with Dyer's analysis of the Christian notion of 'embodiment', which regards the body as the base container of a superior spirit (1997: 14–40) — a notion that he shows to be central to the repeated association of whiteness with death (1997: 207–23). Only by suppressing the body can fulfilment be attained. It is this that allows ¡Harka! to present Santiago's and Carlos's homoerotic bond as in no way transgressive. On the contrary, their homoerotic bond is what marks them out as superior to the other Spanish officers, for it renounces bodily gratification. Elena has noted that Santiago is driven by an urge to self-punishment (1997: 134). Although Andrade's relationship with Halima is clearly sexual, it is 'purified' by the fact that it appears to be a form of self-abasement, aimed at working through his complex about his mixed-race origins. Near the start of the film, Andrade is depicted as experiencing mystical ecstasy when he tests a knife by cutting his forearm whilst looking heavenward; the fact that the knife has been given him by a Berber brings a colonial dimension into this rapture. Andrade's Christ-like death brings him ultimate purification from the taint of Halima. The death drives of both Santiago and Andrade construct them as white heroes. If both Halima and Ahmed shrink from whiteness as the colour of death, by the end of *La llamada de África* Ahmed has, it seems, learnt from Ochoa's example that whiteness signifies a superior embrace of death.

In loving Africa, Santiago and Carlos and Andrade and Ochoa are in love with the desert. On the one hand, the desert beckons with the glorious promise of death. *La llamada de África* has recurrent images of men — including the dying Andrade at the end — sifting the sand through their fingers like an hourglass. On the other hand, the desert can be seen as an image of the voiding of the self for which the white male military heroes of these films are striving. In both ¡Harka! and *La llamada de África* the 'call of Africa' is, in the end, not so much the lure of Arab culture as the call of whiteness: a whiteness that can be attained only by rejecting the love of white women — and, for that matter, the love of coloured women — for love of the desert.

Works Cited

AIDI, HISHAAM D. 2006. 'The Interference of al-Andalus: Spain, Islam, and the West', *Social Text*, 24.2: 67–88.

ARÉVALO, CARLOS (dir.). 1941. ¡Harka! (Cifesa)

—— (dir.). 1942. *Rojo y negro* (Cepicsa)

BHABHA, HOMI. 1994. *The Location of Culture* (London: Routledge)

DOMÍNGUEZ RODIÑO, ENRIQUE, and CARLOS VELO (dirs). 1939. *Romancero marroquí / Der Stern von Tetuan* (Alta Comisaría de España en Marruecos / CEA / Tobis Kunst)

DYER, RICHARD. 1997. *White* (London: Routledge)

ELENA, ALBERTO. 1997. '¡Harka!, 1941', in *Antología crítica del cine español, 1906–1995*, ed. by Julio Pérez Perucha (Madrid: Cátedra), pp. 132–34

——. 2001. 'Cámaras al sol: Notas sobre el documental colonial español', in *Mirada, memoria y fascinación: Notas sobre el documental español*, ed. by Josep Maria Català, Josetxo Cerdán, and Casimiro Torreiro (Málaga: Festival de Cine Español), pp. 115–24

——. 2004. *'Romancero marroquí': El cine africanista durante la Guerra Civil* (Madrid: Filmoteca Española)

——. 2010. *La llamada de África: Estudios sobre el cine colonial español* (Barcelona: Bellaterra)

EVANS, PETER. 1995. 'Cifesa: Cinema and Authoritarian Aesthetics', in *Spanish Cultural Studies: An Introduction*, ed. by Helen Graham and Jo Labanyi (Oxford: Oxford University Press), pp. 215–22

FERNÁNDEZ ARDAVÍN, CÉSAR. 1951. *La llamada de África* (filmscript) (Madrid: Imp. Laguno)

—— (dir.). 1952. *La llamada de África* (Hesperia Films)

—— (dir.). 1953. *Con los hombres azules* (Hesperia Films)

FERNÁNDEZ ARDAVÍN, EUSEBIO (dir.). 1949. *Neutralidad* (Valencia Films)

GENINA, AUGUSTO (dir.). 1936. *Lo squadrone bianco* (Roma Film)

GODA, NORMAN J. W. 1999. 'Franco's Bid for Empire: Spain, Germany, and the Western Mediterranean in World War II', in *Spain and the Mediterranean since 1898*, ed. by Raanan Rein (London: Cass), pp. 168–94

GONZÁLEZ ALCANTUD, JOSÉ ANTONIO. 2003. *Marroquíes en la guerra civil española: Campos equívocos* (Barcelona: Anthropos)

HAY, JAMES. 1987. *Popular Film Culture in Fascist Italy: The Passing of the Rex* (Bloomington: Indiana University Press)

LABANYI, JO. 1997. 'Race, Gender and Disavowal in Spanish Cinema of the Early Franco Period: The Missionary Film and the Folkoloric Musical', *Screen*, 38.3: 215–31

LANDY, MARCIA. 1998. *The Folklore of Consensus: Theatricality in the Italian Cinema, 1930–1943* (Buffalo, NY: SUNY Press)

MADARIAGA, MARÍA ROSA DE. 2002. *Los moros que trajo Franco... La intervención de tropas coloniales en la guerra civil española* (Barcelona: Martínez Roca)

MARTIN-MÁRQUEZ, SUSAN. 2008. *Disorientations: Spanish Colonialism in Africa and the Performance of Identity* (New Haven, CT: Yale University Press)

REIN, RAANAN. 1999. 'In Pursuit of Votes and Economic Treaties: Francoist Spain and the Arab World, 1945–56', in *Spain and the Mediterranean since 1898*, ed. by Raanan Rein (London: Cass), pp. 195–215

REY, FLORIÁN (dir.). 1939. *La canción de Aixa* (Hispano Film Produktion)

SÁENZ DE HEREDIA, JOSÉ LUIS (dir.). 1941. *Raza* (Cancillería del Consejo de la Hispanidad)

TAUSSIG, MICHAEL. 1993. *Mimesis and Alterity* (New York: Routledge)

THEWELEIT, KLAUS. 1989. *Male Fantasies*, vol. II: *Male Bodies: Psychoanalyzing the White Terror*, trans. by Stephen Conway, Chris Turner and Erica Carter (Cambridge: Polity)

VISCARRI, DIONISIO 2002. '¡Harka!: Representación e imagen del africanismo fascista', *Revista de Estudios Hispánicos*, 36.2: 404–24

ZUMALDE ARREGI, IMANOL. 1997. 'La llamada de África, 1952', in *Antología crítica del cine español, 1906–1995*, ed. by Julio Pérez Perucha (Madrid: Cátedra), pp. 309–11

PART V

Cinema of the 1970s to 1990s

CHAPTER 19

Fetishism and the Problem of Sexual Difference in Buñuel's *Tristana* (1970)

> Every perversion is an attempt to unsettle the boundaries
> between the real and the not-real. (Louise Kaplan 1991: 119)

Buñuel chose to film Galdós's 1892 novel *Tristana* because its heroine has her leg amputated (Sánchez Vidal 1984: 330). While acknowledging the recurrence of foot fetishism in Buñuel's work, critics have largely seen his insistence on Tristana's mutilated stump and artificial leg as a critique of a 'castrating' traditional society — a reading encouraged by Buñuel's surrealist iconoclasm and political exile, plus the scandal over the only other film he made in Franco's Spain, *Viridiana*, which was stripped of its Spanish nationality and banned in Spain after winning the Palme d'Or at the 1961 Cannes Film Festival as Spain's official entry. *Tristana* too had problems with the Francoist censors, who withdrew permission for Buñuel to shoot it in Spain in 1964 and several times more in 1969, when they finally relented (Buñuel 1971: 8–9). Buñuel changed the location from 1890s Madrid to Toledo (seat of the Catholic Church in Spain and site of the Military Academy famously besieged by the Republicans during the Civil War) in the years 1929–35 (the Primo de Rivera dictatorship and the Republic) — a period marked, in Buñuel's words, by 'overt social unrest' (Buñuel 1982: 239). Numerous sequences open with shots of passing civil guards or priests or nuns. But, as Linda Williams (1981) has argued in relation to other films by Buñuel, *Tristana* is not a clear-cut denunciation of authority but an exploration of the collusion between desire and repression.

Buñuel (1982: 238–39) liked Galdós's ambiguous depiction of the film's protagonist Don Lope as patriarchal tyrant and anarchic subversive. In film and novel, Tristana learns her desire for independence from him. And in the film, unlike the novel, Tristana succeeds in escaping Don Lope's home and chooses to return to it. More fundamentally, the amputation of Tristana's leg, while physically 'castrating' her, gives her a newfound power over men. Peter Evans (n.d.) rightly notes that the film is less concerned with Don Lope's curtailing of Tristana's freedom than with his anxieties about his masculinity. The images of Tristana's 'castration' have to be taken together with those of Don Lope's severed head. The scene where Tristana on the balcony exposes her 'castrated' body to a terror-struck Saturno on the ground directly enacts the scenario which Freud posited as the origin of fetishism (foot fetishism in particular), in which the boy looks up as his mother's genitals from below and is seized by the 'horror' of sexual difference (the mother's lack of a penis, interpreted as a castration). As Freud put it in his 1927 essay 'Fetishism': 'Probably no male human being is spared the fright of castration at the sight of a female genital' (1981: 354). The fetish, he suggested, functioned as a reassuring substitute for the woman's 'missing penis', allowing the man to disavow (deny/affirm) the woman's 'castration': Tristana's artificial leg, sometimes attached to her body, sometimes not, plays this double function. The complementary images of Don Lope's severed head enact Freud's 1922 essay 'The Medusa's Head', where he argued that the Medusa's decapitated head functioned as a fetishistic disavowal of male castration anxiety provoked by the 'horrific' sight of the 'castrated' female genitals, since the snakes round it functioned as a sign of her missing penis and as a compensatory replacement, 'petrifying' the male spectator in the double sense of terrifying him and giving him a 'hard-on' (1940: 273–74). Buñuel's Medusa's head is male, making it clear that that this is a fantasy of male castration. As Laura Mulvey puts it in her essay on fetishism: 'fundamentally most male fantasy is a closed-loop dialogue with itself, as Freud conveys so well in the quotation about the Medusa's head. Far from being a woman, even a monstrous woman, the Medusa is the sign of a male castration anxiety' (1989: 11). Freud's theory of fetishism has particularly provoked feminist critics because it supposes that women are 'castrated' not by patriarchal authority but by their own biology: the theory itself mimics the fetishistic disavowal process by affirming women's disempowerment while exonerating men from blame and making women the cause of masculine insecurity. In this essay, I shall read *Tristana* through successive feminist re-readings of Freud's theory of fetishism for, like Freud, Buñuel posits the castrated woman as a castrator of men. I am not concerned here with the wider notion (Metz 1982; Williams 1981) that film, providing gratification through looking, is by definition a fetishistic medium — what interests me is Freud's notion that fetishism is a response to the 'horror' of sexual difference.

Laura Mulvey stresses that fetishism, supposing possession of a penis as the norm, specularizes women's bodies by turning them into 'fantasy male anatomies' (1989: 13). Buñuel's film shows how the 'castrated' Tristana, with her 'substitute penis' (artificial leg), functions as a fantasy image for males beset by castration anxiety (the ageing Don Lope, the adolescent Saturno constantly scolded for masturbating). But it also asks disturbing questions about who is in whose fantasy. Tristana steps out of the role that Don Lope has fantasized for her, using it to assert her independence; and she, as his fantasy object, fantasizes his castration (her visions of his severed head). Tristana wakes up twice from her repeated nightmare of Don Lope's severed head; the continuity editing makes it impossible to know at what point the dream sequence began, and on the final occasion at least, as Don Lope lies dying, her nightmare seems to be a projection of his terrors. Conversely, we cut from Tristana and Horacio's kiss to Don Lope waking, unsure whether any or all of the previous sequence was or was not dreamt by him. All of these surrealist breakdowns of the boundary between dream and reality erode male ontological security, as women refuse to remain fantasy objects dreamed by men and male anxieties become nightmares dreamed by women.

Mulvey notes that the goal of male fetishism is to create stiff, phallic images of women that immobilize them, reassuring men that women are not so frighteningly different while denying the latter agency (1989: 6–13). Woman is given a substitute penis to symbolically castrate her: the phallic woman and the woman in bondage are identical. Mulvey also notes that the fetish functions as a detachable body part, signifying that the woman does and does not have a penis. Tristana's detachable artificial leg both counters and signals her disablement. In an unfilmed scene in the script, the artificial leg is described lying on her bed, seen by her lover Horacio as he carries her to it, excited and repelled by her 'lack'. Its calf is ultra-feminine, its thigh ultra-phallic while also signifying Tristana's bondage: 'Amongst the silk and lace underwear we see an artificial leg, the lower part of which is perfectly shaped and clad in a fine silk stocking and a charming little patent leather shoe. The part corresponding to the thigh, however, is a mass of aluminium, straps and padding' (Buñuel 1971: 124). The straps here remind one of the snakes around the Medusa's head. Tristana's fetishistic function is reinforced by the stiffness of Catherine Deneuve's acting. Almost from the start, Don Lope dresses her in smart clothes that require a rigid posture. He is not responsible for the amputation of her leg but his exclamation on first hearing she has a tumour is telling: 'This time she won't escape' (Buñuel 1971: 113).

Horacio, too, fetishizes Tristana by turning her into a specularized fantasy image, in his case by painting her portrait. Early in the film, Tristana polishes the portrait frame of one of Don Lope's former conquests, presaging her own reduction to possessed object. We are not allowed to see Horacio's portrait of her. On her visit to his studio he talks of wanting to finish her portrait, but when we glimpse the canvas on his easel it is a view of Toledo — appropriately, for in painting her he turns her into a 'view': his view.

However, the film is not about Tristana's disablement but about her progressive empowerment through 'castration' and fetishization. E. Ann Kaplan observes that Freud's notion of the fetish as a substitute penis creates a masculinized female image with which female spectators can identify as an expression of their own desires for empowerment (1983: 5). Tristana's fetishization both confirms that she is a 'castrated' woman and denies her sexual difference by masculinizing her. The first sign of her newfound authority is the stick she bangs on the ground from her wheelchair, echoing the stick which is an essential part of Don Lope's public masculine 'equipment'. The script stresses the hardening of Tristana's features after her operation. Antonio Monegal has suggested that the amputation of her leg deprives her of her femininity (1993: 174). In fact, her 'castration' confirms her sexual difference from men, while her acquisition of an artificial leg plus stick masculinizes her. Like Don Lope, she now has three legs. Indoors, Don Lope loses his stick as he does in his confrontation with Horacio. But if in public Tristana has one real leg, an artificial leg, and a stick, indoors she retains three legs: one leg and two crutches. It is the sound of her crutches stomping up and down the corridor that most memorably conveys her power over the ageing Don Lope. She is also on her crutches when she exposes herself to Saturno. One is reminded of the Sphinx's riddle, 'What walks on four legs in the morning, two at noon, and three in the evening?'. Oedipus solved the riddle by answering, 'Man', like Freud, leaving woman out of the picture. The Sphinx's riddle is, of course, about the ageing process. The passing of power from Don Lope to Tristana via his fetishization of her can be seen as the counter-productive result of his attempt to compensate for his phallic decline through ageing.

Tristana's three legs, over-compensating — as in Freud's theory of the fetish — for the leg she has lost, are echoed by her three-legged grand piano. The first time we see Tristana after her operation, Buñuel indulges his love of visual puns, shooting Tristana's stump and one leg from under the piano so that the latter forms a triad framed by two piano legs, matched by the three-legged piano stool. The proliferation of wooden legs functions, like the snakes around the Medusa's head, as a fetishistic reminder/denial of the woman's 'castration'. The symbolic link between the piano and Tristana's 'castration' is clear: it is wheeled in as the doctor writes his 'sentence', and the film cuts from the doctor touching her leg to the maid Saturna polishing the piano. Here Buñuel is giving visual form to the verbal puns in Galdós's novel, where the piano is explicitly referred to as an 'organ': a 'little organ' ('organito') and a 'superior organ' ('órgano expresivo de superior calidad'; Pérez Galdós 1987: 153, 168), for it signifies Tristana's 'lack' while providing a phallic compensation for it. The film clearly relates to the 1640 'miracle of Calanda' (Buñuel's birthplace in Aragón), when the Virgin restored the amputated leg of a male peasant who each day had rubbed his stump with holy oil, as Buñuel never tired of telling (Buñuel 1982: 21). In addition to polishing the piano which functions as a fetishistic displaced image of Tristana's 'castration', Saturna later offers to 'rub' her mutilated body.

The fetishization of Tristana's wooden leg is paralleled by the camera's fetishization of male feet. When Don Lope visits Horacio after Tristana's operation, the camera closes on Horacio's boot being polished by a bootblack, legs again being associated with rubbing. Don Lope tells Horacio that Tristana 'is missing something': his boot represents the penis Tristana 'lacks' because he has the phallus denied her. The camera also insists on Don Lope's tatty, floppy slippers, undermining the stiff, 'upright' posture he maintains in public. Tristana puts his slippers on his feet as he reads a newspaper article about the need to 'cure' Spain's 'gangrene', echoing the demands for an 'iron surgeon' to 'amputate' the nation's 'diseased limbs' that plagued left- and right-wing Spanish political rhetoric from 1900 until Franco took the metaphor literally. The newspaper Don Lope is reading is *El Socialismo Español*: the power he derives from Tristana putting on his slippers is subverted by their association with political demands for the 'castration' of the patriarchal order he represents. Tristana later rebels by throwing the slippers in the rubbish bin. The shots of the spaces left on the walls by the absent fencing rapiers and portraits of Don Lope's earlier female conquests, as these have to be sold off, also suggest that, beneath the virile public facade, Don Lope is — like Tristana — characterized by 'lack'. His fetishization of her is a defence as much against the very real possibility of his own 'castration' — the workers' rioting signals the end of his gentlemanly order and he cannot escape the ageing process — as against the imaginary threat of castration represented by women's bodies.

Barbara Creed (1993) has suggested that Freud's theory of fetishism posited the notion that men fear women because they see them as castrated, in order to mask a deeper fear of woman as castrator. Noting that in many horror movies the monster is female, she argues that if men react to the female genitals with horror it is not because these are perceived as lacking a penis but because they are imagined as a dismembering and engulfing *vagina dentata*. The problem is still the horror of sexual difference but Creed's explanation restores agency to women. She suggests that Freud's own difficulties in accepting women's agency made him posit the father as the source of the castration feared by the son, demonstrating that Freud overlooked the evidence in his case studies that it was the mother who threatened to castrate the child for masturbating (1993: 121). Creed notes that Freud's archetype of the phallic woman and that of the castrating woman 'are quite different and should not be confused; the former ultimately represents a comforting phantasy of sexual sameness, and the latter a terrifying phantasy of sexual difference' (1993: 157–58).

Creed's inversion of Freud's explanation of the male horror of sexual difference fits with the emphasis in *Tristana* on male castration. The creaking sounds as Don Lope's decapitated head swings from the rafters are almost a parody of the horror genre. It is possible to read *Tristana* as a horror film in which Tristana's increasing domination of Don Lope is caused not by his fetishization of her, endowing her with a substitute penis, but by her 'monstrous' female power. The film does, after all, end with her hastening his death. In this reading the amputation of her leg, and its replacement by an artificial one plus stick and crutches, would signify not her castration but her 'monstrousness': witches have sticks. Tristana becomes increasingly vampire-like towards the film's end, her pallor emphasized by her garish make-up (indicated in the script) and her black shawl echoing Dracula's cape, particularly in the final scene where she leans over the dying Don Lope like a vampire over its prey. This scene visually reverses the earlier shot of her leaning over Cardinal Tavera's tomb, suggesting the vampire's habit of drawing its strength from the dead. As she bends over the dying Don Lope, as when exposing herself to Saturno on the balcony, her over-painted red lips part in a monstrous smile, revealing her white teeth in an image of the *vagina dentata*. In the balcony scene, this image functions as a direct substitute for the sight of her genitals, granted to Saturno but denied the spectator. It is logical that Saturno should see the female genitals as castrating rather than castrated, since throughout he is violently reprimanded for masturbating by his mother Saturna. The film's two female characters, Tristana and Saturna, are both constructed as castrators of men.[1] The film is also about a man's fear of ageing: the monstrous-feminine and the (male) fear of ageing are both stock themes of the horror genre. In *The Hunger* (Tony Scott, 1983), Catherine Deneuve would later act the role of vampire in a classic horror film playing on these two terrors.

---

1   Evans (n.d.: 98) notes that Saturna, as devouring mother, is a female version of Goya's painting *Saturn Devouring his Children*. However, Buñuel inherited her name from Galdós's novel, where she has no such role.

Louise Kaplan has similarly suggested that Freud's theory of fetishism is a cover for a male fear of women's agency, but rather than reject his theory she rewrites it. Defining perversion as 'a mental strategy that uses one or another social stereotype of masculinity and femininity in a way that deceives the onlooker about the unconscious meanings of the behaviours she or he is observing', she argues that Freud's essay on fetishism 'makes use unconsciously of the perverse strategy and is itself a fetishistic document' (1991: 9, 55). Kaplan's notion that perversion is a strategy of deception designed to distract attention from a deeper anxiety is particularly useful when dealing with a director like Buñuel who so perversely delights in misleading the spectator. As Kaplan notes, perversions are fictitious enactments or performances. The fetishist directs his/her own scenario, designed to 'screen out' what is really going on. Fetishism is a visual activity not because the fetishist is disavowing his horror on seeing the female genitals, but because he (or she, for Kaplan insists that women are also fetishists) is directing everyone's gaze at the 'screen' of surface appearance.

Kaplan's main thesis is that perversions are not so much sexual problems as 'pathologies of gender stereotyping' (1991: 196). Freud's 'Fetishism' is, for her, a fetishistic text because it sets up norms of masculinity and femininity to 'screen out' the troublesome evidence, recognized by him elsewhere, that 'gender normality' is an unattainable imaginary construct. Kaplan argues that standard notions of masculinity and femininity are themselves perverse enactments, and that fetishism, while apparently deviant, is in fact acting out a reassuring fiction of 'gender normality'. Thus, male fetishism enacts a fantasy of phallic performance, while female fetishism acts out a masquerade of stereotypical femininity. But since fetishism, as a form of disavowal, is about having it both ways, there are further levels to the pretence. The man who subordinates himself to a phallic woman is allowing himself to satisfy the feminine (passive) side of himself that society makes him feel ashamed of, while pretending that he is being forced into it and anyway it is 'only an act'. At the same time this enactment enables him to perform sexually as a phallic man, reassuring him that he is in control because he is paying the woman to act his script. If the performance takes place with a fetish object, the sense of being in control is even greater. This complex transaction allows the man to have it both ways by simultaneously living out his feminine and masculine drives, while appearing on the surface to conform to the stereotype of the phallic man.

Kaplan suggests that, if perversion is regarded as an overwhelmingly male practice, this is because it has been seen as a sexual problem rather than one of gender stereotyping. If male perversion consists in impersonating masculinity so as to secretly indulge one's femininity, female perversion consists in impersonating a socially acceptable femininity so as to secretly indulge unacceptable masculine desires. The female fetishist turns herself into a fetish for men in order to exert power over them while appearing to be stereotypically feminine. Male and female fetishists are in collusion. As Kaplan notes, the feminine stereotype offers women many ways of disabling themselves as a mask for being in control: by dressing up as an object of desire, by being frigid, by obsessively cleaning (to take three examples relevant to *Tristana*).

Kaplan's argument is enormously suggestive as a way of reading Buñuel's film. All the film's main characters are male 'male impersonators' or female 'female impersonators', enacting a socially acceptable pretence of masculinity or femininity. This is evident even with Saturna and Saturno. The former, described in the script as 'rather masculine in appearance' (Buñuel 1971: 15), rules the household by playing the role, with some telling lapses, of dutiful servant. Saturno's obsessive locking himself in the lavatory allows him to assert his phallic prowess (everyone, including the spectator, assumes he is masturbating interminably) while getting out of the masculine obligation to work. In an unfilmed scene in the script, his bricklayer uncle says 'he's not cut out for working on a site' because he is 'soft' (Buñuel 1971: 88).

This same-sex impersonation is particularly clear in the case of Don Lope, whom we repeatedly see 'making himself up' (literally and figuratively) in the bathroom. He is as specularized by his image in the mirror as Tristana in the scene where she makes up before exposing herself to Saturno. The gap between Don Lope's public image as a paragon of upstanding virility and his private reality when laid low with a cold or surprised in his longjohns 'can only be described as lamentable', to quote the script (Buñuel 1971: 84). What Don Lope seems to be ashamed of is not so much unacknowledged feminine desires as loss of virility with old age. With a typically perverse logic, he will justify standing down from his former role as duelling second by arguing that other men have become effeminate, freeing himself from the demands of masculinity while presenting himself as the only 'real man' left. It could be argued that Tristana's increasing domination of him is the counter-productive result of his fetishization of her, not because his 'sadistic' reduction of her to 'bondage' masculinizes her by endowing her with a substitute penis, but because — in a brilliantly perverse strategy designed to make his decline into 'feminine' vulnerability less humiliating — he creates a masochistic scenario that allows him to delude himself that she is 'forcing' him into submission, while continuing to believe that he is 'really' in control because he has written the script and is paying for the costumes. In which case, he is indeed deluding himself because the fantasy is real.

On Horacio's first appearance, the script indicates that he is 'dressed as an artist, the stereotyped image of the painter' (Buñuel 1971: 63–64). He and Don Lope, despite their apparent scorn for convention, represent two contrasting masculine stereotypes: the gentleman and the bohemian. Horacio's concern throughout is to turn human beings into 'models'. When we first see him, he is 'fixing' his male model in a ludicrously stereotypical pose of 'erect' peasant virility, with *gorro catalán*, wineskin, and donkey. His first reaction on meeting Tristana is to ask if she will be his model.

Tristana complies with her fetishization because the elegant clothes Don Lope buys her make her not only hyper-feminine but also classy and superior, fixing her in a frigid pose just as when she 'poses' for Horacio. She is also shown cleaning and ironing (in the novel, her mother was an obsessive cleaner); this allows her to play the feminine subordinate role while subverting it, as when she throws Don Lope's slippers out in the name of hygiene. Ginette Vincendeau has observed that Catherine Deneuve's star image embodies the stereotype of the French woman as sexy but impeccably dressed. Deneuve's first collaboration with Buñuel in *Belle de jour* (1967), which made her an international star, initiated a longstanding partnership with Yves Saint-Laurent; she has also modelled for Chanel (Vincendeau 1994: 43–44). *Tristana* draws on Deneuve's star image to show how stereotypical femininity can be used as a perverse cover for masculine agency.[2] Vincendeau notes that Deneuve would, in the 1980s and 1990s, exploit her elegant image to play overtly strong female parts, and quotes her co-star Gérard Depardieu as saying: 'Catherine Deneuve is the man I would have liked to be' (1994: 47).

Tristana does not choose to have her leg amputated but, in turning this imposed restraint to her advantage by making increased feminine dependence a cover for increased masculine control, she perfectly illustrates Kaplan's definition of female perversion. Kaplan notes that fetishism replaces living human beings by dehumanized objects, and that the fetish 'holds together a body that is experienced as a container for leaking, fragmented parts' (1991: 33, 37). Tristana's artificial leg, with its straps to be fixed round the thigh, fulfils both functions. Much the same could be said of Don Lope's stiff suits which function as masculine 'straitjackets'.

Kaplan notes that the nineteenth century's increased emphasis on conformity to gender stereotypes created the category of the perverse: the 'abnormal' requires the concept of the 'normal'. She also observes that the late twentieth century's 'commercialization and standardization of so-called deviant sexuality' is 'a last-ditch effort to contain and regulate the gender ambiguities that are the lot of human beings' (1991: 6). One has to ask whether Buñuel's film contributes to this particularly devious form of gender normalization. There are two interesting things in Galdós's novel that Buñuel suppresses. The first (its main theme, for it belongs to the 1890s European cycle of 'New Woman' novels) is that of Tristana's desire for emancipation, not in the sense of power over men, but in that of earning one's living like a man. Her long discussions on the subject, particularly with Horacio, are reduced in the film to one brief comment: 'I want to be free, I want to work' (Buñuel 1971: 88). The second omitted aspect occurs in the novel's epistolary section which Buñuel found weak (Buñuel 1982: 238–39). In terms of gender, it is the most interesting part because, in it, an extraordinary homoerotic relationship develops between Don Lope and Horacio. Don Lope starts by helping the invalid Tristana write her love letters to the absent Horacio, and ends up taking over the writing entirely. When Horacio comes to visit Tristana after her operation, he finds himself increasingly curtailing his meetings with her to chat with Don Lope. The two men's mutual attraction is made clear. Freud suggested that one of the functions of fetishism was to disavow homosexual inclinations by masculinizing the woman's body (1981: 353). Buñuel's *Tristana* can, like Freud's 'Fetishism', be called a fetishistic text because its exposure of the perverse enactment of stereotypical gender roles masks full acknowledgment of the gender ambiguity that the novel shows to be present in both women and men.

2   Kaplan's analysis suggests that the sexual perversions indulged in by Deneuve in *Belle de jour* should not be seen as the repressed 'other' to her role as bourgeois wife, but as an indicator that her conventional femininity is itself a perverse enactment. See Evans 1995: 151–72.

Kaplan notes that the pervert has often been seen as a 'culture hero' whose transgressions subvert conventional morality. Perversion is, she argues, about 'unsettling reality' but 'the rebellion and the bravery are deceptions. For the pervert is rigid and conservative' (1991: 41–42). Her analysis explains how Don Lope can, to his friends' surprise, uphold traditional values while being a sexual non-conformist: his refusal of marriage and monogamy may shock society but it confirms his stereotypical masculinity by freeing it from the taint of feminine domesticity (in public, at least, for he still has his slippers). Kaplan's insistence that perversion is a product, rather than a subversion, of the rigid gender stereotypes developed during the nineteenth century echoes Foucault's argument (1987) that Victorian morality did not so much repress sexuality as create it, by talking obsessively about it. Foucault turns on its head the idea that repression is in opposition to desire and that, to free the latter, one has only to abolish the former, suggesting more uncomfortably that desire is dependent on repression.

Thus, Don Lope, as Tristana's guardian (legal but not natural father) and seducer (natural but not legal husband), is having it both ways by enjoying patriarchal power while indulging in scandalous sexual relations that proclaim publicly that he is a 'real man'. His notion of freedom is a perverse strategy that uses gender stereotypes to feign deviance while maintaining male authority. When he claims that he and Tristana are happy because they respect each other's freedom, he means that he does not want to curtail his freedom by marrying her, and that he is confident enough of her feminine compliance not to need to resort to coercion, though he will if necessary. As his authority wanes with age, he turns to the institutional props he had previously despised, marrying Tristana and frequenting the company of priests. This loss of authority is presented as an emasculation. Unable to perform as a 'real man', he abandons the public, masculine space of the café and retreats into 'feminine' domesticity, surrounded by men in skirts (they sit sipping chocolate like old ladies). The abandonment of deviance involves abandonment of the pretence of conforming to the phallic stereotype.

The fact that Buñuel, unlike Galdós, allows Tristana to leave with Horacio, only to decide freely to return to her patriarchal tyrant when ill, implies that the freedom she was seeking was illusory and that desire depends on restraints. This suggests that desire is either perverse or is not at all, since it must simultaneously acknowledge and deny repression. Buñuel's conventional framing of characters while they are staring at something offscreen encapsulates the perverse logic that makes desire dependent on its negation. The film opens with Tristana and Saturna walking outside the city walls to meet Saturno; the final reprise ends with them walking back to where they came from: this open space, like the space to which Tristana escapes with Horacio, must be outside the film because it is unrepresentable. Tristana meets Horacio in a walled courtyard in the process of being rebuilt, another perverse combination of openness with closure. The same effect is produced by the emphasis throughout on exterior locations such as walled streets and colonnaded squares or courtyards that have the effect of interiors; and by the converse use of interiors that have a doorway, window or corridor opening up on to a space beyond. The scene where Don Lope shuts the door in our face as he takes Tristana into the bedroom makes the point, while also teasing us, that desire can be realized only in a closed space.

Any political reading of the images of police, Church and patriarchal repression in *Tristana* must take into account the film's demonstration, through its treatment of fetishism, that deviance and restraint go together. Fetishism is also, of course, a Marxist concept. Marx's definition of commodity fetishism as a concern with the surface appearance of 'things' that masks the underlying social relations between them is close to Kaplan's notion of perversion as a deception designed to distract the viewer's gaze from what is really going on.[3] In a kind of disavowal, things are worshipped as commodities while their commodity status is denied. It could be argued that Don Lope's acquisition and fetishization of Tristana is linked to his denial of the socio-economic relations governing his household (left to Tristana) and his society (he declares work to be a 'curse', and making money to be a 'dirty business' best left to 'Jews' like the dealer to whom he sells the family silver). In the film, unlike the novel, he inherits money from his sister ('Men make the laws,' she protests) just before Tristana returns: Tristana is another piece of property reverting to its 'rightful owner', like the silver which he buys back. (His phallic trophies — the fencing rapiers and portraits of his conquests — are never recovered.) Don Lope has originally 'inherited' Tristana from her mother, regarding it as 'natural' that she pass to a male owner. The Marxist theory of fetishism can be used to supplement Freud's analysis of the fetishistic disavowal of sexual difference, for it allows us to see how Don Lope takes advantage of the gender relations involved in commodity exchange while wilfully ignoring their gendered basis.

Fetishism is so appealing to a director who, like Buñuel, had his origins in surrealism because its use of objects as decoys, designed to distract attention from the real source of anxiety, invests 'things' with a perverse symbolic significance. The symbolic meaning of a fetish is always likely to be the opposite of what one thinks; indeed, it may have no 'deep' symbolic significance but function as a 'screen' diverting attention from what is really going on. Buñuel consistently resisted critics' attempts to explain the symbolism of his images. They, like fetishes, are perverse because they are 'screen images' analogous to the 'screen memories' analysed by Freud: diversionary tactics designed to frustrate the search for meaning. Such seems to be the function of the shell that Horacio clutches, or the various dogs in the film: the rabid dog shot by a Civil Guard as Tristana meets Horacio; Tristana's fox-terrier, a perfect image of displacement always being picked up and put down somewhere else.[4] Other elusive images function as enactments of the mechanism of disavowal, simultaneously affirming and denying difference: the visual rhymes between disparate objects that look alike (the cut from Don Lope's brazier to the similarly round, metallic *barquillero*'s wheel); Tristana's game of distinguishing between identical objects (columns, chickpeas, streets); the final reprise that ends by playing backwards the film's opening shot, except that Tristana and Saturna are facing the

3   For Marx's theory of commodity fetishism, see McClellan 1977: 435–43.
4   Sánchez Vidal (1984: 336) notes that, when he visited Buñuel in Mexico, he had a fox-terrier named Tristana.

other way (the same yet different). Resistance to intelligibility is created by the use of deceptive continuity editing, and by the converse strategy of cutting the opening establishment shot and closing frames of almost every sequence (Buñuel 1971: 10). Saturno's lack of speech and hearing (Buñuel's invention; in the novel, where Saturno barely figures, some deaf-mutes walk by as Tristana and Saturna meet him) foregrounds the resistance to meaning, as does Tristana's recourse to piano playing both to express and distract attention from her frustrated feelings. The sound of bells ringing is heard over the opening credits: the bell-ringer later tells Tristana that people no longer understand the language of bells.

The soundtrack over the final reprise consists of the opening bell-ringing played backwards, reinforcing the effect of a film rewinding and reminding us that what we have been watching is simply a 'screen image'. *Tristana* is a 'fetishistic' film because its use of deceptive 'screen images' exposes the characters' perverse masquerade of masculinity and femininity which simultaneously allows and denies gender ambiguity, while itself delighting in the perversity. It is also a fetishistic text because, like Freud's essay on fetishism, it reinforces gender stereotypes in the process of deconstructing them. Whether we interpret Tristana's increasing domination of Don Lope as the triumph of the monstrous-feminine or as the counter-productive result of his fetishization of her, we have the story, not of a woman but of a man's fantasies of Woman. In either reading, the man's belief that he is in control is a delusion because he is finally destroyed by a woman. For all its sensitivity to the perverse games men and women play to reconcile their contradictory desires for domination and submission with acceptable norms of masculinity and femininity, *Tristana* in the end sends us back to Freud's notion that the basis of fetishism is man's 'inevitable' terror of woman.

Works Cited

AMORÓS, ANDRÉS. 1977. 'Tristana, de Galdós a Buñuel', in *Actas del Primer Congreso Internacional de Estudios Galdosianos* (Las Palmas de Gran Canaria: Cabildo Insular de Gran Canaria), pp. 319–29

BUÑUEL, LUIS (dir.). 1970. *Tristana* (Época Films / Talía Films / Selenia Cinematográfica / Les Films Corona)

——. 1971. *Tristana*, ed. by J. Francisco Aranda, trans. by Nicholas Fry, Modern Film Scripts (London: Lorrimer Publishing)

——. 1982. *Mi último suspiro (Memorias)* (Barcelona: Plaza & Janés)

CAESARMAN, FERNANDO. 1976. *El ojo de Buñuel: Psicoanálisis desde una butaca* (Barcelona: Anagrama)

CREED, BARBARA. 1993. *The Monstrous-Feminine: Film, Feminism, Psychoanalysis* (London: Routledge)

EDWARDS, GWYNNE. 1982. *The Discreet Art of Luis Buñuel* (London: Marion Boyars)

——. 1994. *Indecent Exposures: Buñuel to Almodóvar* (London: Marion Boyars)

EVANS, PETER W. N.D. 'Buñuel and *Tristana*: Who is Doing What to Whom', in *Carnal Knowledge: Essays on the Flesh, Sex and Sexuality in Hispanic Letters and Film*, ed. by Pamela Bacarisse (Pittsburgh, PA: Ediciones Tres Ríos), pp. 91–98

——. 1995. *The Films of Luis Buñuel: Subjectivity and Desire* (Oxford: Oxford University Press)

FOUCAULT, MICHEL. 1987. *The History of Sexuality: An Introduction*, trans. by Robert Hurley (Harmondsworth: Penguin)

FREUD, SIGMUND. 1940. 'The Medusa's Head', in *The Standard Edition of the Complete Psychological Works*, vol. XVIII (London: Hogarth Press), pp. 273–74

———. 1981. 'Fetishism', in *Pelican Freud Library*, vol. VII: *On Sexuality* (Harmondsworth: Penguin), pp. 345–58

GALEOTA, VITO. 1988. *Galdós e Buñuel: Romanzo, film, narratività in 'Nazarín' e in 'Tristana'* (Naples: Instituto Universitario Orientale)

HARVARD, ROBERT. 1982. 'The Seventh Art of Luis Buñuel: *Tristana* and the Rites of Freedom', *Quinquereme*, 5: 56–74

KAPLAN, E. ANN. 1983. *Women and Film: Both Sides of the Camera* (New York: Methuen)

KAPLAN, LOUISE J. 1991. *Female Perversions* (London: Penguin)

LARA, ANTONIO. 1981. 'Lectura de *Tristana*, de Luis Buñuel, según la novela de Galdós', in *La imaginación en libertad: Homenaje a Luis Buñuel*, ed. by Antonio Lara (Madrid: Universidad Complutense), pp. 97–246

MCCLELLAN, DAVID (ed.). 1977. *Karl Marx: Selected Writings* (Oxford: Oxford University Press)

MELLEN, JOAN. 1973. 'Buñuel's *Tristana*', in *Women and Their Sexuality in the New Film* (New York: Horizon Press), pp. 191–202

——— (ed.), 1978. *The World of Luis Buñuel: Essays in Criticism* (New York: Oxford University Press)

METZ, CHRISTIAN. 1982. *Psychoanalysis and Cinema: The Imaginary Signifier*, trans. by Celia Britton, Annwyl Williams, Ben Brewster and Alfred Guzzatti (London: Macmillan; first publ. 1977)

MONEGAL, ANTONIO. 1993. *Luis Buñuel, de la literatura al cine: Una poética del objeto* (Barcelona: Anthropos)

MULVEY, LAURA. 1989. *Visual and Other Pleasures* (London: Macmillan)

PARTRIDGE, COLIN. 1995. *'Tristana': Buñuel's Film and Galdós's Novel: A Case Study in the Relation between Literature and Film* (Lewiston, NY: Edwin Mellen)

PÉREZ GALDÓS, BENITO. 1987. *Tristana* (Madrid: Alianza)

SACKETT, THEODORE, 1976. 'Creation and Destruction of Personality in *Tristana*: Galdós and Buñuel', *Anales Galdosianos* (anejo), 71–90

SÁNCHEZ VIDAL, AGUSTÍN. 1984. *Luis Buñuel: Obra cinematográfica* (Madrid: Ediciones JC)

SCOTT, TONY (dir.). 1983. *The Hunger* (Metro-Goldwyn-Mayer)

VINCENDEAU, GINETTE. 1994. 'Catherine Deneuve and French Womanhood', in *Women and Film: A Sight and Sound Reader*, ed. by Pam Cook and Philip Dodd (London: Scarlet Press), pp. 41–49

WILLIAMS, LINDA. 1981. *Figures of Desire: A Theory and Analysis of Surrealist Film* (Urbana: University of Illinois Press)

———. 1987. 'The Critical Grasp: Buñuelian Cinema and its Critics', in *Dada and Surrealist Film*, ed. by Rudolf E. Kuenzli (New York: Willis, Locker and Owens), pp. 199–206

CHAPTER 20

The Ghosts of the Past and the Seductions of Psychoanalysis: *El desencanto* (Jaime Chávarri, 1976)[1]

My title refers to two kinds of ghosts of the past. First, the ghost of Francoism, represented by the figure of Franco as the all-powerful absent father — the subject of *El desencanto* (*The Disillusionment*) according to most of the critics who have discussed the film. Second, the ghosts of the Transition to democracy, in the sense of the phantasmatic (largely psychoanalytic) projections onto that period that have taken Chávarri's film as the supposed symbolic expression of sociopolitical processes that occurred after its release in 1976. In the second case, the film functions as something like a ghost of the future; specifically, of a future predetermined by a past with which it had supposedly broken. The interpretations of the Transition that I will question, and that have previously been critiqued by Paul Julian Smith (2006),[2] were chiefly — though not exclusively — developed in critical studies published in Spain but authored by scholars of Spanish origin working in the United States academy, at a time when psychoanalysis was in vogue as a theoretical framework. In noting this, I do not wish to subscribe to the frequent denigration of scholars who write on Spain from overseas: first, because I am also a foreign scholar (from the United Kingdom and now based in the United States); and second, because the studies I mention are major monographs by scholars I admire. It is one thing to engage in personal criticism, and another to question intellectual premises that become hegemonic in certain disciplines at certain historical moments, and that subsequently can be challenged.

In an interview posted on YouTube, apparently introducing *El desencanto* on television, Jaime Chávarri voiced his irritation at the film's retrospective conversion into an analysis of Spain's supposed disenchantment with democracy: 'y yo decía, ¿pero qué democracia? Sólo llevamos un año.' ('and I kept saying, but what

1   The original Spanish version of this essay was written as part of the project "Los medios audiovisuales en la transición española (1975–1985): las imágenes del cambio democrático" (CSO2009–09291) directed by Manuel Palacio of the Universidad Carlos III de Madrid and funded by the Spanish Ministry of Science and Innovation.
2   For Smith, the Transition, far from being marked by an unresolved process of mourning for, or melancholic fixation with, the dead father, for many Spaniards supposed the possibility of pleasure.

democracy? We've only had democracy for a year.') Indeed, shooting of the film began in August 1974, ending in late 1975. The editing — fundamental to the process of creating meaning out of the many hours of footage of conversations with the poet Leopoldo Panero's widow and sons — was done in early 1976, with the film being released in September 1976, just ten months after Franco's death. Thus, most of the film was shot while Franco was still alive.[3] To convert the poet Leopoldo Panero, who died in 1962, into a symbol of Franco as the all-powerful dead but ever-present father is to pay scant attention to chronology. But if this reading does not work as a historical interpretation, it does reveal a desire to project a Freudian narrative onto the country's historical and cultural situation. If the oedipal reading of the film became consecrated in critical studies published in the late 1990s and first years of the new millennium (notably, in the monographs of Teresa Vilarós and Alberto Medina), the film had in fact already started to be read in psychoanalytic terms, as the staging of a love–hate relationship to the father, in contemporary reviews such as those published in *Triunfo* by Fernando Lara and Eduardo Haro Ibars in October and December 1976 respectively.[4] Lara, for example, praised the film for deconstructing the 'mito del padre' ('myth of the father'), which he saw as the 'soporte inconsciente' ('unconscious buttress') of Francoism. Haro Ibars found the Panero family members depicted in the documentary 'monstrous' for centering their existence on a dead father. But Haro Ibars also noted that the film is more than a straightforward allegory of Francoism, since the Panero family, in airing their dirty laundry, do something that would never be done by a Francoist bourgeois family 'que basa toda su escala de valores morales en lo privado, en lo secreto, en el disimulo' ('that bases its whole gamut of moral values on privacy, on secrecy, on dissimulation'; 78). Haro Ibars raises the possibility that the Panero family are dissimulating in their own way; in that case, he observes, the film should be read not as a 'document' but as a 'fiction' (78). Two observations are in order here. First, contemporary reviews of *El desencanto* offer more or less explicit oedipal readings of the film but related to Francoism and not the Transition. Second, Haro Ibars's acute observation reminds us that the reality represented in a documentary film is staged — especially when, as is the case here, those being interviewed know they are acting for the camera.

Haro Ibars tells us that Leopoldo Panero's widow, Felicidad Blanc, prepared her interventions in the film, in some cases scripting them in advance. Her later autobiography, *Espejo de sombras* (1981), disconcertingly repeats verbatim some of the dialogue in *El desencanto*; the autobiography describes the same situations narrated in the film, sometimes citing the film explicitly, as if Felicidad Blanc's involvement in the film had been conceived by her as the rough draft of an autobiographical text. In 1977, the Fotogramas de Plata award for best actor in a Spanish film was given to the members of the Panero family who appear in the film, recognizing that their interviews in the documentary are a performance.

3   According to Minguet Batllori (1997: 74), Chávarri and the producer Elías Querejeta, who suggested the project to him, reduced the footage to some ten hours that were felt to be usable, which were then edited to produce the final ninety-five-minute version.
4   The article by Haro Ibars reviews the screenplay, published by Elías Querejeta Ediciones in 1976.

In the same YouTube interview, Chávarri describes *El desencanto* as 'un documental rodado como si fuera un melodrama' ('a documentary shot like a melodrama'), and expresses his admiration for the Panero family for their adoption of roles or 'máscaras' ('masks') that they succeeded in sustaining throughout the film: roles or masks that do not coincide with the image that Chávarrri — a friend of the youngest son, Michi Panero — has of these individuals in real life. In effect, the oedipal interpretation is introduced into the film by the second son, Leopoldo María, a well-known poet who spent much of his life in psychiatric hospitals, and whose writing takes oedipal scenarios to the limit. Leopoldo María is the only member of the family who looks straight at the camera, indicating his desire to interpellate the viewer. And one of the moments when Leopoldo María seeks out the camera's gaze — our gaze — is when he says he would like to sleep with his mother. Although Leopoldo María stresses that this is the opposite of the Oedipus myth, since Oedipus committed incest unknowingly, the result is an explicit invitation to the viewer to read the family's love–hate relationships in the light of Freudian theory. We might then ask: why does Leopoldo María want to turn his family relationships into a Freudian scenario? One possible reply is that the protagonist of the oedipal narrative is the son;[5] Leopoldo María's attempt to make himself the protagonist of the family history is evident, dominating the other family members when they appear together on screen, and presenting himself as the scapegoat onto which they project their hatreds — a position that conveniently gives the impression that he is the center of his mother's and brothers' existence.[6]

Indeed, as Juan Egea has noted in an excellent analysis of *El desencanto* (2004), the film's protagonist is not the absent dead father so much as Leopoldo María, the absent son whom they all talk about until he appears in the second part of the film, where he dominates the screen. The film's protagonist is, then, the son who, thanks to his clinical experience, is saturated with psychoanalytical interpretations, which he projects onto the other family members. In the previously-mentioned interview, Chávarri points out that the reason that Leopoldo María only appears in the second half of the film is because he did not agree to participate in the shooting until it was well underway; however, Chávarri could have edited the film differently. The late appearance of Leopoldo María, the best-known member of the family thanks to his literary standing (in the 1970s no one was reading the poetic corpus of the dead father, Leopoldo Panero, and the youngest brother Michi recognizes in the film that the poetry of the eldest brother, Juan Luis, never enjoyed much success), gives the documentary a melodramatic twist when the 'ogre' they have all been talking about in the first part suddenly shows up. The only appearance of Leopoldo María in the film's first part is an image, inserted into Michi's opening conversation with Juan Luis, which depicts him walking in a cemetery, like a character from a Gothic drama. Indeed, Leopoldo María's arrival turns what begins as the narration of a

5   In the same year 1976 when *El desencanto* was released, Leopoldo María Panero published a short story collection entitled precisely *El lugar del hijo* (*The Place of the Son*). The stories are based on the desire for death through sexual intercourse with the "madre devoradora".

6   It seems significant that Leopoldo María never shares the screen with his elder brother Juan Luis, his rival as a poet, like his father.

family history into a drama, acted out before our eyes and given an oedipal slant by Leopoldo María's dominance on screen. We may also note that the family drama enacted in the film's second half is based not on the figure of the absent father, but on that of the very-present mother, Felicidad Blanc.

In her book *Blood Cinema*, Marsha Kinder proposed that the frequency in Spanish cinema of castrating mothers and matricide suggests the existence of a Spanish Oedipus complex whereby the desire to kill the father is projected onto the mother, given the impossibility under the dictatorship of committing parricide. For Kinder, this psychic structure can still be seen in the cinema of the democratic period, as a legacy of the repressive past. If we accept this analysis, we could read *El desencanto* as the dramatization of an oedipal desire for the mother — mixed with a strong dose of hatred — that is an indirect expression of fear of castration by the father. Such a reading does not convince me: first, because I find attempts to psychoanalyze a national psyche dangerous (the abuse of the notion of a national character or national spirit in Francoist ideology is all too well known); and second, because I find it offensive to reduce the mother to the status of mere symbolic substitute for the father. The drama of Felicidad Blanc, as both she and her youngest son Michi say in the film, is that, while her husband was alive, she had no life of her own. An obvious reading of the film, which needs no psychoanalytic explanation, would be to see it as the drama, not of the sons' love–hate relationship towards the phantasmal figure of the dead father, but of the conflictive relationship between mother and sons: a relationship in which she intervenes actively in the film, compensating for her previous subordination by sharing the limelight with her sons — despite the attempts of Leopoldo María, with his oedipal narration, to hijack the camera's attention. If she was the only member of the family who prepared her interventions, we may suppose that the film meant for her a chance to prove that she was capable of playing an active role — literally turning the film into her own script. We may or may not like the female role she scripted for herself, but the fact is that she wrote it. If the film can be seen as representative of the Transition, why not see it as a reflection of the changes in the situation of women that were already visible in the early 1970s thanks to women's efforts, contradicting the notion that the political scene was dominated by the omnipotent presence of the all-powerful dying father?

As Felicidad Blanc herself says in the film, after talking of how she 'resucitó' ('came back to life') after her husband's death: 'el mundo ha cambiado' ('the world has changed'). Despite critics' attempt to impose an oedipal reading on the film, turning it into an expression of the impossibility of breaking with the father, Felicidad Blanc shows that she did succeed in breaking with the past — perhaps because the only thing her husband bequeathed to her, despite his status as 'glorioso poeta nacional' ('glorious national poet'), was the straitened economic situation that forced her to work, as she had done before marriage as a nurse in wartime Republican Madrid. We could say that she succeeds in breaking with the past imposed by her husband by returning to a period prior to her marriage, illustrated in the film by the photograph of a young, sportive Felicidad Blanc in a mountain landscape. As she recognizes herself, the story of Felicidad Blanc is that of a 'niña bien' who lost her independence on marriage, coinciding with the start of the dictatorship, and who recovered it, at least partly, on becoming a widow in 1962, without having to wait for the death of any all-powerful symbolic father. And if she did not manage to recover the happiness of her life before marriage, it was not because she continued to be overshadowed by the ghost of her husband, but because of the problems that her sons would give her, especially Leopoldo María who, in her own words, 'fue el gran problema de mi vida' ('was the great problem of my life'). If Leopoldo María was the 'great problem' of Felicidad Blanc's life, I suggest that the oedipal discourse that Leopoldo María insists on imposing on the family narrative is the 'great problem' of the film.

In his previously-mentioned article, Juan Egea has insisted that it would be useful to 'subrayar todo lo que Leopoldo Panero no tiene de trasunto simbólico de Franco y hacer asismismo hincapié en lo que en el filme hay de texto que no lo necesita como referencia' ('stress all the ways in which Leopoldo Panero does not function as a symbolic stand-in for Franco and to highlight those textual aspects of the film that do not need him as a reference point'; 85). On the one hand, Egea observes that the sons talk not of an official poet, much less of an exemplary father, but of a father who was cruel and habitually drunk. The sons also complicate the image of official poet generated by the shot of Leopoldo Panero's statue at the film's start and end, by mentioning his attempts, during his time in London as Director of the Instituto de España, to secure a rapprochement with Republican exile poets. A despotic father, yes; but a model Francoist father, no; and a stalwart supporter of the Franco dictatorship, not without qualifications. Egea notes, rightly, that in the film the Panero family talks as much if not more about Leopoldo María (both when he is absent in the film's first half and when he is present in its second half) than about the dead father Leopoldo. The opening conversation between the eldest and youngest brothers, Juan Luis and Michi, which we deduce must have been filmed at a later stage in the shooting since it reflects on how the film would have been different had Leopoldo María been present throughout, insists that Leopoldo María is 'uno de los temas indudablemente más importantes de la película. Vamos, que significa o cristaliza, si quieres, la ruptura de una serie de cosas' ('one of the obviously most important themes of the film. Meaning that he represents or, if you like, crystallizes the break with a whole series of things'; qted, by Egea, 2004: 85). For Michi, it is 'una cosa bastante obvia' ('pretty obvious') that 'el hecho de Leopoldo' ('the fact of Leopoldo') is more important than 'la muerte de papá' ('our dad's death'). We may note that, for Michi, his brother Leopoldo María signifies a break ('ruptura'): the opposite of possession by the dead father. Effectively, the first thing recalled by Leopoldo María when he enters the film are his periods in jail on account of his communist militancy; later he talks of 'la muerte feliz de nuestro padre' ('the godsend of our father's death'). Michi, who was very young when his father died, insists that his death did not make much of an impact on him. It is Leopoldo María who, with his psychoanalytic discourse, accuses his brothers of having wanted to take the dead father's place, exempting himself from the accusation because he never wanted his father's position as the regime's 'official poet' or as an authoritarian figure, though he does insist on his desire to sleep with his mother. Michi never adopts this oedipal discourse, though Juan Luis, Leopoldo María's literary rival, does — again, in the sexual terrain rather than that of authority — by recounting how it excited him when sometimes, in the street, he would be mistaken for his mother's lover. The memory of the father turns out to be a desire for intimacy with the mother.

In practice, it is the film's director, Chávarri, who imposes an oedipal reading, not only by giving a central role to Leopoldo María but above all by framing the footage of the family's conversations with the opening and closing shots of the statue of Leopoldo Panero, as official poet of the regime, at the moment of the inauguration of the monument to him in his native Astorga in 1974. The brilliant decision to show the statue trussed up in a white dust sheet (and later covered with the national flag) before being officially unveiled has encouraged readings of the film as a reflection on the all-powerful absent father whose power remains alive after his death: that is, a reflection on the ghost of Francoism that supposedly continues to cast its shadow over the Transition — which, we should remember, had not happened at the time of the statue's inauguration and was only just beginning at the time of the film's release. However, in the previously mentioned interview, Chávarri insists that this was not his intention but that 'la figura del padre iconográficamente ya estaba puesta en la película como alguien atado y envuelto que no se podía defender' ('iconographically, the figure of the father was already positioned in the film as someone tied and bound who couldn't defend himself') — a somewhat ambiguous statement that seems to vindicate Leopoldo Panero.

Egea notes that Chávarri is responsible for the only mention in the film of the word 'desencanto', since Michi's discussion of the word evidently responds to a question by Chávarri as interviewer that was edited out. This makes it clear that Chávarri did intend his film to be a meditation on 'desencanto' (he would, after all, give his film that title), but a disillusionment related to Francoism rather than the Transition. Alberto Medina, who accepts the oedipal reading of the film, suggests that the other all-powerful absent father in the film is Chávarri, who throughout the film suppresses the questions that he directs to the characters and which condition what they say. This suppression of the interviewer's voice is a technique of classic griersonian documentary, used especially in the English-speaking world from the 1920s as a way of abolishing the distance between the viewer and the subjects on screen, and thereby reinforcing the feeling of 'authenticity'. Since the 1950s, especially in France, the documentary genre has resorted increasingly to self-reflexive techniques that make the interviewer visible and sometimes even the camera, making viewers aware that they are watching a mise-en-scène.[7] As Egea

---

7   See, for example, Winston 1995. A frequent self-reflexive technique is parodic use of the "voice-of-God" voice-over that characterized early documentary and newsreels. Chávarri's filming of the inauguration of Panero's statue in Astorga includes fragments of the official speeches, which inevitably remind the viewer of the "voice-of-God" voice-over of the official Francoist newsreel NO-DO, as Minguet Batllori has observed (1997: 745). However, by suppressing his own voice, which is directing the conversation of his informants, Chávarri reintroduces the authoritarianism

indicates, Chávarri's intervention, which can be deduced from Michi's reply, results in Michi's rejection of the director's attempt to impose a reading of the film as a meditation on 'desencanto' in relation to Francoism. Michi astutely replies: 'para estar desencantado hace falta antes haber estado encantado. Yo, desde luego, no recuerdo nada más que cuatro o cinco momentos muy frágiles, muy huidizos de mi vida de haber estado encantado. Yo diría mejor, ilusionado' ('to be disillusioned one first has to have been enthusiastic about something. As far as I'm concerned, I can only remember four or five brief, insubstantial moments in my life when I felt enthusiastic. Or rather, when I felt it was possible to be enthusiastic'). Michi explains his 'desilusión' ('disillusionment') or 'aburrimiento' ('disaffection') (what Chávarri calls 'desencanto') as a result of the fact that 'yo simplemente, como en todo, he participado como espectador, nada más' ('as in everything, I've participated merely as an onlooker, that's all'). This description of the negative effects of Francoism seems much more convincing than any oedipal explanation, seeing them as the result of the impossibility of any kind of civic engagement, producing a sense of impotence and paralysis. Indeed, if on the one hand *El desencanto* gives us a depressing view of the last years of Francoism and the first months after the dictator's death (the period covered by the shooting of the film), on the other hand, as Egea observes, the film offers us a 'modelo de ruptura, de discontinuidad y de confrontación' ('a model of rupture, discontinuity, and confrontation'; 2004: 89) by recording the Panero family's venting of its family hatreds.

So, one has to ask why the film has been seen, by all of its critics apart from Egea, as the representation of the climate of 'desencanto' that supposedly marked the Transition. Egea traces the creation of the topos of 'desencanto' in the press of the Transition years, noting the word's first use in the financial press in July 1976, two months before the film's release, and then a gap of two years until the word started to appear in op-eds, especially in the daily *El País*, in relation to the debate on the 1978 Constitution (Egea 2004: 82). From that time on, peaking in the years 1979 and 1980, the idea that Spaniards were suffering from 'desencanto', and that this disillusionment found its maximum expression in Chávarri's film despite the fact that it was made at an earlier moment, became a commonplace. Alberto Medina, in his 2001 book *Exorcismos de la memoria: Políticas y poéticas de la melancolía en la España de la transición* (*Exorcisms of Memory: The Politics and Poetics of Melancholy in Spain of the Transition Period*), has proposed that this disillusionment was not a reaction against the consensus politics that made the Transition possible, but a topos created strategically by those in power — Egea would say by *El País* as the mouthpiece of the Socialist Party (PSOE) — since it was convenient for politicians of the time to have a passive public that would not ask for radical change. However, Medina, after proposing that 'desencanto' was a response generated by neo-liberalism, falls back into the idea that, in at least some cases, it was also the expression of a melancholic inability to break with the past. For Medina, the emblematic representation of this psychoanalytic discourse is Chávarri's film, which he sees as a 'monumento al padre' ('monument to the father'; 2001: 68–80, 135–51). In this respect, Medina's analysis

that he parodies in his filming of the inauguration.

recalls that of Teresa Vilarós's earlier book, *El mono del desencanto: Una crítica cultural de la transición española* (*Disenchantment as Withdrawal Symptom: A Cultural Critique of the Spanish Transition*, 1998). Medina quotes the passage in which Vilarós uses Lacanian theory to theorize a disillusionment seen as an unconscious return to the past, resulting from the withdrawal symptoms — the 'mono' of her book title — experienced, on Franco's death, by a 'cuerpo social' ('social body') shaped by the dictatorship's repressive structures and unable to adjust to the new freedoms:

> Entre este mañana que no puede escribirse y el ayer borrado se encripta el fantasma del pasado, convirtiéndose para el inconsciente colectivo un eco de lo que Jacques Lacan denominó 'la Cosa', evocación de algo ominoso al que es difícil acceder porque queda siempre fuera del significado.' (Vilarós 1998: 11; qted. in Medina 2001: 79)

> (Between this tomorrow that can't be written and the past that has been erased, the specter of the past encrypts itself, becoming for the collective unconscious an echo of what Jacques Lacan called 'the Thing,' the evocation of something sinister that is hard to access because it lies always beyond signification.')

It makes sense that, for Vilarós, *El desencanto* should be the maximum expression of this psychological paralysis, despite the fact that, as she recognizes, the film precedes the phenomenon it supposedly depicts. The same idea was previously expressed in Joan Minguet Batllori's chapter on Chávarri's film in the *Antología crítica del cine español* published by Cátedra in 1997, for whom *El desencanto* 'se convierte, a raíz de su estreno en septiembre de 1976, en una suerte de metáfora ejemplar del desaliento, de la frustración que la política española tras la muerte del Dictador había generado en los sectores más esperanzados con el cambio político' ('became, on its release in September 1976, a kind of exemplary metaphor of the dejection, of the frustration that Spanish politics after the Dictator's death generated in those sectors most invested in political change'; 744). For Minguet Batllori this was a metaphorical function made possible by the film's treatment of 'el conflicto edípico y la muerte simbólica del padre' ('the oedipal conflict and symbolic death of the father') in relation not just to the poet Leopoldo Panero but also to the 'dictador, padre putativo de todos los Panero y, por desgracia, de tantos otros españoles' ('dictator as alleged father of all the Paneros and, unfortunately, of so many other Spaniards'; 745). In her later book of 2002, *Cultura herida* (*Wound Culture*), Cristina Moreiras Menor proposed that the literature and cinema of democratic Spain — after the Transition — is marked by something even worse: a trauma so serious that the effects of the repressive past continue to be felt even though its traces are no longer represented.

What, we may ask, is the impulse driving this repeated tendency to explain the Transition — and even the following years when democracy had been fully assumed — in terms of a hangover or melancholy or trauma caused by the death of the Father? A partial explanation, as suggested at the start of this essay, might be the hegemony of psychoanalysis in the critical discourse of literature departments in the US academy (and in the English-speaking world generally) in the 1990s and the early years of the new century, whose scholars were frequently formed in the psychoanalytic discourse practiced in Film Studies and especially in Women's Studies. But if psychoanalysis was dominant in feminist academic discourse, why did no one notice the role in *El desencanto* of Felicidad Blanc, whose problem in 1976 is not her dead husband, represented by the ghostly monument that opens and closes the film, but her sons, and especially Leopoldo María who insists on seeing everything through a psychoanalytic lens? And since the oedipal interpretation of the film is not exclusive to scholars in the US academy, though they have taken it furthest, why did no one, before Egea's 2004 article, question this interpretation and the retrospective maneuver that turns the film into the expression of a disillusionment that supposedly characterized the subsequent years of the Transition?

On the one hand, the discourse of disillusionment that became hegemonic in the op-ed column of *El País* during the Transition and that was back-projected onto Chávarri's film shows that the Transition was not mythified at the time as an exemplary political model — the accusation made so often today. That mythification process came later, once democracy was consolidated. The fact that the discourse of 'desencanto' was seen as having been prefigured by the film of the same name, which documents a family's memories of the past, also suggests a need to question the equation of the Transition's politics of consensus with a 'pacto del olvido' ('pact of forgetting') — another topos that became hegemonic thanks to Paloma Aguilar Fernández's 1996 book *Memoria y olvido de la guerra civil española* (*Memory and Amnesia: The Role of the Spanish Civil War in the Transition to Democracy*, as its 2002 English translation was entitled). That the critical studies whose psychoanalytical discourse I have questioned were made possible by Aguilar's book is shown by the fact that they see the impossibility of breaking with the ghosts of the past as a return of the repressed: that is, as the consequence of an attempt to forget. Chávarri's film is, in fact, an unsuitable example of this supposed psychic process because it documents a family that does nothing but remember — which, we may note, did not prevent Leopoldo María from breaking politically with the past nor the whole family, with the possible exception of the eldest brother Juan Luis, from breaking with the dead father that Chávarri insists on depicting as eternally present.

This does not mean that the members of the Panero family succeeded in life: they are clearly a family of failures. But to attribute this failure to a fixation with the dead father is to ignore the evidence given in the film: it is a failure caused by the collapse of the family finances on the death of a father whose passing no one regrets. If we want to make a symbolic reading of the film, I suggest that we read it not through an oedipal lens but through the concept of disillusionment articulated by Michi: a disillusionment not in the sense of a loss of illusions but one that is the result of growing up in an atmosphere where it was not possible to have illusions about anything — that is, where belief in the possibility of creating a future had been lost. Even the political rebellion of Leopoldo María is remembered by Michi via a revealing incident in which he led his fellow demonstrators down a blind alley, where they were all arrested by the police. Not so much possession by the ghosts of the past, then, as living in an empty present with no sense of a future. It is common today to criticize the Transition for being so focused on the future that it refused to take stock of the past. Although the responsibility for a repressive past must be tackled, Chávarri's film — with its devastating depiction of a family whose empty lives are devoid of illusions whether past or present, for whom the past was better only in a material sense, and who have no faith in the future — leaves one with a sense of the political importance of belief in the possibility of a better future. And it is not true that the Transition was characterized only by disillusionment: it was the actions of workers' movements and the parties of the left that forced the heirs of Francoism to pact with them, as Molinero has shown. To convert *El desencanto* into a symbolic representation of the Transition is to forget those who were its real protagonists and to suppose, in keeping with certain narratives of the Transition circulating today, that it was the product only of the political families associated with the dictatorship.[8] Chávarri's portrait of a family previously linked to the regime and now in total decline is remarkable but it should not be read as more than what it is. Above all, it should not be forgotten that, if the Panero family talks about the past and, on occasions, about the dead father, it is because Chávarri asked them to do so.

Works Cited

Aguilar Fernández, Paloma. *Memoria y olvido de la guerra civil española*. Madrid: Alianza, 1996.

Blanc, Felicidad. *Espejo de sombras*. Barcelona: Argos Vergara, 1981.

Chávarri, Jaime, dir. *El desencanto*. Élias Querejeta P.C., 1976.

Egea, Juan. '*El desencanto*: La mirada del padre y las lecturas de la transición.' *Symposium* 58.2 (2004): 79–92.

Haro Ibars, Eduardo. '*El desencanto* y el ilusionismo.' *Triunfo* 723 (4 December 1976): 77–78.

Kinder, Marsha. *Blood Cinema: The Reconstruction of National Identity in Spain*. Berkeley: U of California P, 1993.

Lara, Fernando. '*El desencanto*, de Jaime Chávarri: La 'célula primaria' del franquismo.' *Triunfo* 714 (2 October 1976): 49.

Medina Domínguez, Alberto. *Exorcismos de la memoria: Políticas y poéticas de la melancolía en la España de la transición*. Madrid: Ediciones Libertarias, 2001.

Molinero, Carme. 'La transición y la 'renuncia' a la recuperación de la "memoria democrática".' *Journal of Spanish Cultural Studies* 11.1 (2010): 33–51.

Minguet Batllori, Joan M. '*El desencanto*, 1976': *Antología crítica del cine español, 1906–1995. Flor en la sombra*. Ed. Julio Pérez Perucha. Madrid: Cátedra, 1997. 743–45.

Moreiras Menor, Cristina. *Cultura herida: Literatura y cine en la España democrática*. Madrid: Ediciones Libertarias, 2002.

8   Molinero's rigorous analysis of the events that comprised the Transition argues that, far from representing a political continuity imposed by the heirs of Francoism on a precarious left, it was a "ruptura pactada" ("negotiated break") made possible by the fact that the former knew, thanks to the pressure exerted by the political opposition and workers' organizations in the preceding years, that they had no option but to agree to a democratic solution. (Author's note to the 2018 English translation for this book: I would today qualify my reading of the Transition, thanks to the information that has emerged in recent years about how the traditional parties of the left [socialist and communist] deactivated groups that were demanding more radical change. But I would maintain the view that it was the strength of the left and of workers' — and, I would now add, citizens' — movements that forced the Francoist political families to accept democracy as the only possible future for the country.)

Smith, Paul Julian. *Spanish Visual Culture: Cinema, Television, Internet.* Manchester: Manchester UP, 2006.

Vilarós, Teresa. *El mono del desencanto: Una crítica cultural de la transición española (1973–1993).* Madrid: Siglo XXI, 1998.

Winston, Brian. *Claiming the Real: The Documentary Film Revisited.* London: British Film Institute, 1995.

CHAPTER 21

Silence, Trauma, and Abjection:
La madre muerta (Juanma Bajo Ulloa, 1993)

La madre muerta is a film that invites and frustrates psychoanalytic explanation. Psychoanalysis has been central to the discipline of film studies since the latter's professionalization in the 1970s, and especially to feminist film criticism, which since 1975 has dominated the field. But its centrality has also been challenged, most notably by Steven Shaviro who has argued for a material reading of the medium. In this chapter, I propose to take Bajo Ulloa's film as a test case for discussing the relative merits of psychoanalytic and material readings. To do so, I shall read it alternately through Julia Kristeva's *Powers of Horror* and Shaviro's *The Cinematic Body*, which discuss abjection from a psychoanalytic and anti-psychoanalytic standpoint respectively. I shall supplement my discussion of abjection with brief reference to writing on trauma.

The hesitation as to whether to read the film psychoanalytically or in material terms derives from the film's refusal to tell us whether the cause of the muteness of the film's protagonist, Leire, is psychological or physical. She is shown to suffer throughout the film from traumatic re-enactments, triggered by the sight of blood, of the moment when, as a young child, she witnessed the murder of her mother by an intruder, Ismael. This encourages us to suppose that her inability to speak is the result of psychological damage. The fact that she whimpers at the sight of blood shows that she can utter sounds. But we also see Ismael put his shotgun to the little Leire's head when she confronts him with her accusing gaze as, after shooting her mother, he takes her half-eaten bar of chocolate, left in the kitchen (more about chocolate later). This moment is followed by a blinding flash, which we provisionally assume is a gunshot — an assumption confirmed towards the end of the film when Ismael parts the now teenage Leire's hair to reveal the scar from the bullet wound. The dialogue never reveals the extent of the brain damage, if any, done to Leire by this gunshot, but it is clear from the positioning of the gun and the scar that the bullet must have entered her brain. It is never clarified whether Leire understands language but is just unable to speak, or whether she has no access to language at all. Indeed, it is not clear whether she has any kind of subjectivity. A noticeable feature of the film is its presentation of Leire as object of the gaze, with only a minimal number of shots taken from her point of view — all of these intercut, through the use of shot/reverse shot, with glimpses of her blank stare.

Thus, these point-of-view shots tell us nothing about Leire's response to what she sees. The fascination of Leire for us and for Ismael is that we are uncertain whether she is a person — able to generate meaning from within — or a body — that is, a blank surface onto which others attempt to project meaning but which resists that attempt.

Shaviro, discussing Warhol's films, talks of the 'primordial *stupidity* of the body, a weird inertness and passivity, something that freely offers itself to all the categories of thought and representation, allows them to invest it and pass through it, yet somehow always effortlessly evades them' (208). Shaviro similarly highlights the evacuation of subjectivity incarnated in the zombie, since they are 'all body' with 'brains but not minds' (86). He insists that this 'abject vacancy' and 'passive emptying of the self' (98) produces not only horror in the spectator, but also fascination. This is a 'disidentification' rather than an identification, since it consists of a sympathetic attraction to the evacuation of subjectivity:

> But such vacuity is not nothingness, for it is powerfully, physically felt... . The hardest thing to acknowledge is that the living dead are not radically Other so much as they serve to awaken a passion for otherness and for vertiginous disidentification that is already latent within our own selves. (99)

Leire is a kind of zombie in that she has 'come back from the dead,' apparently brainless, after being shot by Ismael as a child. But unlike the classic zombie she is beautiful, increasing the attraction to her evacuation of subjectivity in a particularly disturbing way.

If we read Leire through Shaviro's analysis of the zombie movie and of Warhol's attempt to evacuate meaning by reducing bodies to an impenetrable surface, she becomes an emblem of the material image that invites but refuses meaning. Thus, she asserts her materiality over any attempt by the spectator to draw it into the symbolic order of language. The key point made by Shaviro in this respect is that such vacuous material images, in resisting spectators' attempts to invest them with meaning, do not distance spectators but allow them to open themselves up to engulfment by what Sartre disparagingly called 'the practico-inert' (Shaviro 202): that is, to enjoyment of the annulment of their subjectivity. In other words, the 'stupid body,' which fascinates and attracts us, allows us to give ourselves up to a state of abjection: invasion of the self by an alien materiality.

Shaviro only once mentions Kristeva's classic study of abjection, *Powers of Horror*, to note that, although its force lies in her analysis of the *jouissance* afforded by giving oneself up to abjection, nonetheless she sees the abject as something that needs to be resisted in order to construct the ego (Shaviro 260). In other words, Kristeva is still operating from within a psychoanalytic concept of the self as a defensive process of boundary formation and policing, necessary to protect the self from engulfment by the Other and from the formlessness that results from any breaching of the self-Other boundary. Her book celebrates the ways in which certain writers have reveled in the abject, abandoning defensive ego-formations, but she nevertheless posits language as their means of conquering the threat of the abject in the process of immersing themselves in it.

Kristeva's discussion is gendered since she assumes that the abject is incarnated in the maternal body, fusion with which produces *jouissance* but also terror of loss of self; and that language is the means of transcending it since language is (to use Lacan's term) the 'Law of the Father' (a curious concept given that, as the phrase 'mother tongue' indicates, language is usually learnt from the mother). Kristeva argues that only male writers explore the terror of the abject, since only they succeed in fully separating from the mother and constructing ego boundaries, through their incorporation into the 'Law of the Father.' Only they can appreciate the terrors of the abject since only they have something to lose — unlike women who occupy the position of the abject anyway. Like Freud and Lacan, Kristeva assumes that the mother stands for the body, and the father for the symbolic order of language, access to which necessarily involves separation from 'the real.' In other words, the symbolic order is constituted by lack. If Freud saw the Oedipus complex in terms of the lack produced by the horror of the mother's 'castrated' body and by the threat of castration by the father for desiring the mother's body, Lacan will recast the psychoanalytic notion of lack in terms of the loss of the real produced by the passage from the pre-oedipal identification with the mother's body to the symbolic order represented by access to language. Kristeva's relation to the Freudian and Lacanian oedipal scenario is complex, since, although she accepts the inevitability of the passage from the pre-oedipal to the oedipal, she also attaches a positive value to the pre-oedipal mother–child bond (Moi 137–213). If Freud saw emergence from the pre-oedipal scenario as necessary to avoid engulfment by the mother, Kristeva will celebrate the primary mother–daughter bond as a fullness inevitably but tragically lost on access to the symbolic order based on lack. In celebrating male writers who have been able to open themselves to the abject, she is celebrating their ability to face the dissolution of the self implied by the primary bond with the mother; that is, male writers who have been able to face the 'horror' of immersion in the maternal body (16–18).

Kristeva insists that abjection — the construction of boundaries through the expulsion of what is perceived as abject — is necessary to culture (2). She takes her analysis of the foundation of culture through abjection from the anthropological work of Mary Douglas. Kristeva's originality lies in her re-reading of Douglas's anthropological analysis of the role of material culture in the formation of collective symbolic systems, through a psychoanalytic exploration of the role of abjection in cultural formation, seen in terms of individual ego formation. This leads her to associate the polluted substances analyzed by Douglas — all of which exit or enter the body, breaching body boundaries — with the maternal or fertilizable body: menstrual blood, milk, and excrement (which comes to be perceived as abject through the toilet training imparted by the mother).

La madre muerta invites a psychoanalytic reading because of its opening scene, before the credits, showing us Leire's violent separation from the mother. The violence of this scene is made more shocking by the initial close-up of the beautiful photograph of the infant Leire in her Madonna-like mother's arms, followed by a slow zoom out and pan of the statues and paintings, mostly of the Madonna, in her mother's art restorer's studio — set to the overwhelmingly beautiful strains of the theme tune. The camera halts — as the violins hit a jarring note — on a painting of the Madonna and Child severed from each other by a diagonal rip in the canvas at the level of the mother's neck. This image was used on the poster for the film (**Figure 21.1**), which placed a metal collar and chain round the Child's neck, prefiguring the collar and chain that Ismael will later use to imprison the teenage Leire as his kidnap victim. All of these Madonna images, including the photograph of Leire in her mother's arms, are filmed in flashes of color, punctuating the blue-tinged dark interior as the intruding Ismael's torch falls on them. This appears to 'reanimate' the images — an impression violently shattered by the ensuing shooting of Leire's mother and, subsequently, Leire herself. Both of these shootings are filmed in blue-tinged monochrome, with one important exception: the blood that we see trickle over Leire's mother's point-of-view shot as, lying dying on the ground, she sees the feet of little Leire approach, cutting to an all-red screen as her vision is blotted out.

But although this violent prologue invites a psychoanalytic reading, given that psychoanalysis posits the separation from the mother as the founding moment of ego formation, it is hard to make such a reading work. In the Freudian and Lacanian accounts, it is the father who severs the mother–child bond. Are we then to see Ismael as the 'Law of the Father'? Leire's actual father is neither seen nor mentioned in the film. The equation of Ismael with the father who separates the daughter from the mother provides an explanation of Leire's curious attraction and self-subordination to him when he kidnaps her years later. But such a reading posits an extraordinarily degraded image of the father, since Ismael is a brutal criminal. Should we read this as a critique of the violence involved in the subordination of the ego — especially the female ego — to the 'Law of the Father'? Such a reading is possible, given the strong critique of patriarchy in Bajo Ulloa's first film, *Alas de mariposa* (*Butterfly Wings*, 1991), which describes a daughter's repudiation from birth for not being a boy, her killing of her younger brother and consequent estrangement from her mother, and her later enforced impregnation through rape. Ismael does in some ways come to occupy the position of father to Leire — twice saving her from the oncoming train under which he vainly attempts to throw her — but this is a murderous father. Susan Martin-Márquez argues that Ismael takes on the role of mother to Leire, attempting to instill in her a notion of what Kristeva calls the 'clean and proper body' (Kristeva 72), by chiding her for eating the bar of chocolate she has dropped in the mud, and subsequently nourishing her with repeated offers of chocolate. But Ismael also seems to live in a state of infantile narcissism, having no super-ego but expecting immediate satisfaction of his desires, and killing or threatening to kill anyone who gets in the way of them (the drug-dealer, Maite) — apart from Leire who instils in him a strange respect because she alone makes no demands on him. The inability to locate Ismael firmly in any one position in the oedipal triad (father, mother, infant) is compounded by the fact that we have absolutely no information about his past history.

Even more problematic is Leire's relation to the oedipal scenario. For, in her case, separation from the mother, far from allowing ego-formation and access to the

FIG. 21.1. Poster for *La madre muerta* (Juanma Bajo Ulloa, 1993, prod. Gasteizko Zinema). Filmoteca Española. © Juanma Bajo Ulloa.

symbolic order of language, leads to autism and an inability to speak. The fact that we first see Leire through her dying mother's bloodstained point-of-view shot invites the suggestion that Leire remains trapped in the mother's viewpoint for ever. This is tantamount to saying that she remains forever trapped within a wounded maternal vision, her development arrested at the point of the traumatic event. According to such a reading, Leire is damaged not by violent separation from the mother, but by being permanently locked, through an act of violence, in the pre-oedipal realm of indifferentiation, prior to language. If, on the one hand, we read Leire's violent separation from her mother as an entry into the oedipal, then this is an oedipal crisis that cannot be resolved for lack of a father (other than Ismael as murderous father substitute). If, on the other hand, we read this violent separation as locking Leire in the pre-oedipal, then this is a pre-oedipal scenario of indifferentiation from the mother, but without the mother. These complications do not necessarily imply that we should abandon a psychoanalytic reading, for it could be argued that the lack of fit between Leire's situation and those of the psychoanalytic oedipal paradigm is precisely the source of her psychic and physical disturbance.

Psychoanalysis has played a major if problematic role in modern Western culture by attributing physical impairment to psychic factors, as in Freud's reading of hysteria, which led him to 'discover' the existence of the unconscious. This gives supremacy to the individual psyche, at the expense of underestimating the role of the material in psychological life. Freud's major breakthrough was his reading of hysteria as a response to a traumatic experience, relegated to the unconscious, and manifesting itself in physical symptoms whose psychic origin had been repressed. As is well known, Freud took further this de-materialization of trauma by rejecting his female patients' claims to have been physically abused by their fathers, interpreting this as a fantasy projection. Freud's discussion of war neurosis, after World War I, forced him to admit that trauma can have a material cause, but nevertheless he argued that the psychic trauma diminishes when there is material mutilation (301–05).

Certain writers on trauma have qualified Freud's interpretation of it as a largely, if not entirely, psychic phenomenon. Ernst van Alphen argues that the traumatic event is not repressed, and that there is strictly no such thing as traumatic memory, for the traumatic event was never experienced in the first place. What van Alphen means by this is that the traumatic event happened to the individual, but could not be registered as an 'experience' because it did not fit the categories of possibility of that individual's culture. For example, the atrocities of the Holocaust could not be registered as 'experiences' since they totally denied our modern Western assumption that the individual is defined by his or her ability to exercise free will. This makes it impossible to 'experience' a situation in which the possibility of exercising free will does not arise, for in such circumstances one is not an individual but a thing; that is, a body. Van Alphen notes how many trauma victims talk of having died at the moment of the traumatic event. Trauma thus registers on the body rather than on the mind. Susan Brison has similarly argued that the compulsive reliving of the traumatic event is not so much the return of a repressed memory as a bodily possession by, and re-enactment of, the past. Although van Alphen and Brison argue that trauma is written on the body — including on vision — rather than on the mind, they both suppose that the trauma can be overcome only by reconstructing an ego whose boundaries are strong enough to incorporate the traumatic event into it as an 'experience.' They do not ultimately challenge the modern Western notion of the free individual, which their theorization of trauma shows to be inadequate in certain situations.

Van Alphen's and Brison's discussions of trauma seem appropriate in Leire's case, for her traumatization consists in her reduction to a thing or body. She does not have flashes of memory of the traumatic event, but it returns to 'possess' her physically at the sight of blood. The trauma thus seems to be written on her body and not on her psyche, for she is a body without any perceptible interiority. She has vision, but her gaze registers events blankly. Her responses are purely physical, with no sign of comprehension: when Maite, bathing her, tells her she is pretty, she plays with the soap suds; when Ismael tries to make her laugh with his clown song, she moves her head to the rhythm but her expression is vacant. She responds physically when Ismael touches her breast, when he masturbates her, and especially when he offers her chocolate — but in each case her gaze remains expressionless. Each time she is offered a chance of freedom, she retreats back to the corner where she had been chained by Ismael, implying that she has no sense of herself as a modern Western individual, defined by free will. Leire's 'thingness' is illustrated strikingly the second time Ismael tries to push her under a train: when she falls after he hits her for whimpering, she gets up not to run away but to move zombie-like towards the approaching train. It is on occasions like this, when Leire responds as a 'thing,' that Ismael shows her tenderness. He may be infuriated by her refusal to offer him any kind of recognition, but he is able to respond to her because, as a 'thing,' she makes no demands on him. This contrasts with his abusive treatment of all the other people he encounters, whom he reduces to the status of 'things' to protect his seemingly fragile ego boundaries against their demands.

Ismael's obsession with Leire takes the form of gazing at her for hours on end. Maite insists that Leire is not the inert object of the gaze, but is controlling Ismael to get her revenge for the film's inaugural act of violence. Whether Leire recognizes Ismael as her mother's killer and her own assailant is never made clear; it is Ismael who insists that she does and that she must be eliminated because she could denounce him. In practice, it is not Ismael who triggers memories of his murder of her mother in Leire, but Leire who triggers memories of it in him. Ismael had originally shot Leire when she challenged him with her accusing gaze as he ate her chocolate. As his kidnap victim, years later, she does not look at him accusingly but blankly (it is not clear how Ismael recognizes her as a teenager, but he appears to connect the fixity of her blank stare at him, as she passes the open door of the nightclub where he is confronting the drug dealer, with the fixity of her accusing stare as a child). Leire's blank stare and Ismael's fascinated staring at her raise the question of the relation between power and the gaze. This is an issue crucial to gaze theory, which has formed the central plank of feminist film criticism.

Shaviro takes gaze theory, as instituted by Laura Mulvey's 1975 article 'Visual Pleasure and Narrative Cinema' and its 1981 sequel 'Afterthoughts on "Visual

Pleasure and Narrative Cinema"' (Mulvey 14–38), to task for assuming that cinematic pleasure comprises a 'masculine' desire (whether exercised by male or female
spectators) to reduce the female characters on screen to the status of 'objects of the
gaze.' Shaviro suggests that such a desire for control is in fact a defense against what
he sees as the principal pleasure offered by cinema: that of abandoning oneself to
possession by the cinematic image (9–17). He argues that Mulvey, while criticizing
the 'masculine' gaze that objectifies women on screen, is herself advocating such
a 'masculine' position by deconstructing cinematic pleasure, thereby refusing to
be seduced by it (12–13). This defensive posture has, he argues, come to constitute
an orthodoxy: 'It seems as if theorists of the past twenty years can scarcely begin
their discussions without ritualistically promising to resist the insidious seductions
of film' (11). He notes that this fear of images is supported by the whole history of
the Western philosophical tradition, which since Plato has 'warned us against being
seduced by reflections and shadows' (15): that is, by cinema. What, Shaviro asks, is
wrong with allowing oneself to be seduced? Might this not be a refusal (whether
by male or female spectators) of the patriarchal order that insists on 'mastery' as the
precondition of being an individual self?

Shaviro notes that Kaja Silverman's later theorization of the gaze from a Lacanian
perspective does allow for a kind of gaze (what she terms 'the look,' to distinguish
it from the controlling 'gaze') that declares its vulnerability in the face of the
power of the image (Shaviro 57–59). Silverman also observes that, by opting for the
position of object of the gaze (that is, by making oneself into a spectacle), one can
exert considerable power over others. Her key example, from Fassbinder's *Fear Eats
the Soul*, is a male character, the Turkish immigrant Ali who is othered not by his
gender but by his ethnicity (Silverman 125–56). Thus, Silverman does not radically
break with the traditional psychoanalytic schema whereby men — driven by lack
through their inscription into the symbolic order — are the owners of desire, and
women — whose entry into the symbolic order remains problematic, since they can
never fully separate from the feminine body — its objects. As Shaviro comments
(59), Silverman is still operating within the framework of psychoanalytic film
criticism which supposes that the medium — which appears to give us the real,
but in fact only gives us a play of shadows on screen — is characterized by lack,
and consequently functions as an emblem of the symbolic order of language which
represents the real while substituting for it.

Shaviro notes that Lacanian psychoanalysis remains within the Platonic tradition
of mistrust of images in that 'it denounces the delusions of the optical system ... and
privileges the Symbolic order of language in opposition to an Imaginary defined
primarily in visual terms' (15). Thus, the cinematic image is treated suspiciously
by psychoanalytic film criticism for giving us representation (surface) rather than
essence (depth). Shaviro asks:

> But is it really *lack* that makes images so dangerous and disturbing? What these
> theorists fear is not the emptiness of the image, but its weird fullness; not its
> impotence so much as its power... . Images are banally self-evident and self-
> contained, but their superficiality and obviousness is also a strange blankness, a
> resistance to the closure of definition, or to any imposition of meaning. Images

are neither true nor false, neither real nor artificial, neither present nor absent;
they are radically devoid of essence. (17)

Leire's blankness, at which Ismael gazes in obsessive fascination, is an embodiment
of this concept of cinematic pleasure, derived from abandoning ego boundaries
rather than asserting them.

Shaviro insists that cinema is an intensely material medium, which overwhelms
us with tactile, corporeal sensations. *The Cinematic Body* is an attempt to engage
with that materiality, and to explore the pleasures that result from abandoning
oneself to it. For Shaviro, the pleasures of the cinematic gaze are derived not from
any attempt to assert control, but from a masochistic immersion in the material
images that overwhelm one's senses. Cinema thus has the merit of 'undoing the
security and possessiveness that have conventionally been associated with the "male
gaze"' (9). Leire — the 'stupid body' which is capable of vision but not of language
— is not only beautiful but incontinent. She thus embodies a cinematic pleasure
that is about opening the body up and admitting its porousness: what Shaviro —
following Deleuze and Guattari's *Anti-Oedipus* — calls a 'radical passivity' (Shaviro
48). Thus, Shaviro defines voyeurism or scopophilia as 'the opposite of mastery: it
is rather a forced, ecstatic abjection before the image' (49).

Both *The Cinematic Body* and *Powers of Horror* are explorations of abjection.
Kristeva's analysis offers itself as a way of making sense of *La madre muerta* because
Leire is marked both by loss of the maternal body and by a fascination with
chocolate, which in turn is associated in the film with mud and excrement, as
Conway (73–100) and Martín-Márquez have noted. Little Leire's accusing stare
at Ismael in the film's prologue is an immediate response, not to his shooting of
her mother, but to his eating of her chocolate. The film's poster (Figure 21.2) is
headed with the words 'Matar es tan fácil como robar un dulce a un niño ... pero
menos peligroso' (Killing is as easy as stealing a sweet from a child ... but less
dangerous). Both Leire and Ismael have a passion for chocolate. Ismael's supplying
of Leire with chocolate while his hostage, and again at the end of the film when
he returns to find her at the clinic for the disabled, can be seen as his way of asking
her forgiveness: a forgiveness which is accepted at a bodily level since Leire takes
the chocolate on every occasion — her one gesture of recognition towards him.
We are told at the start by Blanca, the nurse at the clinic, that Leire is diabetic. If
she cannot assimilate sugar, this would explain her craving for chocolate. What the
film does not explain is how, if Leire is diabetic, she does not become ill during
the several days when she is held hostage by Ismael, given that she is not receiving
insulin and is being plied with chocolate regularly. A physical explanation in terms
of her love of chocolate does not fully work. A psychoanalytic explanation suggests
itself through the association of chocolate with mud and excrement, allowing it to
figure the pre-oedipal state of union with the mother, before the child has learnt
to distinguish the contours of its 'clean and proper body' through toilet training
and learning what food may and may not be eaten. 'Es caca' ('It's shit'), Ismael tells
Leire when she picks the chocolate up from the mud by the railway tracks and puts
it in her mouth. A similar association of chocolate with what should not be taken

into the mouth is set up in the scene when the nurse Blanca, having broken into the house where Leire is held captive, hides behind the wardrobe and watches, horrified, as Leire appears to go towards Ismael to suck his penis; in the following shot — seen by the spectator and not Blanca — Ismael zips up the bottom pocket of his leather jacket and we realize she has been sucking the chocolate he has taken out of his pocket to give her.

This scene started with Blanca, who we are told at the start has bladder problems, involuntarily urinating. Incontinence — lack of control over the body — is thus associated with a 'normal' character as well as with the disabled and/or traumatized Leire. Blanca's killing by Maite is represented obliquely through the image of her urine on the ground mixing with a pool of blood. Ismael's brutal killing of the drug dealer early in the film is a reversal of this incontinence, with liquid breeching the body's boundaries by entering it rather than leaving it, as Ismael pours beer into his mouth until he suffocates.

The film's powerful final scene as, in the pouring rain, Leire takes the bar of chocolate held out by Ismael, prostrate on his knees before her, links chocolate with dissolution — and with mud as Leire, pulled away by the Directora of the clinic, drops the chocolate in the mud in which Ismael is lying, pinned down by the male nurses. When Leire breaks free from the Directora to go back to Ismael, we expect a redemptive end — brutally frustrated as Leire bends to pick up the chocolate from the mud and go back to the Directora, leaving Ismael — immersed in the mud, in his mud-brown leather jacket — to his fate. In this final scene, the chocolate is also associated with blood, as Leire wipes chocolate over her cheeks, only to discover the blood left on her face by the caress of Ismael's wounded hand.

During this embrace, Ismael presses his face to her breast, screwed up like that of a newborn infant — an expression he adopts again at the end as, Leire having retrieved the chocolate and abandoned him, he sinks his head back into the mud. This final sequence follows an unexplained scene in a railway carriage — separated from the previous and succeeding scenes by abrupt editing, disrupting our sense of time and place. In the previous night-time scene, Ismael, shot in the hand by Maite and having left Leire — also shot by Maite — at the hospital unconscious, had leapt into a goods wagon to escape the police. We cut to Ismael sitting in a passenger carriage (on the same train?), in daylight, his hand bandaged. The previous scene by the railway tracks when Maite shot Leire and Ismael was covered by autumn leaves; outside the train carriage we see snow on the ground. There seems to have been a break in time or place. The following scene cuts to Ismael back outside the clinic, with leaves again on the ground, his hand still bandaged and bleeding but Leire apparently recovered from what appeared to be a gunshot wound in the body. The dislocation and temporal incoherence is increased by the unexplained events in the intermediate scene in the passenger carriage, as Ismael finds himself sitting next to a woman, wearing a blue shawl like the Madonna, holding an infant in her arms. An unidentified man sits down opposite her, wrinkles his nose (as does Ismael) at the smell, and the woman takes off the male baby's diaper to reveal a wad of excrement looking much like a half-melted bar of chocolate. She gives the soiled diaper to the unknown man, who exchanges looks with Ismael, huddled in his chocolate-brown (excrement-colored) leather jacket. At this point we cut to Ismael outside the clinic, stalking Leire. The film's closing scenes set up a correlation between blood, chocolate, mud, and excrement which inevitably recalls Kristeva's analysis of the abject as that which threatens body boundaries by entering or leaving the body (blood, chocolate, excrement), or through its formlessness (mud). Most pertinent here is Kristeva's observation that such abject substances are associated with the maternal body: in *La madre muerta* the blood is reminiscent, not of menstrual blood, but of the blood that we — and Leire — saw trickle over her dying mother's face.

La madre muerta is a thriller, with an intensely Gothic visual style. It is, in other words, a film about horror. Its images are also — like its female protagonist — strikingly beautiful, as is its musical soundtrack. As previously noted, Kristeva argues that writers have been able to give themselves up to the abject through language, which permits them to 'master' it while exploring the pleasures — and terrors — of release from ego boundaries. But what happens when the exploration of the abject takes place not through language (Leire cannot speak and Ismael speaks very little) but through images and music? While Ismael is driven crazy by the fact that Leire never laughs — i.e. never acknowledges his capacity to affect her — he is quite happy that she does not speak: 'hablar no es importante' (talking isn't important), he insists. Ismael's relationship to Leire is also mediated by smell: at first he is repelled by the smell of excrement as she soils herself; later he sniffs her body and exclaims, ¡Qué bien hueles, hueles a chocolatina!' ('You smell so nice, you smell of chocolate drops!'). It is possible to read the film as a demonstration of Kristeva's theorization of the abject as a zone of bodily exclusions, related to the need to separate from the maternal body, whose exploration can produce an ecstatic release from ego boundaries as well as horror. Thus, Ismael's screws up his face like a newborn baby both when he presses it to Leire's breast and when he sinks it into the mud, as if returning to the pre-oedipal symbiosis with the mother. Such a reading fits with Kristeva's insistence on the abject as a 'sacred configuration' (6); that is, a kind of secular redemption in a world devoid of religious belief. The repeated images of Madonna and child in the film — in Leire's mother's studio at the start, later visited by Blanca who takes the photograph of Leire in her mother's arms home with her; and in the abandoned cathedral where Ismael and Maite take refuge with Leire after killing Blanca — suggest such a sacred space: a space of bonding with the maternal. Kristeva notes that Christianity, through the figure of the Virgin Mary, introduces the maternal into a previously paternal monotheism (116). But, for Kristeva, Christianity links the abject to the sacred through the practice of confession which makes 'spoken sin' into 'fortunate sin.' In other words, language — the 'Law of the Father' — allows one to take abjection upon oneself in order to purge oneself of it. Kristeva notes that the Christian practice of confession was responsible for creating the modern Western notion of the individual self, through this interiorization of abjection in order to triumph over it (130–32).

It is not clear whether *La madre muerta* can be read as a redemption narrative. Any redemptive message it may offer comes not from language, but from the beauty of its images and musical soundtrack; that is, from those aspects of cinema that impress themselves on the body. This is a kind of redemption that comes not from transcending the abject but from plunging into it. The cathedral is derelict, and the Madonna images are associated with violence. The final scene, set to the swelling violins of the theme tune, appears to offer Ismael redemption as Leire accepts his offer of chocolate and caresses his head as he presses it to her bosom — only to leave him abandoned in the mud, making it clear that what mattered to her was the chocolate (Martin-Márquez; Jordan and Morgan-Tamosunas 192). This devastating end dispels any illusions on the spectator's part that Leire may have acquired a degree of subjectivity — a capacity to love — through her abject experience of captivity: her only capacity for love remains a physical craving for chocolate. Blanca and Maite are dead, the latter by her own hand as she realizes Ismael cares more for Leire than her. Leire walks off to a presumed future as the adoptive daughter of the Directora (who at the start told Blanca she was thinking of adopting her), whose institutional status and somewhat rigid body language suggest a future in which Leire will be trained to adhere to the 'clean and proper body.' This, if we accept Kristeva's analysis, means putting behind her the bond with the 'dead mother' whose absent presence dominates the film — not least through its title. In other words, learning to 'grow up,' for Leire's 'abnormality' consists of continuing to behave like an infant, prior to language and the formation of ego boundaries.

The film's stylized images are built around the colors blue and red. Its director of photography and cameraman, Javier Aguirresarobe, has noted that most of the frames contain a red object, which stands out against the pale or gloomy background like a gash or wound (Seguin 934). The most obvious examples are the balls that the Directora of the clinic and the nurse Blanca are clutching during their first meeting; Maite's sweater, cardigan, handbag or underwear; the fruit in Maite and Ismael's kitchen; the lipstick with which Ismael daubs his face in his clown act; the red of Maite's gloves as she prepares to shoot Leire; the tartan blanket in the cathedral; the red front of the second train under which Ismael tries to throw Leire; the red lining of Ismael's leather jacket; and above all the red wall behind the bed where Leire is chained as Ismael's hostage (the room also has a red lamp and red curtains). These splashes of red remind us of the blood we saw trickle over the face of Leire's dying mother; the credits after the film's violent prologue also place the actors' names over a growing pool of red. In the ripped painting of the Madonna and Child on which Ismael's torch alights in this prologue, the Madonna's veil is — unusually — red rather than blue. As Martin-Márquez notes, the gash in this painting is echoed by the crack in the red wall of the room where Leire is held hostage. We are introduced to this room by the shot of a hand (which the zoom-out reveals to be Leire's) fingering the crack, as if lingering on the open wound of her mother's death.

A large number of scenes are filmed through a blue filter, the color blue being associated with the Madonna's veil — as in the statues and paintings of the Madonna in Leire's mother's studio (apart from the red-veiled Madonna in the ripped canvas), and as in the statue of the Madonna in the derelict cathedral. The color blue is also traditionally associated with melancholy, as here through its juxtaposition with the wistful theme tune; this melancholic association links the Madonna with the theme of the lost mother. In addition to the monochrome blue of the violent prologue (apart from the Madonna images illuminated by Ismael's torch and the drop of blood falling over Leire's mother's point-of-view shot), certain scenes in the Gothic mansion where Ismael and Maite are squatting are also filmed in monochrome blue or have a blue tint (mostly interrupted with a splash of red). The most striking moments when the screen is flooded with blue are the two night-time scenes by the railway tracks, when Ismael first drags Leire there to throw her under a train, and later when he leaps into a goods train; plus the whole of the sequence when Ismael and Maite take Leire to the abandoned cathedral. Both locations — the railway tracks and the cathedral — are given an apocalyptic feel by the intensity of the blue light, which turns scenes of devastation and impending doom into scenes of stunning visual beauty. This is a beauty which does not allow detached aesthetic contemplation, but which overwhelms us physically.

The physicality of the film's striking images is compounded by the soundtrack. In the cathedral, Ismael furiously pedals the organ bellows, filling its derelict space with a nightmarish, swelling cacophony. In the second scene by the railway tracks, filmed in daylight with a slight blue tint, a similar effect of horror is created by the sound and then sight of the sparks produced by the overhead electric cables, as the approaching (red-fronted) train hurtles towards Leire and Ismael — and us. Shaviro recalls the physical shock produced in spectators by the approaching train in the first Lumière Brothers' film (33). The electric charges given off by the cables in this scene subject the audience to a series of acoustic and visual shocks. Something similar happens when we are first introduced to the Gothic mansion where Ismael and Maite are squatting: the long traveling shot around its corridors is interrupted by the sound and sight of shattering glass as Ismael thrusts Maite's head through an interior window. Bajo Ulloa has said that, in filming *La madre muerta*, 'busqué una razón muy fuerte para contar algo que a mí pudiera hacerme daño como espectador' ('I strove for a powerful rationale that would justify narrating something that could hurt me as a spectator'; Heredero 48): the film is an assault on the spectator's hearing and vision. The film's use of long traveling shots is worthy of comment, given that Giuliana Bruno has, like Shaviro, argued that cinema spectatorship is primarily a physical, tactile experience, since the movements of the camera — particularly in a traveling shot — take us into the image. The physicality of the two scenes by the railway tracks is heightened by the long tracking shots as we follow Ismael dragging Leire to her intended death.

Equally physical in its effects is the film's theme tune, composed by Bingen Mendizábal. First heard in the prologue, its subsequent reprises take the spectator back to this inaugural moment of violence, its haunting phrases acting as a constant reminder of the loss of the mother. The jarring note struck by the violins in this prologue as Ismael's torch falls on the ripped canvas of the Madonna and child is also reprised as the train approaches on the first occasion when Ismael attempts to throw Leire under it. Throughout the film there is a striking lack of synchronicity between the editing of image and soundtrack: frequently, the theme tune continues over two or more disparate sequences, providing a kind of *enjambement* that works against the often-violent visual cutting. For example, the theme tune which plays over the final scene where Ismael returns to Leire at the clinic had already come in at the end of the previous scene with the mother changing the baby's diaper on the train.

Particularly striking is the use of editing to start a scene, not with an establishing shot, but with that of a body part, whose identity is only later revealed through a zoom-out. This technique is in place from the moment of the film's opening close-up of the photograph of Leire with her mother, revealed to be a photograph as the camera pulls away. It could be argued that this focus on body parts provides an external correlate to Leire's infantilized vision, whose interiority is never revealed to us. But it also seems to correspond to the vision of Ismael — as, for example, when he comes round from unconsciousness to see the disembodied face of the dead Señora Millas, only then taking in the whole scene in her kitchen, in which she lies dead artistically positioned amid the spilt Bovril and chopped vegetables. This focus on body parts is especially evident in the scene when Ismael touches Leire's breast — the same left breast on which the camera focused in its opening close-up of the photograph of Leire's mother with the infant Leire in her arms.

Carlos Heredero (46) compares the camerawork of Bajo Ulloa's first film *Alas de mariposa* to that of Robert Bresson, in its concern with the material image — despite the fact that Bajo Ulloa claimed not to know Bresson's work. (*La madre muerta* does, however, pay tribute to François Truffaut when Ismael and Maite go to watch one of his films.) Shaviro's last chapter on Bresson notes: 'It is only through an intense and precise attention to the body that Bresson broaches his ultimate religious themes of loss and redemption' (242). What Shaviro means by this is that Bresson, like Warhol, evacuates his characters' subjectivity and finds redemption in abjection. This is a different kind of redemption from that which Kristeva describes as achieved by transcending the abject. Here there is no transcendence but just the flesh, not organized by any controlling subjective vision. Shaviro notes that Bresson often focuses on hands and feet, as body parts which 'are not conventionally taken to signify inner states' (243), while the facial expressions of his characters are blank. Both of these techniques characterize *La madre muerta*. Shaviro finds Bresson's evacuation of subjectivity 'redemptive' in that it rescues his characters from any subordination to a spectatorial controlling gaze, since they simply 'are,' in their enigmatic materiality. This is redemption in the sense of an acceptance of the body 'in which grace is indistinguishable from suffering and abjection' (Shaviro 252).

Shaviro's chapters all end with the word 'abjection': 'passivity and abjection,' 'new ecstasies of abjection,' 'opening to abjection,' 'self-abandonment and abjection,' 'ecstasy and terror of abjection,' 'secret pleasures of abjection,' 'embarrassment and abjection,' 'a vision in which grace is indistinguishable from suffering and abjection' (the chapter on Bresson), 'affirmation and abjection.' This is an abjection that can provide redemption from the straitjacket of the modern Western self, which defines itself through its exclusions. Most radically, it involves abandoning the privileging of self over matter. As Shaviro notes:

> In Western thought, the body has generally been regarded as an affront to the intelligence, an obstacle to both thought and action. The body is passive matter

> waiting to be shaped by the logos's articulating form. Or it is something that
> needs to be regulated and contained — this is why it is subjected to the canons
> of representation. (257)

Cinema, Shaviro argues, can get beyond the Cartesian dualism of mind and body
by thinking through, rather than against, the body. This is another way of saying
that cinema creates its effects through the corporeal qualities of images and sound.
In other words, cinema does not function as a language in the Lacanian sense of
loss of the real but gives us the real in the form of the material. As Shaviro puts it:
'Cinema allows me and forces me to see what I cannot assimilate or grasp. It assaults
the eye and ear, it touches and it wounds... . This touch, this contact, is excessive:
it threatens my very sense of self' (260).

   Heredero notes that, despite the acclaim granted to Bajo Ulloa's first film *Alas de
mariposa*, *La madre muerta* flopped at the box office (46). Critics have mostly ignored
it (at the time of writing this essay, the MLA international bibliography lists not a
single article on it), though in its year of release (1993) it won an impressive number
of awards at international film festivals: in Puerto Rico, the International Critics'
Prize for Best Film and the Public's Prize for Best Film; in Stockholm, the Critics'
Prize for Best Film and the Prize for Best Actress (Ana Álvarez); and in Montreal,
the Prize for Best Director. In the wake of this international acclaim, the film was
released on video with English subtitles. As a result of the film's lack of popularity
with Spanish audiences, Bajo Ulloa radically changed his style, making the hugely
successful comedy *Airbag* (1997) and then abandoning cinema altogether (he worked
with Julio Medem on *Tierra* in 1996, and Medem conversely worked with Bajo
Ulloa on *Airbag*). One senses that the Spanish critics that have written about *La
madre muerta* are disconcerted by the film's refusal of a symbolic reading — such
as those that can be given to Medem's films, for example. In particular, critics
seem to have found this hard to accept of a young Basque director, whose work
they are keen to interpret as in some way 'Basque.' Although *La madre muerta* was
filmed in Vitoria-Gasteiz and Salvatierra-Agurain (Álava) — as well as Miranda de
Ebro in Burgos — there is nothing in the film that allows a reading in terms of
Basque politics. Jean-Claude Seguin, however, has attempted one, suggesting that
'el mundo claustrofóbico de la película es a su vez metáfora de Euskal Herria... .
Detrás del destino trágico de los personajes ... ¿cómo no vislumbramos la imagen
de una sociedad traumatizada por sus propios terrores y sus propios demonios?'
('the claustrophobic world of the film is also a metaphor for the Basque Country... .
Behind its characters' tragic fate ... how can we fail to glimpse the image of a society
traumatized by its terrors and demons?'; 935).

   Seguin has, I would suggest, missed the point of Bajo Ulloa's insistence on
the corporeal nature of the cinematic image and soundtrack, which pre-empt
psychologized and symbolic readings. We can appreciate *La madre muerta* better if
we abandon the attempt to read coherent meaning into it and give ourselves up
to its visual and acoustic pleasures. This does not mean abandoning analysis, but
analyzing the film in terms of what it does to us: that is, as performative rather
than representational.

Works Cited

BAJO ULLOA, JUANMA, dir. *Alas de mariposa*. Gasteizko Zinema, 1991.

——, dir. *La madre muerta*. Gasteizko Zinema, 1993.

BRISON, SUSAN J. 'Trauma Narratives and the Remaking of the Self.' *Acts of Memory: Cultural Recall in the Present*. Ed. Mieke Bal, Jonathan Crewe, and Leo Spitzer. Hanover: UP of New England, 1999. 39–54.

BRUNO, GIULIANA. *Atlas of Emotion: Journeys in Art, Architecture, and Film*. New York: Verso, 2002.

CONWAY, MADELINE RUTH. 'Representing Difference: A Study of Physical Disability in Contemporary Spanish Cinema.' Diss. U of London, 2001.

DELEUZE, GILLES, and FÉLIX GUATTARI. *Anti-Oedipus: Capitalism and Schizophrenia*. Trans. Robert Hurley, Mark Seem, and Helen R. Lane. Minneapolis: U of Minnesota P, 1989.

DOUGLAS, MARY. *Purity and Danger*. London: Routledge & Kegan Paul, 1969.

FREUD, SIGMUND. 'Beyond the Pleasure Principle.' *On Metapsychology*. The Penguin Freud Library. Vol. 11. London: Penguin, 1984. 269–338.

JORDAN, BARRY, and RIKKI MORGAN-TAMOSUNAS. *Contemporary Spanish Cinema*. Manchester: Manchester UP, 1998.

KRISTEVA, JULIA. *Powers of Horror: An Essay on Abjection*. Trans. Leon S. Roudiez. New York: Columbia University Press, 1982.

MARTIN-MÁRQUEZ, SUSAN. 'Disability, Maternity, and Abjection in *Mater amatísima* and *La madre muerta*.' King Juan Carlos I of Spain Center, New York University. 30 September 2002. Unpublished talk.

MOI, TORIL, ED. *The Kristeva Reader*. Trans. Seán Hand and Léon S. Roudiez. New York: Columbia UP, 1986.

MULVEY, LAURA. *Visual and Other Pleasures*. London: Macmillan, 1989.

SEGUIN, JEAN-CLAUDE. '*La madre muerta*, 1993.' *Antología crítica del cine español, 1906–1995*. Ed. Julio Pérez Perucha. Madrid: Cátedra, 1997. 933–35.

SHAVIRO, STEVEN. *The Cinematic Body*. Minneapolis: U of Minnesota P, 1993.

SILVERMAN, KAJA. *Male Subjectivity at the Margins*. New York: Routledge, 1992.

VAN ALPHEN, ERNST. 'Symptoms of Discursivity: Experience, Memory, and Trauma.' *Acts of Memory: Cultural Recall in the Present*. Ed. Mieke Bal, Jonathan Crewe, and Leo Spitzer. Hanover: UP of New England, 1999. 24–38.

PART VI

Historical Memory

CHAPTER 22

❖

History and Hauntology; or, What Does One Do with the Ghosts of the Past? Reflections on Spanish Film and Fiction of the Post-Franco Period

In this essay I shall link a number of films and works of fiction produced in Spain from the 1970s to the mid-1990s.[1] The question I shall be asking is what does a society — in particular, Spanish society of the Transition and since — do with history? that is, what does it do with the ghosts of the past? Given the criticisms of contemporary Spanish culture triggered by the 1992 quincentennial commemorations for refusing to confront the traumas of the past, this is an important question. While agreeing that, in many respects, contemporary Spanish culture — obsessed with creating the image of a brash, young, cosmopolitan nation — is based on a rejection of the past, I want to stress the engagement with the past by a considerable number of directors and writers, both older and young; and also to suggest, tentatively, that the current postmodern obsession with simulacra may be seen as a return of the past in a spectral form.

Just as there are many kinds of ghosts — I shall be talking about werewolves, vampires, Frankenstein's monster, as well as the politically displaced or 'desaparecidos' ('disappeared') — so there are various ways of dealing with them. One can refuse to see them or shut them out, as the official discourses of the state have always done with the various manifestations of the popular imaginary, where for good reasons ghost stories are endemic. One can cling to them obsessively through the pathological process of introjection that Freud called melancholia, allowing

1   First published in 2000, this essay only considers works produced up to 1994, before the beginnings of the memory boom that started in Spain around 1998, snowballing from 2000 with the first public exhumation of a mass grave from the wartime and postwar Francoist reprisals. I leave it unchanged to illustrate how literary and cinematic approaches to the need to acknowledge the victims of Francoism have evolved over the years. Retrospectively, what is most striking is how films and novels about Spain's difficult mid-twentieth-century past prior to the memory boom take on the challenge of finding forms of representation adequate to conveying the spectral presence of the past, by contrast with the overwhelming recourse to realism in the vast corpus of novels and films on the Civil War produced post-2000 in consonance with political demands to "recover the past" and with neo-liberal bestseller culture.

the past to take over the present and convert it into a 'living death.' Or one can offer them habitation in order to acknowledge their presence, through the healing introjection process that is mourning, which, for Freud, differs from melancholia in that it allows one to lay the ghosts of the past to rest by, precisely, acknowledging them as past. The first two options — denying the existence of ghosts, becoming possessed by them — in different ways result in a denial of history, whether through repression or through paralysis. The last option — accepting the past as past — is an acknowledgment of history, which allows one to live with its traces. As Derrida nicely puts it in *Specters of Marx*, ghosts must be exorcised not in order to chase them away but in order 'this time to grant them the right ... to ... a hospitable memory ... out of a concern for justice' (175). For ghosts, as the traces of those who have not been allowed to leave a trace (Derrida's formulation again), are by definition the victims of history who return to demand reparation; that is, that their name, instead of being erased, be honored. This concept helps explain why the term 'los desaparecidos' ('the disappeared') so caught the imagination at the time of the military take-overs in Chile, Argentina and Uruguay: for it constructs the dead, by virtue of the fact that they have not just 'disappeared' but have 'been disappeared,' as ghosts or *revenants* (to use the French term) who refuse to have their presence erased but insist on returning to demand that their name be honored. Derrida has proposed the term 'hauntology' as a new philosophical category of being — a variant on ontology — appropriate to describe the status of history: that is, the past as that which is not and yet is there — or rather, here. That this 'virtual space of spectrality' (Derrida 11) is somehow related to the simulacra of postmodernism is an idea that immediately suggests itself.

In their book *Memory and Modernity: Popular Culture in Latin America*, William Rowe and Vivian Schelling recount a startling anecdote:

> There are conditions under which a massive erasure of memory can occur. A study, begun in 1985, of *villas miserias* (shanty towns) in Córdoba, Argentina, has revealed an absence of memory of the period of military government (1976–85), as compared with the years preceding it. This silence is not the result of fear: informants were not hesitant with information about their activities in the preceding period, details of which could equally be considered 'subversive.' Nor does it indicate a lack of knowledge, since the issue was what they remembered not about the country or the government but about their own lives (119–20).

Rowe and Schelling suggest that the reason for this traumatic erasure of memory was the lack, during the period of military dictatorship, of any form of collective sphere other than that imposed by surveillance; that is, the lack of any space in which memories could be articulated. What is so striking about this anecdote is that the casualty of this suppression of all forms of collective discourse should have been private memories. For popular memory — relying on oral rather than written transmission — requires some kind of collective space, even if it be reduced to that of the family (which is never a purely private sphere). When teaching adult Spanish students who grew up under Francoism, I have frequently been struck by the fact that the only historical knowledge they had about Spain's immediate past was transmitted to them by their families ('family' here means a collective, extended family network).

Interesting work has been done in France by Pierre Nora on the notion of 'lieux de mémoire' or 'memory places': that is, the dependence of memories on attachment to some concrete site; for example, a monument or a landscape. This concept has also been developed by Raphael Samuel in his wonderful book *Theatres of Memory*. The sense of place in the films of Víctor Erice or the novels of Juan Marsé and Julio Llamazares is extraordinarily strong but, in all cases, these are spaces where the possibility of collectivity and communication is denied or at best curtailed. One thinks of the oppressive silences in Erice's *El espíritu de la colmena* (*The Spirit of the Beehive*, 1973) and *El sur* (*The South*, 1983); the image of snow blotting out the traces of landscape and with it memory in Llamazares's *Luna de lobos* (*Wolf Moon*, 1985) and *Escenas de cine mudo* (*Scenes of Silent Cinema*, 1994), plus in both novels the image of the mine which forces memory underground into a disaster-prone space that threatens, and frequently causes, obliteration; while in Marsé's novels the *barrio* succeeds in keeping popular memory alive only in the form of dispersed, discontinuous, phantasmatic fragments. It is also worth noting that *El sur* and Marsé's novels focus on Andalusian migrants in the north, while Llamazares's novels deal with the Leonese *maquis* forced into hiding or (in *Escenas de cine mudo*) a series of travelers who pass through the Leonese mining village, while Llamazares is himself coming to terms with his own uprooting from his Leonese village now submerged beneath a *pantano* (one of the many reservoirs that Franco was famously filmed inaugurating in the state newsreel NO-DO). In *Beatus ille* and *El jinete polaco* (*The Polish Rider*), Antonio Muñoz Molina similarly recreates his fictional Mágina — modeled on his own former hometown, Úbeda — through a return to roots by his protagonists from economic exile in Madrid and New York respectively. In all these cases, there is a traumatic crisis of memory related to a geographical displacement or 'loss of place.'

In *El sur*, Erice's disagreement with his producer halfway through making the film resulted in the scenes due to be shot in 'the south' never being completed, with the felicitous result that, contrary to Adelaida García Morales's story where Estrella goes to Seville and meets her father's former lover, in the film 'the south' remains a ghostly presence, felt but invisible. In evoking 'the south,' Estrella is, of course, conjuring up the ghost of her dead Sevillian father, whose memory lives in her through the pendulum whose function is to divine the presence of that which is invisible — that is, ghosts. The film also changes the profession of her father's former lover to that of film star, reinforcing the notion of the past as ghost, for the human figure on screen is, literally, a shadow: a spectral presence that is and is not there. The cinema is also central to the topography of the *barrio* in Marsé's novels, where its spectral images form the basis of the construction of popular memory, allowing the past to endure as a ghostly presence that cannot be suppressed precisely because it lacks tangible form. The jumble of film images and snatches of historical memory in the adventure stories ('aventis') told by the boys in *Si te dicen que caí* (*The Fallen*, published in Mexico in 1973 and in Spain in 1976 after Franco's death) makes the point that the status of history, particularly but not only under censorship, is that of ghost haunting the present: not there but there. The first of the family photographs on which Llamazares's *Escenas de cine mudo* is based consists in the young Julio standing in front of the stills outside of the village cinema. It is the film stills, rather than the films themselves, that leave their trace in Marse's work, as images of a spectral past that, unlike official versions of history, is discontinuous, lacking in causal logic, and for that very reason offers a space to let the ghosts of the past in, allowing popular memory to elaborate the ghost stories that are the stuff of oral history. Indeed, the boys' stories in *Si te dicen que caí* are attempts to conjure up the ghosts of the 'desaparecidos' Marcos and Aurora/Carmen. The spectral quality of the film image is, I suggest, one of the reasons why it so 'haunts' fiction of the post-Franco era, as the expression of a history that can be recovered only in spectral form. In this sense, one could argue that even those writers who, in true postmodernist fashion, replace history with a series of film images are, despite their apparent historical evasion, at least acknowledging the existence of ghosts. The phrase 'post-Franco era,' after all, defines it as a period haunted by a spectral Francoist past.

Photographs, like film stills, play an important role as images of a fragmentary, discontinuous, spectral past in *Si te dicen que caí*, as they do in Muñoz Molina's *Beatus ille* and especially *El jinete polaco*, in which the past emerges from the gaps in between the photographs of Mágina's local studio photographer, Ramiro Retratista. Echoing Barthes's famous essay on photography, Ramiro Retratista perceives his photographs as ghostly images of the dead: 'cuando examinaba una foto recién hecha pensaba que a la larga sería, como todas, el retrato de un muerto, de modo que lo intranquilizaba siempre la molesta sospecha de no ser un fotógrafo, sino una especie de enterrador prematuro' ('whenever he examined a recently-taken photograph, he would think that, in the long run, it would, like all the others, be the portrait of someone dead and gone, which accosted him with the disturbing suspicion that he was not a photographer but a kind of premature gravedigger'; 93). But this is the case only because the photograph has the capacity to immortalize its subjects after death, in 'una clandestina y universal resurrección de los Muertos' ('a clandestine and universal resurrection of the Dead') bringing back to life 'aquellas vidas que luego no quiso nadie recordar' ('those lives that later no one wanted to remember'; 495). Indeed, as the narrator's girlfriend Nadia comments, the only person who cannot be brought back from the dead is the photographer himself, absent from his photographs (499). Ramiro Retratista's key photograph is, of course, that of the mummified body — a literal embodiment of a returning past — of the mysterious 'emparedada' ('walled-up woman'), stories of whose discovery 'haunted' the protagonist's childhood: a mummified corpse later replaced by a wax simulacrum, but nonetheless kept 'alive' in the collective imaginary. Similarly, history enters *El espíritu de la colmena* as a ghostly presence via the prewar photograph of Ana's father with Unamuno. In *Escenas de cine mudo*, the 'silent cinema' of the title consists in Llamazares's narrative animation of the 'stills' comprised by the family snapshots kept by his mother.

Walter Benjamin has described the historian as collector or *bricoleur*, in the sense that he rummages around in the debris or litter left by the past and reassembles the fragments in a new 'constellation' that permits the articulation of that which has been left unvoiced (45–104; Frisby 187–265). Benjamin's historian — who looks for significance in fragments and details normally overlooked — is a historian of popular culture: that is, of trivia, for it is trivia that give us the 'structure of feeling' that Raymond Williams saw as the key to understanding a particular period of history. Benjamin is to cultural history what Eisenstein is to film: that is, the theorist of montage. According to Benjamin's theory of cultural history as montage, the historian not only collects bits of rubble from amid the ruins of the past but reduces the past to ruins and rubble — that is, broken bits and pieces — so it can be reassembled to create new meanings through the dialectical confrontation of fragments that normally are separate. One thinks here of the anarchist leader Durruti's magnificent reply to a foreign journalist during the Civil War, reminding him that the workers, as builders, will know how to build a new future from the ruins of war: 'We're not afraid of ruins' (qted by Cleminson in Graham and Labanyi 117). The historian's task is, thus, not to put the uprooted fragments of the past back into their context, but to decontextualize even that which has not been reduced to ruins and rubble, allowing new relationships to be created. This, one may note, is exactly what the boys do with their *aventis* in Marsé's *Si te dicen que caí*, and what the protagonist and Nadia do as they rummage through the photographs and other objects in the trunk of the now dead Ramiro Retratista in Muñoz Molina's *El jinete polaco*. As excavator of ruins and 'rubbish collector,' Benjamin's cultural historian is a topographer, but one who defamiliarizes the maps made by official surveyors (whose function is to put everything in its 'proper place') in order to create an alternative, phantasmagorical topography that can recover, not just things, but the dreams and desires attached to them which did not find realization as 'fact': that is, popular history. Another image used by Benjamin is that of the photographer who produces a photographic negative in which light and dark are reversed (this, one may note, turns human figures into ghosts), and who can focus on a detail, or extract a detail and amplify it, destroying illusory official notions of history as continuity and allowing that which is normally overlooked to speak. Benjamin saw this as a materialist history, but it is also a history that, in acknowledging that which is normally rendered invisible (what Benjamin calls the 'optical unconscious'), gives habitation to ghosts.

Ghosts, as Avery Gordon notes in her suggestive book *Ghostly Matters: Haunting and the Sociological Imagination*, give 'embodiment' to those figures from the past who have been rendered invisible; that is, 'desaparecidos.' Likewise, Benjamin's dialectical method of montage 'animates' the fragmentary debris of history. Animation is precisely what Llamazares does to the snapshots that form the basis of *Escenas de cine mudo*, and also what Marsé does to the reproduction of Torrijos's execution on the carpet in *Si te dicen que caí*: in turning photographs and the figure in the carpet into a form of silent cinema, they are giving the past a ghostly embodiment. Animation and montage are the cinematic techniques used by Basilio

Martín Patino in his historical documentary films *Canciones para después de una guerra* (*Songs for after a War*, 1971, authorized for release 1975) and *Caudillo* (1976; named after Franco's official military title), which construct an alternative history through the articulation of popular memory, combining voice-over personal memories with a varied range of cultural trivia (advertisements, comics, and above all popular film and song), intercut with newsreel footage which concentrates on images of the debris of war and, above all, of the 'desaparecidos' leaving for exile. The popular songs sing overwhelmingly of loss and absence, conjuring up the ghosts of history that have been rendered invisible. Martín Patino's brilliant use of superimpositions and dissolves give the human figures in the documentary footage a ghostly quality appropriate to this evocation of the 'disappeared,' while reducing Franco and other official figures to the same ghostly status. But as ghosts, both the victims and the victors of history are a living presence that we are forced to acknowledge: the animation of newsreel footage or children's comics depicting Franco not only makes him ridiculous but reminds us that ghosts can be placated only if their presence is recognized. For these two films, Martín Patino did a huge amount of archival work, 'digging up' in Berlin previously unknown film footage in an excavation of popular memory that Benjamin would surely have admired. Worthy of Benjamin also is Martín Patino's dialectical concept of montage which intercuts sequences moving in different directions (from right to left, from left to right), in a rapid succession of visual fragments lifted out of context and reorganized into a new constellation releasing alternative meanings. It is worth noting that *Caudillo* opens with an evocative sequence of ruins, including human ruins, left by the Civil War, leading directly into a pictorial representation of Franco, thereby constructed as a specter inhabiting the ruins of the past.

For ruins are the favorite habitat of ghosts. The boys in *Si te dicen que caí* conjure up the ghosts of the past in the ruins of the crypt of the appropriately named church Las Ánimas ('All Souls'), also frequented by Rosita in the later novella *Ronda del Guinardó* (1984). The fugitive or 'desaparecido' in *El espíritu de la colmena* materializes as an apparition from an unknown past in a ruined, abandoned hut. As Paul Julian Smith has noted (34–35), Erice's film insists on the time-ravaged texture of walls and faces, giving both things and adult humans the quality of ruins: that is, relics haunted by the memory of the past. Like Benjamin, Raphael Samuel describes the historian of popular memory as a rubbish collector 'scavenging among what others are busy engaged in throwing out or consigning to the incinerator' (20). The American historian of popular culture, Greil Marcus, in his collection of essays *The Dustbin of History*, bewails the contemporary tendency, in our obsession with the new, to scorn the past, as in phrases such as 'It's history', which, as he notes, is a kind of contagious 'language-germ' that means the opposite of what it says: 'It means that there is no such thing as history, a past of burden and legacy', for 'once something ... is "history", it's *over*, and it is understood that it never existed at all'; 'Gone — it's history.' (22–23) As he comments, 'The result is a kind of euphoria, a weightless sense of freedom.' Marcus notes that the phrase 'dustbin of history' was coined by Trotsky in 1917 when he said of the Mensheviks: 'you are bankrupts;

your role is played out. Go where you belong from now on — into the dustbin of history'. Since then, as Marcus wryly notes, we have been busy consigning history's losers to the 'dustbin of history' in our mania for recording only success stories and our embarrassment at the existence of losers who contradict our Western obsession with progress. Marcus's essays in popular culture are an attempt to write from inside the dustbin of history; that is, from inside the 'historical hell' to which history's losers are assigned as ghostly 'shades' or 'shadows'; a dustbin or hell that is 'a wasteland in which all are distant from each other, because this is a territory, unlike history, without any borders at all — without any means to a narrative, a language with which to tell a story' (18). As Marcus puts it: 'written history, which makes the common knowledge out of which our newspapers report the events of the day, creates its own refugees, displaced persons, men and women without a country, cast out of time, the living dead' (17). What makes these 'refugees from history' (one thinks of the refugee in *El espíritu de la colmena*, who leaps from a train, the latter being a classic metaphor of history as progress) the 'living dead' is the fact that they are denied memory: not only because their story is not recorded by others, but because 'the shame of stories they cannot tell and that no one would believe if they could' means that they 'can barely credit even their own memories' (20). It is crucial that the refugee in *El espíritu de la colmena* has no articulated or articulatable past. It is also important that, in *Beatus ille*, we have no way of knowing how much of the historical reconstruction that we are reading is the account written by the officially dead Solana — who 'appears" to the protagonist Minaya in a cemetery — and how much of the narrative is written by Minaya. The novel's final postmodern twist, in which Solana reveals that he has trapped his autobiographer Minaya in his own narrative, but in which he also bequeaths his text (and his lover Inés) to Minaya, to be completed by him, foregrounds the impossibility of history's losers making public their own historical accounts, and the ethical imperative of future generations taking up their ghostly legacy, as an act of historical reparation.

As Marcus insists, the stories of such 'refugees from history' do not make sense; they puncture the continuity of what we take for history as if they were 'stories told by cranks' (37). Marcus notes that thriller writers have been able to capture the horror of the Holocaust in a way that historians rarely have, because they are not bent on explaining it; as Marcus comments, one does not explain an abyss, one locates it (59–62). It is the strong sense of place in Erice's films and Marsé's novels that captures the horror of a historical period traumatized by the prohibition on recalling the past through memory and narrative. Marsé's novels are 'stories told by cranks,' while Erice's films are focalized through the eyes of female children or adolescents who have not yet learnt to explain horror away. Marcus has Walter Benjamin in mind when he warns us to 'Beware of the smooth surface of history, looking backwards, making everything make sense,' because 'It made no sense at the time, like a random series of jump cuts' (1994: 18): the first time Erice shows us the ruined hut where the 'desaparecido' will materialize from nowhere, he does so through a series of jump cuts. In *El jinete polaco*, the protagonist compares his experience of history to that of watching a film lacking in continuity editing

(247) or where the images succeed each other so fast that one loses the thread and cannot make out the connections (248); his reconstruction of the past, as he attempts to fill in the gaps between Ramiro Retratista's photographs, highlights these discontinuities rather than ironing them out. Here Muñoz Molina conforms to Marcus's insistence on the need to counter the deceptive seamlessness of what goes down as history (what Marcus calls 'history as disappearance'), which edits out the bits that do not fit the master narrative of success stories, by letting in through the cracks and disturbances (through the jump cuts) those parts of history that 'survive only as haunts and fairy tales, accessible only as spectres and spooks' (24). *El jinete polaco* 'resurrects' a past kept alive through the ghost stories told to the narrator as a child, just as *Beatus ille* literally 'resurrects' its hero Solana, officially declared dead by the Civil Guard in the 1940s. Marcus's epigraphs include the Sex Pistols' line 'We're the flowers in your dustbin' and Bakhtin's dictum 'Nothing is absolutely dead; every meaning will have its homecoming festival.'

Bakhtin, of course, is the chronicler of the popular cultural forms that, from the Renaissance onwards, were gradually forced underground by the growing division between 'high' and 'low' culture. In writing from inside the 'dustbin of history,' Marcus is constructing an alternative history from discontinuous fragments of popular culture: pop music, pop art, and popular literary forms such as the thriller. In much the same way, Martín Patino's *Canciones* creates a discontinuous alternative history out of snatches of popular song, rescued from the dustbin to which popular culture is so often consigned and recycled to form a 'usable past'; indeed, the film shows how, in 'los años del hambre' ('the years of hunger') after the war, history's losers themselves recycled songs from earlier periods or songs written by the victors, investing them with alternative meanings as a strategy for coping with loss and bereavement. Snatches of popular song are also woven into the 'aventis' told by the boys in *Si te dicen que caí*, whose leader is Java, a 'trapero' (ragpicker) who recycles trash; indeed, many of the stories are told in his 'trapería' ('junk store'), which is also reputedly the hideout of the 'desaparecido' Marcos, quite literally walled up in the 'dustbin of history' (one thinks here of the 'emparedada,' another of history's losers, in *El jinete polaco*). Images of rubbish and of hell run throughout *Si te dicen que caí* and *Ronda del Guinardó*; I would read these images not just as signs of moral and physical degradation, but as a metaphorical figure of the consignment of history's losers to the 'dustbin of history' which at the same time is a 'historical hell' inhabited by the living dead.

Which brings me to vampires, werewolves, and other forms of the 'undead.' In Chapter 21 of *Si te dicen que caí*, on the pretext of Luisito's death from tuberculosis, the boys tell the story of his visit to the Siamese Consulate, at the time of his father's second 'disappearance,' where his mother has been summoned to receive news of 'un hermano desaparecido en la Guerra' ('a brother disappeared in the War'). The boys recount this episode in the form of a vampire story, which mobilizes the genre's diverse connotations.[2] Just before this vampire story starts, we are told of the tramp Mianet's stories of 'niños que raptaban para chuparles la sangre' ('children

2   For an excellent exploration of the symbolic potential of the vampire genre, see Gelder.

kidnapped to suck their blood'): a 'story told by a crank' which 'explains' the prevalence of tuberculosis in 'los años del hambre' as the vampirism of the poor by the wealthy who, in drawing blood from kidnapped children to prolong their own life, turn them too into vampires who waste away for lack of lifeblood. The same popular explanation of tuberculosis is related in Muñoz Molina's *El jinete polaco* (77). Such popular 'explanations' do not explain horror away; indeed, what could be more appropriate to capture the horror of the immediate postwar period than a horror story? True to form, the vampire in the boys' story appears to the tubercular Luisito immediately after he coughs up blood. It has been noted that stories of vampires (and of the kidnapping of children for organ transplants) have been rife in Peru and other parts of South America in recent decades as a way of dealing with historical trauma (Kraniauskas 1998). The notion of the wealthy (particularly the moneylender) as vampires draining the poor is an old one, evidenced in Galdós's *La desheredada* where Juan Bou calls the rich 'sanguijuelas del pueblo' ('bloodsuckers who prey on the people').[3] At the Siamese Consulate, not only does the torturer El Tuerto, with his vampire-like dead eye, drain Luisito of his lifeblood but 'también la memoria le vaciaron, el pobre nunca más llegó a acordarse de nada' ('they also drained his memory, after that poor Luisito could never remember anything'; 319). For vampires are the 'living dead' because they have no memory (and thus no shadow or reflection): the disease with which Luisito is infected is that of the amnesia enforced by the regime, which the boys' stories, keeping the 'desaparecidos' alive through narrative, are an attempt to stave off. It is loss of historical memory that allows the boys' fathers to degenerate from urban guerrillas into petty criminals. Manuel Vázquez Montalbán has also described the effects of Francoist repression and censorship as a 'vampirización de la memoria' ('vampirization of memory'). Sarnita, the chief teller of 'aventis,' in later life becomes a morgue attendant, who accompanies the dead in their historical underworld, keeping their memory alive through his own remembrance.

As all writers on the subject insist, vampires are close relatives of the werewolf, for both are human and yet non-human predators on the living. Vampire stories are complicated because the vampire turns his victims into vampires too; indeed, many vampire stories express pity for the vampire who is condemned to a living death (in *Si te dicen que caí*, El Tuerto has become a vampire because he previously was the victim of torture at the hands of Marcos and Aurora). Llamazares's *Luna de lobos* casts in the role of werewolf the rural guerrillas forced into clandestinity in the Cantabrian mountains after the Civil War: predatory loners not of their own choosing. If the vampire has no memory, Llamazares's werewolves depend on memory: not their own but that of the collective in the form of the villagers and the Civil Guards who, out of love or terror, keep them alive as ghosts of the past through the stories they tell about them. In struggling to survive in the snow, the

---

3   Tannahill (167–88) shows that the vampire myth, often but not only in this sense, predates its nineteenth-century literary manifestations by several centuries in the popular imagination, notably in the "vampire epidemic" that swept Hungary, Moravia, Silesia, and Poland in the late seventeenth and first half of the eighteenth centuries.

maquis are struggling against the threat of oblivion (whiteness/blankness). Greil Marcus laments the recent prevalence of apocalyptic narratives that assign the past to 'history' in the sense of non-existence. It is important that Llamazares's novel is open-ended: the last of the *maquis* is expelled from the memory of his loved ones in the village and is left with no alternative but to 'disappear' into exile, but at the end of the novel he is still alive and, most importantly, is telling his story.

The centrality to *El espíritu de la colmena* of Frankenstein's monster has been much commented on. While the monster has mostly been seen as an embodiment of the 'otherness' that the Franco regime sought to repress by demonizing it — an association made explicit by Ana's equation of the monster with the refugee or 'desaparecido' — it has also been connected with Ana's father, seen as an embodiment of patriarchal authority (Evans 1982). Ana's father's connection with the monster is clear from the scene when he is filmed via his shadow in a retake of Murnau's classic vampire film *Nosferatu*. But there are problems with this interpretation, not so much because it casts the monster in the role of both victim and oppressor (we have seen how vampires are both), as because Ana's father — played by Fernando Fernán Gómez who, although never a political activist, had since the 1950s moved in opposition cultural circles — is a kindly figure, whose prewar association with Unamuno casts him as a Republican intellectual. I should like to suggest a different reading of the monster image in the film, whereby he represents not so much the demonization of the 'other' as their assignment to the status of 'living dead': Frankenstein created his monster out of body parts taken from a collection of corpses. In this sense, the monster stands as the embodiment, which returns to haunt the present, of a collective living death, which includes Ana's father as Republican intellectual denied self-expression except through his private diary, just as Ana's mother can tell her story only through letters to a disappeared loved one. There is no suggestion in the film that the fugitive is Ana's mother's former lover, as some critics have assumed, but they both share the 'condition of being ghosts of history'.[4] In offering the fugitive hospitality, Ana is carrying out Derrida's moral imperative of granting ghosts 'the right ... to ... a hospitable memory ... out of a concern for justice' — indeed, by giving him her father's watch, she is reinserting him into historical time. Ana is right to see the fugitive as the embodiment of the monster in James Whale's film for, as we have seen, films do not so much represent reality as embody it in the form of shadows or ghosts. Appropriately, the body of the 'desaparecido' is laid out beneath the screen where the film *Frankenstein* had previously been shown. As in Martín Patino's *Canciones*, *El espíritu de la colmena* insists on shots of the cinema audience watching the shadows on the screen, showing how ghosts are given embodiment in the collective memory which, after the show is over, can continue to tell their story.

The final words of the film, 'Soy Ana' ('It's me, Ana'), have encouraged readings which minimize its political significance by seeing it as a Freudian narrative of Ana's

---

4   If one pauses the film at the moment when she throws her last letter in the fire, we can make out on the envelope the female name "Sole", c/o the International Red Cross, Nice, France, which acted as a clearing house for missing persons after the Civil War.

oedipal trajectory, as she learns to separate from parental figures and establish an autonomous identity. Avery Gordon, in her book *Ghostly Matters* (50–58), notes that Freud, while acknowledging the importance of haunting in his work on mourning and melancholia, nevertheless de-historicizes it by theorizing it as a psychological projection. Indeed, she observes that Freud's early anthropological reading of spirits as a kind of animism, whereby men introject the dead into themselves in the form of totemism, was leading him towards a historical theory of hauntology, but that he stepped back from this (just as he stepped back from acknowledging that his female patients were the victims of real seduction by the father), instead positing ghosts as a purely imaginary externalization of the inner contents of the unconscious. Derrida makes similar points about Marx's use of spectral imagery to figure the psychological projection that is bourgeois ideology (171–72). Gordon and Derrida insist that ghosts are not psychic projections, but the form in which the past lives on in the present. In this sense, Gordon insists that haunting is 'neither pre-modern superstition nor individual psychosis' but 'a constituent element of modern social life' (7). Faced with such a phenomenon, sociology — traditionally based on facts and statistics — does not know what to do and thus has joined the censors by insisting that ghosts do not exist. How, Avery asks, 'do we reckon with what modern history has rendered ghostly? How do we develop a critical language to describe and analyze the affective, historical, and mnemonic structures of such hauntings?' (18). Her answer is found through readings of literature: Luisa Valenzuela's narratives of the 'desaparecidos'; Toni Morrison's stories of the returning ghosts of earlier generations of black slaves. I suggest that Erice's representation of Frankenstein's monster likewise makes the point that ghosts, while they require remembrance in human consciousness, have an objective existence as the embodiment of the past in the present. As Derrida reminds us, ghosts are not just the object of the gaze for they look at and summon us (7). This point is made by the culminating sequence in *El espíritu de la colmena* in which Frankenstein's monster appears to Ana, and in which something extremely important happens. The sequence starts with the subjective point-of-view shot so characteristic of the film, which constructs the monster as a psychic projection of Ana; but as it slips into a re-take of the scene from James Whale's *Frankenstein* — seen earlier in the film by us and Ana — in which the monster appears to the little girl by the lake, the camera suddenly changes position, filming both Ana and the monster from behind, from an objective vantage-point that belongs to no character. Thus, the monster cannot be explained away as a projection of Ana's fantasy: it is 'really there.' Or rather, as befits a ghost of the past, it is and is not there, for it is a cinematic shadow: intangible but nonetheless embodied. The monster is thus a perfect illustration of the hauntological status of history in the present.

In *Ghostly Matters*, Gordon condemns the hypervisibility and superficiality of contemporary postmodern culture: 'No shadows, no ghosts' (16). But the recent burst of writing on hauntology can be seen as related to 'the return of the real' which some critics (notably Hal Foster in the book of that title) have proclaimed as the underside of the postmodern emphasis on simulacra. For the ghost is an embodiment of the real in the form of the simulacrum; which is to say that postmodernity's conversion of reality into simulacra does not after all mean the death of history but rather its return in spectral form. The term Hal Foster gives to this phenomenon is 'traumatic realism' or, using a Lacanian pun, 'troumatic realism' in the sense of a 'trou' or gap in reality, for Lacan defines the traumatic as a missed encounter with the real (130, 132, 136). Ghosts are, precisely, the 'might have beens' of history that return as an actualizable, embodied alternative reality. Fredric Jameson says something similar with his suggestive phrase 'Spectrality is ... what makes the present waver' (Gordon 168); that is, it opens up a hole in reality as we like to think we know it. As the monster appears to Ana, it troubles her image (his image) in the water, opening up a hole in comfortable notions of what is self and what is out there, what is present and what is an apparition of the past. Derrida insists that, just as there is a mode of production of the commodity, so there is 'a mode of production of the phantom,' through the process of mourning which, unlike melancholia which has no direct object, is always triggered by a trauma (97). Foster reminds us that the word 'trauma' means 'wound' (153): when the 'desaparecido' vanishes out of Ana's life, he leaves behind the tangible evidence of the blood from his wounds. The wounds of the dead body which we and Rosita confront at the end of *Ronda del Guinardó* do not help establish the victim's identity but nevertheless provide tangible evidence of the historical fact of repression.

Haunting, as Gordon puts it, is the result of 'improperly buried bodies' (16): that of the unclaimed torture victim in *Ronda del Guinardó* whom the police want to see 'dead and buried' in the sense of consigned to oblivion; that of the unknown fugitive in *El espíritu de la colmena*; that of the 'emparedada' in *El jinete polaco*, or that of the officially dead Solana in *Beatus ille*; that of the 'desaparecidos' evoked in the songs and images of *Canciones para después de una guerra*; that of the miners buried beneath the slagheaps in *Escenas de cine mudo*. But what should one do with improperly buried bodies: give them proper burial, or learn to live with their ghosts? Derrida advocates the second option: a 'being-with specters' that is a '*politics* of memory, of inheritance, and of generations' (xix). In *El jinete polaco*, the 'emparedada' and the doctor Don Mercurio (described in his old age as a living corpse) are revealed at the end to be the protagonist's great-great-grandparents, thus inserting the ghosts of the past into the family. The narrator's girlfriend Nadia inherits Ramiro Retratista's photographs from her recently deceased father, again stressing the importance of personal inheritance. As Barthes notes (7), the photographs that most move us are family photographs. *El espíritu de la colmena*, *El sur*, and *Si te dicen que caí* rely on family photographs to bring back to life a past — that of the Republic and the Civil War — that has been consigned to oblivion. The structuring of *Escenas de cine mudo* around the photographs in the family album assembled by the narrator's mother, inherited by him on her death, provides an image of history as discontinuous fragments held together by personal inheritance, just as the text of *Beatus ille* is made possible by Minaya's acceptance of the officially dead Solana's legacy, in the form of his story or voice. In *El jinete polaco*, it is the protagonist's postmodern profession as international interpreter — second-hand transmitter of a global Babel of voices — that enables him to respond to the summons of the ghosts of the past, which, via Ramiro Retratista's photographs, beckon him back to the historical roots he had attempted to leave behind him. The novel's first part is titled 'El reino de las voces' ('The Realm of Voices'), for to hear voices is analogous to seeing ghosts. But ghosts cannot make their own voice heard: they rely on an interpreter to speak for them. The postmodern stress on the impossibility of direct access to the past may be a response to the ubiquitousness of the media and the advertising and heritage industries, which convert history into a consumer commodity; but it can also be seen as a recognition of the spectral quality of the traces left by the past on the present, and of the particular need to bear witness to 'the traces of those who were not allowed to leave a trace' — namely, ghosts. In a country that has emerged from forty years of cultural repression, the task of making reparation to the ghosts of the past — that is, to those relegated to the status of living dead, denied voice and memory — is considerable. Derrida's notion that history occupies in the present a 'virtual space of spectrality' abolishes the supposed opposition between postmodernism and history. The fact that Spain returned to democracy at the height of the postmodern vogue for 'virtual reality' should not necessarily be bemoaned as having prevented an engagement with the past. Perhaps instead we should consider the ways in which postmodernism, by breaking with empiricist concepts of mimesis, allows us to recognize the existence and importance of ghosts.

Works Cited

BARTHES, ROLAND. *Camera Lucida*. Trans. Richard Howard. London: Fontana, 1984.

BENJAMIN, WALTER. *One-Way Street*. Trans. Edmund Jephcott and Kingsley Shorter. London: Verso, 1997.

DERRIDA, JACQUES. *Specters of Marx: The State of the Debt, the Work of Mourning, and the New International*. Trans. Peggy Kamuf. New York: Routledge, 1994.

ERICE, VÍCTOR, dir. *El espíritu de la colmena*. Élias Querejeta, 1973.

——, dir. *El sur*. Élias Querejeta, 1983..

EVANS, PETER W. '*El espíritu de la colmena*: The Monster, the Place of the Father, and Growing up in the Dictatorship'. *Vida Hispánica* 31.3 (1982): 13–17.

FOSTER, HAL. *The Return of the Real: The Avant-Garde at the End of the Century*. Cambridge, MA: MIT Press, 1996.

FRISBY, DAVID. *Fragments of Modernity*. Cambridge, UK: Polity Press, 1988.

GELDER, KEN. *Reading the Vampire*. London: Routledge, 1994.

GORDON, AVERY F. *Ghostly Matters: Haunting and the Sociological Imagination*. Minneapolis: U of Minnesota P, 1997.

GRAHAM, HELEN, and JO LABANYI, eds. *Spanish Cultural Studies: An Introduction. The Struggle for Modernity*. Oxford: Oxford UP, 1995.

KRANIAUSKAS, JOHN. '*Cronos* and the Political Economy of Vampirism: Notes on a Historical Constellation.' *Cannibalism and the Colonial Order*, co-ed. Francis Barker, Peter Hulme, and Margaret Iverson. Cambridge, UK: Cambridge UP, 1998. 142–57.

LLAMAZARES, JULIO. *Escenas de cine mudo*. Barcelona: Seix Barral. 1994.

——. *Luna de lobos*. Barcelona: Seix Barral, 1985.

MARCUS, GREIL. *The Dustbin of History*. London: Picador, 1994

MARSÉ, JUAN. *Ronda del Guinardó*. Barcelona: Seix Barral, 1984.

——. *Si te dicen que caí*. Barcelona: Seix Barral, 1976.

MARTÍN PATINO, BASILIO, dir. *Canciones para después de una guerra*. Francisco Molero, 1971.

——, dir. *Caudillo*. Retasa, 1976.

ROWE, WILLIAM, and VIVIAN SCHELLING. *Memory and Modernity: Popular Culture in Latin America*. London: Verso, 1991.

SAMUEL, RALPH. *Theatres of Memory*. London: Verso, 1994.

SMITH, PAUL JULIAN. *The Moderns: Time, Space and Subjectivity in Contemporary Spanish Culture*. Oxford: Oxford UP. 2000.

TANNAHILL, REAY. *Flesh and Blood: A History of the Cannibal Complex*. Rev. ed. London: Abacus, 1996

VÁZQUEZ MONTALBÁN, MANUEL. *Crónica sentimental de España: Una mirada irreverente a tres décadas de mitos y de ensueños*. Barcelona: Planeta, 1980.

CHAPTER 23

Testimonies of Repression:
Methodological and Political Issues

The number of historical studies on the Civil War and ensuing Dictatorship published in Spain since General Franco's death in 1975 is now massive; these have been published throughout the post-dictatorship period. The mid-1980s additionally saw the emergence of a number of novels and feature films on the war (Labanyi, 'Memory'), followed in the mid-1990s by a flurry of early Francoist memorabilia and related reminiscences (Harvey). It was only in the late 1990s, however, that historical studies, novels, and documentary and feature films started to focus overwhelmingly on the wartime and postwar Francoist repression.[1] A key text was Santos Juliá's 1999 edited volume *Víctimas de la guerra civil* (*Victims of the Civil War*) which established a paradigm for discussing the Civil War and Dictatorship in terms of victimhood. This emphasis on victimhood was given additional impetus by the exhumations of victims of the Francoist repression set in motion by Emilio Silva's first public excavation of a mass grave in 2000, and his consequent founding of the Asociación para la Recuperación de la Memoria Histórica (ARMH). In the wake of this new focus on victimhood, the years 2000–03 saw the appearance, in rapid succession, of a number of collections of testimonies. From 2003, following the first two documentaries by Montse Armengou and Ricard Belis on the victims of Francoist repression, *Els nens perduts del franquisme* (*The Lost Children of Francoism*, 2002, with the collaboration of historian Ricard Vinyes) and *Les fosses del silenci* (*The Graves of Silence*, 2003), made for Televisió de Catalunya, television largely took over responsibility for airing testimonies of victims. Since that date, only a trickle of print testimonies has been published, contrasting with the production of an impressive body of documentary film, most of it made for television, based on interviews with eyewitnesses or surviving relatives of the wartime or postwar repression (Resina; Herrmann).

This essay discusses a selection of the testimonies that were issued in book form between 2000 and 2003. Passing reference will be made to the earlier collections of testimonies published in the late 1970s and 1980s by Fraser, Leguineche and Torbado, and Cuevas; and to the books that accompanied Armengou and Belis's

---

1   Loureiro notes how representations and studies of the Spanish Civil War prior to the late 1990s emphasized it as a heroic struggle, giving way in recent years to a stress on victimhood. As he points out, this shift in the last decade to a view of history as grievance is not limited to Spain.

above-mentioned television documentaries. I shall be concerned not with the question of whether these testimonies are helpful to their narrators as a form of memory-work — something that their compilers (with the exception of Armengou and Belis) have not seen fit to address in their eliciting or editing of the narratives — but rather with the question of whether their presentation encourages contemporary Spanish readers to think about the war in helpful ways. My argument will be that these edited collections, while valuable in making readers — especially the vast majority born after the war — appreciate the extent of the wartime and postwar repression, nonetheless help to construct a form of collective memory that obscures the key political issues: issues both about the past and about how we deal with it in the present. For memory is the afterlife of the past in the present.

We can bear in mind here the American feminist lawyer Bonnie Honig's suggestion in her book *Democracy and the Foreigner* (mentioned in another context in Chapter 8) that the most appropriate genre for narrating the nation is not romance but the Gothic, for democracy does not mean living happily ever after with those you love, but learning to live non-violently with those you would rather not live with, and who may fill you with terror (107–22). To do this, one needs to know about the events that have caused this terror, and to understand terror as an emotion. The current discourse on terrorism — as in 'the war on terror' — encourages us to forget that terror is an emotion and not an act or fact. In this essay I will argue that the main value of testimonies is not the legal function of establishing what happened (though that has to take place too), but the insight they give us into emotional attitudes towards the past in the present time of the speaker. Only if this is borne in mind can testimonies serve not only to recognize past injustices, but also to work for a future that is not determined by them.

Testimony (*testimonio*) has become a privileged genre in Latin America for making state terror known to the public. It has mostly been promoted by Marxist critics, largely in the United States, who have seen in its first-person micro-histories a way of saving Marxist political commitment while also acknowledging the postmodern critique of 'master narratives.' The titles of the key critical works in the field are eloquent: John Beverley's 2004 *Testimonio: On the Politics of Truth*; Georg Gugelberg's 1996 edited volume *The Real Thing: Testimonial Discourse in Latin America*. For the word *testimonio*, as is made even clearer by the English 'testimony,' has a legal origin: it is the eyewitness account of someone testifying to a court of law in order to establish who was guilty of a crime. In other words, its purpose is to establish the facts so that justice may prevail. This involves not only legal recognition of what was unjustly suffered by the victim but also the entitlement to reparation and, most importantly, punishment of the perpetrator of the crime. *Testimonio* became a literary genre in Latin American countries ruled by repressive regimes (Guatemala, Argentina, Uruguay, Chile, especially) where such firsthand evidence could not be made public through the legal system. We may note that, in Spain, the 1977 Amnesty Law ruled out the possibility of bringing to trial perpetrators of violence during the Civil War and Franco dictatorship, thus opening up a space for alternative forms of testimony.[2] There are differences between *testimonio* and oral history, as all writers on the former insist, in that the *testimonio* is denouncing an injustice and thus has a particular urgency. But there are also significant overlaps between the two. In both *testimonio* and oral history, the eyewitness report reaches us via the mediation of an interviewer, who presents it to the public in edited form. In both cases, it is usually the interviewer who solicits the account. And, in both cases, we have a form of memory-work. Memory is notoriously unreliable but, as Shoshana Felman and Dori Laub have shown in their classic study of Holocaust testimonies, *Testimony: Crises of Witnessing in Literature, Psychoanalysis, and History*, what memories give us, especially when they are unreliable, is an insight into the emotions in the present attached to the past events that are recalled.

The volumes of testimonies of wartime and postwar atrocities published in Spain from 2000 to 2003 have been compiled by journalists, and sometimes historians, concerned — as befits their profession — with the truth value of these testimonies as historical evidence. It seems significant that such volumes multiplied under the last years of the Partido Popular Government of 1996–2004 which consistently refused to support the excavation of mass graves or the opening of archives to the public. These testimonies function as a supplement to the demands by historians and activists for open access to material evidence. But, in the process, they risk becoming construed as material evidence in their own right. The works which use testimonies most responsibly are those where the first-person memory narratives are backed by historical evidence. Particularly impressive examples are Montse Armgengou and Ricard Belis's two books based on their earlier documentary films for Televisió de Catalunya's program *30 minuts: Los niños perdidos del franquismo* (2003), co-authored with the historian Ricard Vinyes, which investigates the postwar separation of babies and young children from their Republican mothers in order to 'save' them from 'ideological contamination,' and *Las fosas del silencio* (2004) which interviews eyewitnesses on the executions carried out by the Nationalists during and after the Civil War. In these documentaries, the testimonies are interspersed with accounts by historians based on archival research, as well as visits to the 'scene of the crime.' The accompanying books include a considerable amount of historical contextualization based on firsthand archival research. Another good example is the oral-history work done by the historian Ángela Cenarro in Aragón, where the

---

2   At the start of September 2008, Judge Baltasar Garzón embarked on compiling a register of deaths as a result of reprisals during the wartime and postwar periods. This exercise was undertaken in response to the many individuals who, appealing to the requirement of the 27 December 2007 "Law of Historical Memory" that official institutions provide information about victims of violence in the Civil War and Franco dictatorship to those requesting it, filed such requests with the Audiencia Nacional (Spanish Supreme Court), on which Garzón served. By 25 September 2008, Garzón had received from assorted associations a total of 130,137 names of victims of Francoist reprisals. However, none of the individuals requesting information about their "disappeared" relatives asked for perpetrators to be brought to trial. See Altozano and Junquera. Garzón would subsequently be barred from pursuing legal proceedings (though exonerated from accusations of legal misconduct on this matter) and banned from legal practice in Spain following a court case brought against him by a far-right organization on a different matter.

testimonies are supported by meticulous historical research ('Memory').[3] In all of these cases, we are dealing with historical investigations which draw on testimonies, rather than the edited collections of testimonies which are the subject of this essay. A noticeable difference is that Armengou and Belis, and Cenarro, analyze critically the testimonies which inform their investigation; no such analysis is found in the many other anthologies of testimonies that have appeared in democratic Spain. This lack of analysis is not only a wasted opportunity but encourages readers to take the stories narrated at face value.

This is not just a difference between the work of journalists and historians: first because Armengou and Belis, although journalists by profession, engage in the firsthand research which one expects of historians; but also because not all historians who draw on testimonies do so with an appreciation of the specific qualities of oral accounts. For example, the British historian Ronald Fraser's otherwise ground-breaking *Blood of Spain* (published in English and Spanish as early as 1979) is highly problematic in its mingling of historical narrative and first-person accounts such that one often is not sure who is speaking. Neither does Fraser tell us anything about the circumstances of the interviews or about the relation of the excerpts cited to the whole transcripts. The principal problem in Fraser's book is that the excerpts from the interviews are selected according to their subject-matter and are then inserted into a chronological historical narrative as if the informants' memories and the historian's account of the war's progress had a similar factual status. This is not how memory — notoriously non-chronological and non-factual — works. Consequently, Fraser's intertwining into his historical account of excerpts from a mass of oral-history interviews brings the history to life and democratizes it by giving us a multiple view 'from below,' but it ignores the specificity of memory as a mental process.

This mining of firsthand testimonies as a 'resource' so as to 'recover' particular events, with the excerpts ordered either chronologically or thematically, is the norm in the collections of testimonies that appeared between 2000 and 2003. I am thinking of Alfonso Bullón de Mendoza and Álvaro de Diego's *Historias orales de la guerra civil* (*Oral Histories of the Civil War*, 2000); Jorge Reverte and Socorro Thomás's *Hijos de la guerra: Testimonios y recuerdos* (*Children of the Civil War: Testimonies and Memories*, 2001); Carlos Elordi's *Los años difíciles: El testimonio de los protagonistas anónimos de la guerra civil y la posguerra* (*The Difficult Years: Testimonies of the Anonymous Protagonists of the Civil War and Postwar*, 2002), which publishes letters and documents sent, by invitation, to his radio program *Hoy por Hoy* (broadcast on Cadena SER), between September 2001 and June 2002; and José María Zavala's *Los horrores de la guerra civil* (*The Horrors of the Civil War*, 2003). The notion of 'recovering' the past is a problematic one: this is achieved when documents from the time are presented for publication — several radio listeners sent in farewell letters written from prison by their fathers on the eve of their execution — but not when we are given a memory narrative spoken or written in the present. Memory is not a slice of the past waiting

---

3   See also Cenarro's current oral history work with individuals institutionalized as children by the Francoist welfare institution Auxilio Social ("Memories of Repression").

hidden to be 'recovered'; it is a process which operates in the present and which cannot help but give a version of the past that is colored by present emotions and affected by all sorts of interferences from subsequent experiences and knowledge. As Elizabeth Jelin has stressed, writing about post-Dictatorship Argentina's handling of the 'dirty war': memory is a form of 'labor' — that is, a process of 'working through' that takes place in the present.

Awareness of this has been strong in the abundant historical and theoretical work on the Holocaust. Armengou and Belis provocatively subtitle their book *Las fosas del silencio* with the question: '¿Hay un Holocausto español?' ('Is there a Spanish Holocaust?') and they title the English version of their documentary *The Spanish Holocaust*, answering their question in the affirmative. The question 'Is there a Spanish Holocaust?' is an important one, not only because an affirmative answer would mean recognition that the victims should receive reparation and that the guilty should be brought to trial, but also because much can be learned in Spain from the debates about how the Holocaust is (or should be) remembered, at both a public and private level. It is necessary that historians and journalists in Spain should first have concentrated on establishing what happened and who was responsible. But if there is to be a further stage of working through those memories of violence in order to achieve a democratic society where different groups agree to cohabit peacefully despite fearing or hating each other, there also needs to be a critical exploration of the feelings in the present of those who offer their testimonies. In his essay 'On Forgiveness,' Derrida notes that official 'forgiveness' ceremonies serve the function of unifying the nation, enforcing homogeneity from above; such instrumental 'forgiveness' is an economic transaction conditional on the repentance — and consequent conversion — of the guilty (31–35). This, of course, was the agenda behind the intermittent offers of pardon by the Franco dictatorship. Derrida argues for a concept of unconditional 'forgiveness' whereby one pardons that which is unforgivable. Whether the victims of Francoist aggression should offer their aggressors unconditional forgiveness is debatable. We can, however, usefully relate Derrida's argument to Honig's insistence that democracy means, not turning hatred and fear into love, but agreeing to live non-violently with those one hates and fears.

A positive feature of Derrida's notion of unconditional forgiveness is that it gives agency to the victims. In some respects, the parallel between the Francoist repression and the Holocaust is unhelpful, since the dominance of the Holocaust in memory studies sometimes risks tipping into an endorsement of victim culture, whereby only the stories of victims are found valid or interesting. Particularly problematic has been the privileging, in writing on Holocaust victims, of trauma: we need to ask why trauma is such a seductive concept, why the stories of trauma victims so often become bestsellers. One cannot help feeling that the attraction may, in at least some cases, be less a desire to know the truth than a disturbing pleasure derived from 'regarding the pain of others' (to cite the title of Susan Sontag's last book).

Trauma is generally defined as the blocking of memory by an event so horrific that it could not be registered and thus recalled. Instead, the traumatic event keeps re-enacting itself for the victim, who is unable to break free of its grip. More radically, Ernst van Alphen has argued that trauma occurs when the event so fails to fit any known category of thought that it cannot even be 'experienced' in the first place, let alone remembered. By this he means that, in modern Western culture, subjecthood is defined in terms of autonomy and agency. Thus, if all autonomy and agency are taken away, it becomes impossible to conceive of oneself as a person. In such cases, one becomes the object of an event, rather than the subject of an experience: he notes how Holocaust survivors tend to recount their horrific experiences in the third person and talk of how they had to 'kill the self' in order to survive. This denial of personhood to Jews, gypsies, homosexuals, and other 'deviants' was precisely what the Holocaust was about: such objectification both allowed the Holocaust to happen and was enacted in its genocidal regime. I shall come back to this loss of personhood at the end of this essay. What I want to note at this point is that the recent proliferation of testimonies about the Civil War shows that we are not dealing here with trauma (blocked memory), for these firsthand accounts remember past events in the most graphic detail. I am not suggesting that there were no genuine trauma victims of the Spanish Civil War but, by definition, they are not the authors of these testimonies. If these eyewitnesses did not tell their story before, the reason is evidently that, for the nearly forty years of the Franco dictatorship, there was not a public sphere — and often not even a private sphere — in which their accounts could be heard by willing listeners. And while censorship was abolished by the 1978 democratic Constitution, Spaniards during the Transition were more concerned with the uncertainties of the future than with a repressive past, which they wished to put behind them. This lack of interlocutors for some sixty years has created habits of silence that are hard to break. This is important since the emphasis on trauma, by attributing the failure to recount past atrocities to the internal psychic mechanisms of the victim, can stop us from looking for social and political explanations of this failure. One is struck by the number of cases when the stories of past atrocities are told, not to children (still too close to events to want to know, or for their parents to want to pass the burden onto them), but to grandchildren (born late enough not to have inherited the legacy of humiliation, shame, and fear).[4]

While the best of these Spanish collections of *testimonios* do serve to give agency — a voice — to those who suffered, there is sometimes a stress on victimhood that, while eliciting sympathy, can encourage a view of Republican supporters as 'helpless' objects of historical events beyond their control. This is tricky, because the 'víctimas de la guerra civil' (to cite the title of Juliá's previously-mentioned pioneering volume) were indeed victims, and often reduced to the status of a thing, if not a corpse. But it is important not to create a landscape of perpetrators and victims as though those were the only historical positions. We need also to pay attention to the immense grey areas in between these two positions: for example, by examining the difficult subject of the responsibility, not just of perpetrators,

4   For a thoughtful discussion of how the third generation (the grandchildren of those who experienced the war) has imbibed its meagre knowledge of the wartime and postwar years, and the problems that are created by this, see Izquierdo Martín and Sánchez León.

but of informers, or those who simply turned a blind eye. This is an area that has barely been broached in Spain — unlike Germany, France, or Holland, where there has been considerable debate on the widespread complicity with Nazism of the population at large. We need also to show that those who were reduced to the status of victim by extreme repression were nevertheless, in other aspects of their lives, individuals with agency.

Here I am arguing against the practice of reproducing only those excerpts from testimonies that recount atrocities perpetrated against victims, and in favor of printing the interview transcript in its entirety (or at least with minimal editing). In this respect, there is a striking contrast between earlier collections of testimonies published in democratic Spain and those that have been published since 2000. I refer here to Manuel Leguineche and Jesús Torbado's pioneering *Los topos*, published in 1977 and reissued in 1999 on the back of the recent 'memory boom'; and to Tomasa Cuevas's collections of testimonies of women activists imprisoned during the war and the Franco dictatorship, *Cárcel de mujeres* (*Women's Prison*, 1985) and *Mujeres en la resistencia* (*Women in the Resistance*, 1986) — reprinted in a single volume in 2004 as *Testimonios de mujeres en las cárceles franquistas* (*Testimonies of Women in Francoist Prisons*). In both cases, the testimonies were mostly gathered before the end of the Dictatorship. In both cases, too, the compilers give us full life histories, each one occupying a separate chapter. This allows their narrators to represent themselves as subjects and not just as victims, since their story is not limited to moments of persecution.[5] In *Los topos*, it is noticeable that the narrators give more space to their wartime exploits — which construct them as historical agents — than to their thirty-or-so years in hiding, when their agency was severely reduced: all of them stress how they kept mentally, if not physically, active in their hideouts. In the testimonies of female members of the Communist Party (including herself) collected by Cuevas, what strikes the reader is the courage of these women who did not abandon their political activism despite their repeated imprisonment and torture. That is, they depict themselves as women who refused to be reduced to object status, despite what was done to them. The narrative form of the testimonies compiled by Leguineche and Torbado, and by Cuevas, is that of the picaresque genre, which insists on the subaltern narrator-protagonist's ability to defy authority by mocking its rules. The result is an insight into the mentality of a series of individuals that impresses, not just because of what they have suffered, but above all because of their resourcefulness and capacity for survival.

By contrast, the testimonies published since 2000 are narrated in the mode of tragedy, for these are stories of victims, as the jacket blurbs stress. These volumes do not give full life histories,[6] but are organized in thematic or chronological chapters,

5   The life histories published by Cuevas are very full and were collected by her personally from fellow communist activists she had encountered in prison; she allows them to stand with little interference from herself as editor. Leguineche and Torbado tell us little about the circumstances of the interviews they conducted, apart from their time span (1969–77), and frequently interrupt the interviews to give information of their own. They have clearly edited the transcripts but nevertheless present each life story as a discrete whole.
6   An exception is José Antonio Vidal Castaño's *La memoria reprimida: Historias orales del maquis*

mixing testimonies from a number of narrators in each chapter in order to construct a composite account of a particular category of atrocity. In the most problematic cases, the interviews are chopped up into snippets, which are then spliced together with snippets on the same topic from other interviews (as previously noted, Ronald Fraser had done this in his 1979 *Blood of Spain*). Reverte and Thomás's *Hijos de la guerra* and Elordi's *Los años difíciles* do not go this far, but they arrange their testimonies in themed or chronologically ordered chapters, edited in such a way that they are devoted almost exclusively to accounts of atrocities.[7] Nonetheless, they print each individual's account (or personal documents submitted to the radio) one at a time, rather than plundering them for 'highlights' that are then cut and pasted in different sections to illustrate different points. This allows them to contribute not just to an understanding of what happened but, at a more fundamental level, to the history of subjectivity.

This practice of organizing the testimonies into composite themed or chronological chapters is also used to mix accounts by both Republican and Nationalist victims. This is a striking feature of most of the collections of testimonies published from 2000 to 2003, the explicit aim being the avoidance of partisanship. There have, to my knowledge, been no attempts in Spain to record life-stories by perpetrators — although Armengou and Belis do a good job of pursuing a perpetrator in *Les fosses del silenci*, and Manuel Rivas's 1998 novel in Galician, *O lapis do carpinteiro* (*The Carpenter's Pencil*) is noteworthy for making a perpetrator its narrator. The earlier 1977 *Los topos* throws in a small number of Nationalist survivors, interviewed just before the publication date (one suspects at the request of the publishers). But in their compilation *Hijos de la guerra*, Reverte and Thomás make a point of mixing testimonies by people who suffered the war as children on both sides, on the grounds that, regardless of their parents' politics, they were equally innocent victims (13). Their explicit aim is to encourage 'el reconocimiento del sufrimento de los demás' ('recognition of the suffering of others', 13): a noble sentiment which nevertheless ends up producing a depoliticized vision in which everyone is a victim. *Los años difíciles* respects the overwhelming predominance of Republican testimonies and documents submitted to Elordi's radio program (as he notes), but it includes several accounts of victims of Republican repression. This is right and proper, but the indiscriminate mixing in the same chapter of accounts by victims on both sides creates the impression that they were all the victims of a 'collective madness' (the phrase is frequently used). Such a notion glosses over the fact that this was a conflict between radically different political visions.

This depoliticizing strategy becomes explicit in the collections of testimonies which overwhelmingly privilege atrocities committed in the Republican zone. *Hist-*

(*Silenced Memories: Oral Histories of the Anti-Franco Resistance*, 2004), which gives full transcripts of extensive life histories. Although the author's analysis of these unstructured interviews tends to mine them for "proof" of what "really happened," their full reproduction allows insights into how key events have been processed psychologically.

7   The chapters in Reverte and Thomás's collection are 'La victoria rápida', 'Bombardeos, huída y exilio', and 'En zona roja' ('Rapid Victory', 'Air Raids, Exodus and Exile', 'In the Red Zone'). Those in Elordi's book are 'La guerra', 'La derrota' (despite including some pro-Nationalist testimonies) and 'La posguerra' ('War', 'Defeat', 'Postwar').

orias orales de la guerra civil, based on nearly a thousand family interviews undertaken by students at the Universidad de San Pablo-CEU in Madrid as an assignment for their History degree, claims to be impartial while admitting, 'Claro que estamos hablando de una universidad católica y de élite' ('Of course, we are talking about an elite Catholic university'; 10). 54.9% of the responses are pro-Nationalist, 12.7% are pro-Republican, and the rest are undeclared. The result is an overwhelming predominance of atrocities committed by Republicans, compounded by the editors' consistent use of the term 'liberation' to refer to Nationalist territorial gains. This volume cuts and pastes snippets from a mass of interviews into its various themed chapters, so that one cannot build up a profile of any of the narrators, which would enable one to interpret what they say. In the absence of any picture of the individual narrators that would reveal their ideological positioning, the reader is encouraged to take the accumulation of snippets as 'fact.' The editors' claim to impartiality is belied by their practice of starting each chapter with accounts of Republican atrocities, plus the overall move of the chapters from the war and repression on both sides to 'Piedad y perdón' ('Compassion and Forgiveness') and 'Guerra y religión' ('War and Religion,' this being an account of persecution of Catholics). It is important to have testimonies from Nationalist supporters but this mix of depoliticization and blatant bias, while claiming objectivity, is dangerous. Much worse is José María Zavala's 2003 *Los horrores de la guerra civil*, which claims to be a 'trabajo exhaustivo y ecuánime' ('exhaustive, impartial study') while offering a lurid gallery of 'fusilamientos, violaciones, mutilaciones y decapitaciones, infanticidios, enterramientos de vivos, cadáveres devorados por fieras' ('executions, rapes, mutilations and decapitations, infanticides, live burials, corpses devoured by wild beasts'; back cover). The book's epigraphs from political figures of the left and right (Manuel Azaña and Dionisio Ridruejo) are chosen to suggest that both sides were equally guilty. The editor's preface, however, clarifies that the book's aim is to combat the pro-Republican bias of post-1975 Spanish historians, concluding that the panorama of 'universal violence' which it will offer is an illustration of Hobbes's dictum that man is a wolf to man. This volume at least makes it blatantly obvious that the presentation of the Civil War as a collective madness is a strategy for avoiding Nationalist responsibility.[8]

Nevertheless, we need to find a way of tackling Nationalist memories if there is to be a working through of old hatreds. It is not surprising that there have been more Truth Commissions than Truth and Reconciliation Commissions, for reconciliation — if it is to be more than an enforced national unification — is not easy. The classic Truth and Reconciliation Commission is that of South Africa, which brought perpetrators and victims together in public, to try to work through their antagonistic feelings with the help of a professional 'comforter.' This process has been criticized as a state-sponsored public performance, which by definition

---

8   In fact, this volume, while claiming to present 'más de doscientos testimonios' ('over two hundred testimonies') consists in a collage of quotes from previously published sources, predominantly but not exclusively pro-Nationalist, inserted into the author's own inflammatory account. Zavala's later book *Los gángsters de la guerra civil* (2006) makes his political stance clear: the 'gangsters' are all Republican historical figures.

skewed the testimonial accounts by forcing them into an overall narrative that had reconciliation as its predetermined end (Castillejo-Cuéllar). Indeed, exemption from prosecution was granted in advance to those who agreed to tell their story in public. Chile's Truth and Reconciliation Commission, which produced the *Informe Rettig*, attempted no such 'working through' and has been dismissed by critics (Richard, Avelar) as an official mourning process designed to lay the past to rest as quickly as possible. The impact of official investigations into state repression in Latin America, and elsewhere in the world, on the current discourses of memory in Spain is evident, to the extent of providing a vocabulary for talking about repression.[9] Not only has Spain not attempted any such reconciliation process but it has not even had a Truth Commission.

This is where testimonies can play a productive role. For what testimonies give us is not so much evidence of what happened, as evidence of what the narrators feel about the past at the present time of speaking. A striking feature of the pro-Republican testimonies in most of the volumes I have mentioned, as the editors often note, is the lack of demand for retribution — though there is a strong demand for official recognition of the crimes committed. It seems that nearly four decades of not being able to voice publicly any demand for justice has led to an overwhelming desire, not to see the guilty brought to trial, but simply to have lifted the burden of humiliation and shame that was imposed on the defeated. But when we read pro-Nationalist testimonies — the volume *Historias orales de la guerra civil* is a frightening example — we cannot help but be struck by the virulence of the hatred for the Left that remains unabated to this day. Effectively, what emerges from these testimonies is that the Right continues to regard the Left as not fully human, as 'rojos' ('reds') denied any subjectivity.[10] In this sense, if we accept van Alphen's definition of the ultimate repression as the denial of personhood, the Right continues — at a figurative level — to exercise the denial of humanity that it enacted materially with the physical repression of the war and its aftermath. It is perhaps impossible to change the mindset of those who for nearly forty years had control over the way the Civil War was remembered. But what can be done is critical analysis of the many testimonies of the Civil War in the public domain, in order to try to understand — and produce public awareness of — the complex structures of present-day feeling that they reveal. This, I would argue, is just as important as using testimonies as evidence of what happened in the past. In saying this, I am arguing for a view of *testimonio*, not so much as a 'politics of truth' (Beverley's definition), but rather as a 'politics of feeling'.

9   For example, Montse Armengou has worked as a journalist in Guatemala and Bosnia. Emilio Silva, founder and president of the Asociación para la Recuperación de la Memoria Histórica (ARMH), has explained how his contacts with Spanish lawyers involved in prosecutions concerning human rights violations under military dictatorship in Chile and Argentina facilitated the ARMH's activities as a political pressure group (Labanyi, 'Entrevista' 147).
10   Emilio Silva similarly concludes that national reconciliation is not possible in Spain since the right does not recognize the suffering of those who supported the Republic (Labanyi, 'Entrevista' 154).

Works Cited

ALTOZANO, MANUEL. 'Garzón lanza la mayor investigación sobre los desaparecidos del régimen de Franco.' *El País* 2 September 2008: 1, 10.

ARMENGOU, MONTSE, and RICARD BELIS, *Las fosas del silencio: ¿Hay un Holocausto español?* Barcelona: Plaza & Janés, 2004.

——, dirs. *Les fosses del silenci*. Televisió de Catalunya, 2003.

AVELAR, IDELBER. *The Untimely Present: Postdictatorial Latin American Fiction and the Task of Mourning*. Durham, NC: Duke UP, 1999.

BEVERLEY, JOHN. *Testimonio: On the Politics of Truth*. Minneapolis: U of Minnesota P, 2004.

BULLÓN DE MENDOZA, ALFONSO, and ÁLVARO DE DIEGO. *Historias orales de la guerra civil*. Barcelona: Ariel, 2000.

CASTILLEJO-CUÉLLAR, ALEJANDRO. 'Knowledge, Experience, and South Africa's Scenarios of Forgiveness.' *Truth Commissions: State Terror, History, and Memory*. Ed. Greg Grandin and Thomas Miller Klubock. Spec. issue of *Radical History Review* 97 (2007): 11–42.

CENARRO, ÁNGELA. 'Memories of Repression and Resistance: Narratives of Children Institutionalized by Auxilio Social in Postwar Spain.' *Remembering and Forgetting on Europe's Southern Periphery*. Ed. Yannis Hamilakis and Jo Labanyi. Spec. issue of *History & Memory* 20.2 (2008): 39–59.

——. 'Memory beyond the Public Sphere: The Francoist Repression Remembered in Aragon.' *Spanish Memories: Images of a Contested Past*. Ed. Raanan Rein. Spec. issue of *History & Memory* 14.1–2 (2002): 165–88.

CUEVAS GUTIÉRREZ, TOMASA. *Cárcel de mujeres*, 2 vols. Barcelona: Sirocco, 1985.

——. *Mujeres de la resistencia*. Barcelona: Sirocco, 1986.

——. *Testimonios de mujeres en las cárceles franquistas*. Ed. Jorge J. Montes Salguera. Re-ed. of *Cárcel de mujeres* and *Mujeres de la resistencia*. Huesca: Instituto de Estudios Altoaragoneses, 2004.

DERRIDA, JACQUES. *On Cosmopolitanism and Forgiveness*. Trans. Mark Dooley and Michael Hughes. London: Routledge, 2001.

ELORDI, CARLOS. *Los años difíciles: El testimonio de los protagonistas anónimos de la guerra civil y la posguerra*. Madrid: Aguilar, 2002.

FELMAN, SHOSHANA, and DORI LAUB. *Testimony: Crises of Witnessing in Literature, Psycho-analysis, and History*. New York: Routledge, 1992.

FRASER, RONALD. *Blood of Spain: The Experience of Civil War*. London: Allen Lane, 1979. Spanish translation: *Recuérdalo tú y recuérdalo a otros: Historia oral de la guerra civil española*. 2 vols. Barcelona: Crítica, 1979.

HARVEY, JESSAMY. 'The Value of Nostalgia: Reviving Memories of National-Catholic Childhoods.' *Journal of Spanish Cultural Studies* 2.1 (2001): 109–18.

HERRMANN, GINA. 'Documentary's Labors of Law: The Television Journalism of Montse Armengou and Ricard Belis.' *The Politics of Memory in Contemporary Spain*. Ed. Jo Labanyi. Spec. issue of *Journal of Spanish Cultural Studies* 9.2 (2008): 193–212.

HONIG, BONNIE. *Democracy and the Foreigner*. Princeton, NJ: Princeton UP, 2001.

GUGELBERGER, GEORG. M. *The Real Thing: Testimonial Discourse and Latin America*. Durham, NC: Duke UP, 1996.

IZQUIERDO MARTÍN, JESÚS, and PABLO SÁNCHEZ LEÓN. *La guerra que nos han contado: 1936 y nosotros*. Madrid: Alianza, 2006.

JELIN, ELIZABETH. *State Repression and the Labors of Memory*. Minneapolis: U of Minnesota P, 2003.

JULIÁ, SANTOS, ed. *Víctimas de la guerra civil*. Madrid: Temas de Hoy, 1999.

JUNQUERA, NATALIA. 'Garzón recibe 130.137 nombres de víctimas y pistas sobre su paradero.' *El País* 22 September 2008: 16.

Labanyi, Jo. 'Entrevista con Emilio Silva.' *The Politics of Memory in Contemporary Spain*. Ed. Jo Labanyi. Spec. issue of *Journal of Spanish Cultural Studies* 9.2 (2008): 143–55.

——. 'Memory and Modernity in Democratic Spain: The Difficulty of Coming to Terms with the Spanish Civil War.' *Poetics Today* 28.1 (2007): 89–116.

Leguineche, Manuel, and Jesús Torbado. *Los topos*. Barcelona: Argos, 1977. Repr. Madrid: El País/Aguilar, 1999.

Loureiro, Ángel. 'Pathetic Arguments.' *The Politics of Memory in Contemporary Spain*. Ed. Jo Labanyi. Spec. issue of *Journal of Spanish Cultural Studies* 9.2 (2008): 225–37.

Resina, Joan Ramon. 'Window of Opportunity: The Television Documentary as "After-Image" of the War.' *Teaching Representations of the Spanish Civil War*. Ed. Noël Valis. New York: Modern Language Association, 2007. 406–24.

Reverte, Jorge M., and Socorro Thomás. *Hijos de la guerra: Testimonios y recuerdos*. Madrid: Temas de Hoy, 2001.

Richard, Nelly. *Cultural Residues: Chile in Transition*. Trans. Alan West-Durán and Theodore Quester. Minneapolis: U of Minnesota P, 2004.

Sontag, Susan. *Regarding the Pain of Others*. New York: Picador, 2003.

Vidal Castaño, José Antonio. *La memoria reprimida: Historias orales del maquis*. Valencia: Universitat de València, 2004.

Vinyes, Ricard, Montse Armengou, and Ricard Belis, dirs. *Els nens perduts del franquisme*. Televisió de Catalunya, 2002.

——. *Los niños perdidos del franquismo*. Barcelona: Random House Mondadori, 2003.

Zavala, José María. *Los gángsters de la guerra civil*. Barcelona, Plaza & Janés, 2006.

——. *Los horrores de la guerra civil*. Barcelona: Random House Mondadori, 2003.

CHAPTER 24

The Languages of Silence: Historical Memory, Generational Transmission and Witnessing in Contemporary Spain[1]

This essay is based on personal stories transmitted orally. Some have been recounted by historians or anthropologists or shown in television or film documentaries; one was collected by one of my undergraduate students; others were told to me in conversation with individuals involved in the current excavation of mass graves from the Francoist repression during and after the Spanish Civil War.[2] What interests me in these stories is their reference to practices of silence. I shall start with one personal story, as a way of introducing some historical and theoretical reflections. The remaining personal stories will be discussed in the second half of the essay.

At a 2005 conference devoted to 'Franco's Mass Graves', I was privileged to have a conversation with the forensic anthropologist Francisco Etxeberria who, since 2000, has collaborated with the Asociación para la Recuperación de la Memoria Histórica (Association for the Recovery of Historical Memory, ARMH) and the Basque Sociedad de Ciencias Aranzadi on the excavation of over one hundred mass graves.[3] He told how, after his mother's death, he came across some documents that revealed that his mother and one of her sisters had been nurses with the Republican army during the Spanish Civil War. Neither his mother nor his aunt had ever talked about having taken part in the war. When Etxeberria telephoned his aunt to find out more, she snapped back, 'How did you find out?' When Etxeberria asked why

1   A shorter version of this essay was given in Spanish at the conference 'La memoria insatisfecha', Universidad de Artes y Ciencias Sociales (ARCIS), Santiago de Chile, 28–29 June 2007.
2   For the exhumations of mass graves that have taken place in Spain since 2000, see Silva and Macías 2003; Labanyi 2008; Ferrándiz 2008. See also Ferrándiz 2014, which appeared after this essay was originally published.
3   'Franco's Mass Graves: An International Interdisciplinary Investigation', University of Notre Dame. 28–29 October 2005. Exteberria has also been invited to participate in exhumations in Chile, including that of President Salvador Allende in 2011. The information given here on the exhumations in Spain in which Exteberria has participated has been updated to cover the period 2000–18.

she and her sister had never talked about this in the family, her immediate reply was, 'To protect you'. Etxeberria was born in 1957, eighteen years after the end of the war. Even in the 1960s, by when Francoism had fully embraced capitalist development, Etxeberria's mother and aunt believed that it would be harmful to their children to know that they were 'hijos de rojos' ('children of reds', the term used for children of Republican supporters throughout the Franco dictatorship).

The straightforward reply of Etxeberria's aunt brought to the surface my increasing disquiet at the dominance in memory studies of trauma theory. This dominance derives from the key importance of the Holocaust for the development of memory studies over the past few decades.[4] Trauma theory attributes silence about a catastrophic event to an inner psychic process responsible for blocking the event's registration in consciousness. Unable to recall the traumatic event voluntarily, the trauma victim is prey to its belated and repeated replay at a physical, sensory level. This psychoanalytical narrative turns survivors of traumatic events into victims of psychic processes they cannot control. I do not, of course, mean to suggest that traumatized individuals do not exist, nor that trauma theory has not been hugely productive in helping us understand the psychological damage suffered by Holocaust survivors and the victims of other kinds of violence. However, in the case of Etxeberria's mother and aunt, silence does not represent a failure of memory but was chosen by them as a strategy. In the oral histories that have been conducted with people who lived through the Civil War and immediate postwar period, what is most striking is their astonishing ability to recall the details of what happened some sixty or seventy years ago.[5] The anthropologist Francisco Ferrándiz — who works with victims' relatives during the exhumations of mass graves from the war and postwar period, a process which encourages them to speak for the first time about the atrocities that they witnessed or that affected them — has observed that some people have difficulty finding words to articulate these previously untold experiences (Lezaiola 2006; Ferrándiz 2006). But this is due not to a blocking or failure of memory, but to the habits of silence acquired over so many years. In other cases when people talk for the first time about what they suffered in and after the war, the capacity for detailed recollection is extraordinary. An example is the case of the daughter of the Nationalist colonel responsible for surrendering Teruel to the Republicans and later shot by them, who told her story for the first time at the age of 86, in the course of an interview conducted by her granddaughter — I shall return to this interview later.

The fact that the Franco dictatorship (1939–75) lasted for almost forty years means that the impact of the silence adopted as a strategy for survival by the war's losers was prolonged over several generations. Etxeberria is an example of a member of the second generation, born in the late 1950s, who chose to break the silence his mother had maintained till her death, by devoting himself to the exhumation and identification of the victims of the Francoist repression. He explained that he had volunteered to work on the excavations out of a retrospective sense of guilt at

4   See especially Felman and Laub 1992; Caruth 1996; LaCapra 2001.
5   See Cuevas Gutiérrez 2004; Leguineche and Torbado 1977; Elordi 2002; Reverte and Thomás 2001; Armengou and Belis 2003.

having done nothing to alleviate his parents' suffering under the Dictatorship. In his view, this kind of guilty conscience was common among members of the second generation, but often it produced a contrary reaction: a desire not to know about the war or subsequent repression. In many cases, those responsible for the 'recovery of historical memory' in Spain today are the grandchildren of the generation that lived through the war, who have reacted against their parents' silence, which perpetuated the silence of the first generation. Although the role of the third generation (the grandchildren) is crucial, the story of Etxeberria's mother and aunt has made me reflect on the need to try to understand the earlier generations that opted for silence. I shall discuss here only the silence of the first generation, since this is documented. The silence of the second generation, which has received practically no attention and for which documentation remains largely unavailable, is a subject urgently requiring future research.

The best-known example of a grandson who took upon himself the recovery of his grandfather's memory is that of Emilio Silva, who (with Santiago Macías) founded the ARMH in response to the many letters he received from relatives of victims of the Francoist repression when, in 2000, he organized the first public excavation of a wartime mass grave, in order to disinter and rebury his murdered Republican grandfather. The phrase 'recovery of historical memory', which has become standard in the Spanish media since the ARMH's creation, is problematic in that it supposes that memory lies buried in the past, awaiting 'disinterment'. If this phrase has caught on, it is because the archaeological metaphor — so beloved of Freud — is seductive in its promise to offer access to a lost past. Freud went so far as to argue that, as with archaeological remains, the deepest layers of memory 'unearthed' by the psychoanalyst are those that remain the most intact — hence his privileging of early childhood memories. Cathy Caruth and Dominick LaCapra have suggested that trauma theory is attractive because it compensates for loss of belief in the possibility of representing the real, since traumatic repetition seems to offer unmediated access to the real without passing through the filter of voluntary memory. Indeed, trauma theory became fashionable in the 1990s, in the wake of post-structuralist theories that questioned the possibility of representation; there is a close correspondence between trauma theory and the Lacanian definition of the real as that which is beyond representation.[6] The phrase 'recovery of historical memory' similarly suggests that memory bypasses representation by giving us a 'piece' of the past, like the human remains being recovered. However, memory is not a 'thing' but a process that necessarily takes place in the present. If memory is a powerful political instrument, it is because it links the past with the moment of recall, producing an engagement with the past in the present. For this reason, it is important that the grandchildren should have taken responsibility for investigating the Francoist repression, re-establishing the process of generational transmission interrupted not only during the Dictatorship, but also during the first twenty-five years of the return to democracy.

6   See, for example, the concept of 'traumatic realism' developed by Foster (1996) in relation to contemporary art.

What is hardest to explain in the Spanish case is why the lack of public debate about the past should have been maintained under democracy until recently. The excavations of mass graves undertaken by the ARMH, a non-governmental organization, have succeeded in breaking the silence in those villages where exhumations have taken place, and have attracted a degree of media attention. But only with the Socialist government of José Luis Rodríguez Zapatero (2004–11) was there an attempt at an institutional level to create a public debate on the repression that took place during the war and Dictatorship, through its sponsorship of a law on the rights of victims, finally approved in December 2007.[7] Despite its timidity, provoking much criticism from the Left, this law, popularly if inaccurately known as the 'Law of Historical Memory' (the title of the original 2004 proposal), provoked a hysterical reaction from the Right, particularly from the main conservative opposition party, the Partido Popular. There is no room here to discuss the different stages through which this ongoing silence about the Francoist repression passed in the period between the end of the Dictatorship and the debates on the 2007 Law of Historical Memory. I shall limit myself to four observations.

First, the Socialist Government of 1982–96 and the subsequent Conservative Government of 1996–2004 coincided in avoiding public debate about the Francoist past: in the former case, to create a modern, emancipated society that broke with the past; in the second, to close the door on the historical responsibility of the Spanish Right; and, in both cases, to promote the values of neo-liberal consumerism, for which only the new matters.

Second, there did exist a *cultural* discourse on the war and dictatorship — intermittent until 1998 when it turned into a 'memory boom', intensifying in the first decade of the twenty-first century. But the existence of a considerable number of historical studies, novels, testimonies, and documentary and feature films on the subject was not enough, in the absence of a parallel political discourse, to create a public debate. It was only with the exhumations and the political debate on the 'Law of Historical Memory' that this cultural production attained widespread — and in some cases mass — public dissemination. It seems that cultural production needs to be supported by political debate to make a public impact. Political debate carries more weight not only because of its institutional backing — I include here the interventions of NGOs, which provoke government responses — but also because it confronts the public with contrary opinions, generating discussion. The polemical nature of the political debate on the Civil War and Dictatorship triggered by the passage through parliament of the 'Law of Historical Memory' seems to me healthy, though one may decry the vituperative tone of the interventions by the political Right. Indeed, it could be said that the debate's aggressiveness has had the advantage of breaking through public indifference, permitting the airing in

---

7   For the text of the law, whose full title is 'Ley por la que se reconocen y amplían derechos y se establecen medidas en favor de quienes padecieron persecución o violencia durante la guerra civil y la dictadura' ('Law Recognizing and Extending Rights and Establishing Measures in Favour of Those who Suffered Persecution or Violence during the Civil War and Dictatorship'), see <https://leymemoria.mjusticia.gob.es/cs/Satellite/LeyMemoria/es/memoria-historica-522007> [accessed 14 January 2019].

the private as well as public sphere of issues that have been relegated to silence for almost seventy years. Another advantage of political debate is that it is transmitted via television. Statistics show that a significant majority of Spaniards depend on television to inform themselves about current affairs (Smith 2006: 5). Television broadcasting is unique among the communications media for its ability to affect the private sphere, since it is viewed in the privacy of the home.

Third, the current Spanish debates on historical memory were triggered to a large extent by the post-dictatorship processes in Latin America's Southern Cone, which offered a vocabulary for framing the issue in terms of a legal discourse on human rights violations. The discourse on the Holocaust — which had previously served that function in the rest of Europe (also emerging belatedly, in the 1970s) — never had a significant impact in Spain, for historical reasons: a general supposition that modern Spain had nothing to do with the Jews, having expelled them in the late fifteenth century, and the persistence of hostile relations towards Israel, fully recognized by Spain only in 1986. But the debates in Latin America were another matter, given a tendency in Spain, still today, to suppose that Spain's former colonies form part of a 'great Hispanic family'. It was no coincidence that the 'memory boom' in Spanish cultural production started in 1998: this was the year when Judge Baltasar Garzón secured the arrest of General Pinochet in London. Garzón's intervention was criticized at the time as an attempt to compensate for, rather than rectify, lack of attention to the repressive past at home.[8] But that very criticism triggered renewed attention to the Francoist repression. From 1998, thanks to Garzón's gesture, the debate on human rights violations in Latin America — known in Spain previously — became something directly related to Spain. Comparisons with the post-dictatorship processes in the Southern Cone allowed a critical reflection on Spain's own Transition to democracy: specifically, the 1977 Amnesty Law which had declared immune from prosecution the political crimes of the Dictatorship, as well as those committed by both sides in the Civil War; and the lack of a Truth and Reconciliation Commission or even of an official report on the disappeared. From this time (1998), the word 'disappeared', coined at the time of Pinochet's coup in Chile, started to be used of the victims of the Francoist repression buried in unmarked graves.

Fourth and most importantly: this long silence, which remained almost intact until the late 1990s, did not mean that the past was forgotten. If that had been the case, the reaction of the Right to the 'Law of Historical Memory', criticized by most

8   In September 2008, Judge Garzón ordered state institutions, the Church and other public bodies to provide information about extra-judicial deaths of civilians on both sides during the Civil War and Dictatorship, in order to compile a definitive list of victims, at the same time ordering several notorious mass graves to be excavated. Garzón's statement publicly indicted Franco and a number of his generals for crimes against humanity — the first time such an allegation had been made by a Spanish judge — while recognizing that they could not be tried since they were all dead. The list of victims of the Francoist repression submitted to Garzón by the ARMH included approximately 130,000 names. Garzón's order was overruled by the Attorney General, who determined that he lacked judicial competence to investigate Francoist crimes and ordered him to refer the matter of exhumations to provincial courts, which mostly failed to take the issue up. See Altozano 2008; Yoldi 2008; Junquera 2009.

of the Left for not going far enough, would not have been so violent. The many existing print and audio–visual testimonies show the strength, still, of the emotions evoked by memories of the war and its aftermath. Paloma Aguilar Fernández's classic 1996 study, *Memoria y olvido de la Guerra Civil española* (*Memory and Amnesia: The Role of the Spanish Civil War in the Transition to Democracy*), important for being the first discussion by a historian of the memory of the Civil War, put about the idea that the politicians of the Transition to democracy negotiated a 'pacto de olvido' (pact of forgetting) in order to reach consensus. I agree with Santos Juliá's view, expressed in his equally pioneering 1999 book *Víctimas de la guerra civil* (*Victims of the Civil War*), that the consensus politics of the Transition were based, not on a pact of forgetting, but on an agreement not to let the past affect the future. Juliá insists that there was not a pact of silence either, since many historians published studies of the war and Dictatorship; but, in practice, the separation of discussion of the past from discussion of the future eliminated the subject of the past from political debate.

Perhaps the most negative consequence of the Transition has been this separation of the future from the past. The idea of the incompatibility of past and future has helped to create the idea that one has to choose between memory and forgetting; as Marc Augé insists in his book *Oblivion* (2004), the two are imbricated. Opting for the future does not necessarily mean that one forgets the past and remembering the past does not necessarily mean that one rejects the future. Indeed, all memory (voluntary memory, at least) is future-oriented, in that one remembers the past so as to satisfy certain needs in the present. The ceremonies held at the exhumations of victims of the Francoist repression, culminating in the subsequent reburial of the human remains in a publicly recognized, marked grave, institute practices of mourning that give closure to the past in the sense of allowing the relatives to reinsert themselves into civic life, free from the stigma of public humiliation which they had to internalize as a result of not being able to talk about their murdered family members.[9] The ability to remember in public is what permits reintegration into a collective future.

In her essay 'Memories between Silence and Oblivion' (2006), the Italian historian Luisa Passerini, a specialist in oral history in contexts of political repression, reminds us that silence can be confused with forgetting only if we equate memory with narration. But a memory does not have to be narrated to exist: silence offers the possibility of reflecting on what is remembered, and memories are transmitted not only through words but also through the body and material culture. An absence of narration does not necessarily mean the existence of a traumatic block, though it may well indicate the existence of some kind of coercion or the lack of adequate conditions for the memory's reception by others. What is tragic in the Spanish case is that the victims of the Francoist repression, and their relatives, had to wait till the twenty-first century — too late, in many cases[10] — for suitable conditions of

9   During the war, relatives of civilians murdered in the Nationalist zone were not even allowed to wear tokens of mourning (Armengou and Belis 2004: 212).
10   Etxeberria has commented that the emergence of human remains at an excavation is often accompanied by laments such as 'What a shame my brother who died three years ago could not be here to see our father!' (Leizaola 2006: 36).

reception to exist for their stories. It seems clear that the reason for their previous silence was not, in the majority of cases, a traumatic blocking of memory but a lack of interlocutors.

Symptomatic in this respect is the above-mentioned case of the daughter of the Nationalist colonel who surrendered Teruel to the Republicans, since her father — and by extension his family — had been repudiated by the Nationalists as a traitor; for obvious reasons, his daughter could not tell her story to Republican interlocutors either. After reading the transcription of the interview that her granddaughter Natalia — a student of mine at the time — recorded with her over the course of a week,[11] I realized that we also need to learn to listen to the stories of those whose political beliefs we do not share — which does not mean justifying their views. Natalia's grandmother is a very specific case, since she was a woman of the Right rejected by her own political class. But her life-story shows that the triumphalist rhetoric of Francoist commemorations of the Nationalist war dead, repeated throughout the Dictatorship, were not able to give closure to mourning for those Nationalist supporters who had lost a loved one in the war, since they allowed no space for personal grief. Natalia's grandmother also lost a brother in the war, who could be mourned openly, unlike her father. Although the family knew about her father's and brother's deaths, she had never talked to them about either of these losses. But for years she had slept with the bloodstained blanket in which her brother's corpse had been wrapped covering her bed, later preserving it in a wardrobe: a graphic example of the ability of a material object to embody memory, compensating for the inability to express personal grief in words. Her conservation of the blanket with the physical traces of her brother's body — as well as several documents relating to her father — in the private space of her bedroom suggests that her silence, as well as being caused by the lack of an interlocutor, meant for her the possibility of tending and being faithful to the memory of her lost loved ones.

Passerini insists on the difficulty of listening to silence — something she learnt to do when writing her first book, an oral history of the working class in Turin under fascism (1987). Initially she was frustrated by how the workers she interviewed skipped over the fascist period as if it did not matter to them. Then she learnt to read this silence as an indication of how difficult it was for them to express the experience of defeat (Turin, Gramsci's city, had had a highly organized working class) (1998: 58–60, 2006: 252). Idelber Avelar has also talked — in the context of the repression suffered under military dictatorship in the Southern Cone and Brazil — of the difficulty of articulating the experience of defeat, which tends to be camouflaged in compensatory heroic narratives (1999: 66–68). Historians of France and Italy have examined how the mythification of the anti-fascist resistance served as a way of silencing other more uncomfortable stories. A considerable number of the novels, films and historical studies produced in Spain from around 1998 depict the anti-Franco guerrilla fighters who kept up their struggle till 1951. It is important to counter the idea that the Spanish people submitted passively to Francoism. Nonetheless, it should be remembered that the history of the anti-

---

11   I thank Natalia for her permission to use her interview with her grandmother in my work.

Franco *guerrilla* is the story of a defeat — as is recognized by the first of these novels, Julio Llamazares's *Luna de lobos* (*Wolf Moon*, 1985).

Passerini insists that silence can mean something more complicated than acceptance of repression (1998, 2006). Under dictatorship, there is no alternative but to internalize repression, but this does not necessarily mean complicity with those in power. Silence can mean respect or fear for the repressive authority, or an attitude of defiance, or a way of safeguarding one's intimacy from ideological colonization by the state — or an ambivalent mixture of these (and other) things. It is important to recognize that silence can have multiple meanings. The interviews conducted by the historian Ángela Cenarro with individuals who as children were institutionalized by Auxilio Social (Social Aid) — the Francoist version of the Nazi Winterhilfe (Winter Aid) — refer repeatedly to the silence enforced in Auxilio Social's children's homes, to prevent the children from developing networks of solidarity, and to keep them ignorant of the other children's family origins, since the goal was to alienate them from their parents (mostly Republican), indoctrinating them with hatred for the 'reds' (Cenarro 2008; also 2006). These interviews show that, although the children never got to know much about their fathers (usually dead; their widows placed their children with Auxilio Social so they would have enough to eat), the fact of having had a Republican father marked their life-choices in adulthood: the silence around their father's identity did not produce a forgetting. The same interviews show how the children did not speak about their fathers' identity, or about their families in general, not only because of Auxilio Social's enforcement of silence on the matter, but also because their mothers had made them promise never to talk of their origins. When the children appeared to be obeying the imposition of silence by Auxlio Social, they were really obeying their mothers. None of those interviewed felt any resentment towards their mothers for having handed them over to Auxilio Social; they understood how terrible it was for their mothers to have to give up their children to a state institution that taught them to repudiate their parents (fortunately, without success), so that they would not go hungry.

Passerini observes that memory depends on a network of articulations, which can be disarticulated or rearticulated. She insists that memory is not so much suppressed as reorganized — that is, the suppression of a particular articulation of memory necessarily creates a new articulation, which generates different memories (2006: 240–41). However, the anthropologist Stephan Feuchtwang notes that memory relies on a series of everyday-life props, whose overwhelming annihilation can make any kind of re-articulation impossible. Here Feuchtwang offers an anthropological explanation, based on the relation between the individual and his or her social environment, of what trauma discourse has explained in psychoanalytical terms as the result of an internal psychic failure. Given the situation of extreme hardship experienced by many Republican women as the family providers in the war and postwar period, it seems likely that in some cases the annihilation of the everyday props of memory may have been so severe as to make any new re-articulation impossible. But the majority of personal stories that have been documented show an extraordinary ability to adjust to the most adverse circumstances, through a re-articulation of memory that makes survival possible.

A poignant case is that of Asunción Álvarez, who appears in the 2003 documentary *Les fosses del silenci* (*The Graves of Silence*) made for Catalan television (TV3) by Montse Armengou and Ricard Belis. Álvarez speaks to the camera as she looks on at an excavation where she hopes to find the remains of her two brothers, executed during the war. She defines herself as a devout Catholic, who dreams only of reburying her brothers' remains in the village cemetery. She recounts how the local falangists (members of the Spanish fascist party, Falange Española, responsible for the majority of the extra-judicial killings that took place in the Nationalist zone during the war), after executing her brothers and other men from the village, celebrated the event with a fiesta, and ordered her to entertain them with a tambourine. She played the tambourine throughout the night, without saying a word or shedding a tear (when she got home, the tears came pouring out). This silence was an act of defiance. If Álvarez could tell this story coherently in 2002, when she was filmed, it is because she had been able to re-articulate her experience so as to make it compatible with her religious belief. She was living in the Nationalist zone where it was normal for the local priest to attend the executions and publicly celebrate the 'crusade' against the 'reds'. Indeed, another eye-witness filmed at the same excavation recalls how, when some dogs partly disinterred the corpses, the village priest declaimed from the pulpit that this was proof of the executed men's wickedness, since the earth, which was God's creation, was rejecting them (Armengou and Belis 2004: 194). Álvarez seems to have strategically 'forgotten' this incident, since she does not mention the village priest in her account. But she does remember that her mother lost her sanity and died shortly after the murder of her two sons. According to Álvarez's account, her mother suffered the total collapse of her everyday-life props, on discovering that her Christian devotion was no use to her and even made her suffering worse: on the one hand, she had to endure the taunts of a neighbour who constantly reminded her that her lifetime of prayer had not saved her sons; on the other hand, her adhesion to Catholic doctrine made her believe that her sons had been condemned to hell because they had died without receiving confession (Armengou and Belis 2004: 195). In these circumstances, Álvarez's mother was unable to make the mental re-adjustment needed to produce a coherent account of her family history. By contrast, her daughter demonstrated an extraordinary capacity for survival. After the exhumation Álvarez, at the age of 87, re-articulated her historical memory again, becoming an activist for the ARMH.

Silva has told the story of another elderly woman who was brought by her daughter to the 2004 concert organized by the ARMH to pay homage to the Republic. On entering the concert venue, seeing it decked with Republican flags, the woman's impulse was to run away, convinced it was dangerous to be seen publicly to identify with the Republic; but her daughter persuaded her to stay. After this event, this woman also became an activist for the ARMH in what Silva described as 'el nacimiento de una ciudadana' ('the birth of a citizen').[12] She too

---

12   Silva told this anecdote at the symposium 'The Politics of Memory in Contemporary Spain', King Juan Carlos I of Spain Center, New York University, 10 November 2006. The concert paying

was able to reorganize the everyday-life props to her memory — a memory of fear inscribed on the body — in order to change the course of her life.

Another impressive but different case has been recounted by Ferrándiz. The excavation of the mass grave at the village of Fontanosas, in the province of Ciudad Real, containing the remains of seven villagers shot two years after the war's end, was undertaken thanks to a letter revealing the existence of the grave, sent by a man who had participated in the firing squad — a secret this man had kept all his life. The excavations carried out since 2000 had produced a climate in which this man was able to reorganize his memory of the past, in order to reveal his guilty secret. The victims' relatives expressed no desire for revenge towards him, which indicates that their memories had also been reorganized over the years. A further story, told by Silva, has a less happy end.[13] A woman interviewed by him at an exhumation in Burgos province recounted how her mother had told her children that their father had abandoned the family. The children grew up hating their father for his irresponsibility. This woman had just discovered that her father's remains were among those found in the grave being excavated outside the village where she had grown up. Her mother had chosen to lie to her children, inventing a story that was humiliating for her and degrading for her husband, so that they would not know they were children of an executed Republican. This example shows how, for the losers in the war, it was not a matter of choosing between a good and bad solution, but of choosing between two bad options. For this woman, it was preferable to have her children hate their father than to expose them to public humiliation and the risk of reprisals. With the discovery of the silenced truth, the lives of both mother and daughter were shattered: the daughter racked with guilt at having hated her father; the mother having to give up a fictitious biography that she had maintained for over sixty years. Both mother and daughter found themselves confronted with the need to reorganize from scratch their memories of a lifetime.

As Passerini notes, it is important to consider not only the internal articulation of memory, but also the articulation (or lack of it) between individual and collective memory (2006: 245). If there is no belief in, or possibility of, some kind of collective identity, generational transmission cannot take place. Passerini describes an oral history project undertaken in post-Soviet Russia with young enthusiasts for the new capitalist system, who talked about the Stalinist past as if it were the past of another country (2006: 246). Until a few years ago, I suspect the same could have been said of the relationship of many young Spaniards to the Francoist past. However, the recent interest in historical memory has its own dangers, as Etxeberria has remarked: the risk of 'patrimonialización' or conversion into a kind of heritage industry (Leizaola 2006: 42–43, 44–45). That is, its trivialization and sanitization through the production of a marketable and institutionally sanctioned memory, whose consumption makes people feel righteous rather than indignant — a danger

homage to the Republic, 'Recuperando memoria', was organized in Rivas-Vaciamadrid on 25 June 2005. Asunción Álvarez spoke at the event, as she did at the first national symposium of the ARMH in Valladolid in 2003 (Silva, Esteban, Castán, and Salvador 2004: 87–88).

13   Conversation with Emilio Silva, New York, November 2006.

that Susan Sontag identified in her last book, *Regarding the Pain of Others*. Passerini describes how the reconstruction of Hiroshima insisted on cleanliness and comfort, erasing any reference to horror (2006: 241). In Spain, the Valle de los Caídos (Valley of the Fallen) is another case of this sanitization of painful memory: a triumphalist monument to the dead in the Civil War that excludes any mention of the Republican dead and converts the Nationalist 'fallen' into 'glorious martyrs'. Additionally, the monument still today silences the story of the Republican prisoners who built the monument, several losing their lives in the process — a historical whitewash reinforced under democracy, in a misguided attempt at political correctness, by the withdrawal from the site's bookstore of publications about Franco.[14]

The Valley of the Fallen endures as a material reminder, set in stone, of the fascist will to power, but it is a material memory that requires interpretation. In some cases, it is more productive to forgo the imposition of an interpretation and invite the spectator to learn to listen to silence, in order to recognize its uncomfortable ambivalence or emotive power. This is done brilliantly by the Austrian filmmaker Günter Schwaiger, in his documentary *Santa Cruz, por ejemplo...* (*Santa Cruz, for example...*). In 2003–04, Schwaiger filmed the excavation of a mass grave at Santa Cruz de Salceda, in Burgos province, interviewing the local inhabitants. In a short sequence near the film's end the camera focuses on four elderly local men sitting on a bench. The director's voice-over asks what they think of the exhumation taking place outside the village. The camera holds on them for several minutes during which they refuse to reply, recording their body language as they try to elude the camera's gaze. The camera finally turns to track one of the men who, after covering his face with his arm, gets up and walks away, unable to bear the camera's scrutiny any longer. In an earlier sequence, the camera confronts us with the body language, still and silent, of a series of relatives of the victims being exhumed, holding the photographs, also still and silent, of their dead loved ones. We see one tiny photo in the palm of a hand; another, large and framed, is clasped against his naked chest by an elderly man. The relatives holding the photos and the dead depicted in them are all looking directly at the camera; that is, at us. From this series of photographs, we pass to a shot of the grave, showing the volunteers bent over the human remains, painstakingly scraping away the earth to make them visible. These human remains are by definition the best example of the silent eloquence of material memories. Earlier in this essay I criticized the concept of the recovery of historical memory, since it supposes that memories exist buried in the past. But there is a sense in which we can say that material remains embody the memory of the past. However, we can say this only if those remains are viewed through the eyes of those who reclaim them in the present as part of their inheritance.

---

14   Recent investigations show that, of the 40,000 to 60,000 bodies entombed in the Valle de los Caídos, there are more Republicans than previously thought. In the haste to procure enough bodies in time for the inauguration in 1959, corpses were disinterred from cemeteries indiscriminately, disregarding the opposition of the majority of relatives of the Nationalist dead (relatives of the Republican dead were not consulted). See Gómez 2007. At the time of writing (2007) the ARMH had started to receive enquiries about how to reclaim bodies buried at the Valle de los Caídos (Labanyi 2008: 155). On the Valle de los Caídos, see Sueiro 2006; Valis 2007.

I should like to end with three short examples of such a reclamation of the dead as part of a personal inheritance: in all three cases, the reclamation is made through a silent bodily gesture. Silva has told how, in a village in Burgos province, the women succeeded repeatedly in preserving the site of a mass grave from building speculators by throwing themselves on the ground so that the bulldozers could not advance.[15] The second example, reported in the national newspaper *El País*, took place in Cuenca, where a mass grave containing over 300 bodies is located in a walled space next to a monastery used as a prison in and after the war. The widows of those executed, unable to gain access to the site, for the whole of the Franco dictatorship threw flowers over the wall (C.E.C. 2006). The last example is a photograph taken by Etxeberria, published in *El País* (Tesón 2006). It depicts a ceremony held at the end of the excavation of a mass grave in Burgos province, when some of the relatives and volunteers decided to re-enact the positions in which the bodies fell. The photograph shows a compact mass of bodies, on top of one another, surrounded by a rope tracing the boundary of the area where the remains were found. As Etxeberria comments in the caption: 'Es una especie de homenaje. Hay quien quiere estar en el lugar en el que estuvo su padre.' ('It's a kind of homage. Some people want to occupy the place occupied by their father.')

Works Cited

AGUILAR FERNÁNDEZ, PALOMA. 1996. *Memoria y olvido de la guerra civil española* (Madrid: Alianza) (English trans. *Memory and Amnesia: The Role of the Spanish Civil War in the Transition to Democracy*, trans. by Mark Gordon Oakley [Oxford: Berghahn Books, 2002])

ALTOZANO, MANUEL. 2008. 'Garzón lanza la mayor investigación sobre los desaparecidos del régimen de Franco', *El País*, 2 September, p. 10

AMAGO, SAMUEL, and CARLOS JEREZ-FARRÁN (eds). 2010. *Unearthing Franco's Legacy: Mass Graves and the Recuperation of Historical Memory in Spain* (South Bend, IN: University of Notre Dame Press)

ARMENGOU, MONTSE, and RICARD BELIS (dirs). 2003. *Les fosses del silenci* (Televisió de Catalunya)

——. 2004. *Las fosas del silencio. ¿Hay un Holocausto español?* (Barcelona: Plaza & Janés)

AUGÉ, MARC. 2004. *Oblivion*, trans. by Marjolin de Jager (Minneapolis: University of Minnesota Press)

AVELAR, IDELBER. 1999. *The Untimely Present: Postdictatorial Latin American Fiction and the Task of Mourning* (Durham, NC: Duke University Press)

CARUTH, CATHY. 1996. *Unclaimed Experience: Trauma, Narrative, and History* (Baltimore, MD: Johns Hopkins University Press)

C.E.C. 2006. 'La mayor apertura de una fosa común en España se para por falta de fondos', *El País*, 19 August, p. 17

CENARRO, ÁNGELA. 2006. *La sonrisa de Franco: Auxilio Social en la guerra civil y en la posguerra* (Barcelona: Crítica)

——. 2008. 'Memory, Repression and Resistance: Narratives of Children Institutionalized by Auxilio Social in Postwar Spain', in *Memory and Forgetting in Southern Europe and the Balkans*, ed. by Yannis Hamilakis and Jo Labanyi (special issue of *History & Memory*, 19.2: 39–59)

15   Conversation with Emilio Silva, Madrid, March 2006.

CUEVAS GUTIÉRREZ, TOMASA. 2004. *Testimonios de mujeres en las cárceles franquistas*, ed. by Jorge J. Montes Salguero (Huesca: Instituto de Estudios Altoaragoneses) (first pub. as *Cárcel de mujeres*, 2 vols [Barcelona: Sirocco, 1985] and *Mujeres de la resistencia* [Barcelona: Sirocco, 1986])

ELORDI, CARLOS. 2002. *Los años difíciles: El testimonio de los protagonistas anónimos de la guerra civil y la posguerra* (Madrid: Aguilar)

FELMAN, SHOSHANA, and DORI LAUB. 1992. *Testimony: Crises of Witnessing in Literature, Psychoanalysis, and History* (New York: Routledge)

FERRÁNDIZ, FRANCISCO. 2006. 'The Return of Civil War Ghosts: The Ethnography of Exhumations in Contemporary Spain', *Anthropology Today*, 22: 7–12

——. 2008. 'Cries and Whispers: Exhuming and Narrating Defeat in Spain Today', in *The Politics of Memory in Contemporary Spain*, ed. by Jo Labanyi (special issue of *Journal of Spanish Cultural Studies*, 9.2: 177–92)

——. 2014. *El pasado bajo tierra: Exhumaciones contemporáneas de la Guerra Civil* (Barcelona: Anthropos)

FEUCHTWANG, STEPHAN. 2006. 'Loss: Transmissions, Recognitions, Authorisations', in *Memory Cultures: Memory, Subjectivity and Recognition*, ed. by Susannah Radstone and Katharine Hodgkin (New Brunswick, NJ: Transaction Publishers), pp. 76–89

FOSTER, HAL. 1996. *The Return of the Real: The Avant-Garde at the End of the Century* (Cambridge, MA: MIT Press)

GÓMEZ, LUIS. 2007. 'El Valle de los desconocidos', *El País*, 21 October, p. 26

JULIÁ, SANTOS (ed.). 1999. *Víctimas de la guerra civil* (Madrid: Temas de Hoy)

JUNQUERA, NATALIA. 2009. 'El tiempo se acaba para las víctimas de Franco', *El País*, 8 June, pp. 40–41

LABANYI, JO. 2008. 'Entrevista con Emilio Silva', in *The Politics of Memory in Contemporary Spain*, ed. by Jo Labanyi (special issue of *Journal of Spanish Cultural Studies*, 9.2: 143–55)

LACAPRA, DOMINICK. 2001. *Writing History, Writing Trauma* (Baltimore, MD: Johns Hopkins University Press)

LEGUINECHE, MANUEL, and JESÚS TORBADO. 1999. *Los topos* (Madrid: El País/Aguilar) (first pub. 1977)

LEIZAOLA, AITZPEA. 2006. 'La antropología a pie de fosa: Diálogo con Francisco Etxeberria y Francisco Ferrándiz sobre la memoria de la Guerra Civil', *Ankulegi: Gizarte Antropologia Aldizkaria / Revista de Antropología Social / Revue d'Ethnologie*, 10: 33–46

LLAMAZARES, JULIO. 1985. *Luna de lobos* (Barcelona: Seix Barral)

PASSERINI, LUISA. 1987. *Fascism in Popular Memory*, trans. by Robert Lumley and Jude Bloomfield (Cambridge: Cambridge University Press)

——. 1998. 'Work Ideology and Consensus under Italian Fascism', in *The Oral History Reader*, ed. by Robert Perks and Alistair Thomson (London: Routledge), pp. 53–62

——. 2005. *Memory and Totalitarianism* (New Brunswick, NJ: Transaction Publishers) (first pub. 1992)

——. 2006. 'Memories between Silence and Oblivion', in *Memory, History, Nation: Contested Pasts*, ed. by Katharine Hodgkin and Susannah Radstone (New Brunswick, NJ: Transaction Publishers), pp. 238–54

REVERTE, JORGE M., and SOCORRO THOMÁS. 2001. *Hijos de la guerra: Testimonios y recuerdos* (Madrid: Temas de Hoy)

SCHWAIGER, GÜNTER (dir. and prod.). 2005. *Santa Cruz, por ejemplo...*

SILVA, EMILIO, and SANTIAGO MACÍAS. 2003. *Las fosas de Franco: Los republicanos que el dictador dejó en las cunetas* (Madrid: Temas de Hoy)

SILVA, EMILIO, ASUNCIÓN ESTEBAN, JAVIER CASTÁN, and PANCHO SALVADOR (eds). 2004. *La memoria de los olvidados: Un debate sobre el silencio de la represión franquista* (Valladolid: Ámbito)

SMITH, PAUL JULIAN. 2006. *Spanish Visual Culture: Cinema, Television, Internet* (Manchester: Manchester University Press)

SONTAG, SUSAN. 2003. *Regarding the Pain of Others* (New York: Picador)

SUEIRO, DANIEL. 2006. *El Valle de los Caídos: Los secretos de la cripta franquista* (Madrid: La Esfera de los Libros) (first pub. 1977)

TESÓN, NURIA. 2006. ' "Estamos recuperando dignidades": El forense Francisco Exteberria ha exhumado más de 500 fusilados de la Guerra Civil', *El País*, 17 December, p. 26

VALIS, NOËL. 2007. 'Civil War Ghosts Entombed: Lessons of the Valley of the Fallen', in *Teaching Representations of the Spanish Civil War*, ed. by Noël Valis (New York: MLA), pp. 425–35

VINYES, RICARD. 2002. *Irredentas: Las presas políticas y sus hijos en las cárceles de Franco* (Madrid: Temas de Hoy)

VINYES, RICARD, MONTSE ARMENGOU, and RICARD BELIS (dirs). 2002. *Els nens perduts del franquisme* (Televisió de Catalunya)

YOLDI, JOSÉ. 2008. 'Garzón atribuye a Franco un plan de exterminio sistemático de los "rojos" ', *El País*, 17 November, p. 12.

INDEX

9 781781 889329